Monetary Policy Transmission in the Euro Area

Proper conduct of monetary policy requires understanding the monetary transmission mechanism, to monitor the economy, make decisions on the stance of policy and explain the policy actions to the public. An urgent task now for the European Central Bank is to gather and analyze evidence on the euro-zone. This book presents the results of the first ever research project on the monetary transmission mechanism in the euro area. The findings are drawn from a multi-year collaborative project by the European Central Bank and the other Eurosystem central banks. The Monetary Transmission Network research team analyzed both macro- and micro-economic data for the area as a whole and for individual countries. The results described in country case studies and overview essays by central bank economists, along with a discussion chapter by eminent academics, provide an essential contribution to the latest research.

Ignazio Angeloni is Deputy Director General for Research at the European Central Bank. He is the co-author of *Monetary Policy in the Euro Area: Strategy and Decision-Making at the European Central Bank* (with Vitor Gaspar, Otmar Issing and Oreste Tristani: Cambridge University Press, 2001)

Anil Kashyap is the Edward Eagle Brown Professor of Economics and Finance at the University of Chicago's School of Business. He is the author of *Corporate Financing and Governance in Japan: The Road to the Future* (with Takeo Hoshi: MIT Press, 2001).

Benoît Mojon is Senior Economist at the General Economic Research Division of the European Central Bank.

Monetary Policy Transmission in the Euro Area

A Study by the Eurosystem Monetary Transmission Network

Edited by

Ignazio Angeloni, Anil K Kashyap
and Benoît Mojon

CAMBRIDGE
UNIVERSITY PRESS

PUBLISHED BY THE PRESS SYNDICATE OF THE UNIVERSITY OF CAMBRIDGE
The Pitt Building, Trumpington Street, Cambridge, United Kingdom

CAMBRIDGE UNIVERSITY PRESS
The Edinburgh Building, Cambridge, CB2 2RU, UK
40 West 20th Street, New York, NY 10011–4211, USA
477 Williamstown Road, Port Melbourne, VIC 3207, Australia
Ruiz de Alarcón 13, 28014 Madrid, Spain
Dock House, The Waterfront, Cape Town 8001, South Africa

http://www.cambridge.org

First published 2003

Printed in the United Kingdom at the University Press, Cambridge

Typeface Plantin 10/12 pt.   *System* LATEX 2_ε [TB]

A catalogue record for this book is available from the British Library

Library of Congress Cataloguing in Publication data
Monetary policy transmission in the Euro area : a study by the Eurosystem
Monetary Transmission Network/edited by Ignazio Angeloni, Anil Kashyap
and Benoît Mojon.
    p.   cm.
Includes bibliographical references and index.
ISBN 0 521 82864 3
1. Monetary policy – European Union countries.   2. Transmission mechanism
(Monetary policy)   3. Euro.   I. Angeloni, Ignazio, 1953–   II. Kashyap, A. K.
III. Mojon, Benoît.   IV. Eurosystem Monetary Transmission Network.

HG3942.M66   2003
332.4'6 – dc21   2003043966

ISBN 0 521 82864 3 hardback

Contents

**Part 4 Monetary policy in the euro area:
summary and discussion of the main findings**

Appendix

Contributors

Anna-Maria Agresti	European Central Bank
Ignazio Angeloni	European Central Bank
Charles Bean	Bank of England
Ben Bernanke	Board of Governors of the Federal Reserve System
Sophocles N. Brissimis	Bank of Greece and University of Piraeus
Paul Butzen	Banque Nationale de Belgique
Jean Bernard Chatelain	Université d'Orléans and CEPREMAP
Jaak Claessens	European Central Bank
Leo de Haan	De Nederlandsche Bank
Michael Ehrmann	European Central Bank
Peter van Els	De Nederlandsche Bank
Luísa Farinha	Banco de Portugal
Xavier Freixas	Pompeu Fabra University
Benjamin Friedman	Harvard University
Catherine Fuss	Banque Nationale de Belgique
Eugenio Gaiotti	Banca d'Italia
Leonardo Gambacorta	Banca d'Italia
Vítor Gaspar	European Central Bank
Andrea Generale	Banca d'Italia
Jürgen von Hagen	University of Bonn
Ignacio Hernando	Banco de España
Ulf von Kalckreuth	Deutsche Bundesbank
Nicos C. Kamberoglou	Bank of Greece
Anil K Kashyap	University of Chicago
Sylvia Kaufmann	Oesterreichische Nationalbank
Jens Larsen	Bank of England
Alberto Locarno	Banca d'Italia
Claire Loupias	Banque de France
Patrick Lünnemann	Banque Centrale du Luxembourg
Jorge Martínez-Pagés	Banco de España

Thomas Mathä	Banque Centrale du Luxembourg
Peter McAdam	European Central Bank
Benoît Mojon	European Central Bank
Julian Morgan	European Central Bank
Kalin Nikolov	Bank of England
Gert Peersman	Bank of England
Carlos Robalo Marques	Banco de Portugal
Frédérique Savignac	Université de Paris XII
Patrick Sevestre	Université de Paris XII
Frank Smets	European Central Bank
George T. Simigiannis	Bank of Greece
Daniele Terlizzese	Banca d'Italia
André Tiomo	Banque de France
Jukka Topi	Suomen Pankki
Maria-Teresa Valderrama	Oesterreichische Nationalbank
Philip Vermeulen	European Central Bank
Jean-Pierre Villetelle	Banque de France
Jouko Vilmunen	Suomen Pankki
Andreas Worms	Deutsche Bundesbank

Foreword

This book presents to the community of central bankers and academics, and to the public at large, the results of the research project undertaken by the Eurosystem Monetary Transmission Network (MTN) on the transmission of monetary policy in the euro area. This is the first comprehensive research project completed jointly by the European Central Bank (ECB) and by the euro area National Central Banks (NCBs) after the introduction, in 1999, of the new single European currency, the euro.

The choice of monetary policy transmission as the topic for this study was a logical and almost a necessary one. The transmission process is a central issue for every central banker. It figures prominently in the preparation, decision-making and communication of monetary policy. Good analysis is needed to get information on the transmission mechanism and to make it systematic and soundly based on economic theory and data evidence. This task was assigned, shortly after the onset of the single European monetary policy, to the Monetary Transmission Network, a team of Eurosystem economists with the proper mix of expertise. Their work lasted some two years. Preliminary results of this research were presented, even before its completion, to a number of academic and policy-making audiences on both sides of the Atlantic. Disseminating in-house research, particularly when the topic is of such policy relevance, is an integral part of central bank communication. This book is part of this communication effort.

Monetary transmission is a difficult subject, for a variety of reasons. It is broad, covering economics almost in its entirety. It crucially hinges on unobservable factors, most notably market expectations. It is even more difficult in this case because the focus is the euro area, a new entity, partly unexplored and not yet richly endowed with statistical information. All this considered, the task assigned to the Monetary Transmission Network was a very challenging one; I am glad to see that the group was able to deliver such impressive results in a relatively short period of time. The experience of the Monetary Transmission Network sets an excellent example of productive cooperation among research staff in a system of central banks.

The success of this effort is owed first to its participants, whose names appear in the introduction of the book and in the individual chapters. All of them contributed with competence and dedication. The Eurosystem research areas – and the Group of Heads of Research, chaired by Vítor Gaspar – contributed with their support and by securing the necessary resources. Finally, a special mention should go to Ignazio Angeloni, who directed the project, Anil Kashyap, who provided relentless stimulus and guidance, and Benoît Mojon, who directed the Network Secretariat. The success of this project owes much to their commitment and determination.

Otmar Issing
ECB Chief Economist and Member of the Executive Board
Frankfurt am Main, November 2002

Acknowledgements

As editors of this book, our gratitude goes first to all the members of the Monetary Transmission Network, each of whom contributed to creating a stimulating environment in which our collective work could develop. We have learned a lot during the course of this project, and, equally important, we have enjoyed it.

For encouragement and support we, and the whole Monetary Transmission Network, are grateful to Professor Otmar Issing, Chief Economist and Executive Board member of the ECB, and to Vítor Gaspar, ECB Director General for Research and Chairman of the Eurosystem Heads of Research Group. The Heads of Research of the Eurosystem were most supportive in providing staff resources. The ECB Governing Council and the ECB President, Wim Duisenberg, provided comments and encouragement on the occasion of a special Governing Council seminar held in April 2002, where the results of the project were presented.

We also thank, without involving them, all those who provided comments and advice during the course of the work and at the concluding conference of December 2001. The list includes: Ernst Baltensperger, Charlie Bean, Ben Bernanke, Steve Bond, Gabe de Bondt, Claudio Borio, Fabio Canova, Bob Chirinko, Rich Clarida, Jean Dermine, Xavier Freixas, Ben Friedman, Jordi Gali, Vítor Gaspar, Luigi Guiso, Jürgen von Hagen, Skander van den Heuvel, Gert Jan Hogeweg, Ken Kuttner, Otmar Issing, Jens Larsen, Jean Charles Rochet, Plutarchos Sakellaris, Christopher Sims and Axel Weber. Our gratitude goes also to the Federal Reserve Board staff, for comments, and especially to Flint Brayton, who conducted the simulations reported in chapter 24. We also thank the Bank of England (Charlie Bean, Jens Larsen and Kalin Nikolov) for their contribution to the conference (chapter 6).

We are grateful to Susana Sommaggio for the central role she played, together with the staff of the ECB Protocol and Conferences Division, in the organisation of the December 2001 conference, to Sabine Wiedemann, who helped the organisation of the regular meetings of the Monetary

Transmission Network, and to Sandra Afonso-Rodrigues and Juliette Cuvry, who edited the manuscript of this book.

Finally, we wish to express appreciation to those who gave us the opportunity to present early parts of this research in seminars and conferences which generated valuable feedback that helped shape this final product. Among them we wish to thank Martin Feldstein and Ben Bernanke, for inviting us to participate in the NBER Summer Institute, Ignazio Visco, for organising a session at the OECD, Jürgen von Hagen, for inviting us to present the work at the 2002 Konstanz seminar, David Cobham, for organising a session at the 2002 Macro Money and Finance workshop, and Carlo Carraro and Thierry Verdier, organisers of the 2002 Annual Congress of the European Economic Association, for hosting an invited session on the project.

Any errors should be attributed to us, first and foremost, and to the other authors of this book.

Abbreviations

AT	Austria
AWM	Area-wide model of the euro area, developed and used by the ECB
BE	Belgium
BIS	Bank for International Settlements
CPI	Consumer price index
DE	Germany
ECB	European Central Bank
EMS	European Monetary System
EMU	Economic and monetary unification of Europe
ES	Spain
FI	Finland
FR	France
FRB	Board of Governors of the Federal Reserve System
FRB-US	Quarterly econometric model of the US economy, developed and used by the FRB
GDP	Gross domestic product
GR	Greece
IC	Investment contribution to the GDP (or aggregate domestic demand) effect of a monetary policy shock
IE	Ireland
IRC	Interest rate channel of monetary policy
IT	Italy
LU	Luxembourg
MTN	(Eurosystem) Monetary transmission network
NCBs	National Central Banks. Together with the ECB, the NCBs of the euro area form the Eurosystem
NIGEM	National institute global econometric model, developed by the National Institute for Economic and Social Research
NL	Netherlands
PT	Portugal
VAR(s)	Vector auto-regressive model(s)
WGEM	Working Group on Econometric Modelling

Introduction

I. Angeloni, A. K. Kashyap and B. Mojon

In 1999 the European Central Bank (ECB), together with the National Central Banks (NCBs) of the countries that had just adopted the euro, launched a major research initiative to study the transmission of monetary policy. The objective was to put together, in a reasonably short time, a comprehensive body of information on how the monetary policy of the newly created central bank would affect the economy of the 'euro area'.[1] In December 2001 this research was presented to academics and central bankers in an international conference at the ECB. This book brings together, in revised and shortened form, all the contributions presented at that conference.[2] It also includes a summary of the discussion and some further papers that, owing to time constraints, could not be presented then. For the reader, this book provides an overview of the project results and access to the most comprehensive set of analyses on the working of the single European monetary policy yet published.

Knowledge of the transmission mechanism is needed to determine how the monetary policy instruments should be set to achieve the desired goals. Interest rate decisions by central banks always rely on some explicit or implicit understanding of the transmission mechanism. Moreover, ideally this understanding suggests also how to *efficiently* achieve the monetary policy goal, i.e. limiting undesired side effects on other economic variables besides the ones the central bank is directly responsible for. Finally, understanding the transmission mechanism is critical for the external communication of policy. A central bank that uses this information well in explaining its actions can normally be more articulate, convincing and effective, other things being equal.

---

[1] The euro area is composed of all the countries that have adopted the euro as their currency. Currently, the area includes twelve of the fifteen countries belonging to the European Union (the exceptions being Denmark, Sweden and the UK). The Eurosystem includes the ECB and the euro area NCBs.

[2] The papers presented at the conference have been published in the ECB Working Paper Series, nos. 91–114. The conference, entitled 'Monetary Policy Transmission in the Euro Area', was held at the ECB on 18 and 19 December 2001. Its program can be accessed at www.ecb.int.

When, in 1999, the ECB Governing Council started making monetary policy decisions for eleven sovereign countries[3] and a community of about 300 million Europeans, information on the euro area monetary policy transmission mechanism was extremely limited. The Bank for International Settlement (BIS) had in 1995 published a systematic set of simulations conducted on central bank econometric models, with harmonised criteria, showing the effects of monetary policy in a broad group of countries, including eight of the present euro area members. Additional research, by academic economists and central bankers, had provided other perspectives. Moreover, the research staff of the NCBs has considerable in-house knowledge of the national economies, much of which was of potentially great value for understanding the transmission mechanism. This expertise, largely unpublished, was available to the ECB decision-making bodies. But other crucial elements were missing. First, many of the existing analyses employed long data samples, going far back in time; this made the results potentially misleading since economic structures and institutions are changing over time. Secondly, most of these analyses, especially some of the studies of micro data, were country-specific, whereas the ECB needs evidence for the euro area as a whole. Lastly, the existing knowledge was fragmented and could not easily be pieced together to form an overall picture. In short, the regime shift entailed by the European Monetary Union (EMU) necessitated a fresh look at the transmission mechanism.

Some strategic choices on the direction of the project were taken at the outset and influenced the whole course of the work. These choices will be discussed in detail in the book, but we will also summarise them here because they help the reader understand the logic of the individual chapters and the links among them. This is the objective of the next section. The following section provides an overview of the results of the whole project and guide the reader through the structure of the book. A short section on the organisation of the research team concludes this introduction.

1 Fundamental issues in studying the transmission of monetary policy in the euro area, and the approach taken by the Eurosystem research team

1.1 Area-wide versus country-level analysis

The ECB aims at maintaining price stability for the euro area over a medium-term horizon. Unnecessary fluctuations in output and other

---

[3] Greece, the twelfth country to adopt the single currency, joined the euro area in 2001.

relevant economic variables should be avoided.[4] This implies that an analysis of monetary policy transmission for the euro area aiming to have policy relevance should, as a matter of priority, yield information on how monetary policy influences euro-area-wide price dynamics over time. Moreover, it should indicate how other relevant economic variables might be affected during the adjustment process following a monetary policy change.

Though the analysis ultimately needs to produce aggregate results, there are several reasons why the problem cannot be approached *only* by a direct analysis of euro area-wide macroeconomic variables (such as money market interest rates, monetary and credit aggregates, output and prices). First, most existing euro area data are aggregations of national variables over a time when countries still conducted independent national monetary policies. Such *synthetic* variables, which include pre-1999 data, are likely to violate the criteria for valid aggregation. Before 1999, even the definition of an area-wide monetary policy stance is problematic. Hence, the analysis conducted with synthetic area-wide variables, while potentially useful, ought to be validated and cross-checked with other analyses.

Second, at present, the richest statistical data for monetary transmission analysis still refer to national economies, not to the euro area. The European statistical office (Eurostat) and the ECB produce only a limited number of harmonised EMU-wide macro series. Many of these series are built up by collecting information that is released at different points in time for individual countries. Thus, policy-makers out of necessity have to interpret national data as they become available in order to make an early assessment of area-wide conditions. This is further complicated because the national statistics themselves are in many cases heterogeneous, in quality and coverage. This calls for econometric analyses at the country level, tailored to the existing statistics. Thirdly, country-level analyses are also justified by the potential existence of national differences in the transmission mechanism, owing to differences in economic and financial structures.

To balance these concerns, euro area-wide data were analysed to obtain estimates of the aggregate impact of monetary policy. These estimates were compared with estimates using national sources to verify the area-wide figures, and to obtain additional details on the distribution of the effects and on the importance of different transmission channels. Moreover, extensive use of national sources permitted the researchers to exploit their country-specific institutional knowledge.

---

[4] See Issing *et al.* (2001) and the January 1999 issue of the *ECB Monthly Bulletin*.

1.2   *Use of pre-EMU data for post-EMU inference*

All the chapters of this book contain empirical analyses using data *prior* to the introduction of the euro in 1999. The aim is to obtain evidence for which one can claim validity *after* 1999. The changeover to a new currency is a policy regime change of major proportion, to which the 'Lucas critique' which states that changes in policy regimes may alter private economic behaviour forcefully applies; this raises serious potential objections to the validity of the results. One obvious response is that there were, and still are, no alternatives to the use of pre-1999 data for a comprehensive investigation of the euro area monetary transmission process while analysis (let alone monetary policy) cannot wait for long data samples to become available. But this cannot be, and in our view is not, the only answer.

A number of elements support the validity of a selective use of pre-1999 data. First, EMU was a gradual process. It included a prior convergence in policies and economic performance during which economic agents had time to prepare and adjust. Much of this adjustment is likely to have occurred before 1999, but some took place even after the new currency was introduced. Data prior to 1999 are likely to contain early information about the new regime. The use of panel data, extensive in parts 3 and 4 of this book, is intended *inter alia* to reduce the need for a long time-series dimension. Moreover, panel data might help in identifying structural parameters that can be viewed as approximately constant during the transition. Furthermore, the approach taken in the project, to cross-check different sources of evidence using alternative methodologies and data, should be of help. In cases where instability is significant, it is likely to induce different effects on different tests; put differently, in cases where many indicators point in a similar direction this is unlikely to be due to chance, while a finding that different indicators yield different conclusions suggests that more cautious conclusions should be drawn. All this said, it is clear that, as more data from the new regime become available, our results and conclusions will require closer and more intense scrutiny. The findings here should be taken as a tentative benchmark for these future investigations.

1.3   *Choice of data and economic sectors under investigation*

In addition to area-wide and national aggregate data the research team also worked extensively with panel data on banks and non-financial firms. These sectors and this type of data were chosen for several reasons. First, the Eurosystem experts had some comparative advantage in using some of the panel data. One source of advantage arises because some of the data, in the case of the supervisory information on banks, are collected by central banks and not typically available to other scholars. In other cases, such as with the firm panels, the NCB economists had extensive experience working with these data. Bank- and firm-level data happen to be potentially very relevant for the transmission of monetary policy. Commercial banks, as described in chapter 14, play a dominant role in the financing of investment expenditures in the euro area, and a small but increasing one in financing consumption. Moreover, the structure of the euro area banking system (characterised on average by small-sized banks and strong bilateral ties with borrowers) creates potentially the conditions for a bank lending channel to be present. The literature in recent years has repeatedly explored this hypothesis, and has provided partly different answers. In any case, a strong focus on banks in this project was a natural choice. Regarding firms, their role in the transmission of monetary policy – determined essentially by the way pricing and expenditure decisions are influenced by monetary policy via interest rate and financial channels – is clearly also a central one.

A third factor was that some other options that might be equally important simply could not be explored because of data problems. In particular this project provides little information on household responses to monetary policy changes. Neither broadly homogeneous households' data panels (as in the case of banks and firms), nor good aggregate national and area-wide series (for example, separating durable from non-durable consumption) are available in the euro area yet. As these data differ significantly across countries in terms of coverage and definitions, the analysis would have lost much of its comparative content and area-wide relevance.

While the joint use of micro and macro data proved very fruitful in this project, such use was not free of difficulties. Micro data do not respect macroeconomic accounting identities, owing to the differences in data sources and coverage, in collection methods, etc. Making the link between the results coming from different data requires judgement. Explicit discussion of the difficulties involved in making these judgements is contained in the summary chapters bringing together different sources of evidence (see especially chapters 7, 14 and 24).

1.4   Choice of the modelling strategy

The choice of data is sometimes linked to that of model specification: for example, for panel data the set of econometric techniques and model specifications is rather standard. When analysing aggregate macroeconomic series, the choice-set is broader. In particular, structural models,

VARs, and various combinations of semi-structural models have all extensively been used for analysing the transmission mechanism.

We do not wish to enter here into the debate on the relative merits of these models. The empirical VAR literature on monetary transmission published in recent years is so vast, and its role in academic and policy discussions so prominent, that VARs had in any case to be part of a comprehensive research on the transmission mechanism. Accordingly, chapters 2 and 3 examine the VAR properties of the area-wide data (with the US results used as a benchmark) and of the national data.

At the same time, given the data limitations and the pitfalls deriving from structural change, VARs, in which the use of theoretical priors is willingly limited, would not alone constitute a sufficient approach. Structural analysis offers a way to incorporate prior knowledge in a systematic manner. Hence, extensive use was also made of a variety of structural econometric models, for the whole area and for the countries separately (chapters 4, 5 and 24), and their results were compared and cross-checked with the VAR results (mainly in chapter 24).

2   Summary of findings

Three chapters in the book (7, 14 and 24) provide partial summaries of the findings. This section puts in a nutshell the main findings of the whole project, reviewing the macroeconomic evidence first, followed by the micro-firm and the micro-bank evidence. We highlight only the findings which were corroborated by different sources of evidence.

Starting from the macro evidence, the analysis suggests that the basic business cycle properties of the aggregate euro area economy appear remarkably similar to those of the USA (chapter 1). Chapter 2 shows that a number of familiar patterns emerge when a standard VAR is fitted to synthetic euro area data, i.e. a tightening of monetary policy leads to a decline in output with the maximum response between one and two years after the policy change. Output returns towards baseline in the long run, as consistent with monetary neutrality, and prices are estimated to decline gradually, responding much more slowly than output. Several structural models yield similar patterns (chapters 4 and 5). The VAR results confirm the fact that the lags with which monetary policy affects prices are long and uncertain, which suggest that monetary policy should take a medium-term orientation and not engage in fine-tuning.

Besides these similarities, there are also two important differences between the ways in which monetary policy appears to operate in the USA and the euro area. First, the estimated impact of the exchange rate on prices and output seems, in the short run, larger for the euro area than for the USA. However, the role of the exchange rate in the transmission of monetary policy should in our view be discounted because there is much uncertainty about the link between monetary policy and the exchange rate (see the discussion in chapters 5 and 24).

Second, the adjustment of euro area output in the wake of a monetary policy change appears to be primarily driven by investment changes. The evidence for the USA is that monetary policy seems to have (relatively) stronger effects on consumption than investment. This difference is being explored in follow-up work.

The country-level macro analysis follows two complementary approaches. First, chapter 3 analyses the impact of monetary policy in euro area countries prior to 1999, using VAR models that explicitly take into account the different nature of the exchange rate constraint faced by each country within the European Monetary System (EMS). The analysis shows how this constraint can be modelled using three different VAR specifications. Second, chapter 5 reports the results of a coordinated simulation of NCBs of their own country for an EMU-like interest rate shock. Both approaches suggest that the results found for the euro area as a whole by and large correspond with those for the individual countries.

Cross-country comparisons of the magnitude of GDP and prices' responses to interest rate shocks are difficult. Previous studies do not agree on these magnitudes for different euro area countries. The rankings based on the VARs and on structural models also differ somewhat. These differing findings could reflect a lack of statistical power, given the myriad special factors during the recent, short sample periods that are typically studied, or may accurately signal that there are no true differences in the effects of monetary policy across euro area countries. As experience with the single monetary policy accumulates, we expect to be able to much more confidently judge the size of these magnitudes and better determine whether or not policy has asymmetric cross-country effects.

The micro evidence on non-financial firms' investment (chapter 7, drawing on chapters 8–13) provides further insight into the response of investment to monetary policy shifts. In particular, firm-level estimates show that the elasticity of the capital stock with respect to the user cost of capital is significant in Austria, Belgium, France, Germany, Italy, Luxembourg and Spain. The point estimates of the elasticity cluster between -0.1 and -0.5, and essentially all of them are significantly lower (in absolute terms) than -1. These findings are important because the macro evidence had suggested that investment responses accounted for a substantial portion of the adjustment after a monetary policy change.

However, the interest rate effects on investment through the user cost of capital are not the only transmission channel. In most countries, cash flow is also a driver of investment. Cash flow effects tend to be stronger for sub-samples of firms with low collateral values. But there is no single sample split of firms that consistently identifies firms with different cash flow sensitivity of investment in all countries. Moreover, chapters 7 and 24 show that the impact of changes in interest rates on the cash flow of firms is not economically significant in all countries.

There are also a number of recurring patterns regarding the response of the lending behaviour of banks to monetary policy shocks (chapter 14 and the country case studies of chapters 15–23). Aggregate national and bank-level estimates show that the long-run effect of an increase in interest rates is to reduce loan growth in most countries (Finland, France, Germany, Greece, Italy, the Netherlands, Portugal and Spain). While this could reflect either loan demand or loan supply, subsequent tests suggest that, in most countries, loan-supply shifts are contributing to this decline.

However, loan-supply effects differ from those that have been shown for the USA. The key factor in Europe seems to be whether banks are holding high or low levels of liquid assets. The banks with more liquid asset holdings show weaker loan adjustments in the wake of changes to the short-term interest rate. But, in contrast to the USA, monetary policy does not have stronger effects on the lending of small banks, or banks with low ratios of capital to assets in most of the European countries studied. These findings could be attributable to a number of the structural characteristics of European banking markets. In particular, the importance of banks' networks, state guarantees and public ownership is likely to weaken the importance of bank size and capitalisation (these aspects are discussed in chapter 14) as determinants of loan-supply shifts in the business cycle.

The overall judgement that emerges concerning the role of financial factors generally, and of the bank lending channel in particular, in the transmission of monetary policy is mixed. On the one hand, the joint reading of the micro and macro evidence (chapter 24) suggests that, both in the euro area and in the majority of the component countries, the classic 'interest rate channel' is sufficient to explain the broad patterns of the responses of the economy to monetary policy. From this viewpoint, the observed pro-cyclical patterns of several monetary and credit aggregates could be interpreted as largely demand-driven. On the other hand, the micro estimates, as we have seen, support the idea that there are systematic cash flow effects on firms' expenditures and that bank lending supply amplifies, at least to some extent and for some types of banks, the effects of monetary policy changes. This suggests that, at least when certain categories of banks meet certain categories of borrowers, financial factors and lending constraints are likely play a role. This evidence could be seen as supportive of an active role of bank balance sheet aggregates in the transmission of monetary policy.

Finally, chapter 6, written by a Bank of England team led by Charlie Bean, was commissioned specifically for the December 2001 conference. This chapter is the only one that does not focus on the euro area, but provides additional perspectives and elements of comparison for the other results presented in the book. Chapter 25 contains an edited transcript of the concluding discussion of the December 2001 conference, with interventions, among others, by Ben Bernanke, Xavier Freixas, Ben Friedman, Vítor Gaspar, Jürgen von Hagen and Christopher Sims. Finally, chapter 26 brings together various pieces of statistical information on the economic and financial structures in the euro area, used as background during the course of the work.

Each chapter in this book is signed by the author, or group of authors, mainly responsible for the analysis and the draft contribution. However, much more than is usually the case in edited volumes, each chapter was subject to intense scrutiny and peer review by the overall team that participated in the project. The summary chapters, in particular, were discussed and reviewed many times. The version in which they appear now is, to a large extent, the result of collective ideas and contribution.

3   Directions for future research

Most findings in this book call for further investigation and confirmation, particularly when longer data samples and richer statistics for the euro area become available. Moreover, there are many aspects that the project, owing to a lack of time or data, left open for the future.

A major area that clearly calls for further work relates to the response of private consumption to monetary policy. The tentative evidence and inference presented in chapter 24 suggests that the response of European consumers to monetary policy changes may be different – and on the whole more muted – than that of the consumers in the USA. Why do the USA and Europe seem to differ with respect to consumption behaviour? Is it a structural difference – linked, for example, to intertemporal preferences, and hence possibly long-lasting – or is it due to other less fundamental and more transient factors? Is convergence to be expected?

A second critical question is why inflation seems to respond so sluggishly to policy shifts. From where do these patterns of persistence originate? Are they more relevant in some countries than in others, and if so, why? Will the present patterns of inflation persistence continue now that a single currency is used across the whole euro area?

Finally, the analysis of euro area monetary transmission will use more and more post-1999 data. Initially, such investigation will concentrate on banking and financial markets, for which high-frequency data exist. Later on, the empirical analysis can gradually be extended to other sectors. It should be of particular interest to look for any changes that may have occurred as a result of the policy regime shift, which may provide a test for the empirical relevance of arguments based on the Lucas critique.

4   Organisation of the research team

The team of researchers who carried out this work, called the 'Monetary Transmission Network', included Ignazio Angeloni, Michael Ehrmann, Reint Gropp, Benoît Mojon, Frank Smets and Philip Vermeulen (ECB); Anil Kashyap (University of Chicago Graduate School of Business and NBER); Paul Butzen and Catherine Fuss (Banque Nationale de Belgique); Heinz Herrmann, Ulf von Kalckreuth and Andreas Worms (Deutsche Bundesbank); Ignacio Hernando and Jorge Martinez-Pagés (Banco de España); Jean-Bernard Chatelain (then at the Banque de France and now at LEO, Université d'Orléans and CEPREMAP), Claire Loupias and André Tiomo (Banque de France); Patrick Sevestre (Banque de France and Université Paris XII Val-de-Marne); Sophocles Brissimis (Bank of Greece and University of Piraeus), Nicos Kamberoglou and George Simigiannis (Bank of Greece); Don Bredin and Gerard O'Reilly (Central Bank of Ireland); Eugenio Gaiotti, Leonardo Gambacorta, Andrea Generale and Daniele Terlizzese (Banca d'Italia); Patrick Lünnemann and Thomas Mathä (Banque centrale du Luxembourg); Leo de Haan (De Nederlandsche Bank); Sylvia Kaufmann and Maria Valderrama (Oesterreichische Nationalbank); Luísa Farinha and Carlos Robalo Marques (Banco de Portugal); Jukka Topi and Jouko Vilmunen (Suomen Pankki). The views expressed in the book should not be attributed to the institution to which the authors are affiliated.

In addition, the following persons participated in one or more meetings: Luigi Guiso (University of Sassari and Ente Einaudi); Jeremy Stein (Harvard University); Raf Wouters and Annick Bruggeman (Banque Nationale de Belgique); Fred Ramb (Deutsche Bundesbank); Gert Peersman (then an intern at the ECB and now at the Bank of England); Juan Ayuso (Banco de España); Anna-Maria Agresti, Gabe de Bondt, Jaak Claessens and Julian Morgan (ECB); Rolf Strauch (then at the Deutsche Bundesbank and now at the ECB); Dario Focarelli, Francesco Lippi and Fabio Panetta (Banca d'Italia); Sandrine Scheller (Banque centrale du Luxembourg); Ad Stokman and Marga Peeters (De Nerdelandsche Bank); and Bernardino Adao (Banco de Portugal).

All participants worked part-time on the project. Ten plenary meetings were held, as well as a number of other smaller or bilateral meetings. Team members communicated mainly by e-mail and using a dedicated intranet website). The editors of this book acted, respectively, as Chairman of the team (Ignazio Angeloni), consultant on the research strategy and on the contacts with the academic community (Anil Kashyap), and head of the Secretariat in charge of the organisation (Benoît Mojon).

In the final stage of the project, the MTN availed itself of the contribution of another group of Eurosystem researchers, the Working Group on Econometric Modelling (chaired by Gabriel Fagan, ECB), which contributed the set of results based on structural econometric models presented in chapter 5. Peter McAdam and Julian Morgan (ECB) prepared a complementary chapter on the simulation of monetary policy shocks in structural models (chapter 4).

Part 1

Macroeconometric evidence on the transmission mechanism in the euro area

1   Some stylised facts on the euro area business cycle

A.-M. Agresti and B. Mojon

1   Introduction

There is a long tradition of describing the main regularities in the economic fluctuations by reporting the standard deviations and cross-correlations of de-trended macroeconomic time series. Economists, originally mostly contributors to the Real Business Cycle (RBC) research programme, have then used these cyclical properties as benchmarks to discriminate across competing theoretical models. Against this background, the cyclical properties of the US economy (Stock and Watson, 1999) and other OECD countries (Baxter, 1995) are well documented. On the contrary, no study has yet described systematically the cyclical properties of the euro area.

This chapter fills this gap by compiling the moments of de-trended euro area macroeconomic time series. For comparison, we also report similar statistics for the USA and for euro area countries.[1]

We find that the cyclical properties of the euro area and the USA are surprisingly similar in mainly three respects: the magnitude of the fluctuations in consumption, investment, prices, inflation, interest rate and monetary aggregates relative to the fluctuations of GDP; the patterns of cross-correlation of GDP components, prices and interest rates with respect to GDP; and the persistence of GDP and of prices.

We also describe the high synchronicity of national cycles and the euro area aggregate cycle. This synchronicity is observed for the main GDP components as well as for the short-term interest rate. It is particularly high for the largest countries of the euro area and for Austria, Belgium and the Netherlands, which belonged to the core ERM.

The authors are extremely grateful to Alistair Dieppe and Jérôme Henry for providing us the data from the euro area AWM, as well as for sharing their procedures to built historical series for the national account variables; and to Don Bredin, Sophocles Brissimis, Raf Wouters and Luisa Farinha for providing us with quarterly national account data for respectively Ireland, Greece, Belgium and Portugal.
[1] There are no quarterly national accounts available for Luxembourg and Irish quarterly national account data are available for too small a sample period.

The analysis is conducted in five steps. We explain how we de-trend the data in section 2. Section 3 briefly reviews the data we use and describes how the area-wide data are constructed. In section 4, we evaluate the synchronicity of the euro area aggregate cycle with the national cycles and compare the cyclical properties of euro area synthetic data constructed with different aggregation approaches. In section 5, we compare the euro area and US business cycles. Section 6 concludes.

2   Our favourite filter for the European macroeconomic time series

To facilitate a comparison with Stock and Watson's (1999) comprehensive study of the US business cycle, we de-trended our data using a band pass filter developed by Baxter and King (1999) (BK). As Stock and Watson note this transformation keeps 'those movements in the series associated with periodicity within a certain range of business cycle duration'.[2] We slightly deviate from Stock and Watson in two respects.

First, we allow the upper bound on the length of the business cycle to be forty quarters (ten years) instead of thirty-two (eight years). We see several reasons why this seems reasonable. To begin, the associated trend we extract is less likely to have a cyclical pattern (Rotemberg, 2002). In addition, while Stock and Watson refer to the NBER business cycle reference dates whereby most cycles from trough to trough experienced by the US economy last between eighteen months and eight years, the euro area only saw three recessions since 1970. And actually, the intervals between the last three US recessions, which took place in 1982, 1991 and 2001, lasted for about ten years. Hence, we felt it was appropriate to include 'frequencies' as low as ten years into our 'business cycle component'. Finally, the spectral densities of GDP growth quarterly time series, reported in figures 1.1 and 1.2, indicates that the peak of the variance has shifted lower when the sample is extended to the second part of the 1990s.[3]

Our second deviation from Stock and Watson is to truncate the band pass filter at eight leads and lags (instead of twelve for Baxter and King and Stock and Watson). As many of the series we consider start only in the 1980s or the mid-1970s, we thought we could not afford a twelve leads and lags truncation because it would mean losing six years of data. The

---

[2] See appendix 2 in Agresti and Mojon (2001) for a brief discussion on recent literature on filtering and a description of the Baxter and King band pass filter.

[3] These spectral densities were estimated with a Bartlett window of width 8. We thank Luca Sala for providing these estimates.

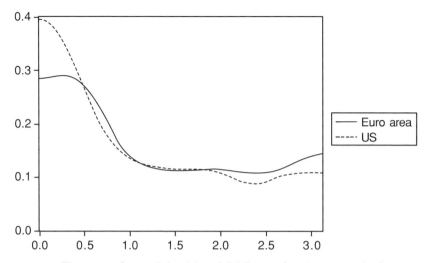

Figure 1.1 Spectral densities of GDP growth, 1970–2000, in the euro area and the USA

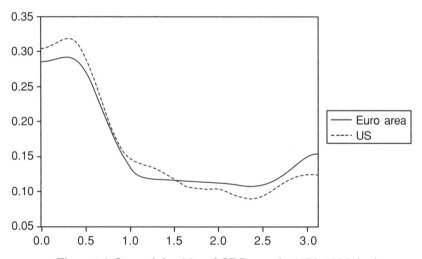

Figure 1.2 Spectral densities of GDP growth, 1970–1995, in the euro area and the USA

sensitivity analysis in Agresti and Mojon (2001) presents the effects of these two deviations from the Stock and Watson version of the Baxter and King filter and also compares the outcome with the Hodrick–Prescott filter applied to the a sub-set of macroeconomic time series. Section 5 also reports robustness checks of some of our results with regards to the method used to de-trend the series.

3   Data

We analyse the business cycle components of twenty-four series for the euro area aggregate and the USA.[4] The variables[5] belong to six main categories: GDP components and other activity indicators such as industrial production and unemployment, price level indices, money and credit aggregates, market and retail bank interest rates, exchange rate and asset prices. At the level of euro area member countries, the analysis is limited to GDP, consumption, investment and short-term interest rates.

Euro area variables are actually euro area aggregates (euro area less Greece, which joined EMU in 2001). These variables come from the current version of the Euro Area Wide model (AWM), which has been constructed by the staff of the Econometric Modelling Division of the ECB. The aggregation has been done with fixed weights, based on 1995 PPP GDP.[6] As a robustness check we also report results series for GDP and the GDP deflator that are aggregated using exchange rate based variable weights as in Beyer, Doornik and Hendry (2001).

All series, except the unemployment rate and interest rates, have been transformed into logarithms before being filtered. The availability and the quality of the data on which the euro area aggregates are based differs from country to country. For instance, a majority of series is available back to 1970, while monetary aggregate series and retail bank interest rates are available only back to 1980. But there are exceptions to these general rules. An exhaustive report of the exact sources and time coverage for each time series is given in the appendix of this chapter.

---

[4] We are grateful to Jérôme Henry and to Alistair Dieppe, of the Econometric Modelling Division of the ECB, for giving us their data for the euro area aggregates and for sharing their procedures to built historical series for the national account variables.

[5] Availability and source are listed in appendix 2 in Agresti and Mojon (2001).

[6] For euro area variables, a complete description of the methodology and the variables used to construct the AWM database is in annex 2 of Fagan, Henry and Mestre (2001). This paper represents the current version of the area-wide model for the euro area that has been developed by the ECB staff in the Econometric Modelling Division.

4   The business cycle in the euro area

4.1   Business cycles of the euro area and EMU countries

We briefly review the correlations of each national business cycle with the aggregate euro area cycle. There are already many studies that have addressed this issue with various methodologies,[7] and reviewing them all is beyond the scope of this chapter.

We just want to stress that Forni and Reichlin (2001) have shown that when the business cycle of European regions is decomposed into a European component, a national component and a regional component, the European component had a larger role than the national ones. The share of the European regions' GDP variance that is explained by the common European business cycle range between 40 and 60 per cent for most countries of the euro area (Portugal and Greece being the exception) while the share of the national components range between 20 and 35 per cent. The rest of the variance is driven by the regions' idiosyncratic components.

To explore these issues further, we report the cross-correlations of the country cycles and the euro area aggregate cycle. We focus on four variables: GDP, consumption, investment and the short-term interest rate.

As can be seen in panel A of table 1.1, the contemporaneous correlations of euro area and national GDP are relatively high, between 0.7 and 0.92 for most of the countries. For Greece, Portugal and Finland, the correlation drops to around 0.4. Panels B and C report similar measures for respectively consumption and investment. Both consumption and investment of most European countries is highly correlated with euro area consumption or investment. Panel D shows the fairly high correlations between short-term interest rates in the euro area.

Two additional results of table 1.1 are worth stressing. First, the high correlations between national GDP, consumption, investment and interest rates with respect to their euro area counterparts do not merely reflect an international business cycle. The last three columns of each

---

[7] First, empirical studies on optimal currency areas have compiled the country pair-wise cross-correlation of VAR-based supply and demand shocks. For a survey of this literature, see Bayoumi and Eichengreen (1996). Second, some studies aim at characterising a European business cycle by weighting countries; business cycles. A recent example of this line of research is the paper of Altissimo *et al.* (2001). The authors apply dynamic factor models to selected series from the six largest euro area countries, and obtain an indicator that tracks the euro area GDP relatively closely. See also Artis, Krolzig and Toro (1999). Third, the literature on international business cycles has produced a number of results on the synchronicity of European business cycles. See for instance the references in Baxter (1995).

Table 1.1 *Synchronicity of fluctuations for selected variables of the Euro area countries*

	Panel A											
	St. dev			Cross-correlation								
	absolute	relative		with euro area GDP $(t + k)$					with GDP (t)			
GDP (t) of		GDP	euro area	k	−4	−1	0	1	4	own	euro area	US
euro area	0.90	1	0.9		−0.20	0.89	1.00	0.89	−0.18	1.00	1.00	0.47
DE	1.06	1	1.0		−0.29	0.69	0.88	0.88	0.06	1.00	0.87	0.57
FR	079	1	0.7		−0.18	0.81	0.89	0.76	−0.18	1.00	0.88	0.36
IT	1.41	1	1.3		−0.18	0.86	0.92	0.76	−0.36	1.00	0.91	0.38
ES	0.85	1	0.8		0.13	0.74	0.71	0.56	−0.15	1.00	0.71	0.18
BE	0.90	1	0.9		−0.14	0.75	0.89	0.84	−0.03	1.00	0.88	0.26
NL	0.65	1	0.7		0.03	0.66	0.69	0.58	0.04	1.00	0.72	0.59
FI	1.42	1	1.3		−0.17	0.37	0.46	0.48	0.31	1.00	0.45	0.21
AT	0.84	1	0.8		0.17	0.72	0.70	0.55	−0.07	1.00	0.69	−0.17
PT	1.08	1	1.0		0.36	0.41	0.40	0.35	0.09	1.00	0.35	−0.45
GR	1.04	1	1.0		0.22	0.44	0.39	0.27	−0.27	1.00	0.35	−0.45
Countries av.*	**1.00**	**1**	**1.0**		**0.00**	**0.64**	**0.69**	**0.60**	**−0.06**	**1.00**	**0.68**	**0.15**
USA	1.35	1	1.5		−0.34	0.25	0.48	0.60	0.29	1.00	0.47	1.00

	Panel B											
	St. dev			Cross-correlation								
	absolute	relative		with euro area investment $(t + k)$					with GDP (t)			
Investment (t) of		GDP	euro area	k	−4	−1	0	1	4	own	euro area	US
euro area	1.99	2.2	1.0		0.05	0.92	1.00	0.92	0.07	1.00	0.86	0.31
DE	2.41	2.3	1.2		−0.27	0.60	0.78	0.82	0.24	0.81	0.67	0.50
FR	2.12	2.7	1.1		0.00	0.75	0.84	0.78	0.10	0.87	0.82	0.30
IT	2.78	2.0	1.4		0.34	0.91	0.86	0.67	−0.19	0.76	0.75	0.22
ES	2.95	3.5	1.5		0.10	0.66	0.72	0.66	0.08	0.82	0.75	0.22
BE	2.62	2.9	1.3		0.17	0.52	0.52	0.45	0.21	0.52	0.57	0.33
NL	2.01	3.1	1.0		0.44	0.52	0.39	0.22	−0.06	0.62	0.50	0.29
FI	4.36	3.1	2.2		0.06	0.56	0.58	0.52	0.13	0.81	0.45	−0.05
AT	2.48	2.9	1.2		0.05	0.52	0.58	0.54	0.05	0.68	0.47	0.06
PT	4.40	4.1	2.2		0.40	0.58	0.42	0.21	−0.22	0.70	0.30	−0.32
GR	2.72	2.6	1.4		0.32	0.26	0.18	0.10	0.15	0.19	0.33	0.29
Countries av.*	**2.88**	**2.9**	**1.4**		**0.16**	**0.59**	**0.59**	**0.50**	**0.05**	**0.68**	**0.63**	**0.26**
USA	4.19	3.1	2.1		−0.08	0.19	0.22	0.22	0.14	−0.40	−0.33	−0.40

Table 1.1 *(cont.)*

Panel C

Consumption (t) of	St. dev absolute	St. dev relative GDP	St. dev relative euro area	k	Cross-correlation with euro area consumption $(t+k)$ −4	−1	0	1	4	with GDP (t) own	euro area	US
euro area	0.59	0.7	1.0		0.08	0.92	1.00	0.92	0.09	1.00	0.79	0.35
DE	0.78	0.7	1.3		0.07	0.57	0.69	0.72	0.32	0.60	0.29	0.29
FR	0.81	1.0	1.4		−0.31	0.44	0.62	0.68	0.28	0.59	0.42	0.35
IT	1.11	0.8	1.9		0.20	0.84	0.80	0.62	−0.21	0.80	0.83	0.23
ES	0.85	1.0	1.4		0.13	0.74	0.71	0.56	−0.15	0.75	0.71	0.16
BE	0.72	0.8	1.2		−0.01	0.57	0.71	0.74	0.29	0.69	0.70	−0.16
NL	0.96	1.5	1.6		0.45	0.64	0.58	0.48	0.17	0.49	0.50	0.03
FI	1.31	0.9	2.2		−0.31	0.24	0.39	0.47	0.33	0.79	0.52	−0.01
AT	0.93	1.1	1.6		0.14	0.47	0.41	0.26	−0.29	0.61	0.35	−0.20
PT	1.51	1.4	2.6		0.64	0.44	0.33	0.22	−0.14	0.50	0.05	−0.56
GR	1.07	1.0	1.8		−0.08	0.18	0.22	0.21	0.10	0.72	0.05	−0.56
Countries av.[*]	**1.01**	**1.0**	**1.7**		**0.09**	**0.51**	**0.55**	**0.50**	**0.07**	**0.65**	**0.44**	**−0.04**
USA	1.03	0.8	1.7		−0.36	0.20	0.35	0.44	0.24	0.85	0.32	0.85

Panel D

Short-term rate (t) of	St. dev absolute	St. dev relative GDP	St. dev relative euro area	k	Cross-correlation with euro area short-term rate $(t+k)$ −4	−1	0	1	4	with GDP (t) own	euro area	US
euro area	1.18	1.3	1.0		−0.28	0.87	1.00	0.87	−0.26	1.00	0.61	0.15
DE	1.47	1.4	1.2		−0.38	0.58	0.81	0.87	0.19	0.55	0.65	0.39
FR	1.44	1.8	1.2		−0.14	0.90	0.94	0.73	−0.45	0.51	0.51	0.04
IT	1.81	1.3	1.5		−0.16	0.74	0.80	0.63	−0.40	0.57	0.38	−0.17
ES	1.62	1.9	1.4		−0.12	0.92	0.87	0.58	−0.66	0.19	−0.11	−0.09
BE	0.79	0.9	0.7		−0.07	0.57	0.56	0.46	−0.07	0.32	0.22	0.22
NL	1.38	2.1	1.2		0.19	0.60	0.55	0.42	−0.19	0.30	0.36	−0.03
FI	1.39	1.0	1.2		−0.21	0.55	0.64	0.63	0.16	0.32	0.37	−0.11
AT	1.03	1.2	0.9		0.24	0.75	0.71	0.57	−0.05	0.05	0.22	0.12
PT	0.71	0.7	0.6		0.01	0.49	0.56	0.54	0.13	0.53	0.69	−0.21
GR	0.55	0.5	0.5		−0.05	−0.55	−0.53	−0.41	0.10	−0.37	−0.35	0.03
Countries av.[*]	**1.19**	**1.3**	**1.0**		**−0.04**	**0.55**	**0.57**	**0.46**	**−0.16**	**0.36**	**0.32**	**0.03**
USA	1.40	1.0	1.2		−0.48	0.01	0.25	0.42	0.40	0.48	0.51	0.48

Notes: Standard deviation of and cross-correlation between the business cycle component (BCC) of individual time series (GDP, Consumption, investment and three-month interest rate of the countries). The BCC was obtained from a band pass filter BPF(6,40,8) *à la* Baxter and King (1999) as described in appendix 1 of Agresti and Mojon (2001). The euro area synthetic data, which were built for the ECB AWM, are aggregates of the eleven countries that initially adopted the euro, in January 1999. The series have not yet been backdated to include Greece, which joined the monetary union in January 2001.

[*] Average of country values with 1995 PPP GDP weights.

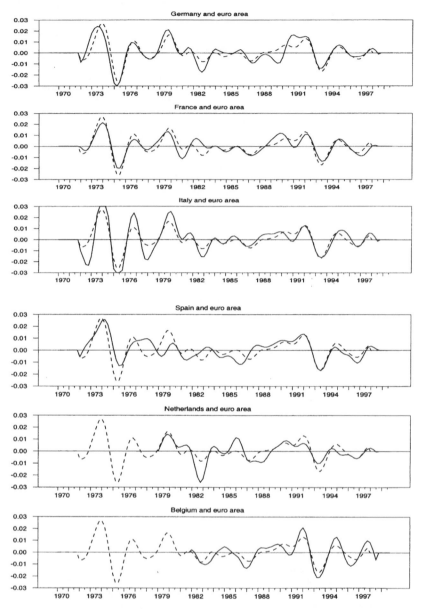

Figure 1.3 Business cycle component (using a Baxter and King (6,40,8) filter) of GDP for EMU countries (solid line) and the euro area (dotted line), 1973–1997

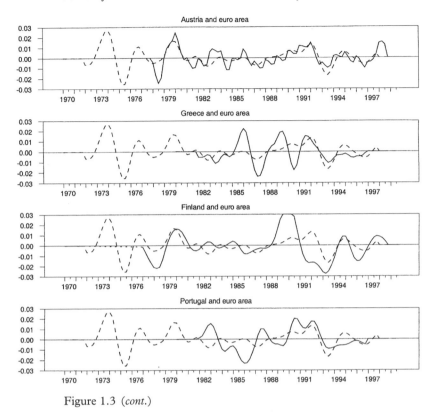

Figure 1.3 (*cont.*)

panel show that the correlation of national cycles with the US business cycle, albeit positive for most countries, is markedly smaller than the ones observed with the euro area cycle.

Secondly, the US norm of consumption being less volatile than GDP and investment being more volatile does not hold for all countries. This puzzling finding, which can partly be explained by the fact that private consumption includes durable consumption is, however, not unusual. Baxter (1995) reports that consumption fluctuations are larger than GDP fluctuations for Japan and for the UK and nearly as large for France.

We now turn to a graphical description of the cyclical components of national and euro area GDP series (figure 1.3). It is particularly interesting to stress some specific periods where each country deviated from the rest of the euro area. For example, during the German reunification, the German cycle diverged significantly from the euro area one. In

France, the most striking deviation occurred around the fiscal expansion undertaken after the 1981 elections. The Spanish business cycle appears to 'converge' with the area cycle after 1986, the date when Spain joined the European Community (EC). The Finnish financial deregulation of the second part of the 1980s and the trade shock after the collapse of the Soviet Union mark the largest deviations of the Finnish business cycle. Italy, although highly synchronised with the area business cycle throughout the sample period, experienced much larger fluctuations in the 1970s. This is probably due to the heavy Italian reliance on imported oil. The Italian fluctuations subsequently decreased as the share of energy-related imports declined dramatically during the 1980s.

Altogether, this evidence suggests that the national and the euro area business cycles are fairly synchronised. Wynne and Koo (2000) have nevertheless stressed that the cross-correlation between the business cycles (of GDP, of prices or of employment) of the twelve US Federal Reserve districts are still much higher than the cross-correlation of the business cycles of the fifteen EU countries. Unfortunately we do not have data to carry out this comparison with the Federal Reserve districts before they integrated a formal monetary union at the beginning of the twentieth century. As conjectured by Bentoglio, Fayolle and Lemoine (2001), the monetary union could lead to an increase in the synchronicity of the business cycle of countries participating in EMU.[8]

4.2   Aggregation

We now show evidence that the aggregation method chosen to build euro area aggregates has only second-order implications for the business cycle properties of the euro area GDP. As discussed in section 3, the aggregation of country macroeconomic variables into euro area aggregates is based on summing national growth rates with weights that are proportional to PPP GDP in 1995. The major drawback of this approach to aggregation is that it may introduce distortions in periods of large changes in 'intra-euro area' exchange rates. Another aggregation approach, using weights that vary over time with the exchange rates, has been proposed by Beyer, Doornik and Hendry (2001) (BDH aggregation in table 1.2).

---

[8] Bentoglio, Fayolle and Lemoine (2001) show that interest shocks tended to be asymmetric across countries in the period prior to EMU. Mojon and Peersman (chapter 3 in this volume) also show that the monetary policy shocks were asymmetric across countries in the early 1990s, especially around the EMS crisis. Angeloni and Dedola (1999) show that the synchronicity between European countries business cycles has increased over time. Finally, Frankel and Rose (2001) show that monetary unions have a stimulating impact on trade among its members.

Table 1.2 *Cyclical properties of the alternative synthetic euro area macroeconomic time series, 1970–2000*

variables (t)	St. dev		Cross-correlation with GDP ($t + k$)								
	absolute	relative/GDP	k	−4	−3	−2	−1	0	1	2	3	4
Alternative aggregations											
GDP, AWM[a], 80:99	0.61	0.7		−0.01	0.30	0.64	0.90	1.00	0.90	0.63	0.29	−0.01
GDP, BDH[b], 80:99	0.62	0.7		−0.04	0.28	0.62	0.88	0.99	0.90	0.65	0.32	0.03
GDP deflator (level) AWM	0.67	0.5		0.00	−0.16	−0.31	−0.42	−0.48	−0.49	−0.46	−0.42	−0.39
GDP deflator (level), BDH	0.45	0.5		0.10	0.05	−0.02	−0.11	−0.21	−0.33	−0.44	−0.53	−0.57
Other economic activity indicators											
Industrial production	1.57	1.9		−0.18	0.16	0.52	0.82	0.96	0.89	0.66	0.35	0.03
Unemployment	4.66	5.6		−0.24	−0.55	−0.79	−0.89	−0.81	−0.58	−0.26	0.08	0.34

Note: See table 1.1.

[a] AWM refers to the Area Wide Model where the aggregation is based on fixed weights as in Fagan, Henry and Mestre (2001).

[b] BDH Aggregation based on variable weights as proposed by Beyer, Dooornik and Hendry (2001).

Table 1.2 shows the cross-correlation of the band pass filtered euro area GDPs obtained with the two alternative aggregation methods over the sample period from 1980 to 1999 with the benchmark euro area GDP filter for the full sample of the last thirty years. It also reports their respective standard deviations. Both the standard deviation and the cross-correlations of the two measures of euro area GDP indicate that the type of weights used in the aggregation have a very small impact on the business cycle fluctuations of the aggregate. This is also reflected in the similarity of the standard deviation and the cross-correlation *vis-à-vis* GDP of the GDP deflator, aggregated following the two methods.

Hence the business cycle properties of the euro area aggregates do not depend on the aggregation method (either fixed or variable exchange rates-based weights to country time series) used to construct these aggregates.[9] This conclusion is further supported by Labhard, Weeken and Westaway (2001), who compared time-series analyses of the euro area economy based on alternative aggregation methods.

Finally table 1.2 also reports evidence of the very high correlation of the euro area GDP aggregate with two other key indicators of economic activity: industrial production and the unemployment rate. Following Stock and Watson (1999), we take this result as a confirmation that euro area GDP is a good benchmark to describe the cyclical properties of other euro area macroeconomic variables.

5   Comparing the euro area and the US business cycle

5.1   *Euro area and* US *growth and business cycle*

To start with, we compare the movements in GDP for the euro area with those for the USA. The average annual GDP growth in the USA from 1970 to 1999 is slightly higher (3.3 per cent against 2.7 per cent). However, for the same period, the growth of the population has been much larger in the USA (34 per cent in total or nearly 1 per cent per annum) than in the euro area (11 per cent in total or 0.3 per cent per annum).

The spectral density of the euro area GDP growth reaches its peak for cycles of five years duration, while for the USA the maximum is reached

---

[9] Actually, the aggregate euro area series built with the two aggregation methods can differ only if major growth or inflation asymmetries across countries have taken place at the time of the largest intra-exchange rate fluctuations. Moreover, these asymmetries should occur for large enough countries to be noticeable at the level of euro area aggregates.

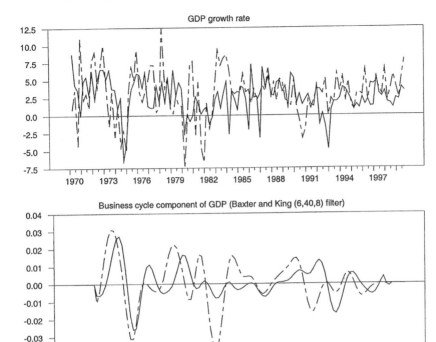

Figure 1.4 Business cycle in the euro area (solid line) and in the USA (dotted line), 1973–1997

at zero frequencies (figure 1.1).[10] The common wisdom, that Europe is less cyclical than the USA (Forni and Reichlin, 2001), is based on sample periods that (as shown in figure 1.2) do not include the second half of the 1990s. As shown in figure 1.4, which reports the growth rate of GDP and the its business cycle component as obtained by the Baxter and King band pass filter, economic activity in the USA has recently been less cyclical than in the euro area and less cyclical than it used to be.[11]

Figure 1.4 also shows the sequence of long periods of increases and short periods of declines of output that characterises these two economies. There are some similarities in the timing of their cyclical patterns as well. They both fell into recession between 1973 and 1975 and the two US

[10] We still obtain a peak at zero frequency when the spectral density is computed on a time series of GDP spanning from 1970 to 2002 Q2, i.e. when including the 2001 US recession.
[11] McConnell and Perez-Quiros (2000) have already described this result.

Table 1.3 Cyclical properties of the euro area, 1970–2000

variables (t)		St. dev		Cross-correlation with GDP (t + k)								
		absolute	relative/GDP	k −4	−3	−2	−1	0	1	2	3	4
GDP	1	0.84	1.0	−0.19	0.18	0.58	0.88	1.00	0.80	0.66	0.40	0.09
Consumption	2	0.55	0.7	−0.13	0.09	0.37	0.63	0.79	0.75	0.51	0.21	−0.09
Investment	3	1.85	2.2	0.06	0.34	0.62	0.81	0.86	−0.19	−0.52	−0.70	−0.70
Cumulated inventories	4	2.40	2.9	0.65	0.83	0.82	0.59	0.22	−0.55	−0.72	−0.76	−0.67
GDP deflator (level)	5	0.58	0.7	0.29	0.27	0.16	−0.04	−0.30	−0.50	−0.66	−0.72	−0.66
CPI (level)	6	0.68	0.8	0.28	0.26	0.16	−0.03	−0.26	−0.52	−0.67	−0.73	−0.66
CPI (inflation)	7	0.31	0.4	0.35	0.34	0.27	0.21	0.20	0.26	0.31	0.30	0.19
Stock prices	8	12.00	0.1	−0.10	−0.07	−0.01	0.05	0.08	0.06	0.01	−0.03	−0.02
Real estate prices	9	1.36	1.6	0.53	0.52	0.50	0.45	0.39	0.31	0.20	0.06	−0.08
Short-term rate nominal	10	1.09	1.3	0.27	0.54	0.73	0.76	0.61	0.30	−0.08	−0.43	−0.67
Short-term rate real	11	0.76	0.9	0.49	0.65	0.68	0.55	0.26	−0.11	−0.43	−0.61	−0.59
Long-term rate nominal	12	0.57	0.7	0.22	0.38	0.48	0.47	0.33	0.09	−0.17	−0.37	−0.46
Yield curve	13	0.83	1.0	−0.20	−0.45	−0.63	−0.68	−0.58	−0.34	−0.01	0.32	0.56
Real ef. exchange rate	14	3.58	4.3	0.22	0.33	0.36	0.30	0.17	0.01	−0.12	−0.18	−0.18
DM–USD exchange rate	15	5.23	6.2	0.13	0.36	0.56	0.61	0.48	0.22	−0.08	−0.34	−0.46
M1	16	1.00	1.2	−0.22	−0.26	−0.20	−0.05	0.16	0.39	0.58	0.68	0.67
M3	17	0.72	0.9	0.45	0.23	0.01	−0.17	−0.26	−0.27	−0.19	−0.06	0.07
Total loans	18	0.85	1.0	0.59	0.55	0.48	0.37	0.23	0.10	0.00	−0.06	−0.08
				Cross-correlation with own (t + k)								
CPI (level)	19	0.68	0.8	0.33	0.55	0.77	0.94	1.00				
GDP deflator	20	0.31	0.4	0.27	0.50	0.74	0.93	1.00				

Note: See table 1.1.

Table 1.4 Cyclical properties of the USA, 1970–2000

variables (t)		St. dev		Cross-correlation with GDP (t + k)								
		absolute	relative/GDP	k −4	−3	−2	−1	0	1	2	3	4
GDP	1	1.34	1.0	−0.09	0.24	0.60	0.89	1.00	0.89	0.59	0.23	−0.09
Consumption	2	1.01	0.8	−0.24	0.03	0.34	0.64	0.84	0.87	0.74	0.51	0.27
Investment	3	3.26	2.4	0.11	0.44	0.75	0.94	0.95	0.80	0.53	0.20	−0.10
Cumulated inventories	4	2.35	1.8	0.74	0.89	0.88	0.69	0.35	−0.02	−0.32	−0.48	−0.48
GDP deflator (level)	5	0.67	0.5	0.00	−0.16	−0.31	−0.42	−0.48	−0.49	−0.46	−0.42	−0.39
CPI (level)	6	1.02	0.8	0.23	0.10	−0.07	−0.24	−0.41	−0.52	−0.56	−0.54	−0.49
CPI (inflation)	7	1.29	1.0	0.48	0.59	0.63	0.56	0.38	0.15	−0.09	−0.25	−0.31
Stock prices	8	7.92	5.9	−0.50	−0.50	−0.37	−0.12	0.16	0.39	0.47	0.40	0.22
Real estate prices	9	2.12	1.6	−0.18	−0.21	−0.16	−0.06	0.08	0.21	0.24	0.17	0.03
Short-term rate nominal	10	1.31	1.0	0.38	0.56	0.68	0.67	0.50	0.21	−0.14	−0.44	−0.62
Short-term rate real	11	1.11	0.8	−0.11	−0.03	0.07	0.14	0.15	0.07	−0.06	−0.22	−0.36
Long-term rate nominal	12	0.82	0.6	−0.03	0.14	0.28	0.35	0.30	0.14	−0.07	−0.28	−0.41
Yield curve	13	0.90	0.7	−0.51	−0.60	−0.63	−0.56	−0.39	−0.15	0.12	0.33	0.45
Real ef. exchange rate	14	2.96	2.2	0.08	0.11	0.08	0.00	−0.07	−0.12	−0.12	−0.08	−0.01
DM–USD exchange rate	15	6.66	5.0	0.19	0.23	0.23	0.23	0.27	0.37	0.45	0.42	0.27
M1	16	1.78	1.3	−0.22	−0.23	−0.18	−0.08	0.05	0.16	0.22	0.24	0.22
M3	17	0.87	0.7	0.25	0.37	0.42	0.39	0.28	0.12	−0.03	−0.13	−0.15
Total loans	18	1.99	1.5	0.75	0.78	0.68	0.48	0.19	−0.11	−0.34	−0.45	−0.45
				Cross correlation with own (t + k)								
CPI (level)	19	1.02	0.8	0.38	0.61	0.81	0.95	1.00				
GDP deflator	20	1.29	1.0	0.35	0.58	0.80	0.95	1.00				

Note: See table 1.1.

recessions of the early 1980s are mirrored by a slowdown in the euro area. There was some divergence in the 1990s, as the American recession in 1991 during the Gulf War did not coincide with a slowdown in the euro area (which was buoyed by the fiscal stimulus in Germany following reunification). However, 1993 was the most severe recession of the post-Second World era for many European countries.

The phases of the two growth cycles are quite similar. The US business fluctuations are more volatile for most of the sample period. The standard deviation of the US GDP business cycle fluctuations is 50 per cent higher than the euro area one. However this seems to have changed after 1992. We also observe that the US cycle tends to lead the euro area cycle. The cross-correlation of the two business cycles is the highest between US GDP (t) and euro area GDP ($t + 2$ or $t + 3$) which is consistent with the euro area business cycle lagging the US cycle by two–three quarters.[12]

5.2   *Further similarities with the US business cycle*

The business cycle properties of a number of euro area variables (table 1.3) are very much like those observed over the corresponding US variable (table 1.4). The following is a list of the characteristics that are similar in the two economies.

First, consumption and investment series are pro-cyclical while inventories[13] are slightly lagging aggregate activity (usually by two–three quarters). Second, consumption is smoother than output while investment is more than twice as volatile as output.[14] Third, the levels of the CPI and GDP deflator are counter-cyclical, while inflation is pro-cyclical. However the correlations with current GDP are hardly significant.[15] The cross-correlation of price levels with future GDP are much larger. Higher price levels are followed, two–three quarters later, by a decline in GDP.

Fourth, the persistence of the price-levels business cycle components is very high. Fifth, all interest rates (short-term nominal, short-term real

---

[12] The leads and lags of two and three quarters are not reported in table 1.1 for the sake of tractability and readability. These results are available from the authors upon request.

[13] In most countries of the euro area are measured as a residual in the national accounts. In Italy, in France and in the Netherlands, inventory series are also based on surveys.

[14] We do not report statistics for imports and exports *vis-à-vis* non-euro area countries because they are available only back to the late 1980s.

[15] The standard deviation of the correlation coefficient is about 0.1 for series available back to 1970 and about 0.16 for variables available only since 1980.

Table 1.5 *Business fluctuations of the euro area*[a]

Euro area economy (1970–2000)

BXKG(6,32,8)*

Variables (t)		St. dev		Cross-correlation with GDP (t + k)				
		absolute	relative/GDP k	−4	−1	0	1	4
GDP	1	0.87	1.00	−0.22	0.88	1.00		
Consumption	2	0.57	0.65	−0.18	0.64	0.80	0.82	0.03
Investment	3	1.91	2.18	0.04	0.82	0.87	0.75	−0.17
CPI (level)	4	0.69	0.79	0.30	−0.07	−0.32	−0.54	−0.59
CPI (inflation)	5	0.95	1.09	0.02	0.69	0.67	0.49	−0.47
Short-term rate nominal	6	1.14	1.30	0.26	0.78	0.63	0.32	−0.65
				Cross-correlation with own (t + k)				
CPI (level)	7	0.69	0.79	0.29	0.93	1.00		

BXKG(6,40,12)*

Variables (t)		St. dev	Cross-correlation with GDP (t + k)				
		relative/GDP k	−4	−1	0	1	4
GDP	1	1.14	1.00	0.23	0.93	1.00	
Consumption	2	0.89	0.78	0.33	0.75	0.81	0.80	0.30
Investment	3	2.92	2.57	0.43	0.90	0.91	0.83	0.19
CPI (level)	4	1.19	1.04	−0.06	−0.38	−0.49	−0.59	−0.61
CPI (inflation)	5	1.43	1.26	0.36	0.61	0.57	0.43	−0.31
Short-term rate nominal	6	1.28	1.13	0.52	0.68	0.53	0.29	−0.47
			Cross-correlation with own (t + k)				
CPI (level)	7	1.19	1.04	0.60	0.97	1.00	

HP filter 1600*

Variables (t)		St. dev	Cross-correlation with GDP (t + k)				
		relative/GDP k	−4	−1	0	1	4
GDP	1	1.05	1.00	0.19	0.86	1.00	
Consumption	2	0.83	0.79	0.26	0.65	0.80	0.74	0.33
Investment	3	2.72	2.59	0.37	0.82	0.89	0.78	0.27
CPI (level)	4	1.10	1.04	0.06	−0.30	−0.45	−0.59	−0.70
CPI (inflation)	5	1.48	1.41	0.23	0.46	0.39	0.28	−0.25
Short-term rate nominal	6	1.30	1.24	0.51	0.66	0.52	0.28	−0.46
			Cross-correlation with own (t + k)				
CPI (level)	7	1.10	1.04	0.55	0.94	1.00	

(cont.)

Table 1.5 *(cont.)*

US economy (1970–2000)

BXKG(6,32,8)*

	St. dev			Cross-correlation with GDP $(t + k)$			
	absolute	relative/GDP	k	-4	0	1	4
1	1.26	1.00		-0.08	1.00		
2	0.97	0.77		-0.19	0.85	0.87	0.18
3	3.18	2.53		0.11	0.95	0.79	-0.18
4	0.99	0.79		0.18	-0.49	-0.58	-0.39
5	1.24	0.99		0.31	0.58	0.41	-0.26
6	1.26	1.00		0.38	0.54	0.26	-0.64

				Cross-correlation with own $(t + k)$			
7	0.99	0.79		0.39	1.00		

BXKG(6,40,12)*

	St. dev			Cross-correlation with GDP $(t + k)$			
	absolute	relative/GDP	k	-4	0	1	4
1	1.76	1.00		0.27	1.00		
2	1 .44	0.82		0.07	0.89	0.93	0.65
3	4.90	2.78		0.33	0.96	0.88	0.35
4	1.70	0.96		0.12	-0.51	-0.63	-0.76
5	1 .34	0.76		0.55	0.58	0.45	-0.02
6	1 .82	1 .03		0.59	0.31	0.07	-0.56

				Cross-correlation with own $(t + k)$			
7	1.70	0.96		0.53	1.00		

HP filter 1600*

	St. dev			Cross-correlation with GDP $(t + k)$			
	absolute	relative/GDP	k	-4	0	1	4
1	1.63	1.00		0.27	1.00		
2	1.36	0.83		0.07	0.87	0.90	0.52
3	4.45	2,72		0.32	0.95	0.85	0.28
4	1.53	0.94		0.10	-0.59	-0.72	-0.69
5	2.00	1.22		0.47	0.47	0.38	-0.16
6	1.80	1.10		0.53	0.34	0.08	-0.56

				Cross-correlation with own $(t + k)$			
7	1.53	0.94		0.50	1.00		

Notes: Standard deviation of and cross-correlation between the BCC of individual time series (GDP, Consumption, Investment and three-month interest rate of the countries). The BCC was obtained from the Band Pass filter BPF(6,40,8), BPF(6,32,8) and BPF(6,40,12) *à la* Baxter and King (1999) as described in appendix 1 of Agresti and Mojon (2001) as well as with the HP filter with a 1600 weight.

and long-term nominal) are pro-cyclical, while the yield curve (long-term rate–short-term rate) is counter-cyclical. The cross-correlation between interest rates and output reaches a maximum positive value near lag zero or a small negative lag.

Sixth, all interest rates lead GDP slowdowns by about a year. Seventh, among the three interest rates, the nominal short-term interest rate appears to have the highest negative correlation with future GDP. Eighth, an appreciation (depreciation) of the US dollar–DM exchange rate leads economic activity in the euro area (the USA) by about three quarters.

Before turning to the differences in the euro area and the US business cycle, it is worth stressing that (as shown in table 1.3) these similarities between the USA and the euro area do not depend on the filter used.

5.3   *Differences with the US business cycle*

There are also some differences between the two economies. First, stock prices are leading GDP by two quarters in the USA but not in the euro area. This is not necessarily surprising if one considers the small role traditionally played by the stock market in continental Europe. We also observe a few other differences (e.g. the correlation between past GDP and current inflation tends to be lower in the euro area; the M1 lead of GDP is much stronger in the euro area than in the USA; and real estate prices are lagging GDP in the euro area but not in the USA). However, these do not lend themselves to straightforward interpretations.

6   Conclusion

This chapter has put together a set of stylised facts about the euro area economy and how these compare to the USA and the individual countries that form the euro area. The main finding is that the business cycle of the euro area aggregate is strikingly similar to the US business cycle in a number of respects. The phase of the business cycle, the magnitude of consumption and investment fluctuations relative to GDPs, the leading, coincident or lagging correlations of GDP with consumption, investment, prices, inflation, interest rates, and finally the persistence of prices are very similar in the USA and in the euro area. We also describe the very high synchronicity between the euro area business cycle and the business cycle of the countries that form the euro area.

Table 1.6 *Summary table on data source and availability*

Definition	Main source[b]	euro area	Austria	Belgium	Germany
National accounts					
GDP REAL	OECD-QNA	70q1–99q4	76q1–00q3	80q1–00q3	70q1–00q3
Private consumption	OECD-QNA	70q1–99q4	76q1–00q3	80q1–00q3	70q1–00q3
Durables	OECD-QNA	na	na	na	na
Non-durables	OECD-QNA	na	na	na	na
Investment	OECD-QNA	70q1–99q4	76q1–00q3	80q1–00q3	70q1–00q3
Residential	OECD-QNA	na	na	80q1–99q3	91q1–00q3
Non-residential	OECD-QNA	na	na	80q1–99q3	91q1–00q3
Change in inventories	OECD-QNA	70q1–99q4	76q1–00q3	80q1–00q3	70q1–00q3
Cumulated change in inventories	OECD-QNA	70q1–99q4	76q1–00q3	80q1–00q3	70q1–00q3
Total (intra- and extra-euro area) exports	OECD-QNA	70q1–99q4	76q1–00q3	80q1–00q3	70q1–00q3
Total (intra- and extra-euro area) imports	OECD-QNA	70q1–99q4	76q1–00q3	80q1–00q3	70q1–00q3
Government consumption	OECD-QNA	70q1–99q4	76q1–00q3	80q1–00q3	70q1–00q3
GDP deflator	OECD-QNA	70q1–99q4	76q1–00q3	80q1–00q3	70q1–00q3
Consumption deflator		70q1–99q4	76q1–00q3	80q1–00q3	70q1–00q3
Other data					
CPI	IMF	70q1–99q4	76q1–00q3	80q1–00q3	70q1–00q3
Industrial production index	IMF	85q1–99q4	76q1–00q3	80q1–00q3	70q1–00q3
Share prices (IMF)	IMF	80q1–99q4			
Share prices (OECD)	OECD		77q1–00q3	85q1–00q3	70q1–00q3
Unemployment (BIS)	BIS	70q1–99q4	77q1–00q3		
Unemployment (OECD)	OECD			85q1–00q3	70q1–98q3
Real estate prices	ECB	80q1–99q4	76q1–99q4	85q1–99q4	72q1–00q3
Interest rates					
Short-term money market	AWM and ECB	70q1–99q4	76q1–00q3	80q1–00q3	70q1–00q3
Long-term bond	AWM and ECB	70q1–99q4	76q1–00q3	80q1–00q3	70q1–00q3
Retail interest rate on house purchase loans[a]	ECB	90q1–99q4	95q1–00q3	80q1–00q3	80q1–00q3
Retail rate on short-term loans to firms[a]	ECB	90q1–99q4	95q1–00q3	80q1–00q3	80q1–00q3
Retail rate on Time deposits[a]	ECB	90q1–99q4	95q1–00q3	80q1–00q3	80q1–00q3
Monetary aggregates					
Total loans	ECB	82q4–99q4	83q1–00q3	83q1–00q3	80q1–00q3
M1	ECB	80q1–99q4	80q1–00q3	80q1–00q3	80q1–00q3
M3	ECB	80q1–99q4	80q1–00q3	80q1–00q3	80q1–00q3
Loans to firms	NCB's	na	81q1–00q3	80q1–00q3	78q1–00q3
Loans to households	NCB's	na	81q1–00q3	80q1–00q3	78q1–00q3
Exchange rates					
Real effective exchange rate	BIS	70q1–99q4	76q1–00q3	80q1–00q3	70q1–00q3
Exchange rates *vis-à-vis* DEM	BIS	na	76q1–00q3	80q1–00q3	na
Exchange rates *vis-à-vis* US Dollar	BIS	79q1–99q4	76q1–00q3	80q1–00q3	70q1–00q3
World market prices, raw materials, total Index	BIS	70q1–00q3	70q1–00q3	70q1–00q3	70q1–00q3
Private loans[c]	ECB	83q1–00q3	83q1–00q3	83q1–00q3	80q1–00q3

Notes: [a] At country level all data come from OECD_qna; except for PT, GR and BE, we received data from the NCBs.

Table 1.6 *(cont.)*

Spain	Finland	France	Greece	Italy	Netherlands	Portugal	United States
70q1–00q3	75q1–00q3	70q1–00q3	80q1–98q4	70q1–00q3	77q1–00q3	80q1–98q4	70q1–00q3
70q1–00q3	75q1–00q3	70q1–00q3	80q1–98q4	70q1–00q3	77q1–00q3	80q1–98q4	70q1–00q3
na	75q1–00q3	70q1–00q3	na	70q1–00q3	na	na	na
na	75q1–00q3	70q1–00q3	na	70q1–00q3	na	na	na
70q1–00q3	75q1–00q3	70q1–00q3	80q1–98q4	70q1–00q3	77q1–00q3	80q1–98q4	70q1–00q3
na	75q1–00q3	70q1–00q3	na	na	77q1–00q3	na	70q1–00q3
na	75q1–00q3	70q1–00q3	na	na	77q1–00q3	na	70q1–00q3
70q1–00q3	75q1–00q3	70q1–00q3	na	70q1–00q3	77q1–00q3	na	70q1–00q3
70q1–00q3	75q1–00q3	70q1–00q3	na	70q1–00q3	77q1–00q3	na	70q1–00q3
70q1–00q3	75q1–00q3	70q1–00q3	na	70q1–00q3	77q1–00q3	na	na
70q1–00q3	75q1–00q3	70q1–00q3	na	70q1–00q3	77q1–00q3	na	na
70q1–00q3	75q1–00q3	70q1–00q3	na	70q1–00q3	77q1–00q3	na	na
70q1–00q3	75q1–00q3	70q1–00q3	na	70q1–00q3	77q1–00q3	na	70q1–00q3
70q1–00q3	75q1–00q3	70q1–00q3	na	70q1–00q3	77q1–00q3	80q1–98q4	na
70q1–00q3	70q1–00q3	70q1–00q3	80q1–98q4	70q1–00q3	77q1–00q3	80q1–98q4	70q1–00q3
70q1–00q3	70q1–00q3	70q1–00q3		70q1–00q3	77q1–00q3	80q1–98q4	70q1–00q3
70q1–00q3	70q1–00q3	70q1–00q3	80q1–98q4	70q1–00q3	77q1–00q3		70q1–00q3
		70q1–00q3				88q1–98q4	
70q1–00q3			80q1–98q4	70q1–00q3	77q1–00q3		
	84q1–00q3	70q1–98q3				83q1–98q4	
70q1–00q3	78q1–00q3	77q1–99q4		70q1–00q3	77q1–00q3	80q1–98q4	80q1–00q3
77q1–00q3	75q1–00q3	70q1–00q3	80q1–98q4	70q1–00q3	77q1–00q3	80q1–98q4	70q1–00q3
78q1–00q3	75q1–00q3	70q1–00q3	85q1–98q4	70q1–00q3	77q1–00q3	85q1–98q4	70q1–00q3
80q1–00q3	80q1–00q3	90q1–00q3	80q1–98q4	89q1–00q3	80q1–00q3	90q1–98q4	
80q1–00q3	80q1–00q3	84q1–00q3	80q1–98q4	89q1–00q3	80q1–00q3	90q1–98q4	
80q1–00q3	80q1–00q3	80q1–00q3	80q1–98q4	89q1–00q3	80q1–00q3	90q1–98q4	
80q1–00q3	80q1–00q3	80q1–00q3	na	83q1–00q3	83q1–00q3	80q1–98q4	
80q1–00q3	80q1–00q3	80q1–00q3	80q1–98q4	80q1–00q3	80q1–00q3	80q1–98q4	70q1–00q3
80q1–00q3	80q1–00q3	80q1–00q3	80q1–98q4	80q1–00q3	80q1–00q3	80q1–98q4	70q1–00q3
83q1–00q3	89q1–00q3	78q1–00q3	80q1–98q4	80q1–00q3	80q1–00q3	80q1–98q4	
83q1–00q3	89q1–00q3	78q1–00q3	80q1–98q4	80q1–00q3	80q1–00q3	80q1–98q4	
70q1–00q3	70q1–00q3	70q1–00q3	80q1–98q4	70q1–00q3	77q1–00q3	80q1–98q4	70q1–00q3
70q1–00q3	70q1–00q3	70q1–00q3	80q1–98q4	70q1–00q3	77q1–00q3	80q1–98q4	70q1–00q3
70q1–00q3	70q1–00q3	70q1–00q3	80q1–98q4	70q1–00q3	77q1–00q3	80q1–98q4	78q1–00q3
70q1–00q3	70q1–00q3	70q1–00q3	70q1–00q3	70q1–00q3	70q1–00q3	70q1–00q3	70q1–00q3
80q1–00q3	80q1–00q3	80q1–00q3	80q1–00q3	83q1–00q3	83q1–00q3	80q1–00q3	70q1–00q3

[b] Eu-11 data come from the AWM, EMD ECB.
[c] For USA, data come from the IMF.

2　The monetary transmission mechanism in the euro area: evidence from VAR analysis

G. Peersman and F. Smets

1　Introduction

There is a large literature that has used identified Vector Autoregressions (VARs) to study the macroeconomic effects of an unexpected change in policy-controlled interest rates in the euro area countries.[1] The use of VARs for the analysis of monetary policy started with the seminal work of Sims (1980). Christiano, Eichenbaum and Evans (1999) and Leeper, Sims and Zha (1998) have reviewed what one has learned from this extensive literature regarding the monetary transmission mechanism in the USA. A large part of the literature on the euro area has focused on trying to identify cross-country differences. In these studies, VARs are estimated for the individual countries of the euro area, and the impulse responses of the main macroeconomic variables to a monetary policy shock are compared.

The focus of this chapter is on what we can learn regarding the area-wide monetary transmission from analysing a VAR estimated on synthetic euro area data from 1980 to 1998. In section 2, we show that using a standard identification scheme as in Christiano, Eichenbaum and Evans (1999) and Eichenbaum and Evans (1995) delivers plausible estimates of the effects of monetary policy in the euro area. An unexpected, temporary rise in the short-term interest rate tends to be followed by a real appreciation of the exchange rate and a temporary fall in output after two quarters. The effect on output reaches a peak after three–five quarters, after which it slowly returns to the baseline. Prices are more sluggish and start to fall significantly below zero only several quarters after GDP. The effect on prices is also more persistent.

In section 3 we perform a number of robustness checks. We show that the impulse responses to a monetary policy shock are relatively stable over time. The results also appear robust to alternative identification schemes,

We thank Don Bredin for valuable input.

[1] For a recent survey, see, for example, Guiso *et al.* (2000).

similar to the ones used in Galí (1992) and Sims and Zha (1998). In section 4, we use the VAR to examine how the various money, credit and GDP components respond to an area-wide monetary policy impulse, as well as some asset prices and labour market variables. Finally, in section 5 we discuss the conclusions.

2 A VAR model for the euro area

2.1 The benchmark specification

In this section we describe two benchmark VAR models that we use to analyse the effects of a monetary policy shock in the euro area. The benchmark VARs have the following representation:

$$Y_t = A(L)Y_{t-1} + B(L)X_t + \mu_t \tag{1}$$

where Y_t is the vector of endogenous euro area variables and X_t is a vector of exogenous foreign variables. Throughout this chapter, the vector of exogenous variables contains a world commodity price index (cp_t), US real GDP (y_t^{US}), and the US short-term nominal interest rate (s_t^{US}):[2]

$$X_t' = \lfloor cp_t \quad y_t^{US} \quad s_t^{US} \rfloor \tag{2}$$

These variables are included to control for changes in world demand and inflation. The inclusion of these variables helps to solve the so-called 'price puzzle' (i.e. the empirical finding in the VAR literature that prices rise following an interest rate tightening).[3] By treating these variables as exogenous, we implicitly assume that there is no feedback from the euro area variables to the foreign variables.[4] We also allow for a contemporaneous impact of the exogenous variables on the endogenous euro area variables.

In the first model, the vector of endogenous euro area variables, Y_t, consists of real GDP (y_t), consumer prices (p_t), the domestic nominal short-term interest rate (s_t) and the real effective exchange rate (x_t):[5]

$$Y_t' = [y_t \quad p_t \quad s_t \quad x_t] \tag{3}$$

In the second model, we also include a broad monetary aggregate (M3) (m_t) in the block of endogenous variables. Historically money developments have played an important role in the monetary policy strategies

---

[2] Each of the VAR models also contains a constant and a linear trend.
[3] For example Sims (1992).
[4] The results are very similar when such a feedback is allowed.
[5] Most of the data used in this paper come from the AWM database. See Fagan, Henry and Mestre (2001).

of some of the countries now participating in the monetary union. The inclusion of a money aggregate could therefore be helpful in identifying monetary policy innovations. In this case, the vector of endogenous variables can thus be written as:

$$Y_t' = [\, y_t \quad p_t \quad m_t \quad s_t \quad x_t \,] \tag{3'}$$

In both cases, the euro area monetary policy shock is identified through a standard Choleski-decomposition with the variables ordered as in (3) and (3').[6] The underlying assumption is that policy shocks have no contemporaneous impact on output, prices and money, but may affect the exchange rate immediately. However, the policy interest rate does not respond to contemporaneous changes in the effective exchange rate. The latter assumption is appropriate for a large, relatively closed, economy such as the euro area as a whole.[7] In section 3, we provide a robustness analysis for alternative identification strategies.

Unless otherwise mentioned, each of the VAR models is estimated in levels using quarterly data over the period 1980–98.[8] In this chapter we do not perform an explicit analysis of the long-run behaviour of the economy. By doing the analysis in levels we allow for implicit cointegrating relationships in the data. A more explicit analysis of the long-run behaviour of the various variables is limited by the relatively short sample available.[9] The data are expressed in logs and seasonally adjusted, except the interest rates, which are in levels. We use the three-month interest rate as the monetary policy rate as this is the only short-term interest rate that is available for all countries over the whole sample period. Standard likelihood ratio tests are used to determine the lag-order of the VARs, which turns out to be of order three. Finally, in order to test the stability of the VAR, we ran sequential Chow break tests starting in 1990:1. There is no evidence of instability at the 5 per cent confidence level.

2.2   Basic estimation results

The results of the two benchmark VAR models for the euro area are shown in the first two columns of figure 2.1. This graph gives the effect of a domestic, one-standard deviation, monetary policy shock on domestic

---

[6] As in Christiano, Eichenbaum and Evans (1999) and Sims (1980).

[7] Eichenbaum and Evans (1995) make the same assumption for the USA. One can argue that the euro area as a whole is more like the USA in terms of openness than like any of its individual members.

[8] We took 1980 as a starting date because some of the data series used are available only from that year.

[9] See Sims, Stock and Watson (1990). Coenen and Vega (1999) estimate a VECM model for the euro area.

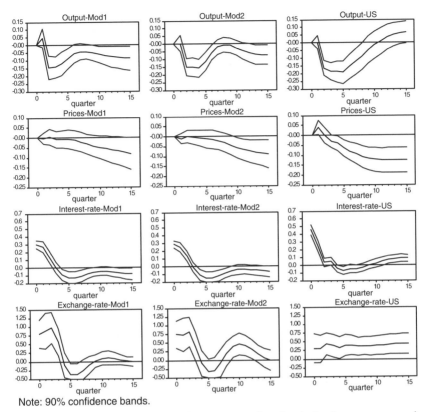

Note: 90% confidence bands.

Figure 2.1 The effects of monetary policy shocks in the euro area and the USA (estimation period 1980–1998), 90 per cent confidence bands

real GDP, domestic consumer prices, the exchange rate and the domestic short-term interest rate, together with a 90 per cent confidence band.[10]

The third column reports the results of a similar exercise for US data. The main difference with the VAR specification for the euro area is that in this case we do not include exogenous variables. Moreover, consistent with many other papers on the USA (e.g. Christiano, Eichenbaum and Evans, 1999), we include commodity prices as an endogenous variable, $Y'_{US,t} = [cp_t \quad y_t \quad p_t \quad s_t \quad x_t]$. The sample period is identical (1980–98) and the identification of the US monetary policy shock is again obtained using a standard Choleski-decomposition.

[10] The confidence band is obtained through a standard bootstrapping procedure with 100 draws. Very similar, though somewhat wider, confidence bands are obtained when Monte Carlo methods are used. See Sims and Zha (1998).

The impulse response patterns reported in the graph are broadly in line with the existing empirical evidence for the USA and many other countries (Christiano, Eichenbaum and Evans, 1999; Gerlach and Smets, 1995). An unexpected, temporary rise in the short-term interest rate tends to be followed by a real appreciation of the exchange rate and a temporary fall in output after two quarters. The effect on output reaches a peak after three–five quarters and returns to the baseline afterwards. Prices respond much more sluggishly, but the effects of the policy shock are more persistent.

A comparison of the first and second column of figure 2.1 shows that overall the results obtained in the euro area models with and without money are very similar. The inclusion of M3 (model 2) does lead to somewhat tighter estimates. The effect of the policy shock on prices is now significant after eight quarters. Also, the initial positive impact on output disappears. In what follows we will therefore use the model with money as our benchmark for the euro area. An analysis of how M3 and its components are affected is given in section 4.3.

Comparing the effects in the euro area and the USA, it is striking how similar the impulse response functions are. A typical monetary policy shock is somewhat greater in the USA than in the euro area (45 basis points compared to 30 basis points), which is reflected in a somewhat stronger impact on output and prices. The impact on prices is, however, much faster in the USA. One explanation for this finding could be that prices are more flexible in the USA. The slower response of prices in the euro area may, however, also be due to aggregation bias, which given the heterogeneity of inflation rates in the individual countries of the euro area could be most severe for prices. The impact on the real effective exchange rate is much smaller, but more persistent in the USA, which is somewhat consistent with the findings of Eichenbaum and Evans (1995).

The size of the policy shock obtained for the euro area is much larger than the one obtained by Monticelli and Tristani (1999), who use a longer estimation period and an identification strategy that combines both short- and long-run restrictions. These authors find that a one-standard deviation monetary shock corresponds to a 10-basis points move in the interest rate. The maximum impact of this shock on GDP is, however, much larger at 0.4 per cent.

Figure 2.2 shows the historical contribution of the monetary policy shocks to the short-term interest rate in the euro area and the USA, whereas table 2.1 provides the contribution of the monetary policy shocks to the variance of the forecast error of output, prices, the interest rate and the exchange rate at various horizons. From figure 2.2, it is clear that periods of easy monetary policy in the euro area can be situated

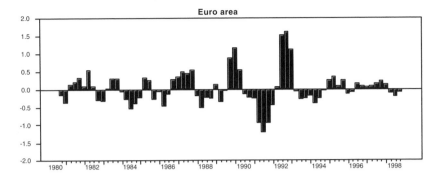

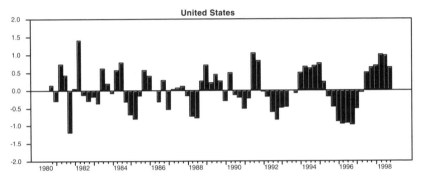

Figure 2.2 Contribution of euro area monetary policy shocks to the short-term interest rate, 1980–1998

at the end of 1984 and in 1991. In contrast, monetary policy was on average relatively tight at the beginning of 1990 (possibly associated with the reunification of Germany) and again during the ERM crisis at the end of 1992 and the beginning of 1993. The timing of these episodes are quite different from those in the USA. In fact, the correlation coefficient between monetary policy innovations in the euro area and the USA turns out to be negative in this sample period (−0.2).

Table 2.1 shows that, as in most of the VAR literature, the contribution of policy shocks to output and price developments is rather limited. This is to be expected as the monetary policy shocks capture deviations of the short-term interest rate from average monetary policy behaviour over the estimation period. In a stable monetary policy regime such deviations should be limited. The fact that the contribution of monetary policy shocks to output and exchange rate developments is larger in the euro area than in the USA is partly due to the fact that the overall variance to be explained is smaller because of the inclusion of exogenous variables in the euro area VAR.

Table 2.1 *Contribution of monetary policy shocks to the forecast error variance of output, prices, the interest rate and the exchange rate in the euro area and the USA (per cent)*

	Horizon				
	1-year	2-year	3-year	5-year	10-year
Euro area					
Output	13	28	34	39	38
Prices	3	7	11	18	23
Interest rate	65	41	29	14	4
Exchange rate	17	21	23	27	33
USA					
Output	4	2	5	10	20
Prices	7	16	18	15	14
Interest rate	50	25	23	21	21
Exchange rate	6	3	2	3	3

3   A robustness analysis

In this section, we analyse the robustness of the results described in section 2. First, we analyse the stability of the impulse responses over different sample periods (section 3). We then provide a robustness analysis for alternative identification schemes. Two alternative strategies are investigated: the Sims and Zha (1998) methodology and an identification strategy using long-run restrictions as in Galí (1992).

3.1   Stability of the impulse responses over time

Using the recursive Chow tests referred to in section 2, the null hypothesis that the benchmark VARs are stable over the estimation period cannot be rejected. In order to test this further, we report in this section impulse responses for both longer and shorter sample periods. Evidence of the stability of the impulse responses over time would suggest that the problems due to aggregation over different monetary policy regimes may be overrated. The recursive impulse responses also allow us to see whether there is any evidence that the transmission mechanism of monetary policy in the euro area has changed over time. Figure 2.3 reports recursive impulse responses to a monetary policy shock based on model 1 for the euro area.[11] The full lines refer to sample periods that start in the 1970s

---

[11] We do this analysis with the benchmark model without money because an area-wide money series is not available before the 1980s.

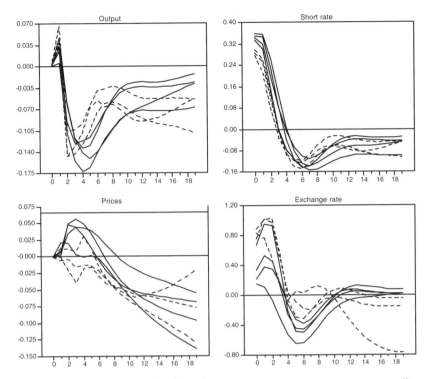

Figure 2.3 Recursive impulse responses to euro area monetary policy shocks, the solid lines refer to the sample periods that start in 1973, 1975, 1977 and 1979; the dashed lines refer to the sample periods that start in 1981, 1983 and 1985, in all cases, the end of the sample period is 1998:4.

(1973, 1975, 1977 and 1979) and end in 1998, whereas the broken lines refer to shorter sample periods that start in the 1980s (1981, 1983, 1985).

Overall, the results confirm the stability of the VAR results. The qualitative effects of a monetary policy shock are quite similar over the different sample periods. There are some quantitative differences, which are unlikely to be significant. The average size of the interest rate shock has fallen somewhat in the latter period, while the associated exchange rate response is clearly larger. The stronger exchange rate effect is translated into a smaller price puzzle in the latter period. Compared to the full sample results, the effect of a monetary policy shock on output has been quicker in the 1980s and 1990s. The peak effect takes places in the second and third quarter, compared to the fourth and fifth quarter for the full sample.

3.2   Alternative identification schemes

It is well known that impulse response functions in VAR analysis can be sensitive to alternative identification schemes. In this section we apply two alternative identification schemes to check the robustness of our previous results. The first is due to Kim and Roubini (1995) and Sims and Zha (1998) and permits a contemporaneous interaction between the short-term interest rate, the exchange rate and the money aggregate. The second is based on Galí (1992) and uses a mixture of long- and short-run restrictions to identify monetary policy shocks.

3.2.1   Permitting a contemporaneous interaction between the short-term interest rate, the exchange rate and the money aggregate

In this section we use a more general identification method suggested by Bernanke (1986) and Sims (1986) and applied by, for example, Kim and Roubini (1995) and Sims and Zha (1998). If μ_t are the residuals from the reduced form estimation of (1), then these residuals can be related to the structural shocks by the following general structural model:

$$A\mu_t = B\varepsilon_t \tag{5}$$

In our basic, recursive identification strategy, A is assumed to be the identity matrix and B is assumed to be a lower triangular matrix. The policy shock then refers to the shock to the interest rate equation. Following Kim and Roubini (1995) and Sims and Zha (1998), an alternative, non-recursive identification scheme allows for a contemporaneous interaction between the short-term interest rate, money and the exchange rate. In the model with money, these authors propose the following restrictions on the A and B matrix:

$$\begin{bmatrix} 1 & 0 & 0 & 0 & 0 \\ a_{21} & 1 & 0 & 0 & 0 \\ a_{31} & a_{32} & 1 & a_{34} & 0 \\ 0 & 0 & a_{43} & 1 & a_{45} \\ a_{51} & a_{52} & a_{53} & a_{54} & 1 \end{bmatrix} \begin{bmatrix} \mu_t^y \\ \mu_t^p \\ \mu_t^m \\ \mu_t^s \\ \mu_t^x \end{bmatrix} = \begin{bmatrix} \varepsilon_t^y \\ \varepsilon_t^p \\ \varepsilon_t^m \\ \varepsilon_t^s \\ \varepsilon_t^x \end{bmatrix} \tag{6}$$

The first two equations represent the sluggish reaction of the real sector (output and prices) to shocks in the monetary sector (money, interest rate and exchange rate). There is no contemporaneous impact of the monetary policy, money demand and exchange rate shock on output and prices. The third equation can be interpreted as a short-run money demand equation. Money demand is allowed to respond contemporaneously

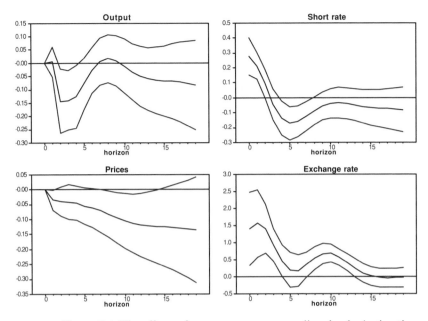

Figure 2.4 The effects of euro area monetary policy shocks (estimation period 1980–1998; Sims–Zha identification), 90 per cent confidence bands

to innovations in output, prices and the interest rate. The fourth row represents the monetary policy reaction function. The monetary authority sets the interest rate after observing the current money stock and the exchange rate, but does not respond contemporaneously to disturbances in output and the price level. The argument is that information about the latter variables is available only with a lag. Finally, the exchange rate, being an asset price, reacts immediately to all the other innovations.

Figure 2.4 shows that the impulse responses obtained with this identification scheme are very similar to those of the basic model. The typical size of the interest rate shock is somewhat smaller, while the exchange rate appreciation is much stronger. Because of this appreciation the effect on prices is more immediate.

3.2.2   A mixture of short- and long-run restrictions   Another possible identification strategy is to combine short and long-run restrictions as in Galí (1992) and Gerlach and Smets (1995). In this case, we assume that the vector of the endogenous variables is given by:

$$Y_t' = [\Delta y_t \quad \Delta p_t \quad s_t \quad \Delta x_t] \tag{7}$$

and the vector of the structural disturbances:

$$\varepsilon_t^Y = \lfloor \varepsilon_t^s \quad \varepsilon_t^d \quad \varepsilon_t^p \quad \varepsilon_t^x \rfloor \tag{8}$$

with ε_t^s denoting a supply shock, ε_t^d a demand shock, ε_t^p a monetary policy shock and ε_t^x an exchange rate shock. A typical restriction consistent with many macroeconomic models is that only supply shocks have permanent effects on output, while demand, monetary policy and exchange rate shocks have zero impact on output in the long run (Blanchard and Quah, 1989). In order to discriminate between the aggregate demand shocks and the two other shocks, we use, as before, the restrictions that the latter two have no contemporaneous impact on output. Finally, in order to distinguish between the monetary policy shock and the exchange rate shock we assume, as in the basic model, that the interest rate is not contemporaneously affected by disturbances in the exchange rate.

The results are reported in Figure 2.5. In the first row, we find the responses of output, prices, the interest rate and the exchange rate to a supply shock. As the textbook model predicts, a supply shock has a positive influence on output and a negative effect on prices. Both variables reach a peak about three years after the shock and stabilise at that level subsequently. In line with lower inflation, the nominal interest rate also decreases following the supply shock. The response to a positive aggregate demand shock is given in the second row. Its effect on output dampens out after four–five years. This shock also leads to a rise in inflation and the nominal interest rate. The impact of a monetary policy shock (third row of figure 2.5) is qualitatively comparable with the previous results. The impact on output is, however, somewhat more prolonged with a peak effect between five and eight quarters. The effect on prices is quantitatively much stronger and more immediate. This appears to be mostly due to the stronger and more persistent appreciation of the exchange rate. These results are broadly consistent with the findings of previous studies using this identification strategy as in Galí (1992) and Gerlach and Smets (1995).

3.2.3   Comparing the monetary policy shocks across models   Table 2.2 reports the correlations of the monetary policy shocks of the alternative identification strategies. Overall, the correlation of these shocks is quite high. The correlation is the weakest between the shocks derived from contemporaneous restrictions and those derived from the mixed short- and long-run restrictions.

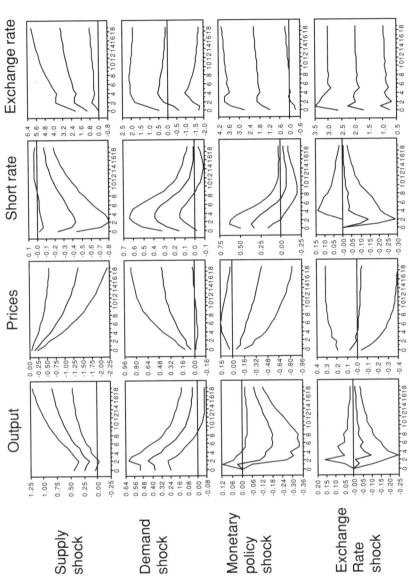

Figure 2.5 The effects of euro area monetary policy shocks (estimation period 1980–1998; short- and long-run restrictions), 90 per cent confidence bands

Table 2.2 *Correlation of euro area policy shocks obtained under alternative identification strategies*

	1	2	3	4
1 Benchmark model 1	1.00	0.95	0.91	0.71
2 Benchmark model 2 (+ money)		1.00	0.85	0.67
3 Sims–Zha (1998)			1.00	0.73
4 Short- and long-run restrictions				1.00

4   The effect of monetary policy on other macro variables

4.1   The extended model

In this section, we discuss the influence of a monetary policy shock on other macroeconomic variables that are not included in the basic model. We do this by extending the basic model as follows:

$$\begin{bmatrix} Y_t \\ Z_t \end{bmatrix} = \begin{bmatrix} A(L) & 0 \\ C(L) & D(L) \end{bmatrix} \begin{bmatrix} Y_{t-1} \\ Z_{t-1} \end{bmatrix} + \begin{bmatrix} B(L) \\ E(L) \end{bmatrix} X_t + \begin{bmatrix} \mu_t^Y \\ c\mu_t^Y + \mu_t^z \end{bmatrix} \tag{9}$$

As before, X_t and Y_t are, respectively, the vector of exogenous and endogenous variables. Z_t is the macroeconomic variable of interest (for example, investment). To keep the policy shock invariant to the inclusion of the different Z_ts, we assume that the macroeconomic variable of interest does not affect the block of endogenous variables, Y_t.[12]

4.2   Components of GDP

Figure 2.6 shows the effects of an area-wide monetary policy shock on *the various components of GDP* (total real GDP, total investment, private consumption and net trade). The impulse response pattern of total investment is similar to the response of real GDP. However, the magnitude of the effect on investment is three times as large as the magnitude of the effect on GDP. After a typical monetary tightening of 30 basis points, investment falls by around 50 basis points. In contrast, the response of private consumption is weaker and slower. Consumption starts decreasing after two quarters and reaches its minimum impact after five quarters. Finally, following an initial negative impact, the net trade

---

[12] We have also estimated alternative VARs where the additional macroeconomic variable is included in the endogenous block of the model. In that case, this variable is ordered as the last one in the recursive structure ($F(L) \neq 0$). The results are very similar.

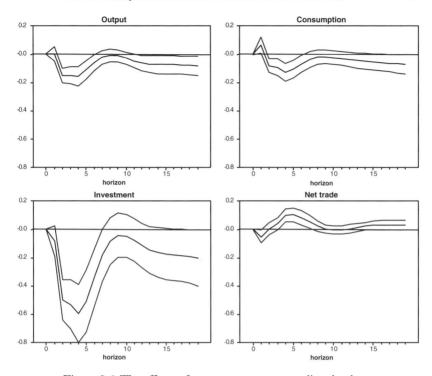

Figure 2.6 The effects of euro area monetary policy shocks on components of GDP (estimation period 1980–1998), 90 per cent confidence bands

position improves significantly in line with the fall in domestic demand and associated imports.

The influence on *total manufacturing and investment and consumption goods* in manufacturing is shown in figure 2.7. As expected, the response of total manufacturing is larger than the response of real GDP (a peak of about 50 basis points after a monetary tightening of 30 basis points). Again, we find a significantly stronger impact on investment goods than on consumption goods.

4.3   *Monetary variables and asset prices*

The impulse response functions of M3, *its components and loans to the private sector* to a contractionary monetary policy shock are presented in figure 2.8. We find a negative, but not very significant, liquidity effect on M1, which appears to be robust to alternative identification schemes.

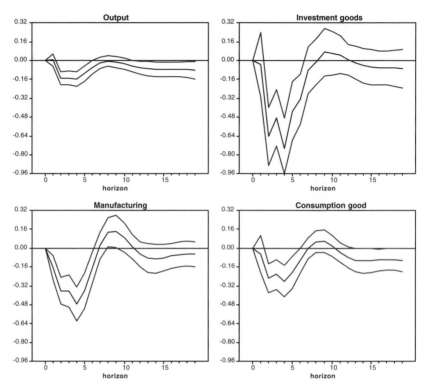

Figure 2.7 The effects of euro area monetary policy shocks on manufacturing (estimation period 1980–1998)

The slow response of M3 is clearly due to the initial increase in the other components of M3. An interest rate tightening gives rise to substitution effects from money components that bear no or regulated interest to time deposits and money market funds that are included in the broader money aggregates. This finding is consistent with the literature on euro area money demand.[13] There is an immediate and negative effect on credit to the private sector.

Figure 2.9 plots the response of various asset prices to a temporary monetary policy tightening. The increase of the short rate by 30 basis points is accompanied by a similar, but smaller increase in the long-term rate by about 10 basis points, as one would expect on the basis

---

[13] For example, Fase and Winder (1993) find a negative relationship between M1 and the short-term interest rate, while the relation between M3 and the short-term interest rate is positive.

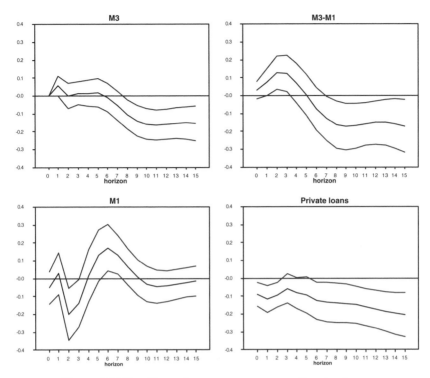

Figure 2.8 The effects of euro area monetary policy shocks on monetary variables (estimation period 1980–1998)

of the expectations hypothesis of the term structure of interest rates. As expected, stock markets fall immediately and quite strongly after a monetary policy tightening. In contrast, house prices fall much more gradually.

4.4 Labour market variables

Finally, figure 2.10 reports the impulse responses to a monetary policy shock of selected labour market variables: employment, labour productivity, unit labour cost and nominal wages. The pattern of employment is very similar to that of output. However, the quantitative effect on employment is less, resulting in a pro-cyclical movement of labour productivity. This pro-cyclical behaviour of labour productivity, together with the slight price puzzle that one can observe in the response of nominal wages, implies that unit labour costs rise quite significantly before falling back below base line.

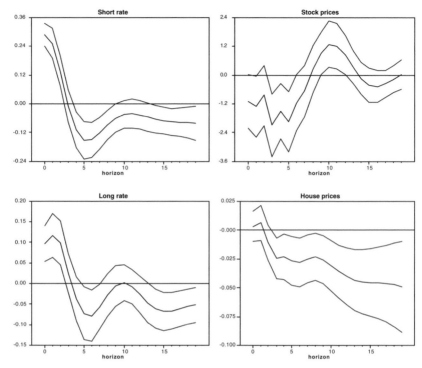

Figure 2.9 The effects of euro area monetary policy shocks on asset prices (estimation period 1980–1998)

4.5   Individual country effects

The results discussed in the preceding sections of this chapter are based on synthetic, euro area-wide time-series variables. Before concluding the analysis, it may be useful to check how output and prices in the individual countries of the euro area are affected by the common monetary policy shock defined in section 2. For that purposes we include output and prices of each country in the extended model of section 4.1. and calculate their response to the identified euro area monetary policy shock.

The results are summarised in figure 2.11. The upper row plots the individual country effects, while the lower row compares the aggregate effects based on the area-wide benchmark model with the aggregation of the individual country effects using similar weights. From the upper part of figure 2.11 it is clear that there is a quite large variability in how output and prices in the individual countries respond to the euro area policy shock. Nevertheless, with a few exceptions, the overall pattern of

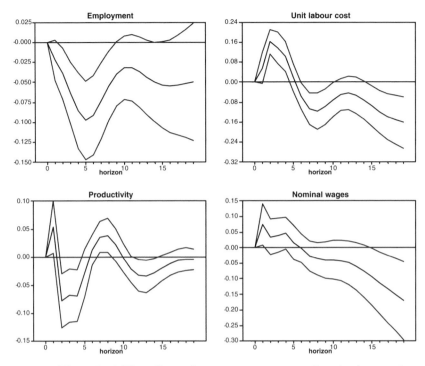

Figure 2.10 The effects of euro area monetary policy shocks on other variables (estimation period 1980–1998)

the responses are similar: output falls quite quickly, while prices take more time to respond. When aggregating those responses across countries, one basically retrieves the area-wide responses discussed in section 2.

5   Concluding remarks

In this chapter, we have estimated an identified VAR on synthetic euro area data from 1980 till 1998 to study the macroeconomic effects of a monetary policy shock in the euro area. Using several standard identification schemes, we uncover plausible impulse responses of the main macroeconomic variables to an unexpected monetary policy tightening in the euro area. A temporary rise in the nominal and real short-term interest rate tends to be followed by a real appreciation of the exchange rate and a temporary fall in output. Prices are more sluggish and start to fall significantly below zero only several quarters after GDP. These results are very similar to those obtained for the US economy using similar

Country effects

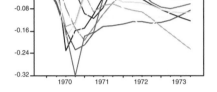

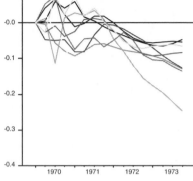

Aggregate euro area effects

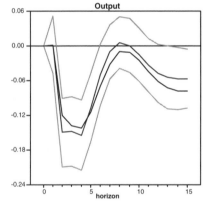

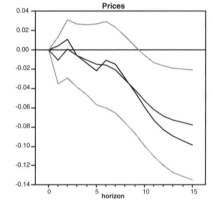

Figure 2.11 The effects of euro area-wide monetary policy shocks on individual countries (estimation period 1980–1998)

methodologies. These results appear to be stable over different sample periods.

We also investigated the reaction of other macro variables and the GDP components to a monetary policy shock. The response of output is mainly due to a decrease in investment which responds with a magnitude three times as large as GDP, and to a lesser extent in private consumption. Employment falls in line with GDP, but less strongly which results in a pro-cyclical response of labour productivity. We find an immediate liquidity effect on M1, but a more gradual decrease of M3 and other credit aggregates. The long-term interest rate shows a muted response to the temporary rise in the short-term interest rate consistent with the expectations theory of the term structure. Share prices fall significantly on impact, while house prices respond more sluggishly.

Overall, these findings are encouraging and show in our view that the results from applying standard techniques to synthetic euro area data can be used as a benchmark for the further theoretical and empirical analysis of the transmission mechanism in the euro area. Of course, the caveats that come with this analysis are even more important in this case. In particular, we know that there was no common monetary policy in the euro area over the estimation period, so that identifying monetary policy innovations on the basis of an aggregate monetary policy reaction function may be problematic. It is therefore important to monitor how these results change as data from the new single monetary policy regime come in. In addition, the aggregate analysis results need to be complemented with a more disaggregated investigation that takes the features of the national monetary policy regimes into account. Recent work in that respect can be found in Ciccarelli and Rebucci (2001), Sala (2000) and in chapter 3 in this volume by Mojon and Peersman.

3 A VAR description of the effects of monetary policy in the individual countries of the euro area

B. Mojon and G. Peersman

1 Introduction

Recent empirical and theoretical studies, mainly focused on the US economy, tend to converge on the view that contractionary monetary policy shocks lead to a temporary decrease in output and to a gradual decline in prices. These results are convincing, and therefore policy-relevant, mainly because they are derived from models that imbed a plausible description of the monetary policy decision process. Chapter 2 showed that the estimation of standard VAR models using euro area synthetic data also delivers this pattern of response of output and prices to identified monetary policy shocks. However, given that this approach is somewhat artificial when considering the euro area economy as a whole before the start of EMU, these results should be complemented with VARs where estimating central bank reaction functions is completely legitimate, i.e. country-level VAR models.

This chapter analyses the transmission mechanism of monetary policy in the ten countries that now form the euro area.[1] We use VAR models, which, as argued in the introduction of the previous chapter, is the most widely used empirical methodology to analyse the transmission mechanism.

In Europe, the perspective of EMU led a large part of the literature to use VARs to evaluate cross-country differences in the transmission mechanism. The typical paper in this literature imposes the same identification of monetary policy shocks across countries, in spite of the differences in

We thank Andres Manzanares for outstanding research assistance and Frank Smets, Ignacio Hernando, Don Bredin and Lutz Kilian for helpful discussions and Ignazio Angeloni, Paul Butzen, Fabio Canova, Fiorela de Fiore, Catherine Fuss, Carlos Robalo, Daniele Terlizzese and Raf Wouters for comments on a previous draft of this chapter.

[1] Luxembourg is not modelled because it formed a monetary union with Belgium, and had no independent monetary policy. Portugal is also excluded because of data limitations.

monetary policy regime of each country within the European Monetary System (EMS).[2] For instance, Germany followed an independent monetary policy as the *de facto* anchor of the EMS while the interest rate of countries of the core EMS was tied by a hard peg to the Deutsche Mark during most of the years following 1980. We propose instead to estimate for each country a model that accounts for the EMS constraint to which the country was subject during the sample period. Most of the VAR studies that have explicitly modelled the EMS context focus on one or on a small number of countries.[3] In contrast, we cover most countries that adopted the euro.

We form three groups of 'monetary policy regime-like countries' depending on the country monetary integration with Germany. As the anchor of the EMS, Germany is a group on its own for obvious reasons. Austria, Belgium and the Netherlands form the second group. We model their monetary policy as if they were in a 'fixed' exchange rate regime with respect to Germany. It follows that there is no autonomous monetary policy shocks in addition to the German ones. All the other countries are modelled as open economies with a flexible exchange rate *vis-à-vis* Germany. The influence of German monetary policy is taken into account by including the German interest rate and the bilateral DM–exchange rate in the model. Although the German interest rate is then a major argument of the reaction function of the central bank, there is room for 'autonomous' domestic monetary policy in the adjustment of domestic interest rate around the German interest rate.

The contribution of the chapter with respect to the existing VAR literature on the transmission mechanism in euro area countries is threefold. First, we show that imposing one of three relatively simple identification schemes[4] leads to well-behaved and qualitatively consistent estimated effects of the monetary policy shocks in all the countries. While

---

[2] For an overview of the empirical literature on the macroeconomic effects of monetary policy shocks in the Euro area countries, we refer to section 2 of working paper version of this paper, available as the ECB Working paper 92, at www.ec.int. and to section 2 of Mojon (1999b).

[3] Three related recent studies use VAR models to evaluate the effect of the single monetary policy in each of the countries. Clements, Kontolemis and Levy (2001) report the effect of monetary policy shocks when the reaction function is constrained to be similar across countries and the intra-EU exchange rates are fixed. Sala (2001) implements dynamic factor models to define common monetary policy shocks for eight countries of the euro area. Peersman (2001) estimates the effects of area-wide monetary policy shocks on the individual countries.

[4] See also Clements, Kontomelis and Levy (2001) for a complementary point of view on the role of the EMS in the transmission mechanism. Their study focuses on the effects of German monetary policy shocks on all the other countries of the euro area.

our models are fairly similar and comparable, we avoid the implausible uniformity of approaches that characterises most of the VAR literature on international comparisons of the transmission mechanism. We also avoid the multiplication of models that confuses the cross-country comparison.

Our results are consistent with the consensus view on the transmission mechanism. A 'contractionary monetary policy shock' is defined as a positive deviation of the interest rate from the average reaction function of the central bank for the sample period. It leads to a temporary fall in GDP that peaks between three and six quarters after the shock and to a gradual decrease in the price level, as well as an appreciation of the exchange rate. We also show that M1 initially decreases and that the response of investment is larger than that of consumption.

Second, the results of the estimations at the country level are consistent with the area-wide results of chapter 2. Third, we show how the monetary policy shocks defined at the euro area level relate to the particular episodes of the domestic monetary policy shocks of the different countries.

The chapter is structured as follows. Section 2 describes the three identification schemes chosen and section 3 the results of their implementation. Finally, section 4 concludes.

2   VAR models for the individual countries in the euro area: identification

In this section we present VAR models for all euro area countries except Luxembourg and Portugal. We discuss the features of the model that are necessary to fit the individual country experiences. In doing so, our objective is to minimise differences in specification across countries, so as to preserve comparability in the outcome of the estimates. We distinguish three groups. The first group is Germany, which played a special role as the *de facto* anchor within the EMS system. The second group is Austria, Belgium and the Netherlands. These countries have maintained their fixed exchange rate parity against the DM during most of the sample period. All the other countries (Finland, France, Greece, Ireland, Italy and Spain) can be described by a similar VAR model. Most of these countries have participated in fixed, but adjustable exchange rate regimes during large parts of the sample period, but nevertheless experienced quite large parity changes. With the exception of France and Ireland, each of these countries also went through a floating exchange rate regime during the sample period.

2.1   Germany

For Germany, we estimate the following VAR model, which is very similar to the benchmark model of the chapter by Peersman and Smets.

$$\begin{bmatrix} X_t \\ Y_t \end{bmatrix} = \begin{bmatrix} A(L) & B(L) \\ C(L) & D(L) \end{bmatrix} \begin{bmatrix} X_{t-1} \\ Y_{t-1} \end{bmatrix} + \begin{bmatrix} a & b \\ c & d \end{bmatrix} \begin{bmatrix} \varepsilon_t^X \\ \varepsilon_t^Y \end{bmatrix} \tag{1}$$

The variables included in the model can be divided into two groups.[5] The first group of variables, X_t, contains a world commodity price index (cp_t), US real GDP (y_t^{US}), and the US short-term nominal interest rate (s_t^{US}). These variables are included to control for changes in world demand and inflation. Moreover, the inclusion of these variables helps to solve the so-called 'price puzzle' (i.e. the empirical finding in the VAR literature that prices rise following an interest rate tightening).[6] In all of the results reported below, we assume that this group of variables is exogenous to the rest of the VAR model. In other words, these variables influence the other variables of the model, y_t, but there is no feedback from the other variables to these variables. Further, we also allow for a contemporaneous impact of the exogenous variables on the endogenous variables. In sum: $b = 0$ and $B(L) = 0$ in equation 1, and:

$$X_t' = \begin{bmatrix} cp_t & y_t^{US} & s_t^{US} \end{bmatrix} \tag{2}$$

The endogenous variables of the benchmark model, Y_t, consist of real GDP (y_t), consumer prices (p_t), the domestic short-term nominal interest rate (s_t) and the real effective exchange rate (x_t):

$$Y_t' = \begin{bmatrix} y_t & p_t & s_t & x_t \end{bmatrix} \tag{3}$$

The main difference of this model with the standard VAR model used to identify monetary shocks either for the US, but also for Germany, is that we do not include money in the model. This omission is mainly motivated by our aim to estimate a model that would be as similar as possible across countries. Because most countries now in EMU had a DM exchange rate target during the period preceding the introduction of the single currency, monetary aggregates have had a secondary role in the monetary policy strategy of these countries. Accordingly, we exclude money aggregates from our benchmark models (including for the results on euro area that we reproduced from the chapter 2 by Peersman and Smets).[7]

---

[5] Each of the VAR models contains also a constant and a linear trend.
[6] For example, Sims (1992).
[7] See also chapter 2 in this volume for a comparison of the response of GDP and prices using alternative identification strategies.

Sensitivity analyses indicated that the inclusion of money in the model did not affect the impact of the German interest rate shock on output and prices. In addition, we also show that the identification of the benchmark model implies that a monetary policy contractionary shock is followed by a fall in money for most of the countries. In other words, our monetary shocks identified in a model without money does not produce a liquidity puzzle.

Turning to the identification of a monetary policy shock, we allow for a contemporaneous interaction between the German interest rate and the real effective exchange rate. Assuming that there is no contemporaneous reaction of the central bank to an exchange rate shock may be appropriate for relatively closed economies such as the euro area and the USA, but is less justifiable for an open economy such as Germany. For example, both Bernanke and Mihov (1997) and Clarida and Gertler (1997) have found a significant contemporaneous response of German interest rates to changes in the exchange rate. Similarly, Smets and Wouters (1999) show that allowing for such a response helps to avoid a price puzzle. Following Smets and Wouters (1999), we solve the simultaneity problem by estimating the reaction coefficient on the exchange rate using the spread between the French and the German long-term interest rate and US dollar/yen exchange rate as instruments.[8]

2.2   Austria, Belgium and the Netherlands

During most of the sample period, Austria, the Netherlands and, to a lesser extent, Belgium, maintained a fixed central exchange rate parity *vis-à-vis* the DM.[9] This implies that, in these countries, the scope for an independent monetary policy was extremely limited and that it is unlikely that we are able to get precise estimates of the effects of *domestic* monetary policy shocks. Instead, most of the policy shocks are likely to be driven by policy innovations in the German interest rate. Moreover, these countries' economies are strongly influenced by economic conditions in Germany. In this case, we therefore modify the benchmark model by including German output, prices, real effective exchange rate and short-term interest rate in the list of endogenous variables and by replacing the effective exchange rate with the bilateral rate versus the DM. In addition, we assume that there is no feedback from the smaller country to

---

[8] See Smets and Wouters (1999) for an explanation on the implementation of this two-step methodology.
[9] The central parity within the EMS changed only in the early 1980s for the Netherlands, and in 1982, 1983, 1986 and 1987 for Belgium. The Austrian exchange rate fluctuated in a very narrow band for the whole sample period.

Germany. The monetary policy shock is identified as the shock to the German interest rate. We can represent this as follows:

$$
\begin{bmatrix} X_t \\ Y_t^{DE} \\ Y_t^j \end{bmatrix} = \begin{bmatrix} A(L) & 0 & 0 \\ D(L) & E(L) & 0 \\ G(L) & H(L) & I(L) \end{bmatrix} \begin{bmatrix} X_{t-1} \\ Y_{t-1}^{DE} \\ Y_{t-1}^j \end{bmatrix} + \begin{bmatrix} a & 0 & 0 \\ d & e & 0 \\ g & h & i \end{bmatrix} \begin{bmatrix} \varepsilon_t^X \\ \varepsilon_t^{DE} \\ \varepsilon_t^j \end{bmatrix} \tag{4}
$$

with

$$
Y_t^{DE} = \begin{bmatrix} y_t^{DE} & p_t^{DE} & s_t^{DE} & x_t^{DE} \end{bmatrix} \tag{5}
$$

$$
Y_t^j = \begin{bmatrix} y_t^j & p_t^j & x_t^j & s_t^j \end{bmatrix}, \quad j = AT, \, NL \text{ or } BE \tag{6}
$$

This implies that we estimate the same monetary policy shocks as in the German case. The response of the German variables to this monetary policy shock is also unchanged. The block-recursive structure of this two countries model closely resembles the one applied by Cushman and Zha (1997) to model the influence of the US economy on Canada. Cushman and Zha consider the effects of an independent monetary policy because of the flexible exchange rate regime that characterises Canada. In contrast, because there was hardly any variation of the DM exchange rate during most of the sample period, we focus on the effects of the German monetary policy shock in Austria, Belgium and the Netherlands.

2.3 Finland, France, Greece, Ireland, Italy and Spain

For all the other countries, we modify the German model in two respects. First, we include the German short-term interest rate in the block of endogenous variables. Second, we replace the real effective exchange rate with the nominal bilateral DM exchange rate given its prominence in the EMS.[10] This leads to the following set of endogenous variables:

$$
Y_t' = \begin{bmatrix} y_t & p_t & s_t^{DE} & x_t & s_t \end{bmatrix} \tag{7}
$$

The German interest rate is included in addition to the bilateral DM exchange rate in order to describe the role of Germany as an anchor of the ERM.[11] Hence we allow for the possibility that the central bank

---

[10] Using an effective exchange rate does not change the results in any significant way. We prefer to include the bilateral DM exchange rate in order to model the specific situation of the EMS.

[11] The macroeconometric model of the Banque de France also defines the reaction function in terms of deviations from the German interest rate. Interestingly, a price puzzle is found for many of these countries when the German interest rate is excluded from the model. This can be explained by mixing up systematic responses of domestic interest rates to German interest rates and the inflationary effects of the ensuing depreciation vis-à-vis the DM as exogenous monetary policy shocks.

systematically reacts to deviations of the exchange rate from the ERM target and to changes in the German short-term interest rate. The monetary shocks associated to this specification of the reaction function correspond to domestic policy decisions taken to fine-tune the pre-EMU process of nominal convergence with Germany.

As before, the domestic policy shock is identified using a standard recursive identification scheme, which corresponds to the ordering of the variables in (7). This means that there is a contemporaneous impact of all the endogenous variables on the monetary policy variable. On the other hand, there is no immediate impact of a monetary policy shock on the other variables. The ordering of the bilateral DM exchange rate before the domestic interest rate is preferable to an alternative ordering of the interest rate and the exchange rate since, in the period, central banks adjusted their interest rate to react to deviations of the exchange rate from the EMS peg. However, the results are robust with respect to a reverse ordering of the domestic interest rate and the bilateral DM exchange rate. Also allowing for a two-way interaction between the exchange rate and the domestic interest rate did not significantly affect the results.

It is important to bear in mind that in the case of Greece, monetary policy was implemented through 'quantity rationing of the banks' so that the three-month interest rate was left unchanged for long periods during the 1980s. The results for this country should therefore be viewed with extra caution.

3   Results

3.1   Estimation

Unless otherwise mentioned, each of the VAR models is estimated in levels over the period 1980–98, which corresponds approximately to the start of the EMS.[12] For Germany, where monetary policy was not constrained by the EMS, we estimated the model for the longest period of data availability, i.e. 1970–98.[13]

The data are seasonally adjusted logs, except the interest rates, which are in levels. We use the three-month interest rate as the monetary policy

[12] Also, we took 1980 as a starting date because some of the data series used are only available from that year.
[13] In this chapter we do not perform an explicit analysis of the long-run behaviour of the economy. By doing the analysis in levels we allow for implicit cointegrating relationships in the data (see chapter 18 in Hamilton, 1994). A more explicit analysis of the long-run behaviour of the various variables is limited by the relatively short sample available. See Ehrmann (2000a) for an explicit cointegration analysis of VAR models for the countries of the euro area.

instrument rate because this is the only short-term interest rate that is available for all countries over the whole sample period. Standard likelihood ratio tests are used to determine the lag-order of the VARs, which usually turns out to be of the order of two or three.

Chow break tests did not reject the overall stability of the various VARs at the 5 per cent confidence level. However, in some countries we detected instability in some of the equations of the VAR. This was in particular the case for Italy where overall stability is rejected at the 10 per cent confidence level. Both the Italian output and exchange rate equation appear to be subject to a significant break in the third quarter of 1992 coinciding with the EMS crisis and the floating of the Italian lira. Also in Finland there is some evidence of instability in the exchange rate equation in the early 1990s. In the case of Germany, it turns out that a longer sample period helps to reduce the weight of the reunification episode, when the monetary policy tightening in the early 1990s coincided with a big positive demand shock due to direct government spending and tax incentives. Estimating the model just for the 1980s and 1990s exacerbates the importance of this event and leads to implausible estimates of the effects of German monetary policy on output and prices.

3.2   The effects of monetary policy on prices, GDP and the exchange rate

The results of the identification schemes described in section 3.1 for each of the individual countries and the euro area (obtained from Peersman and Smets, chapter 2 in this volume) are shown in figure 3.1. This figure summarises for each of the countries the effects of a one-standard deviation monetary policy shock on domestic real GDP, domestic consumer prices, the exchange rate (effective real exchange rate in the case of the euro area and Germany, the bilateral DM exchange rate in the case of the other countries), and the domestic short-term interest rate. We report the OLS estimate-based impulse response function together with 90 per cent confidence bands. Figure 3.1 shows that in each of the countries, a monetary policy tightening eventually leads to a fall in output and prices.[14] It is remarkable that these fairly simple identification schemes allowed us to compile well-behaved responses of GDP and prices to domestic monetary policy shocks. Moreover, these responses are qualitatively consistent with the area-wide results. However, some additional features are worth noting.

---

[14] The exception is the impact of monetary policy on output in Ireland. This effect, which disappears if we use industrial production instead of GDP, seems to be due to export patterns involving the UK.

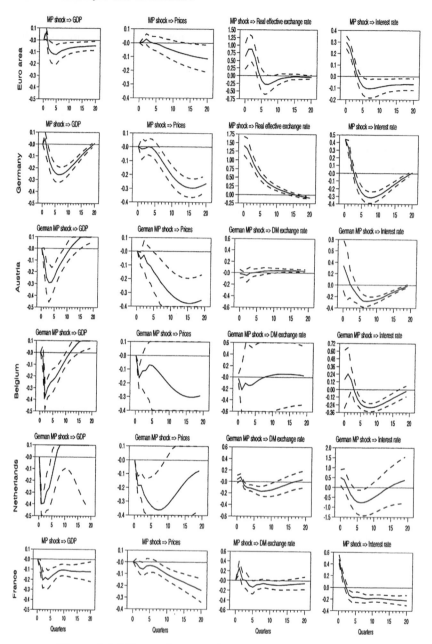

Figure 3.1 Effects of country-level monetary policy shocks (dotted lines = 0.05 and 0.95 percentiles; full line = IRF)

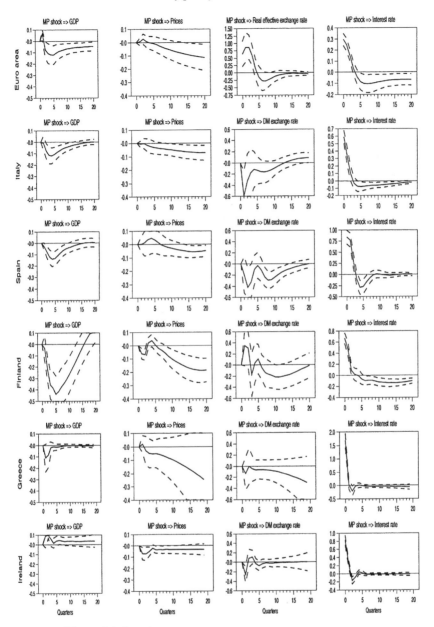

Figure 3.1 (*cont.*)

First, the effects on output and on prices measured at the country level are larger than at the euro area level. This may be due to the adjustments that took place through trade between countries prior to the adoption of the euro. These effects are expected to disappear in the new monetary policy regime. Second, while the overall pattern for output and prices is quite similar across countries, the effects on the exchange rate are less consistent across countries. For Belgium and the Netherlands the lack of response of the exchange rate to the German monetary policy shock reflects the full credibility of the EMS for those countries. In France, Ireland, Greece, Germany and Austria the monetary policy shock triggers an appreciation of the exchange rate. Finally, in Italy and Spain, we find the so-called 'exchange rate puzzle', i.e. a tightening of the monetary policy stance leads to a (only slightly significant) depreciation of the exchange rate. Given the shifts in exchange rate regime in these countries, the finding of erratic exchange rate responses should not be too much of a surprise.[15] More interesting is the fact that the different patterns in the exchange rate responses are not reflected in the responses of prices and output. It is likely that the exchange rate response for one country has often coincided with a similar change of the exchange rate of other European countries in a similar direction so that the effective exchange rate of the country was less affected. Moreover, the 1980s and 1990s were characterised by a negative correlation between the DM exchange rate and the dollar exchange rate of the European currencies.

Third, we show that in the countries of the third group, domestic monetary policy shocks that were orthogonal to the German interest rate have had the 'typical' effects of monetary policy on both output and on prices. These effects reflect the actions taken by central banks in these countries to stimulate nominal convergence with Germany. They may also pick up the effects of the EMS crisis on the 1993 recession and disinflation that followed.

Fourth, the comparison of our results to the estimates of a representative set of previous studies indicates that, taken globally, the literature does not point to any country as experiencing either weaker or larger effects of monetary policy than the loose average of the countries. This is consistent with our (and Kieler and Saarenheimo's, 1998) finding of qualitatively similar results across countries and high uncertainty on the size of the effects. Most studies report that, overall, countries experience

---

[15] While some studies (Gaiotti, 1999; Hernando, 2000; Smets, 1997) have shown that other identification schemes can alleviate this exchange rate puzzle, we prefer to stick to our 'simple' model that performs well in terms of GDP and prices, for the sake of comparability with the other countries.

a fall in output (either GDP or industrial production) after a contractionary monetary policy shock. An overview of the maximum impact on output is provided in table 3.1. The studies present, however, different rankings of the potency of monetary policy across countries. Some countries are documented to be more sensitive to a monetary policy shock in one study, but less in another. For example, Barran, Condert and Mojon (1997) find the largest impact in Germany and the weakest impact in Italy, while Peersman and Smets (1999) find the opposite. Actually, the difference in size and inertia of the estimated monetary policy shock hinders comparisons across countries. While the monetary policy shocks could in principle be harmonised by imposing the same reaction functions across countries, we believe that the estimated parameters of the model are not necessarily invariant to the specification of the policy rule.[16]

Moreover, for any of these studies, the confidence bands around these responses are such that the differences across countries are not significant. In addition, Kieler and Saarenheimo (1998) show that by screening the full space of observationally equivalent identifications of monetary policy shocks for Germany, France and the UK, one can build very similar impulse responses of GDP and prices to monetary policy shocks.

Given the limited power of quantitative comparisons of impulse responses to monetary policy shocks across countries, it is not surprising that the findings are not robust across studies. This is partially confirmed by a recent study that has attempted formally to test the cross-country differences in the transmission mechanism. Ciccarelli and Rebucci (2002) estimate a dynamic heterogeneous panel on a sample that pools macroeconomic data for Germany, France, Italy and Spain. They show that the cumulative impact of monetary policy on economic activity is not significantly different across countries.

3.3   Pre-EMU 'euro area monetary policy' and national monetary policy histories

One interesting outcome of a monetary policy identification exercise is that it allows a retrospective view on when the monetary policy shock

---

[16] This is illustrated by the two variants of Gerlach and Smets (1995). In the first case (a one standard deviation monetary policy shock), the response of output looks similar across Germany, France and Italy, while in the second case (a one-percentage point, eight-quarters sustained increase of the interest rate), German GDP moves by almost twice as much as that of France and Italy. To justify this latter type of analysis, however, we have to assume that the estimated parameters of the model are invariant to the specification of the policy rule, and we are confronted with the Lucas critique. For further discussion, see also Guiso et al. (2000).

Table 3.1 *Effects of monetary policy shocks on output: a comparison across available studies*

	Germany	France	Italy	Spain	Finland	Belgium	Netherlands	Austria	Ireland	Portugal
Mojon and Peersman (2001)	-0.20	-0.20	-0.12	-0.14	-0.44	-0.32	-0.45	-0.25	-0.32	
BIS: National central banks[b]	-0.37	-0.36	-0.44	-0.25		-0.23	-0.18	-0.14		
BIS: FRB multi-country[b]	-0.72	-0.70	-0.44							
Gerlach and Smets (1995) 1	-0.28	-0.19	-0.31							
Gerlach and Smets (1995) 2[b]	-1.00	-0.50	-0.50							
Barran, Condert and Mojon (1997)	-0.65	-0.46	-0.30	-0.55	-0.36		-0.35	-0.48		
Britton and Whitley (1997)	-0.60	-0.62								
Ramaswamy and Sloek (1997)	-0.75	-0.48	-0.50	-0.28	-0.85	-0.95	-0.60	-0.70		
Ehrmann (2000a)[a]	-0.90	-0.40	-0.42	-0.22	-0.60	-0.36	-0.10	-0.05	-0.30	-0.40
Dedola and Lippi (2000)[a,c]	-1.61	-0.66	-1.07	-1.54						
Dornbusch, Favero and Giarazzi (1998)	-1.40	-1.54	-2.14							
Mihov (2001)[b]	-0.55	-0.35	-0.40				-0.30	-0.35		
Peersman and Smets (1999)	-0.87	-1.15	-1.85			-1.80	-1.00	-0.93		
Clements, Konto and Levy (2001)	-0.80	-2.20	-1.10	-1.30	-1.70	-1.40	-1.10	-1.00	-1.20	
Sala (2001)[a]	-0.40	-0.56	-0.32	-0.52		-0.28	-0.22	-0.31	-0.30	-0.33
Peersman (2001)	-0.28	-0.19	-0.17	-0.22		-0.18	-0.11	-0.17		

Notes: Maximum impact; data not comparable across studies. DE = Germany, FR = France, IT = Italy, ES = Spain, FI = Finland, BE = Belgium, NL = the Netherlands, AT = Austria, IR = Ireland, PT = Portugal.
[a] effect of monetary policy on industrial production.
[b] effect of a 100-basis points, eight-quarters sustained increase of the interest rate.
[c] effect of a one-percentage point increase in the short-term rate.

contributed to the evolution of the variables of the model. More importantly, we can relate the evolution of the monetary policy stance of the euro area in the pre-EMU period of the sample to the monetary policy histories of the individual countries.

Figure 3.2 plots the historical contribution of the shocks to the domestic interest rate for the euro area, France, Germany and Italy. The bars are the contribution of the monetary policy shocks to the (domestic) short-term interest rate, whereas the full line is the contribution of the accumulation of all shocks to the short-term interest rate.

The contribution of those shocks to interest rate developments is not uniform. For the euro area as a whole, the years 1987, 1990 and 1992–3 appear as periods of relatively tight monetary policy, whereas in 1984 and 1991 policy is estimated to be relatively loose. Overall, it is not the case that these three periods of tight and two periods of loose monetary policy are observed consistently for Germany, France and Italy. In particular, the experience of the three countries is contrasted during the EMS crisis.

Then, the monetary policy tightening in France, Italy, and other countries – not shown in figure 3.2 to save space – is consistent with the sharp tightening observed at the euro area level. On the contrary, German monetary policy was not too restrictive during the period 1992–3. This means that the high interest rate in Germany after the reunification can be explained by the endogenous response of the Bundesbank to a booming economy. For the other countries, the stance of monetary policy, conditional on the state of the economy, was more restrictive than for the rest of the sample period.

Another remarkable feature is that the contribution of the monetary policy shocks to the accumulated shocks of all the variables is very low in Germany, Belgium, the Netherlands and Austria. Most changes in the German interest rate are due to systematic response to price and output, while most changes to the Belgian, Dutch and Austrian interest rate are due to systematic response to the exchange rate. In contrast, monetary policy shocks explain a large share of the variance of the interest rate of other countries.

Cross-country comparison of the shocks is put into sharper focus in table 3.2, which reports the correlations of the identified monetary policy shocks across countries and with the euro area. The monetary policy shocks that can be identified for the euro area aggregate (see Peersman and Smets, chapter 2 in this volume) are highly correlated to the ones identified for Germany, Italy and France. The correlation of the area-wide shocks with these three national monetary policy shocks is, respectively 0.66, 0.49 and 0.51.

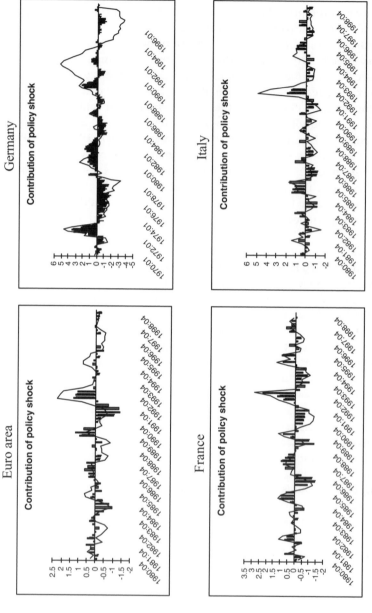

Figure 3.2 Monetary policy shocks' contribution to the short-term interest rate for the euro area, Germany, France and Italy

Table 3.2 *Correlation of country-level monetary policy shocks*

	Euro	Germany	Italy	France	Spain	Finland	Portugal	Greece	Ireland
Euro area	1.00	0.66	0.51	0.49	0.46	0.13	0.08	−0.07	0.30
Germany		1.00	0.16	0.21	0.09	0.19	0.22	0.08	0.14
Italy			1.00	0.34	0.30	0.08	0.11	−0.07	0.24
France				1.00	0.21	0.01	−0.12	−0.29	−0.27
Spain					1.00	0.07	−0.03	−0.20	0.29
Finland						1.00	0.53	−0.15	−0.03
Portugal							1.00	0.06	0.16
Greece								1.00	−0.27
Ireland									1.00

3.4   Further evidence on the effects of monetary policy shocks

In this section, we discuss the effects of monetary policy shocks on other macroeconomic variables that are not included in the basic model. We have done this by estimating the following equations:

$$
\begin{bmatrix} X_t \\ Y_t \\ Z_t \end{bmatrix} = \begin{bmatrix} A(L) & 0 & 0 \\ D(L) & E(L) & 0 \\ G(L) & H(L) & I(L) \end{bmatrix} \begin{bmatrix} X_{t-1} \\ Y_{t-1} \\ Z_{t-1} \end{bmatrix} + \begin{bmatrix} a & 0 & 0 \\ d & e & 0 \\ g & h & 1 \end{bmatrix} \begin{bmatrix} \varepsilon_t^X \\ \varepsilon_t^Y \\ \varepsilon_t^Z \end{bmatrix} \quad (8)
$$

The system of equations (8) is very similar to (1). X_t is still the block of exogenous variables and Y_t the endogenous block. Let Z_t be another macroeconomic variable (for example, investment). Again, we suppose that neither contemporaneous nor lagged values of the endogenous variables has an influence on the exogenous block. This is also the case for our variable under interest. However, following Evans and Marshall (2002), we suppose the same for our macroeconomic variable, Z_t, with respect to our endogenous block of variables, Y_t, i.e. there is no impact of the variable under investigation on the other variables in the system. This assumption ensures that the shocks are invariant to the choice of the macroeconomic variable added to the original model.

3.4.1   The impact on GDP components   Figure 3.3 presents for each individual country the response of respectively investment, consumption and export to a monetary policy shock. With the notable exception of Greece and Ireland, the response of investment is at least twice as large as the response of consumption. Investment response is, however, insignificant in both countries, and the response of consumption is insignificant for Greece. These results are broadly consistent with the ones of Barran,

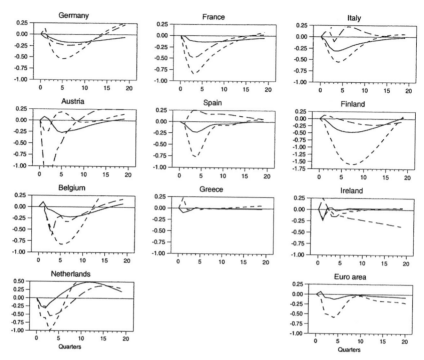

Figure 3.3 Effects of country-level monetary policy shocks on consumption (full line), investment (dotted line) and exports (broken line)

Condert and Mojon (1997) for models estimated on a sample period spanning from 1975 to 1993. They reflect the fact that consumption is smoother than investment over the business cycle, but also possibly the income effects of monetary policy, whereby net-debtor investors revise their expenditure plans more than net-creditor consumers. These results are also consistent with the area-wide results obtained in Peersman and Smets (chapter 2 in this volume).

For most countries, we find a strong impact of a monetary policy shock on exports. For instance, Austrian, Belgian and Dutch exports are affected by the appreciation of the real effective German exchange rate, while their nominal exchange rate *vis-à-vis* Germany hardly moves (Belgium and the Netherlands) or slightly appreciates (Austria). In these three countries, as well as in Germany and in France, the dampening effect of contractionary monetary policy shocks on exports is larger than the one observed on GDP. In Finland, exports decrease as well and this fall is slower and smaller than the one observed for GDP. Finally, for Italy and Spain, we do not find a negative impact of contractionary monetary

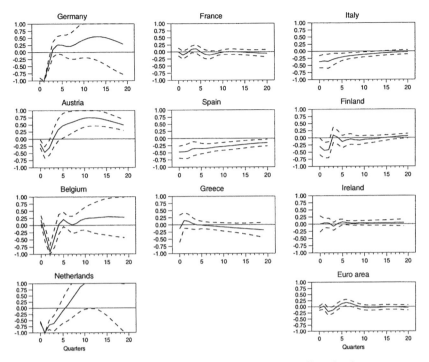

Figure 3.4 Effects of country-level monetary policy shocks on money (M1) (dotted lines = 0.05 and 0.95 percentiles; full line = IRF).

policy shocks on exports. The impact is even significantly positive in the latter country. This finding is not surprising given the exchange rate puzzle in these countries. However, the positive response of exports is not large enough to make the response of Spanish and Italian GDP deviate from the 'typical' responses of GDP observed in most countries and at the euro area level.

3.4.2   No 'liquidity puzzle'   We have not considered money in our identification of monetary policy shocks because it had a much less important role than the exchange rate for all the countries, which were targeting a fixed exchange rate with the DM within the EMS. We nevertheless check that our identification is not characterised by a 'liquidity puzzle'. This 'puzzle' stresses the risk of confusing money demand shocks and money supply shocks. A positive shock to money, which would be accompanied by a rise in the interest rate, is more likely to correspond to a money demand shock than to a monetary policy shock.

We estimated the response of M1 to the monetary policy shock identified in section 3.1. The central bank can better control this narrow aggregate than M3 because the yield on bank deposits and on money is correlated to the short-term interest rate. As expected, the monetary policy shock triggers an immediate fall of M1 in all countries except France, Greece and Ireland (figure 3.4). This further confirms the validity of our identification scheme.

4   Concluding remarks

In this chapter, we have used VAR models to analyse the effects of monetary policy shocks in the individual countries of the euro area in the pre-EMU period. First, we show that three, relatively simple, identification schemes depending on the monetary policy decision process in the EMS, obtain well-behaved and qualitatively consistent effects of the monetary policy shocks in all the individual countries of the euro area. We confirm that, for these countries, the qualitative effects of monetary policy are quite similar to the ones described in a large literature for the USA and by Peersman and Smets in chapter 2 for the euro area aggregates. A contractionary monetary policy shock leads to a temporary fall in GDP that peaks between three and six quarters after the shock and a gradual decrease in the price level. The investment response and the export response are larger than the one of GDP while the response of consumption is smaller. We show also that the shocks are initially accompanied by a decline in a narrow monetary aggregate. The effect on the exchange rate is somewhat more mixed. For some countries, we find an exchange rate puzzle. However, the temporary depreciation of the DM exchange rate observed in these countries does not seem to affect the response of GDP nor the response of prices. Second, this analysis allows us to compare the 'artificial' monetary policy shocks measured for the euro area with those of the individual countries. In particular, the early 1990s appear as a contraction for the euro area and for most of the individual countries while the Bundesbank was just reacting to the reunification boom.

The chapter argues that the comparison of the effects of monetary policy across countries is hardly feasible. One cannot use VAR models to conclude that some countries are characterised by larger effects of monetary policy than others because the confidence bands around the estimated impulse responses are very large. It is also important to bear in mind that the harmonisation of the size and the inertia of the estimated monetary policy shocks, of which the difference hinders comparisons across countries, requires that the estimated parameters of the model are invariant to the specification of the policy rule, an assumption subject to the Lucas critique.

4   Analysing monetary policy transmission at the euro area level using structural macroeconomic models

P. McAdam and J. Morgan

1   Introduction

This chapter examines the monetary policy transmission mechanism at the euro area level using macroeconomic models and considers some of the issues raised by such an undertaking. The aim is to assess how important various aspects of model and simulation design are in determining the results. To illustrate the importance of these issues, we report results using the ECB's Area Wide Model (AWM) and the National Institute Global Economic Model (NiGEM).[1]

The AWM is a single-country model of the euro area using aggregated euro area data – a full description of the model is provided by Fagan, Henry and Mestre (2001). There is no country disaggregation so the AWM treats EMU members as one country. NiGEM, by contrast, models each individual country separately and the euro area results that we report are based on a static aggregation of individual country results (NIESR, 2001). Nevertheless, it is possible to run the model consistent with a monetary union in the euro area and thereby ensure common interest rate and exchange rate paths for countries within the euro area.

The chapter takes as its starting point the last major study of comparative properties of central bank models (BIS, 1995). The BIS study examined cross-country differences in the transmission mechanism of monetary policy and considered the extent to which these could be due to differences in financial structure. Simulation experiments were undertaken on the models involving a 100-basis point increase in the short-term policy interest rate for two years.[2] In this chapter we undertake simulations similar to those undertaken in the BIS (1995) exercise, but our focus is at the euro area level.

We thank, without implicating, Gabriel Fagan, Ricardo Mestre, Carlos Robalo-Marques and Christopher Sims. The opinions expressed are not necessarily those of the ECB.
[1] The April 2001 release of NiGEM was used.
[2] The results were summarised by Smets (1995).

1.1   The monetary policy transmission mechanism[3]

In this section we review the transmission of monetary policy in the AWM and NiGEM, initially with common aspects before turning to specific features of each model. In most large-scale macroeconomic models the transmission mechanism of monetary policy takes place through the interest rate. The central bank chooses the short-term policy interest rate, which has a pass through to other market yields, asset prices and the exchange rate. Following these financial linkages, the 'real economy' effects typically emerge via the impact on domestic spending (private investment and consumption) and on the external sector through export and import volumes. These effects are highlighted to differing degrees in both models.

As regards financial market linkages, both models embody forward-looking uncovered interest parity (UIP) for exchange rate determination. This implies that the expected appreciation of the home currency exchange rate is set equal to the differential between the home and foreign short-term interest rates. Long-term interest rates can be determined in a backward or forward-looking manner. The former involves a weighted moving-average of past short (R) and long-term (RL) interest rates. For the AWM and NiGEM, respectively, they are:[4]

$$RL_t = 0.25 \cdot R_t + 0.25 \sum_{i=1}^{3} RL_{t-1} \tag{1}$$

$$\Delta RL_t = RL_{t-1} + 0.8 \Delta R_t + 0.2(R_{t-1} - RL_{t-1} + 0.5)^5 \tag{2}$$

In both models the forward-looking determination of long rates is:

$$\log(1 + RL_t/100) = \frac{1}{40} \sum_{j=0}^{39} \log\left(1 + \frac{R_{t+j}}{100}\right) \tag{3}$$

That is to say, both models embody a ten-year bond term structure.

In terms of the determination of short-term interest rates, both models incorporate the same 'Taylor rule':

$$R_t = \alpha_1 + \alpha_2 \tilde{\Pi}_t + \alpha_3 \tilde{Y}_t \tag{4}$$

Where Π is current inflation, Y is the real output gap, a tilde indicates deviation from the (baseline) target and α_2, α_3 are set at standard weights.

---

[3] McAdam and Morgan (2001) provide a more formal representation of the transmission mechanism in structural macroeconomic models using an illustrative maquette.
[4] The backward-looking long-rate equation used in the AWM is not standard and thus is used purely for illustrative purposes.
[5] The risk premium from holding bonds is assumed to be 0.5 per cent.

Both models also incorporate a fiscal closure rule to maintain a deficit–output ratio to the baseline by changes in the direct tax rate.

Following these financial market interactions there will be a reaction in the rest of the economy. A change in the nominal long rate (negatively) affects capital accumulation through the increased user cost of financing new investment. There can be a direct 'substitution' effect on consumption since the real lending rate can proxy its opportunity cost. There can also be an indirect effect of long-term interest rates on consumption through changes in net wealth. The net-wealth effects typically stem from such sources as changes in the stock of public debt, the capital stock, monetary aggregates and changes in equity prices. In the latter case, a rise in interest rates is usually considered to lead to lower equity prices and lower net wealth. In relation to government debt, a rise in long-term interest rates will lead to a downward revaluation of holdings of government debt and hence lower net wealth. Finally, there may be a role for interest rates to directly affect the monetary aggregate, which feeds into government debt stock with a negative coefficient and thereby affects net wealth.

There are also a number of ways in which changes in interest rates can have an impact on income and cash flows. Government interest payments typically depend on long-term interest rates reflecting the term structure of government debt. In addition to affecting the government budget balance, government interest payments feed into personal income (thereby affecting consumers' expenditure) and into the debits of interest, profits and dividends (thereby affecting net overseas asset accumulation – a component of net wealth).

The discussion thus far describes the transmission channels and structure involved in the AWM fairly well, although inevitably some exceptions apply. First, *short (rather than long) rates* enter consumption and drive the user cost of capital (short rates being preferred on statistical grounds). Second, there is no *endogenous foreign rate* and thus the exchange rate (though modelled as UIP) is purely driven by movements in short-run rates relative to the baseline. Third, the *income effect* is determined via the impact on government interest payments which are linked to changes in long-term interest rates. Finally, the *wealth effect* is embodied through the capital stock and public debt. For public debt, as before, interest payments are linked to long-term interest rates. In the case of wealth through capital accumulation, the accumulation of investment defines the capital stock.

In relation to NiGEM, it is important to note that, although similar, the set-up in each of the national economies within the euro area can be somewhat different. This reflects the deliberate design of the model as the larger economies are modelled in somewhat more detail than the smaller ones, but also econometric evidence, as interest rate effects have been found to be present in some equations in some countries but not in others. A good example of this is a direct interest rate effect in consumption, which is present only in the consumption functions of Italy, the Netherlands and Ireland. The interest rate used is also different, being the short rate in Italy and the long rate in the Netherlands and Ireland – although in all three cases the coefficient is negative implying that a rise in interest rates has a direct effect in terms of lowering consumers' expenditure.[6]

In NiGEM, the standard model also allows for model-consistent forward-looking behaviour in equity prices, in the inflation terms used in monetary policy rules and in the wage equations.[7] In relation to the wage equations, when these equations were estimated they typically allowed for the possibility that past, current and future inflation developments could have an impact on current wages.[8] In estimation a significant role for expected inflation was found in some – but not all – countries. When the model is used in simulation mode it is possible to choose between a term for expected inflation based on backward-looking variables or alternatively to allow for a truly forward-looking expected inflation term based on the model generated values for inflation in the next quarter. This choice has an impact on the dynamics of wages but leaves their long-run level unaffected.

2   Design of monetary policy transmission simulation experiment.

This section briefly discusses how key aspects of both model construction and the design of simulation experiments have an important bearing on the estimated size of monetary policy effects in structural macroeconomic models. The first issue we address is whether monetary policy can be treated as exogenous or whether it is more appropriate to treat policy as endogenous via a policy rule. In the former case, monetary policy experiments can involve a shock to the policy interest rate. In the latter case, it is common to undertake monetary policy experiments via a shock to the policy rule – e.g. a change in the target for the inflation rate or the

---

[6] McAdam and Morgan (2001) provide more details on the transmission mechanism of monetary policy in NiGEM.

[7] More details on the approach taken to modelling forward-looking variables are given in the NIESR (2001).

[8] In the long run, real wages are determined by labour productivity and the unemployment rate.

money stock. In principle, the shock to the policy rule can be calibrated in such a way as to yield the same change in the policy interest rate that could be imposed if the interest rate were treated as exogenous. However, it is important to bear in mind that when comparing results across models, a common shock to a policy rule can produce very different reactions of policy interest rates.[9]

An interesting and related question is whether to keep monetary policy endogenous or exogenous after the completion of the initial monetary policy shock. If it is kept exogenous there may be prolonged periods of disequilibria in many macroeconomic models. For this reason, there may be a case for allowing endogenous monetary policy following the completion of the initial (fixed) monetary policy experiment. The drawback of such an approach is that it renders the results sensitive to the policy rule used and therefore limits the comparability of results across models if each incorporates a different monetary policy response.

The use of fiscal policy rules in macroeconomic models raises some similar issues. It has long been recognised (e.g. Christ, 1968) that the government budget constraint is important. If a government deficit emerges in a simulation, it is necessary to have some financing assumption. Therefore, many models now incorporate fiscal closure rules, which aim to maintain some level of fiscal solvency through adjusting fiscal variables (often the direct tax rate but sometimes government expenditure) to achieve a target specified either in terms of the deficit or debt stock. Both models incorporate such a rule which targets the baseline deficit ratio by changes in the direct tax rate. In some situations, particularly in models with many forward-looking elements, such rules can help stabilise the model. The main argument against incorporating fiscal reaction functions is that they would undermine the comparability of the results across models.

An important feature of model design that will significantly affect the results of simulations is the treatment of expectations of variables such as long-term interest rates, the exchange rate and inflation. A traditional way of dealing with expectations in macro models was to assume that they are determined as a function of current and lagged values of some observed variables – often in the form of adaptive expectations. However, reflecting the increased popularity of the notion of rational expectations in recent decades there has been a move to including expectations that are genuinely forward-looking in the sense that they are consistent with the future outcomes generated by the model ('model-consistent' expectations). As already discussed, the AWM and NiGEM models allow, albeit

[9] For examples of this issue see Church *et al.* (2000) and Mitchell *et al.* (1998).

to varying degrees, for forward-looking behaviour. In section 3 we explore the implications of changing the extent of forward-looking behaviour in the models.

3   Simulation experiments using the AWM and the NiGEM models

To illustrate the importance of the issues raised in section 2, we now turn to a comparison of the results of a number of simulation exercises using both models. As a starting point we followed BIS (1995) and undertook a monetary policy experiment involving an increase of the short-term policy interest rates by one percentage point for two years (simulation 1). Thereafter a return to baseline values was assumed and no monetary policy rules were implemented. No fiscal rules were in operation either and the models were run in an entirely backward-looking mode with a fixed nominal exchange rate. Simulation 2 was identical to simulation 1, except that a monetary policy rule was implemented at the end of the two-year initial shock. The form of the monetary reaction is the Taylor rule specified in (4) with Π^d and Y^d (desired values) set at their baseline values. Simulation 3 was identical to simulation 2 but a fiscal policy rule was allowed to operate from the start of the simulation. The fiscal rule adjusts the direct tax rate to achieve a target for the government budget balance as a proportion of GDP. Simulation 4 was identical to simulation 3 but it allowed all the forward-looking elements of the models, as described in section 1, to operate.

3.1   *The results*

The results of the simulation experiments are shown in table 4.1 In *simulation 1*, the rise in short-term interest rates induces a rise in long-term interest rates in both models but the pattern is rather different – reflecting the differences in the backward-looking equations for the long rate (see (1)–(3)). In NiGEM, the long rate increases by nearly as much as the short rate in the first two years and then immediately returns to close to the baseline thereafter. In the AWM, the initial rise in the long rate is much smaller than the rise in the short rate.

In terms of activity, both the maximum and the average loss of output over the first three years are quite similar, but there are differences in the timing. With the NiGEM simulation, output falls by 0.09 per cent in the first year, dropping by 0.36 per cent and 0.44 per cent in the second and third years, respectively. In the AWM simulation, the initial impact is somewhat larger with a fall in output of 0.23 per cent in year 1 reaching to 0.46 per cent in year 2 before moderating to 0.39 per cent in the third year. Thereafter, in both models, there is a tendency for output to return to the baseline, and then to remain above the baseline for some time. However, while both models exhibit such a tendency, the reversion to base is more protracted in the AWM due to the fact that this model contains relatively weaker feedback and error corrections leading to a slower speed of adjustment.

The government budget balance worsens in both models as lower output leads to lower tax receipts and higher government transfers due to higher unemployment. However, the deterioration of the fiscal position in the first two years is more pronounced in NiGEM despite a more modest output loss over this period compared with the AWM. This reflects a greater sensitivity of the fiscal variables to changes in economic activity in NiGEM than in the AWM. It is also the case that changes in economic activity exert a larger impact on unemployment in the AWM, albeit with a somewhat longer lag than in NiGEM. After three years, the unemployment rate is 0.35 of a percentage point higher in the AWM compared with a rise of 0.19 of a percentage point in the NiGEM simulation. This is despite the fact that in year 3 output is further below its baseline in the NiGEM simulation than in the AWM one. However, the longer lag in the impact on unemployment is indicated by the fact that the peak in the rise in unemployment occurs after the trough in the fall in output in the AWM, in contrast with the NiGEM results when both effects occur in the same year.

The response of prices reflects the developments in output, albeit with a marked lag due to conventional sticky price mechanisms in models. In NiGEM, prices do not fall significantly in the first couple of years, but by year 3 they are 0.12 per cent below base and in year 5 they are 0.34 per cent below and thereafter they return to the base-line. In the AWM the fall in prices is more marked in the first two years (reflecting the larger initial output loss) and continues to gather pace during the reporting period for the simulation and in year 5 prices are 0.40 per cent below the base-line. In the longer term, prices will return to their baseline levels because of the assumption of a fixed nominal exchange rate. The initial fall in domestic prices means that there is depreciation in the real exchange rate, which ultimately boosts output and prices.

In *simulation 2*, the first two years are identical but in year 3 the Taylor rule begins to operate. Because output and prices are both below the baseline there is a decline in the short-term interest rate in year 3 in both models. In NiGEM the Taylor rule leads to a decline in short-term interest rates of 38 basis points while in the AWM the decline is more modest. As the parameters of the Taylor rules are identical the difference

Table 4.1 *Effects of euro area monetary policy shocks in NiGEM and AWM simulations[d]*

	GDP[a,b]	PCE[a,b]	U[a,c]	S-Rate[a,c]	L-Rate[a,c]	Nom XR[a,b]	Real XR[a,b]	TBR[a,c]	GBR[a,c]
Simulation 1									
				NiGEM					
1	−0.09	0.00	0.03	1.00	0.85	0.00	0.00	0.03	−0.21
2	−0.36	−0.03	0.15	1.00	0.94	0.00	0.00	0.11	−0.45
3	−0.44	−0.12	0.19	0.00	0.12	0.00	−0.02	0.11	−0.44
5	0.08	−0.34	−0.07	0.00	0.02	0.00	−0.17	−0.01	−0.19
				AWM					
1	−0.23	−0.03	0.07	1.00	0.24	0.00	−0.04	0.17	−0.10
2	−0.46	−0.11	0.25	1.00	0.36	0.00	−0.15	0.27	−0.29
3	−0.39	−0.21	0.35	0.00	0.17	0.00	−0.24	0.13	−0.39
5	−0.17	−0.40	0.19	0.00	0.02	0.00	−0.45	0.01	−0.40
Simulation 2									
				NiGEM					
1	−0.09	0.00	0.03	1.00	0.85	0.00	0.00	0.03	−0.21
2	−0.36	−0.03	0.15	1.00	0.94	0.00	0.00	0.11	−0.45
3	−0.40	−0.12	0.18	−0.38	−0.20	0.00	−0.02	0.10	−0.36
5	0.20	−0.30	−0.12	0.08	0.05	0.00	−0.14	−0.03	−0.08
				AWM					
1	−0.23	−0.03	0.07	1.00	0.24	0.00	−0.04	0.17	−0.10
2	−0.46	−0.11	0.25	1.00	0.36	0.00	−0.15	0.27	−0.29
3	−0.33	−0.20	0.33	−0.23	0.11	0.00	−0.23	0.09	−0.37
5	−0.09	−0.36	0.12	−0.10	−0.03	0.00	−0.39	−0.03	−0.32

Simulation 3

NiGEM

1	-0.10	0.00	0.04	1.00	0.85	0.00	0.00	0.04	-0.17
2	-0.44	-0.03	0.18	1.00	0.94	0.00	0.00	0.14	-0.27
3	-0.59	-0.15	0.26	-0.52	-0.32	0.00	-0.02	0.15	-0.06
5	0.02	-0.46	-0.05	-0.13	-0.14	0.00	-0.19	0.02	0.14

AWM

1	-0.23	-0.03	0.07	1.00	0.24	0.00	-0.04	0.17	-0.10
2	-0.48	-0.11	0.26	1.00	0.36	0.00	-0.15	0.28	-0.27
3	-0.42	-0.22	0.37	-0.31	0.09	0.00	-0.25	0.16	-0.28
5	-0.37	-0.49	0.33	-0.38	-0.12	0.00	-0.56	0.11	-0.05

Simulation 4

NiGEM

1	-0.24	-0.05	0.08	1.00	0.10	1.11	1.05	0.05	-0.16
2	-0.31	-0.08	0.15	1.00	-0.01	0.26	0.13	0.04	-0.16
3	-0.19	-0.15	0.08	-0.24	-0.06	-0.16	-0.33	0.06	0.07
5	-0.09	-0.31	0.00	-0.12	-0.02	0.20	-0.15	0.03	0.05

AWM

1	-0.41	-0.10	0.12	1.00	-0.31	0.88	0.80	0.24	-0.05
2	-0.86	-0.24	0.47	1.00	-0.40	-0.05	-0.35	0.47	-0.11
3	-0.83	-0.39	0.72	-0.60	-0.40	-0.42	-0.90	0.36	0.00
5	-0.61	-1.02	0.70	-0.86	-0.16	0.88	-0.24	0.11	0.17

Notes: [a] GDP is real GDP, PCE is the consumer's expenditure deflator, U is the standardised unemployment rate, S-Rate is the three-month interest rate, L-Rate is the ten-year interest rate, Nom XR is the nominal exchange rate, Real XR is the real exchange rate, TBR is the real trade balance and GBR is the government budget balance to GDP ratio.
[b] GDP, PCE, Nom XR and Real XR are all expressed as a percentage difference from baseline.
[c] The remaining variables are expressed as an absolute difference from baseline.
[d] A fall in the nominal or real exchange rate is a depreciation.

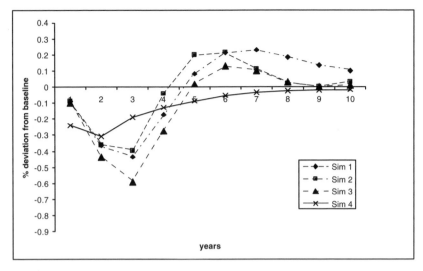

Figure 4.1 Euro area GDP response in NiGEM to the four monetary policy experiments

in outcomes is due to the fact that when the rule begins to operate the output loss and fall in inflation are both greater in NiGEM than in the AWM.

Inevitably, the lower interest rates from year 3 onwards reduce the magnitude of the subsequent output losses – although the initial impact is not that large. In year 3, the output loss is reduced by about 0.05 per cent in both the NiGEM and AWM simulations when compared with simulation 1. Some interesting contrasts then emerge between the results from the two models. In NiGEM short-term interest rates are close to the baseline by year 5, but this return to the baseline takes longer in the AWM, reflecting the fact that output and prices are below the baseline for longer. In both models the Taylor rule speeds the return of GDP towards the baseline. As both also generate a period of above-baseline GDP (as shown in figures 4.1 and 4.2), the Taylor rule then works to reduce towards the baseline by raising short-term interest rates.

In *simulation 3*, with the fiscal policy rule, the effects on output are larger in the first few years as the fiscal rule seeks to close the widening government deficit by raising direct taxation. The initial impact of the fiscal rule on output is not that large, but it does increase in importance. The effect of the fiscal rule is initially slightly larger in NiGEM. This is because, as already discussed, the monetary policy shock has a larger initial impact on the public finances in NiGEM than in the

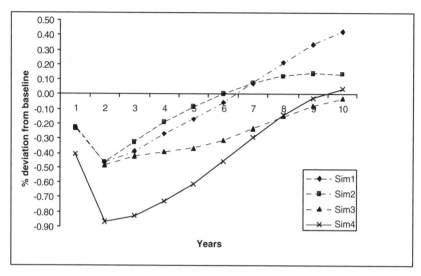

Figure 4.2 Euro area GDP response in the AWM to the four monetary policy experiments

AWM – reflecting a greater cyclical sensitivity of the fiscal variables in NiGEM. In year 3 output is 0.59 per cent below the baseline in NiGEM while in the AWM it is 0.42 per cent below the base-line. Thereafter, the standard pattern of output returning to the baseline more quickly in NiGEM than in the AWM reasserts itself.

One notable feature of this simulation is that the fall in the price level is somewhat more pronounced. Reflecting the lower output induced by the fiscal contraction, the response of the Taylor rule is to lower interest rates by a larger amount – 52 basis points in NiGEM and 31 basis points in the AWM – in year 3.

In *simulation 4*, with forward-looking behaviour, the results are quite different from the preceding three backward-looking simulations. A marked contrast is the reaction of long-term interest rates. This is not due to a different equation for long-term interest rates as the forward-looking condition is the same in both models. The reaction of long-term interest rates in NiGEM is much more subdued – a rise of 10 basis points in year 1 and a return to the baseline in year 2. The forward-looking condition takes into account that the initial hike in short-term interest rates will last for only two years. In addition, the Taylor rule will subsequently ensure that interest rates fall below the baseline for a period after the initial rise. However in the AWM model the long rate actually falls significantly in year 1 – by 31 basis points rising to 40 basis points in year 2 – as the forward-looking long rate reacts to the larger and protracted falls in short-term interest rates from year 3 onwards.

An important factor underlying these results is that the impact of long-term interest rates is different in the two models. In NiGEM, long-term interest rates affect investment (via the user cost of capital), consumption in some countries and also affect some financial variables. A rise in long-term interest rates will tend to lower economic activity through lower investment and to some extent also lower consumers' expenditure. In the AWM, the only impact of the long-rate is on financial variables and in particular government interest payments to the personal sector. Nevertheless, the impact of this change in government interest payments generates strong income effects in the AWM. This means that a rise in long-term interest rates can have surprisingly strong *positive* short-term effects on personal income and thereby also economic activity.

The rise in short-term interest rates now leads to a year-1 appreciation in the exchange rate of 1.11 per cent in NiGEM and 0.88 per cent in the AWM.[10] In terms of its effect on output in year 1, the exchange rate appreciation more than offsets the effect of lower long-term interest rates and output falls by 0.24 per cent in NiGEM. Thereafter, output effects are smaller and the return to something closer to the baseline is markedly faster and smoother in this simulation. This can be seen in figure 4.1, which compares the GDP response in simulations 1–4. In the forward-looking simulation there is a much smoother return towards the baseline without the overshooting seen in the other three simulations.

In the AWM, the initial output effect is also much larger due to the exchange rate appreciation and the fall in the long rate. Since the long-rate feeds only into public debt-related income-bearing assets the immediate effect is to reduce households' public debt-related income through lower interest repayments. Since – in the current version of the model – all such income is held domestically, this is clearly a significant (negative) channel. Output falls by 0.41 per cent in year 1 and by 0.86 per cent in year 2 before gradually moving towards the baseline thereafter. The results from the simulations using the AWM are shown in figure 4.2. Although superficially, the AWM results look different from the NiGEM results there is a similar broad pattern. Output effects in the forward-looking simulation are initially more pronounced than in simulation 3,

---

[10] In the longer term, the nominal exchange rate remains permanently appreciated in both models. It is noteworthy that in the NiGEM model the long-run nominal exchange rate appreciation is reached more quickly than in the AWM, which experiences a temporary period of cycling in the exchange rate. The reasons for this are discussed in McAdam and Morgan (2001). The role played by the nominal exchange rate in each model in the adjustment process is somewhat different (for details see Fagan, Henry and Mestre, 2001, McAdam and Morgan, 2001).

but the forward-looking simulation settles down at the baseline level more quickly.[11]

The considerably faster reaction of NiGEM in the forward-looking scenario reflects the far larger number of forward-looking elements within NiGEM. As already discussed, in addition to forward-looking long-term interest rates and the exchange rate, NiGEM incorporates forward-looking behaviour in wage formation equity prices and the Taylor rule takes into account expected prices. It is well known (e.g. Fisher, 1992) that more forward-looking models tend to exhibit faster reactions compared to models with fewer forward-looking elements. In the absence of substantially more forward-looking elements in the AWM, the relatively large initial demand effects in simulation 4 take some time to die out. Investigating the degree to which more forward-looking elements can be put in the AWM is the subject of ongoing research.

3.2   Channels of transmission

The above simulations show only the overall effect of a change in monetary policy on the endogenous variables. But, as discussed in McAdam and Morgan (2001), it is standard practice when reporting such results to decompose them into their various (transmission) channels. We identify the following channels: (1) an *income/cash* flow channel, which measures the effect of interest rates on net interest payments; (2) a *wealth channel*, to capture the impact of interest rates on wealth; (3) a direct interest channel on *consumption*; (4) a *cost of capital* channel, to capture the effect of interest rates on investment and (5) an *exchange rate* channel, to capture the effects of changes in the exchange rate due to changes in interest rates. The results for GDP and prices are shown in table 4.1.[12]

As shown in table 4.2, in the case of NiGEM, the clear message is that in the initial period the exchange rate channel is the most important, accounting for 0.15 per cent of the 0.24 per cent fall in output in year one. Thereafter it gradually diminishes in importance reflecting the fact that the real exchange rate rapidly returns close to its baseline level. From year 2 onwards the domestic channels – and most notably the cost of capital in investment channel – gradually gain in importance. The direct

---

[11] In the case of the AWM, the final reversion to baseline can not be seen clearly in figure 4.2 as it occurs after ten years. A chart comparing the reversion to the baseline over a long time horizon is available upon request.

[12] McAdam and Morgan (2001) also report results for the channel decomposition with what they term as a 'channel-dependent' monetary policy, where the interest rate rule response is allowed to be different for each of the channels. The general pattern of results is not significantly altered when using a channel-specific monetary policy, although the income channel significantly diminishes in importance in the AWM.

Table 4.2 *Decomposition of channels of transmission in NiGEM and the AWM*

	Total	Income effect	Wealth	Consumption effect	Cost of capital	Exchange rate channel
GDP effects				*NiGEM*		
1	−0.24	−0.02	−0.02	−0.01	−0.06	**−0.15**
2	−0.31	−0.05	−0.04	−0.03	**−0.10**	−0.07
3	−0.19	**−0.06**	−0.02	−0.03	−0.03	0.03
5	−0.09	−0.05	0.03	0.00	**0.07**	−0.02
				AWM		
1	−0.41	−0.05	0.00	−0.06	**−0.21**	−0.08
2	−0.86	−0.16	−0.01	−0.04	**−0.57**	−0.06
3	−0.83	−0.25	−0.02	0.06	**−0.60**	0.02
5	−0.61	**−0.29**	−0.06	0.05	−0.12	−0.06
Price effects				*NiGEM*		
1	−0.05	0.00	0.00	0.00	0.02	**−0.08**
2	−0.08	−0.01	−0.01	−0.01	0.03	**−0.12**
3	−0.15	−0.02	−0.03	−0.02	−0.02	**−0.12**
5	−0.31	−0.05	−0.03	−0.03	−0.08	**−0.13**
				AWM		
1	−0.10	−0.01	0.00	−0.01	−0.02	**−0.07**
2	−0.24	−0.03	0.00	−0.02	**−0.12**	−0.07
3	−0.39	−0.09	0.00	−0.02	**−0.26**	−0.01
5	−1.02	−0.30	−0.03	0.01	**−0.55**	−0.11

interest effect in consumption has only a modest impact, reflecting the fact that such an effect is present in only three countries of the euro area. Nevertheless, the effects of the wealth channel are not that much larger, while the income channel assumes greater importance from year 3.

For the AWM, the cost of capital channel is also the most important domestic channel in the first three years but unlike NiGEM it is more important than the exchange rate channel for the whole of the reporting period. This reflects the fact that the elasticity of the user cost of capital in investment is quite high in the AWM. As indicated in Fagan, Henry and Mestre (2001) a 100-basis point rise in the real interest rate will lower investment by around 10 per cent after ten years. The impacts of a 100-basis point rise in the user cost of capital on investment in NiGEM vary between countries, but are generally well below 10 per cent after ten years.

One interesting contrast is the magnitude of the income effects in the two models as the effects are much larger in the AWM. Both models take into account the effects of changes in interest rates on government interest payments. This should have a broadly neutral long-run effect in that it boosts interest payments received by the personal sector but also induces a fiscal reaction as the government seeks to adjust taxes in response to the change in interest costs. However, as already discussed, in the AWM the initial impact of the fall in long-term interest rates induced under simulation 4 is strongly negative, which is a somewhat counter-intuitive result. The reason is that the income loss is experienced immediately while it takes time for the fiscal rule to react and reduce taxation to restore the government budget balance to its baseline level. Nevertheless, the magnitude of this negative income effect from falling long-term interest rates appears large in the AWM and is much larger than NiGEM would generate for a similar path of long-term interest rates. However, in this case, the negative income effect in NiGEM is not from this source as long-term interest rates do not fall in the NiGEM simulation. In NiGEM the negative income effect stems principally from the fact that this model takes into account the fact that the domestic interest payments to foreigners increase following the rise in short-term interest rates, which leads to a worsening in the current account and net wealth.

In terms of the impact on prices, the exchange rate channel tends to dominate initially with both models, as the change in exchange rate has a direct and rapid impact on import prices. Thereafter the exchange rate channel remains dominant for the NiGEM results, reflecting the fact that there is a permanent nominal appreciation, accompanied by a permanent fall in prices, while most variables, which have the potential to impact on prices, have returned to their baseline levels. In the case of the AWM the cost of capital channel takes over in year 2, reflecting the larger and more persistent output gap that emerges in this case.

4   Conclusions

In this chapter we have examined some of the issues faced by macroeconomic model builders in analysing the monetary transmission mechanism using the AWM and NiGEM models. Our results highlighted the importance of various aspects of model and simulation design in affecting the results from such exercises. From this, we draw a number of conclusions.

The NiGEM and AWM models yield broadly similar results for the effects of monetary policy on output for years 2–3 when the forward-looking elements of the models are not used. Both the maximum and average loss of output over years 1–3 are quite similar, although there are differences in timing. This holds true when monetary and fiscal policy rules are introduced into the simulations. The models have quite different properties thereafter, reflecting different adjustment speeds in the two models. The considerably faster reaction of NiGEM is due to relatively stronger feedback and error correction mechanisms, leading to a faster speed of adjustment within NiGEM.

Permitting forward-looking behaviour tends to increase the initial impact of the monetary policy exercise but also hastens the return to the baseline. Once the forward-looking elements of the model are allowed to operate, the impact in the AWM is clearly stronger than in NiGEM. The output losses in the AWM are approximately twice as large in each of the first three years. A major factor behind this is the particularly large adverse income effects stemming from the fall in long-term interest rates generated by the forward-looking simulation.

In both models, the user cost of capital tends to be the dominant channel of transmission in terms of its impact on GDP. The main exceptions are that in year 1 in NiGEM the exchange rate channel is dominant whilst the income channel grows in importance in later years in both models. The user cost of capital and income effects tend to be larger in the AWM than in NiGEM. In the former case, this is due to a higher sensitivity to changes in the user cost of capital. In the latter case it is due to a particularly marked income effect from the impact of changes in long-term interest rates on government interest payments. In terms of the impact on prices, the exchange rate channel plays an important role in both models given the direct impact on import prices stemming from changes in the exchange rate.

5   The effects of monetary policy in the euro area: evidence from structural macroeconomic models

P. van Els, A. Locarno, J. Morgan and J.-P. Villetelle

1   Introduction

The purpose of this chapter is to analyse the monetary transmission mechanism in the euro area through the use of large-scale macroeconomic models at the disposal of the European Central Bank (ECB) and the National Central Banks (NCBs) of the Eurosystem. The results reported in this paper are the fruit of cooperation within the Working Group on Econometric Modelling (WGEM) and are based on a carefully designed common simulation experiment.

The last major study of comparative properties of central bank models in terms of monetary transmission was carried out by the BIS in 1994 (BIS, 1995). The experiment involved a one-percentage point increase in the policy interest rate for two years and the results were summarised by Smets (1995). There are a number of important reasons why it is timely to re-examine the transmission mechanism rather than relying on the BIS results. First, there is evidence that the monetary transmission mechanism may change considerably even in a short period of time.[1] Second, it is now possible to undertake this experiment for all twelve members of the euro area rather than the eight EU countries included in the BIS exercise. In addition, a further new model that can now be used in such an exercise is the ECB's Area Wide Model (AWM) which is a model of the aggregate euro area economy (as detailed in Fagan, Henry and Mestre 2001).

Third, although the aim was to undertake a comparable simulation across countries in the BIS exercise, there were nonetheless important

---

[1] Taylor (1995) provides some evidence that in the USA, Japan and Germany the impact of a monetary policy action has changed with respect to the 1970s. Galí, Lopez-Salido and Valles (2000) compare the pre-Volcker and the Volcker–Greenspan period and detect significant differences in the response of the economy as well as the US Federal Reserve to technology shocks. Boivin and Giannoni (2001) have tried to assess on quantitative grounds whether the way in which monetary policy impulses are transmitted has changed since the 1980s.

differences. For example, some central banks undertook the simulations with fixed intra-European exchange rates while others allowed these exchange rates to vary as a result of the change in monetary policy. This significantly affects the comparability of the results for the euro area countries and limits their usefulness in the current environment of monetary union.

This final point leads to one of the key aspects of this study – namely the consistency of the experiment undertaken on the models. Considerable attention was paid to undertaking a genuinely comparable monetary policy experiment on all models that reflects the realities of monetary union in the euro area. In addition, unlike BIS (1995), the exercise using national models is conducted on the basis that the change in monetary policy has taken place simultaneously in all euro area countries. In the BIS (1995) study the exercise was conducted in isolation in each of the NCB's models.

2   Channels of transmission

The transmission of monetary policy impulses may be described as developing in three phases. First, a change in the policy instrument is transmitted to the whole set of interest rates and exchange rates. Second, the movements in financial prices interact with the spending behaviour of households and firms. Third, the ensuing change in the output and unemployment gaps induces wages and prices to adjust in order to restore a new equilibrium. The changes in prices and quantities feed back into the financial system, inducing modifications in the composition of balance sheets which may exert second-round effects on interest rates, thus setting in motion an interaction between the real and the financial side of the model. The process through which interest rates affect aggregate demand – the second phase – can, somewhat arbitrarily be, grouped into transmission channels, which single out the components of aggregate spending which are affected by the policy action and the processes which drive these shifts. In this chapter, five channels are identified, which are present in most of the participating models.

The exchange rate channel – in most models of exchange rate determination, a monetary policy tightening appreciates the currency. A stronger exchange rate exerts a widespread influence on both the real and the financial side of the economy. It causes a fall in exports, partially compensated by the parallel contraction in import volumes via the multiplier effect, and an increase in consumer spending, induced by the positive real income effect which follows an appreciation. It also yields a fall in the price level, directly since it reduces the cost of imported goods and the size of the mark-up and indirectly since it worsens the competitive position of domestic firms and hence net exports.

The substitution-effect-in-consumption channel – the real interest rate represents the relative cost of present versus future consumption. Following a policy tightening, it becomes more rewarding to delay consumption and increase saving, which exerts a negative impulse on the current level of economic activity.

The cost-of-capital channel – the rise in the real interest rate is reflected in the real cost of capital. The optimal capital–output ratio falls and therefore the pace of capital accumulation slows. A similar mechanism operates for investment in housing and structures and for inventories' accumulation. The rental cost of durable goods moves in parallel with the cost of capital and also causes a contraction in consumer spending.[2]

The income and cash-flow channel – a rise in financial yields increases the disposable income of net lenders and worsens the cash flows of net borrowers. The effects are stronger the higher the portfolio share of short-term and floating rate securities. The relevance of the cash-flow channel is strictly linked to the financial structure of the economy and depends also on the relative propensity to spend of borrowers and lenders.

The wealth channel – a deterioration in borrowing conditions reduces the discounted value of future expected payoffs of physical and financial assets. The market value of households' net wealth adjusts to incorporate capital losses, constraining the opportunity set of consumers, and household spending falls accordingly.

Not every channel can be identified in all models. The combined *cash-flow/income channel* does not exist in the models for Greece and Ireland. In the case of the Netherlands the income channel includes the effects of portfolio reallocation by households and firms. The *wealth channel* is not present in the models for Austria, Germany, Greece, Spain, France and Portugal. Finally, there are a number of country-specific channels that are not reported here. In the German model there is a separate monetary channel which transmits interest rate impulses to inflation via the price gap, i.e. the deviation of the actual price level from the equilibrium price level (P-star).[3]

---

[2] Since most econometric models used in the experiment do not distinguish between the consumption of durables and non-durables, to permit comparisons the response to the monetary policy shock of durables' spending has been allocated not to the cost-of-capital channel but to the substitution-effect channel.

[3] More information on how differences across models may impact on the results of the monetary policy experiment is provided in van Els *et al.* (2001).

3   The monetary policy experiment

This section summarises the design of the standard simulation experiment that was undertaken using the models. The details relate to the treatment of monetary and fiscal policy, long rates, exchange rates, international spillovers and wage policies. The aim was to minimise differences due to simulation design so as to allow meaningful cross-country comparisons and to provide a reliable assessment of the effects of a common monetary policy action.

A common procedure for preparing an out-of-sample baseline for each model was undertaken, full details of which are provided in van Els *et al.* (2001). Following BIS (1995), the monetary policy shock was a two-year increase in the short-term policy interest rate by one percentage point from 2001:Q1–2002:Q4. From and including 2003:Q1 a return to baseline values was assumed.[4] This means that no monetary policy rules were implemented. Whether this choice is appropriate or not is questionable. It could be argued that a story of the transmission mechanism which does not include a description of the central bank's reaction function is incomplete and a policy rule may be helpful for achieving model stability. However, if a common policy framework is to be imposed, the policy rule must respond, not to domestic, but to area-wide variables, whose path represents the output of the experiment and is therefore not known when the national models are simulated. No fiscal policy rules (e.g. targeting a specific government budget or debt stock target) were used in the simulations. The issues surrounding the use of policy rules in structural macroeconomic models are considered in greater depth in chapter 4 in this volume.

Under the assumption that the policy action was perfectly anticipated by financial markets, asset prices moved according to arbitrage conditions. The term structure was modelled using the expectations hypothesis, while exchange rates were determined by an uncovered interest parity (UIP) condition. The bilateral exchange rate between third-country currencies (e.g. USD versus JPY) was assumed to remain unchanged. Clearly there was also no change in the bilateral exchange rates for the residual currencies of the euro area. Models were initially operated in 'isolated' mode without international spillovers (e.g. changes in foreign demand).

---

[4] This means that the experiment was a temporary one. An alternative approach would have been a permanent shock such as a permanent shift in a policy rule. For example, Church *et al.* (2000) examine monetary policy through a permanent change in the inflation target. Unfortunately such an approach would not have been possible in this exercise as a common change in a policy rule would have induced differing interest rate reactions in each country – which would not have been compatible with monetary union.

However, such effects were taken into account in a second round when the trade figures from the first run of all models in isolated mode were incorporated in each model.[5]

Despite the need for a wide-ranging agreement on the details of these simulations, many differences remained in model design. For example, some models incorporated – to a greater or lesser extent – forward-looking behaviour in financial markets and the real economy.

4   The results

The results presented here relate to full model simulations based on the common design of the experiment, and using the 'flag' method of channel decomposition which is described in Altissimo, Locarno and Siviero (2001).[6] The common assumptions underlying the response pattern of the euro exchange rate *vis-à-vis* non-euro countries entail that the interest rate shock is accompanied by an appreciation of the euro with respect to non-euro currencies of 1.6 per cent on average in year 1 and 0.6 per cent in year 2. However, the size of this change in terms of the national effective exchange rates depends on the weights of the non-euro countries in the international trade of the respective economies.[7]

4.1   Impact on prices

Figure 5.1 provides an overview of the aggregate effects for the euro area on four price variables: the deflators of private consumption, real GDP, exports and imports. Figures 5.2 and 5.3 show the effects of the monetary policy shock on the private consumption deflator according to the national models, the aggregate euro area response from these models (see line 'aggregate'),[8] as well as the euro area response according to the AWM.

Focusing on the evolution of the *consumption deflator*, there are a number of noteworthy features in these results. With the exception of Finland,

[5] This process could be repeated a number of times until the spillover effects appear to have settled down. The results presented in this chapter are those obtained after one round of iteration as after close inspection it was concluded by the Working Group that more rounds of iteration were not required as no further meaningful changes in the results were anticipated.

[6] A more comprehensive and detailed presentation of the results is provided in van Els *et al.* (2001). However, it should be noted that this paper incorporates revised results for Austria, Greece and Portugal.

[7] The response profiles of exchange and interest rates and the trade weights are reported in van Els *et al.* (2001).

[8] Aggregate effects for the euro area are GDP-weighted averages of national effects.

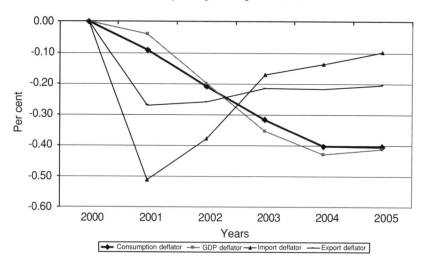

Figure 5.1 Impact of monetary policy shocks on aggregate euro area prices according to NCBs' models

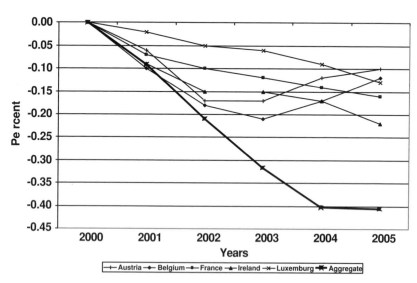

Figure 5.2 Impact of monetary policy shocks on the consumption deflator: countries with moderate effects

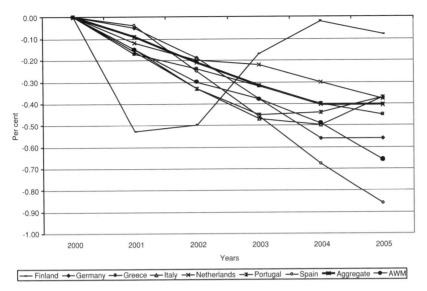

Figure 5.3 Impact of monetary policy shocks on the consumption deflator: countries with larger effects

price-level effects are persistent over the time horizon shown. There are a number of countries for which price effects are relatively moderate (figure 5.2), with consumer prices falling 0.25 per cent below the baseline at the maximum: this group includes Belgium, France, Ireland, Luxembourg and Austria. At the other extreme, there are Germany, Italy and Spain, where price effects exceed the aggregate response (figure 5.3). The AWM model shows a price response for the euro area as a whole which is somewhat higher than the one obtained by aggregating country evidence. In terms of timing, Finland is the only country where a particularly marked short-term impact arises (−0.5 per cent). The maximum aggregate response of consumer prices in the euro area is 0.4 per cent below the baseline, an effect that is reached in the fourth year. Note that this aggregate timing profile masks differences between countries. In Greece, Spain, France, Ireland, the Netherlands and the AWM prices are still decreasing in the fifth year.

Although not shown here, the initial impact of the shock is larger on the trade deflators compared with the GDP and consumption deflators. The developments driving the response of domestic prices have not yet had a noticeable effect, whereas the exchange rate shock has a direct and immediate impact on the trade deflators. As expected, the trade deflators are more markedly affected in the countries that are more open to trade

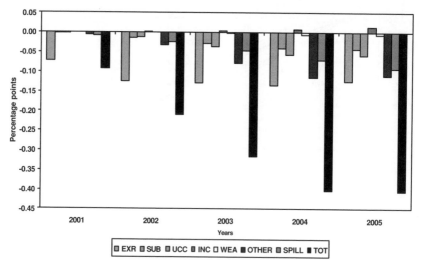

Figure 5.4 Decomposition of the effects of monetary policy shocks on the consumption deflator (according to NCBs' models). TOT is the total effect, EXR the contribution of the exchange rate channel, SUB the substitution channel, UCC the user cost of capital channel, INC the combined income and cash-flow channel, WEA the wealth channel, OTHER the combined contribution of the monetary channel (Germany) and the expectations channel (Italy), and SPILL the contribution of the international spillovers

outside the euro area. The difference in the evolution of domestic prices compared to trade prices leads to a loss of competitiveness.[9] The biggest impact on domestic prices appears in Finland, the model where the labour market reacts most rapidly to the shock. In all countries the initial change in the consumption deflator is almost exclusively due to the exchange rate response and its impact on the import deflator. This is confirmed by the decomposition which shows that other channels of transmission make at most a negligible contribution to the change in the consumption deflator. Figure 5.4 reports on the decomposition of the aggregate effects on the private consumption deflator according to the NCB models.[10]

Overall the exchange rate channel is the most important channel in the determination of prices throughout the simulation period, particularly

[9] Because of the delayed response of employment to the change in activity, the reduction in activity can lead to a temporary fall in productivity compared to baseline, leading to a rise in unit labour costs and hence, in some cases, in the output price.

[10] Full details of the channel decomposition at a national level are provided in van Els et al. (2001).

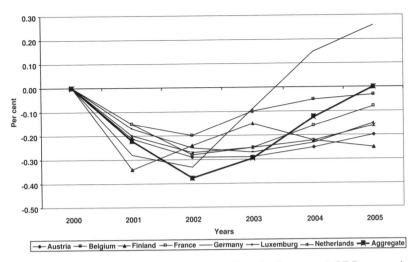

Figure 5.5 Impact of monetary policy shocks on real GDP: countries with moderate effects

in the short run (Figure 5.4). Nevertheless, in the medium term other channels increase in importance. As reported in van Els *et al.* (2001), the monetary channel is important in the German case; the expectations channel in the Italian case; the cost of capital channel in Spain and Italy; and the substitution channel in Greece, Ireland, France and again Portugal. Moreover, international spillovers provide a significant propagation mechanism in all countries. In general, the income/cash-flow and the wealth effects do not play any significant role in the determination of prices, except in the case of Italy where the income/cash-flow channel explains part of the drift in the price level. To some extent this will be due to the offsetting effects of changes in interest rates on the income of lenders and the cash flow of borrowers, as discussed earlier.

4.2   Impact on real activity

Figures 5.5 and 5.6 summarise the main findings in terms of real GDP. In the first year real, GDP falls on average by 0.2 per cent relative to the baseline according to the aggregate response of the national models (see line 'aggregate'). The maximum average reduction in real GDP of 0.4 per cent is obtained in year 2. Thereafter, with nominal short-term interest rates returning immediately to the baseline, real GDP also starts its return to the baseline, which is reached by year 5 (2005). These 'aggregate' results contrast with those obtained by the AWM. The latter show

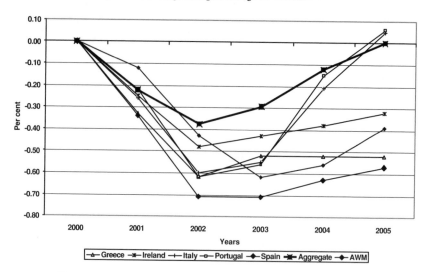

Figure 5.6 Impact of monetary policy shocks on real GDP: countries with larger effects, 2000–2005

a stronger impact of the monetary policy action, in both the short and in the medium term. The AWM requires a monetary policy rule to be in place in order to speed the adjustment towards a stable equilibrium. Without imposing such a rule the AWM shows a more persistent deflationary spiral. In this respect, the AWM differs from most of the national models.

Across countries, differences may be noted. Effects on real GDP are modest for Austria, Belgium, Germany, France, Luxembourg, the Netherlands and Finland, with maximum effects in absolute terms under 0.35 per cent (see figure 5.5). For the other countries the effects on real GDP are between −0.35 per cent and −0.6 per cent (figure 5.6). Differences also occur in terms of timing and cycling. In nine out of twelve euro-countries the negative impact on real GDP is strongest in year 2. In Finland the impact on output is faster, whereas in Luxembourg and Spain it takes about three years to reach the maximum response. Cycles, in the sense that the initial reduction in real GDP bottoms out and output starts moving to above baseline levels within five years, occur in Germany, Portugal and Italy.

In common with the impact on prices, the exchange rate channel is crucial in the transmission of monetary policy onto aggregate euro area output in the short run (figure 5.7). This is also the case for the AWM simulations. However, in the medium and long term, the cost-of-capital channel and the direct-substitution channel account for most of the downward

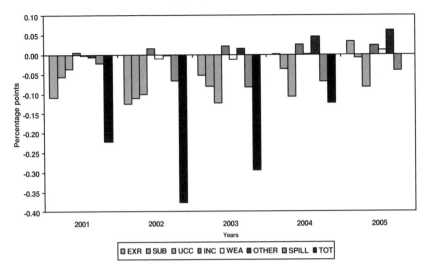

Figure 5.7 Decomposition of the effects of monetary policy shocks on real GDP according to NCBs' models, TOT is the total effect, EXR the contribution of the exchange rate channel, SUB the substitution channel, UCC the user cost of capital channel, INC the combined income and cash-flow channel, WEA the wealth channel, OTHER the combined contribution of the monetary channel (Germany) and the expectations channel (Italy), and SPILL the contribution of the international spilllovers

pressure on real GDP. Another perhaps remarkable result, given the increased importance of stocks and bonds in portfolios of households and firms, is the fairly modest role of the wealth channel. In the case of France, the issue is controversial and the evidence supporting the existence of a wealth channel is not very robust (see Artus, Legros and Nicolaï, 1989 and Bonnet and Dubois, 1995). The absence of wealth as a separate transmission channel in Germany and the fact that in France wealth does not seem to be very important at least in the short run finds support in an IMF study by Edison and Sloek (2001). Another reason why wealth and valuation effects would be moderate, even if accounted for in the models, relates to the fact that, by assumption, the interest rate shock is a temporary one so that forward-looking long-term interest rates respond only partially, mitigating the impact on asset prices.

The same mechanism weakens the strength of the substitution- and cost-of-capital channels in Germany and the Netherlands, where long rates rather than short rates affect investment and private consumption. This is in line with the fact that firms and households in these countries prefer long-term over short-term debt as a means of financing spending (see table 26.4, p. 444). A further argument for Germany is the existence of 'relationship banking', entailing close ties between corporations and banks, such that changes in the cost of capital have a relatively small impact. Further evidence on this is documented in Ehrmann and Worms (2001).

Qualitatively, the contribution of the income/cash-flow channel of transmission depends on the financial position of households and firms (table 26.5, p. 447). In Italy, the positive contribution of the income channel reflects the fact that households are net creditors, and raise consumption in response to the increase in interest payments received on holdings of government debt. In Finland and the Netherlands, households are net debtors. Hence, the income channel tends to reinforce the drop in output in these countries.

It is informative to compare our results with those of the BIS (1995). However, it should be borne in mind that, because of the differences in the design of the exercise, and because models have undergone changes in the course of time (partly reflecting changes in economic and financial structures but also revisions of old data), the comparison of the new results with BIS (1995) is a precarious exercise.[11] Some tentative conclusions can, however, be drawn. First, in a number of countries the positive output effect of the income channel in the BIS results has become smaller, or in some cases disappeared altogether. One general reason for this is a weakening of the financial position of households and firms. Second, it might have been expected that this comparison exercise would reveal an increased importance of the wealth channel. However, no clear evidence in favour of this propostion has been found. For Germany and France the empirical evidence in support of (increased) wealth effects is weak or not very robust. This may be due to the fact that the holding and valuation of wealth components have been changing rapidly and becoming more important only since the mid-1990s, which may be insufficient time for a wealth effect to become detectable in these countries.

5   Validation of the results and policy issues

To assess the validity of the results presented in the previous sections, it is worth considering whether they are consistent with the stylised facts reported in the literature, how they compare with other studies and also whether or not cross-country differences in the channel decomposition correspond to differences in the economic structures.

---

[11] More information is provided in van Els *et al.* (2001).

According to Bernanke and Gertler (1995), who mainly rely on VAR evidence, the following stylised facts characterise the response of the economy to monetary policy shocks: (i) a monetary tightening induces, in the short run, a sustained decline in both output and the price level; (ii) the fall in aggregate demand leads the contraction in production; (iii) residential investment reacts promptly to the deterioration in financing conditions, while the response of consumer spending and particularly fixed business investment is smaller and more delayed.[12] Most of these features are also reflected in the results presented above, with the only significant difference involving capital accumulation. In our results, business investment rather than residential investment is most immediately and to the greatest extent affected by the rise in interest rates, which may well reflect the fact that within the euro area the elasticity of investment to the cost of capital is quite high.

The results also share some common features with the evidence presented in Peersman and Smets (chapter 2 in this volume). A direct comparison is difficult because the size of the shock and the implied profile of the interest rate are different.[13] However a number of similarities are worth mentioning. In both cases, output starts declining well in advance of prices. With the VAR results, a trough is reached by the end of year 1, but with the macromodel results the trough is reached between year 2 and year 3 due to the more sustained nature of the monetary shock. In both cases, prices respond more sluggishly and continue to fall until year 4 or year 5 (depending on the model considered). If a simple adjustment for the size of the monetary policy shock is made, the size of the output and price effects can be seen as broadly comparable.

Concerning channel decomposition, table 5.1 reports the ranking for each country and lists a few variables which may be used to cross-check our findings. The ranking is computed in terms of the (cumulated) output losses caused by each channel in the first five years of the simulation. A few results are worthy of comment. As expected the spillover channel is relevant for Belgium, Luxembourg and the Netherlands, where intra-EU trade is a large share of GDP; despite its openness to trade, this is not true

---

[12] Such a response of fixed business investment – in terms both of timing and size – is possible if capital accumulation has a zero (or very low) elasticity to the cost of capital or, alternatively, if the cost of capital is not affected, even in the short-run, by changes in the monetary policy stance: investment would then move only because of the accelerator effect and because there exists a credit channel. This is by no means a piece of undisputed empirical evidence. Taylor (1995), for instance, forcefully rejects this claim.

[13] The monetary policy shock, corresponding to one standard deviation, lasts one period and amounts to roughly 30 basis points. The working of the policy rules induces some persistence in the response of the interest rate, which returns to the baseline only in the third period.

Table 5.1 *Decomposition of channels of transmission in the NCBs' models*

	E[a]	C	S	W	I	SP	Intra EU-15 export share 1990	2000	Labour share[b] 1990	2000	Short-term debt (firms)[c] 1990	2000	Import share[d] 1990	2000	Interest inc. (households)[e] 1990	2000
Belgium	2	3	5	6	4	1	44.6	52.4	0.52	0.51	33.2	29.8	59.2	76.1	9.8	7.7
Germany	1	4	3		5	2	16.9	15.5	0.56	0.54	26.6	22.1	23.2	31.7	−1.2	−2.5
Greece	4	3	1			2	6.5	4.7	0.32	0.33		70.3	22.3	32.1		
Spain	3	1	4		5	2	7.7	14.2	0.50	0.50		50.0	17.8	32.5	3.1	0.5
France	4	3	1	5	5	2	11.3	14.4	0.52	0.52	21.4	27.8	18.9	27.2	0.7	1.3
Ireland	2	1	3	5	5	4	39.1	47.2	0.46	0.40	19.3	20.8	51.0	87.3		
Italy	4	1	2	6	6	3	9.6	11.4	0.46	0.41	65.7	57.2	21.1	28.5	10.4	5.4
Netherlands	3	2	5	4		1	33.4	31.4	0.51	0.51	23.8	34.0	47.8	61.4	−3.9	−7.1
Austria	2	4	1		5	3	17.5	20.8	0.53	0.52		28.7	35.4	47.6		
Portugal	4	2	1		5	3	18.6	17.5	0.44	0.42		19.8	36.4	45.9		0.4
Finland	2	1	5	6	4	3	11.7	20.0	0.56	0.47		73.0	26.3	35.1		−2.6

Notes: [a] The channels have been coded as follows: E stands for exchange-rate, C for cost-of-capital, S for substitution-in-consumption, W for wealth, I for income and SP for spillover. In a few cases, figures for Belgium aggregate data for Luxembourg as well.
[b] The starting value for DE is 1991, for LUX, the NL, PT and GR is 1995; the ending figure for PT is 1999.
[c] The starting value is 1991 for DE, 1995 for FR and 1994 for NL; the ending date for AT is 1999; for ES the figure refers to credit which is at variable rates and for PT debt is considered short term if it falls due within a year.
[d] The starting value for PT is 1995.
[e] Net interest payments as a share of GDP, households. The starting value for DE is 1993 and for NL is 1995; the ending figure for DE, BE and IT is 1999.

for Ireland, presumably reflecting the high trade with the UK for which no spillover effects are included. The size of the self-employed sector, proxied by the (complement to the) labour share, is large in Greece and Portugal, where the consumption channel is the most important, and is sizeable also in Italy and Ireland, where it ranks second and third, respectively.[14] The share of short-term liabilities in firms' balance sheets helps explain the magnitude of the cost-of-capital channel in Finland, Italy, Spain and the Netherlands, but does not contribute to explaining the results for Greece. The import share supports the influence of the exchange rate in Belgium and Ireland, but is not helpful in understanding why this channel is so important in Germany. Finally, the amount of interest payments to households is consistent with the relatively larger role played by the income channel in Belgium.

The move to a single currency and the centralisation of the responsibility of policy decisions has made the understanding of the transmission mechanism a key issue. As shown clearly in figures 5.2–5.6, the responsiveness of output and prices to a standardised increase in the monetary policy instrument is not uniform across the euro area. The distinction, made in a number of previous studies, between a 'core' region and a 'periphery', is partially consistent with the evidence presented here, though in fact more than two clusters are present. At one extreme there are countries, such as Germany, Benelux and Finland, where a policy tightening is effective in curbing inflationary pressures at modest costs in terms of output losses, while in Greece the increase in interest rates engenders a marked contraction in economic activity and only a modest restraint on price developments. The remaining countries are located in between, though somewhat closer to the core region.

6   Conclusions

This chapter has reported the results of a common monetary policy experiment that has been undertaken using large-scale macroeconomic models at the disposal of the ECB and the NCBs of the Eurosystem. As discussed in the chapter, considerable attention has been paid to undertaking a genuinely comparable experiment that reflects the existence of monetary union.

---

[14] The larger the share of self-employment, the largelabour income uncertainty. If autonomous workers are more sensitive to interest rates changes, possibly through the interaction of liquidity constraints and precautionary saving, the share of the self-employed sector is not just an amplification mechanism, but rather affects the relative size of the substitution-in-consumption channel.

On the basis of the results provided a number of conclusions can be drawn. In terms of the impact of monetary policy on output, a one-percentage point rise in short-term interest rates is found to have a maximum aggregate effect in NCBs' models of −0.4 per cent after two years. The maximum aggregate effect on prices is also −0.4 per cent but in this case it occurs two years later, reflecting the fact that in most of the models prices react more slowly and largely in response to changes in economic activity. The dominant channel of transmission in years 1 and 2 – in terms of its impact on both output and prices – is the exchange rate channel. However, from the third year of the simulation onwards the user cost of capital channel determines most of the contraction in output.

Inevitably these aggregate responses mask some notable variations in the results across models. There are variations with respect both to the magnitude and timing of the effects and the relative contributions of each of the channels of transmission. The impacts on output and prices were found to be relatively modest in Belgium, France, the Netherlands and Luxembourg and relatively strong in Italy, Spain, Portugal and Greece. Some models also incorporate special features not included in the other models – for example the 'P-star' effects included in the German model – which lead to differences in the patterns of adjustment to the monetary policy experiment. There are also noteworthy differences between the aggregate results from the NCBs' models and the results from the ECB's AWM. The latter tends to show more pronounced and prolonged impacts of monetary policy on economic activity and prices.

6 Financial frictions and the monetary transmission mechanism: theory, evidence and policy implications

C. Bean, J. Larsen and K. Nikolov

1 Introduction

There is little doubt that central bankers pay considerable attention to the activities of commercial banks and other financial intermediaries. So in a survey of eighty-nine central banks on the key ingredients for a successful monetary framework, Fry *et al.* (2000) found that out of twenty-one possible factors 'analysis of the banking sector' came seventh on average, even ranking ahead of 'analysis of the real sector'. Of course central banks will usually have an interest in the behaviour of financial intermediaries for financial stability reasons and indeed 'analysis of domestic financial stability' was ranked fifth on average in the same survey. But even for the sixteen central banks that cited an inflation target as the most important ingredient and for whom understanding the transmission mechanism would be key, the categories relating to the banking sector received high ranking.

The traditional textbook models that are routinely used for the analysis of monetary policy, such as IS-LM, usually do not spell out the assumptions that underpin the transmission mechanism and, in so far as they do, they usually pay little attention to the role of financial intermediaries. New Keynesian models of the sort set out in Clarida, Galí and Gertler (1999) often build on more explicit microfoundations, and usually assume that capital markets are free of frictions and complete. In such a world the behaviour of financial intermediaries would be of only rather limited interest. This neglect of financial intermediaries and their impact

We are grateful to Anna-Maria Agresti, Peter Andrews, David England, Jordi Galí, Simon Hall, Anil Kashyap, Vincent Labhard, Lavan Mahadeva, Steven Millard, Katharine Neiss, Gert Peersman, Laura Piscitelli, James Proudman, Rachel Reeves, Gabriel Sterne, Frank Smets, Peter Westaway, the editors and an anonymous referee for helpful comments. Thanks also go to Kosuke Aoki, Luca Benati and Jan Vlieghe for help with the estimation and simulation work, and to Ed Dew and Richard Geare for research assistance. The views expressed are those of the authors and do not reflect and views of either the Bank of England or the Monetary Policy Committee.

is at odds not only with the survey evidence on the attitudes of central bankers, but also with episodes such as the Asia crisis and the current Argentinean experience where developments in financial markets have been central.

In this chapter we discuss the impact and implications of frictions originating in financial markets for the transmission of monetary policy. Within the broad class of financial market imperfections, we consider those that drive a wedge between internal and external sources of finance, and those that result in rationing of credit. Our focus is primarily on the transmission mechanism in a developed economy operating in normal circumstances; we thus avoid discussion of financial crises, liquidity traps and similar issues. But even with such a relatively narrow focus, a comprehensive survey of the literature is well beyond the scope of this chapter. Excellent surveys of this territory can be found in Bernanke, Gertler and Gilchrist (1999), Christiano, Eichenbaum and Evans (1999) and Clarida, Galí and Gertler (1999).

The remainder of the chapter is organised as follows. Section 2 discusses the theoretical underpinnings for a role for financial frictions in the monetary transmission mechanism. Section 3 then summarises some of the associated empirical evidence. Section 4 turns to the question of how the presence of financial frictions might impact on the design and implementation of monetary policy, focusing in particular on the added uncertainty they introduce into the transmission mechanism. A brief concluding section follows.

2   Competing views of the monetary transmission mechanism

Under the classical view of the monetary transmission mechanism, interest rates influence economic activity by altering various relative prices in the economy. The primary channels of influence on aggregate demand are threefold. First, variations in the real interest rate induce intertemporal substitution in consumption, as well as affecting the valuation of human and financial wealth. Second, they affect the cost of capital and thus impact on fixed investment and inventory accumulation. Finally, in an open economy subject to the international mobility of capital they impact on the real exchange rate and net trade via the uncovered interest parity (UIP) condition. In addition they may have consequences for aggregate supply, for instance via intertemporal substitution in labour supply and, in open economies, by altering the wedge between consumer and producer prices and thus the equilibrium wage. This is a fairly broad description of the 'classical interest rate channel' – it essentially encompasses most mechanisms that are not associated with financial market frictions.

But even such a broad characterisation of the transmission mechanism appears potentially incomplete. Christiano, Eichenbaum and Evans (2001) show that a calibrated dynamic stochastic general equilibrium model with sticky wages, variable capacity utilisation and adjustment costs in consumption and investment can match the estimated response of the US economy to a monetary policy shock, but only with a very large elasticity of investment to the long-term interest rate. However, studies of investment spending usually find only a rather weak role for the cost of capital (Chirinko, 1993). Furthermore, Euler equation studies typically find that intertemporal substitution in consumption is also rather limited, suggesting that interest rate movements have only limited effects on consumer spending (Hall, 1988). Finally, for open economies, UIP *cum* rational expectations does rather a poor job of explaining exchange rate movements (Meese and Rogoff, 1983), and the pass-through from exchange rates to final domestic prices also appears to be incomplete. As a consequence that part of the transmission mechanism that operates via net trade also appears to be rather weak.

Bernanke and Gertler (1995) encapsulate the shortcomings of the classical view of the interest rate channel in three main puzzles:

- *Composition.* Why do temporary movements in short-term interest rates appear to affect expenditure on durable goods, which presumably should depend on the long rate?[1]
- *Propagation.* Why do real variables continue to adjust long after a change in short rates has been reversed?
- *Amplification.* Why do changes in interest rates lead to such pronounced movements in output while 'cost of capital' measures appear to be insignificant in explaining movements in individual expenditure components?

To these puzzles, Kocherlakota (2000) adds *asymmetry* as another facet of monetary transmission that cannot be readily explained through the interest rate channel.

Much recent research has attempted to explain these puzzles by appealing to various frictions in financial markets, all of which generate departures from the Modigliani–Miller axioms so that finance is more than just a veil. The theoretical literature has identified two main ways in which

---

[1] This puzzle presumes that there are frictions in durable/capital goods markets: if there are perfect second-hand markets and firms and individuals face no costs of adjusting their stock of durables/capital, then the opportunity cost of holding the good is given by the *short* interest rate.

the financial system can act to amplify and propagate the effect of monetary shocks: the 'bank-lending' channel; and the 'broad credit channel'. The first applies to models that focus on the behaviour of financial intermediaries in affecting the quantity of credit. The latter applies to models that focus on the nature of the relationship between borrowers and lenders, and consequently on the terms under which loans are supplied.

2.1   The bank-lending channel

The bank-lending channel attributes the effects of monetary policy to movements in the supply of bank credit. The first generation of bank-lending models motivated the departures from the Modigliani–Miller axioms on the basis of asymmetric information between borrowers and lenders about the characteristics of individual projects. Stiglitz and Weiss (1981) assume that entrepreneurs have private information about their projects, which have the same expected return but different probabilities of success. Because of limited liability borrowers can default on their loans in the event that the project does not succeed. Hence, at high-levels of interest rates, the only entrepreneurs who would find borrowing attractive are high-risk ones, with a low probability of repayment. Consequently there is a problem of adverse selection and the resulting equilibrium is characterised by credit rationing and under-investment[2].

However, subsequent research has shown that the Stiglitz–Weiss result is not robust once sorting devices are allowed. The credit rationing result is an example of a pooling equilibrium. Following Rothschild and Stiglitz (1976), Spence (1973) and others, such equilibria can be eliminated by the use of a suitable sorting device, which forces agents to reveal their types. Bester (1985) and others have shown that collateral can be used as a sorting device, since safe borrowers will be more willing to undertake secured borrowing than risky ones. The resulting separating equilibrium involves no credit rationing.

Later contributions focus on the imperfect substitutability between retail deposits and wholesale deposits or debt on the liability side of the banks' balance sheets. In the model of Bernanke and Blinder (1988), a number of borrowers are bank-dependent in the sense that their only providers of outside finance are banks. Furthermore, banks themselves are assumed to suffer from information problems in the market for

---

[2] DeMeza and Webb (1987) consider a different form of uncertainty in which successful projects deliver the same *ex post* return. They show this leads to over- rather than under-investment, with projects with a high probability of success subsidising low-probability ones.

equity and corporate debt, which implies that they cannot just raise extra outside capital fully to replace any lost retail deposits. This imperfect substitution between retail and wholesale deposits (or debt) means that a fall in retail deposits induced by a monetary contraction tends to be followed by a decline in loans rather than an offsetting increase in the quantity of wholesale deposits. Bernanke and Blinder (1988) show that such structures tend to amplify the effects of monetary policy shocks.

A recent strand of the literature provides an alternative explanation for a bank-lending channel. Van den Heuvel (2001) examines bank behaviour in the presence of a 'capital-adequacy ratio' and a constraint on the ability to issue new equity. He shows that following a shock to the value of their equity, banks will contract potentially profitable lending if they get sufficiently close to the capital-adequacy ratio. And since banks hold short-term liabilities and long-term assets, monetary policy shocks will generate movements in bank equity. Furthermore, this 'bank-capital channel' works in a highly non-linear fashion, implying the potential for asymmetries in monetary transmission.

The key feature of the bank-lending channel is therefore that, by altering the quantity of base money, the central bank can influence the supply of credit from financial intermediaries, thus raising the (shadow) cost of capital to bank-dependent borrowers. This effect is additional to that induced by the change in the official interest rate operating via the interest rate channel.

For a special role for banks in monetary transmission we need some borrowers in the economy to be dependent on banks for their external finance. Fixed costs to direct financial market participation is a frequently cited motivation for the existence of such bank-dependent borrowers. Banks can economise on the fixed costs of monitoring, which makes them the natural provider of finance for borrowers that are too small for it to be economical for them to issue securities directly. Hence, any changes in banks' willingness to lend will influence such borrowers directly. And minimum capital requirements offer one plausible mechanism that may affect banks' willingness to lend when their capital is close to the regulatory minimum.

The quantitative significance of the bank-lending channel will depend partly on the size of the contraction in deposits for a given monetary policy shock. This contraction will be greater, the more interest-elastic is the demand for money. With elastic money demand, deposits (and hence loans) will show more variation in response to a policy shock. Furthermore, the larger is the pool of bank-dependent borrowers, the bigger the effect of the lending contraction on the real economy.

2.2   The broad credit channel

Much of the recent theoretical literature on the role of credit in economic fluctuations has focused on moral hazard problems in the principal–agent relationship that characterises debt contracts. These models derive a role in the monetary transmission mechanism for credit in general, and not just bank lending. Bernanke, Gertler and Gilchrist (1999) and Carlstrom and Fuerst (2000) are perhaps the most widely cited papers in this literature. In their models, there are 'bad' states of the world, in which it is efficient for firms to default on their debts. But because of limited liability, borrowers may prefer to default on their borrowings in other states of the world too. Furthermore lenders have to pay a cost to ascertain whether the true state of the world warrants default or not. Lenders therefore demand an external finance premium in steady state to compensate them for this state verification cost. The consequence of these credit market imperfections is that firms find it cheaper to invest out of retained funds than out of borrowed funds. Hence, stronger firm cash flow leads to higher investment. In general equilibrium, this mechanism has the potential to provide amplification and propagation, because aggregate demand shocks will affect firm cash flow, causing persistent movements in firms' average cost of capital and investment.

Kiyotaki and Moore (1997) assume incomplete contract enforceability and show that entrepreneurs will be credit constrained. They argue that if the value of investment projects is highly dependent on human/entrepreneurial capital, lenders will issue loans only up to the value of physical capital. The reason for this is that physical capital can be foreclosed on, unlike human capital. The aggregate consequences are similar to that of Bernanke, Gertler and Gilchrist (1999): investment is highly dependent on the value of collateral, which can generate amplification and persistence following monetary shocks.

Cooley, Quadrini and Marimon (2001) also assume incomplete enforceability and examine the structure of long-term incentive-compatible contracts between entrepreneurs and lenders. They find that the incentive-compatible contract involves higher investment and growth by new firms than by old, and that the investment of new firms depends on cash flow. The intuition is the following: when the firm is 'young' and/or current cash flow is high, there is an incentive for the entrepreneur to repudiate the contract and appropriate the entire cash flow. Hence, the optimal contract has to provide sufficient incentive to the entrepreneur not to default. This is achieved through growth in the value of the firm, which is achieved through higher investment. In general equilibrium, the incentive-compatible financial contract prolongs and amplifies shocks.

The broad credit channel influences economic conditions by leading to variations in a firm's cost of capital in line with its financial health. Hence this transmission channel will be quantitatively stronger when the terms of debt contracts are re-negotiable. For example, floating rate loans/bonds at a fixed spread over government or money market instruments will not be affected by deterioration in credit quality; the bondholder will realise a loss on his initial investment instead. On the other hand, loans/bonds where lenders can frequently change the spread, such as those with embedded options, will be affected in line with the predictions of credit channel theories. But even when most loans are at a fixed rate, the effect of the credit channel will be increasing in the 'churn' in the debt stock, i.e. the proportion of the debt stock that is new each period.

3   Empirical evidence on the role of financial frictions

In section 2 we showed that there were two main ways that financial frictions could impact on the monetary transmission mechanism and thus address some of the limitations to the classical interest rate view. The bank-lending channel predicts that banks will contract the supply of loans following a monetary shock. And the broad credit channel predicts that financial factors such as cash flow and net worth will be among the determinants of firms' expenditure. In this section we review some of the main empirical findings relating to these propositions.

3.1   Evidence for the bank-lending channel

The bank-lending view of monetary transmission is partly motivated by the observation that many borrowers are dependent on banks for their external finance. Kashyap and Stein (1995), using data for 1991 from the *Quarterly Financial Report* for US manufacturing firms, found that small firms were dependent on banks for 82.9 per cent of their external finance. For medium-sized firms, the share of bank debt was almost as high, at 77 per cent. This evidence by itself suggests that the behaviour of banks may be important for the transmission of monetary policy.

A number of papers have studied the co-movement of output and bank lending following a monetary policy shock. Bernanke and Blinder (1992) show that bank loans decline following a contractionary monetary policy shock and argue that this provides evidence for the existence of a bank-lending channel. Aggregate lending to corporates in the UK is also positively correlated with investment, and leads GDP growth.

There is, however, a serious identification problem in econometric work that uses aggregate data. Since loan demand is a function of the interest rate even under the classical interest rate view, the latter is also capable of explaining the fall in lending aggregates following a monetary policy shock. What bank-lending channel proponents need to demonstrate is that the fall in the quantity of lending was caused by a fall in loan supply (which is consistent with the bank-lending view) rather than by a fall in loan demand (which would be the case with frictionless capital markets).

Kashyap, Stein and Wilcox (1993) attempt to solve this identification problem by looking at the relative movements of bank lending and commercial paper issuance. Their results show that the ratio of commercial paper to bank loans rises following a monetary policy contraction. They argue that because large companies that are unlikely to be credit constrained issue commercial paper, this form of non-bank borrowing can provide a proxy for changes in the demand for loans. Hence changes in the composition of debt indicate a contraction of the supply of bank loans, consistent with the operation of a bank-lending channel.

However, Oliner and Rudebusch (1995) argue that, rather than indicating a contraction in bank loan supply, the results of Kashyap, Stein and Wilcox (1993) are driven by a rise in commercial paper issuance, and a reallocation of bank lending from small firms to large firms. Hence, according to Oliner and Rudebusch (1995), there is no evidence of a reduction in the supply of bank lending across the board, although there is some evidence that certain types of firms (e.g. small firms) do suffer a reduction in lending following monetary contractions.

In line with the rest of the literature on financial market frictions, that on bank lending has resorted to microeconomic data to get a better understanding of their role in the transmission mechanism. Kashyap and Stein (2000) examine a large panel of US banks spanning twenty years of quarterly data. They examine the way bank lending responds to changes in monetary policy and find significant links between the size of a bank's lending contraction and the bank's liquidity position as measured by the ratio of securities to total assets. The authors argue on the basis of their results that up to a quarter of the response of lending to a monetary shock is due to banks' liquidity constraints. That suggests the bank-lending channel plays a significant role in the monetary transmission mechanism.

3.2   *Evidence for the broad credit channel*

Although bank lending is a very important source of external finance for firms, it is not the sole one, and much of the empirical literature on credit frictions has concentrated on identifying the importance of credit in general and not just bank lending.

The behaviour of financial variables provides one possible source of information that could be used to identify the effects of financial market frictions. Bernanke, Gertler and Gilchrist (1999) show that corporate spreads over risk-free government rates increase sharply in response to a contractionary monetary shock – this behaviour is a key element of their theory of the credit channel.

But even taken at face value, the results of Bernanke, Gertler and Gilchrist (1999) do not lend convincing support to the broad credit channel. Corporate spreads will fluctuate even in the absence of credit frictions, simply because corporate risk or the market price of risk changes. In addition, as Cooper, Hillman and Lynch (2001) show, evidence from corporate bond spread indices is suspect, because individual spreads are a highly non-linear function of individual debt-to-equity ratios. Consequently changes to the financial health of a small sub-sample of firms could affect aggregate spreads, while being entirely consistent with frictionless credit markets.

But by far the largest literature on credit constraints has grown out of the failure of the standard Q-model of investment to match the data. According to neo-classical investment theory under adjustment costs, investment should depend on marginal Q – the ratio of the additional value created by a unit of capital to the cost of capital. And, as shown by Hayashi (1982), under constant returns to scale and with perfectly competitive product markets marginal Q will be equal to Tobin's (average) Q – the ratio of the stock market value of the firm to the replacement cost of its capital stock. This result has motivated a number of authors to test whether movements in Q can adequately account for firms' investment behaviour. But the results of these tests have not been encouraging, with the regressions having low explanatory power and small, insignificant coefficients on average Q.

These poor empirical results are, in some studies, taken as evidence of misspecification caused by the omission of the effects of credit constraints on investment. If variables such as cash flow turn out to be significant in explaining investment, this is interpreted as evidence in favour of a broad credit channel. Obviously, any test here is a joint hypothesis of the assumption of no credit frictions *and* the remaining assumptions underpinning the Q model: there is plenty of scope for other types of misspecification (see Hubbard, 1998, for a recent survey).

The main approach to assessing the significance of credit constraints on investment has been to split firms into those that are constrained and those that are unconstrained on *a priori* grounds. The significance of financial variables in explaining the investment decisions of each group is then examined, with the unconstrained firms essentially acting as a control group.

In a pioneering study, Fazzari, Hubbard and Petersen (1988) split their sample of US firms into firms that pay high dividends and/or issue new shares (the unconstrained firms) and into firms that pay low dividends and do not issue new shares (the constrained firms). They find that the constrained firms are more sensitive to cash flow than the unconstrained firms. Devereux and Schiantarelli (1990) split their sample of UK firms according to size. However, their results are more mixed, with large firms more sensitive to cash flow than small ones. Others, such as Gilchrist and Himmelberg (1995), avoid using measures of average Q derived from the stock market. Instead they obtain forward-looking proxies for future profits using VAR forecasts and find the results similar to the rest of the literature. Finally, Bond and Meghir (1994) allow firms to be subject to time-varying credit constraints according to their financial policy. The authors find that the investment of firms that pay low dividends and do not issue new equity remains more sensitive to cash flow than the investment of other (unconstrained) firms.

The literature has also studied the behaviour of lending after changes in monetary policy. Oliner and Rudebusch (1996) find that the link between cash flow and investment becomes stronger for small firms following a monetary tightening, but does not change following a monetary expansion. At the same time, they find that the role of cash flow for the investment decisions of large firms is unrelated to monetary policy. Oliner and Rudebusch interpret their results as evidence for the operation of the broad credit channel.

Recent contributions to the literature have offered an alternative interpretation of the significant cash flow effect on investment. Bond and Cummins (2000) and Cummins, Hasset and Oliner (1999) have argued that the above studies use the wrong measure of average Q. Measures derived from the stock market will be good proxies for the investment opportunities of firms only if the stock market valuation reflects the net present value of firms' future profits. If equity prices are noisy, for instance because of the presence of bubbles, they will provide only an imperfect measure of the correct economic concept of average Q. The authors construct an alternative measure of average Q based on the profit forecasts of investment analysts, and find that it is significant while cash flow becomes insignificant. So the significance of cash flow may simply be down to it proxying for unobserved (to the econometrician) future profit opportunities. But studies such as Bond and Meghir (1994) suggest the story may be more complex than this: cash flow is more significant for firms that are likely to be credit constrained, so the standard interpretation may nevertheless be correct.

3.3   Summing up

This brief survey of the empirical literature has noted some, albeit controversial, evidence for the existence and importance of a credit channel. A number of studies find that credit effects are particularly important for small firms during periods of monetary tightening. These results are appealing from a theoretical point of view since small firms are the most likely to face informational problems, and consequently to suffer credit constraints. Moreover, there are clear links between bank lending behaviour and bank balance sheet liquidity, which suggests that the bank-lending channel may turn out to be a significant source of monetary transmission when the banking system is relatively illiquid.

4   Consequences for the conduct of monetary policy

In this section we shift the discussion to the implications of credit frictions for the conduct of monetary policy. One might be tempted to argue that if there is a stable empirical relationship between the policy instrument and the target variable(s), then there is no reason why monetary policymakers need be concerned with the details of the transmission mechanism and whether or not financial market frictions matter. But the nature of such frictions is such that their impact is likely to vary over time depending on the history and state of the economy. Furthermore their potential presence is likely to generate extra uncertainty about the impact of monetary policy on activity and inflation. So we centre the discussion on two issues. First, how might the presence of frictions in financial markets modify the conduct of an optimal monetary policy? And, second, how should any consequent uncertainty about the timing and magnitude of the impact of interest rate changes on the economy affect policy design?

4.1   The model

To analyse these questions we utilise a New-Keynesian-style model of a closed economy in which the specification of aggregate demand is modified to allow for the impact of financial frictions.[3] In particular, we assume that some firms and some households face quantitative credit constraints

---

[3] We are grateful to our discussant, Jordi Galí, for encouraging us to develop a model with explicit microfoundations.

as in models of the bank-lending channel, while the cost of borrowing for firms that do have access to financial markets carries an external finance premium as in models of the broad credit channel. We then study the behaviour of the economy under different degrees of financial frictions and ask how this in turn might affect the optimal monetary policy.

In this economy the unconstrained households consume according to a standard intertemporal optimality condition:

$$E_t c_{t+1}^u - c_t^u = \sigma(R_t - E_t \pi_{t+1}) \tag{1}$$

where C_t is consumption in period t, R_t is the nominal interest rate in period t, π_{t+1} is the inflation rate between period t and $t + 1$, E_t denotes an expectation at time t and σ is the intertemporal elasticity of substitution in consumption. A u superscript will be used to denote unconstrained households or firms, and a c superscript will be used to denote constrained households or firms. We shall be considering deviations around a fixed steady state, and lower-case letters will generally be used to denote proportional deviations from that steady state, i.e. $c_t = (C_t - C)/C$ where C is the steady-state value of consumption. Without loss of generality the steady-state interest and inflation rates, R_t and π_{t+1}, will also be set to zero so they can interchangeably be thought as levels and deviations from their steady state.

Credit constrained households have no access to financial markets and just consume the labour income they received in the previous period:

$$c_t^c = w_{t-1} \tag{2}$$

where W_t is labour income in period t and for simplicity we will assume that labour income is a constant fraction of output, Y_t. If the (time-invariant) fraction of constrained households is λ, then aggregate consumption:

$$c_t = \lambda c_t^c + (1 - \lambda)c_t^u \tag{3}$$

Unconstrained firms invest according to a Q-equation, which is consistent with the behaviour of a neo-classical firm with convex adjustment costs for the capital stock:

$$i_t^u = \eta q_t \tag{4}$$

where I_t is investment in period t and Q_t is marginal Q in period t, i.e. the ratio of the market valuation to the replacement cost of an additional unit of capital. The elasticity of investment with respect to the valuation of capital, η, is equal to the inverse of the elasticity of the marginal capital adjustment cost with respect to the investment–capital ratio. In theory (4) should relate the investment–capital ratio, rather than investment itself, to Q. But we ignore capital stock variations on the grounds that they do not contribute much to variations in the investment–capital ratio at business cycle frequencies. Marginal Q evolves according to a no-arbitrage condition that sets the real return on debt equal to the return on equity, comprising dividends and expected real capital gains:

$$R_t^f - E_t \pi_{t+1} = \psi y_t + E_t q_{t+1} - q_t \tag{5}$$

where R_t^f is the nominal interest rate paid by firms on debt in period t. For simplicity dividends are assumed to be proportional to output, and ψ is thus the dividend per unit of capital.

Although these firms are unconstrained, there is nevertheless a broad credit channel in operation so that the market interest rate is higher than the risk free rate by an amount that depends on the quantity of real debt, B_t, i.e. there is an external finance premium:

$$R_t^f = R_t + v b_t \tag{6}$$

Modelling the debt–equity choice in this environment is complex. For simplicity we therefore assume that as well as paying interest on outstanding debt, firms simply repay a fraction of old debt that is increasing in both their profits (which vary with output) and the amount of debt outstanding:[4]

$$B_{t+1}^u = \left(1 + r_t^f\right) B_t^u - \left(\chi Y_t + \delta B_t^u\right) \tag{7}$$

where $r_t^f = R_t^f - E_t \pi_{t+1}$ is the real return on corporate debt. Log-linearising around the steady state then gives:

$$b_{t+1}^u = (1 + r^f - \delta) b_t^u - (\chi Y / B^u) y_t + \left(R_t^f - E_t \pi_{t+1}\right) \tag{8}$$

where variables without time subscripts denote steady-state values. This specification for the behaviour of unconstrained firms therefore implies that a high value of initial debt, e.g. because of past low output, depresses the share price and investment.

The investment of constrained firms is determined by their liquid resources, and so depends on retained profits from the previous period (proportional to output) less interest payments on outstanding debt. We

---

[4] We abstract from the issue of who holds the debt. Implicitly we therefore assume that the asset position of the household sector does not affect consumption decisions.

assume that the real debt burden of constrained firms is fixed at B^c because they are for the most part excluded from debt markets. So the investment of constrained firms is given by:

$$I_t^c = \varepsilon Y_{t-1} - B^c \left(R_t^f - E_t \pi_{t+1} \right) \tag{9}$$

This leads to the corresponding expression in terms of deviations around the steady state:

$$i_t^c = (\varepsilon Y/I) y_{t-1} - (B^c/I) \left(R_t^f - E_t \pi_{t+1} \right) \tag{10}$$

Aggregate investment is then given by a weighted average of the expenditure of constrained and unconstrained firms:

$$i_t = \mu i_t^c + (1 - \mu) i_t^u \tag{11}$$

where μ is the share of unconstrained firms.

Finally, the national income identity gives aggregate output as a suitably weighted average of consumer, investment and government demand:

$$y_t = s_c c_t + s_i i_t + s_g g_t \tag{12}$$

where g_t is government expenditure in period t and s_c, s_i and s_g are the shares in output of consumption, investment and government spending, respectively. The term in g_t also functions as a generic shock to aggregate demand.

The key feature of this specification of credit frictions is that more widespread credit constraints raise the degree of persistence in the economy as a greater fraction of current spending depends on past levels of activity while a smaller fraction depends on expectations of future economic conditions. Thus the model addresses the second of Bernanke, Gertler and Gilchrist's (1999) puzzles (propagation). The model is also capable of addressing the third (amplification), although whether it does or not depends on the calibration chosen. Constrained households will actually be *less* sensitive to current movements in interest rates than unconstrained ones, but the same may or may not be true of firms, depending on the parameters chosen.

The specification of aggregate supply is as in many existing New-Keynesian models and contains both forward- and backward-looking elements:

$$\pi_t = \alpha E_t \pi_{t+1} + (1 - \alpha) \pi_{t-1} + \kappa y_t + u_t \tag{13}$$

where u_t is a supply (cost) shock and α indexes the degree of forward-looking behaviour in wage- and price setting. One rationalisation for such an equation would be a world where there are overlapping wage contracts of the Buiter–Jewitt (1981)/Fuhrer–Moore (1995) variety.

To complete the model we need to describe the behaviour of the monetary authorities. We assume that they care about the variability of output, inflation and the nominal interest rate with the following loss function, L_t:

$$L_t = \sum_{j=0} \beta^{t+j} \left(\pi_{t+j}^2 + \theta y_{t+j}^2 + \gamma R_{t+j}^2 \right) \tag{14}$$

where β is a discount factor and θ and γ are policy weights.

As far as possible we calibrate the model in line with the existing literature, with a period corresponding to a quarter. For the elasticity of intertemporal substitution, σ, there is a substantial range of estimates available. Those for the USA run from 0.16 (McCallum and Nelson, 1999) as far as 6 (Rotemberg and Woodford, 1997). The real business cycle literature normally sets a value of unity corresponding to logarithmic preferences. We pick a benchmark value of 0.4, in line with Nelson and Nikolov (2002), but later consider the implications of values between 0.1 and 1.5, encompassing all but the very largest estimates for the USA or the UK.

There is also little consensus on the appropriate value of η, the elasticity of investment with respect to the value of capital. Bernanke, Gertler and Gilchrist (1999) calibrate $1/\eta$, the elasticity of the marginal adjustment cost with respect to the investment to capital ratio, equal to 0.25, implying an investment elasticity of 4. However, empirical estimates of the sensitivity of investment to cost of capital measures are very low and range from zero to 0.15. In a model of the financial accelerator for the household sector, Aoki, Proudman and Vlieghe (2001) set η equal to 2 in order to match the relative variability of house prices and housing investment. We calibrate our parameter in the same spirit by reconciling the relative volatilities of detrended UK stock prices (used as a proxy for Tobin's Q) and detrended UK investment. This method gives a value for η equal to 0.36 (the standard deviation of stock price is around 14 per cent while the standard deviation of investment is around 5 per cent). For simplicity, we set our baseline value equal to 0.4 – the same as the intertemporal elasticity of consumption. So our baseline value of η is slightly above most empirical estimates, but substantially below calibrated values for the USA. We later conduct policy experiments over a range of 0.1–1.5, encompassing most of these estimated and calibrated values.

There is even less evidence on the degree of credit constraints in the economy. We consider both a 'strong-credit frictions' world with λ and μ set to 0.8 and a 'no-credit frictions' world with λ and μ set to zero, as well as intermediate possibilities. In the former (latter) case we also set υ, the elasticity of the external finance premium with respect to firms' debt stock, equal to 0.05 (zero) following Bernanke, Gertler and Gilchrist (1999). As debt in our model effectively performs the same role as net worth in standard financial accelerator models, we set the debt–output ratio at 0.5 for unconstrained firms, in line with Bernanke, Gertler and Gilchrist's (1999) value for corporate gearing. The amount of principal repaid in each period by unconstrained firms, δ, is set to 0.05. There is no obvious evidence to draw on for constrained firms, so we set the debt–output ratio for constrained firms equal to 0.25, reflecting their more limited access to debt markets. We note below the consequences of choosing a larger value for this parameter.

The other demand-side parameters are mainly calibrated with reference to national accounts data. The consumption, investment and government spending shares in GDP are set at, respectively, 0.6, 0.2 and 0.2. Both χ and ε are set to 0.36, and the dividend–capital ratio, ψ, is set to 0.05. Finally the shocks, u_t and $s_g g_t$, are assumed to be serially and mutually uncorrelated, with standard deviations equal to 0.5 per cent.

As far as the supply side goes, the weight on expected inflation in the supply curve, α, is set to 0.2 in line with Batini and Haldane (1999) and Batini and Nelson (2000). The response of inflation to activity, κ, is set to 0.1, which is broadly consistent with the estimates of Bean (1998) for the UK. Finally, with regard to the policymaker's preferences, we set θ to unity and γ to 0.25, implying some concern about interest rate variability, but to a much lesser extent than for the variances of output and inflation. The discount rate, β, is set to 0.99, implying a steady-state real interest rate of approximately 4 per cent per annum.

Although one could certainly take issue with many of these choices, our purpose is primarily to draw some generic lessons about the impact of financial frictions on policy design. We would expect the main lessons we draw below to be robust to reasonable variation in the parameters of the model.

4.2   Optimal monetary policy under different degrees of financial friction

We now consider how the extent of financial frictions affects the optimal monetary policy around a fixed steady state; we do not consider the more complex question of how policy should respond during the transition from one steady state to another, e.g. during a financial liberalisation. Throughout we assume the policymaker has access to an appropriate commitment technology and, following Woodford (1999), study the optimal commitment equilibrium (also described as the 'timeless perspective' by McCallum and Nelson, 2000) which involves minimisation of the expected value of the loss function at 'the beginning of time'. This gives

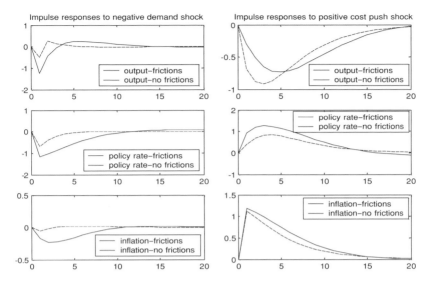

Figure 6.1 Impulse responses of output, inflation and the policy rate to a 'demand' and a 'supply' shock

an optimal contingent plan for the interest rate, which by assumption the policymaker can then commit to. Because the model contains forward-looking elements the policymaker would have an incentive to deviate from this equilibrium in the absence of a suitable commitment technology.

The model is solved by minimising the expected value of the loss function (14), evaluated at date zero, subject to the linearised laws of motion of the economy given by the system (1)–(13). We first examine the dynamic response of the variables of interest to demand and cost shocks. Figure 6.1 shows the responses for the two polar sets of parameters corresponding to a frictionless world; and a world of strong financial frictions.

Figure 6.1 shows that, as expected, movements in both output and inflation are somewhat more persistent when there are financial frictions present. Interestingly, though demand shocks have a greater short-run effect on output when frictions are present, the opposite is true for a cost shock. This is because of the extra inertia in output induced by the frictions. In the absence of frictions agents are less responsive to current economic conditions and more influenced by future movements in output and real interest rates, and this tends to depress consumption and investment more strongly in the short term.

The behaviour of policy is also affected substantially. When frictions are present the nominal interest rate changes more and that change is

Table 6.1 *The effects of financial frictions on welfare, inflation, output and the interest rate*

	Financial frictions	No financial frictions
Expected loss	384.6	261.4
Standard deviations (%):		
Inflation	4.91	4.15
Output	1.24	1.14
Interest rate	7.63	4.42

also more persistent. Again this is related to the fact that in the absence of frictions, future developments, including future policy movements, have a greater impact on agents' decisions. Thus a commitment by the policymaker to alter the level of future interest rates in response to the current shock will affect current spending. Consequently the current interest rate needs to be changed less in order to stabilise output and inflation. The presence of this 'expectations channel', which is more powerful in the absence of frictions, effectively increases the potency of monetary policy, allowing the central bank to stabilise output and inflation with lower instrument variability. In contrast, when financial markets are subject to significant imperfections, monetary policy needs to be rather more aggressive in order to prevent persistent fluctuations in inflation and output.

Table 6.1 shows the associated expected values of the loss function.[5] as well as the standard deviations of the key endogenous variables in the model. The value of the loss function is significantly higher when frictions are present. Table 6.1 also shows that the main effect of financial frictions is to increase the variability of interest rates, output and inflation. Intuitively, when significant financial frictions are present, policymakers must take care not to permit large fluctuations in current output as these are costly to correct subsequently. The costs of such a strategy are more volatile interest rates and a more gradual return of inflation to target.

However, inflation and output volatility are relatively unaffected by financial frictions if we assume a larger leverage ratio for constrained firms.[6] In this case, the cash flow and investment expenditure of constrained firms becomes more sensitive to the interest rates, and the power of monetary policy is thus enhanced. The monetary authority is then able

---

[5] Of course, this expected loss considers only the impact of inflation, output and interest rate *volatility* on welfare. It does not take account of the possibly large effects on welfare of the *lower* level of national income that may result from the presence of financing constraints.

[6] Recall that in our baseline calibration constrained firms are less leveraged than the average.

to offset the impact of shocks more easily. By the same token, monetary policy shocks – not present in our analysis – would also have a substantially larger destabilising impact.

4.3   Policy when the impact of financial frictions is uncertain

In this section, we recognise that there is considerable uncertainty about the impact of financial frictions on the transmission mechanism and explore the consequences for policy design. Of course, even if policy affects the economy solely through the classical interest rate channel, there may still be uncertainty about the interest elasticity of demand and other key parameters. But as more evidence accumulates one might hope to pin these down more precisely. By contrast, the potentially asymmetric and episodic nature of financial frictions is likely to lead to uncertainty that cannot be resolved purely through the passage of time and the accumulation of more aggregate data. There are at least two reasons for this. First, credit constraints are fundamentally an asymmetric propagation mechanism that will bind most often in a downturn when households and firms wish to increase borrowing. But ascertaining the extent to which they bind really requires detailed microeconomic evidence on the financial position of households and firms that is unlikely to be available to the policymaker. Secondly, the supply of credit is likely to be influenced by the health of the financial system as well as the shocks hitting it at any point in time. Again this requires access to detailed data on the health of individual financial institutions.

The standard approach to policy design under parameter uncertainty assumes that the policymaker knows the statistical distribution of any unknown parameters; optimal control procedures can then be applied in the usual way (see the classic paper by Brainard, 1967). But in practice the policymaker may not feel sufficiently well informed to formulate such a distribution. This is particularly relevant in the current context where microeconomic evidence might be required to formulate such a distribution. For that reason we adopt a robust control approach, along the lines of Giannoni (2001) and Hansen and Sargent (2001). They assume the policymaker knows the range of possible parameter realisations, but is not in a position to formulate a probability distribution over that range. The robust policy rule in these circumstances is the one that minimises the objective function in the worst-case scenario (the min-max Nash equilibrium). Effectively this can be thought of as a game between the policymaker and a Malevolent Nature, with the policymaker choosing a policy that minimises the loss function, and Malevolent Nature picking a parameter combination designed to maximise the loss, given that policy is conducted optimally.

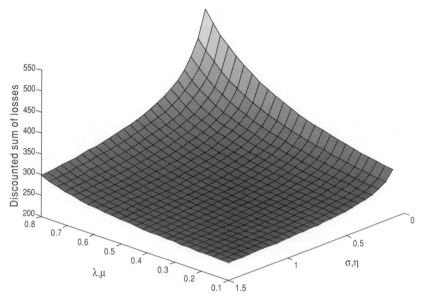

Figure 6.2 The optimal commitment loss surface

There are a large number of parameters in our model, each of which might be uncertain. In order to keep things simple, we focus just on uncertainty about the extent of credit constraints (given by λ and μ) and about the impact of interest rates on demand (given by σ and η). Moreover to keep the dimensions down and facilitate graphical display of the results, we set $\lambda = \mu$ and $\sigma = \eta$. We thus consider variation in just two key parameters, one corresponding to the extent of credit constraints and the other to the impact of interest rates on demand. Drawing on our earlier discussion of the calibration of the model, we then define feasible ranges for the proportion of credit constrained firms and consumers ($\lambda = \mu \in [0.1, 0.8]$) and for the interest elasticity of demand ($\sigma = \eta \in [0.1, 1.5]$). We then compute the expected loss in the commitment equilibrium for each feasible parameter combination.

Figure 6.2 gives a diagrammatic representation of the solution, with each point on the chart corresponding to the minimised expected loss conditional on a given set of parameters. It is easy to see from figure 6.2 that a Malevolent Nature would pick $\lambda = \mu = 0.8$ and $\sigma = \eta = 0.1$, the parameters which give the highest minimised expected loss. Consequently, a robust policymaker would conduct policy as if the economy was characterised by these worst-case parameter values.

This scenario corresponds to the case where most agents are credit constrained, with their expenditure being driven by past income, while the few agents that are unconstrained are not very responsive to monetary policy, and are consequently unable to absorb the slack left by constrained agents. So the economy is characterised by significant endogenous propagation through credit constraints coupled with limited efficacy of monetary policy. That makes output and inflation very difficult to control, amplifying volatility and reducing welfare.

4.4   *Robustness versus performance*

The robust policy derived above ensures relatively good outcomes in the worst-case scenario. But it may produce relatively poor outcomes for other realisations of the parameters. And in many cases, including that considered here, the robust policy optimises performance at extreme ends of the parameter range. It is consequently very sensitive to where these boundaries are located. There is something rather unsatisfactory in assuming that the policymaker can say with great confidence what the range of feasible parameter values is, while at the same time positing total ignorance about the relative likelihood of different parameter values occurring within that range. What we seek, therefore, is a suitable halfway house.

Suppose the policymaker is prepared to assert that the 'most likely' realisation of the parameter values corresponds to our baseline values for the interest elasticity of demand, $\sigma = \eta = 0.4$, and an intermediate value for the extent of credit constraints, $\lambda = \mu = 0.5$. Now as an alternative strategy – we make no claims for optimality here – consider setting policy to minimise the expected loss assuming that the parameters take these values; call this the 'Modal rule'. The first panel in figure 6.3 [7] shows the relative welfare loss (on the vertical axis, in log differences) of the Robust rule compared to the Modal rule across the feasible parameter space. Negative values in the figure indicate that the Robust rule delivers lower expected loss than the Modal rule (and vice versa). The key conclusion to be drawn is that the Modal rule performs better than the Robust rule for most of the parameter space, but that its performance deteriorates rapidly as monetary policy loses its potency and credit constraints bite. However, the deterioration occurs only when $\sigma \ (= \eta)$ is below 0.2, while the proportion of constrained agents, $\lambda (= \eta)$, is over 70 per cent – i.e. at one extreme of the parameter ranges.

Now suppose that the policymaker has *some* prior knowledge on the distribution of the parameters, but is unwilling or unable to fully specify it. A natural extension of the robust control approach is to assume that the policymaker is prepared to make some statement about the relative likelihood of different parameter values, and that Malevolent Nature then

---

[7] Note that the orientation of the axes is different from figure 6.2.

Density

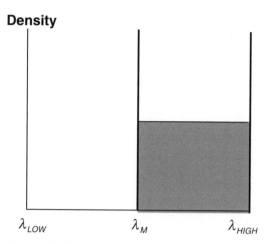

λ_{LOW} λ_M λ_{HIGH}

Figure 6.3 The worst-case distribution

chooses the *worst possible distribution*. The policymaker then minimises the expected loss given that distribution using the standard approach.

Suppose, then, that the policymaker knows the most likely outcome of λ $(= \mu)$, denoted λ_{MODE}, and its support, $[\lambda_{LOW}, \lambda_{HIGH}]$, but not the shape of the associated distribution. However, he is prepared to assert that values closer to the mode are at least as likely as values further away from the mode. As discussed above, the conduct of policy becomes more difficult for larger values of λ. So, Malevolent Nature would like to place as much probability as possible into the upper tail of the distribution of λ. But she is constrained in her choice of distribution, because values closer to the mode must be at least as likely as values further away from the mode. Then it is easy to see that the worst distribution Malevolent Nature can inflict upon the policymaker is a uniform distribution over the support $[\lambda_{MODE}, \lambda_{HIGH}]$; see figure 6.3. A similar argument applies for σ $(= \eta)$. Conditional on the joint distribution of λ and σ, the policymaker then solves a standard optimal control problem over the relevant sub-set of the parameter space. We refer to this policy as the Intermediate rule, as it combines elements of both standard policy optimisation and robust control.

To see what effect this might have in the present model, assume that the modes and supports of λ $(= \mu)$ and σ $(= \eta)$ are as above. Then Malevolent Nature picks a uniform distribution for λ $(= \mu)$ over the range [0.5, 0.8] and a uniform distribution for σ $(= \eta)$ over the range [0.1, 0.4]. The policymaker then minimises the expected loss, given these parameter distributions. This last step is somewhat complex in even this simple

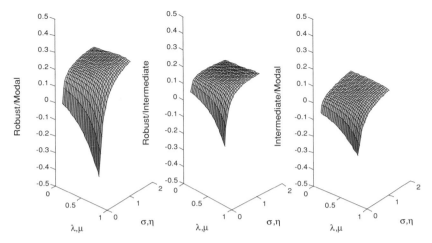

Figure 6.4 Welfare differences under the Robust, Modal and Intermediate rules

set-up, but to get a feel for the implications of the approach we calculate the expected welfare losses when policy is constructed assuming that λ ($= \mu$) and σ ($= \eta$) are equal to their means with respect to the distribution selected by Nature, i.e. $(\lambda_{MODE} + \lambda_{HIGH})/2$ and $(\sigma_{MODE} + \sigma_{LOW})/2$ respectively. Call this the 'Intermediate rule'. This policy does not, of course, strictly correspond to the optimal rule calculated over the entire feasible sub-space, but is probably a reasonable approximation.

The third panel in figure 6.4 compares the performance of the Modal and Intermediate rules over the feasible parameter range. The Intermediate rule gives roughly comparable performance to the Modal rule, while still providing some insurance against the worst-case scenario. Of course, as the second panel in figure 6.4 comparing the Robust and Intermediate rules shows, this insurance is not complete: the Robust rule still performs better in the worst case. But the Intermediate rule performs better than the Modal rule over a wider range of parameter values than the Robust rule, and is hence less sensitive to extreme values.

5   Concluding remarks

In this chapter we have surveyed the ways that financial frictions augment the classical interest rate channel of monetary transmission. The difficulty of providing a satisfactory explanation for the magnitude and persistence of the impact of changes in the official interest rate relying solely on the classical channel suggests that financial frictions may be an important part of the transmission mechanism. However, these frictions may be manifested in a variety of ways, as witnessed by the variety of theoretical models in the credit channel and bank-lending literatures.

Sorting out the relative importance of these different channels is hampered by the fact that the competing theories often have similar implications, at least on aggregate data. However, the microeconomic evidence does suggest that both the credit channel and bank-lending channel are operative.

With respect to the implications for the conduct of monetary policy, a key feature of financial frictions is that they tend to increase persistence and also amplify the effect of changes in official interest rates. In our New Keynesian macroeconomic model, the presence of such frictions means that policy has to be rather more aggressive. This is because the forward-looking elements in the transmission mechanism are relatively less important when there are frictions, so that expectations of future movements in interest rates have a more muted effect on the economy today.

The nature of these financial frictions, and their potentially asymmetric and episodic character, are also likely to introduce (even greater) uncertainty into the magnitude and timing of the response of the economy to changes in monetary policy. Here we drew on the recent robust control literature to explore how optimal policy might be affected. That approach suggests that the policymaker should act on the assumption that credit constraints are important, but that demand is not very responsive to interest rates. Arguably, the robust control approach places too much weight on avoiding bad outcomes in extreme cases. We therefore considered a case that is intermediate between robust control and standard optimal control. In that intermediate case the policymaker can say something, but not everything about the nature of the uncertainty facing him. That approach potentially moderates the sensitivity to extreme outcomes found under the standard robust control approach.

Clearly there is still much more that could – and no doubt will – be said and written on the topic of financial frictions and their role in the transmission mechanism. But one thing is certain: the empirical studies that comprise the bulk of this volume have added immeasurably to our knowledge in this   area.

Part 2

Firms' investment and monetary policy: evidence from micro economic data

The macroeconomic evidence in Part 1 suggests that an important part of the output adjustments that are induced by monetary policy are ultimately due to changes in investment. The chapters in this section of book use firm level data to better understand the investment dynamics. A survey paper by J. B. Chatelain, A. Generale, I. Hernando, P. Vermeulen and U. von Kalckreuth is followed by country specific analyses focused on Belgium, Germany, France, Italy, Luxembourg and Austria.

The motivation for using firm-level data is two fold. First, using micro data may make it possible to side step some of the problems associated with studies that rely on aggregate data. Specifically, the simultaneity problem that plagues macroeconomic studies of investment is of particular concern for inferences regarding monetary transmission. Since short term interest rates tend to move counter-cyclically, there will be a natural tendency for interest rate changes to appear to have limited effects on investment. It is extremely difficult to find any econometric instruments that could be used to solve this problem.

The studies in this project largely identify the link between investment and the user cost of capital off of cross-firm variation in the user cost, much which of which is due to tax differences and other sources of asymmetry in firm-specific interest rates. These differences give rise to exogenous cross-firm variation that can be exploited in the estimation. Moreover, other firm-level instruments are often available for the endogenous components of the user cost. Therefore, it may not be surprising that these studies typically find significant, and relatively precisely estimated, elasticities of investment with respect to the user cost of capital.

A second motivation is to explore other channels (besides via the user cost) through which monetary policy might affect investment. The main interest is in assessing the importance of capital market imperfections and we follow the literature in trying to search for cross-firm differences that might be expected if borrowing constraints are important. A number of country-specific studies in this part identify significant and sizeable cash-flow or liquidity effects on investment. The initial summary chapter explores the comparative dimension across the large countries in the area, reaching similar results.

7 Firm investment and monetary policy transmission in the euro area

*J. B. Chatelain, A. Generale, I. Hernando,
P. Vermeulen and U. von Kalckreuth*

1 Introduction

Monetary policy is generally thought to be able to affect business investment through multiple channels. First, a traditional 'interest rate channel' is identified, whereby changes in market interest rates imply changes in the cost of capital, which in turn affect investment. However, the difficulties of using aggregate data to find clear evidence of this channel are well known. Second, changes in market interest rates affect the net cash flow (i.e. cash flow after interest payments) available to a firm. Given imperfect capital markets, the availability of net cash flow will have an effect on investment. This is generally referred to as the 'broad credit channel'.

This chapter provides an investigation of those two channels based on results from a unique comparative study of the four largest euro area countries.[1] Using rich firm databases for each country, standardised regressions were run to make comparison across countries feasible. Although, for confidentiality reasons, individual data could not be pooled – making formal statistical testing impossible – the standardisation of the analysis should still allow asymmetries in the working of these channels to be detected. In particular, reliance on firm data should make it possible to identify whether there are differences in the behaviour of firms with otherwise similar characteristics. This has a distinct advantage over the inference based on aggregate data in which 'true' differences in behaviour are potentially confounded by differences due to composition of the firms in the aggregate.

We would like to thank the participants of the monetary economics workshop at the NBER Summer Institute 2001 and Bob Chirinko for helpful discussions and feedback, and Daniele Terlizzese for his very helpful comments.
[1] Mojon, Smets and Vermeulen (2002) investigate the elasticity of investment with respect to its user cost using industry data on the same four countries. The MTN project has led to a number of complementary companion papers on investment and monetary policy: Butzen, Fuss and Vermeulen (2001), Chatelain and Tiomo (2001), Gaiotti and Generale (2001), von Kalckreuth (2001), Lünneman and Mathä (2001) and Valderrama (2001b).

The rest of the chapter is structured as follows. In section 2 we motivate the analysis and spell out the relevant questions that can be answered by comparing the results across countries. In section 3 we describe the theoretical framework. In section 4 we present our data. In section 5 we present the regression results. In section 6 we test whether a broad credit channel is operative in the euro area. In section 7 we investigate the links between monetary policy, user cost and cash flow.

2   Motivation of the analysis

Since the beginning of monetary union in Europe, a large body of empirical analysis has been devoted to the transmission mechanism of monetary policy. These analyses are usually justified by the observation that a common monetary policy affects economies characterised by a high degree of heterogeneity.

This chapter is a contribution to the discussion of monetary policy transmission in the euro area; it focuses on the four major euro area countries by using data collected at the national level. Our perspective is at once wider and narrower than the one motivating previous research. It is narrower in that we limit our attention to a specific channel of monetary policy, firms' investment spending. It is wider in that, by using micro data, we try to take into account the relevance of firms' balance sheet conditions in the transmission of monetary policy. The contribution of the chapter consists mainly in an assessment of the main determinants of investment spending in each of the countries.

Interest in the transmission mechanism is motivated by a variety of reasons that also can have policy implications. First, for a careful assessment of the monetary stance in the area, it is important to know if the pure interest channel is the only channel at work. If agents' financial conditions are shown to be important, then knowing these conditions proves to be important for the policymaker; at the same time this knowledge helps better to forecast the likely effects of a monetary policy decision.

As it is well known, the main channels of monetary policy transmission have been thoroughly examined mainly using macro information (see the survey in Guiso *et al.*, 1999). These kind of analyses have, on the one hand enabled regularities and differences across the countries of the euro area to be uncovered; on the other hand, they have proved to be limited in many respects. First of all, it is known that aggregation can blur the differences in the transmission of monetary policy and impede the identification of important parts of the transmission mechanism. Hence, recourse to micro data is often motivated in the literature by the recognition of the limits of aggregate studies. In their US study on the relationship between investment spending and the user cost of capital, Chirinko, Fazzari and Meyer (1999) motivate the use of micro data by the very fact that studies at the aggregate level often fail to find an economically significant relationship between these two variables. As the authors note, this failure could have been due 'to biased estimates due to problems of simultaneity, capital market frictions, or firm heterogeneity that may be better addressed with micro data'.

Moreover, micro data are also needed because of the 'extensive variation [in micro data that] will likely provide better instruments [for instrumental variable estimation] than can be obtained at the aggregate level.' The motivation for employing micro data can be generally ascribed to the advantages of panel data estimation versus time series estimation, that is to use 'information on both the intertemporal dynamics and the individuality of entities being investigated' (Hsiao, 1986). Moreover, in our analysis on the determinants of investment, the use of micro data permits firm-level measures of the user cost, sales and cash flow, thus taking into account the fact that the transmission of monetary impulses occurs at the firm level.

In fact, as is well known and indeed very well explained by Chirinko, Fazzari and Meyer (1999), one of the difficulties found in the empirical analysis of the relationship between investment and the user cost is that these estimates usually turn out to be very low. They report that this may be due to simultaneity bias, arguing that 'investment comprises a volatile component of aggregate demand, positively correlated with the business cycle, and business cycle movements correlate with interest rates. Positive investment shocks, for example, can cause positive movements in output and the demand for credit that affect the required rates of return on debt and equity. Conventional wisdom suggests that simultaneity between investment shocks and interest rates biases the user cost elasticity towards zero.' In this respect, a source of cross-sectional variation comes from the tax component in the user cost variable that we use in the estimation; this component can be regarded as an exogenous source of variation, thus allowing us better to identify the effects of the cost of capital on investment. Moreover, simultaneity problems are reduced by IV or GMM estimation. Hence, the combination of instrumental variable estimation and the exogenous source of variability ensured by tax variations should improve our ability properly to identify user cost effects.[2]

---

[2] It has to be clarified that we are not pursuing the strategy of research adopted by Cummins, Hassett and Hubbard (1994, 1996) that stretched this line of identification as far as to measure investment elasticities to the user cost in years of major tax reform. At any rate, it is important for us to be sure of having a sufficient amount of variability in the data due to this tax component.

Finally, micro data permit us to uncover the existence of a broad credit channel, i.e. the second channel of monetary transmission.

The literature on the broad credit channel of monetary policy has emphasised the relevance of information asymmetries in the transmission of monetary policy. In particular, the difficulty faced by lenders in monitoring the projects of 'opaque' firms implies that firms' financial conditions are important for the availability and cost of external finance. These firms are likely to be more exposed to problems of asymmetric information and they might react more to a monetary tightening (Gilchrist and Zakrajsek, 1995). Analysing the reaction to a common shock of groups of firms characterised by weaker balance sheets and comparing it to other firms that are in a better financial position solves the identification problems encountered with the use of macro data. There are also drawbacks in using micro data. They mainly consist in the difficulty of recovering aggregate effects from micro estimations. This is mainly caused by the fact that usually shorter time periods are available in panels, thus implying that variation in the monetary policy stance can be more limited than with time-series data, and that samples are often biased towards specific types of firms. We are aware of these difficulties: as documented in the data set description, we are confident that the sample chosen is quite representative of the firms' characteristics in each country; moreover, in comparison to other contributions on panel analysis, we have panels that are quite long. A high degree of heterogeneity seems to characterise these economies in particular with regard to firms' financial structure, the availability of external funds and the industrial structure. Table 7.1 illustrates some of these differences.

On the real side, the distribution of firms by size turns out to be quite dissimilar: in Germany only 48 per cent of total turnover of non-financial firms pertained to firms with fewer than 250 employees, whereas, at the other extreme, in Italy such firms accounted for 71 per cent.

As to financial structure, firms differ markedly with respect to both the availability of external funds and the composition of their financial debt. Table 7.1 shows that reliance on bank credit is highest in Italy, partly reflecting the more limited role of equity in firm financing; it is much more limited in the other countries. Spain, a country in an intermediate position as to dependence on bank debt, also shows a high share of equity financing, in terms of both capital's and reserves' share of firms' total liabilities and of stock market capitalisation as a percentage of GDP. More importantly, for the transmission of monetary policy impulses, the share of short-term debt differs markedly across countries, with higher values in Italy and Spain. Looking at recent transaction data, flows in bank loans have substantially exceeded flows in shares and other equity in Germany,

Table 7.1 *Financial structure, capital markets and real indicators in the euro area*

	Germany	France	Italy	Spain
Financial structure of manufacturing firms (1)				
as % of total liabilities, 1997				
Bank credit	6.2	7.2	21.2	11.0
Of which:				
Maturity of less than 1 year	3.7	3.3	14.3	6.6
Maturity of more than 1 year	2.5	3.9	6.9	4.4
Bonds	0.2	1.9	0.9	0.1
Trade credit	12.8	24.2	26.2	23.9
Other debt	16.0	23.8	15.8	14.9
Provisions	31.9	4.9	7.8	4.4
Capital and reserves	32.9	38.0	28.1	45.7
External financing transactions of non-financial corporations (2)				
as % of nominal GDP, average 1996–9				
Loans	4.5	2.0	2.0	5.4
Securities other than shares	−0.1	0.6	0.0	−0.1
Shares and other equity	1.5	3.4	1.3	2.7
Other liabilities	0.8	0.7	1.2	6.3
Capital markets (2)				
as % of nominal GDP, 1997				
Total financial liabilities of non-financial firms	128.8	268.4	135.0	209.6
Stock market capitalisation	39.9	49.5	30.6	56.2
Bonds of non-financial firms	0.1	.	1.6	2.7
Real indicators (3)				
as % average 1996–2000				
Investment/GDP	22.2	19.0	19.4	23.3
Share of total non-financial firms' turnover attributable to firms fewer than 250 employees 1997 (2)	48.0	56.0	71.0	62.0

Notes:
(1) *Source:* BACH data set (European Commission).
(2) *Source:* Eurostat.
(3) *Source:* OECD and Eurostat.

Italy and Spain. France is the exception to this pattern. It seems to be the country with a lower dependence on bank debt, corroborated by its relatively high stock market capitalisation.

One obvious question that arises when looking at cross-country differences, then, is whether these broad institutional characteristics are conducive to a different reaction to monetary policy. It needs to be clarified that the research strategy adopted in this chapter is able to address only partially the issue of asymmetries across countries. We are in fact mainly interested in documenting the importance of the different transmission mechanisms in each country. Our research strategy is the following: we first estimate investment equations for each country, giving us the sensitivity of investment to its main determinants: the user cost, sales and cash flow. This permits an assessment of the relative importance of the different channels in each country. Moreover, by calculating the response of investment determinants to monetary policy we obtain a measure of the elasticity of investment to monetary policy. The comparison of the results obtained across countries is needed to understand how the transmission of monetary impulses takes place at the country level. Moreover, it gives a rough indication of the existence or absence of asymmetries. For confidentiality reasons, cross-country comparisons are not performed on a pooled data set, thus impeding a formal test on the significance of the differences.

We believe, though, that examining the main channels of transmission in each country is only a first step in assessing the relevance of asymmetries. Consider the case of the broad credit channel: if financial variables prove to be important in a given country, then there is evidence that differences in access to financial markets in this country play a role. But, at the country-by-country analysis stage, finding larger effects of financial variables in one country does not mean that a broad credit channel is at work. One way partly to address this issue consists in performing a test of the differences in reaction to investment determinants for firms that are more likely to be subject to information asymmetries. The detection of significant differences within each country permits us to highlight how widespread heterogeneous behaviour is in the countries we examine. Future research in the field should seek to carefully assess the quantitative importance of the eventual differences found and try to trace the observed differences back to the presence of heterogeneity in behaviour or in the composition of the firms in the economy.

3   The theoretical framework

The investment model we use is derived from the neo-classical demand for capital. It has recently been estimated using panel data by, among others, Bond *et al.* (1997), Chirinko, Fazzari and Meyer (1999) and Hall, Mairesse and Mulkay (1999, 2001). Abstracting from irreversibility, uncertainty, delivery lags and adjustment costs, the first-order condition for a firm's optimisation problem leads to the equality between the marginal product of capital and the user cost of capital UC_{it}:

$$F_K(K_{it}, L_{it}) = UC_{it}, \tag{1}$$

where i stands for firm, and t stands for time.

Following Auerbach (1983) and Hayashi (2000), we obtain a weighted average definition of the user cost of capital where the cost of debt and equity are weighted with their respective share of the total liabilities of the firm. We use the accounting proportions of debt and equity which affects taxation:

$$UC_{it} = \frac{P_t^I}{P_{st}} \frac{(1 - itc_t - \tau_t z_s)}{(1 - \tau_t)} \left[AI_{it} \left(\frac{D_{it}}{D_{it} + E_{it}} \right) (1 - \tau_t) \right.$$
$$\left. + (LD_t) \left(\frac{E_{it}}{D_{it} + E_{it}} \right) - (1 - \delta_s) \frac{\Delta P_{t+1}^I}{P_t^I} + \delta_s \right] \tag{2}$$

where s is the sector-specific index, P_{st} the price of final goods, P_t^I the price of capital goods, τ_t the corporate income tax rate, against which interest payments and depreciation are assumed to be deductible, z the present value of depreciation allowances and itc the investment tax credit. AI is the apparent interest rate, measured as interest payment over gross debt, LD the long-term debt rate used as a proxy for the opportunity cost of equity, E the book value of equity and δ_s the industry-specific rate of economic depreciation.

In contrast to the King and Fullerton (1984) approach, as used by Harhoff and Ramb (2001) and von Kalckreuth (2001), this user cost of capital does not take into account the differences for dividends and retained earnings for households; income tax and the distinction between different capital goods for the computation of the net present value (NPV) of depreciation allowances.[3]

Following Eisner and Nadiri (1968), we parameterise the production function by a constant elasticity of the substitution production function:

$$F(K_{it}, L_{it}) = TFP_i A_t \left[\beta_i L_{it}^{\frac{\sigma-1}{\sigma}} + \alpha_i K_{it}^{\frac{\sigma-1}{\sigma}} \right]^{\frac{\sigma}{\sigma-1} \nu}, \quad \alpha_i + \beta_i = 1 \tag{3}$$

where σ is the elasticity of substitution between capital and labour, ν represents returns to scale, $TFP_i A_t$ is total factor productivity (TFP), which we assume to have two components: a firm-specific one and a year-specific one. Substituting the marginal productivity of capital in equation (1) yields:

$$k_{it} = \theta y_{it} - \sigma uc_{it} + h_{it} \tag{4}$$

---

[3] The user cost variable in von Kalckreuth (2001) models additional details of the German tax code. However, results in that paper are qualitatively similar to the results presented here.

where

$$\theta = \left(\sigma + \frac{1-\sigma}{\nu}\right) \quad \text{and} \quad h_t = \log\left[(TFP_i A_t)^{\frac{\sigma-1}{\nu}} \cdot (\nu\alpha_i)^\sigma\right] \quad (5)$$

y_{it} represents sales (small letters are logs). The variable h_{it} depends on the time-varying term A_t and the firm-specific term TFP_i. The elasticity of capital to sales is unity ($\theta = 1$), if the production function has constant returns to scale ($\nu = 1$), or if its elasticity of substitution is unity ($\sigma = 1$), that is, in the Cobb–Douglas case.

We do not assume that (4) always holds; instead, we assume that the firm changes its capital stock in the direction of a long-run target value k^*:

$$k_{it}^* = \theta y_{it} - \sigma uc_{it} + h_{it} \quad (6)$$

The long-run target value for capital, k^*, is not observable, which means that to go from (6) to an empirical specification, we need to specify an adjustment process. We specify an autoregressive distributed lag model (ADL(3,3)[4]):

$$\begin{aligned}
k_{it} = {} & \omega_1 k_{it-1} + \omega_2 k_{it-2} + \omega_3 k_{it-3} + \theta_0 y_{it} + \theta_0 y_{it-1} + \theta_2 y_{it-2} \\
& + \theta_3 y_{it-3} - \sigma_0 uc_{it} - \sigma_1 uc_{it-1} - \sigma_2 uc_{it-2} - \sigma_3 uc_{it-3} \\
& + \phi_0 h_{it} + \phi_1 h_{it-1} + \phi_2 h_{it-2} + \phi_3 h_{it-3}
\end{aligned} \quad (7)$$

where we have used lower-case letters to refer to the corresponding level variables in logs. In the long-run, the effects of a permanent change in the explanatory variables in (7) are assumed to add up to the effect given by (6). This implies that we can identify the long-run elasticities of sales and user cost. The long-run user cost elasticity with respect to the stock of capital is given by $\sigma = (\sigma_0 + \sigma_1 + \sigma_2 + \sigma_3)/(1 - \omega_1 - \omega_2 - \omega_3)$ and the long-run sales elasticity with respect to the stock of capital is $\theta = (\theta_0 + \theta_1 + \theta_2 + \theta_3)/(1 - \omega_1 - \omega_2 - \omega_3)$. Some caution has to be taken in interpreting these long-run coefficients. The ADL model is a reduced form of some underlying unknown structural model of adjustment of the capital stock. As such the long-run coefficients can contain both expectational and technology parameters. At this stage, there are two possible strategies. The first one transforms the ADL model into an error correction model (Hall, Mairesse and Mulkay, 1999). The second strategy consists of first differencing the ADL model (Chirinko, Fazzari and Meyer, 1999). The possibility of firm-specific effects not only on the level of productivity but also on its growth rate may justify this second strategy on panel data. For simplicity, we will use only the second strategy. We leave the possible comparison between the two approaches to companion country papers of

---

[4] Hall, Mairesse and Mulkay (1999) consider an ADL(2,2) but do not include the user cost of capital.

the Monetary Transmission Network (MTN). First-differencing and using the approximation $k_t - k_{t-1} = I_t/K_{t-1} - \delta$, and replacing productivity by time dummies, a firm-specific effect f and a random term ε yields:

$$
\frac{I_{it}}{K_{it-1}} = f_i + \omega_1 \frac{I_{it-1}}{K_{it-2}} + \omega_2 \frac{I_{it-2}}{K_{it-3}} + \omega_3 \frac{I_{it-3}}{K_{it-4}} + \theta_0 \Delta y_{it}
$$
$$
+ \theta_1 \Delta y_{it-1} + \theta_2 \Delta y_{it-2} + \theta_3 \Delta y_{it-3} - \sigma_0 \Delta uc_{it} - \sigma_1 \Delta uc_{it-1}
$$
$$
- \sigma_2 \Delta uc_{it-2} - \sigma_3 \Delta uc_{it-3} + time\ dummies + \varepsilon_{it} \qquad (8)
$$

We estimate (8). In addition, to be in line with the literature, we also estimate an extension of (8). It has been argued frequently that a measure of liquidity should enter the model to account for access to internal funds that might affect investment in the presence of financing constraints. Liquidity is usually measured as cash flow (CF). For comparison with the existing literature, and to avoid unit problems, cash flow enters relative to the existing capital stock.

$$
\frac{I_{it}}{K_{it-1}} = f_i + \omega_1 \frac{I_{it-1}}{K_{it-2}} + \omega_2 \frac{I_{it-2}}{K_{it-3}} + \omega_3 \frac{I_{it-3}}{K_{it-4}} + \theta_0 \Delta y_{it}
$$
$$
+ \theta_1 \Delta y_{it-1} + \theta_2 \Delta y_{it-2} + \theta_3 \Delta y_{it-3} - \sigma_0 \Delta uc_{it}
$$
$$
- \sigma_1 \Delta uc_{it-1} - \sigma_2 \Delta uc_{it-2} - \sigma_3 \Delta uc_{it-3}
$$
$$
+ \phi_0 \frac{CF_{it}}{p_{st}^I K_{i,t-1}} + \phi_1 \frac{CF_{i,t-1}}{p_{s,t-1}^I K_{i,t-2}}
$$
$$
+ \phi_2 \frac{CF_{i,t-2}}{p_{s,t-2}^I K_{i,t-3}} + \phi_3 \frac{CF_{i,t-3}}{p_{s,t-3}^I K_{i,t-4}} + time\ dummies + \varepsilon_{it}
$$

$$(9)$$

The parameters ϕ measure the sensitivity of investment with respect to cash flow movements.

4   Data set description

In this section an overview is given of the individual country data used in the regressions. Definitions of the variables used were made as comparable as possible between the different countries. National data sets do differ in many respects. First of all, the way in which data are collected in each country is not the same. The fact that the prerequisites for entering in the sample are different implies that the representativeness of each sample differs across countries. In general, the samples are skewed towards larger firms. Moreover, every sample is unbalanced and differs in the degree in which firms enter and leave the sample.

In Germany, the Bundesbank's corporate balance sheet database constitutes the largest collection of accounting data for German non-financial firms.[5] On the whole, every year around 70,000 annual accounts were collected,[6] on a strictly confidential basis, by the Bundesbank's branch offices. The German data set is skewed towards large firms since, according to the turnover tax statistics, these firms represented roughly 75 per cent of the total turnover of the West German manufacturing sector, albeit only 8 per cent of the total number of firms.

In France, the data source consists of compulsory accounting tax forms[7] and of additional information taken from surveys collected by the Banque de France (the database 'Centrale des Bilans'). Since these data are collected only from firms who are willing to provide them, French data are likewise skewed towards large firms.[8]

Data for Italy are drawn from the Italian Company Accounts Data Service (Centrale dei bilanci), that, considering the whole period 1983–99 and all non-financial enterprises, contains around 692,000 observations, for around 40,000 firms per year. For Italy there also exists a bias towards large firms: the prerequisite for entering the sample is that each firm has to be indebted with a bank; moreover, preference is given to firms with multiple lending relationships.[9]

The Spanish data were obtained from the Central Balance Sheet Office of the Banco de España (CBBE), and, in particular, from the Annual Central Balance Sheet Database (CBA); this database is compiled through the voluntary collaboration of non-financial firms and is edited by means of contacts with them. Thus, it covers only those firms that voluntarily complete the questionnaire and is biased towards large firms. The initial database included 115,980 observations corresponding to 22,014 firms over the 1983–99 period. In 1994, its coverage of the non-financial firms sector, in terms of value added, was around 35 per cent.[10]

For the econometric analysis, a smaller data set was used in each country. The loss in observations was due to the following reasons. First, we limited the analysis to the manufacturing sector.[11] Second, applying the perpetual inventory formula and using investment over lagged capital as

---

[5] A detailed description is contained in Deutsche Bundesbank (1998); see also Friderichs and Sauvé (1999) and Stöss (2001).

[6] The collection of financial statements originated from the Bundesbank's function of performing credit assessments within the scope of its rediscount operations.

[7] They are collected by the Banque de France in the database FIBEN.

[8] Small firms of fewer than twenty employees are under-represented. No statistical sampling procedure has been used to correct this bias.

[9] Moreover, since the information collected is meant to be a service for banks in deciding their credit policies, the sample is biased towards firms that are creditworthy. A detailed description can be found in the Centrale dei bilanci website: www.cntbil.it.

[10] For a more detailed description of this database, see Banco de España (2000a).

[11] The calculation of the capital stock at replacement cost presumably is more reliable for the manufacturing sector.

a regressor meant dropping the first year-firm observations. Third, trimming and selecting firms which are consecutively present in the sample at least during five years in order to use a sufficient number of lags as explanatory variables led to the final sample in each country.[12]

In general, we ended up with samples that, though skewed towards larger firms, are still representative of the manufacturing sector of each economy. Their coverage, calculated on the total number of employees in the manufacturing sector, ranges from 19 per cent for Spain to somewhat less than 45 per cent for Germany. The corresponding figures for France and Italy are 27 per cent and 21 per cent, respectively. Moreover, very often, balance sheet data contain only large and listed firms, whereas in our sample the median number of employees is 118 in Germany, 31 in Italy, 50 in Spain, and 55 in France. This means also that the data set covers unlisted companies, which are probably the best candidates to test for balance sheet effects, quite well; listed companies represent less than 4 per cent of the sample in Spain, less than 2 in Italy, and less than 6 in Germany and France. Moreover, firms are spread throughout the sectors of manufacturing.[13]

In each country, the period covered by the samples used in estimation is 1985–99, with the exception of Germany for which the time period available for estimation is 1988–97. The total number of observations and the number of years available are comparable to or higher than those of the sample used by Chirinko, Fazzari and Meyer (1999) for US firms.[14]

Table 7.2 shows the investment–capital ratio, real sales growth, real user cost growth, cash flow on capital and log of the user cost level in each country. Overall, as is usually the case with panel data, there is a

---

[12] Some specificities in each country are worth mentioning: for the German sample, which originally contained unincorporated businesses, we have excluded sole proprietorships and unincorporated partnerships because of differences in accounting rules; this permits a higher degree of comparability with the other countries. All publicly owned enterprises were discarded, too, as they might not be profit-oriented. Again for reasons of comparability, we consider only West German manufacturing firms, and we confine ourselves to the years 1988–97. Earlier years are affected by the radical regulatory changes in accounting introduced in 1985, triggered by an EU Directive on the harmonisation of financial statements. In Italy, we discarded the firms for which information to construct the user cost (i.e. fiscal data) was not available. More details can be found in Chatelain and Tiomo (2001), Gaiotti and Generale (2001) and von Kalckreuth (2001).

[13] The wider time dimension of these databases makes them preferable to other data sets containing a larger number of firms, which are often available in the countries examined. For example, in Italy the CERVED database contains information on balance sheet and profit and loss accounts of all firms excluding sole proprietorships (roughly 500,000 firms), but the first year available is 1993.

[14] They had a sample of 26,071 observations ranging from 1981 to 1991 with a total number of firms of 4,095.

Table 7.2 *Summary statistics: complete cleaned panels of individual firms*

Var. Country	Mean	Std dev.	Minimum	25%	Median	75%	Maximum
$It/Kt-1$							
Germany	0.181	0.219	0.000	0.059	0.116	0.216	2.291
France	0.122	0.141	0.000	0.039	0.080	0.151	1.430
Italy	0.124	0.155	0.000	0.040	0.080	0.151	3.300
Spain	0.186	0.217	-0.033	0.049	0.117	0.240	1.560
$\Delta \log St$							
Germany	0.021	0.158	-0.596	-0.058	0.021	0.107	0.828
France	0.029	0.153	-1.780	-0.051	0.029	0.112	1.360
Italy	0.034	0.196	-2.400	-0.060	0.035	0.131	3.000
Spain	0.043	0.171	-0.660	-0.051	0.041	0.136	0.780
$\Delta \log Uct$							
Germany	0.025	0.110	-0.356	-0.044	0.025	0.091	0.422
France	-0.009	0.140	-0.339	-0.107	-0.014	0.089	0.362
Italy	-0.012	0.263	-2.100	-0.150	-0.008	0.126	1.700
Spain	0.006	0.150	-0.380	-0.107	0.011	0.113	0.510
$CFt/Kt-1$							
Germany	0.276	0.464	-1.191	0.109	0.188	0.325	9.268
France	0.330	0.330	-0.450	0.160	0.260	0.410	4.320
Italy	0.196	0.220	-1.200	0.090	0.152	0.244	4.500
Spain	0.370	0.469	-1.100	0.126	0.256	0.471	5.000
Log Uct							
Germany	-1.865	0.182	-2.572	-1.984	-1.859	-1.738	-1.126
France	-1.770	0.140	-2.260	-1.860	-1.770	-1.670	-1.270
Italy	-1.870	0.272	-3.500	-2.000	-1.860	-1.710	-0.900
Spain	-1.742	0.185	-3.351	-1.851	-1.736	-1.613	-0.984

	No. obs.	No. firms	Years
Germany	40,362	5,876	1989–97
France	61,237	6,946	1985–99
Italy	94,523	8,019	1985–99
Spain	19,025	2,034	1985–99

wide dispersion of the variables used in all countries. The mean of the investment capital ratio is higher in Germany (0.181) and Spain (0.186) than in France (0.122) and Italy (0.124). The high mean of the investment capital ratio in Spain is matched by a high average sales growth (0.043). This contrasts with Germany where average sales growth is the lowest of all four countries (0.021). Average user cost growth over the period differs quite substantially across the four countries. In Germany user costs increased on average by 2.5 per cent, while in Italy they decreased

Table 7.3 *ADL models of investment demand – 3 lags WITHIN estimates, dependent variable:* $I_{i,t}/K_{i,t-1}$

Explanatory variable	Germany	France	Italy	Spain
$\Delta\log S_{i,t}$	0.126 (0.008)**	0.107(0.005)**	0.075 (0.004)**	0.080(0.014)**
$\Delta\log S_{i,t-1}$	0.121 (0.009)**	0.099 (0.005)**	0.072 (0.003)**	0.077 (0.013)**
$\Delta\log S_{i,t-2}$	0.097 (0.097)**	0.059 (0.005)**	0.048 (0.004)**	0.042 (0.013)**
$\Delta\log S_{i,t-3}$	0.064 (0.008)**	0.040 (0.005)**	0.031(0.003)**	0.038(0.012)**
Long-term sales elasticity	**0.407 (0.022)****	**0.305 (0.011)****	**0.228(0.010)****	**0.237 (0.033)****
$\Delta\log UC_{i,t}$	−0.230(0.013)**	−0.211(0.007)**	−0.144 (0.003)**	−0.187(0.029)**
$\Delta\log UC_{i,t-1}$	−0.213 (0.014)**	−0.110(0.007)**	−0.095 (0.003)**	0.024 (0.030)
$\Delta\log UC_{i,t-2}$	−0.107 (0.013)**	−0.046 (0.007)**	−0.052 (0.003)**	0.048 (0.030)
$\Delta\log UC_{i,t-3}$	−0.080 (0.080)**	−0.015 (0.006)*	−0.020 (0.002)**	0.023 (0.026)
Long-term user cost elasticity	**−0.630(0.022)****	**−0.382 (0.013)****	**−0.318(0.010)****	**−0.092 (0.064)**
No. of obs.	22,734	33,453	62,447	8,855
No. of firms	5,876	6,946	8,019	2,034

Note: * Significant at the 5% level; ** significant at the 1% level; time dummies are included.

on average by 1.2 per cent. On average, the ratio of cash flow over capital is higher in Spain (0.37) and France (0.33) than in Germany (0.276) and Italy (0.196).

5   Regression results

In this section we present regression results for the specifications reported in (8) and (9). We first present estimation results using the WITHIN estimator. We then present estimation results using the GMM estimator developed by Arellano and Bond (1991).

Table 7.3 reports the results obtained with the WITHIN estimator. We include a full set of time dummies. These will capture the effect of macro influences on firm-specific investment. We dropped the lagged dependent variable for two reasons. First, it is known that the WITHIN estimator is biased with certainty when lagged dependent variables are present (Nickell, 1981). This bias is due to the correlation of the transformed residual with the transformed lagged dependent variable. Second, in this way we can directly compare our WITHIN estimation results with those obtained for US data by Chirinko, Fazzari and Meyer (1999) using a panel of 4,095 manufacturing and non-manufacturing firms from

1981–91 representing 48 per cent of aggregate US non-residential investment in 1987. (See their table 2, p. 62, for the WITHIN results.)

For all countries, sales have a substantial effect in the long run on the capital stock. We obtain long-term sales elasticities ranging from 0.407 in Germany to 0.228 in Italy. Also for all countries, the contemporaneous effect of sales is the largest, ranging from 0.126 in Germany to 0.075 in Italy. All lags of sales growth (up to $t - 3$) have a significant effect on investment. This could be due to many different reasons, including installation lags or adjustment cost. Chirinko, Fazzari and Meyer (1999) found a rather similar long-run sales elasticity of 0.322 with a contemporaneous effect of 0.120 for the USA. Note that our specification abstracts from possible irreversibility of investment. Under irreversibility the sales growth and user cost growth could have a non-linear effect on investment. For all countries except Spain, also the user cost has a significant effect on the capital stock in the long run. We obtain user cost elasticities ranging from –0.63 in Germany to −0.318 in Italy.[15] Chirinko, Fazzari and Meyer (1999) found a long-run user cost elasticity of −0.721. In every country (including the USA), except for Spain, these long-term user cost elasticities are even higher than the long-term sales elasticities. Again, the contemporaneous effect is the largest and past user cost changes are generally significant. This provides evidence against simple sales–accelerator models that include only sales and exclude user costs. It is important to note that even for Spain, although the long-run user cost elasticity (UCE) is not significant, the contemporaneous user cost effect is clearly negative and significant. Moreover, in a more parsimonious specification, removing the insignificant lags, the point estimates of the remaining regressors do not significantly change and the long-run UCE is larger, in absolute value, and significant.

Owing to simultaneity between investment and the user cost, the WITHIN estimates might be biased towards zero. This problem, of course, can be generalised to a potential simultaneity between all variables in the regression.

Therefore, we also present the results using the GMM first-difference estimator of Arellano and Bond (1991). This time we include the lagged dependent variable. We use as instruments the lagged variables used in the regression from $t-2$ onwards. The results are in table 7.4.

For all countries, with the partial exception of Spain, the long-run sales elasticities are similar to the WITHIN results. The point estimates increase somewhat for Germany, France and Italy, and decrease for Spain,

---

[15] The sign and dimension of these two effects are similar to those obtained using specifications with a different lag structure and are similar to those reported in the paper by Gaiotti and Generale (2001) that employs a data set that contains non-manufacturing Italian firms as well.

Table 7.4 *ADL models of investment demand – 3 lags GMM estimates, dependent variable:* $I_{i,t}/K_{i,t-1}$

Explanatory variable	Germany	France	Italy	Spain
$I_{i,t-1}/K_{i,t-2}$	0.142 (0.017)**	0.024 (0.061)	0.176 (0.007)**	0.123 (0.019)**
$I_{i,t-2}/K_{i,t-3}$	0.010 (0.009)	0.050 (0.011)**	0.022 (0.005)**	−0.004 (0.014)
$I_{i,t-3}/K_{i,t-4}$	0.008 (0.007)	0.029 (0.006)**	0.017 (0.005)**	0.001 (0.012)
$\Sigma\, I_{i,t-n}/K_{i,t-n-1}$	**0.160 (0.026)****	**0.103 (0.031)****	**0.215 (0.013)****	**0.120 (0.035)****
$\Delta\log S_{i,t}$	0.162 (0.053)**	0.073 (0.035)**	0.117 (0.032)*	0.038 (0.064)
$\Delta\log S_{i,t-1}$	0.106 (0.013)**	0.086 (0.009)**	0.062 (0.005)**	0.041 (0.017)**
$\Delta\log S_{i,t-2}$	0.069 (0.011)**	0.137 (0.008)**	0.033 (0.005)**	0.027 (0.014)*
$\Delta\log S_{i,t-3}$	0.042 (0.010)**	0.014 (0.006)**	0.013 (0.005)**	0.018 (0.012)
$\Sigma\, \Delta\log S_{i,t-n}$	**0.379 (0.062)****	**0.310 (0.024)***	**0.224 (0.039)****	**0.124 (0.075)***
Long-term sales elasticity	**0.452 (0.073)****	**0.346 (0.036)***	**0.286 (0.049)****	**0.141 (0.085)***
$\Delta\log UC_{i,t}$	−0.286 (0.089)**	−0.055 (0.026)**	−0.045 (0.016)**	−0.274(0.135)**
$\Delta\log UC_{i,t-1}$	−0.170 (0.029)**	−0.045 (0.019)**	−0.027 (0.008)**	−0.003 (0.041)
$\Delta\log UC_{i,t-2}$	−0.072 (0.021)**	−0.002 (0.011)	−0.011 (0.005)*	0.032 (0.035)
$\Delta\log UC_{i,t-3}$	−0.029 (0.015)	0.007 (0.007)	−0.004 (0.004)	0.017 (0.028)
$\Sigma\, \Delta\log UC_{i,t-n}$	**−0.557 (0.134)****	**−0.095 (0.037)***	**−0.087 (0.030)****	**−0.228(0.177)**
Long-term user cost elasticity	**−0.663 (0.167)****	**−0.106 (0.048)***	**−0.111 (0.039)****	**−0.259 (0.201)**
No. of obs.	16,858	33,453	62,447	8,855
No. of firms	5,876	6,946	8,019	2,034
Sargan-Hansen test	69.81 (p=0.29)	105.12 (p=0.09)	126.80 (p=0.09)	127.26 (p=0.09)
AR(1)	13.74**	−6.51 **	−30.90**	−14.37**
AR(2)	−2.03 (p=0.04)*	−2.17 (p=0.03)*	3.08 (p=0.99)	−0.19 (p=0.85)

Notes: Estimation method: two-step GMM estimates, including time dummies
* significant at the 5% level; ** significant at the 1% level.
Instruments: Germany: lags 2 and earlier of I/K, $\Delta\log S$ and $\Delta\log UC$: France: I/K lags 3 to 5; $\Delta\log S$ lags 2 to 4 and $\Delta\log UC$ lags 2 to 5; Italy: I/K lags 2 to 6; $\Delta\log S$ and $\Delta\log UC$ lags 2 to 4.; Spain: lags 2 to 5 of I/K, $\Delta\log S$ and $\Delta\log UC$.

but the effect of sales on capital remains statistically significant. The effect of sales on investment is clearly a robust feature in every country.

What is striking, however, is how the point estimates of the long-run UCEs change when moving to GMM. These differences are non-uniform across countries. The GMM results show a slightly higher point estimate of the long-run UCE for Germany (−0.663), a dramatically lower one for France (−0.106) and Italy (−0.111) and a dramatically higher one for Spain (−0.259).

So far, these are the results obtained by means of a common specification. Before proceeding it is worth mentioning some robustness checks made for each country. Comparison with other results is obtained either by running regressions with a slightly modified set of instruments (results not shown) or by taking stock of the results presented in the companion papers of the MTN project.

For Germany, the AR(2) statistics in the specification presented in table 7.4 show that there might be an autocorrelation problem in the residuals. It is interesting to note that, using King–Fullerton (1984) user costs, von Kalckreuth (2001) obtains a smaller UCE of 0.522 for the same model. For France, the significance level of the elasticity of I/K to the user cost turns out to be dependent on the choice of instruments. For Italy, a sensitivity analysis of the results obtained with this specification was conducted by trying different instrument sets. By using a more parsimonious set of instruments, excluding lags 2 and 3 of the user cost, the long-run effect of the user cost is −0.234, more similar to the outcome of the WITHIN regression. Moreover, the Sargan test accepts the set of instruments at a higher confidence level. The effect of sales is similar to the one observed in table 7.4. For Spain, the use of a more parsimonious specification again leads to more precise estimates. When removing insignificant lags, the point estimates of the remaining regressors do not significantly vary and the standard errors for the long-run elasticities are significantly lower. In particular, the point estimate for the long-run sales elasticity is 0.098 with a standard error of 0.039, and the point estimate of the long-run UCE is −0.273 with a standard error of 0.131.[16]

It is important to investigate whether the sales and UCEs are sensitive to adding cash flow to the regression. Since Fazzari, Hubbard and Petersen (1988) it is usual to enter cash flow in the regression to allow for liquidity constraints. The results estimated by GMM are presented in table 7.5.

As is generally the case in the empirical literature, the cash flow capital ratio enters significantly and with a positive sign. The total effect of cash flow on I/K ranges from a low of 0.079 in Germany to a high of 0.301 in Italy. The higher coefficient with respect to those obtained in the other countries could indicate that firms' balance sheet conditions are relatively important in Italy.[17] Also, the sales elasticity declines

---

[16] Results not shown are available from the authors.

[17] On the other hand, as is well discussed by Bond *et al.* (1997), a positive effect of cash flow on investment does not necessarily reflect the presence of financial constraints. If higher cash flows are a good predictor of high activity in the future, it may very well be that a positive relationship between investment and cash flow does not reflect the existence of financial constraints. To partially address this criticism, the regression for Italy was re-run using liquidity stock as a measure of firms' balance sheet conditions. This variable should be less correlated with expectations of future demand conditions: results (not reported) indicate that liquidity, too, has a positive and significant effect on capital formation; in the regression the sign and significance of sales and the user cost remain unchanged.

Table 7.5 *ADL models of investment demand including cash flow – 3 lags GMM estimates, dependent Variable:* $I_{i,t}/K_{i,t-1}$

Explanatory variable	Germany	France	Italy	Spain
$I_{i,t-1}/K_{i,t-2}$	0.124 (0.017)**	0.086 (0.010)**	0.168 (0.011)**	0.120 (0.021)**
$I_{i,t-2}/K_{i,t-3}$	0.002 (0.009)	0.016 (0.007)*	0.024 (0.006)**	0.007 (0.014)
$I_{i,t-3}/K_{i,t-4}$	0.005 (0.007)	0.014 (0.006)*	0.018 (0.005)**	0.010 (0.012)
$\Sigma\, I_{i,t-n}/K_{i,t-n-1}$	**0.131 (0.026)****	**0.116 (0.033)****	**0.206 (0.016)****	**0.137 (0.038)****
$\Delta\log S_{i,t}$	0.142 (0.054)**	0.031 (0.040)	0.045 (0.033)	−0.043 (0.063)
$\Delta\log S_{i,t-1}$	0.097 (0.014)**	0.055 (0.009)**	0.039 (0.006)**	0.028 (0.018)
$\Delta\log S_{i,t-2}$	0.061 (0.011)**	0.017 (0.007)*	0.018 (0.005)**	0.014 (0.014)
$\Delta\log S_{i,t-3}$	0.036 (0.010)**	0.007 (0.005)	0.007 (0.004)	0.016 (0.013)
$\Sigma\, \Delta\log S_{i,t-n}$	**0.338 (0.068)****	**0.110 (0.039)****	**0.109 (0.040)****	**0.015 (0.075)**
Long-term sales elasticity	**0.387 (0.077)****	**0.124 (0.046)****	**0.138 (0.050)****	**0.018 (0.087)**
$\Delta\log UC_{i,t}$	−0.220 (0.080)**	0.002 (0.030)	−0.079 (0.021)**	−0.279 (0,126)**
$\Delta\log UC_{i,t-1}$	−0.151 (0.028)**	−0.030 (0.03)	−0.055 (0.017)**	−0.018 (0,040)
$\Delta\log UC_{i,t-2}$	−0.060 (0.020)**	0.002 (0.013)	−0.021 (0.013)	0.036 (0.034)
$\Delta\log UC_{i,t-3}$	−0.021 (0.015)	0.002 (0.007)	−0.006 (0.005)	0.021 (0.027)
$\Sigma\, \Delta\log UC_{i,t-n}$	**−0.452 (0.124)****	**−0.024 (0.032)**	**−0.161 (0.048)****	**−0.240 (0,171)**
Long-term user cost elasticity	**−0.521 (0.148)****	**−0.027 (0.039)**	**−0.204 (0.060)****	**−0.278 (0.198)**
$CF_{i,t}/K_{i,t-1}$	0.043 (0.036)	0.056 (0.030)*	0.255 (0.035)**	0.121 (0.032)**
$CF_{i,t-1}/K_{i,t-2}$	0.011 (0.012)	0.091 (0.015)**	−0.025 (0.019)	0.037 (0.022)*
$CF_{i,t-2}/K_{i,t-3}$	0.011 (0.006)	0.018 (0.007)**	0.008 (0.007)	−0,019 (0,009)**
$CF_{i,t-3}/K_{i,t-4}$	0.004 (0.005)	0.008 (0.005)	0.000 (0.006)	−0.006 (0.008)
$\Sigma\, CF_{i,t-n}/K_{i,t-n-1}$	**0.069 (0.027)***	**0.173 (0.030)****	**0.238 (0.022)****	**0.133 (0.032)****
Long-term cash flow sensitivity	**0.079 (0.031)***	**0.196 (0.939)****	**0.301 (0.028)****	**0.153 (0.037)****
No. of obs.	16,858	33,453	62,447	8,855
No. of firms	5,876	6,946	8,019	2,034
Sargan-Hansen test	91.80 (p=0.29)	133.40 (p=0.43)	127.20 (p=0.40)	149.81 (p=0.17)
AR(1)	13.72**	−24.60**	−30.10**	−14.62**
AR(2)	2.08 (p=0.04)*	1.21 (p=0.23)	−0.18 (p=0.86)	0.13 (p=0.90)

Estimation method: two-step GMM estimates, including time dummies
* Significant at the 5% level; ** significant at the 1% level.
Instruments: Germany: lags 2 and earlier of all explanatory variables; France: lags 2 to 5 of I/K, CF/K and $\Delta\log S$, and lags 3 to 5 of $\Delta\log UC$; Spain: lags 2 to 5 of I/K, CF/K and $\Delta\log UC$, and lags 2 to 4 of $\Delta\log S$; Italy: I/K lags 2 to 6; $\Delta\log S$ lags 2 to 4; $\Delta\log UC$ lag 4; CF/K lags 2 to 5.

substantively for all countries. Since cash flow might be a proxy for future profitability and future sales, this result was to be expected. Likewise, in the former regression, the sales variable might have picked up some effects that should really have been attributed to liquidity and profits. The long-run UCEs are different with respect to the former GMM results. They are lower for Germany and Italy if for those countries we compare the results obtained using the same set of instruments, and they are close to zero for France.

The change in the long-run UCE when cash flow is entered into the regression can be explained by how the user cost was constructed. The apparent interest rate variable used for constructing the user cost of capital is interest payments divided by the amount of debt. This induces a correlation with cash flow, of which interest payments also are an important part.[18]

Overall, the results in tables 7.3–7.5 suggest that sales, user cost and cash flow are all important determinants of investment. That user cost enters significantly in investment regressions is an important result, since it is the prerequisite for an interest rate channel. The finding that (for most countries) the UCE varies substantially according to estimation method and specification is less satisfying. (Note that this is also the case for the USA in Chirinko, Fazzari and Meyer, 1999.) However, given the difficulties encountered in the empirical literature for this kind of estimation this is not too surprising. In addition one needs to cautiously interpret the UCEs as stemming from pure interest rate effects. Since the firm-specific user cost could change when the firm's risk premia changes over the cycle, part of the user cost change might reflect risk premia changes and hence be ascribed to a balance sheet channel.[19] Adding additional collateral variables besides cash flow to the regression would potentially alleviate this problem.

6   The broad credit channel in the euro area

In this section we test whether small and large firms show different investment behaviour. We are especially interested in differences in the coefficient estimates of the cash flow capital ratio. By testing whether the long-run effect of the cash flow capital ratio is significantly different for small firms than for large firms, we are able to compare the behaviour of firms that are likely to be characterised by weaker balance sheets with that of other firms.

It is well known that 'models that incorporate financial frictions are more relevant for certain types of agents, certain classes of borrowers,

---

[18] As noted by Chirinko, Fazzari and Meyer (1999) 'in the regression without cash flow the estimated sum of coefficients of the user cost captures both the conventional substitution effect as well as the income effect induced by financing constraints, which affect investment in the same direction'.

[19] However this potential problem might not be too large. Mojon, Smets and Vermeulen (2002) reject that changes in the user cost following changes in the market interest rate are different for small and large firms.

and certain sectors of the economy' (Gilchrist and Zakrajsek, 1995). Moreover, as these authors note: 'because of the difficulties associated with formulating and estimating true structural models, empirical exercises seeking to establish the validity of either a credit channel or a financial accelerator must make comparisons against benchmarks where such credit effects are less likely to be relevant.'

Sample comparisons using size as a discriminating characteristic of the balance sheet conditions of firms are commonly used in the empirical literature that has examined the link between financial constraints and investment spending (see Schiantarelli, 1995, for a discussion). Smaller firms are more likely to be less collateralised, to be more opaque towards external investors and, insofar as age is correlated with small size, have less established contacts with lenders, thus making it more difficult to distinguish between good and bad firms. Other characteristics that have been commonly used in these tests are dividend payout behaviour, group membership, the nature of the bank–firm relationship and the degree of ownership concentration. In particular circumstances and in some countries, these characteristics may very well be more important than size. In fact, as Schiantarelli (1995) notes, one problem with splitting the sample along one firm characteristic is that '[this] single indicator may or may not be a sufficient statistic for the existence of liquidity constraints'.

Analysis of the institutional characteristics that in each country can blur the relevance of the size split is beyond the scope of this chapter. In the companion papers that focus on single country evidence, other firm characteristics that might prove relevant for the transmission of monetary policy shocks via the balance sheet are analysed. We present here only the size-split results since these are probably more easily comparable across countries.

Table 7.6 contains the regression results of (9) when allowing for different coefficients for user cost growth, sales growth and the cash flow capital ratio for large and small firms. With the exception of Italy, we find no systematic differences between large and small firms across countries. This is the case for both the sales and user cost elasticities and for the effect of cash flow. The point estimates of the differences in elasticities are non-systematically positive or negative and usually non-significant.

For Italy, the sum of the cash flow coefficients for small firms is significantly higher than for large firms. The fact that balance sheet conditions are more important for firms that are probably more exposed to problems of information asymmetries seems to confirm the existence of a broad credit channel in Italy. These results seem robust to different

Table 7.6 *Long-term elasticity of sales and user cost and long-term effect of cash flow on large and small firms. GMM ADL(3) with CF/K*

	Germany	France	Italy	France
log S large firms	0.337 (0.086)**	0.073 (0.032)*	0.108 (0.051)*	0.040 (0.012)**
Diff. Small – Large	−0.029 (0.125)	0.042 (0.040)	0.027 (0.079)*	−0.031 (0.021)
log UC$_{i, large firms}$	−0.512 (0.173)**	−0.053 (0.040)	−0.238 (0.060)**	−0.153 (0.082)*
Diff. Small – Large	0.063 (0.255)	0.057 (0.180)	0.024 (0.098)	0.072 (0.167)
CF/K large firms	0.092 (0.038)*	0.221 (0.030)**	0.196 (0.027)**	0.116 (0.021)**
Diff. Small – Large	−0.050 (0.050)	−0.035 (0.031)	0.144 (0.045)**	0.030 (0.033)

* Significant at the 5 per cent level. ** Significant at the 1 per cent level.

model specifications, such as the error correction model estimated in Gaiotti and Generale (2001).

We think, however, that it would be too early to conclude that the broad credit channel is operative only in Italy. Clearly, more sophisticated sample splits might provide significant differences across firms belonging to different groups. The results in table 7.6 do indicate that identifying the broad credit channel by taking into account only the size classification might be an over-simplification in most euro area countries. Size might not be a sufficient or even a correct indicator for some countries of informational asymmetries that are the basis for broad credit channel effects.

Indeed, as already noted above, the companion papers to this research project address the issue of heterogeneity across firms under many other different dimensions. For Germany, when firms' ratings are used as a proxy of financial constraints, it turns out that those with a lower rating are more sensitive to financial variables (von Kalckreuth, 2001). For France, firms belonging to the equipment goods sector, firms with a lower rating and firms with a high share of trade credit in the balance sheet are also more sensitive to cash flow (Chatelain and Tiomo, 2001). In addition, for France, the introduction of dummy variables which isolate firms that are more sensitive to cash flow has the effect of shifting back the UCE to its level obtained without cash flow, i.e. a significant value below −0.1. For Italy, firms with a high share of intangible assets over total assets, an indication of the extent of asymmetric information, respond more to variables that approximate their financial condition (Gaiotti and Generale, 2001). Moreover, results for other countries that we do not analyse by means of a common specification point to the presence of heterogeneity. For Austria, the existence of a 'Hausbank' (main bank) significantly affects the transmission of monetary impulses. Valderrama (2001b) finds that firms having closer relationships with the main bank react less to cash flow and more to the user cost than firms with less 'intense' relationships. In Luxembourg, younger firms seem more exposed to liquidity constraints, measured by means of various financial ratios (Lünnemann and Mathä, 2001). For Belgium, Butzen, Fuss and Vermeulen (2001) document a high degree of heterogeneity in firms' reaction to monetary policy depending on the sectors in which the firms operate.

7 User cost, cash flow, sales and monetary policy: a simulation exercise[20]

In this section, we first analyse the dynamics of the regression equation. We then perform a more complicated simulation exercise to determine the elasticity of investment with respect to user cost, sales and cash flow. We finally determine the elasticity of investment with respect to the market interest rate.

We use the point estimates of the coefficients as presented in table 7.5. In the following, we present the short-run time profile of I/K in the presence of simple shocks to the explanatory variables and compare these profiles over the four European countries.

Consider the following experiment. Imagine a firm for which user cost growth, sales growth, CF/K and I/K are all at their steady-state path. Next, imagine one single shock at time t to user cost growth, e.g. user cost growth at time t is equal to its steady-state path value plus 0.01, and that after time t user cost growth is again at its steady-state path. What happens to I/K at time t, $t + 1$, etc. assuming the paths of the other variables, i.e. real sales growth and CF/K, are held constant at their steady-state path? A similar experiment can be performed for real sales growth (again holding the other variables at their steady state), or for CF/K.

Note that one could object to this type of analysis on multiple grounds. First, user cost growth, sales growth and CF/K are all endogenous, implying that shocks to one variable might have immediate or lagged effects on the other variables. Basically, the regression equation is just one equation describing I/K. In reality, the behaviour of all relevant variables should be described with a multi-equation system. This, however, is outside the scope of this chapter. Second, the regression equation contains the capital stock at both the left-hand side and right-hand side (I/K and CF/K). Since movements in I/K will ultimately move K, CF/K will also change (unless CF moves by the same amount as K). In this first exercise, we also

---

[20] We want to thank Daniele Terlizzese for a patient and productive discussion of the issues involved.

Table 7.7 *Change in I/K after a one-time 1% or one-standard deviation increase in the user cost growth*

	Germany		France		Italy		Spain	
	(1)	(2)	(1)	(2)	(1)	(2)	(1)	(2)
t	−0.22	−2.33	0.00	0.03	−0.08	−2.06	−0.28	−4.05
$t+1$	−0.18	−1.88	−0.03	−0.41	−0.07	−1.78	−0.05	−0.75
$t+2$	−0.08	−0.84	0.00	−0.01	−0.03	−0.90	0.03	0.40
$t+3$	−0.04	−0.38	0.00	0.02	−0.01	−0.39	0.02	0.31

Notes: A one-standard deviation increase in the user cost growth is equal to 0.106 in Germany, 0.137 in France, 0.261 in Italy and 0.145 in Spain.

Figures in columns (1) and (2), respectively, represent the deviation of I/K in percentage points after a 1% and one-standard deviation increase in the user cost growth.

abstract from this second objection (hence implicitly letting CF move at the same rate of K when holding CF/K constant.).

Given the above two objections, we still believe the experiment to be of value. First, it provides a description of the dynamics of the equation concentrating on one variable at a time. Second, more complicated experiments in which shocks to certain variables coincide with (lagged) shocks to other variables are just linear combinations of the above simple experiments. For instance, if one considers a simultaneous shock to sales growth and CF/K, then one can simply add the effects on I/K.

We consider two types of shocks for this experiment. We first consider a shock of 1 per cent (i.e. the explanatory variable at time t has the value of its steady state plus 0.01). It is necessary to see that such a *transitory* shock to the growth rates of user costs or sales corresponds to a *permanent* shock to the level of this variable. We next consider a shock which has a magnitude of one standard deviation of the within-firm variation of the variable. We find this last shock especially appealing because it represents a shock relative to the 'normal' variation present in the variable in our data. We indeed find that the within-firm variation of user cost growth, sales growth and CF/K is much larger than 1 per cent and differs substantially across variables and across countries.

Tables 7.7–7.9 present the deviation of I/K from its steady-state path after those two types of shocks, adopting as a benchmark the specification presented in table 7.5. Table 7.7 shows the change in I/K after a 1 per cent (column (1)) or one-standard deviation shock (column (2)) in user cost growth. Most of the effects take place within the first two years. A 1 per cent increase in user cost growth has the largest effect

Table 7.8 *Change in I/K after a one-time 1% or one-standard deviation increase in sales growth*

	Germany		France		Italy		Spain	
	(1)	(2)	(1)	(2)	(1)	(2)	(1)	(2)
t	0.16	2.26	0.03	0.44	0.05	0.84	−0.04	−0.68
$t+1$	0.12	1.77	0.06	0.81	0.05	0.87	0.02	0.36
$t+2$	0.08	1.16	0.02	0.32	0.03	0.50	0.02	0.26
$t+3$	0.04	0.59	0.01	0.15	0.01	0.25	0.02	0.28

Notes: A one-standard deviation increase in sales growth is equal 0.145 in Germany, 0.141 in France, 0.187 in Italy and 0.159 in Spain.
Figures in columns (1) and (2), respectively, represent the deviation of I/K in percentage points after a 1% and one-standard deviation increase in sales growth.

Table 7.9 *Change in I/K after a one-time 1% or one-standard deviation increase in CF/K*

	Germany		France		Italy		Spain	
	(1)	(2)	(1)	(2)	(1)	(2)	(1)	(2)
t	0.04	1.28	0.06	1.29	0.26	3.90	0.12	3.74
$t+1$	0.02	0.47	0.10	2.21	0.02	0.27	0.05	1.59
$t+2$	0.01	0.40	0.03	0.63	0.02	0.26	−0.01	−0.37
$t+3$	0.01	0.17	0.01	0.29	0.01	0.12	−0.01	−0.18

Notes: A one-standard deviation increase in the cash flow capital ratio is equal to 0.305 in Germany, 0.231 in France, 0.153 in Italy and 0.309 in Spain.
Figures in columns (1) and (2), respectively, represent the deviation of I/K in percentage points after a 1% and one-standard deviation increase in the cash flow capital ratio.

in Spain and Germany. Misleadingly, the magnitude of the effect seems small. However, in the data, a one-standard deviation change in the user cost growth rate is much larger than 1 per cent; it is 10.6 per cent in Germany, 13.7 per cent in France, 26.1 per cent in Italy and 14.5 per cent in Spain. In the first period, a rise in the user cost growth in Germany of one standard deviation depresses I/K by 2.33 percentage points. Given the level of average gross investment per unit of capital of 0.181 in Germany, this translates into a drop to 0.1577 (i.e. 0.181 − 0.0233). Similar larger effects can be observed in Italy and Spain. The comparison between columns (1) and (2) reveal some interesting features of the data and the regression result. We can interpret the regression equation as a description of investment behaviour in the period of investigation.

Then it is clear that two distinct features have determined this behaviour: the magnitude of the reaction of the I/K ratio to shocks to the explanatory variables, and the magnitude of those shocks. For instance, whereas the contemporaneous reaction to identical user cost growth shocks in Italy was much smaller than in Germany (as evidenced in column (1)) Italian user cost growth shocks were on average much larger than German shocks. Combining those two features implies similar behaviour of the I/K ratio after a one-standard deviation shock (as evidenced in column (2)) Note that our regressions are conditional on the historical variation in the data. This historical variation from the time before EMU could be quite different from future variation.

Table 7.8 shows the change in I/K after both a 1 per cent (column (1) or one-standard deviation shock (column (2)) in sales growth. Again, the largest effects can be observed in the first two years. The sales effect is largest in Germany. A one-standard deviation increase in the growth rate of sales increases the I/K ratio by 2.26 per cent in the same year.

Table 7.9 shows the change in I/K after a 1 per cent (column (1)) or one-standard deviation shock (column (2)) in the CF/K ratio. The contemporaneous effects are quite large. They are the smallest in Germany. Investment in Italian and Spanish firms, in particular, seems to move quite strongly simultaneously with CF/K movements.

The regression equation 'explains' I/K in terms of user cost growth, sales growth and the CF/K ratio. However, the reader might find it more natural to think of the level of investment in terms of the level of user cost, sales or cash flow. After some algebra, the regression equation can also be used to calculate the elasticity of investment (I) with respect to the user cost, sales or cash flow. For example, by the elasticity of investment with respect to the user cost, we mean the percentage change of investment (i.e. I, not I/K) due to a 'permanent' 1 per cent change (from the base path) in the user cost level. The wording 'permanent' is important here. As in the first set of simulations given by tables 7.7–7.9, a permanent change in the user cost level (from the base path) is given by a one-time 1 per cent change in the growth rate (from the base path) of user costs.[21]

Tables 7.10– 7.11 provide the elasticity of investment with respect to (the levels of) user cost, sales and cash flow. A substantive elasticity of investment with respect to its user cost is a necessary condition for an interest channel to be operative. As evidenced in Table 7.10, the elasticity of contemporaneous investment with respect to the user cost is quite large in Germany (−1.21), Italy (−0.63) and Spain (−1.49). It is negligible in France (0.02), but becomes non-negligible in the year after (−0.24). The

---

[21] Appendix C in the working paper version provides details about the calculation.

Table 7.10 *Elasticity of investment with respect to user cost*

	Germany	France	Italy	Spain
t	−1.21	0.02	−0.63	−1.49
$t+1$	−1.17	−0.24	−0.59	−0.48
$t+2$	−0.79	−0.03	−0.36	−0.05
$t+3$	−0.61	0.00	−0.21	−0.06

Table 7.11 *Elasticity of investment with respect to sales*

	Germany	France	Italy	Spain
t	0.86	0.25	0.36	−0.23
$t+1$	0.82	0.50	0.40	0.09
$t+2$	0.69	0.25	0.27	0.08
$t+3$	0.54	0.15	0.17	0.10

Table 7.12 *Elasticity of investment with respect to cash flow*

	Germany	France	Italy	Spain
t	0.06	0.15	0.40	0.24
$t+1$	0.10	0.42	0.46	0.38
$t+2$	0.13	0.54	0.52	0.39
$t+3$	0.16	0.60	0.55	0.42

elasticity at time $t+1$ remains substantive in Germany, Italy and Spain, but is smaller. Overall, table 7.10 provides evidence of a strong and rapid reaction of investment to user cost changes.

Table 7.11 presents the elasticity of investment with respect to sales. The contemporaneous elasticities are 0.86 for Germany, 0.25 for France, 0.36 for Italy and −0.23 for Spain. Surprisingly in Germany, Italy and Spain, investment seems to have a lower contemporaneous elasticity with respect to sales than with respect to its user cost. Given the emphasis on the sales accelerator model and the general ignoring of user cost in the investment literature, this is a provocative result. Although sales growth does undeniably have a positive effect on investment, one should not ignore user costs.

Table 7.12 provides the elasticity of investment with respect to cash flow. Due to the past CF/K ratios in the regression, the effect of a permanent increase in cash flow gradually evolves and accumulates over time. The picture that emerges is mixed. In Germany and France the elasticity is generally lower than the sales elasticity. In Italy and Spain it is generally higher.

To understand the effect of monetary policy on investment tables 7.10–7.12 are not sufficient. A relevant question is: 'How do market interest rates affect user costs and cash flow in those four euro area countries'?[22] Essentially, the interest channel or 'cash flow channel' works through two stages. In the first stage, the market interest rate has to change firm fundamentals (user cost, and cash flow). In the second stage, these firm fundamentals have an effect on investment with the elasticities as presented in tables 7.10–7.12. Below we present some evidence on the first stage and show how, combined with the second stage, the channels of monetary policy differ across countries.

We first investigate the effect of market interest rate changes on the user cost. The first important fact that should be noted is that interest rates form a part of the user cost of capital. The importance or weight of this part depends on the importance of the other parts such as depreciation and relative price changes. Since the user cost directly contains an interest rate in its definition, the elasticity of the user cost with respect to the interest rate can therefore be calculated directly. It is equal to:

$$
\frac{\partial UC_{it}}{\partial i} * \frac{i}{UC_{it}}
$$

$$
= \frac{AI_{it}\left(\dfrac{D_{it}}{D_{it}+E_{it}}\right)(1-\tau_t) + (LD_{it})\left(\dfrac{E_{it}}{D_{it}+E_{it}}\right)}{AI_{it}\left(\dfrac{D_{it}}{D_{it}+E_{it}}\right)(1-\tau_t) + (LD_{it})\left(\dfrac{E_{it}}{D_{it}+E_{it}}\right) - (1-\delta_s)\dfrac{\Delta P^I_{st+1}}{P^I_{st}} + \delta_s}
$$

$$(10)$$

The elasticity is simply the weight of the interest rate in the user cost definition. Hence, if depreciation or changes in relative prices are large, interest changes will have a small effect on the user cost. Table 7.13 shows the relative importance of the interest rate in the user cost definition in the

---

[22] Another relevant question is: 'How do market interest rates affect sales?' We do not attempt to answer that question. Interest rate shocks do not have a 'mechanical' effect on sales in the same way as interest rate shocks have on user cost and cash flow (interest rates are part of user costs, and interest payments are part of cash flow). Although interest rates can influence firm-specific demand (e.g. for investment goods- or durable consumer goods-producing firms), this demand effect is much more difficult to quantify. Trying to do this here would require a whole new paper.

Table 7.13 *Elasticities of the user cost and of cash flow with respect to interest rate*

	Germany	France	Italy	Spain
(1) $\frac{\partial uc}{\partial i} * \frac{i}{uc}$	0.32	0.58	0.70	0.65
(2) $\frac{\partial CF}{\partial i} * \frac{i}{CF}$	−0.32	−0.28	−0.60	−0.47

Table 7.14 *Elasticity of investment with respect to interest rate through user cost*

	Germany	France	Italy	Spain
t	−0.39	0.01	−0.44	−0.97
$t+1$	−0.38	−0.14	−0.41	−0.31
$t+2$	−0.25	−0.02	−0.25	−0.04
$t+3$	−0.19	0.00	−0.15	−0.04

different countries for an average firm in the data set. It is relatively high in Spain and Italy, somewhat lower in France and lowest in Germany. Market interest rate changes will therefore have larger effects on user cost in Italy and Spain than in France and Germany. Note that these elasticities are historical, i.e given our data. They are dependent on the historical level of interest rates, debt–equity levels, tax rates, investment good inflation and depreciation rates. Where monetary union cause the yield curve to be identical across member countries, differences in the effect of market interest rate changes on the user cost could still come from differences across members countries in the above other variables, such as corporate tax rate.

We now consider the effect of a permanent 1 per cent change in the market interest rate through the user cost. Note that by this we mean, for example, a change in the interest rate from 5 per cent to 5.05 per cent, not from 5 per cent to 6 per cent. Table 7.13 shows us how much the user cost will change permanently. So, for instance, a 1 per cent permanent increase in the market interest rate leads to a user cost change of 0.32 per cent in Germany and 0.70 per cent in Italy. Combining this with the results of table 7.10 gives us the dynamic effects on investment of a 1 per cent change in the market interest rate. The results are presented in table 7.14.

We find relatively large effects in Germany, Italy and Spain. If one were to consider, e.g., a 50-basis points increase in a market interest rate from 5 per cent to 5.50 per cent, one would have to multiply the

Table 7.15 *Elasticity of investment with respect to interest rate through cash flow*

	Germany	France	Italy	Spain
t	−0.02	−0.04	−0.24	−0.11
$t+1$	−0.03	−0.12	−0.28	−0.18
$t+2$	−0.04	−0.15	−0.31	−0.18
$t+3$	−0.05	−0.17	−0.33	−0.20

numbers in table 7.14 by 10. Such a policy experiment would lead to contemporaneous 3.9 per cent decrease in investment in Germany, 4.5 per cent in Italy, 9.8 per cent in Spain and no effect in France.

We also investigate the effect of a permanent change in the market interest rate on cash flow. Since interest payments are a flow, they decrease cash flow. When firms have higher interest payments to make, they have lower cash flow, *ceteris paribus*. The elasticity of cash flow with respect to the interest rate can also be calculated directly. It is equal to:

$$\frac{\partial CF_t}{\partial i_{t-1}} * \frac{i_{t-1}}{CF_t} = -\frac{(1-\tau)i_{i,t-1}D_{i,t-1}}{(1-\tau)(pY - Costs - i_{i,t-1}D_{i,t-1})}$$

The elasticity is equal to the inverse coverage ratio, i.e. interest payments over cash flow. The higher the inverse coverage ratio is, the higher the effect of interest payments will be on cash flow. Table 7.12 shows the elasticity of cash flow with respect to the market interest rate for the average firm in the samples. Italy and Spain again display higher values for this elasticity. Presumably this is due to high nominal interest rates for both countries during the years of investigation.

Table 7.15 presents the effect on the growth rate of the capital stock (or investment) of a transitory increase of 1 per cent of the interest rate through the effect on cash flow. The effects are in general relatively small in all countries. Consider again a 50-basis points increase in a market interest rate from 5 per cent to 5.50 per cent. Such a policy experiment would lead, after the first year, to a contemporaneous 0.2 per cent decrease in investment in Germany, 0.4 per cent in France, 2.4 per cent in Italy and 1.1 per cent in Spain.

8   Conclusion

This chapter presents a comparable set of results on the monetary transmission channels on firm investment for the four largest countries of the euro area. We focus on two different channels that affect investment. The interest channel is operative when market interest fluctuations change the user cost of capital and hence investment. The broad credit channel is operative when market interest fluctuations change the balance sheet condition and the available cash flow of firms and, through this, investment. This chapter is the first to provide an investigation of those two channels for the four largest economies of the euro area, based on results from a unique comparative study using large firm databases for each country, containing a total of over 215,000 observations from 1985 to 1999. Its emphasis on using large micro datasets makes this exercise an important complement to the vast macro literature in which euro area countries are compared.

We find investment to be sensitive to user cost changes in all those four countries. Most of the effect of user cost changes is borne within the first two years. This implies an operative interest channel in these euro area countries. We also find investment in all those countries to be quite sensitive to sales and cash flow movements. Furthermore, we have investigated whether significant differences exist between large and small firms in investment behaviour. We find that only in Italy do smaller firms react more to cash flow movements. We argue that size might not be the right indicator in all countries to investigate the broad credit channel.

8 Business investment and monetary transmission in Belgium

P. Butzen, C. Fuss and P. Vermeulen

1 Introduction

This chapter investigates how monetary policy affects business real fixed investment in Belgium, through the interest rate channel and the broad credit channel. These channels are roughly associated with the effects that operate through the user cost of capital and the cash flow–capital ratio. An extensive version of this chapter can be found in Butzen, Fuss and Vermeulen (2001).

Our analysis relies on firm-level annual accounts data. To our knowledge, there is no firm-level evidence so far on the interest rate channel for Belgium. Only a few papers explicitly introduce the user cost of capital in their specification. One example is the cointegration analysis of Gérard and Verschueren (2000) on industry-level data that reveals differences in long-run elasticity of investment to the user cost across Belgian industries.

A couple of papers assess the relevance of financial constraints for particular groups of Belgian firms. The existence of these constraints is a necessary condition for the broad credit channel to be at work. Using an Euler equation framework Vermeulen (1998) finds that only firms that entirely depend on banks as providers of external funds are financially constrained. Deloof (1998) stresses the role of holding companies and corporate groups as providers of intra-group funds. Barran and Peeters (1998) show that firms affiliated to a coordination centre (a particular form of group membership, see section 2, p. 166) are less financially constrained than other firms. In contrast with this evidence, Bond *et al.* (1997) find no significant effect of financial variables in Belgium. Our contribution to the literature is threefold. First, to our knowledge, this is the first paper that focuses on both the broad credit channel and the interest rate channel of monetary policy transmission in Belgium using panel data. To investigate the interest rate channel, we include a firm-specific user cost of capital in the investment equation, a feature which is absent from other panel data studies for Belgium. Second, we make use of an extremely representative data set: the Belgian annual accounts data base. Since the reporting of annual accounts is a legal requirement for (nearly) all firms in Belgium, this data base, indeed, covers (almost) the complete population of Belgian firms. Our data base, hence, differs from data bases in other countries, which are often collected on a voluntary basis and/or are intended to serve a particular purpose. Therefore, compared to previous panel data studies, including those on the Belgian economy that generally restrict their focus to a limited sample of large and/or manufacturing firms, we include in our study firms of all sectors and sizes. We thereby avoid a representation bias.[1] Third, again thanks to the scope of our data set, we are able to evaluate the effects of an interest rate change on the investment behaviour of firms in different size classes and/or operating in different sectors of the economy. By doing so, we can analyse the distributional effects of monetary policy.

This chapter is organised as follows. Section 2 describes our data set and some features of corporate finance in Belgium. Section 3 presents the estimates of the investment equation. Section 4 computes the long-run impact of monetary policy on the stock of capital. Finally, in section 5, we formulate our conclusions.

2   Description of Belgian data

Our analysis rests on the annual accounts data base collected by the National Bank of Belgium. Since in Belgium almost every non-financial firm is required to deposit its annual accounts, the data base covers nearly the entire population of firms. In 1998, for instance, 228,566 firms complied with the regulations. Our unbalanced panel is also relatively extensive in the time dimension as it draws on a period of fifteen years (1985–98). This permits us to study the dynamic properties of investment. From the initial data base, we drop missing values, remove outliers[2] and select firms with enough consecutive observations for our dynamic model. The final sample contains 157,547 observations representing 29,600 firms; that is around 12 per cent of the initial data base.[3] Although there is

---

[1] In Butzen, Fuss and Vermeulen (2001) we show that using pooled data does not produce significant effects of user cost fluctuations on the investment rate, and formal tests show that this results from a specification bias.

[2] We exclude firm years for which at least one of the variables of interest (except value added, which is scale-dependent) belongs to the first or 99th percentile, where percentiles were computed year by year and for large and small firms separately.

[3] 97 per cent of the observations of the initial sample refer to firms that may be considered as 'profit-maximising'. 90 per cent of the annual accounts are satisfactory in the sense that total assets, total liabilities, real fixed assets and depreciation rate are strictly positive. After requiring that data are available for the level and first difference of all RHS and LHS variables, there remains only 52 per cent of the sample. Almost 10 per cent is again lost

a small bias towards 'large' firms,[4] the number of very small firms is still considerable. Around 10 per cent of the firms have only one employee, and 44 per cent of the firms employ at most five persons. At the sector level, manufacturing industries and construction are slightly overrepresented,[5] but this should not be harmful to our results as we analyse each sector separately. All in all, compared to other data sets used in the literature, our sample is very representative of the Belgian private sector.

The corporate finance structure of Belgian firms has evolved over the last decade, as shown in table 8.1. In particular, the size (as measured by total assets over the number of firms) of large service firms has exploded: on average, total assets are now 2.5 times higher than at the beginning of the period. Large service firms also control relatively less real fixed assets and inventories (two times less), and relatively more financial assets and other assets than in the past. The rise of the share of financial assets is even more remarkable in manufacturing and for small service firms (at least two times). On the liability side, firms rely less on trade debt than in the past, which points to a more efficient use of funds. Furthermore, for large service firms, equity has become more important: the share of equity rose by 30 per cent over the period. The share of long-term bank credit has been almost halved while non-bank loans have exploded, especially in the manufacturing and construction sector where this share more than doubled. Small firms, on the other hand, have kept roughly the same leverage as fifteen years ago, but have shifted primarily from trade debt towards long-term bank financing. Small firms are more dependent on bank debt than large firms and have further increased their share of bank debt over the period by 30 per cent (up to 40 per cent – 60 per cent for long-term bank debt).

These patterns can be explained by (changes in) the institutional features of Belgian financial markets. In Belgium, firms' direct access to capital markets has always been limited. Instead, Belgian corporate finance is characterised by large shareholders, such as holding companies, which control firms through complex ownership structures. Holding companies may substitute for poorly developed corporate capital markets and can

---

owing to trimming for outliers. Finally, we loose 30 per cent more by requiring a sample with enough consecutive annual accounts to estimate an ADL(4).

[4] A company is regarded as 'large', in 1999, either when the yearly average of its workforce is at least 100 or when at least two of the following thresholds were exceeded: (1) yearly average of workforce: 50, (2) turnover (excluding VAT): EUR 6,250,000, (3) balance sheet total: EUR 3,125,000. In general, the values of the latter two thresholds are modified every four years in order to take account of inflation.

[5] The share in total value added for the manufacturing sector is 18.9 per cent according to the national accounts, whereas it is 43.8 per cent in our sample. For construction the values of these shares are, respectively, 4.8 per cent and 7.7 per cent.

Table 8.1 *Financial structure of Belgian firms, 1987–1998*

| | Manufacturing | | | | Construction | | | | Service | | | |
| | Large firms | | Small firms | | Large firms | | Small firms | | Large firms | | Small firms | |
	1987	1998	1987	1998	1987	1998	1987	1998	1987	1998	1987	1998
Number of firms (000)	2.8	3.4	10.3	16.5	0.5	0.7	9.0	19.9	6.0	9.1	55.7	133.2
Total assets (million euro)	19.6	35.1	0.5	0.6	10.8	13.7	0.3	0.3	12.9	32.3	0.3	0.5
Assets as % of total												
Real fixed assets	24.0	19.3	29.5	33.8	8.3	10.8	23.2	28.9	19.7	10.0	35.2	40.1
Financial assets	14.1	34.0	1.8	4.9	7.8	9.8	1.8	3.0	22.9	31.5	3.9	11.5
Inventories	21.3	13.5	20.9	16.3	35.8	32.4	17.5	16.4	11.0	5.8	20.1	12.1
Trade credit – total	24.4	17.9	28.7	25.2	31.5	27.4	34.7	28.6	21.5	13.8	19.9	15.5
Other assets	16.1	15.4	19.1	19.9	16.5	19.5	22.8	23.2	25.0	38.9	20.9	20.8
Liabilities as % of total												
Loans of credit Institutions	13.7	10.1	16.7	21.4	6.1	7.8	13.0	18.6	23.5	15.7	18.4	24.7
– Maturity < 1 year	5.7	4.4	5.3	6.0	3.0	3.5	4.9	6.0	9.5	8.8	5.4	5.7
– Maturity > 1 year	7.9	5.7	11.3	15.4	3.0	4.3	8.0	12.6	14.0	7.0	13.0	19.0
Other financial debt	8.0	17.5	2.4	3.7	1.1	2.6	1.6	3.0	8.3	14.8	3.3	5.0
(Debt securities and other loans)												
Trade debt	17.9	14.2	24.1	20.2	25.6	21.9	27.2	23.2	17.4	10.4	22.4	14.4
Other debt	17.4	13.8	19.7	20.1	41.5	42.2	18.5	19.9	14.8	12.9	18.7	20.7
Equity and reserves	36.1	37.5	35.6	32.7	21.8	21.5	37.8	33.5	32.5	43.8	35.4	33.3
Other liabilities	7.0	6.9	1.7	1.9	3.9	4.1	1.9	1.8	3.5	2.4	1.8	2.0
Flows as % of assets												
Interest charges	2.2	1.7	2.9	2.9	0.9	0.8	2.1	2.4	2.3	1.9	2.8	2.9
Net operating profit	6.3	4.7	7.7	5.1	1.2	2.0	7.4	5.4	3.0	1.6	5.9	4.3
Gross investment	8.1	5.0	12.6	10.9	2.8	4.3	10.2	9.8	4.0	2.3	11.5	7.4
Cash flow	12.4	11.0	12.2	10.5	4.9	6.2	11.1	10.3	7.5	8.4	9.3	7.6

Source: Annual Accounts.

alleviate financial constraints for the firms they control. Furthermore, since 1982, large multinationals have been allowed to set up a so-called 'coordination centre', which provides support and financial services to their affiliated firms on a low-tax basis. This may provide an additional manner to reduce financial constraints of affiliated firms. Coordination centres have become the main source of external finance for their members. Capitalisation of the coordination centre by multinationals may explain the rise in equity. Firms have also replaced bank credit by intragroup loans, afters bank credit became relatively more expensive.[6]

3   Investment behaviour of Belgian firms

In order to evaluate the interest rate and credit channels we estimate a reduced form investment equation derived from the neo-classical model.[7] Hence it includes value added (VA_{it}) and a firm-specific user cost of capital (UCC_{it}). This equation is augmented with the cash flow–capital ratio ($cash_{it}/K_{it-1}$) as in Fazzari, Hubbard and Petersen (1988) in order to capture financial constraints,[8] and with lagged variables which reflect adjustment costs and future expectations. In contrast to Bond *et al.* (1997) or Mairesse, Hall and Mulkay (1999), who apply the same strategy, we explicitly introduce a firm-specific user cost of capital.[9] This permits us to analyse the interest rate and broad credit channels through the user

---

[6] See, for example, Tychon (1997) for an overview of the financial structure of Belgian firms, Barran and Peeters (1998) for a short description of coordination centres.

[7] The Lucas critique (Lucas, 1976) has stimulated an alternative approach, i.e. an Euler type of equation (e.g. Barran and Peeters, 1998, for Belgium). Although from a theoretical point of view it seems more appealing, it has often failed to produce significant adjustment cost parameters. Moreover, even in this approach the variables that are assumed to represent financial constraints are entered in an ad hoc way (see the criticism of Vermeulen, 1998).

[8] Interpreting the investment–cash flow sensitivity as an indication of the degree of financial constraints may be misleading, as argued by Kaplan and Zingales (1997). One reason is that cash flow may also capture profit expectations. For example, the results of Deloof (1998) for Belgium suggests that his finding of a higher cash flow sensitivity may reflect over-investment rather than financial constraints. See also Fazzari, Hubbard and Petersen (2000) and Kaplan and Zingales (2000) over this controversy.

[9] Note that our measure of the user cost is based on a firm-specific depreciation rate. Furthermore, it is based on an apparent interest rate, defined as the ratio of interest charges over debt, rather than on the short- and long-term market interest rates weighted according to the debt structure. Although this definition is closer to the average interest rate than to the marginal one, we think that it may be more relevant than that based on the market interest rates. The latter is closer to the marginal rate paid by the firm but omits important firm-specific factors such as the risk premium, which is embedded in the apparent interest rate. The latter explains a large part of the heterogeneity of the user cost between firms. In our sample, the standard deviation of the user cost of capital is almost three times larger when it is based on the apparent interest rate than on the market interest rate.

cost of capital and the cash flow variables, respectively. Our investment equation becomes:[10]

$$
\begin{aligned}
(I_{it}/K_{it-1}) = {} & \omega_1 \cdot (I_{it-1}/K_{it-2}) + \cdots + \omega_p \cdot (I_{it-p}/K_{it-p-1}) \\
& - \sigma_0 \cdot \Delta\log(UCC_{it}) - \cdots - \sigma_p \cdot \Delta\log(UCC_{it-p}) \\
& + \theta_0 \cdot \Delta\log(VA_{it}) + \cdots + \theta_p \cdot \Delta\log(VA_{it-p}) \\
& + \phi_0 \cdot (cash_{it}/K_{it-1}) + \cdots + \phi_p \cdot (Cash_{it-p}/K_{it-p-1}) \\
& + (1 - \omega_1 - \cdots \omega_p) \cdot \delta_i + \text{time dummies} + \varepsilon_{it}
\end{aligned}
\tag{1}
$$

We exploit the extremely broad scope of our sample to analyse the investment behaviour of different sub-groups. We consider firms of different sizes and sectors separately. This allows us to avoid aggregation biases due to heterogeneous behaviour of firms across groups. Differences across firms of different size have been widely documented in the literature.[11] Small firms are assumed to face stronger financial constraints. So, assuming that differences in investment–cash flow sensitivity capture differences in the degree of financial constraints, we expect the cash flow coefficients to be smaller for large firms. Also, investment by large firms is, in general, smoother than that by small firms because it results from an aggregation over several plants and projects (see Doms and Dunne, 1998). For small firms, bursts of investment in one year may not spill over to the following years. Differences across sectors may also induce different investment behaviour. Owing to differences in the nature of their activities or in their production technology, one may expect sectors to face a different degree of financial constraints, and/or to have different sensitivities to the cost of capital.

Table 8.2 summarises the second step robust results of the GMM Arellano–Bond (1991) estimator of (1).[12] We consider as instruments the second lag and beyond of all RHS variables. The estimation runs over the period 1991–8. We first focus on the distinction between small

---

[10] See Chatelain *et al.* (chapter 7 in this volume) for a detailed model description. Unlike their chapter, we estimate an ADL(4) and proxy output by value added. First, Wald tests, reported in the tables, show that, in most of the cases, lag four is significant. Furthermore, preliminary estimates indicate that an ADL(3) model is misspecified for small firms (in the sense that the Sargan statistic rejects the model). Second, we use value added because small Belgian firms do not have to report sales. If we make the assumption that value added is proportional to sales, the coefficient for output in (1) keeps the same structural interpretation.

[11] For Europe, see, for instance, Guiso (1997) for Italy, Mörttinen (2000) for inventories in Finland, Vermeulen (2000) for Germany, France, Italy and Spain and Wesche (2000) for Austria.

[12] We present the second-step estimates rather than the first-step estimates. Although the second-step t-statistics may be upwards biased, the consistency of the point estimates improves, provided that the sample is large, which is the case in our study.

Table 8.2 *ADL(4) model of investment by sector – long-run effects, Belgium*

Large firms	Manufacturing		Construction		Services	
	coef.	t-stat	coef.	t-stat	coef.	t-stat
I_{t-1}/K_{t-2}	0.039***	2.899	0.049***	3.235	0.066***	4.703
$\Sigma(I_{t-j}/K_{t-j-1})$	0.015	0.455	0.000	−0.011	0.010	0.338
$\Sigma\Delta\log(UCC_{t-j})$	−0.032***	−3.181	−0.093***	−2.800	0.013	0.567
Long-run elasticity	−0.032		−0.093		0.013	
$\Sigma\Delta\log(VA_{t-j})$	0.309***	4.403	0.008	0.118	0.183**	2.543
Long-run elasticity	0.313		0.008		0.185	
$\Sigma(cash_{t-j}/K_{t-j-1})$	0.207***	4.524	0.134***	6.676	0.083***	4.815
Long-run elasticity	0.211		0.133		0.084	
# obs. # firms	8158	1529	2720	452	16624	2826
Sargan (p-value)	119.50	0.62	118.82	0.64	118.96	0.64
m1 (p-value)	−11.72	0.00	−8.01	0.00	−17.40	0.00
m2 (p-value)	0.36	0.72	−1.22	0.22	−0.72	0.45

Small firms	Manufacturing		Construction		Services	
	coef.	t-stat	coef.	t-stat	coef.	t-stat
I_{t-1}/K_{t-2}	−0.029*	−1.910	−0.034**	−2.320	0.018	1.456
$\Sigma(I_{t-j}/K_{t-j-1})$	−0.113***	−2.736	−0.158***	−4.755	−0.023	−1.157
$\Sigma\Delta\log(UCC_{t-j})$	−0.097*	−1.949	−0.099	−1.293	0.022	0.985
Long-run elasticity	−0.088		−0.086		0.022	
$\Sigma\Delta\log(VA_{t-j})$	0.289***	2.656	0.208**	2.079	−0.012	−0.148
Long-run elasticity	0.260		0.180		−0.012	
$\Sigma(cash_{t-j}/K_{t-j-1})$	0.200***	3.479	0.266	4.375	0.374***	6.826
Long-run elasticity	0.180		0.230		0.365	
# obs. # firms	14856	3040	25444	4648	88220	16954
Sargan (p-value)	121.65	0.57	114.52	0.74	130.06	0.36
m1 (p-value)	−15.66	0.00	−19.15	0.00	−34.80	0.00
m2 (p-value)	1.35	0.18	−1.78	0.08	−1.87	0.06

Notes: 2nd-step first-difference GMM Arellano–Bond estimates of the investment equation
(1) over 1991–98 instrument set: lags two and beyond of all RHS variables.
* Significant at the 10% level; **Significant at the 5% level; *** Significant at the 1% level.

and large firms. The coefficient of lagged investment is negative for small
firms (from −0.29 to −0.34), while it is positive for large firms (from
0.04 to 0.07). This finding is consistent with our priors: aggregation over
plants and projects results in a smoother investment pattern for large
firms. Small firms also tend to react more sharply to changes in the user
cost of capital, but only in the manufacturing sector. In this sector a 1
per cent increase in the user cost of capital growth rate causes the investment rate to decrease in the long run by around 0.1 per cent for

small firms and by only 0.03 per cent for large firms. In the other sectors, however, this elasticity takes the same value for both size classes: about −0.1 in construction and close to zero and not significant in services. Finally, the investment–cash flow sensitivity is considerably higher for small firms than for large firms (except in manufacturing where it has the same magnitude for both groups of companies, i.e. about 0.2): the elasticity ranges from 0.08 for large service firms to 0.37 for small service firms. The latter evidence suggests that small firms in services or construction face stronger financial constraints.[13] Summing up, small firms seem to invest once they have the opportunity, available internal finance or cheap external financing, and then wait for some time for new investment opportunities and funding.

Comparing estimates across sectors, table 8.2 indicates that manufacturing firms are the most affected by demand fluctuations. A 1 per cent increase in value added growth rate increases the investment rate of manufacturing firms by around 0.30 per cent in the long run. In the other sectors, the rise in the investment rate is limited to a range between zero and 0.2 per cent. The effect is not significant for small service firms and large construction firms. With respect to the user cost, construction firms are very sensitive, while service firms are insensitive.[14] A further breakdown into sub-sectors as in Butzen, Fuss and Vermeulen (2001) suggests that the investment sensitivity to changes in the user cost of capital is directly related to degree of capital intensity.

4   Evaluating the interest rate channel of monetary policy on the capital stock

The results of section 3 suggest that small firms face stronger financial constraints than large firms, especially in the service sector, and with the exception of the manufacturing sector. This evidence supports the existence of a broad credit channel in Belgium. In the short run, a monetary contraction would reduce investment of small firms by a larger extent. Small service firms would be the most affected by such a policy, while the effect would be close to zero for large service firms. Except for service

---

[13] This result is also consistent with other evidence: e.g. Gaiotti and Generale (chapter 11 in this volume), Guiso (1997) Kremp and Stöss (2000), Tychon (1997) and Vermeulen (2000).

[14] When disaggregating the sample further into twenty-three branches, the user cost elasticity of investment is insignificant for most of the service branches (see Butzen, Fuss and Vermeulen, 2001). Given the dominance of the service sector in the Belgian economy, this may explain why aggregate studies often fail to find significant interest rate effects in investment equations.

firms, there is also clear evidence of the existence of an interest rate channel: the long-run effect of a change in the user cost on the investment rate is negative and significantly different from zero.

Next, we evaluate the long-run effects of monetary policy on the capital stock that operate through the interest rate channel.[15] The former results are, however, only a first step towards such an evaluation. For our purpose, we additionally need to combine the parameter estimates of the investment equation with a measurement of the impact of a change in the market interest rate on the user cost of capital. Hence, the long-run elasticity of capital to the market interest rate is equal to:

$$\varepsilon_{r_t}^{K_{it}} = \varepsilon_{UCC_{it}}^{K_{it}} \cdot \varepsilon_{i_{it}}^{UCC_{it}} \cdot \varepsilon_{r_t}^{i_{it}} \tag{2}$$

where ε_y^x is the long-run elasticity of x with respect to y, i_{it} is the apparent interest rate faced by firm i, and r_t the three-month market interest rate. This expression consists of three elements. The first element is the long-run elasticity of capital with respect to the user cost, which is given by the estimates in section 3. The second element is the elasticity of the user cost with respect to the apparent interest rate, which can be derived analytically from its definition[16]:

$$\varepsilon_{i_{it}}^{UCC_{it}} = \frac{i_{it}}{i_{it} + \delta_i - (1 - \delta_i) \cdot \frac{\Delta P_{st+1}^I}{P_{st}^I}} \tag{3}$$

where δ_i is the firm-specific depreciation rate and P_{st}^I the sector-specific deflator on gross capital formation. We approximate these elasticities by taking mean values by sector and size. Finally, we have to quantify the elasticity of the apparent interest rate with respect to the market interest rate. Since we are interested only in the interest rate channel, this is a challenging task. A change in monetary policy stance may, indeed, affect firms' apparent interest rates through both the interest rate and credit channel. By convention the interest rate channel, on the one hand, captures the impact of an increase in the market interest that is identical for all firms. The credit channel, on the other hand, measures its effect on the firm-specific risk premium. To isolate the interest rate channel

---

[15] In this section, we restrict ourselves to the interest rate channel. Since the cash flow–capital ratio enters the investment equation in levels and not in first differences, the long-run elasticity of the capital stock with respect to cash flow cannot be derived directly. A possible solution to this problem might be to perform a simulation exercise as in Chatelain *et al.* (chapter 7 in this volume), Gaiotti and Generale (chapter 11 in this volume) and von Kalckreuth (chapter 9 in this volume).

[16] See Butzen, Fuss and Vermeulen (2001) for the definition of the variables.

Table 8.3 *The long-run effects of the interest rate channel on the stock of capital, Belgium*

	Manufacturing	Construction	Services
Elasticity of the user cost of capital with respect to the market interest rate			
Large firms	0.304	0.232	0.185
Small firms	0.403	0.347	0.335
Long-run elasticity of capital with respect to the market interest rate			
Large firms	−0.010	−0.022	0.002
Small firms	−0.035	−0.030	0.007

Source: Authors' calculations combining (1) and (3).

effect we fix the elasticity of the apparent interest rate with respect to the market interest rate to 1 for all firms.[17]

Table 8.3 reports the elasticity of the user cost of capital with respect to the apparent interest rate as well as the elasticity of the capital stock with respect to the market interest rate. In addition to a stronger investment sensitivity to changes in the user cost of capital (especially in the manufacturing sector, as shown in section 3), small firms also have higher elasticity of the user cost of capital to the market interest rate. Therefore, small firms cut their capital stock more sharply following an interest rate increase than large firms do. Apart from service firms which do not respond to changes in the user cost, a 1 per cent interest rate increase leads to a reduction in the capital stock of around 0.01 per cent–0.02 per cent for large firms to around 0.03 per cent for small firms. The effect of the interest rate channel also differs across sectors.[18] For both small and large firms, the effect is stronger in the construction sector; this is not too surprising, as demand in this sector is interest-sensitive.

Our outcome for the Belgian manufacturing sector is consistent with Wesche's (2000) results for Austria and with Ehrmann's (2000) conclusions for Germany. Other contributions to this volume also highlight distributional effects of monetary policy. In particular Gaiotti and Generale, for Italy, and von Kalckreuth, for Germany, point to differences across firms of different size.

---

[17] Since the time dimension of our panel is relatively short, we prefer to fix rather than estimate this coefficient. By doing so, we avoid using unprecise estimates due to low degrees of freedom.

[18] The results reported in Butzen, Fuss and Vermeulen (2001) indicate that, apart from construction, the interest rate channel triggers stronger effects in capital-intensive sectors than in labour-intensive sectors.

5   Conclusion

This chapter investigates the effects of monetary policy on firms' investment behaviour in Belgium that operate through the user cost of capital and through cash flow, and that, with some reservation, can, respectively, be associated with the interest rate and credit channels of monetary transmission.

The analysis relies on the use of a comprehensive data base of Belgian firms over the period 1985–98, covering all sectors of economic activity, and firms of all sizes. This data base enables us to investigate this issue for each sector – manufacturing, construction and services – and for large and small firms separately. Taking into account heterogeneity across firms enables us to avoid aggregation biases and to find evidence of distributional effects of monetary policy across sectors and sizes.

We proceed as follows. First, we estimate an ADL(4) version of a reduced form investment equation, derived from the neo-classical model, including the firm-specific user cost of capital and augmented with cash flow. This equation is estimated with the Arellano and Bond (1991) GMM first-difference procedure. Our results show that the investment behaviour of manufacturing and construction firms corresponds to theoretical priors. They react negatively to user cost changes, and positively to value added growth and cash flow changes. Small firms in these sectors show stronger user cost and cash flow effects, and less smooth dynamics. Service firms seem not to react to user cost changes. Small service firms do not react to value added growth either, but they do respond strongly to contemporaneous cash flow changes, in contrast to large service firms.

We then calculate the elasticity of the user cost of capital with respect to the market interest-rate and combine it with the estimated effect of the user cost in the investment equation. This computation allows us to evaluate the long-run elasticity of capital with respect to the market interest rate, but only through the interest rate channel. The results show that the interest rate channel is more important for small firms than for large firms. Moreover, it affects construction firms the most, while service firms are essentially insensitive.

In general, the results support the hypothesis of an interest rate and a credit channel in Belgium. The impact of these channels differs across sectors and sizes. We can thus conclude that monetary policy produces distributional effects.

9 Investment and monetary transmission in Germany: a microeconometric investigation

U. von Kalckreuth

1 Introduction

This chapter takes a closer look at the monetary transmission mechanism in Germany, focusing on investment demand. For a more detailed econometric analysis with further results see von Kalckreuth (2001) as well as Deutsche Bundesbank (2002b) and von Kalckreuth (2002). The aim of this chapter is to look at the interest channel and the balance sheet channel in Germany separately and to compare their relative strength. We follow the methodology introduced in Chatelain *et al.* (chapter 7 in this volume). The interest channel is evaluated on the basis of the estimated long-run user cost elasticity of capital demand, whereas the broad credit channel hypothesis is tested by comparing cash-flow sensitivities of financially constrained and unconstrained firms. This chapter has two distinct features. First, we employ a very direct and reliable measure for financial constraints: creditworthy and not creditworthy firms are distinguished using rating data generated by the Deutsche Bundesbank in order to judge the quality of trade bills. Chatelain and Tiomo (chapter 10 in this volume) use a similar methodology in a study of French firm investment.

The second important feature of this chapter is that it uses theoretical user costs of capital constructed according to King and Fullerton (1984), under the assumption that the neo-classical model is true and that everybody has equal access to the financial markets. This reflects the pure price effects more accurately than a user cost variable relying on apparent interest rates, i.e. the ratio of interest paid to total debt. Using average market

This chapter represents the author's personal opinion and does not necessarily reflect the views of the Deutsche Bundesbank. I am grateful to Ignazio Angeloni, Andreas Blochwitz, Nick Bloom, Steve Bond, Jean-Bernard Chatelain, Bob Chirinko, Judith Eigermann, Andrea Generale, Jürgen von Hagen, Dietmar Harhoff, Heinz Herrmann, Ignacio Hernando, Andreas Hertkorn, Anil Kashyap, Benoît Mojon, Daniele Terlizzese, Karl-Heinz Tödter, Christian Upper, Philip Vermeulen, Andreas Worms and Gerhardt Ziebarth. My special thanks go to Fred Ramb, who gave me access to his routines and data necessary to compute firm-specific user costs of capital. Fred's help was crucial and decisive.

rates, theoretical user costs are not affected by endogenous reactions to firm-specific financial constraints. Furthermore, they might be better indicators of the cost of *new* financing in a given year instead of reflecting the cost of credit contracted in previous periods.

The rest of this chapter is structured as follows. Section 1 introduces to some specific features of the corporate sector and the financial structure in Germany. Section 2 describes the data set. Section 3 shows the empirical results with respect to the interest rate channel and the broad credit channel; section 4 evaluates and concludes.

2   Corporate sector and financial structure in Germany

Germany, with a GDP of €1,920.6 billion in 2001, is the largest of the eurozone economies, accounting for 30.4 per cent of overall eurozone GDP. Historically, Germany has specialised in industrial production. Even today, manufacturing, energy and mining still account for 25.2 per cent of GDP (2001 figures) as opposed to 21.4 per cent for the rest of the eurozone. Nevertheless, the corporate sector is characterised by small and medium-sized enterprises (SMEs). In 1997, more than 60 per cent of turnover subject to value added tax was generated by enterprises with total sales of less than DM 500 million (€256.6 million), and 42.0 per cent of total turnover was generated by partnerships and sole proprietorships.[1]

This strong role of smaller and individually owned firms has important implications for the financing of firms.[2] Compared with other industrialised countries, particularly the Anglo-Saxon countries, there are two structural features of indebtedness in Germany that stand out. One is that bonds and money market paper play a rather insignificant role in corporate financing, and the other is that bank debt securities are used intensively to refinance lending, which leads, on balance, to indirect borrowing on the capital markets with intermediation by banks. This makes it a mixture between a purely 'capital market-oriented' system in which firms sell securities to non-banks and a 'bank-based system' in which firms use mainly bank credit and banks rely on deposits for their refinancing.

It is instructive to look at the structure of consolidated non-financial corporations' debt finance according to the financial accounts statistics (table 9.1). In 2000, domestic bonds and money market papers issued by

---

[1] *Source:* Federal Statistics Office. See Deutsche Bundesbank (2000a).
[2] For an introduction to the German financing system see Deutsche Bundesbank (2000a). A detailed description of the balance sheet structure of German firms is given in Deutsche Bundesbank (2002a).

Table 9.1 *Sectoral debt structure of non-financial corporations in Germany, 1998–2000*

	1998	1999	2000
Total debt (€ million)	1,381,247	1,509,166	1,753,593
Debt structure:			
Bonds and money market papers	3.4%	2.9%	3.0%
Loans, total	72.9%	72.9%	73.1%
By resident banks	59.5%	55.2%	50.4%
By resident insurance companies	0.8%	0.6%	0.5%
Other	12.7%	17.1%	22.2%
Of which: by non-residents	10.7%	14.3%	20.2%
Liabilities arising from pension commitments	11.2%	10.7%	9.5%
Other liabilities, including trade credits from other sectors	12.5%	13.5%	14.3%
Sum of shares:	100.0%	100.0%	100.0%

Source: Financial accounts statistics, Deutsche Bundesbank, June 2002.

non-financial corporations accounted for only about 3 per cent of debt. This contrasted with bank loans at 50.4 per cent, credit from foreign sources at 20.2 per cent, and pension provisions amounting to 9.5 per cent of total debt. In Germany, firms regularly form pension provisions in their balance sheets and use these funds for investment purposes. This is a form of debt that is equivalent to internal finance from an informational point of view. It is noteworthy to see that the importance of bank finance for the corporate sector has decreased considerably since the late 1990s, although part of that decrease is due to special influences. To an increasing extent, German companies are raising finance abroad via foreign subsidiaries.

So-called 'house banking relationships' are an important and characteristic feature of the German banking system.[3] According to Elsas and Krahnen (1998. 1312), a house banking relationship is 'an information intensive lender–borrower relationship, entailing implicit insurance by the lender. Based on superior information, the lender stands ready to support the financing needs of the borrower, in a situation of financial strain. Such an insurance is not costless, giving rise to specific long-term pricing policies.'

According to a survey by Harhoff and Körting (1998), 40 per cent of the SMEs surveyed have one banking connection only. Three-quarters

---

[3] On the German house banking system, see Deutsche Bundesbank (2000b), Elsas and Krahnen (1998) and Harhoff and Körting (1998).

of overall indebtedness to credit institutions, on average, is concentrated on that enterprise's 'house bank'. A house banking relationship does not necessarily preclude credit relationships with other banks, as Elsas and Krahnen (1998) show. Firms may have a multitude of lenders but no more than one house bank.

3   Financial statements, creditworthiness data and user costs of capital

The Bundesbank's corporate balance-sheet statistics (Unternehmensbilanzstatistik, UBS), a collection of financial statements, constitutes the largest source of accounting data for non-financial firms in Germany.[4] This collection of financial statements originates from the Bundesbank's function of performing credit assessments as part of its rediscount-lending operations, through which the Bundesbank purchased trade bills issued by non-financial firms from credit institutions. When a bill was presented to the Bundesbank, the creditworthiness of the presenting firm, as well as all other firms that have held this bill, needed to be determined.[5] In the case of default, under German law liability for payment of the bill falls on any firm that has held the bill. The judgement of creditworthiness was made on the basis of these accounting data, using discriminant analysis methodology. Firms are placed in three mutually exclusive categories: 'good standing', 'indifferent standing' and 'endandgered standing'. For the details, see appendix B of von Kalckreuth (2001), as well as Deutsche Bundesbank (1999).

The Bundesbank's branch offices collected about 70,000 financial statements per year on a strictly confidential basis. These data were initially subjected to a computer check for logical errors and missing data. Approximately 15,000 statements had to be excluded from the database because of incompleteness, or because they are consolidated statements, or submitted by firms in sectors for which no meaningful results can be generated owing to the small amount of available data. Additional checks and corrections for errors were undertaken in the Statistical Department at the Bundesbank's Central Office in Frankfurt. Only a part of the database can be used for estimation. Because their tax treatment

---

[4] On investment demand, the data base has been utilised by Harhoff and Ramb (2001) in a user cost study, and by von Kalckreuth (2000) in a study on investment and uncertainty. Detailed descriptions are presented by Deutsche Bundesbank (1998), Friderichs and Sauvé (1999) and Stöss (2001).

[5] Since the implementation of monetary union on 1 January 1999 the Bundesbank assesses corporate credits as part of the Eurosystem monetary policy operations but trade bills are no longer rediscounted.

differs, we excluded partnerships and sole proprietorships. Also for reasons of comparability, the data set used in estimation contains only firms located in the former Western Germany. The sample further shrinks because of data cleaning, outlier control (the upper and lower 1 per cent tails of sales growth, cash flow divided by the capital stock and the overall rating ratio discussed, and the upper 2 per cent tail of the investment–capital ratio), first-differencing, missing values and the necessity of lag lengths and contiguous observations. We thus have at our disposal a data set comprising 44,345 firm/year observations for 6,408 firms. The data set covers the period from 1988 to 1997. For 1996, these data represent 42 per cent of the total turnover of the Western German manufacturing sector.

The user costs of capital are constructed along the lines of King and Fullerton (1984), building upon prior work by Harhoff and Ramb (2001) and Ramb (2003). In a world with distortionary taxation, the nominal discount rate depends on whether the marginal source of funds is from retained earnings, debt finance or new share issues. Taxing at both the personal and the business level potentially leads to vast differences in discount rates. King (1977) and King and Fullerton (1984) have derived a general expression for the discount rate in the presence of distortionary taxes and income taxation at the level of the individual investor see also Chenells and Griffith, 1997 or OECD, 1991. When calculating the user costs, it is necessary to take account of specific features of the German system of capital taxation. From 1977 to 2000 the system of capital income taxation in Germany was a split-rate system with full imputation. The shareholder – provided that s/he was a German resident – received a tax credit in the amount of the corporation tax on distributed profits paid. Ultimately, the tax on capital income on distributed profits was equal to the marginal tax on capital income. Furthermore, the effective tax rate on accrued capital gains was zero, as capital gains were not taxed after a holding period of one year or more.

In a system with full imputation, the two types of outside finance are equivalent (see Sinn, 1984 and especially 1987). The user costs are calculated as a firm-specific weighted sum where the weights reflect the usage of internal and external finance. The weights are based on the flow of the sources of funds in a given year. In von Kalckreuth (2001), a second user cost variable is constructed weighting the costs of internal and external finance by balance sheet proportions. The interest rate is the average yield on industrial obligations of all maturities issued by German residents. For more details on the empirical implementation see von Kalckreuth (2001), especially appendix B.

Table 9.2 *Summary statistics for the overall sample of German firms*

Variable	Mean	Std dev.	Min.	25%	Median	75%	Max.
I_t/K_{t-1}	0.1813	0.2200	0	0.0585	0.1161	0.2157	2.2139
$\Delta\log S_t$	0.0206	0.1597	−0.5960	−0.0654	0.0214	0.1068	0.8309
CF_t/K_{t-1}	0.2843	0.4941	−1.9143	0.1091	0.1887	0.3308	9.2678
$\Delta\log UC_t$	0.0222	0.0717	−0.3478	−0.0178	0.0094	0.0644	0.4991
UC_t	0.1587	0.0182	0.0859	0.1468	0.1583	0.1704	0.2682

Table 9.3 *German firms, sample composition and means*

Variable	'Small'	'Large'	Endangered standing	Indifferent standing	Good standing
Number of firms	3,053	3,355	1,131	893	4,384
Number of obs.	20,452	23,893	7,489	6,029	30,827
I_t/K_{t-1}	0.1981	0.1669	0.1776	0.1891	0.1806
$\Delta\log S_t$	0.0232	0.0184	0.0111	0.0265	0.0218
CF_t/K_{t-1}	0.3253	0.2492	0.1563	0.2262	0.3267
$\Delta\log UC_t$	0.0229	0.0216	0.0217	0.0228	0.0222
UC_t	0.1559	0.1611	0.1584	0.1579	0.1589

Table 9.2 contains summary statistics for the variables entering the regression. The user cost variable is presented in both levels and growth rates. Tables 9.3 and 9.4 complement this information with a description of the sample composition with regard to size and rating categories, both showing the mean value of the variables for the various groups and a cross-tabulation. In the group of small firms, there are slightly more firms grouped as being of endangered credit standing. Table 9.4 presents the size distribution of the firm/year observations by mean employment, and documents the representation of small firms in the UBS database. The median and mean number of employees is 119 and 405, respectively. Nearly one-half of the observations pertain to firms with 100 employees or fewer. Table 9.5 shows the size distribution of German firms.

4   Empirical results: the interest rate channel and the credit channel

The investment equation used here is identical to the standard specification in this book. It defines a desired capital stock in terms of user cost

Table 9.4 *Cross-tabulation of groups of German firms*

	Endangered standing (%)	Indifferent standing (%)	Good standing (%)	All firms (%)
'Small' firms	646 (21.1)	472 (15.5)	1,935 (63.4)	3,053 (100)
'Large' firms	485 (14.5)	421 (12.57)	2,449 (73.0)	3,355 (100)

Table 9.5 *Size distribution of German firms and observations by mean employment*

	$n < 20$	$20 < n \leq 100$	$100 < n \leq 250$	$250 < n < 500$	$n > 500$	Sum
No. of firms	616	2437	1626	828	901	6408
(%)	9.61	38.03	25.37	12.92	14.06	100
No. of obs.	3,989	16,463	11,372	5,936	6,589	44,345
(%)	9.00	37.12	25.64	13.39	14.85	100

and sales variables having separate elasticities.[6] This demand for the stock of capital is translated into a demand for the flow of investment by relating the percentage change in capital (or the investment/capital ratio less depreciation, I/K) to the current and lagged percentage changes in the user cost (UC) and sales (S). To allow for a general pattern of dynamic responses, lagged dependent variables are included. We also enter current and lagged values of a financing variable, the ratio of cash flow to the capital stock (CF/K), to capture the effects of financing constraints. The long-run user cost elasticity (UCE) is the long-run percentage change in the capital stock as a reaction to a permanent increase in the level of its user cost, given by a one-percentage point blip in the growth rate, $\Delta \log$ UC. It is given as the sum of the coefficients on the user cost variables divided by one minus the sum of the coefficients on the lagged dependent variables. For details and a derivation of the estimation equation, see chapter 7 in this volume or von Kalckreuth (2001).

In our investment model, the interest rate channel operates via the user cost of capital, and our results show that there is a statistically significant relation between the user cost and investment. Table 9.6 presents a

---

[6] This model was developed over several years by Bischoff (1969); Coen (1969); Eisner (1969, 1970); Eisner and Nadiri (1968, 1970); Hall and Jorgenson (1967, 1969, 1971); and Jorgenson (1963).

Table 9.6 *ADL(3) models of investment demand, GMM estimates, Germany, dependent variable:* $I_{i,t}/K_{i,t-1}$

Explanatory variable	(1) CF/K included	(2) CF/K excluded	(3) Trimmed eq.
$I_{i,t-1}/K_{i,t-2}$	0.131 (0.016)**	0.148 (0.016)**	0.136 (0.014)**
$I_{i,t-2}/K_{i,t-3}$	−0.002 (0.009)	0.005 (0.009)	
$I_{i,t-3}/K_{i,t-4}$	0.005 (0.007)	0.009 (0.007)	
$\Sigma\, I_{i,t-n}/K_{i,t-n-1}$	**0.135 (0.025)****	**0.163 (0.025)****	**0.136 (0.014)****
$\Delta\log S_{i,t}$	0.161 (0.055)**	0.191 (0.055)**	0.141 (0.052)**
$\Delta\log S_{i,t-1}$	0.095 (0.014)**	0.115 (0.013)**	0.090 (0.014)**
$\Delta\log S_{i,t-2}$	0.065 (0.011)**	0.080 (0.011)**	0.062 (0.011)**
$\Delta\log S_{i,t-3}$	0.033 (0.010)**	0.041 (0.010)**	0.034 (0.009)**
$\Sigma\Delta\log S_{i,t-n}$	**0.354 (0.068)****	**0.427 (0.064)****	**0.328 (0.065)****
Long-run eff. sales	**0.409 (0.077)****	**0.510 (0.076)****	**0.380 (0.075)****
$\Delta\log UC_{i,t}$	−0.206 (0.071)**	−0.232 (0.073)**	−0.209 (0.069)**
$\Delta\log UC_{i,t-1}$	−0.163 (0.038)**	−0.190 (0.039)**	−0.167 (0.031)**
$\Delta\log UC_{i,t-2}$	−0.014 (0.034)	−0.037 (0.034)	
$\Delta\log UC_{i,t-3}$	0.038 (0.027)	0.022 (0.028)	
$\Sigma\Delta\log UC_{i,t-n}$	**−0.347 (0.125)****	**−0.437 (0.126)****	**−0.376 (0.088)****
Long-run eff. user cost	**−0.401 (0.144)****	**−0.522 (0.151)****	**−0.435 (0.103)****
$CF_{i,t}/K_{i,t-1}$	0.070 (0.034)*		0.094 (0.024)**
$CF_{i,t-1}/K_{i,t-2}$	0.013 (0.014)		
$CF_{i,t-2}/K_{i,t-3}$	0.005 (0.005)		
$CF_{i,t-3}/K_{i,t-4}$	0.005 (0.004)		
$\Sigma CF_{i,t-n}/K_{i,t-n-1}$	**0.093 (0.025)****		**0.094 (0.024)****
Long-run eff. cash flow	**0.108 (0.029)****		**0.109 (0.027)****
No. obs.	18713	18713	18713
No. firms	6408	6408	6408
Sargan–Hansen, p-value	0.075	0.048	0.092
LM(2), p-value	0.165	0.240	0.118

Notes: $I_{i,t}$: real gross investment; $K_{i,t}$: real capital stock at replacement value, $S_{i,t}$: real sales; $CF_{i,t}$: real cash flow, calculated as profit plus tax depreciation, $UC_{i,t}$: user cost of capital. Additional regressors: a constant and year dummies. Estimation method: two-step GMM first-differenced. Instruments: the undifferenced values of all regressors lagged at least two periods, and earlier when feasible (i.e., $I_{i,t-m}/K_{i-1-m}$, $\Delta\log S_{i,t-m}$, $\Delta\log UC_{i,t-m}$, $CF_{i,t-m}/K_{i,t-1-m}$ for $m \geq 2$, where the maximum value of m is as large as possible given data availability), as well as a constant and year dummies. The Sargan–Hansen statistic is a test for over-identifying restrictions proposed by Sargan (1958) and Hansen (1982). The LM(2) statistic is the Lagrange Multiplier statistic for second-order serial correlation proposed by Arellano and Bond (1991). The long-run effects of the explanatory variables are defined as the sum of the coefficients of the explanatory variable divided by one minus the sum of the coefficients on the lagged dependent variables; for sales and user cost this is to be interpreted as a long-run elasticity of the capital stock, whereas for cash flow this is a long-run derivative (see von Kalckreuth, 2001, section IV). The standard error is computed using the delta method. Robust standard errors from the second-step estimation are in parentheses; ** significant at the 1% level; * significant at the 5% level.

complete list of coefficient estimates, their sums and associated p-values for a third-order autoregressive distributed lag model that has been chosen on the basis of a prior specification search. The coefficients for the user costs drop sharply, and most of the impact of the user costs is transmitted to investment after two years. The lagged dependent variable moderately contributes to the long-run elasticity, raising it by about 15 per cent.

Column (2) of table 9.6 explores the interaction between the cash flow and user cost variables. In our baseline specification, the cash-flow variable is included to capture expectation and short-term financing effects. If the cash-flow coefficients are now constrained to zero, the user cost elasticities rise by 12 percentage points. The estimates in Chatelain and Tiomo (chapter 10 in this volume) and Chatelain *et al.* (chapter 7 in this volume) come to similar conclusions. This effect and the same magnitude have been observed previously in US data by Chirinko, Fazzari, and Meyer (1999), who argue that it was due to an 'income effect' induced by financing constraints.

To obtain more precise estimates, we proceed to remove those variables in column (1) of table 9.6 whose *p*-value is greater than or equal to 0.10. The results are shown in the last column of table 9.6. The point estimates for the long-run effects are almost unchanged, and the standard deviations are much lower. The UCE is measured at −0.43. This is our preferred estimate. These results have been subjected to a large number of robustness checks involving different measures for the user costs and varying lag lengths, specifications and estimation methods. The estimated UCEs usually stay within one standard error of our preferred estimate.

The UCE for our preferred estimate is slightly lower than the −0.52 measured by Chatelain *et al.* (chapter 7 in this volume) using apparent interest rates, and almost exactly equal to the −0.42 elasticity found by Harhoff and Ramb (2001) using King and Fullerton (1984) user costs in an investment equation without lagged endogenous variables. Mojon, Smets and Vermeulen (2001), using BACH data on German firms, do not find a significant UCE.

In order to test the credit channel hypothesis, we sort the firms in our data set by two characteristics that might identify access to external funding – creditworthiness according to the results of the discriminant analysis done by the Deutsche Bundesbank, and firm size. As is standard in the literature, our estimation strategy is to sort the data set by these characteristics and evaluate whether investment spending is 'excessively sensitive' to cash flow for the firms that are believed to be financially constrained. Given our user cost data and the interest channel that we have identified, we can also examine whether the UCE varies systematically.

Table 9.7 Long-run effects for groups of German firms

Explanatory variable	(1) All firms	(2) Good standing	(3) Endangered standing	(4) Difference	(5) Large firms ($n \geq 100$)	(6) Small firms ($n < 100$)	(7) Difference
User costs, $\Delta\log$ UC	-0.435**	-0.524**	-0.054	0.470*	-0.277**	-0.564**	-0.287
	(0.103)	(0.115)	(0.194)	(0.225)	(0.104)	(0.167)	(0.197)
Real sales, $\Delta\log$ S	0.380**	0.467**	0.103	-0.363**	0.375**	0.334**	-0.040
	(0.075)	(0.083)	(0.095)	(0.126)	(0.077)	(0.100)	(0.127)
Cash-flow relation, CF/K	0.109**	0.086**	0.175**	0.089*	0.078**	0.126**	0.048
	(0.027)	(0.026)	(0.033)	(0.042)	(0.030)	(0.030)	(0.043)
No. firms	6,408	4,384	1,131	.	3,355	3,053	.

Notes: In all cases, the specification is equivalent to the trimmed equation shown in table 9.6, column (3). Variables: $I_{i,t}$: real gross investment; $K_{i,t}$: real capital stock at replacement value, $S_{i,t}$: real sales; $CF_{i,t}$: real cash flow, calculated as profit plus tax depreciation, $UC_{i,t}$: user costs of capital. Additional regressors: a constant and year dummies. Estimation method: two-step GMM first-differenced. Instruments: the undifferenced values of all regressors lagged at least two periods, and earlier when feasible (i.e., $I_{i,t-m}/K_{i,t-1-m}$, $\Delta\log S_{i,t-m}$, $\Delta\log UC_{i,t-m}$, $CF_{i,t-m}/K_{i,t-1-m}$ for $m \geq 2$, where the maximum value of m is as large as possible given data availability), as well as a constant and year dummies. The Sargan–Hansen statistic is a test for overidentifying restrictions proposed by Sargan (1958) and Hansen (1982). The LM (2) statistic is the Lagrange Multiplier statistic for second-order serial correlation proposed by Arellano and Bond (1991). The long-run effects of the explanatory variables are defined as the sum of the coefficients of the explanatory variable divided by one minus the sum of the coefficients on the lagged dependent variables; for sales and user cost this is to be interpreted as a long-run elasticity of the capital stock, whereas for cash flow this is a long-run derivative (see von Kalckreuth, 2001, section IV). The standard error is computed using the delta method. Robust standard errors from the second step estimation are in parentheses: ** significant at the 1% level; * significant at the 5% level.

Columns (2)–(4) of Table 9.7 present estimates of the trimmed model where the firms are classified as being creditworthy or not creditworthy. Classification depends on the state in the year before the first investment–capital ratio enters the regression. For our model, this is the third year of the cleaned sample. Firms that are in the indeterminate category are excluded from these regressions. Two results stand out. First, the coefficients on the cash-flow term are larger for the unfavourably rated firms. The long-term effect of cash flow is twice as large for these firms, and the difference is statistically significant at the 5 per cent level. For those firms with an endangered standing and a presumably higher cost of external finance, investment seems to be excessively sensitive to internal funds.

Furthermore, unfavourably rated firms also demonstrate a smaller sensitivity to the user cost. For these firms, the long-run effect of user cost changes is insignificantly different from zero. Thus, because of financial constraints, these firms show little response to the price incentives associated with variations in interest rates. It is interesting to speculate on this reduced sensitivity to price variations. The underlying reason might be that the badly rated firms are financially 'paralysed' – at the margins, they are unable to adapt their capital stock to changing economic circumstances. Looking at the sales coefficients confirms this explanation: the sales sensitivity of badly rated firms is drastically reduced compared with firms having a good credit standing.[7] Using the firm-specific values of the discriminant function for creditworthiness as an additional regressor in the investment function corroborates this evidence for financial constraints (see von Kalckreuth 2001).

Columns (5)–(7) in table 9.7 sort the sample by number of employees. A firm is categorised as 'small' if it has fewer than 100 employees on average. It has frequently been hypothesised that small firms will face financing problems because they have less visibility in external capital markets and are poorly placed to bear the overhead cost associated with external finance. As nearly half of our firms have fewer than 100 employees, we should be able to detect small-firm financing problems if they exist. The estimated long-run effects of a cash-flow shock are slightly higher for small firms. The difference, however, is insignificant, and has to be seen in conjunction with the slightly worse average rating of small firms as documented in table 9.4. The user cost coefficients seem to be more negative for the small firms, but again the difference is not significant.

---

[7] There is, however, a competing explanation. Badly rated firms might experience disproportionately frequent episodes of decreasing sales. Because of irreversibility and the fact that we do not observe sales of capital goods, the measured reaction may be weak compared to favourably rated firms.

It emerges that being 'small' is something essentially different from being badly rated and credit constrained in Germany. Whereas our sample split according to rating was able to detect clear signs of credit constraints (which was to be expected), the sample split according to size did not. These results might indicate that the German house banking system efficiently surmounts the barriers to external finance that could otherwise have constrained small and therefore 'opaque' firms in the capital market. These results are compatible with the role of the house banking system in Germany as described by, for example, Deutsche Bundesbank (2000b).

5   Evaluating the channels and conclusion

Looking back at table 9.6, it seems that the income effect is important for the influence of monetary policy on financially constrained firms. We want to assess the importance of this 'income channel' for monetary policy and compare it with the strength of the interest rate channel. We assume a transitory increase in nominal capital market rates by 100 basis points, starting from a level of 7 per cent. The change is reversed after two years. It is important to note that this thought experiment does *not* attempt to simulate the effects of a monetary policy shock. First of all, the nominal long-term rate is not a monetary policy instrument, and second, an analysis of a monetary contraction would have to take account of interest rate-structure effects, effects on sales growth and effects on expected prices. A thorough analysis of this kind is provided in Angeloni *et al.* (chaper 24 in this volume). Here, we want to use the dynamic characteristics of our investment equation to reach a conclusion on the relative importance of the interest channel and the credit channel, restricting ourselves strictly to evaluating partial effects.

In order to look at the interest channel first, we need to evaluate the dependence of (log) user costs on nominal interest rates. For each firm, this semi-elasticity is computed using the definition of the user cost. Second, we use the coefficients of the preferred estimate, which is column (3) in table 9.7. Finally, dividing by the mean of the investment–capital ratio, we convert these deviations into relative deviations of gross investment from baseline.

The results are shown in figure 9.1. The assumed temporary increase in nominal interest rates translates into a temporary growth of user costs of 3.4 per cent. In the first year, this causes gross investment to fall by 3.90 per cent of baseline in the first year. In the second year, the difference from baseline is still 3.65 per cent. In the third year, then, the interest rates – and with them the user costs – return to their old level. This means *negative* growth of user costs. Investment rates rise above baseline for a

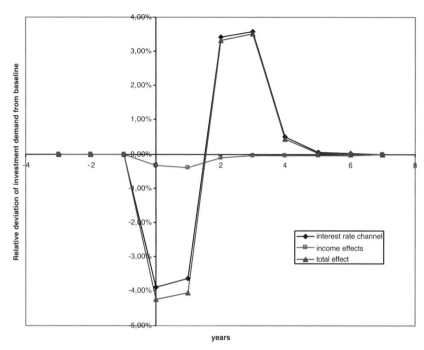

Figure 9.1 Relative strength of interest rate channel and income effects for German firms' investment, transitory increase of the nominal capital market rate from 7 per cent to 8 per cent for two years: Interest rate channel via user costs of capital, income effects via cash flow and total effect.

couple of periods. In the long run, however, the effect of a temporary interest rate hike via the interest rate channel is nil.

In order to evaluate the income effects of an interest rate hike, we will make the extreme assumption that the *entire* effect of cash flow, as shown in table 9.6, is due to financial constraints. It might as well be argued that only the difference between the effects for favourably and unfavourably rated firms is of relevance here. We further assume that the time to maturity of long-term debt (with a maturity of more than one year) is distributed evenly over the next five years. The effect on the cash-flow capital ratio depends on the corporate profit tax and the degree to which the capital stock is financed through debt. The latter is evaluated separately for each firm. Alongside with the interest channel, figure 9.1 shows the income effects of a change in interest rates. In the first period, investment decreases by 0.34 per cent of its baseline value, and by 0.41 per cent in the second year. After that, the effect peters out. The effects via the interest rate channel within the same two years are almost exactly ten times as high! At least the direct 'income effects' of increased interest payments do not seem to be of overwhelming quantitative importance. There may, however, be indirect effects on the creditworthiness of firms that serve to depress investment further.

With respect to investment, the interest rate channel seems to give a good account of monetary transmission in Germany. There is a sizeable UCE, and the effect of an interest rate change is dominated by substitution effects rather than by income effects that work through scarcer internal finance. There is a clear excess sensitivity with respect to internal finance for firms with a shaky credit standing, but at least on the margins size does not seem to create insupportable financial constraints.

It is natural to interpret these results in the light of the special features of the German financial markets, namely the house banking system as sketched in the introduction. However, one has to keep in mind that overcoming the barrier of information asymmetry in marginal financing by the house banking system is by no means cost-free. It will be interesting and important to study the consequences of the ongoing transformation of the financial markets in Germany and Europe for monetary transmission and investment behaviour.

10 Monetary policy and corporate investment in France

J. B. Chatelain and A. Tiomo

1 Introduction

In this chapter, which is a summary of Chatelain and Tiomo (2001), we complete the presentation and discussion of the estimated effects of monetary policy on French corporate investment reported in Chatelain *et al.* (chapter 7 this volume). We focus on the measurement of the impact of the cost of capital channel and the credit channel of monetary policy on individual firms' investment.

On the one hand, the available macroeconomic level evidence shows that the cost of capital channel of monetary policy has no or little effect on corporate investment in France. For instance, neither Amadeus (INSEE), nor Mosaïque (OFCE) nor the model developed by the Banque de France, three French forecasting models developed in the 1990s, include the cost of capital effect on investment. INSEE's Metric model adds a relative factor cost whose parameter is small and not significant (see Assouline *et al.*, 1998). Herbet (2001) published a recent estimation of macroeconomic investment and recognised its failure to incorporate interest rate or user cost effects.

On the other hand, some of the studies that have used sectoral-level data find large and significant investment elasticity to the user cost of capital. Using the BACH European database 'aggregated by size and sector', Mojon, Smets and Vermeulen (2001) obtained an elasticity for the user cost of -0.75. Duhautois (2001), who used data aggregated by sector and size from 1985 to 1996 on the basis of the INSEE BIC-BRN, found a real interest rate elasticity of -0.38 for the period 1985–90 and of -0.27 for the period 1991–6. However, Beaudu and Heckel (2001), who also used BACH, found a zero elasticity.

We would like to thank Steve Bond, Paul Butzen and Philip Vermeulen for their contributions to the previous versions of this chapter, as well as Ignazio Angeloni, Andrea Generale, Ignacio Hernando, Ulf von Kalckreuth, Anil Kashyap, Benoît Mojon and Daniele Terlizzese for their helpful comments.

Finally, Crépon and Gianella (2001), who used a sample of individual firm accounts (INSEE BIC database), obtained a user cost elasticity (UCE) of −0.63 for industry and of −0.35 for services for the two years 1990 and 1995.

These studies show that we obtain a high UCE if (1) the sample period is short and/or (2) the cash flow or the growth of sales is omitted from the regression and/or (3) WITHIN estimates are used instead of dynamic panel data estimates, as in the generalised method of moments (Arrelano and Bond, 1991) and/or (4) when defining the user cost, the marginal cost of debt is computed by a proxy at the firm level instead of an interest rate at the national level.

Turning to the credit channel, several studies have indirectly addressed its relevance in France by testing the existence of liquidity constraints on individual firms' investment. The main result is that financial variables (notably cash flow) affect the investment of groups of firms that are likely to be financially constrained (see Chatelain, 2002). Several studies have tested excess sensitivity of investment to liquidity variables, such as cash flow, the stock of cash, leverage and the coverage ratio (see the references in Bond *et al.*, 1997 and Hall, Mairesse and Mulkay, 1999, 2001).

Crépon and Rosenwald (2001) showed that the leverage parameter was lower for small firms during the years of sustained activity. This means that the agency premium was lower for these firms at that time. The neoclassical demand for capital estimated by Beaudu and Heckel (2001) led to greater investment cash-flow sensitivity for small firms during years of monetary restriction. In Duhautois (2001), leverage explains small firms' investment from 1985 to 1996 in a regression where sales growth is an omitted variable. Using Euler investment equations, where the cost of debt increases with leverage, Chatelain and Teurlai (2000) showed a cash flow misspecification (which is an indirect test of investment cash flow excess sensitivity) for firms with a low dividend/payout ratio or a low investment/retained earnings ratio. Finally, Chatelain and Teurlai (2001) found that small firms with a high variation of debt and a high share of capital financed by leasing displayed an investment leverage excess sensitivity during economic downturns.

The contribution of this chapter is first to allow a greater precision in the estimation of user cost effects by building firm-specific measures of the user cost of capital and allowing for heterogeneity in the UCE across firms. Second, we are able to isolate three groups of firms for which investment is more sensitive to cash flow: firms facing a high risk of bankruptcy, firms belonging to the capital goods sector (which are more sensitive to business cycle fluctuations) and firms making extensive use of trade credit, a potential substitute for short-term bank credit.

The remainder of this chapter is organised as follows. In section 2, we provide an overview of the institutional and macroeconomic background to French corporate investment and financing in the 1990s. Section 3 shows how we obtain a greater precision of the user cost and the financial variable effects on investment, after isolating the heterogeneity in investment demand across different types of firms as precisely as possible. Section 4 compares the effects of a change in monetary policy on investment via the user cost and credit. Section 5 sums up the main conclusions.

2   Institutional and macroeconomic background

Financial deregulation in France occurred in the mid-1980s. This led to considerable changes in financial markets. New financial instruments appeared on the scene, and new equity markets were set up ('second marché'). Quantitative credit regulation of banks by the central bank was stopped. All these reforms reduced both the control of the central bank on the quantity of credit supplied by banks and the dependence of non-financial corporations on banks.

The depressed economic activity of the first half of the 1990s put on hold the development of financial innovations that had benefited small and medium-sized firms (SMEs). The 1993 recession led to a high number of failures, a large amount of bad loans for banks – many of which were triggered by the collapse of the corporate real estate bubble. In addition, the implementation of the capital adequacy ratios further limited banks' willingness and ability to extend corporate loans. Finally, financial innovation that increased the scope of external finance instruments available to the corporate sector resumed after 1996. In particular, it is worth stressing that venture capital finance, promoted by government policies, grew sharply from 1996 to 2000.

We now briefly review the macroeconomic developments of the 1990s. First, the share of corporate profit in value added, which had increased since 1983, consolidated at historically high levels over the 1990s. This feature, combined with low demand owing to low-activity years and low investment, had a remarkable effect. The loss of sales affected aggregate profits far less than aggregate investment. Therefore, a high self-financing ratio prevailed over the period except for the years 1998–2000. For instance, the aggregate retained earnings–investment ratio exceeded 100 per cent for several years of the decade. A direct consequence of this flow of internal income and, perhaps, of 'high' real interest rates for some firms in the early 1990s, was a decrease in leverage, and, in particular, of the share of bank debt in total liabilities. Conversely, this meant an increase of the share of equity. Furthermore, the fall in interest rates from 1995 to 1999 and the decrease of debt led to a decrease in aggregate debt repayments, which in turn further increased aggregate retained earnings.

Second, we note relatively high aggregate investment in the first year (1990) and the last years (1998 and 1999) of the sample period our study, based on. Between these dates, low investment prevailed: low aggregate investment during the years 1991, 1992, 1996 and 1997, with slightly higher investment in 1994 and 1995, which followed an exceptionally low investment level during the 1993 recession. Monetary policy shifted from high nominal short-run interest rates from 1990 to 1993 to falling rates from 1994 to 1999. This fall was anticipated on the bonds market, so that there was an inversion of the yield curve from 1991 to 1993. The high return from short-run debt caused some firms to delay investment and to accumulate cash during this period.

3   Do some firms experience a tighter liquidity constraint?

This section complements the results presented in chapter 7[1] by investigating the reasons why the introduction of cash flow or cash stock (cash in hand) as an explanatory variable of investment drives the user cost elasticity down to zero.[2]

First, we define the user cost as a linear function of a microeconomic apparent interest rate, which includes an agency premium. According to the broad credit channel theory (see Gertler and Hubbard, 1988), this agency premium decreases with respect to collateral, which depends on expected profits, which in turn are very much dependent on expected sales, among other factors (for example, Oliner and Rudebush, 1996 state that the agency premium increases with the risk-free interest rate). Owing to the correlation between future profits and past profits, a potential explanation of the decline in the UCE, when cash flow is added to the regression, may lie in the joint correlation between cash flow, sales and the apparent interest rate (hence user cost). We may hence face a

---

[1] We use an autoregressive distributed lag (ADL) model written in levels instead of in first differences as in Chatelain et al. (see chapter 7 in this volume, which also presents our data). The major difference is that the ADL in levels and its related error correction model have a 'higher autoregressive component' than the ADL in first differences. Consequently, the ADL in levels has a tendency to lead to higher long-run estimates for other explanatory variables compared to the ADL in first differences. However, these differences are not always statistically significant in our sample (Chatelain and Tiomo, 2001).

[2] This result is robust to model and instrument selection using GMM including optimal upward-testing procedures (Andrews, 1999; Chatelain, 2001).

collinearity problem which is not solved by the generalised method of moments (GMM).

A second explanation relates to a heterogeneity bias and to the prevalence of self-financing during the 1990s for some firms observed in the descriptive statistics, at both the macroeconomic and microeconomic level: some firms may depend much more on cash flow than others. In that case, the presence of such firms in the sample may lead to biases in the estimated coefficient and the standard error of the UCE. This is what we investigate in this chapter.

We found three sample-split criteria such that the long-run investment cash-flow excess sensitivity *differential* coefficient across the two groups of firms is significantly different from zero. A first set of results on these sample splits is presented in table 10.1. Three sample splits, according to the level of trade credit in the firm's liabilities, the level of credit risk of the firm and its sector appeared relevant. Furthermore, in contrast with other countries, sample separation with respect to size, the share of intangibles and the dividend pay out ratio did not yield relevant statistical and economic results.

Estimates allowing for different coefficients across sub-samples defined along these three criteria are shown in table 10.2. First, we considered different coefficients for firms in the upper quartile with respect to the share of trade credit in total liabilities. Given the very high financial cost of trade credit, such firms are likely to experience difficulties in securing external finance. Investment cash flow sensitivity is 0.25 for firms with high trade credit–total liabilities ratios, whereas it is zero for other firms, which is consistent with the above interpretation. For all firms, sales growth elasticity is 0.43, but the UCE is not significantly different from zero.

Second, we introduced a dummy variable relative to the capital goods-producing sector, which is more sensitive to business cycle fluctuations than other sectors. Long-run investment cash-flow sensitivity is 0.42 for the capital goods sector, whereas it is only 0.07 for firms in other industrial sectors. Long-run sales growth elasticity is 0.29. It is also remarkable that the user cost is now significant for all firms with a long-run elasticity of -0.26.

Third, we separated firms on the basis of their Banque de France 'score', which is an evaluation of the credit risk of the firm. Risky firms, whose score function is below -0.3, present a long-run investment cash-flow sensitivity of 0.24, whereas it is only 0.02 for other firms. Sales growth elasticity is now 0.65. Again, as for the regression allowing for a capital goods sector 'heterogeneity', the UCE is significant for all firms with a long-run value of -0.21.

Table 10.1 *Descriptive statistics of various groups of French firms (average values, number of observations: 61,237)*

		No. of firms	Main variables						
			$I(t)/K(t-1)$	$\Delta \log S(t)$	$\Delta \log UC(t)$	$CF(t)/K(t-1)$	$\log S(t)$	$\log UC(t)$
Sectors	All sectors	**6946**	**0.122**	**0.0296**	**-0.009**	**0.33**	**8.83**	**-1.77**
	Food products	929	0.12	0.01	-0.014	0.27	9.3	-1.8
	Intermediate products	3371	0.11	0.04	-0.005	0.29	8.8	-1.7
	Equipment goods	1227	0.12	0.04	-0.008	0.37	8.7	-1.8
	Consumption goods	1286	0.15	0.01	-0.02	0.47	8.7	-1.8
	Car industry	133	0.12	0.03	-0.02	0.31	9.8	-1.8
Scoring function	No score	481	0.12	0.003	0.004	0.30	9.0	-1.8
	Risky Firms	1293	0.12	0.03	-0.008	0.30	8.6	-1.8
	Neutral Firms	1169	0.11	0.01	-0.007	0.28	8.5	-1.7
	Riskness Firms	4003	0.13	0.04	-0.01	0.36	8.9	-1.8
Trade credit	<Q3	5910	0.13	0.06	-0.003	0.33	8.8	-1.8
	>Q3	1736	0.12	0.02	-0.011	0.33	8.8	-1.8

Note: I/K: investment over capital; *S:* sales; *CF/K:* cash flow over capital; *UC:* user cost.

Table 10.2 *ADL model of the firms' investment with log(K) as endogenous variable, France*

	Coeff.	T-stats	Coeff.	T-stats	Coeff.	T-stats
Log $K(t-1)$	0.822	31.370	0.835	34.427	0.827	30.713
Log $K(t-2)$	−0.050	−5.670	−0.052	−6.206	−0.066	−5.339
Log $S(t)$	0.075	2.788	0.041	1.743	0.091	3.210
Log $S(t-1)$	0.023	0.826	0.022	0.944	0.064	2.697
Log $UC(t)$	−0.035	−1.306	−0.049	−3.019	−0.034	−1.824
Log $UC(t-1)$	0.003	0.226	−0.007	−0.777	−0.016	−1.707
$CF(t)/K(t-1)$	0.058	2.406	−0.004	−0.185	−0.015	−0.636
$CF(t-1)/K(t-2)$	−0.001	−0.033	0.018	2.025	0.019	2.147
Differential coeff. for:	*Low trade credit*		*Equipment goods*		*Risky firms*	
Log $K(t-1)$	0.003	0.195	0.026	0.901	−0.050	−0.689
Log $K(t-2)$	0.000	0.598	0.001	0.717	0.086	1.542
Log $S(t)$	0.004	0.919	0.004	0.411	0.014	0.401
Log $S(t-1)$	−0.004	−0.236	−0.008	−0.322	−0.046	−1.489
Log $UC(t)$	−0.011	−0.481	0.004	0.172	0.023	1.067
Log $UC(t-1)$	−0.002	−0.195	−0.001	−0.067	0.007	0.425
$CF(t)/K(t-1)$	−0.083	−3.413	0.082	3.260	0.077	2.328
$CF(t-1)/K(t-2)$	0.026	1.392	−0.014	−0.903	−0.034	−2.114
Long-term eff. sales	0.43*		0.29*		0.65*	
Long-term eff. user cost	−0.14		−0.26*		−0.21*	
Long-term eff. cash flow	0.25*		0.07*		0.02*	
Differential coeff. for:	*Low trade credit*		*Equipment goods*		*Risky firms*	
Long-term eff. sales	0.01		0.02		−0.04	
Long-term eff. user cost	−0.06		−0.02		0.11	
Long-term eff. cash flow	−0.25*		0.36*		0.22*	
AR2	−2.266	p = 0.023	−2.077	p = 0.038	−1.993	p = 0.046
Sargan	288.22	p = 0.088	275.48	p = 0.204	300.91	p = 0.031

Note: Instruments used in the regressions are all explanatory variables lagged 2 to 5.

Finally, we report the results obtained by using the risky firm dummies when the cash stock replaces the cash flow. For some authors, investment cash-flow excess sensitivities are not valid measures of the financing constraint (see Kaplan and Zingales, 1997). Like the cash flow, the stock of cash held by the firm is an indicator of the firm's ability to shield future investment from an expected tightening of borrowing conditions. However, the stock of cash may be less affected by the difficulty in interpreting investment cash-flow sensitivity, as liquidity is less likely to be a proxy of expectations of future profits. The use of the stock of cash also alleviates risks of multi-collinearity in the estimation of the investment equation because it is less correlated with sales than cash flow.

Table 10.3 *ADL model of the firms' investment with log(K)*
as endogenous variable and cash stock as the liquidity
'constraint' variable, France

	Coeff.	T-stats
	Low risk firms	
Log $K(t-1)$	0.785	36.2
Log $K(t-2)$	−0.053	−4.4
Log $S(t)$	0.094	3.79
Log $S(t-1)$	0.106	4.80
Log $UC(t)$	−0.053	−3.01
Log $UC(t-1)$	−0.011	−1.12
Cash$(t)/K(t-1)$	−0.007	−0.42
Cash$(t-1)/K(t-2)$	0.041	2.93
Differential coeff. for:	*High risk firms*	
Log $K(t-1)$	−0.033	−0.54
Log $K(t-2)$	0.055	1.10
Log $S(t)$	0.029	1.02
Log $S(t-1)$	−0.091	−3.38
Log $UC(t)$	0.006	0.31
Log $UC(t-1)$	0.011	0.67
Cash$(t)/K(t-1)$	0.022	1.02
Cash$(t-1)/K(t-2)$	−0.021	−1.13
	Low risk firms	
Long-term eff. sales	0.743*	
Long-term eff. user cost	−0.238*	
Long-term eff. cash stock	0.125*	
Differential coeff. for:	*High risk firms*	
Long-term eff. sales	−0.339*	
Long-term eff. user cost	n.s.	
Long-term eff. cash Stock	n.s.	
AR2	−1.694	p = 0.090
Sargan	292.01	p = 0.066

Note: Instruments used in the regressions are all explanatory variables
lagged 2 to 5 (n.s.: not significant).

When the stock of cash replaces the cash flow in the investment regression and when dummy variables relative to credit risk are added to
the regression, the UCE also becomes significant, reaching a nearly unchanged estimate of −0.23 (see table 10.3). This is an additional robustness check for the user cost elasticity. The previous year's cash stock is
a significant determinant of current investment, as a proportion of the

Table 10.4 *Contemporaneous elasticity of firms' investment with respect to market interest rate through user cost, France*

T	-0.16
$T + 1$	-0.23
$T + 2$	-0.20
$T + 3$	-0.18

previous year's cash may finance this year's investment. However, unlike investment cash-flow excess sensitivity, investment cash-stock excess sensitivity is not significant for high risk firms. At the same time, firms' elasticity of investment with respect to sales is significantly lower than that of other firms. This can either mean that the investment of risky firms reacts much less to sales than that of other firms, or that the test of the financial constraints in the investment equation is misspecified.

4   Monetary policy and investment

The final step in our analysis is to connect investment to monetary policy actions. We do so starting from what we see as our most sensible results, i.e. the regression with the risk dummy variable. Following, Chatelain *et al.* (chapter 7 in this volume), we focus on the time pattern and the lags in the reaction of investment to monetary policy shocks. We first consider the effect on investment of a permanent 1 per cent change in the market interest rate through the user cost (table 10.4). The elasticity is now different from zero for France, but France still remains the country where the elasticity of investment with respect to the market interest rate is the lowest in the second year (Spain: -0.31; Germany: -0.38; Italy: -0.41; see table 7.11 in Chatelain *et al.* (chapter 7 in this volume)).

Table 10.5 provides the yearly elasticity of *contemporaneous* investment with respect to cash flow for the group of risky firms (which represents 19 per cent of firms in our sample) and for the other group. In the case of risky firms, the elasticity of investment with respect to cash flow in France follows a similar path to that in Italy and Spain. Low risk French firms, in contrast, are quite similar to German ones (see table 7.3).

We then consider the effect of a permanent change in the market interest rate on cash flow. The higher firms' interest payments, the lower their cash flow, *ceteris paribus*. Table 10.6 presents the effect on the growth rate of the capital stock (or investment) of a transitory 1 per cent increase in

Table 10.5 *Contemporaneous elasticity of investment with respect to cash flow, France*

	Not risky (81%) – Risky (19%)	
T	0.00	0.19
$T+1$	0.06	0.33
$T+2$	0.11	0.44
$T+3$	0.16	0.53

Table 10.6 *Elasticity of firms' investment with respect to market interest rate through cash flow, France*

	Not risky (81%) – Risky (19%)	
T	0.00	−0.05
$T+1$	−0.02	−0.09
$T+2$	−0.03	−0.12
$T+3$	−0.04	−0.15

the interest rate through the cash flow. Again, the pattern for less risky French firms is close to the German ones, while that for risky French firms is close to the Italian or Spanish patterns (cf. table 7.10). These effects are, in general, relatively small in all countries. However, there is also an indirect effect of the market interest rate on sales and hence on cash flow, which is not evaluated here.

5   Conclusion

We reach two major conclusions. First, by allowing heterogeneity across some groups of firms, we isolate more precisely firms sensitive to cash flow and we improve the precision of the results presented in chapter 7 for France. *The user cost elasticity with respect to investment is at the most 0.26 in absolute terms for all the firms of our sample.* Unlike the recent papers which assess user cost effects at the firm level in France, this result is obtained using GMM estimates, which are the only appropriate estimates for dynamic panel data. Our results thus confirm the direct effect of the interest rate channel on investment, operating through the cost of capital.

Second, we find three groups of firms for which investment is more sensitive to cash flow: firms facing a high risk of bankruptcy, firms belonging to the capital goods sector (which are more sensitive to business cycle fluctuations) and firms making extensive use of trade credit, a potential substitute for short-term bank credit. *The rather high investment cash flow sensitivity of these firms (between 0.24 and 0.42), which represents about 20 per cent of our sample, confirms the existence of a broad credit channel operating through corporate investment in France.* For other firms, investment cash-flow sensitivity is close to zero.

11 Monetary policy and firms' investment in Italy

E. Gaiotti and A. Generale

1 Introduction

In this chapter, we study the effects of monetary policy on Italian firms' investment. A broader analysis is in Gaiotti and Generale (2001, 2002).

The available evidence on the effect of monetary policy on investment in Italy is mostly at the macroeconomic level (Banca d'Italia, 1986), and it indicates that a 1 percentage point increase in the interest rate has a negative impact on non-residential investment of the order of 2–3 percentage points each year (Nicoletti Altimari *et al.*, 1995).

At firm level, the empirical literature is extensive, but it only indirectly addresses the effects of monetary policy. The main result is that financial variables (notably, cash flow) affect investment, particularly for small firms (Bianco, 1997; Franzosi, 1999; Galeotti, Schiantarelli and Jaramillo, 1994; Rondi, Sembenelli and Zanetti, 1994; Schiantarelli and Sembenelli, 2000); this is consistent with the existence of a broad credit channel of monetary transmission. Rondi *et al.* (1998), using time-series data for large and small firms, also find that following a tightening episode, small firms report a steeper fall in sales.[1] These results, however, at most give a qualitative hint of monetary policy's impact on different classes of firms.

The contribution of this chapter is to offer a more precise assessment of these effects. The improved precision comes from explicitly modelling the different channels through which monetary policy can affect investment and estimating the channels using panel data on firms' investment.

We thank Stefania De Mitri for invaluable research assistance and Ulf von Kalckreuth and Plutarchos Sakellaris for discussions of previous versions of this chapter. We are also indebted to Jean Bernard Chatelain, Anil Kashyap, Libero Monteforte, Alessandra Staderini, Daniele Terlizzese and Philip Vermeulen for helpful comments.

[1] Also see Dedola and Lippi (2000), who explain the cross-industry differences in policy transmission in terms of financial characteristics of each sector, and Bagliano and Sembenelli (2001), who find a significant effect of leverage on inventory behaviour of Italian, French and British firms (particularly young and small ones) in the recession of the early 1990s. See also Guiso *et al.* (1999).

One channel is through the user cost of capital. The firm-specific user cost that we construct follows Chirinko, Fazzari and Meyer (1999), but contrary to most prior research it also includes an interest rate that is firm-specific. The tax effects, together with the interest rate variation, as well as the variation in depreciation rates and prices of capital goods, permit us tightly to estimate the investment elasticity to the user cost. We also allow for monetary effects to operate through financial variables (cash flow, liquidity) and through sales.[2] We then test whether the financial effects are larger for groups of firms that can be thought of as being more subject to financial constraints. Finally, we report the relative sizes of the effects coming through sales, the user cost and financial variables.

The remainder of this chapter is organized as follows. In section 2 we review the exclusive characteristics of our data on Italian firms. We then briefly describe the financial structure of Italian firms according to their size and report the features of the Italian business cycle for the sample period used in our estimation. Section 3 shows the baseline estimates of the investment equation. Section 4 presents the evidence on heterogeneity in investment demand across different types of firms. Section 5 apportions the effects of a change in monetary policy to the different channels mentioned above. Section 6 summarises the main conclusions.

2   Firm-level data in Italy

Italy is an interesting country to study, given the predominance of small and medium-sized enterprises (SMEs) and the distinguishing characteristics of firms' financial structure. As regards size, in the 1990s 95 per cent of the firms had fewer than ten employees and their share over total employment was 47 per cent as opposed to slightly more than 20 per cent in Germany and France. As regards the financial structure, the share of debt in firms' liabilities is higher than in the euro area (30 per cent as opposed to 25 per cent, according to financial accounts for 2000), and most of debt is bank loans (about 70 per cent in 2000). Compared with other industrial countries, a large portion of loans is short term (60 per cent in 2000).

Moreover, the large variability of the tax policy environment in Italy since the 1980s helps properly to measure the cost of capital. The tax rate on profits varied through time and across regions; the tax deductibility of depreciation charges and investment tax credit were also differentiated by

---

[2] See Bernanke, Gertler and Gilchrist (1996). See chapter 7 in this volume for a survey of the literature on the credit channel of monetary transmission.

region or sector; the provisions for tax reduction for reinvested earnings depend on firms' characteristics.[3] We combine these institutional features with a rich data set including a large number of Italian firms, which permits a detailed reconstruction of tax factors in determining the user cost of capital, as well as of firm-specific *ex post* interest rates.

The firms studied are a sub-set of the non-financial firms included in the Italian Company Accounts Data Service (*Centrale dei Bilanci*). The full data set covers balance sheets and income statements for some 35,000 non-financial firms from 1982 to 1999, for a total of 590,000 observations. The financial statements are collected by a consortium of banks; firms enter by borrowing from one of the banks in the consortium, but the coverage is broadly in line with the overall economy. Besides the standard financial variables, the database contains balance sheet items, as well as information on firms' characteristics (year of foundation, location, type of organization and ownership status, group membership), employment, flow of funds and a firm's credit score, computed by the *Centrale dei Bilanci*. The sample has much broader coverage than most data sets used in economic research, since it includes a large number of unlisted companies and many very small firms.[4] This sample has been used for many and diverse applications.[5] Since the data set is used by banks as one of their tools to analyse firms' outlook and the consistency of the data is checked by them, the quality of information is high. Moreover, with respect to the sample of Italian firms maintained by the Chambers of Commerce (CERVED), that has a broader coverage in terms of number of firms, the Company Accounts Data Service covers a longer time period (from 1982, as opposed to from 1993 for CERVED) and has much more

[3] For the effects of tax reforms on corporate financial policy, see Staderini (2001). For a complete description of the methodology used to calculate the user cost of capital for Italian firms, see De Mitri, Marchetti and Staderini (1998) and Gaiotti and Generale (2001).

[4] As discussed by Guiso *et al.* (1999), the sample may be biased towards firms with multiple banking relationships, which are in turn more likely to be large firms. On the basis of the 1996 census, the total database of the Company Accounts Data Service accounted for approximately 46 per cent of total value added of the economy. Firms in the database accounted for 13.9 per cent of the total value added of all firms with up to 49 employees, 80 per cent of that of firms with between 50 and 199 employees, 80.2 per cent of that of firms with between 200 and 499 employees and 87 per cent of that of firms with more than 499 employees.

[5] Studies using this data set are Pagano, Panetta and Zingales (1998), on the motives for firms going public, Guiso and Parigi (1999) on investment and uncertainty, Pozzolo and Nucci (2001) on exchange rate movements and investment, Marchetti and Nucci (2001) on technology shocks and sticky prices, Guiso, Sapienza and Zingales (2002) on differences in local financial development and Guiso, Pistaferri and Schivardi (2001) on insurance mechanisms within the firm.

Table 11.1 *Financial structure of Italian firms*

	Manufacturing		Services		
	Small	Large	Small	Large	All firms
(as % of total liabilities)					
Loans of credit institutions	25.26	19.02	23.42	14.09	19.74
With maturity < 1 year	18.76	11.77	17.42	6.07	12.69
With maturity > 1 year	6.50	7.25	6.00	8.02	7.05
Debt securities	1.20	1.06	0.84	3.87	1.74
Trade debt	27.47	22.32	33.21	18.17	24.69
Equity and reserves	25.56	32.27	20.04	30.12	27.09
(as % of total assets)					
Gross investment	5.23	5.25	3.88	7.73	5.38
Cash flow	7.20	9.49	5.23	12.49	8.53
Interest and similar charges	2.81	2.33	2.80	2.02	2.53
Leverage	*57.0*	*47.1*	*62.5*	*49.2*	*53.5*

Source: Company Accounts Data Service (*Centrale dei Bilanci*). Averages weighted with total assets.

detailed breakdowns. On the other hand firms that are not creditworthy are under-represented in the *Centrale dei Bilanci*.

Summary statistics for the full sample are shown in table 11.1. There is substantial heterogeneity among firms with respect to size and small and large firms differ in several key dimensions. Small firms are more leveraged, more dependent on banks and on short-term debt, and have a smaller cash flow and heavier interest burden. In 1997–8, for small firms, leverage was 57 per cent in the manufacturing sector and 62 per cent in services and commerce, as opposed to 47 and 49 per cent respectively, for large firms. Bank loans were around 25 per cent of total liabilities, as opposed to between 14 and 19 per cent for large firms; the proportion of short-term debt was also higher (74 per cent of total bank debt, compared with about 50 per cent for large firms). Small firms also featured larger interest expense as a ratio of total assets and a lower cash-flow/capital ratio.

Our estimates are based on a sub-sample, composed of 7,026 firms and 43,912 annual observations. Most of the sub-setting occurred because we had to drop firms that were missing the information needed to construct the tax adjustment for the user cost; the remaining loss is due to the fact that the dependent variable is obtained as a ratio between investment and lagged capital, to outliers' deletion, and because of requiring firms to be continuously present for at least six years, so that enough lags were present to capture the dynamics and properly to instrument.[6]

A complete definition of the firm-specific variables used in the regression is illustrated in detail in Chatelain *et al.* (chapter 7 in this volume) and in Gaiotti and Generale (2001). As mentioned, the user cost of capital is constructed at the firm level. It is based on sector-specific depreciation rates and prices of output, on firm-specific interest rates and on a mix of tax effects. In particular, the tax rate on profits is defined at the economy-wide level, with some regional differentiation, while the tax deductibility of depreciation charges is related to a firm's industry, and the investment tax credit created by the Tremonti Law (1994–6) differs by firm.

The firm-specific interest rate is the ratio of interest expense to financial debt. Although this is an average interest rate, for most Italian firms it should be very close to the marginal borrowing rate because most debt is either short term (about 60 per cent of total) or floating rate.[7]

The full sample covers the period 1982–99, when the Italian economy experienced *three recessions* and *three full monetary policy cycles*. The conventional dating of Italian recessions are 1980:3–1983:3, 1992:3–1993:7 and 1995:11–1996:11 (see Altissimo, Marchetti and Oneto, 2000), while Gaiotti (1999) reviews the conduct of Italian monetary policy and notes that the Banca d'Italia tightened policy in 1986–7, 1992 and 1994–5. An anecdotal look at these episodes indicates that, after a tightening, cash flow and investment decreased, although with varying lags; the decrease was usually more pronounced for small firms.

3   Baseline regression results

Table 11.2 presents the estimates of our version of the baseline regression equation used in this book: the investment–capital ratio is regressed on the change in sales, on the change in the user cost and on a financial variable (for details, see either Chatelain *et al.*, chapter 7 in this volume or Gaiotti and Generale, 2001). Two financial variables (scaled relative to capital) are considered. *Cash flow* is the one traditionally employed in the empirical literature. This variable has also the advantage of fitting easily

---

[6] About 34 per cent of omitted observations is due to the lack of information on the user cost; 30 per cent is due to the omission of the first year for each firm, in order to construct the ratio between investment and lagged capital; 28 per cent is due to trimming for outliers, leaving out six lags for instruments and requiring firms to be present for at least six years; the remaining portion is attributable to discarding the first two years of the sample in order to construct the stock of capital.

[7] In the appendix to Gaiotti and Generale (2001), we show that in our sample the behaviour of firms' interest expense is consistent with a rather high elasticity of the firm-specific debt rate to the policy interest rate, between 0.6 and 0.8.

Table 11.2 *Investment equations and liquidity constraints, Italy*

Dependent variable: $I(t)/K(t-1)$
Sample: 1989–99 – 7026 firms – 43,912 obs.

	GMM(1) (1)	Fixed effect (2)	GMM(2) (3)	Fixed effect (4)
$I_{(t-1)}/K_{(t-2)}$	0.133**	−0.019**	0.162**	−0.014
	(0.027)	(0.008)	0.013	0.008
$I_{(t-2)}/K_{(t-3)}$	−0.009	−0.096**	0.014	−0.092**
	(0.019)	(0.006)	0.008	0.006
$I_{(t-3)}/K_{(t-4)}$	−0.006	−0.078**	0.013*	−0.076**
	(0.015)	(0.007)	0.006	0.006
$\Delta s_{(t)}$	0.018	0.040**	0.036	0.054**
	(0.035)	(0.004)	0.033	0.004
$\Delta s_{(t-1)}$	0.044**	0.040**	0.045**	0.055**
	(0.011)	(0.004)	0.006	0.004
$\Delta s_{(t-2)}$	0.037**	0.030**	0.0298**	0.046**
	(0.011)	(0.004)	0.005	0.004
$\Delta s_{(t-3)}$	0.016**	0.024**	0.0179**	0.038**
	(0.005)	(0.003)	0.005	0.004
$\Delta uc_{(t)}$	−0.104**	−0.124**	−0.124**	−0.124**
	(0.026)	(0.004)	0.037	0.004
$\Delta uc_{(t-1)}$	−0.057*	−0.081**	−0.06*	−0.08**
	(0.022)	(0.004)	0.03	0.004
$\Delta uc_{(t-2)}$	−0.054*	−0.051**	−0.036	−0.047**
	(0.022)	(0.004)	0.026	0.004
$\Delta uc_{(t-3)}$	−0.012	−0.029**	−0.007	−0.026**
	(0.008)	(0.003)	0.010	0.003
$CF(t)/K(t-1)$	0.273**	0.104**		
	(0.041)	(0.011)		
$CF(t-1)/K(t-2)$	−0.006	0.041**		
	(0.038)	(0.009)		
$CF(t-2)/K(t-3)$	−0.004	0.035**		
	(0.043)	(0.009)		
$CF(t-3)/K(t-4)$	0.103*	0.034**		
	(0.052)	(0.008)		
$Liq(t)/K(t-1)$			0.11**	0.025**
			0.032	0.006
$Liq(t-1)/K(t-2)$			−0.011	0.032**
			0.018	0.006
$Liq(t-2)/K(t-3)$			−0.006	0.014*
			0.007	0.006
$Liq(t-3)/K(t-4)$			0.006	0.028**
			0.007	0.006

Table 11.2 (cont.)

	GMM(1) (1)	Fixed effect (2)	GMM(2) (3)	Fixed effect (4)
m_2	−0.104	−0.074	−0.668	−0.225
	($p = 0.917$)	($p = 0.941$)	($p = 0.504$)	($p = 0.822$)
Sargan test	142.0($p = .066$)		104.9($p = 0.228$)	
Total effect of sales	0.130**	0.112**	0.159**	0.163**
	(0.050)	(0.010)	(0.051)	(0.009)
Total effect of	−0.26**	−0.24**	−0.28**	−0.23**
user cost	(0.077)	(0.012)	(0.110)	(0.012)

Notes: ** Significant at the 1% level; * significant at the 5% level.
I/K: investment over lagged capital at replacement value; uc: log of the user cost; s: log of sales; CF/K: cash flow over capital; Liq/K: liquidity over capital; k: log of capital. m_2 is the test of second-order autocorrelation (p-value in parenthesis); Sargan is the test of over-identifying restrictions (p-value in parenthesis). (1) Instruments: I/K ($t-2$ to $t-9$); $\Delta s(t-2$ to $t-4$); $\Delta uc(t-4$); CF/K ($t-2$); control for time and industry dummies. (2) Instruments: I/K ($t-2$ to $t-4$); $\Delta s(t-2$ to $t-4$); Δuc ($t-4$); Liq/K ($t-2$ to $t-4$); control for time dummies.

in our monetary policy exercise in section 4. However, its interpretation is subject to well-known problems.[8] The stock of a *firm's liquidity* (cash in hand and bank accounts), conceptually, plays the same role as the cash flow, as it is an indicator of the firm's ability to shield investment from tightened borrowing conditions. The stock of liquid assets may be less affected by the difficulties in interpreting the sign of the cash flow coefficient, as liquidity is less likely to be a proxy of expectations of high future activity.[9]

We report results obtained using estimation via both OLS fixed effect and GMM first differences.[10] All the estimates feature a statistically significantly negative effect of changes of the user cost on the investment

[8] See Kaplan and Zingales (1997, 2000).
[9] According to the results of Gilchrist and Himmelberg (1998) on a panel of US firms, the present value of future cash flows is highly correlated with the present value of future marginal products of capital (thus giving rise to difficulties in interpreting its economic meaning) while this is not the case when stock measures of the financial status are used. In our sample the correlation between lagged cash flow and sales is around 0.17, whereas it is only 0.03 between lagged liquidity and sales.
[10] GMM first differences eliminates the firm-specific effects by differencing the equations, and then uses instruments, since differencing induces serial correlation in the residuals, which would yield inconsistent estimates when the lagged dependent is included (Bond et al., 1997).

over capital ratio (with a long-run elasticity around -0.25).[11] There are two ways to view these estimates of the elasticity of investment with respect to the user cost. One on the hand, they are relatively precise and consistently statistically negative. This is unusual in this literature. For instance, the finding of Rondi *et al.* (1998) of no significant role for the interest rate in a fixed investment equation estimated separately for small and large firms is representative of past studies; although Rosolia and Torrini (2001) find estimates that are similar to ours. On the other hand, the low elasticity we find[12] contrasts with the assumption of a unit elasticity, common in the Italian macro modelling literature (as in Banca d'Italia, 1986 and in subsequent work).

It is worth discussing the features of our data set which drive the finding of a significant user cost elasticity (UCE). Fiscal factors are the main, but not the only, source of variability in the measure of the cost of capital in our sample. When fiscal data are not used in the construction of the user cost, its overall variance decreases by about 50 per cent. The tax component induces a higher variation of the user cost at both the aggregate and the firm-specific level.[13]

The role played by fiscal information in capturing the effect of the cost of capital can be gauged by estimating the investment equation using as an explanatory variable a measure of the user cost which does not take fiscal factors into account. The user cost elasticity remains significant, but falls from -0.25 to about -0.15.

The long-run effect of changes in sales is of the order of 0.15. This estimate is much lower than the unit elasticity that characterises aggregate models of investment in Italy (Banca d'Italia, 1986; Parigi and Siviero, 2000). By contrast, a low elasticity to sales is consistent with previous estimates based on Italian panel data, as in Schiantarelli and Sembenelli (2000).

---

[11] The long-run elasticity is defined as the sum of the coefficients on the lags of the user cost, divided by the coefficient on the lagged dependent variables.

[12] The small effect of the user cost on investment that emerges from the estimation of simple accelerator models could be due to non-linearities in the adjustment of firms' investment spending stemming from investment irreversibility (Abel and Eberly, 1996; Barnett and Sakellaris, 1998). However, Rosolia and Torrini (2001) also check the different reaction to the user cost, distinguishing periods in which demand expands from those in which it contracts. They find that investment reaction to the user cost is stronger in expansionary periods, but the differences found with respect to the baseline model (that does not take into account these non-linearities) is rather limited.

[13] The user cost calculated taking into account the tax component shows a within-firm standard deviation of 0.027 as opposed to 0.018 when the user cost definition abstracts from the fiscal treatment. These values are; respectively, 0.025 and 0.019 when the between standard deviation is considered.

Table 11.3 *Investment equations and sample splits, Italy*

Dependent variable: $I(t)/K(t-1)$
Sample: 1989–99 – 7,026 firms – 43,912 obs.

	Large firms (a) (1)	Small firms (b) (2)	((b) − (a)) (3)	Low share of intangible assets (c) (4)	High share of intangible assets (d) (5)	((d) − (c))
$I_{(t-1)}/K_{(t-2)}$	0.133** (0.028)	0.090** (0.041)	−0.043 (0.050)	0.117** (0.029)	0.069** (0.031)	−0.048 (0.043)
$I_{(t-2)}/K_{(t-3)}$	0.004 (0.019)	−0.045 (0.029)	−0.049 (0.034)	−0.008 (0.021)	−0.044* (0.022)	−0.036 (0.030)
$I_{(t-3)}/K_{(t-4)}$	−0.016 (0.013)	−0.026 (0.021)	−0.010 (0.024)	−0.012 (0.018)	−0.029 (0.015)	−0.017 (0.024)
$\Delta s_{(t)}$	−0.009 (0.034)	0.030 (0.042)	0.039 (0.054)	0.086** (0.029)	0.053 (0.038)	−0.033 (0.049)
$\Delta s_{(t-1)}$	0.069** (0.013)	0.053** (0.016)	−0.016 (0.020)	0.056** (0.012)	0.069** (0.013)	0.013 (0.018)
$\Delta s_{(t-2)}$	0.018 (0.013)	0.052** (0.014)	0.034 (0.018)	0.048** (0.011)	0.048** (0.013)	0.000 (0.017)
$\Delta s_{(t-3)}$	0.009 (0.008)	0.015** (0.007)	0.006 (0.010)	0.024** (0.006)	0.005 (0.007)	−0.019* (0.009)
$\Delta uc_{(t)}$	−0.125** (0.027)	−0.153** (0.043)	−0.028 (0.051)	−0.124** (0.030)	−0.114** (0.035)	0.010 (0.047)
$\Delta uc_{(t-1)}$	−0.060** (0.022)	−0.103** (0.039)	−0.043 (0.044)	−0.063** (0.028)	−0.093** (0.027)	−0.030 (0.039)
$\Delta uc_{(t-2)}$	−0.016 (0.019)	−0.105** (0.036)	−0.089* (0.041)	−0.036 (0.026)	−0.089** (0.027)	−0.053 (0.038)

	(1)	(2)	(3)	(4)	(5)	(6)
$\Delta uc_{(t-3)}$	0.002	-0.033*	-0.035*	-0.003	-0.025*	-0.022
	(0.008)	(0.013)	(0.015)	(0.010)	(0.011)	(0.015)
$CF(t)/K(t-1)$	0.103*	0.245**	0.142*	0.119*	0.264**	0.145*
	(0.047)	(0.050)	(0.069)	(0.054)	(0.042)	(0.060)
$CF(t-1)/K(t-2)$	0.047	0.038	-0.009	0.019	0.062	0.043
	(0.029)	(0.050)	(0.058)	(0.034)	(0.042)	(0.050)
$CF(t-2)/K(t-3)$	0.055	0.012	-0.043	-0.030	0.069	0.099
	(0.043)	(0.053)	(0.068)	(0.001)	(0.051)	(0.065)
$CF(t-3)/K(t-4)$	0.075	0.178*	0.103	0.102	0.196**	0.094
	(0.043)	(0.077)	(0.087)	(0.058)	(0.055)	(0.082)
m_2	0.953 ($p=0.341$)			-0.127 ($p=0.899$)		
Sargan test	177.9 ($p=0.037$)			263.3 ($p=0.046$)		
Total effect of sales	0.099	0.153*	0.054	0.237**	0.174*	-0.063
	(0.053)	(0.077)	(0.077)	(0.046)	(0.067)	(0.067)
Total effect of the user cost	-0.226**	-0.402**	-0.175	-0.250**	-0.320**	-0.069
	(0.076)	(0.134)	(0.134)	(0.088)	(0.088)	(0.125)

Notes: Standard errors in parentheses. ** significant at the 1%, level; significant at the 5% level. I/K : investment over lagged capital at replacement value; uc: log of the user cost; s: log of sales; CF/K: cash flow over capital; m_2 is the test of second-order autocorrelation (p-value in parenthesis); *Sargan* is the test of over-identifying restrictions (p-value in parenthesis). GMM estimation. Instruments: $\Delta s(t-2$ to $t-4)$; Δuc $(t-4)$; CF/K $(t-2)$; control for time dummies (common to all regressions); $I/K(t-2$ to $t-4)$ (for large/small); $I/K(t-2$ to $t-9)$ (high/low intangibles).

Cash flow significantly enters the equation, with the expected positive sign. When liquidity is used instead, (see columns (3) and (4) of table 11.2) the sign and statistical significance of the various coefficients is not greatly affected; the degree of a firm's liquidity does affect investment with a positive sign. A notable consequence of replacing the cash flow with liquidity is that the elasticity to sales is now slightly larger and more precisely estimated than before. It is also notable that financial constraints still matter in determining investment demand, when we explicitly include the user cost in the regression (see the discussion in Chatelain *et al.* (chapter 7 in this volume).

4   Do some firms experience a tighter liquidity constraint?

While the statistical significance of the financial variable may point to the existence of a broad credit channel, a proper test of the latter involves assessing whether the effect of cash flow on investment is larger for firms that are *a priori* thought to be more financially constrained. To this end, in table 11.3, we separately consider *small firms* (which we define as firms with fewer than 200 employees), as well as *firms with a high proportion of intangible assets on their balance sheet* (firms whose ratio of intangible assets to total assets is higher than 75 per cent of the distribution in at least one year). The former are traditionally considered more subject to liquidity constraints and information asymmetries. The latter are thought to be operating in activities where intangible capital is more important, making them more subject to information asymmetries (Giannetti, 2000).[14]

For each of the regressions, column (3) reports the difference between the coefficient for firms in the second and in the first sub-group. The bottom panel of each table also reports the total effects of the user cost and sales.

Overall, the coefficients on the user cost and sales are relatively robust to the sample split. The impact of the *cash flow* on investment, as expected, is significantly stronger for firms facing more information asymmetries, both small firms and firms with intangible assets. As mentioned in the introduction, the finding that small firms are more sensitive to cash flow is common to several papers on investment in Italy, namely, Bianco (1997), Franzosi (1999), Galeotti, Schiantarelli and Jaramillo

---

[14] Intangible assets include R&D expenditures, patents, development and advertising costs and similar items recorded on the assets side. Firms recorded in this group have an average ratio of intangible assets to total assets ten times greater than that for the other firms (3 per cent against 0.3 per cent). This corresponds to a ratio of intangible assets to the sum of intangible assets and fixed assets equal to 12.4 per cent for this group, against 3 per cent for the others.

(1994), Rondi, Sembenelli and Zanetti (1994), Schiantarelli and Sembenelli (2000).

The results obtained using liquidity instead of cash flow also indicate a higher total elasticity of investment to liquidity for firms with intangible assets. In contrast, no statistically significant difference in this coefficient can be detected for small firms.

5   Monetary policy and investment

The final step in our analysis is to connect monetary policy actions to investment. To do this we model the impact of monetary policy on the determinants of investment. Having modelled these linkages we can then compare the importance of the various channels through which monetary policy operates (a similar exercise is performed by Fazzari, 1993). Contrary to the approach followed in Chatelain *et al.* (chapter 7 in this volume), our simulation approach hinges on macroeconomic evidence on the links between monetary policy and investment determinants that we obtain from the quarterly model of the Italian economy (Banca d'Italia, 1986). We are able to exploit the fact that the quarterly model includes macroeconomic variables that closely correspond to the user cost, cash-flow and sales variables that appear in the investment equations (7)–(9) in chapter 7 in this volume. Therefore, our results provide independent, complementary evidence to that reported in Chatelain *et al.* (chapter 7 in this volume).

The top panel of table 11.4 is obtained from a simulation of the quarterly model of the Italian economy. It shows that a temporary increase in the nominal interest rate by 1 percentage point generates a 3 per cent increase in the user cost of capital over the same period.[15] Firms' cash flow (as a proportion of the stock of capital) deteriorates by about 3.4 per cent, owing to the effect of higher interest rates on both value added and interest expense.[16] Value added (the closest macroeconomic equivalent to the 'sales' variable in section 4) decreases by about 0.7 per cent.

We ran a simulation combining the macro effects of monetary policy on investment determinants and the micro investment equations previously estimated. The exercise is based on a 1 per cent temporary increase

---

[15] Considering that the average interest rate in the sample period was about 10 per cent, this corresponds to an elasticity of about 0.3; such a small elasticity depends on the assumption that long-term interest rates are determined by the expectation theory. Thus, a temporary shock to the short-term rate has only a limited effect on long-term rates.

[16] In Banca d'Italia (1986), cash flow (variable *autimpd*) is defined as value added, less labour income, less direct taxes, less interest expense. This definition is conceptually equivalent to the one we used for our data set.

Table 11.4 *Effects of a temporary increase in policy rates, Italy*

Effect of a temporary increase in policy rates on investment determinants[a], (per cent)

	Resulting change in:		
	User cost (%)	Value added (%)	Cash flow/K (%)
	3.2%	−0.7%	−3.4%

Effect of a temporary increase in policy rates on investment, [b] (in the second year; percentage points)

	Effect due to:			
	Total effect	User cost	Sales growth	Cash flow/K
All firms	−3.9	−2.3	−0.2	−1.4
Large	−3.4	−2.6	−0.1	−0.7
Small	−5.3	−3.7	−0.2	−1.4
Low share of intangibles	−3.7	−2.6	−0.4	−0.7
High share of intangibles	−5.0	−3.1	−0.4	−1.5

Notes: [a] Effect of a 1 percentage point increase in policy rates after two years. Simulation of the quarterly model of the Italian economy.
[b] Effect on I/K after two years, divided by the average I/K ratio, of a percentage point increase in policy rates sustained for two years. Joint simulation of the macro equations and of the micro investment equations.

in the policy rate, sustained for two years – similar to the experiments analysed in Van Els *et al.* (chapter 5 in this volume). The percentage effect on investment in the second year is reported in the bottom panel of table 11.4,[17] both the total and the portion transmitted through three channels: the user cost, sales and cash flow.

For the whole sample of firms, investment decreases by about 4 per cent in the second year after the monetary restriction, an effect that is broadly consistent with the outcome of the macro models of the Italian economy. The decrease is larger for small firms and firms with a larger share of intangibles. The difference between the response of investment in large and small firms is 1.9 percentage points; the investment of firms with a larger share of intangibles decreases by 1.3 points more than for the other group. The differences are not negligible, considering that gross

[17] The effect on investment is approximated by the effect on I/K, divided by the average I/K ratio.

fixed capital in Italy grew at an average annual rate of 2.4 per cent over the period 1985–2000.

Most of the effect of monetary policy is transmitted through the user cost variable. This variable explains between 65 and 70 per cent of the total effect of monetary policy on investment. The effect transmitted through the cash flow is, however, substantial.

6   Conclusions

We reach three major conclusions. First, unlike the standard finding in the literature on firm-level investment, we find significant effects of the user cost of capital on investment. This appears to be partly due to our unique data, in particular the detailed information on the fiscal component of the cost of capital that we are able to reconstruct.

Second, we found that the conclusion, common in the Italian empirical literature, that cash flow matters in determining firms' investment is confirmed, even when the firm's user cost is properly measured and included in the estimation. This result was also not to be taken for granted, considering the high correlation between these two variables.

The significant coefficient on the cash flow variable is likely to capture a broad credit channel effect: this is suggested by the robustness of the result to the choice of alternative measures of the firm's financial constraints, as the cash stock, in place of the cash flow. The same conclusion is suggested by the finding that the elasticity of investment to cash flow is larger for small firms and firms which invest in intangible assets, which should be *a priori* more exposed to agency problems.

Finally, our monetary policy exercise has shown that, while the larger part of the effects of monetary policy on investment should be attributed to a neo-classical, cost of capital mechanism, a significant portion (about one-third) is transmitted through the exacerbation of financial constraints.

12 Monetary transmission: empirical evidence from Luxembourg firm-level data

P. Lünnemann and T. Mathä

1 Introduction

This chapter presents empirical results of the monetary policy transmission process for Luxembourg based on firm-level data. It is the first empirical analysis of this kind for Luxembourg. We investigate whether Luxembourg firms' investment is sensitive to the user cost of capital, to what extent the user cost is affected by changes in the monetary policy indicator and whether the broad credit channel is relevant in Luxembourg.

Following the approach presented in Chatelain *et al.* (chapter 7 in this volume), we estimate a sales accelerator model of investment. These estimates permit us to analyse the effects of monetary policy on firms' investment decisions through the user cost of capital. In addition, we investigate whether firms' investment behaviour is significantly affected by the strength of their balance sheets, as indicated by the cash level–capital ratio. In order to analyse the presence of differential effects between firms, we examine the role of other firm-specific characteristics, such as age.

2 A brief account of some Luxembourg peculiarities

Luxembourg is one of the original member states of the European Community (EC) and, with an estimated population of approximately 440,000 people and a share of around 0.3 per cent in euro area GDP, the smallest economy in today's European Union. The average annual growth of real GDP was around 5.4 per cent between 1990 and 2000. The rapid expansion of the Luxembourg economy owes much to the developments in the financial sector, which started in the early 1980s. On 31 December 2001, the Luxembourg financial centre counted 189 banks and 618 monetary and financial intermediaries (MFIs) (BCL, 2002a). They

We would like to thank Jean Bernard Chatelain, Leo de Haan, Paolo Guarda, Ignacio Hernando, Plutarchos Sakellaris, Jean-Pierre Schoder, Patrick Sevestre, Philip Vermeulen and Ulf von Kalkreuth for their constructive criticism and suggestions. Special thanks to Maria Valderrama for providing detailed comments and helpful suggestions on various drafts.

accounted for about 6.5 per cent of the total number of MFIs in the euro area. The importance of the financial services sector in Luxembourg is reflected by its contribution to GDP, currently standing at about 40 per cent.

In 1997, the market share of large banks (i.e. banks with total assets larger than EUR 6 billion) was 61.7 per cent. This seems to be relatively high considering the presence of about 200 banks. According to the Herfindahl index, the Luxembourg banking sector does, however, not appear to be particularly concentrated. In 1997, the market concentration in the Luxembourg banking sector was *as if* the total market was divided equally between 34.5 banks. This is among the least concentrated market outcomes in the euro area.[1] Also, the Luxembourg banking sector is characterised by a relatively low degree of state influence. State influence in 1995, measured as the percentage of assets of the top ten banks owned or controlled by the government, was 5.1 per cent and among the lowest in the euro area.

The corporate finance structure in Luxembourg is characterised by strong bank-lending relationships. In the second half of the 1990s, the share of outstanding loans to the non-financial corporate sector in GDP was around 25 per cent, thereby exceeding total gross fixed capital formation on average by 16 per cent. On the contrary, financing investment via stock markets is only of secondary importance, as is reflected by the low number of publicly traded companies. Only 60 out of the approximately 20,000 Luxembourg firms were listed on the Luxembourg stock exchange in 2000. Equally, corporate bonds exhibit only a minor role for Luxembourg firms' financing. This underpins the high relevance of bank lending in Luxembourg.[2]

3   Data, variables and estimation methodology

3.1   Data

The data are taken from Luxembourg firms' annual, consolidated where available, balance sheets as published by *Bureau Van Dijk* (Belgium) and refer to the period from 1992 to 1998.[3] The database initially covers 266 firms.

---

[1] See table 14.2 in Ehrmann *et al.* chapter 14 in this volume.
[2] More background information on financial structures in Luxembourg can be found in BCL (2002b).
[3] In order to prolong the panel, data from the *BELFIRST* and the *AMADEUS* data set were merged. The *BELFIRST* database is a sub-set of the *AMADEUS* database that includes Belgian and Luxembourg firms' balance sheets only. For the purpose of the analysis, data from both databases were made compatible. We took into account, as far as possible, the merging activities of firms.

We decided to identify outliers along the time-series dimension at the individual firm level and not as a function of a multiple of the interquartile range around the median. The reason is that the data panel contains a relatively small number of firms from very different industries revealing large discrepancies with respect to size, age or legal form, which may justify significant differences in investment structures. For example, young firms may display much higher investment or sales growth rates. Also, the investment ratio of a manufacturing firm may be very different form that of a real estate agent.[4] A firm-year observation is therefore identified as implausible if the year-on-year change exceeds a pre-specified threshold value. To ensure that true underlying changes, as opposed to data errors, do not lead to the exclusion of an otherwise impeccable observation, implausibility additionally requires the subsequent year-on-year change to exceed the threshold value. The threshold level is initially set to ±40 per cent. Also worthwhile noting is the fact that the plausibility check was run on the raw data and not on the variables included in the estimation.

3.2   Variable definitions

Our empirical analysis is based on the sales accelerator specification derived in detail in chapter 3 in this volume (equation 9). Estimates of the firm-specific capital stock have been obtained by using the perpetual inventory method. As a benchmark, the depreciation rate is assumed to be 6 per cent. The investment–capital stock ratio is defined as $I_{i,t}/K_{i,t-1}$, where I_t and K_{t-1} denote nominal investment and capital stock, respectively. Sales are approximated by firms' turnover, as genuine sales data were not available. Factors feeding into the user cost are the monetary policy indicator, which is of particular interest to this study, as well as economic variables, such as the depreciation rate and the expected future price level. The user cost of capital definition is given in (1) as

$$UC_{i,t} = \frac{p_t^I}{p_t}\left(wr_{i,t} + d_i - (1 - d_i)\frac{\Delta p_{i,t+1}^I}{\Delta p_{i,t}^I}\right) \tag{1}$$

---

[4] Unless applied to well-defined intra-homogeneous sub-samples, the removal of outliers based on multiples of the interquartile range does not discriminate between different industries and their characteristics, and may therefore eliminate firms from the sample for the wrong reason. Furthermore, such a method may not identify implausible jumps in the firms' individual investment behaviour through time, as no connection is made between individual firms and time. As our panel is compact, splitting into sub-samples as required by any sensible removal of outliers based on percentiles is infeasible.

UC, p^I, p, d and wr, respectively, represent the user cost of capital, the price level of investment, the economy-wide price level, depreciation in percentage terms and the weighted average cost of capital.[5] The user cost of capital measure is dynamic in the sense that it includes price expectations. The firm-specific weighted cost of capital, wr, is obtained in weighting the gross debt share by the apparent interest rate $ar_{i,t}$ and the own funds share by the equity interest rate $er_{i,t}$. The apparent interest rate is a proxy for interest paid on debt. It is a firm-specific variable and defined as the ratio of debt charges over gross debt. The equity interest rate is defined as $er_{i,t} = dr_{i,t}^{long} + ep$, where $dr_{i,t}^{long}$ denotes the long-term debt rate, which we take to be the ten-year Government bond in Luxembourg. ep denotes the equity premium, which is assumed to be 6 per cent.

Table 12.1 *Summary statistics on variables used in investment demand estimation, Luxembourg*

	Tangible assets$_t^a$	I_t/K_{t-1}	Sales$_t^a$	Δlog Sales$_t$	UC_t	Δlog UC_t	$Cash_{t-1}/K_{t-1}$
Mean	24822	0.052	57384	0.003	0.106	−0.052	0.822
Maximum	1309611	2.331	513958	0.646	0.196	1.408	36.643
Minimum	34	−0.654	3883	−1.221	0.022	−1.597	0.000
Std dev.	116401	0.227	75101	0.180	0.031	0.347	3.313
Obs.	517	436	429	349	445	365	285
Cross-sections	80	80	80	80	80	80	80

Note: [a] In EUR 1000.

Table 12.1 provides descriptive statistics of the benchmark sample used in the regressions. Owing to data limitations investment had to be calculated as the difference in tangible fixed assets between two years from the asset and liability statement.[6] We use the level of cash rather than cash flow as our primary balance sheet indicator since cash levels say little about the quality of future investment projects and their profitability.

[5] The user cost does not include any taxation term owing to data unavailability.
[6] This is somewhat unsatisfactory, but inevitable, given that data on genuine investment were not available from the income statement. The benchmark depreciation rate is set to be 6 per cent. As noted above, this yardstick also enters the capital-stock equation. Its underlying assumption may be meaningful from a macroeconomic perspective, but may not correspond to the accounting practice of firms, which, at least in part, may explain the low investment ratios obtained. If this was the case, one may argue that the bias is constant over firms and time and hence subsumed into the constant.

3.3   Differential effects

We analyse the presence of differential effects by using interaction variables. All exogenous variables are interacted with a dummy variable, indicating whether or not a firm meets some kind of *ex ante* specified age criterion.[7] The working hypothesis is that young firms have different sales growth, user cost and cash-stock sensitivities.

3.4   Estimation methodology

The inclusion of a lagged dependent variable in dynamic panel data estimation results in OLS estimates being biased and inconsistent, as not only the dependent, but also the lagged dependent variable is a function of the firm-specific error term η_i. Hence, the lagged investment ratio is correlated with the error term (e.g. Baltagi, 1995). Estimation by means of generalised methods of moments (GMM) provides consistent and unbiased estimates (e.g. Arellano and Bond, 1991). However, owing to the rather short and wide nature of the panel, the loss of observations in using lagged variables as instruments, either in levels or in first differences, would be extremely high. Also, GMM estimates might be unreliable in cases where no appropriate instruments are available.

Sevestre and Trognon (1985) show that in theory the consistent estimator lies in between the OLS and WITHIN estimates. The OLS estimator over-estimates the true coefficient, while the WITHIN estimator under-estimates the true coefficient. In light of the severe sample-size restrictions, we present both OLS (upper-bound) and WITHIN (lower-bound) estimates. This may prove a valid alternative, in particular if the estimated coefficients are close to each other.

As the coefficients of the lagged sales growth, user cost and balance sheet variables are not significantly different from zero, the sales accelerator specification, presented in chapter 3 (9) (p. 141) reduces to (2), with CS denoting cash stock:

$$\frac{I_{it}}{K_{i,t-1}} = f_i + \omega_1 \frac{I_{it-1}}{K_{i,t-2}} + \theta_0 \Delta y_{it} - \sigma_0 \Delta uc_{it} + \phi_0 \frac{CS_{it}}{K_{i,t-1}} + \varepsilon_{it} \quad (2)$$

4   Empirical results

This section presents the empirical results. Firstly, regression (I) provides the empirical estimates of the basic sales accelerator specification

---

[7] We also analysed whether small, private liability and unquoted firms, as well as service sector firms reveal different cash-stock sensitivities. The results are less clear and for the sake of brevity not discussed here. These estimates are presented in detail in Lünnemann and Mathä (2001).

augmented by the lagged cash stock–capital ratio. Regression (II) explores differences between various sub-samples. Regression (III) presents selected results with regard to monetary policy changes and its impact on the user cost of capital. The notation (i) and (ii) refers to OLS and WITHIN estimates, respectively.

4.1   Regression (I): the benchmark regression

The results of regression (I) in table 12.2 provide partial evidence in favour of the sales accelerator mechanism. The sales growth coefficient is positively significant in the OLS estimations while it is not significant in the WITHIN estimations.[8] The low magnitude of the sales growth coefficient in the OLS estimation, ranging around 0.08, as well as its insignificance in the WITHIN estimation, may be related to the short sample period, not capturing a full business cycle.

The results with regard to the user cost of capital are as expected. The coefficients range between -0.084 and -0.152 and are significant at the 5 per cent level or better, regardless of whether referring to the OLS or the WITHIN estimation. The size of the estimated coefficients seems to be on the low side compared to other studies in the literature (e.g. Harhoff and Ramb, 2001). Also worthwhile noting is that the differences between the estimated coefficients in the respective OLS and WITHIN estimations are relatively small.[9]

With regard to the lagged cash–capital ratio, the WITHIN estimations seem to provide stronger results. The estimated coefficient is 0.025 and significant in regression (Ib-ii). This result supports the idea that the strength of the balance sheet influences the investment of firms, which is consistent with the arguments forwarded by the broad credit channel theory. Bearing in mind that the coefficients should not be taken at face value, the inclusion of the balance sheet indicator does not affect the sales growth or user cost coefficients in a significant way, as is confirmed by a simple Wald test. This can, however, not be said for the lagged investment ratio coefficient.

---

[8] We refrain from providing the long-term elasticities of the individual coefficients. This is because our lagged dependent variable is often insignificant, the regressions do not contain any lags and the period under investigation does not cover a full business cycle. The interested reader may easily compute the long-term coefficients by dividing the individual coefficients by 1 minus the coefficient of the lagged dependent variable.

[9] However, the theoretically derived property that the OLS over-estimates the true coefficient while the WITHIN estimator under-estimates it, does not seem to hold for the estimated user cost and cash–capital ratio coefficients, as the coefficients are smaller in the OLS regression than in the WITHIN regression.

Table 12.2 *Firms' investment and differential effects for young firms, Luxembourg*

Regression method	(Ia-i) OLS	(Ia-ii) WITHIN	(Ib-i) OLS	(Ib-ii) WITHIN	(IIa-i) OLS	(IIa-ii) WITHIN	(IIb-i) OLS	(IIb-ii) WITHIN	(IIc-i) OLS	(IIc-ii) WITHIN
Dep. var.	I_t/K_{t-1}		I_t/K_{t-1}		I_t/K_{t-1}		I_t/K_{t-1}		I_t/K_{t-1}	
Cross-sections	80	80	80	80	78	78	78	78	78	78
Obs.	257	257	195	195	191	191	191	191	191	191
I_{t-1}/K_{t-2}	0.082	−0.061	0.245***	−0.126*	0.256***	−0.107	0.271***	−0.114	0.250***	−0.099
	0.052	0.040	0.074	0.073	0.078	0.075	0.081	0.079	0.082	0.081
Δlog $SALES_t$	0.079**	−0.042	0.081**	0.002	0.068*	−0.015	0.061*	−0.014	0.065*	−0.029
	0.035	0.039	0.038	0.050	0.036	0.050	0.037	0.050	0.038	0.051
Δlog UC_t	−0.099**	−0.084***	−0.152***	−0.125***	−0.156***	−0.123***	−0.148***	−0.119***	−0.162***	−0.123***
	0.039	0.027	0.049	0.032	0.050	0.032	0.051	0.034	0.055	0.033
$CASH_{t-1}/K_{t-1}$			0.002	0.025***	0.001	0.018**	0.002	0.019***	0.002	0.023***
			0.003	0.008	0.003	0.007	0.003	0.007	0.003	0.008
Interaction var. Threshold value					*Age* <7 years		*Age* <8 years		*Age* <11 years	
I_{t-2}/K_{t-2}					−1.098***	0.638***	−0.602***	0.126	0.041	−0.060
					0.358	0.220	0.161	0.138	0.238	0.233
Δlog $SALES_t$					0.595***	0.290***	0.321	0.355**	0.100	0.231
					0.158	0.080	0.319	0.147	0.167	0.142
Δlog UC_t					−0.588***	−0.078	−0.303***	0.049	0.022	−0.029
					0.136	0.140	0.086	0.080	0.134	0.068
$CASH_{t-1}/K_{t-1}$					0.057***	0.055***	0.052***	0.054***	0.034	0.068***
					0.007	0.007	0.012	0.009	0.0326	0.022
R2	0.054	0.482	0.163	0.626	0.198	0.645	0.204	0.644	0.181	0.646
Adj. R2	0.043	0.237	0.145	0.346	0.163	0.357	0.169	0.356	0.145	0.360
F-statistic	4.788***	8.080***	9.258***	61.948***	5.617***	27.237***	5.830***	27.146***	5.035***	27.409***

Notes: Standard errors below coefficient in smaller type. ***, ** and * denote significance at the 1%, 5% and 10% level, respectively. Estimates are heteroscedasticity consistent and obtained using the plausibility threshold of ±40%, the dynamic user cost, the apparent interest rate in the *wr* definition and a depreciation rate of 6% in the capital-stock calculation.

4.2   Regression (II): differential effects

Regression (II), presented in table 12.2, analyses the existence of differential effects between different types of firms. Due to the short and narrow data set, an interaction variable approach was selected instead of separately estimating various sub-samples. We analyse whether young firms are different in terms of investment behaviour, since according to advocates of the credit channel theory, younger firms may be financially more constrained.

The results obtained strongly support the idea of younger firms being financially more constrained than older firms. The results suggest that the tightness of the constraint declines with increasing age, as the magnitude of the coefficients and their significance generally seem to decrease as higher age thresholds are selected. It thus seems that younger firms are more dependent on internal liquidity to finance their investment decisions and more sensitive to changes in the user cost of capital.

4.3   Regression (III): the effect of monetary policy on the user cost

Regression (III), presented in table 12.3, briefly explores the relationship between the user cost of capital and the monetary policy indicator. Monetary policy signals have the expected positive impact, i.e. a positive change

Table 12.3 *Monetary policy indicator and firms' user cost of capital, Luxembourg*

Regression	(IIIa-i)		(IIIa-ii)
Method	OLS		WITHIN
Dep. var.		$\Delta\log UC_t$	
Cross-sections		80	
Obs.		303	
$\Delta\log MPI_t$	0.951***		0.952***
	0.142		0.132
$\Delta\log MPI_{t-1}$	0.696***		0.689***
	0.266		0.241
R2	0.230		0.308
Adjusted R2	0.225		0.055
F-Statistic	44.84***		98.58***

Notes: Standard errors below coefficient in smaller type. ***, denotes significance at the 1% level. Estimates are heteroscedasticity consistent and obtained using the plausibility threshold of ±40%, the dynamic user cost, the apparent interest rate in the *wr* definition and a depreciation rate of 6%.

in the three-month money market interest rate implies a positive change in the user cost. Also the lagged value of the monetary policy indicator is positively significant. This result complements the results obtained in previous regressions, where it was shown that the user cost of capital is a robust determinant of firms' investment behaviour.

4.4   Some sensitivity tests

The results indicate strong robustness, in particular with respect to the user cost. Despite several modifications undertaken, such as changing the threshold value to 20 per cent, changing the equity premium or the depreciation rate to 3 per cent or 8 per cent, respectively, the coefficients of the user cost and sales growth, as well as the lagged cash–capital ratio keep their sign and remain significant. The exception is the regression with an 8 per cent depreciation rate, where the sales growth coefficient fails to be significantly positive. Furthermore, the magnitude of the individual coefficients is very similar to those in regression (I). If a depreciation rate of 8 per cent instead of 6 per cent is assumed, the user cost and cash–capital coefficients seem to be somewhat higher than those shown in regression (I).

The results also suggest that using the dynamic user cost of capital proxy seems to yield stronger results than using static proxies. The results obtained, using the dynamic user cost of capital proxy with the three-month money market rate instead of the apparent interest rate, are similar to those obtained in regression (Ib).

5   Concluding remarks

The main aim of this chapter was to present first results on the monetary transmission process for Luxembourg. It is the first empirical analysis conducted for Luxembourg firm-level data. Despite the severe sample-size restriction, we obtain indicative results. The results suggest that the sales accelerator mechanism may be at work. Its magnitude is, however, very low. This may be due to the fact that the period under investigation does not capture a full business cycle. The strength of the balance sheet and even more so the user cost of capital are significant and robust determinants of the investment behaviour of Luxembourg firms. Furthermore, young firms in particular show signs of being financially more constrained, as their investment behaviour is more sensitive to changes in the user cost of capital changes and/or internally generated liquidity. These results are consistent with the broad credit channel theory.

13 The role of trade credit and bank lending relationships in the transmission mechanism in Austria

M.-T. Valderrama

1 Introduction

This chapter attempts to analyse the strength of the credit channel using a data set of Austrian firms. In Austria the issuance of equities and bonds has played a minor role in the external financing of firms, while relationships with other firms and the house bank principle have been the dominant financing strategy. Owing to their importance in the financial structure of Austrian firms, trade credit and the house bank principle merit a detailed analysis of their role in the transmission mechanism. While evidence is still mixed the majority of studies have found that the use of trade credit weakens the credit channel. The hypothesis is that if firms face lower loan supply, they may be able to circumvent such a credit squeeze through trade credit. Studies that analyse the role of bank-lending relationships have found that if banks do not reduce their supply of loans even when the monetary stance changes, because of a long-term relationship, then the credit channel will also be weaker but the interest rate channel does not necessarily become weaker.[1]

Following the methodology of the accompanying studies in this volume, the approach used here is to include the firm's specific user cost of capital and the liquidity ratio[2] in a neo-classical investment demand equation. The distributional effects on investment are first studied by splitting the sample according to size and age. In a second step the sensitivity of investment to its components is made dependent on the firm's access to funds.

Special thanks go to my referee Jean Bernard Chatelain and my discussant Kenneth Kuttner for very helpful comments.
[1] See Elliehausen and Wolken (1993), Kohler, Britton and Yates (2000), Marotta (1997) and Nilsen (1999), for studies relating trade credit and the transmission mechanism and Conigliani, Ferri and Generale (1997), Degryse and Van Cayseele (1998), Dell'Ariccia and Marquez (2001), Elsas and Krahnen (1998) and Petersen and Rajan (1994), for the role of lending relationships.
[2] Instead of the cash flow as is done in the other studies in this volume. The liquidity ratio is defined as the ratio of liquid assets to capital stock. 'Liquid assets' include securities, cash, and other liquid assets.

This is done by interacting the parameters of the baseline equation with variables that account for the firm's usage of trade credit or the existence of a house bank. Using this approach it is possible not only to analyse the cross-sectional differences that arise owing to the existence of trade credit or a house bank but also to differentiate the distributional effects depending on the degree of access to the capital market, without losing too many observations.

The chapter is organised as follows. Section 2 contains a short description of the development of investment spending and financing in Austria, followed by a description of the database and the indicators used in the empirical part (section 3). Section 4 describes the results obtained using the baseline investment equation. Section 5 focuses on the role of trade credit and the house bank on the transmission mechanism. Finally, some conclusions are drawn based on these findings (section 6).

2   Investment financing and spending in Austria

Before entering the European Monetary Union (EMU) Austria's monetary policy had followed a fixed exchange rate regime, which pegged the Schilling to a basket of currencies in 1973 and to the Deutsche Mark from 1981 onwards. Owing to the success of this peg, Austria was considered to form a *de facto* monetary union with Germany. Besides this strategy Austria followed a policy of subsidising credit. As a result, the money and the interest rate channels were not important for the transmission mechanism of monetary policy.[3] Therefore, the main influences on investment activity were sales and earnings expectations as well as the existing capital stock and its utilisation.[4]

Partly owing to the structure of the financial system, the universal banking principle and the law which mainly protects creditors, the issuance of bond and commercial paper by non-financial institutions in Austria has also been very small.[5] Corporate finance in Austria has thus been characterised by the strong dependence of firms on bank lending. Capital markets are narrow and under-developed and have been used mostly by public authorities and financial institutions, while the issuance of debt by

---

[3] See Glück (1995) and Gnan (1995) for an explanation of why interest rate changes were perceived as short-lived episodes to stabilise the exchange rate, which made investment less sensitive to the interest rate.

[4] For more details on institutional features and empirical data on all the above points see Pech (1994).

[5] 'the law allows nearly all of a company's assets to be used as collateral against lending, without any formal regulation. The assignment of assets is a means of providing collateral that is widely used in the German (and Austrian) financing system. This reduces the firm's need to have high levels of equity' (Delbreil *et al.*, 2000:35).

private non-financial institutions has been negligible: equity ownership is one of the lowest in Europe, while the ratio of total debt to total assets of Austrian firms of around 75 per cent on average is relatively high compared to other European countries.[6] The share of bonds in GDP issued by non-financial corporations was only 2.8 per cent in 1997, compared to a share of 31 per cent issued by credit institutions and 30 per cent issued by the government.[7] Other reasons for the low development of the capital market, besides the legal system, are the predominance of small and medium-sized firms (SMEs), a relatively strong but declining presence of the state and a high concentration of ownership. This last point also reinforces the importance of bank debt, since banks are both important direct and, through holdings, indirect owners of many firms.[8]

After bank lending and other debt, the most important item in the composition of liabilities is trade credit (see Valderrama 2001b). In 1999 this item amounted to 11 per cent of total liabilities while securities issuance was less than 1 per cent. It is also worth mentioning that on the asset side trade credit also amounts to an important share of the assets of non-financial institutions. Moreover, the developments of trade credit and trade debt closely follow the evolution of inventories on the balance sheet of non-financial corporations. Given the importance of inventories on total investment, trade debt seems to be an important source of investment financing for Austrian firms. In the sample used in this chapter and described later on, the average share of trade credit on short-term debt is 37.4 per cent and this becomes even more important for small firms which show an average share of 44.2 per cent, while this share is 35.4 per cent for young firms.[9]

At the same time, the banking sector is one of the most over-banked in Europe, characterised by many small banks and a very low degree of concentration.[10] There are 123 banks per million inhabitants in Austria, compared to 45 in Germany and 25 in France,[11] while the largest five banks account for less than 50 per cent of the market.[12] Bank relationships have been characterised by the presence of a 'house-bank'.[13] Although difficult to verify in empirical work, the practice of long-standing loyalty to one bank prevails in Austria and has often been held responsible for the absence of a credit channel. The foundations of this relationship lie

---

[6] Gnan (1995), IMF (1998) and Quehenberger (1997).
[7] See table 14.2 in Ehrmann et al. (chapter 14 in this volume).
[8] Gugler (1997).   [9] Valderrama (2001b).
[10] See Kaufmann (2001) for a description of the Austrian banking system.
[11] See table 14.2 in Ehrmann et al. (chapter 14 in this volume).
[12] IMF (1998).   [13] Delbreil et al. (2000).

in the specific banking practices that are governed by the commercial law that systematically protects creditors, which allows firms to hold little equity.[14]

3   Database and indicators[15]

The Oesterreichische Nationalbank (OeNB) collects data on balance sheets and income statements of Austrian firms in the course of its re-financing activities, in order to check the solvency of non-financial enterprises involved in the collateralisation of monetary policy operations. These annual accounts are submitted to the OeNB by the enterprises themselves or by commercial banks doing business with the enterprises in question. Consolidated financial statements are collected only in exceptional cases.[16]

The OeNB database cannot be considered as a statistical sample and is biased, too. Commercial banks usually present collateral from companies which they expect will satisfy the OeNB's solvency requirements. Sound enterprises are thus over-represented in the sample. The bias becomes more severe when only those firms for which longer time series exist are included, since these are mostly large firms. In fact only 17 per cent of the firms in this sample can be classified as small firms, while young firms account for only 12 per cent of the firms in the sample.

In addition to the balance sheet data, the OeNB collects monthly data from banks for each extended loan of more than ATS 5 million. Using this database, which is available only from 1994 onwards, it becomes possible to construct proxies for the existence of a house bank. The existence of a house bank has usually been measured by the duration of the lending relationship.[17] However, owing to the short time span of this database it was not feasible to construct such an indicator. On the other hand, given the large number of banks per inhabitant in Austria and the rather strong competition in this sector, a high share of loans from a single bank in total loans from banks could be taken as an indicator of a close lending relationship.[18] In this sample 53 per cent of the firms show a share of loans from one bank in total loans above 70 per cent.

---

[14] Ibid.

[15] Refer to Valderrama (2001b) for details on the database and the sample used, as well as a description of the variables.

[16] The individual data are strictly confidential and have to be aggregated for any publication in order to comply with data secrecy legislation.

[17] Conigliani, Ferri and Generale (1997), Degryse and Van Caryseele (1998), Dell'Ariccia and Marquez (2001), Elsas and Krahnen (1998) and Petersen and Rajan (1994).

[18] In Valderrama (2001b) three additional indicators, which take into account the maturity of the loan, are also investigated. The results are very similar.

4   Baseline equation

The empirical results are based on the investment equation presented in chapter 7 in this volume. The estimation of the investment demand was done using two-step Arellano–Bond (1991) GMM estimators, which control for biases due to unobserved firm-specific effects and lagged endogenous variables.[19] The estimations were carried out using first differences to remove the firm-specific effects and time dummies were included to control for exogenous shocks in the data. Several estimations, which are not presented, were carried out to determine the number of lags of the variables. All lagged levels of the investment ratio and the predetermined variables are used as instrumental variables.[20] The validity of the instruments was tested with a Sargan test of over-identifying restrictions and tests of serial correlation in the residuals.

The results of the estimation of the baseline equation are shown in table 13.1.[21] The sample was split according to size and age, which are usually used to take into account information asymmetries.[22] The Sargan test does not reject all three estimations and there is no evidence of second-order serial correlation.

These results confirm the perception that growth of net sales is an important determinant of investment, except for small firms, while the user cost of capital is only significant for large, old and small firms. On the other hand, the long-run elasticity of sales growth is highest for younger firms (29.8 per cent) while the sensitivity of investment demand to the user cost of capital is highest for old firms (−33.3 per cent). This last counterintuitive result could be due to omitted variables or to misspecification.

The remaining columns show the results of a regression which takes into account the liquidity ratio. As it is often found in similar studies, the growth of sales and the user cost of capital lose their significance in the presence of a financial variable. The highest long-run elasticity of the liquidity ratio is observed for young firms (30.8 per cent), while the lowest long run elasticity of the liquidity ratio is found for small firms (12.2 per cent).

From these results it can be concluded that the financial position of the firm does seem to play an important role in the determination of investment, in particular for young firms and to a lesser degree for small

---

[19] Arellano and Bond (1991).

[20] Tests not shown here were also done with different lags. The results, however, do not change significantly with different number of lags on the instrument matrix.

[21] For a comprehensive discussion of the results refer to Valderrama (2001b).

[22] See Wesche (2000) and Valderrama (2001a) for more evidence on the role of size and age on the credit channel in Austria.

Table 13.1 *Baseline equation of firms' investment demand, Austria*

	All	Large	Old	All	Large	Old
	p-values of Coeff. χ^2 test	p-values of Coeff. χ^2 test	p-values of Coeff. χ^2 test	p-values of Coeff. χ^2 test	p-values of Coeff. χ^2 test	p-values of Coeff. χ^2 test
I_{t-1}/K_{t-2}	0.130 0.034	0.183 0.043	0.121 0.033	0.057 0.041	0.101 0.044	0.076 0.042
Long-run elasticity[a]						
Growth of sales	0.266 (0.017)	0.247 (0.010)	0.191 (0.066)	0.015 (0.837)	0.020 (0.750)	0.041 (0.484)
Change in user cost	−0.139 (0.394)	−0.219 (0.050)	−0.333 (0.004)	−0.044 (0.724)	−0.094 (0.289)	−0.040 (0.627)
Liquidity ratio				0.285 (0.000)	0.254 (0.000)	0.224 (0.000)
		Small	*Young*		*Small*	*Young*
I_{t-1}/K_{t-2}		−0.291 0.149	−0.001 0.116		−0.220 0.133	−0.303 0.122
Long-run elasticity[a]						
Growth of sales		0.068 (0.467)	0.298 (0.007)		0.013 (0.789)	0.219 (0.001)
Change in user cost		−0.156 (0.096)	0.047 (0.689)		−0.070 (0.368)	0.122 (0.043)
Liquidity ratio					0.122 (0.001)	0.308 (0.000)
Long-run differential coefficient						
Growth of sales		−0.18	0.11		−0.01	0.18
Change in user cost		0.06	0.38		−0.02	0.16
Liquidity ratio					0.13	0.08
No. of obs.	2,652	2,652	2,652	2,652	2,652	2,652
Wald test	30.96	40.44	61.85	39.62	57.68	105.14
Sargan test	24.32	37.64	49.81	39.74	70.00	70.34
p-value	0.500	0.901	0.481	0.229	0.410	0.399
m_1	−9.98	−9.66	−9.87	−8.03	−8.90	−8.39
p-value	0.000	0.000	0.000	0.000	0.000	0.000
m_2	1.78	1.66	1.35	1.35	1.39	0.96
p-value	0.075	0.097	0.176	0.176	0.165	0.337

Notes: Small firms: firms with fewer than 55 employees, young firms: firms established in the last ten years. Time dummies and a constant were included but not reported. Instrumental variables: all lagged levels of endogenous and of all predetermined variables.
[a] Evaluated at the mean of the interaction term.

firms. The user cost of capital is, however, often not significant, and even positive. This could be an indication that this specification does not adequately reflect investment behaviour in Austria. Therefore, in section 5 an attempt is made to improve the estimation.

5 Role of trade credit and bank-lending relationships

In this section an attempt is made to capture the effect that varying access to external funds has on investment demand (tables 13.2, 13.3). The method used here models the effect on investment of growth of sales, the user cost of capital and the liquidity ratio conditional on the firm's access to external financing. The hypothesis is that for firms which are able to circumvent a credit squeeze the dependence on sales and on liquidity as well as the effect of user cost of capital will be different than if these firms faced binding credit constraints. Therefore, the effect of a monetary tightening will be smaller for firms which are able to substitute bank lending by other types of external funds or for firms for which asymmetric information issues are of less relevance. If this hypothesis is confirmed, monetary policy will have distributional effects and the credit channel will be weaker for this type of firms.

In order to test for such distributional effects the variables that account for the access of the firm to external financing are interacted with the determinants of investment. The equation to be estimated can be written as:

$$
\begin{aligned}
\frac{I_{it}}{K_{it-1}} = &\sum_{p=1}^{T} \omega_p \frac{I_{it-p}}{K_{it-p-1}} + \sum_{j=0}^{T} \theta_j \Delta y_{it-j} + \sum_{h=0}^{T} \sigma_h \Delta u c_{i,t-h} \\
&+ \sum_{m=0}^{T} \phi_m \frac{LA_{it-m}}{p_{st}^I K_{it-m-1}} + \phi T_{it}^G + \sum_{p=1}^{T} \omega_p \frac{I_{it-p}}{K_{it-p-1}} T_{it}^G \\
&+ \sum_{j=0}^{T} \theta_j \Delta y_{it-j} T_{it}^G - \sum_{h=0}^{T} \sigma_h \Delta u c_{i,t-h} T_{it}^G \\
&+ \sum_{m=0}^{T} \phi_m \frac{LA_{it-m}}{p_{st}^I K_{it-m-1}} T_{it}^G + \eta_i + \nu_t + \varepsilon_{it}
\end{aligned}
\tag{1}
$$

where $\frac{I_{it}}{K_{it-1}}$, is the investment ratio, y_{it} is the logarithm of net sales, uc_{it} is the user cost of capital, $\frac{LA_{it-m}}{p_{st}^I K_{it-m-1}}$ is the liquidity ratio, and T_{it}^G is the interaction term that takes into account the firm's access to external funds.[23]

---

[23] The variables studied here are: share of trade credit as a percentage of short-term liabilities and two variables that measure the existence of a 'house bank'.

Table 13.2 *Firms' investment demand with an interaction term: share of trade credit in short-term debt, Austria*

	p-values of Coeff. χ^2 test		p-values of Coeff. χ^2 test		p-values of Coeff. χ^2 test	
	All		*Large*		*Old*	
I_{t-1}/K_{t-2}	−0.068	0.100	0.011	0.079	−0.034	0.077
Long-run elasticity[a]						
Growth of sales	0.053	(0.249)	0.050	(0.159)	0.024	(0.435)
Change in user cost	0.081	(0.311)	−0.099	(0.032)	−0.092	(0.052)
Liquidity ratio	0.156	(0.001)	0.156	(0.000)	0.138	(0.000)
Interaction term (IT)	0.160	(0.099)	−0.044	(0.452)	−0.011	(0.776)
Mean of (IT) (%)	37.42		36.07		37.71	
			Small		*Young*	
I_{t-1}/K_{t-2}			−0.446	0.122	−0.413	0.137
Long-run elasticity[a]						
Growth of sales			−0.005	(0.501)	0.156	(0.000)
Change in user cost			−0.049	(0.158)	0.079	(0.011)
Liquidity ratio			0.072	(0.032)	0.163	(0.000)
Interaction term (IT)			0.021	(0.477)	−0.002	(0.943)
Long-run differential coefficient						
Growth of sales			−0.055		0.132	
Change in user cost			0.050		0.172	
Liquidity ratio			−0.084		0.025	
Interaction term (IT)			0.064		0.008	
Mean of (IT) (%)	37.42		44.18		35.37	
No. of obs.	2,645		2,645		2,645	
Wald test	65.64		288.36		608.24	
Sargan test	69.92		131.43		149.49	
p-value	0.704		0.906		0.588	
m_1	−8.68		−8.57		−8.64	
p-value	0.000		0.000		0.000	
m_2	0.81		0.78		0.63	
p-value	0.420		0.434		0.531	

Notes: Small firms: firms with fewer than 55 employees, young firms: firms established in the last ten years. Time dummies and a constant were included but not reported. Instrumental variables: all lagged levels of endogenous and of all predetermined variables.
[a] Evaluated at the mean of the interaction term.

Notice than in this case the interactive variables do not take values of 1 or 0, but rather values between 0 and 1, since these are shares. Thus, it does not only capture the existence of trade credit or a house bank, but also differentiates according to the strength of this relationship. Also, since these variables interact with every parameter of the investment equation, as well as the autoregressive term, the interactive variable affects both the

Table 13.3 *Firms' investment demand with an interaction term: share of loans from one bank on total loans, Austria*

	p-values of Coeff. χ^2 test		*p*-values of Coeff. χ^2 test		*p*-values of Coeff. χ^2 test	
Interaction term	*Largest share of total loans from one bank*					
	All		*Large*		*Old*	
I_{t-1}/K_{t-2}	−0.250	0.198	−0.326	0.149	−0.463	0.149
Long-run elasticity[a]						
Growth of sales	0.043	(0.320)	−0.014	(0.460)	0.074	(0.014)
Change in user cost	0.072	(0.365)	−0.047	(0.399)	−0.057	(0.291)
Liquidity ratio	0.061	(0.327)	0.209	(0.000)	0.107	(0.001)
Interaction term (IT)	0.026	(0.746)	0.036	(0.406)	−0.036	(0.361)
Mean of (IT) (%)	69.90		67.61		70.46	
			Small		*Young*	
I_{t-1}/K_{t-2}			0.185	0.196	0.281	0.189
Long-run elasticity[a]						
Growth of sales			0.006	(0.069)	0.048	(0.320)
Change in user cost			−0.063	(0.094)	0.102	(0.025)
Liquidity ratio			0.075	(0.000)	0.094	(0.003)
Interaction term (IT)			0.088	(0.069)	−0.004	(0.934)
Long-run differential coefficient						
Growth of sales			0.008		−0.026	
Change in user cost			−0.017		0.159	
Liquidity Ratio			−0.134		−0.013	
Interaction term (IT)			0.052		0.032	
Mean of (IT) (%)	69.90		84.08		65.93	
No. of obs.	2,327		2,327		2,327	
Wald test	33.54		654.12		335.74	
Sargan test	76.35		138.26		140.45	
p-value	0.499		0.814		0.776	
m_1	−8.25		−7.49		−7.75	
p-value	0.000		0.000		0.000	
m_2	0.97		0.53		0.72	
p-value	0.331		0.598		0.469	

Notes: Small firms: firms with fewer than 55 employees, young firms: firms established in the last ten years. Time dummies and a constant were included but not reported. Instrumental variables: all lagged levels of endogenous and of all predetermined variables.
[a] Evaluated at the mean of the interaction term.

slope and the intercept of the investment demand function. Therefore, even if the interactive term is not significant, it cannot be concluded that the variable is not relevant. As long as there are differences in at least some parameters compared to the baseline equation, there is an improvement achieved by including this interaction term. What is more important is whether the estimation of the long-run elasticity is improved.

The calculation of the long-run elasticity of the user cost of capital, for example, will be given by:

$$
\varepsilon_{UC}^{LR} = \frac{\left(\sum_{h=0}^{T} \sigma_h + \sum_{h=0}^{T} \sigma_h^G \overline{T}_{it}^G \right)}{\left(1 - \sum_{p=1}^{T} \omega_p - \sum_{p=1}^{T} \omega_p^G \overline{T}_{it}^G \right)}
\tag{2}
$$

where $\overline{T}_{it}^G$ represents the mean of the interaction term.

5.1   Trade credit

When owing to credit market imperfections a bank reduces its supply of loans for some firms, these may draw on trade credit to overcome liquidity shortages. During a period of monetary tightening credit to small or young firms will be more likely to be rationed, while this is not the case for large or old firms. Therefore, it can be expected that trade credit will be an important source of short-term financing for small and young firms. For small or young firms it may be easier to have access to trade credit because the financing firm has more information about the debtor firm and also has an advantage in terms of the collateral. However, trade credit is usually more expensive than bank lending.[24] Thus, in this section the following hypothesis is tested:

H1: the long-run elasticity of the user cost of capital in the investment demand function will be higher and the long-run elasticity of the liquidity ratio in the investment demand function will be lower for firms with a higher share of trade credit in short-term debt.

To test these hypotheses, a variable that indicates the share of trade credit in short-term debt is used. As seen in table 13.2, making the function conditional on the share of trade credit in the regression does not contribute to increase the significance of growth of net sales on the demand equation. However, it does cause the user cost of capital to become significant for large and old firms. The long-run elasticity of the user cost of capital is similar for both groups of firms (−9.9 per cent for large firms and −9.2 per cent for old firms).

Most importantly, it contributes to reduce the long-run elasticity of the liquidity ratio. This effect is, as expected, especially important for young and small firms. The long-run elasticity of the liquidity ratio falls from 30.8 per cent to 16.3 per cent for young firms and from 12.2 per cent to 7.2 per cent for small firms. This elasticity remains the lowest for small

[24] Elliehausen and Wolken (1993)

firms. Small firms are also the group with the highest value for the mean of the interaction term (44.2 per cent).

This evidence supports the hypothesis that small and young firms are able to overcome liquidity constraints by using trade credit. However, the evidence that the sensitivity to the user cost of capital is higher for firms with higher trade credit is not conclusive. The user cost of capital is significant only in the case of large and old firms and the long-run elasticity is lowest for old firms which on average show a higher share of trade credit on short-term debt.

5.2   Bank-lending relationships

Bank-lending relationships have been often made responsible for a weak credit channel. The assumption is that firms which are able to rely on a 'house bank' will suffer less from credit constraints because the problem of asymmetric information is overcome through a long-standing relationship. Thus, such firms may have to rely less on internal funds than firms that are not certain of getting special treatment during periods of tighter monetary stance. The 'house bank', however, does not isolate the client firm from changes in the interest rate since it has a monopolistic power over their clients.[25] Thus, the hypothesis tested here is:

H2: investment demand of firms which have a 'house-bank' is more sensitive to the user cost of capital and less sensitive to the liquidity ratio.

The long-run elasticity of growth of sales becomes significant for old firms, and becomes insignificant for young firms. The total long-run elasticity of the user cost of capital is significant only for small and young firms. In the case of young firms this elasticity is still positive. In the case of small firms, this value of −6.3 per cent seems low compared to the values obtained before for large and old firms. It is worth mentioning that the average share of loans from one bank of total loans is the highest for small firms (84.1 per cent) and lowest for young firms (65.9 per cent).

The elasticity of the liquidity ratio is still positive and significant for all sub-groups but not for the whole sample. This elasticity is still high compared to the other elasticities but much smaller than in the baseline equation. The largest change is observed from small and young firms. In this case the long-run elasticity of the liquidity ratio is highest for old and large firms and not for young firms as in the baseline equation. As before, including this variable in the regression seems to affect mostly small and young firms.

---

[25] Petersen and Rajan (1994). Dell'Ariccia and Marquez (2001), Delbreil *et al.* (2000), Elsas and Krahnen (1998) and Quehenberger (1997).

6   Summary and conclusions

Owing to Austria's monetary policy and financial structure it is widely believed that the effects of monetary policy through the credit channel are much more important than those predicted under the traditional monetary view. This is confirmed here with a sample of Austrian firms for the period 1994–9. Here it is found that the liquidity ratio and the firms' access to external financing are significant determinants of investment demand and also that considerable differences exist across groups of firms.

Contrary to what had been suggested before, growth of sales contributes to explain investment behaviour only as long as the liquidity ratio is not taken into account. In general not only the significance but also the long-run elasticity of sales growth diminishes when this variable or an interaction term are included in the regression. There are also differences across groups of firms: young firms are more dependent on sales than other groups of firms. This may be due to the larger informational asymmetries that young firms face.

The interest rate channel is weak, but it does exist for some groups of firms. The size and significance of the effect of the user cost of capital on investment depends not only on the type of firm, but also on other variables which capture informational asymmetries and access to capital markets. The direction of the change, however, is ambiguous. As in the case of sales, the effect of the user cost of capital on investment diminishes with the presence of financial variables, but does not necessarily decrease with size or age.

The liquidity ratio seems to be the most important determinant of investment demand. It is almost always significant and the size of the effect is also much larger than the effect of the other variables. However, its long-run elasticity is conditional on characteristics of the firms studied here. It is found that firms may be able to diminish their dependence on internal funds by using trade credit or having close relationships to a house bank.

Although these relationships seem to weaken the credit channel, they do not necessarily weaken the interest rate channel when such a channel exists. This confirms the view that trade credit and the house bank principle help overcome liquidity constraints but do not dampen the effect of the interest rate on investment.

Part 3

The role of banks in the transmission: evidence from microeconomic data

The chapters in part 2 have shown that liquidity factors are likely to play a role in the investment decisions of firms in a number of euro area countries, in addition to interest rates and the cost of capital. This suggests that financial conditions may matter in the transmission of monetary policy. Banks, which occupy a central position in the euro area's financial system, are a natural focus of attention here. The chapters that follow contain a summary of evidence of the impact of monetary policy on the lending behaviour of banks. An opening summary chapter by M. Ehrmann, L. Gambacorta, J. Martínez-Pagés, P. Sevestre and A. Worms (chapter 14), brings together the evidence for the euro area, followed by more specific studies on Germany, Spain, France, Greece, Italy, the Netherlands, Austria, Portugal and Finland.

The vast international literature on the role of banks in monetary policy transmission in recent years has yielded a number of conclusions. First, there seems to be conclusive evidence that changes in policy-driven interest rates are followed by significant adjustments in bank balance sheets. Bank lending normally tends to contract after a montary policy restriction. Likewise, the most liquid components of bank liabilities (such as checking and demand deposits) also tend to fall with some lag. The effect on total deposits is more uncertain, as some redistribution takes place towards longer-term deposits. While these are established regularities, the exact causal chain of these movements is much more uncertain, owing to the difficulty of identifying movements coming from the demand and the supply side. In fact, however, such identification is crucial to understanding the role (passive in the first case, active in the second) that banks play in the transmission process.

Panel data have been successfully used, in the USA and in some European countries, to help solve the identification problem. This is the approach taken in most of the chapters that follow. In particular, the rich cross-section dimension of the panels available in the National Central Banks that participated in the project has been used to analyse cross-sectoral differences in the movement in bank balance sheets following montary policy shocks.

In the national studies, the research team adopted the model specification and sample period that best fitted the specifics of each country. In the summary chapter, a homogeneous specification was fitted to the group of large countries together, and the results contrasted with the findings of the national studies.

Taking together all pieces of evidence, three main conclusions can be drawn. First, bank lending unambiguously reacts, with a negative sign, to changes in central bank-controlled short-term interest rates, thus confirming the earlier findings. Second, the size of the bank and the size of its capital, often found in the literature on the USA to be correlated with the intensity of this response, do not seem capable of explaining the cross-country differences observed in the euro area. Finally, a systematic negative relation is found, instead, in almost all countries between the loan response and the degree of liquidity of the bank's asset side. The possible interpretations and motivation of this finding are discussed in detail in the national contributions, and, for the euro area, in the summary chapter.

14 Financial systems and the role of banks in monetary policy transmission in the euro area

M. Ehrmann, L. Gambacorta, J. Martínez-Pagés, P. Sevestre and A. Worms

1 Introduction

Following the microeconometric analysis of firms' investment using firm-level data in part 2 of this volume, part 3 focuses on the microeconometric investigation of the role of banks in monetary transmission in the euro area. While theory offers a wide array of different transmission channels, those that attribute an important role to banks are of special interest here, mainly for two reasons.

First, most European countries rely much more heavily on bank finance than, for example, the USA (see table 14.1). Comparing the ratio of bank total assets to GDP across the four largest countries of the euro area[1] and the USA it turns out that banks are much less important in the USA than in any of the European countries. Accordingly, the financial structure of the corporate sector in Europe relies much more heavily on bank loans, with the mirror image of this being the larger stock market capitalisation and the more prominent role of debt securities issued by the corporate sector in the USA.

Second, beyond the high overall level of bank dependence there are also some notable differences at the country level. We document the differences in a comprehensive fashion in table 14.2, and in what follows concentrate on the gaps that may have implications for the transmission of monetary policy.

We try to quantify the importance of these considerations by focusing on three questions: (1) what is the role of banks (i.e. bank loans) in monetary transmission in the euro area, (2) are there differences in this respect

We would like to thank the participants of the monetary economics workshop at the NBER Summer Institute 2001, Ignazio Angeloni, Sophocles Brissimis, Skander van den Heuvel, Anil Kashyap, Claire Loupias, Benoît Mojon, Ignacio Hernando, Carlos Robalo Marques, and Fred Ramb for their comments and suggestions.

[1] These four countries, which form the group of countries studied in section 5, contribute approximately 80 per cent to euro area GDP.

Table 14.1 *Financial structures in the euro area and the USA (% of GDP), 2001*

	Euro area	France	Germany	Italy	Spain	USA
Bank total assets[a]	267.1	276.7	304.3	154.4	199.6	78.0
Bank loans to corporate sector	42.6	35.7	38.9	42.3	46.4	18.8
Outstanding debt securities of non-financial corporate sector	6.5	17.0	2.8	2.4	2.6	28.9
Stock market capitalisation	71.7	90.6	58.1	48.7	80.9	137.1

Note: [a] Monetary and Financial Institutions (MFIs), excluding the Eurosystem for the euro area; credit institutions and other MFIs for the countries of the euro area; commercial banks, savings institutions and credit unions for the USA.
Source: Eurosystem, BIS, World Federation of Exchange, Federal Reserve Flow of Funds.

across the member countries of EMU and (3) are there distributional effects of monetary policy on different types of banks?

These issues have already been addressed in several recent studies on the monetary transmission process at the aggregate level.[2] However, clear-cut conclusions can hardly be drawn from these studies, mainly because of the wide confidence intervals that are normally associated with such macro time-series estimates. By using the cross-sectional information of data on individual banks, we hope to get more precise estimates, thus allowing for better inference on differences across countries.

The central task in this effort is to identify the reaction of loan *supply* to monetary policy actions. This is important since bank loans are the main link between banks and private non-banks, and because bank loans very often cannot be easily replaced by other forms of finance on the borrower's side. There is ample evidence that aggregate bank loans decline following a monetary contraction.[3] However, such a decline can in principle be caused by both, loan demand and loan supply, and hence sorting out the cause is important.[4]

To discriminate among loan supply and loan demand movements, the recent literature has generally focused on cross-sectional differences

[2] For example, Ciccarelli and Rebucci (2002); Clements, Kontolemis and Levy (2001); Mihov (2001); Sala (2001). For a model which explicitly takes into account the effect of differences in the bank lending channel on monetary policy, see Gambacorta (2001a and 2003).

[3] Bernanke and Blinder (1992); for the euro area, see Peersman and Smets (chapter 2 in this volume) and Mojon and Peersman (2001).

[4] For a definition of the bank lending channel see Bernanke and Blinder (1988).

Table 14.2 *The structure of national financial systems*

	Austria	Belgium	Finland	France	Germany	Greece	Ireland	Italy	Luxembourg	Netherlands	Portugal	Spain
Importance of banks for firms' financing[a]	Very important	Important	Important	Important	Very important	Very important	Important	Very important	Important	Important	Important	Very important
Fraction of short-term loans[b]	Average	Average	Low	Low	Low	High	Low	High	NA	Low	Low	High
Fraction of loans at variable interest rates[c]	Low	High	High	Average	Low	High	High	High	NA	Low	High	High
Relationship lending	Very important (house banks)	Not very important (many SMEs, family-owned, less prone to traditional relationship lending)	Important, but declining	Not important except for small firms	Very important (house banks)	Not important any more	Very important for commercial lending	Very important	NA	Important	Not important (firms often initially borrow from a single bank, but then switch to borrowing from several banks)[g]	Not important
Market concentration[d]	Medium	High	High	Medium	Low	High	High	Low	Low	High	High	Medium

(*cont.*)

Table 14.2 (cont.)

	Austria	Belgium	Finland	France	Germany	Greece	Ireland	Italy	Luxembourg	Netherlands	Portugal	Spain
State influence[a]	Strong (public guarantees for most savings banks)	Medium	Strong (blanket public guarantee in the aftermath of the banking crisis)	Medium	Strong (public guarantees in the savings banks' sector)	Strong	Weak	Strong, but declining	Weak	Weak	Medium	Weak (no public guarantees of savings banks)
Deposit insurance[f]	Average (approx. 15,000 Euros in 1990, 20,000 in 1998)	Average (approx. 12,500 Euros per depositor until 1998, 15,000 in 1999, 20,000 Euros since)	High initially, average now (practically complete in 1990, approx. 25,000 Euros in 1998)	High (76,000 Euros since 1999; at a similar level, but not unified across banks before)	Effectively complete	Average (20,000 Euros, complete for deposits with the Postal Savings bank)	Average (20,000 Euros)	High (103,000 Euros; until 1996 also 75 per cent coverage between 103,000 and 516,000 Euros)	Average (approx. 12,500 Euros per account)	Average (approx. 18,000 Euros in 1990, 20,000 since 1995)	Average (15,000 Euros fully insured, second 15,000 Euros 75 per cent, third 15,000 Euros 50 per cent)	Modest (9,000 Euros per depositor in 1990, 15,000 Euros in 1998, 20,000 Euros now)
Bank networks of independent banks	Very important (most banks are in a network,	Not important (Credit Agricole consists of two member banks,	Very important (the vast majority of banks is organised	Important	Very important (most banks are in a network, with very	Not important (no networks)	Very important (for retail banks)	Very important (most banks are in a network,	Not important (network of mutual agricultural	Not important (bank groups like, e.g., ABN Amro,	Not important (network of mutual agricultural credit	Not important (they exist but weak links between

member banks and head institution)

banks supplies data on the aggregate level)

Rabo or ING have consolidated balance sheets, and can thus be regarded as one bank)

credit banks supplies data on the aggregate level)

with links to the head institution)

strong links to the head institution)

in groups with very close ties between banks)

Credit Professionnel has weak links)

with very strong links to the head institution)

[a] See Ehrmann *et al.* (2001), table 2 . The ranking is based on 1997 data. Countries ranked 'very important' are those that comply with all of the following four conditions: debt securities to GDP <4%, debt securities to bank loans <10%, stock market capitalisation to GDP <60% and funds raised through securities issuance <50%. Countries that fail to comply with at least one of those conditions are ranked 'important'. No country was ranked as 'less important', which would apply, for example, for the USA.

[b] Source: Borio (1996). 'low': fraction of short term loans <20%; 'high': >35%

[c] Source: Borio (1996). 'low': fraction of loans at variable interest rates <40%; 'high': >50%. Source in case of Germany: Bundesbank internal paper, based on survey data for 1997.

[d] Concentration is ranked low when Herfindahl index and the market share of the five largest banks (*Source:* Corvoisier and Gropp, 2001) are in the range of 30 or below. It is ranked high when the Herfindahl index stands at around 100, and the market share of the five largest banks does not give conflicting evidence. It is ranked medium for intermediate cases.

[e] Countries are ranked according to the percentage of the assets of the top ten banks controlled by the government (*Source:* La Porta, Lopez–de–Silanes and Shleifer, 2002): 'strong' (>30%), 'medium' (between 10% and 30%) and 'weak' (<10%). This is checked to be consistent with other available information on public guarantees or ownership. The evaluation refers roughly to the first half of the 1990s. State influence declined steadily during the sample period in almost all countries. Therefore, the present ranking is based on a rough average for the sample period considered in the estimates and does not necessarily reflect the ranking at the end of the sample period.

[f] Source: Eurosystem. 'Average' for values around 20,000 Euros.

[g] See Farinha and Santos (2000).

NA: Not available.

between banks.[5] This identification strategy assumes that a monetary policy tightening leads to a drop in the availability of core deposits, which affects banks' ability to make new loans. If it is possible to single out bank characteristics that are related to a bank's ability to compensate for this drop of funds and at the same time determine its lending behaviour after a monetary tightening, loan-supply effects can be identified. Of course, this assumes that a bank's loan demand is independent of these characteristics. The earlier literature has proceeded by positing several differences that could shape loan-supply sensitivity to monetary policy. One strand of this literature checks whether poorly capitalised banks have a more limited access to non-deposit financing and as such should be forced to reduce their loan supply by more than well-capitalised banks (e.g. Kishan and Opiela, 2000; Peek and Rosengren, 1995; Van den Heuvel, 2001). The role of size has been emphasised, for example, in Kashyap and Stein (1995): small banks are assumed to suffer from informational asymmetry problems more than large banks, and therefore find it more difficult to raise uninsured funds in times of monetary tightening. Again, this should induce them to reduce their lending relatively more when compared to large banks. Another distinction is often drawn between more and less liquid banks (e.g. Ashcraft, 2001; Kashyap and Stein, 2000; Stein, 1998). Whereas relatively liquid banks can draw down their liquid assets to shield their loan portfolio, this is not feasible for less liquid banks.

In the spirit of this approach, we investigate whether there are certain types of banks whose lending is more responsive to monetary policy impulses. In section 2 we will provide a description of the banking systems in the countries of the euro area. We will argue that these characteristics are important for the role of banks in monetary policy transmission, and that some of the results found for the USA are not likely to be applicable to the euro area. Mainly, we believe that the size criterion is not necessarily a good indicator for distributional effects across banks. Our predictions will be tested in the empirical analysis, where we consider which bank characteristics – i.e. size, liquidity or capitalisation – distinguish banks' responses to changes in the interest rates in Europe. In this chapter, we will perform regressions for the euro area as a whole and for Germany, France, Italy and Spain, the four largest countries of the euro area, and furthermore draw on the results obtained in the other chapters of part 3. The main aim of this chapter is to provide an overview of those results obtained at the national level, to produce an exactly comparable set of results by performing regressions in a harmonised approach and

---

[5] Contributions that use macro data are, e.g., Bernanke and Blinder (1992); Brissimis and Magginas (2002) or Kashyap, Stein and Wilcox (1993, 1996) .

to broaden the focus to the euro area as a whole. The other chapters in part 3 provide more detailed and country-specific analyses for nine of the twelve countries of the euro area.

The remainder of the chapter is organised as follows. Section 2 describes the structure of the banking sector in the euro area and the consequences it might have for the role of banks in monetary policy transmission. The theoretical model underlying our analysis is introduced in section 3. Section 4 presents results for the entire euro area using individual bank balance sheet data provided by BankScope. Section 5 presents evidence on a national basis using databases on the full population of banks collected by the respective national central banks. Section 6 summarises the main conclusions.

2   The structure of the banking system and monetary policy transmission

2.1   *Characteristics of the banking system in the euro area*

This section provides a short description of the structure of the banking system in the euro area. As a background, table 14.2 reports a number of qualitative indicators on the banking market in the individual euro area countries – for example, the importance of bank finance for firms, measures of concentration, the role of the government in banking and the importance of bank network structures. Table 14.2 shows that bank finance, as stated in the introduction, is of primary importance in most countries of the euro area, and gives some indication as to the heterogeneity of banking structures.

We believe several features of national banking structures to be important for the response of bank lending to a monetary policy action, and for the assessment of the macroeconomic importance of such responses. In the following, we highlight the most distinctive patterns that might be relevant in this context and refer the interested reader to the subsequent chapters in this volume, which elaborate in more detail on the main features of the respective national banking systems.

2.1.1   *Importance of banks for firms' financing*   As mentioned in section 1, banks play an important role in firms' financing. Market financing of the corporate sector is less developed than in the USA. Even in France, where it is more important than in many countries of the euro area (see table 14.1), only the largest firms can issue debt securities, and the role of banks in financing firms is still much more dominant than in the USA. The business sector has therefore been heavily dependent on

bank credit. This indicates that changes in bank loan supply affect firms relatively strongly, since they cannot easily find substitutes for the bank finance. Table 14.2, which presents a qualitative ranking of the euro area countries, shows that banks are important in every single country.

2.1.2   Maturity of loans, collateralisation   The loans supplied by Italian banks are to a large extent short term and come with variable interest rates. The same tendency is present in Spain. This can accelerate the transmission of monetary policy impulses to lending rates and thus borrowing costs. On the other hand, countries like Austria and the Netherlands have a longer maturity of loans and a higher share of fixed rate contracts.[6] In countries such as Italy, where a high percentage of loans is backed by collateral, the response of bank loans to monetary policy could be furthermore accentuated through the so-called 'balance sheet channel'.[7] The ranking in table 14.2 shows considerable heterogeneity across the euro area countries in these two respects.

2.1.3   Relationship lending   In several European countries, the market for intermediated finance is characterised by relationship rather than arm's-length lending. It is very common that bank customers establish long-lasting relationships with banks, a prominent example being the German system of 'house banks', in which firms conduct most of their financial business with one bank only.[8] With most German banks operating as universal banks, and therefore supplying their customers with the full range of financial services, this implies a much closer linkage to a single bank than in many other countries. For the creditor, this could also imply an implicit guarantee to have access to (additional) funds even if the central bank follows a restrictive monetary policy, or that interest rate increases are not passed through immediately, thus leading to smoother interest rates variations on such loans.[9] In such a case, the reaction of bank loan supply to monetary policy should be at least muted. Typically, house bank relationships exist between relatively small banks – which owing to their presence in local markets are able to entertain personal contacts and for which the loan business with non-banks is still a central activity – and their customers. Italy shows a similar pattern, where many small banks entertain close relationships with their customers, especially with small firms.[10] This is true for France as well, where most small firms

---

[6] Borio (1996).
[7] See, among others, Bernanke and Gertler (1995); Kashyap and Stein (1997); Mishkin (1995) and Oliner and Rudebusch (1996).
[8] See, e.g., Elsas and Krahnen (1998).   [9] See, e.g., Rajan and Zingales (1998).
[10] Angelini, Di Salvo and Ferri (1998).

have business relationships with one bank only. A qualitative ranking of the importance of relationship lending is provided in table 14.2.

2.1.4   Market concentration and size structure   The banking markets in the countries of the euro area were characterised by a steadily increasing concentration during the 1990s. It stands at different levels in the various countries, however. According to the Herfindahl index, Germany and Italy are at the lower end of market concentration in the euro area, as opposed to Belgium, Greece, the Netherlands, and especially Finland (for details, see table 26.2 (p. 438) for a ranking, see table 14.2).

Table 14.3 provides another detailed comparison of the size structure in the four largest countries of the euro area. Our samples of banks are split into small and large banks with respect to a relative national threshold.[11]

For all countries, a small number of large banks holds a major share in both the loan and deposit markets: the 75 per cent smallest banks hold only around 8 per cent–15 per cent of deposits, and account for around 5 per cent–12 per cent of loans, whereas the 5 per cent largest banks hold around 52 per cent–71 per cent of deposits and have a market share of around 56 per cent–77 per cent in loans. Table 14.3 reports similar data on the USA as a benchmark. Also there, the 75 per cent smallest banks account for a small market share in terms of total assets, loans and deposits, whereas the top 5 per cent account for the lion's share in each respect.

The structure of these small banks varies considerably across countries. Whereas French, Italian and Spanish small banks are on average very liquid, there does not seem to be a systematic difference in the degree of liquidity of banks of different size in Germany. Similarly with capitalisation, where small banks are on average better capitalised in France, Italy and Spain, whereas in Germany there is only a small difference in the level of capitalisation among banks of different size.

German banks are the least capitalised. The low degree of capitalisation in Germany is usually explained by the low riskiness of the asset structure of German banks in an international comparison: on average, German banks hold more public bonds and other less risky assets such as, for example, interbank assets (see also table 14.12 in the statistical appendix). It is interesting to note that in Italy, the small banks hold a much larger market share in the deposit market than in the loan market. This gap is much less pronounced in the other countries.

---

[11] A similar table with a split according to a criterion in terms of the absolute value of their total assets is provided in Ehrmann *et al.* (2001).

Table 14.3 *Data description with respect to relative size* [a], *December 1998*

	France			Germany			Italy			Spain			USA (1993)		
	Small	Large	Total	Small	Large	Total	Small	Large	Total	Small	Large	Total	Small	Large	Total
Number of banks	249	16	332	2405	160	3207	578	36	759	182	12	243	8404	561	11206
Mean assets (billion Euros)	0.770	92.33	6.398	0.161	24.49	1.591	0.138	28.90	1.863	0.498	43.67	3.612	0.045	4.82	0.32
Share of total assets	0.090	0.695	1	0.076	0.768	1	0.057	0.736	1	0.103	0.597	1	0.105	0.755	1
Mean deposits	0.492	44.89	3.393	0.123	7.311	0.628	0.070	9.705	0.646	0.292	18.70	1.773	0.039	3.44	0.24
Market share of total deposits	0.109	0.638	1	0.147	0.581	1	0.083	0.713	1	0.123	0.521	1	0.12	0.72	1
Mean loans	0.343	37.91	2.576	0.095	7.673	0.588	0.055	12.31	0.762	0.246	17.65	1560	0.024	2.84	0.19
Market share of total loans	0.100	0.709	1	0.121	0.651	1	0.055	0.766	1	0.118	0.559	1	0.10	0.77	1
Liquid assets/total assets	0.416	0.294	0.401	0.337	0.333	0.342	0.421	0.257	0.399	0.424	0.337	0.407	0.44	0.36	0.37
Loans/total assets	0.411	0.358	0.403	0.580	0.394	0.563	0.387	0.405	0.388	0.450	0.466	0.459	0.53	0.59	0.58
Deposits/total assets	0.581	0.438	0.585	0.781	0.423	0.747	0.550	0.346	0.508	0.625	0.490	0.614	0.88	0.71	0.75
Capital and reserves/total assets	0.106	0.037	0.089	0.059	0.041	0.055	0.122	0.068	0.112	0.154	0.049	0.132	0.10	0.07	0.08

Note: [a] Source: Eurosystem data, Kashyap and Stein (2000). The data sets are corrected for corrupt observations, such as banks with total assets smaller or equal to zero. A 'small' bank is situated below the third quartile of the distribution of total assets, while a 'large' bank is situated above the 95th percentile. Data for the USA refer to 1993 and are expressed in billion US dollars. Liquid assets for the USA are calculated as cash, securities and federal funds lent. Note that the table does not report numbers for medium-sized banks, such that the total is not equal to the sum of the reported figures for small and large banks.

2.1.5   State influence and ownership structure   Although steadily declining over time,[12] the role of the government in banking markets is an important issue in Europe. State influence, exerted through direct public ownership of banks, state control, or public guarantees, has been much more common than in the USA, as is documented in La Porta, Lopez-de-Silanes and Shleifer (2002). Public ownership of banks was, during the sample period studied, most widespread in Austria, but significant also in most other countries of the euro area. In Finland, the government issued a guarantee for all bank deposits following the banking crisis of the early 1990s, and maintained it until 1998. In Greece, the market share of the state-controlled banks is currently around 50 per cent, down from 70 per cent in 1995. In other countries, the influence of the state is rather limited, as for example in Spain, where state-owned banks represented 13 per cent of total loans and 3 per cent of total deposits at the start of the sample period (1988), but were completely privatised by the end of the sample. Savings banks in Spain are not publicly guaranteed, despite the involvement of some local governments in their control. This heterogeneity is shown in the qualitative comparison of table 14.2.

2.1.6   Deposit insurance   The degree of effective deposit insurance differs considerably across European countries during the sample period studied. Table 14.2 provides a cross-country comparison. Deposit insurance in Spain covered all deposits of non-financial entities up to a relatively modest amount (9,000 Euros per depositor in 1990 and 15,000 Euros in 1998). In Germany, on the other hand, the statutory deposit insurance system, a private safety fund as well as cross-guarantee arrangements in the savings banks' and in the cooperative banks' sectors, respectively, effectively amount to a full insurance of all non-bank deposits.[13] France appears to be in an intermediate position with a complete insurance for deposits up to 76,000 Euros per depositor.

2.1.7   Bank failures   In most countries of the euro area, bank failures have occurred much less frequently than in the USA.[14] Around 1,500 bank failures were reported for the USA for the period 1980–94. Even between 1994 and 2000, i.e., in an economic boom, there were seven

---

[12] For example, in Italy the share of total assets held by banks and groups controlled by the State went from 68 per cent in 1992 to 12 per cent in 2000.
[13] See, for example, Deutsche Bundesbank (2000b).
[14] A direct comparison of these numbers is complicated by the fact that the definition of 'bank failures' might be different across countries. Numbers on prevented bank failures are especially difficult to obtain for the euro area countries. Some cases are listed in Gropp, Vesala and Vulpes (2001).

bank failures per year on average.[15] This is a considerably higher fraction of the banking population than, for example, in Germany, where only around 50 private banks have failed since 1966. Also in Italy many fewer bank failures occurred.[16] In Spain, two banking crises have occurred since 1975. The first (1978–85) was more widespread, affecting fifty-eight banks (accounting for 27 per cent of deposits), while the second (1991–3) affected very few banks but involved one of the biggest institutions. In both cases, owing to the potential systemic implications, most of the banks were either acquired by other solvent institutions, or the government intervened, so that depositors' losses were very limited. Besides these two periods, there was only one failure of a very small bank in Spain. A banking crisis was also experienced in Finland during the early 1990s. However, because of strong government intervention, only one bank failure materialised.

2.1.8   Bank networks   Bank networks exist in several countries of the euro area. The savings banks and credit cooperatives are frequently organised in networks, although with a varying degree of collaboration in the different countries. To give an example, in Germany most banks (the vast majority of small banks) belong to either the cooperative sector (in the 1990s about 70 per cent of all banks) or the savings banks' sector (almost 20 per cent). Both sectors consist of an 'upper tier' of large banks serving as head institutions. The 'lower-tier' banks generally entertain very close relationships to the head institutions of their respective sector, leading to an internal liquidity management: on average, the 'lower-tier' banks deposit short-term funds with the 'upper-tier' banks, and receive long-term loans in turn.[17]

Similar structures can be found in many countries of the euro area (for an overview, see table 14.2). In Austria, 750 of 799 banks in 1996 belonged to either the savings banks' or the credit cooperatives' network, which have structures comparable to those described for Germany. In Finland, cooperative banks are organised in the OKO Bank group, which has a centralised liquidity management. In Spain, on the other hand, savings and cooperative banks' networks exist, but their central institutions play only a relatively minor role.

---

[15] See Federal Deposit Insurance Corporation (1998) for 1980–94, and www.fdic.gov.

[16] In the period 1980–97, forty (in almost all cases very small mutual) banks were placed in administrative liquidation. The share of deposits of failed banks was always negligible and reached around 1 per cent only three times, namely in 1982, 1987 and 1996 (see Boccuzzi, 1998).

[17] See Upper and Worms (2001a and 2001b) and Deutsche Bundesbank (2001).

2.2   Some conjectures on the role of banks in monetary policy transmission

The structure of the banking markets in the individual countries is likely to determine the response of bank lending to monetary policy. Several features of European banking markets are significantly different from those found in the USA. It is therefore most likely that the distributional effects across banks that have been documented for the USA will not be identical to those we can expect for the countries of the euro area. Additionally, there are significant differences across European countries, such that we would not necessarily expect results to be identical for the various countries.

One important issue is the relevance of informational frictions in the banking markets. If depositors and players in the interbank markets face strong informational asymmetries, then distributional effects are likely to occur between banks that are informationally opaque to different degrees. This would suggest the use of the size, liquidity and capitalisation criteria as in the existing literature. However, several of the features mentioned above are capable of reducing significantly the extent to which informational frictions exist. A first indication that in general, informational asymmetries are less pronounced is the relatively low risk involved in lending to banks, given the few bank failures experienced in many countries.

The role of governments in the banking markets similarly reduces the risk of depositors: an active role of the State in the banking sector may obviously reduce the amount of informational asymmetries. Publicly owned or guaranteed banks are therefore unlikely to suffer a disproportionate drain of funds after a monetary tightening, and distributional effects in their loan reactions are hence unlikely to occur.

Under a government guarantee, it is also possible that weaker banks engage in a 'gamble for resurrection' by extending their loan portfolio despite potential increases in its riskiness. Evidence for this is provided in Vihriälä (1997), who detects such a pattern among cooperative banks in Finland during the early 1990s. He finds that, the lower the degree of capitalisation of a bank, the more expansionary was its loan supply.

There are also factors that offset the importance of a bank's asset size. One example is deposit insurance. The extensive degree of effective deposit insurance in countries such as Germany and Italy makes it furthermore difficult to believe that deposits at small or less capitalised banks are riskier than deposits held at large or better capitalised banks.

The network arrangement between banks can also have important consequences for the reaction of bank loan supply to monetary policy. In networks with strong links between the head institutions and the lower tier, the large banks in the upper tier can serve as liquidity-providers in times of a monetary tightening, such that the system would experience a net flow of funds from the head institutions to the small member banks. Ehrmann and Worms (2001) show that in Germany, indeed, small banks receive a net inflow of funds from their head institutions following a monetary contraction. This indicates that the characteristics of a single-member bank need not be a good proxy to assess distributional effects of monetary policy across banks, but that the position of the network as a whole, or of the head institution, might become more relevant.[18]

Additionally, banking networks frequently contain mutual assistance agreements, as is the case, for example, for the Austrian and German credit cooperative sectors. These help to diminish informational asymmetries for a single bank, since it is the sector as a whole rather than the single bank that determines the riskiness of a financial engagement with a member bank.

Lastly, under the assumption that relationship lending implies that banks shelter their customers from the effects of monetary policy to some degree, we would expect that those banks show a muted reaction in their lending behaviour. Since it is often small banks which maintain these tight lending relationships, it might very well be that smaller banks react less strongly to monetary policy than large banks (which would be the opposite to the findings for the USA). At least, size does not always need to be a good indicator for distributional effects across banks. However, this notion is at odds with the usual assumption that smaller banks find it more difficult to maintain their loan portfolio after a monetary tightening. Relationship lending can explain why these banks have an incentive to maintain the portfolio, but it does not explain how this can be achieved where informational asymmetries are present. Small banks do therefore need to have the necessary sources of funds at hand to maintain their loan portfolio even in times of monetary tightenings. This can be either achieved through a higher degree of liquidity of those banks (like, for example, in Italy or in France) through the liquidity provisions within the bank networks (as, for example, in Germany) and/or thanks to a better capitalisation (as in France, Italy and Spain).

Tests of the bank lending channel do therefore have to be interpreted in the light of the institutional peculiarities of each country.[19] Doing so leads us to several conjectures on the role of banks in monetary policy

---

[18] A related idea has been documented for the USA in Campello (2002). He shows that internal capital markets in financial conglomerates can dampen bank lending channel effects to some extent.

[19] Several papers have already ranked countries with respect to the effectiveness of a bank lending channel (Cecchetti, 2000; De Nederlansche Bank, 2000; Kashyap and Stein, 1997). They rely on indicators from three main categories: the importance of small banks, bank health and the availability of alternative finance. Despite differences with

transmission. Overall, we would expect informational frictions to be less important in most countries of the euro area than they are in the USA. Several institutional features could imply that banks can shield their loan portfolio from monetary policy shocks. The reaction of a bank's lending might thus depend much more on the importance it attributes to maintaining a lending relationship than on the necessity to fund a certain loan portfolio. In most European countries, size and capitalisation need not be bank characteristics that explain differential loan-supply reactions to monetary policy. However, there may still be distributional effects, which depend on other factors. For example, in some European countries, some groups of small banks have traditionally acted as collectors of retail deposits to the whole banking system. Consequently, those banks tend to be more liquid on average. It may be the case that these banks react differently to monetary policy changes.

3   The model

The basic idea of our empirical test can be illustrated with a simple model of a profit-maximising bank; a more elaborate model of the bank lending channel has been developed, for instance, in Stein (1998). The balance sheet identity of bank i is defined as:

$$L_i + S_i = D_i + B_i + C_i \tag{1}$$

where L_i is the volume of loans, S_i securities, D_i the volume of (secured) deposits, B_i the level of non-secured funding and C_i the capital of bank i. Bank i acts on a loan market characterised by monopolistic competition. The demand for (nominal) bank loans L_i^d is given by:

$$L_i^d = -a_0 \cdot r_{L,i} + a_1 \cdot y + a_2 \cdot p \tag{2}$$

The bank–individual loan rate is given by $r_{L,i}$. y denotes aggregate real output, p the price level. All coefficients are assumed to be positive: a_0, $a_1, a_2 > 0$.

For simplicity, we assume that bank capital is linked to the level of loans (as in the Basle requirements) and banks' holding of securities to the level of deposits (liquidity risk):

$$C_i = k \cdot L_i \tag{3}$$

$$S_i = s \cdot D_i \tag{4}$$

respect to some countries, the rankings reach relatively similar conclusions. For the four largest economies, both Cecchetti (2000) and Kashyap and Stein (1997) rank Italy as the strongest, France and Germany in the mid-range, and Spain as the country with the least exposure to a bank-lending channel.

Deposits D_i are secured, but do not bear interest. They are demanded because of their role as a means of payment. Deposit demand is therefore, according to a 'money-demand'-type function, negatively related to the interest rate of an alternative risk-free asset, r_s, which we take to be the monetary policy rate:

$$D = -b_0 \cdot r_S \tag{5}$$

where $b_0 > 0$. Since banks do not remunerate these deposits, they cannot influence the amount of deposits held at the single bank, D_i. This is exogenous to the bank and it will drop after a monetary tightening (i.e. after an increase in r_s).

However, banks have access to an alternative source of funds, which is unsecured and for which the bank has to pay interest. Banks are perceived to be risky, and the suppliers of unsecured finance to banks therefore ask for an external finance premium. The interest rate they pay, $r_{B,i}$, is thus the risk-free rate r_s plus this premium. The external finance premium depends on a signal of the bank's health, x_i, which can be observed by all market participants. The higher the x_i, the lower the external finance premium:

$$r_{B,i} = r_S \cdot (\mu - c_0 \cdot x_i) \tag{6}$$

where $\mu - c_0 \cdot x_i \geq 1 \; \forall i$. Bank i cannot raise unsecured funds if it offers less than $r_{B,i}$, whereas it can raise any amount of funds if it pays at least $r_{B,i}$. Given $r_{B,i}$ is a cost factor, bank i will not be ready to pay more than $r_{B,i}$.

The profit of bank i, π_i, is given by[20]:

$$\pi_i = L_i \cdot r_{L,i} + S_i \cdot r_S - B_i \cdot r_{B,i} - \Psi_i \tag{7}$$

where Ψ_i captures bank-specific administrative costs and the remuneration costs for the required capital holdings. Inserting (1)–(5), and assuming equilibrium in the loan market, yields:

$$\pi_i = L_i \cdot \left(-\frac{1}{a_0} \cdot L_i + \frac{a_1}{a_0} \cdot y + \frac{a_2}{a_0} \cdot p \right) + s \cdot D_i \cdot r_S$$
$$- ((1 - k) \cdot L_i - (1 - s) \cdot D_i) \cdot r_{B,i} - \Psi_i \tag{8}$$

Setting the first-order condition to zero, and inserting (6) yields:

$$L_i = \frac{a_1}{2} \cdot y + \frac{a_2}{2} \cdot p - \frac{a_0 \cdot \mu \cdot (1 - k)}{2} \cdot r_S$$
$$+ \frac{a_0 \cdot c_0 \cdot (1 - k)}{2} \cdot x_i \cdot r_S - \frac{a_0}{2} \cdot \frac{\partial \Psi_i}{\partial L_i} \tag{9}$$

---

[20] We are also assuming $B_i > 0$.

In the traditional 'money view' there are no informational asymmetries and, hence, no external finance premia. $r_{B,i}$ is equal to r_s for all banks and there are no differences in the response to monetary policy across banks. A monetary policy tightening (i.e. an increase in r_S) leads to a reduction in deposits according to (5). Banks can keep the asset side of their balance sheet unchanged only if they increase other sources of funding B_i accordingly. But, the interest rate a bank has to pay for these funds was increased by the monetary policy tightening according to (6). Banks pass at least part of this higher cost to their loan rate ($r_{L,i}$), which in turn reduces loan demand. In our model, this implies a negative coefficient of r_S in (9).

However, if a bank-lending channel is at work, the costs faced by a bank for raising non-secured funds should depend on the degree to which it suffers from informational frictions in financial markets. In the model, this implication is mirrored by the assumption that different banks face different costs for raising non-secured deposits (i.e. $c_0 > 0$). This differentiation would force some banks to reduce their lending by more, namely those that face higher costs of raising non-secured deposits because they have a low value of the bank characteristic x_i. If, as we assume in the model, loan demand is homogeneous across banks, regardless of their value of x_i, a differential loan reaction to monetary policy identifies a loan-supply movement. Whether such a differential reaction is present, can be seen by looking at the coefficient on the interaction term $x_i \cdot r_s$,

$$\frac{a_0 \cdot c_0 \cdot (1 - k)}{2}.$$

If this coefficient is significantly positive, the assumptions of the model imply that monetary policy affects loan supply.

The assumption of a homogeneous reaction of loan demand across banks is therefore crucial for the identification of loan supply effects of monetary policy. It excludes cases where, for example, large or small banks' customers are more interest rate-sensitive. Given that bank loans are the main source of financing for firms in the euro area, and readily available substitutes in times of monetary tightenings are very limited even for relatively large firms, we see this as a reasonable benchmark for most countries.[21]

For the cases of size and liquidity, we will furthermore estimate a model with double interactions, i.e. we include both bank characteristics $x_{1,i}$

---

[21] Several of the subsequent chapters improve on this identification issue by including bank-specific loan-demand proxies that permit differences in loan demand across banks. The results seem to be rather robust to these changes (see, for example, chapter 15 on Germany).

and $x_{2,i}$, the single interaction with the interest rates, $x_{1,i} \cdot r_s$, and $x_{2,i} \cdot r_s$, and furthermore a double interaction $x_{1,i} \cdot x_{2,i} \cdot r_s$, as well as the interaction of the bank characteristics, $x_{1,i} \cdot x_{2,i}$. With this extended model, it is possible to test whether the effect of liquidity depends on the size of banks (and vice versa). The underlying idea is similar in spirit to Kashyap and Stein (2000), and assumes that the relief a bank gets from additional liquidity should be the larger, the smaller the bank.

Our regression model is based on (9), with slight modifications. Beyond interacting the bank characteristic with interest rates, we furthermore interact it with GDP and prices. This way, we allow banks with different values of the bank characteristic x_i to respond differently to the business cycle. Furthermore, we assume that once we have controlled for other cyclical effects through the inclusion of GDP and prices, the estimated effects of the interest rate truly capture monetary policy effects.[22] We also introduce some dynamics and estimate the model in first differences.[23] The regression model is therefore specified as in (10):

$$
\begin{aligned}
\Delta\log(L_{it}) = a_i &+ \sum_{j=1}^{l} b_j \Delta\log(L_{it-j}) + \sum_{j=0}^{l} c_j \Delta r_{t-j} \\
&+ \sum_{j=0}^{l} d_j \Delta\log(GDP_{t-j}) + \sum_{j=0}^{l} e_j infl_{t-j} + f x_{it-1} \\
&+ \sum_{j=0}^{l} g_{1j} x_{it-1} \Delta r_{t-j} + \sum_{j=0}^{l} g_{2j} x_{it-1} \Delta\log(GDP_{t-j}) \\
&+ \sum_{j=0}^{l} g_{3j} x_{it-1} infl_{t-j} + \varepsilon_{it}
\end{aligned}
\tag{10}
$$

with $i = 1, \ldots, N$ and $t = 1, \ldots, T_i$ and where N denotes the number of banks and l the number of lags. L_{it} are the loans of bank i in quarter t to private non-banks. Δr_t represents the first difference of a nominal short-term interest rate, $\Delta\log(GDP_t)$ the growth rate of real GDP, and $infl_t$ the inflation rate. The bank-specific characteristics are given as x_{it}.

---

[22] As a robustness check, we estimate a second model with a complete set of time dummies instead of macro variables. The results are robust to this alternative model specification. They are presented in Ehrmann et al. (2001).

[23] The underlying idea is that banks react to a change in the interest rate by adjusting new loans. Since the average maturity of loans in Europe is longer than one year, the level of loans approximates the stock of loans for both quarterly and annual data, whereas the flow can be approximated by the first difference. In the estimates below, the exact specification may change from country to country, depending on the empirical properties of the data (see appendix, p. 268, for the exact specification in each case).

The model allows for fixed effects across banks, as indicated by the bank specific intercept a_i.[24]

A negative coefficient on the interest rate implies that loans fall after a monetary contraction. For tests of distributional effects, we would expect positive coefficients on the interaction term of the bank-specific characteristic with the monetary policy indicator.[25]

This model has been used with slight modifications in most of the subsequent chapters in part 3, whereas others (Brissimis, Kamberoglou and Simigiannis (chapter 18), Farinha and Robalo Marques (chapter 22)) opted for a more structural approach. Since the latter is more demanding in terms of data requirements, it has not been chosen as the standard specification. Other chapters consider extensions of (10), for example, Kaufmann (chapter 21), who additionally tests for the existence of asymmetries over time. Again, such a test has not been performed in most other studies owing to the data requirements this creates.[26]

As a monetary policy indicator, we use the short-term interest rate. Following the literature, we consider three measures for bank characteristics: size (S), liquidity (Liq) and capitalisation (Cap). Size and capitalisation are obvious measures of a bank's health that can affect the external finance premium. Liquidity may also be, but even if it is not, to the extent that it allows the bank to draw on it instead of going to the market, it reduces the increase in the marginal cost of funds after a monetary tightening. They are defined as follows:

$$S_{it} = \log A_{it} - \frac{1}{N_t} \sum_i \log A_{it}$$

$$Liq_{it} = \frac{L_{it}}{A_{it}} - \frac{1}{T} \sum_t \left(\frac{1}{N_t} \sum_i \frac{L_{it}}{A_{it}} \right)$$

$$Cap_{it} = \frac{C_{it}}{A_{it}} - \frac{1}{T} \sum_t \left(\frac{1}{N_t} \sum_i \frac{C_{it}}{A_{it}} \right)$$

---

[24] We have chosen not to interact the lagged endogenous variables with the bank characteristics. Such an interaction would be justified if either the serial correlation in the disturbances or the average duration of a bank's loans were systematically linked with the bank characteristics, which we do not necessarily believe to be a realistic assumption.

[25] However, a non-significant coefficient for the interaction term may indicate either the absence of a bank-lending channel or that our chosen characteristic does not appropriately discriminate banks according to their external finance cost.

[26] Note also that our model assumes only linear effects of the underlying bank characteristics on the lending decisions. Of course, non-linearity effects could exist. For example, it is possible that there are threshold effects: once a bank has reached a certain level of capitalisation, the market perceives it to be well capitalised. Or, similarly, once a bank has passed a certain size threshold, it is not subject to higher informational asymmetry problems than any other bank of that size class. Such hypotheses would have to be tested with grouped data, or by explicitly modelling threshold effects.

Size is measured by the log of total assets, A_{it}. Liquidity is defined as the ratio of liquid assets L_{it} (cash, interbank lending and securities) to total assets,[27] and capitalisation is given by the ratio of capital and reserves, C_{it}, to total assets.

All three criteria are normalised with respect to their average across all the banks in the respective sample in order to get indicators that sum to zero over all observations. The average of the interaction term $x_{it-1} \Delta r_{t-j}$ is therefore zero, too, and the parameters c_j are directly interpretable as the overall monetary policy effects on loans. In case of size, we normalise not just with respect to the mean over the whole sample period, but also with respect to each single period. This removes unwanted trends in size that arise because size is measured in nominal terms.

Owing to the inclusion of lags of the dependent variable, we use the GMM estimator suggested by Arellano and Bond (1991). This ensures efficiency and consistency of our estimates, provided that instruments are adequately chosen to take into account the serial-correlation properties of the model (the validity of these instruments is tested for with the standard Sargan test). To ensure econometrically sound estimates for each country, the harmonised model needs to be amended slightly for each country, e.g., by choosing the appropriate treatment of seasonality, lag structure and an adequate set of instrumental variables. The actual regression models for each country are therefore slight modifications of (10).

We have estimated model (10) using two different data sets. The first is BankScope, a commercially distributed database provided by the rating agency Fitch Ibca that covers balance sheet data on banks in all the euro area countries, although not the full population in each. These data are available on an annual basis only. They have been used in all previously published papers for the euro area that are based on micro data on banks. The second data set consists of bank balance sheet data collected by the national central banks of the euro area. These data are likely to be of a better quality, because they are available at least on a quarterly basis and initially cover the full population of banks in a country. To provide a comprehensive picture and to enable an assessment of the adequacy of BankScope for this type of exercise, we will make parallel use of both types of data sets. This will give an indication as to the representativeness of the BankScope results.

---

[27] Alternatively, liquidity may also be measured by the ratio of liquid assets to liquid liabilities. We do not consider this variant in our econometric analysis, since it turned out to have an excessive variability in the short term.

Table 14.4 *Comparison of the coverage of the BankScope data[a] with the full population of banks, 1998*

		France	Germany	Italy	Spain
No. of banks	BankScope	456	2,021	576	159
	Eurosystem data sets	*1,191*	*3,246*	*918*	*396*
Average total assets	BankScope	9,997	3,413	3,657	8,422
(million euros)	*Eurosystem data sets*	*2,365*	*1,583*	*1,671*	*2,283*
Median total assets	BankScope	1,180	364	216	1,599
(million euros)	*Eurosystem data sets*	*164*	*182*	*141*	*302*

Note: [a] The use of consolidated balance sheet data in BankScope, by counting also bank holdings abroad, leads to the sum of total assets for some countries exceeding the actual sum of total assets within that country.

4　Evidence from BankScope data

The existing studies on the euro area show rather inconclusive results. Whereas Favero, Giavazzi and Flabbi (2001) do not find evidence for a bank lending channel in Europe, Altunbas, Fazylow and Molyneux (2002), De Bondt (1999) and King (2000) do. However, the latter studies report conflicting findings: whereas King's results support the existence of the bank-lending channel in France and Italy, the evidence on these two countries appears particularly weak in de Bondt. Altunbas, Fazylow and Molyneux (2002), on the other hand, show that undercapitalised banks tend to respond more to monetary policy in the euro area as a whole – however, looking at single countries, they find the bank lending channel to be at work only in Italy and Spain.

Beyond the differences in specification, these contrasting results may be attributed to two intrinsic weaknesses of the BankScope data. First, the data are collected annually, which might be too infrequent to capture the adjustment of loans following a change in interest rates. Second, the sample of banks available in BankScope is biased toward large banks. This is shown for the four largest countries of the euro area in table 14.4. The coverage of the population of banks ranges from about 40 per cent in France and in Spain to slightly more than 60 per cent in Italy and in Germany. However, the median and average bank size is several times larger in BankScope than in the actual population.

In terms of market share this poses less of a problem, since, as described on p. 243, the larger banks make up a disproportionately larger fraction of the total loans. The biases are, however, stronger for the beginning of the sample, since the coverage of BankScope has improved markedly over the years.

BankScope data offer the choice between consolidated and unconsolidated balance sheets. For the purposes of this chapter, we opted for consolidated balance sheets whenever available, and unconsolidated balance sheets otherwise. In order to assess financial constraints and informational asymmetries of a bank, it is important to know whether a bank is in fact a subsidiary of another, potentially larger or better capitalised, bank. In such a case, using the subsidiary's unconsolidated balance sheet would lead to a biased measurement of the informational problems of the bank. However, this choice is not without drawbacks. Consolidated balance sheets can potentially exaggerate the size of a bank, especially if a bank is internationally oriented, and has bank holdings abroad. This might create problems when looking at individual countries, where the mismeasurement owing to international operations of domestic banks is larger than when looking at evidence on the euro area aggregate level.

To assess the role of banks in monetary transmission at the euro area level, we begin by estimating (10) with the full BankScope data set, making no distinction based on the nationalities of the banks. However, in order to proxy loan demand and the monetary policy changes for each bank as closely as possible, we regress the loan growth of a bank on its national GDP growth, inflation rate and the interest rate change.

The main results are summarised in table 14.5. Each column presents the results from one of the specifications – first models with one of the bank characteristics each, then one model with all three characteristics simultaneously, and last a specification where size and liquidity enter, in both single and double interactions.

We report the estimated long-run coefficients only. These are calculated as the sum of the coefficients of the various lags of the indicated variable, divided by one minus the sum of the coefficients on the lagged endogenous variable.

The model with size as the only bank characteristic performs best – size dominates all other characteristics, both in the specification with all three of them and in the one with double interactions. The average bank reduces lending after a monetary tightening by 1.3 per cent following a 100-basis point increase in interest rates. Smaller banks, however, reduce their lending by more than large banks do.

Whereas capitalisation does not enter the models significantly, liquidity at first sight seems to be a good discriminatory device to trace the

Table 14.5 *Loan equations: long-run coefficients, BankScope data for the euro area*

	Models estimated with the following bank characteristic variables				
	Size	Liquidity	Capitalisation	Size Liquidity Capitalisation	Size Liquidity
Monetary policy	−1.321***	−0.527**	−0.309	−1.539***	−1.494***
	0.000	*0.040*	*0.151*	*0.000*	*0.000*
Real GDP	1.881***	0.885**	1.369***	1.689***	1.550***
	0.000	*0.023*	*0.002*	*0.000*	*0.000*
Prices	1.947***	0.105	0.642	0.846*	0.861**
	0.000	*0.812*	*0.111*	*0.083*	*0.047*
Char1*MP	0.231**	−5.105***	4.293	0.416***	0.408***
	0.050	*0.003*	*0.167*	*0.004*	*0.003*
Char2*MP				−1.392	−1.686
				0.430	*0.398*
Char3*MP				3.875	
				0.248	
Char1*Char2*MP					0.422
					0.605
p-val Sargan	0.069	0.631	0.753	0.558	0.320
p-val MA1, MA2	0.000 0.453	0.000 0.325	0.000 0.948	0.000 0.860	0.000 0.897
No of banks, obs.	3,029 9,662	2,637 7,963	2,990 9,507	2,474 7,370	2,579 7,766

Notes: *, ** and *** denote significance at the 10%, 5% and 1% level. Numbers in italics are *p*-values.

differential loan response of banks, too, given the highly significant interaction term; but this coefficient has an unexpected negative sign. Moreover, this model is not robust to replacing the macro variables by time dummies.[28]

5   Evidence from Eurosystem data sets

In this section, we employ the Eurosystem data sets for national models for France, Germany, Italy and Spain, the four largest countries of the euro area. Owing to confidentiality restrictions, it was not possible to pool the data, so that we are limited to a country-by-country analysis. The results are presented in tables 14.6–14.9.[29]

The long-run effects of monetary policy on loans of an average bank are negative in all countries, indicating that restrictive monetary policy

[28] This result might be driven by the fact that a liquidity measure is provided only for relatively few banks in some countries covered in BankScope. For example, only one-third of observations are available in the Italian case.

[29] A description of the sample periods, the outlier detection methods and the exact specifications can be found in the appendix.

Table 14.6 *Loan equations: long-run coefficients, national data set for France*

				Size Liquidity	Size
	Size	Liquidity	Capitalisation	Capitalisation	Liquidity
Monetary policy	−1.564**	−2.131***	−1.823***	−1.969***	−2.221***
	0.765	0.736	0.701	0.566	0.697
Real GDP	3.239***	3.999***	3.788***	2.975***	2.523***
	0.578	0.493	0.503	0.374	0.470
Prices	−2.850***	−4.173***	−3.701***	−3.678***	−3.147***
	0.742	0.692	0.689	0.512	0.644
Char1*MP	−0.458	4.030	3.547	−0.063	−0.184
	0.553	4.734	15.236	0.218	0.235
Char2*MP				8.106***	7.070***
				1.931	2.010
Char3*MP				2.304	
				7.007	
Char1*Real GDP	−0.262	−1.255	−16.48		
	0.785	7.508	25.648		
Char1*Prices	−0.070	−1.637	5.303		
	0.714	6.143	24.351		
Char1*Char2*MP					0.390
					1.228
p-val Sargan	0.142	0.233	0.111	0.231	0.075
p-val MA1, MA2	0.014 0.451	0.006 0.326	0.017 0.542	0.000 0.387	0.000 0.450
No. of banks, obs.	312 5,327	312 5,327	312 5,327	312 5,327	312 5,327

Column group header: *Models estimated with the following bank characteristic variables*

Notes: *, ** and *** denote significance at the 10%, 5% and 1% level. Numbers in italics are standard errors.

reduces bank lending in the long run. As we had conjectured in section 2, size does not emerge as a useful indicator for the distributional effects of monetary policy. In the specifications with size only, we find it to be insignificant in France, Germany and Italy, but with a negative coefficient in Spain.[30] Hence, the role of size as an indicator of informational asymmetries appears irrelevant in all countries. This is consistent with the conjectures raised on pp. 247–8, that several features of the banking markets in the euro area decrease the degree of informational frictions, and as such the usefulness of size as an indicator for the bank-lending channel. The same applies to capitalisation, which does not play an important role in distinguishing banks' reactions. Its interaction with the monetary policy indicator is insignificant in all countries, both when used by itself as well as in the complete specification with all three criteria.

---

[30] For Italy, this is consistent with previous work analysing lending rates, e.g., Angeloni *et al.* (1995) and Cottarelli, Ferri and Generale (1995).

Table 14.7 *Loan equations: long-run coefficients, national data set for Germany*

	Size	Liquidity	Capitalisation	Size Liquidity Capitalisation	Size Liquidity
			Models estimated with the following bank characteristic variables		
Monetary policy	−1.662***	−0.857***	−0.695***	−0.526***	−0.679***
	0.737	0.238	0.239	0.202	0.205
Real GDP	0.071	0.119	−0.034	0.079	0.008
	0.296	0.163	0.167	0.135	0.138
Prices	3.120***	2.039***	1.965***	1.662***	1.842***
	0.803	0.347	0.350	0.280	0.286
Char1*MP	−0.117	3.547***	1.935	−0.044	0.003
	0.127	1.100	6.300	0.036	0.045
Char2*MP				3.936***	4.689***
				0.883	0.885
Char3*MP				−0.469	
				5.340	
Char1*Real GDP	0.167	−2.960*	1.533		
	0.167	1.398	10.293		
Char1*Prices	−0.561***	2.872	9.328		
	0.252	2.405	14.320		
Char1*Char2*MP					−1.082*
					0.551
p-val Sargan	1.000	1.000	1.000	1.000	1.000
p-val MA1, MA2	0.000 0.184	0.000 0.421	0.000 0.276	0.000 0.351	0.000 0.344
No. of banks, obs.	2,689 48,402	2,693 48,474	2,708 48,744	2,651 47,718	2,659 47,862

Notes: *, ** and *** denote significance at the 10%, 5% and 1% level. Numbers in italics are standard errors.

This could, however, also be caused by several reasons not specified on pp. 247–8. For example, the measure of capitalisation we use could be too crude to capture the riskiness of a bank, and is thus not indicative for the informational asymmetry problems. This concern arises because our capitalisation variable is derived from balance sheets without considering the structure of the loan portfolio or its risk characteristics. It might therefore not be capturing a risk-based measure that is compatible with the Basle capital requirement.[31]

[31] The BIS ratio measure cannot be obtained from the available data sets for all the four largest countries over the same sample period. Using a similar framework over the period 1992–2001, Gambacorta and Mistrulli (2003) find that capital holdings in excess of the minimum required by prudential regulation standards enable Italian banks to contain the effect of a deposit drop on lending; well-capitalised banks can better shield their lending from monetary policy shocks as they have, consistently with the 'bank-lending channel' hypothesis, an easier access to non-deposit funds.

Table 14.8 *Loan equations: long-run coefficients, national data set for Italy*

	Size	Liquidity	Capitalisation	Size Liquidity Capitalisation	Size Liquidity
				Models estimated with the following bank characteristic variables	
Monetary policy	−0.703***	−0.529***	−0.695***	−0.825***	−0.675***
	0.103	0.102	0.102	0.127	0.113
Real GDP	1.363***	1.879***	1.419***	1.389***	1.084***
	0.175	0.162	0.173	0.213	0.175
Prices	0.230	−1.931***	0.101	−0.622	−0.264
	0.302	0.307	0.308	0.386	0.338
Char1*MP	−0.009	2.593**	4.226	0.079	−0.046
	0.025	1.284	2.818	0.054	0.073
Char2*MP				2.278***	2.058***
				0.831	0.574
Char3*MP				3.616	
				3.099	
Char1*Char2*MP					−1.238
					0.845
p-val Sargan	0.196	0.079	0.186	0.077	0.062
p-val MA1, MA2	0.000 0.110	0.000 0.246	0.000 0.116	0.000 0.128	0.000 0.156
No. of banks, obs.	587 25,241	587 25,241	587 25,241	587 25241	587 25,241

Notes: *, ** and *** denote significance at the 10%, 5% and 1% level. Numbers in italics are standard errors.

An alternative explanation could be that all banks are operating at levels of capitalisation sufficiently high to prevent market participants' doubts on the soundness of a bank. As mentioned above, in such a case capitalisation does not determine a bank's reaction to monetary policy any longer. Loupias, Savignac and Sevestre (chapter 17 in this volume) have estimated a model with a double interaction of size and capitalisation with monetary policy. This is a way to check whether, after a monetary policy tightening, small and under-capitalised banks restrict their loan supply by more than large banks. They do not find any significant coefficient, thus confirming that capitalisation does not affect bank loan supply in a significant way in France. Moreover, when comparing the level of capitalisation of European banks with those in the USA (see table 14.3), it can easily be seen that banks in Europe are much better capitalised (with the notable exception of Germany where, as stated in section 2, the asset structure of banks is less risky).

The third bank characteristic, the degree of liquidity, turns out to be a highly significant indicator for distributional effects across banks in Germany, Italy and Spain (tables 14.6–14.9). In the specifications with all

Table 14.9 *Loan equations: long-run coefficients, national data set for Spain*

	Models estimated with the following bank characteristic variables				
	Size	Liquidity	Capitalisation	Size Liquidity Capitalisation	Size Liquidity
Monetary policy	−0.993**	−1.862***	−1.314***	−1.510***	−1.593***
	0.453	0.441	0.487	0.433	0.422
Real GDP	2.022***	1.689***	1.878***	1.695***	1.818***
	0.359	0.347	0.357	0.326	0.327
Prices	−1.092***	−1.979***	−0.985***	−2.074***	−2.066***
	0.315	0.465	0.368	0.387	0.414
Char1*MP	−0.253**	6.061***	0.365	−0.214*	−0.153
	0.114	2.072	8.393	0.128	0.109
Char2*MP				3.986**	5.277***
				1.905	1.879
Char3*MP				−11.304	
				9.112	
Char1*Char2*MP					2.010*
					1.161
p-val Sargan	0.852	0.838	0.888	1.000	1.000
p-val MA1, MA2	0.374 0.952	0.264 0.770	0.130 0.967	0.458 0.913	0.499 0.880
No. of banks, obs.	210 4,012	210 4,012	210 4,012	210 4,012	210 4,012

Notes: *, ** and *** denote significance at the 10%, 5% and 1% level. Numbers in italics are standard errors.

three bank characteristics, it dominates the other characteristics for those countries, and also emerges as the significant and dominant characteristic also for France.

Looking at the more detailed analysis in the subsequent chapters, the results for Spain (Hernando and Martínez-Pagés, chapter 16 in this volume) appear to be less robust than in the case of the other countries. Indeed, the liquidity effect disappears when looking at the response of different types of loans and at the response of loans to an exogenous shock to deposits. Therefore, in the case of Spain, the distributional effects across banks with different degrees of liquidity do not appear to be related to loan-supply effects.

On the other hand, the results for the other countries are very robust. For Germany, it turns out that the result is driven by the short-term interbank deposits that many small banks with a network affiliation hold with their head institutions (Worms, chapter 15 in this volume). For Italy, the analysis is extended to the role of deposits and liquidity. It is shown that deposits drop most sharply for those banks that have fewer incentives to shield their deposits, such as, for example, small banks with a deposits to loan ratio larger than one. The analysis supports the idea that banks use their liquidity to maintain their loan portfolio (Gambacorta, chapter 19 in this volume). For France, too, this conclusion appears to be robust, to both different measures of the liquidity ratio and to the specific treatment of mutual and cooperative banks' networks (Loupias, Savignac and Sevestre, chapter 17 in this volume).

The positive coefficient on the interaction of the monetary policy indicator with the degree of liquidity in France, Germany and Italy means that less liquid banks show a stronger reduction in lending after a monetary tightening than relatively more liquid banks. The underlying reasoning is that banks with more liquid balance sheets can use their liquid assets to maintain their loan portfolio and as such are affected less heavily by a monetary policy tightening. The robustness of these results can be checked through the last column of tables 14.6–14.9 that includes the double interaction between size and liquidity. The double interaction has the expected negative sign only for Germany and Italy, but is insignificant in the case of Italy and only weakly significant for the case of Germany. Hence, there is no strong evidence that the effect of liquidity is stronger for smaller banks; the conclusion that size is not the dominant characteristic that distinguishes banks' responses to monetary policy does therefore obtain further support.

In order to see whether an analysis with BankScope data leads to results that are consistent with those obtained with the more comprehensive databases used in this section, we have performed a set of country-by-country regressions with those data.[32] The results generally do not coincide. For most of the estimated BankScope models, a tightening of monetary policy leads to the expected decrease of loans. However, with the exception of Germany, the results lack significance and robustness. The most extreme case is France, where not a single coefficient turns out to be significant and several coefficients even change sign across different model specifications. Also in Spain and Italy, the coefficients on the macro variables depend on the exact model specification, and frequently change sign.

The lack of robustness and of significance of the estimates and especially the few cases of results that are consistent with those reported in this section cast some doubt on the adequacy of BankScope to capture the *distributional* effects of monetary policy across banks. The Eurosystem data sets, through their much larger variation across both banks and time,

---

[32] The detailed regression results can be found in the working-paper version of this chapter, Ehrmann *et al.* (2001).

and because they do not suffer from BankScope's composition bias towards large banks, seem, in this respect, to be superior to the BankScope data. However, when estimating the *macroeconomic* importance of the bank-loan response, this bias is less important: since the coverage of large banks is relatively good, both the estimates with BankScope and those with the complete population of banks arrive at quantitatively similar conclusions.[33]

The results presented in the chapters devoted to the other countries are also compatible with the conjectures of part 2 that national banking structures matter for the reaction of banks to monetary policy. De Haan (this chapter 20 in volume) finds for the Netherlands that interest rate increases reduce unsecured bank lending, and provides evidence that size, degree of liquidity and capitalisation all matter for a bank's reaction in this market segment. Looking at table 14.2 (p. 237), these findings are compatible with the weak role of the government in the Netherlands, such that banks cannot rely on government guarantees to attract financing. There are also no important bank networks in the Netherlands. The Netherlands thus appears to be a case where the usual informational asymmetry problems may play a bigger role than in many other countries of the euro area.

Chapter 22 in this volume on Portugal (Farinha and Robalo Marques) finds similarly that monetary policy tightenings reduce bank lending. Here, the capitalisation of banks plays an important role for the way banks respond to interest rate changes, whereas size and liquidity do not. They report, furthermore, that the models were subject to a structural break when Portuguese banks had the possibility to access funds from foreign EU banks. Interestingly, during this period the growth rate of loans increased relative to the growth of deposits, suggesting that this improved availability of funds matters for the growth rate of lending.

Brissimis, Kamberoglou and Simigiannis (chapter 18 in this volume) investigate the Greek case, and conclude that both the size and the liquidity of a bank determine distributional effects. Despite a strong government involvement, proxies for informational asymmetries seem to be important in Greece. This is consistent with the absence of bank networks, so that each bank's own creditworthiness is relevant.

Kaufmann (chapter 21 in this volume) looks at Austrian data, and detects distributional effects across banks only for sub-periods of the sample. When they are found, it is the degree of liquidity that matters rather than size. This is in line with our results for Germany, and consistent with the similarity of the two banking systems, as revealed in

---

[33] For details see the working-paper version of this chapter Ehrmann *et al.* (2001).

table 14.2. Interestingly, monetary policy is effective only in times of economic slowdowns, as opposed to times of high growth.

Looking at the case of Finland, an extremely concentrated market (see table 14.11 in the statistical appendix), Topi and Vilmunen (chapter 23 in this volume) find that bank lending contracts after interest rate increases. Monetary policy does seem to affect all banks alike, however. Only liquidity is marginally significant in its interaction with monetary policy. This is in line with our conjecture of section 2, that the State guarantees in the aftermath of the banking crisis, which were maintained in parts of the sample period they study, changed the lending behaviour of banks. The authors provide further evidence in this direction: a dummy variable for the state guarantees enters significantly in their regressions, indicating that these measures themselves might have contributed to the increase in the growth rate of loans.

6   Conclusions

This chapter has investigated the role of banks in monetary policy transmission in the euro area. It has been shown that bank lending contracts significantly after a monetary tightening on both the euro area aggregate and the country level.

Using micro data on banks, it is found that factors such as the size or the degree of capitalisation of a bank are generally not important for the way a bank adjusts its lending to interest rate changes. This is opposed to findings for the USA, where small and less capitalised banks show a disproportionately strong response to monetary policy. We explain the absence of size and capitalisation effects by a lower degree of informational asymmetries: the role of the government, banking networks, as well as the low number of bank failures in the countries of the euro area contribute to a reduction in informational frictions. Proxies for informational asymmetry are therefore less informative in the European case than they are in the USA.

Whereas size and capitalisation do not shape the response of a bank to monetary policy, liquidity does. Banks with a relatively low share of liquid assets reduce loan supply by more than more liquid banks on average. Obviously, they draw on their liquid assets to maintain their loan portfolio. A reason for doing this could be the existence of relationship lending in several euro area countries, where bank customers are shielded to some extent from monetary policy effects.

We have worked with two different types of data sets. The publicly available database BankScope, used in earlier studies, suffers from a composition bias. Since small banks are not covered adequately, the *microeconomic* distributional effects are estimated on a biased sample of banks. This might explain the contradictory findings in the previous literature as well as in some of the analysis in this volume. When estimating the *macroeconomic* importance of the bank loan response, this bias is less important, however: since the coverage of large banks is relatively good, both the estimates with BankScope and those with the complete population of banks arrive at quantitatively similar conclusions.

Several issues deserve further study at this point. The estimated models assume a linear relationship between bank characteristics and the effects of monetary policy. It would be useful to assess the robustness of our findings with respect to this assumption. Furthermore, as more data become available, it will be interesting to update the analysis with more observations after the formation of EMU. Finally, the macroeconomic importance of the bank-lending channel merits further study, with the aim of gaining a sense of its contribution to the overall effects of monetary policy.

STATISTICAL APPENDIX: DATABASES AND ESTIMATION METHODS

A.1   The samples

A.1.1   Data sources

Eurosystem data sets for France, Italy and Spain: respective national banks' supervisory reports. Eurosystem data set for Germany: Bundesbank banks' balance sheets statistics. BankScope: Fitch Ibca. The Eurosystem data sets are on a quarterly basis while BankScope provides annual data. BankScope data are consolidated balance sheets when available (84 per cent of all banks in the sample), and unconsolidated balance sheets otherwise (16 per cent).

A.1.2   Merger treatment

For all countries, mergers have been treated by a backward aggregation of the entities involved in the merger. Other kinds of treatments (such as ignoring the merger, or eliminating the merging banks from the sample following the merger, and considering the merged bank as a new bank)

Table 14.10 *Initial sample coverage of the panels of individual banks*

	Period	No. of banks
BankScope	1992–9	4,425
France	1993:Q1–2000:Q3	496
Germany	1993:Q1–1998:Q4	3,281
Italy	1986:Q4–1998:Q4	785
Spain	1991:Q1–1998:Q4	264

have been shown to have little impact on the econometric results. There is no merger treatment with the BankScope data.

A.1.3   Criteria defining banks and sample initial coverage

Credit-specialised financial institutions are excluded from the sample in France, Italy and Spain. For Spain, branches of foreign banks are also excluded from the sample. For France, each mutual bank network (except for one of them) is considered as an aggregate bank.

A.1.4   Trimming of the sample/outlier elimination

For Italy and Spain, only banks with both non-zero loans and deposits are kept in the sample. Given the focus on loans in this chapter, this positivity condition applies only to loans for Germany and the BankScope data (table 14.11). For France, banks with deposits representing less than 10 per cent of their total liabilities (which are mostly foreign banks) are discarded from the sample, as well as banks with loans accounting for less than 1 per cent of their total assets. Before the necessary trimming of the samples, but after the merger treatment, the coverage is as in table 14.10.

A.1.5   Number of consecutive lags required:

Owing to the model specification as well as the estimation methods requiring numerous lags, we required a minimal number of consecutive observations of the first difference of the log of loans (and correspondingly for the other variables in the model): 2 lags for BankScope, 5 for France, 4 for Germany, 12 for Italy and 9 for Spain.

Table 14.11 *Criteria defining outliers*

	First difference in logs is, for each period, below (above)	First difference in the ratio of liquidity and capitalisation over total assets is, for each period, below (above)
BankScope	Fourth (96th) percentile for loans, deposits and total assets	Fourth (96th) percentile
France	Second (98th) percentile for loans, deposits and total assets	First (99th) percentile
Germany	Second (98th) percentile for loans and First (99th) percentile for total assets	First (99th) percentile of the ratios level
Italy	First (99th) percentile for loans	
Spain	Second (98th) percentile for total assets and Third (97th) percentile for loans	Second (98th) percentile or Third (97th) percentile of the ratios level

Note: For Germany and Italy, banks with one outlier or more are completely removed from the sample. Moreover, for Germany and BankScope, different samples have been built for size, liquidity and capitalisation.

Table 14.12 *Sample coverage of the cleaned panels of individual banks*

	Estimation period	No. of banks	No. of obs.
BankScope	1993–9	Around 3,000	Around 9,700
France	1994:Q3–2000:Q3	312	5,327
Germany	1994:Q1–1998:Q4	Around 2,700	Around 48,000
Italy	1988:Q1–1998:Q4	587	28,763
Spain	1991:Q1–1998:Q4	210	4,012

The final composition of the samples used for econometric estimations is thus as in table 14.12.

A.2   Variable definitions

A.2.1   Loans

For all countries, loans are those to the non-financial private sector. For statistical reasons, bad loans are excluded in Italy and France.

A.2.2   Liquidity

The liquidity ratio is computed by dividing liquid by total assets. The precise definition of liquidity changes slightly from country to country, owing to differences in the available information. In France, it is constructed as cash and interbank deposits. In Germany, it includes cash, short-term interbank deposits and government securities. In Italy, it comprises cash, interbank deposits and securities and repurchase agreements at book value. In Spain, liquid assets include cash, interbank lending and government securities. For BankScope, it generally includes cash, short-term interbank deposits and government securities. For all countries, the ratio liquidity–total assets is centred with respect to its overall sample mean.

A.2.3   Capitalisation

For all countries, capitalisation is defined as the sum of capital and reserves divided by total assets. For BankScope, it is defined as the ratio of capital to total assets. Capitalisation has also been centred with respect to its overall sample mean.

A.2.4   Size

For all countries and BankScope, size is defined as the log of total assets. This variable is centred with respect to each period's mean.

A.2.5   Monetary policy indicator

In each country but Italy, the monetary policy indicator is the three-month interest rate. In Italy, it is the interest rate on repurchase agreements between the central bank and credit institutions.

A.3   Model specification and estimation methods

For France, model (10) is directly estimated with the contemporaneous value and four lags of the macro variables and interaction terms. Instruments are second and third lags of the first difference of log of loans, the second lags of the characteristics included in the equation: size and/or liquidity and/or capitalisation, and the monetary policy indicator which is assumed exogenous. All these instruments are multiplied by time dummies 'à la Arellano-Bond'.

For Germany, all bank-specific variables have been seasonally adjusted on a bank-individual basis (multiplicative seasonal adjustment with seasonal factors based on a moving average). The first-difference operator has been applied to the model before estimation. The model has four lags. Instruments are the macro variables themselves, lags $t - 2$ to $t - 5$ of the first difference of the log of loans, and lags 2 to 5 of all other (interaction) variables in the model. No contemporaneous variables enter the models. Seasonal dummies are included.

For Italy, model (10) is directly estimated. Instruments are lags of the first difference of log of loans and of the characteristics included in the equation. Inflation, GDP growth and the monetary policy indicator are considered as exogenous variables. The model has four lags, and no contemporaneous variables.

For Spain, model (10) is estimated in fourth logs of the first differences. This eliminates the seasonal individual effects existing in the model in first differences. Estimation is done in a model with contemporaneous values and four lags, with the GMM method proposed by Arellano and Bond (1991), using as instruments lags 5 through 8 of the first difference of loans and bank characteristics. Macroeconomic variables are instrumented by themselves and their interactions with bank characteristics are instrumented by the same macro variable interacted with the characteristic at time $t - 5$.

For BankScope, the model is estimated with one lag of the endogenous variable, and either the contemporaneous values or one lag (if contemporaneous values are not significant) for the other explanatory variables. Estimation is performed in first differences. Instruments are the second and consecutive lags of the first difference of log of loans, the bank characteristics and the interaction terms.

15 The reaction of bank lending to monetary policy measures in Germany

A. Worms

1 Introduction

So far, empirical evidence of a credit channel in Germany is inconclusive, irrespective of the methodology or the type of data used. For example, while Favero, Giavazzi and Flabbi (2001), Guender and Moersch (1997), Stöss (1996) and Tsatsaronis (1995), do not find a credit channel, de Bondt (1999, 2000), Kakes and Sturm (2001), Küppers (2001), Hülsewig, Winker and Worms (2001) and Worms (1998), find evidence in support of it.[1] This ambiguity in the results reflects the fundamental problem of identifying monetary policy-induced shifts in loan supply. In order to tackle this problem, most of the recent empirical literature on this issue has turned to micro data.[2]

Along these lines, this study uses individual bank balance sheets in order to test for the existence of a credit channel in Germany.[3] In contrast to the above listed studies, it covers the entire German banking population on an individual basis and it explicitly takes into account bank–individual seasonal patterns. While the results for Germany that are presented in Ehrmann *et al.* (chapter 14 in this volume) are also based on a data set characterised by these two features, this chapter extends the analysis in two directions. First, it uses bank-specific income and risk variables to improve the control for differential movements in loan demand. Second,

I would like to thank J. Breitung, M. Ehrmann, D. Focarelli, H. Herrmann, U. von Kalckreuth, A. Kashyap, B. Mojon, D. Terlizzese, F. Panetta, P. Vermeulen and especially R. Gropp and F. Ramb for their suggestions and support. This chapter has benefited from discussions at the Deutsche Bundesbank, the Oesterreichische Nationalbank and the Universities of Mannheim, Frankfurt/Main and Regensburg. All computations were carried out with STATA and/or DPD for Ox.

[1] For an overview of the empirical literature on the credit channel in Germany, see Worms (2002).

[2] For an overview, see, for example, Cecchetti (1995). von Kalckreuth (chapter 9 in this volume) looks at micro data on German firms to detect possible distributional effects of monetary policy.

[3] This chapter is a summary of Worms (2001a, 2001b). For more detailed information, see these two papers.

it takes into account the network structures of the German banking system by explicitly looking at the role short-term interbank deposits play for banks' loan reaction to monetary policy. Moreover, the results of several robustness checks are reported.

The main finding is that the average bank's reaction to monetary policy does not depend directly on its size – which is the bank-specific factor mainly used as the discriminating variable in the literature – but rather on its share of short-term interbank deposits in total assets. A significant size effect can be found only when controlling for this dominating influence. This result can be interpreted as evidence supporting the existence of the credit channel, although – given the dominating role of short-term interbank deposits – it should be viewed as being only of 'second-order importance'.

This chapter is structured as follows: section 2 looks more closely at banks and the role of bank loans in Germany. Subsequently, the database and the necessary data transformations are described (section 3). Section 4 concentrates on the estimation specification. The estimation results are presented in section 5. Section 6 concludes.

2   Banks and bank loans in Germany

Several authors, for example, Cecchetti (1999) and Kashyap and Stein (1997), have argued that the credit channel should be highly effective in the euro area. Generally, two observations gave rise to this assessment: on the one hand, the euro area banking system is characterised by a large number of comparatively small banks – which are assumed to reduce loan supply by more than large banks in reaction to a monetary policy tightening. On the other hand, bank loans are the most important means of external finance for firms and households, so that a monetary policy-induced reduction in bank loan supply should have a strong effect on aggregate demand.

Particularly in Germany,[4] the volume of bank loans to domestic firms and households relative to nominal GDP is high compared with other countries (see Ehrmann *et al.*, chapter 14 in this volume) and increased steadily during the 1990s. Starting from 54 per cent for firms (incl. self-employed persons) and 29 per cent for households (incl. non-profit organisations) in 1991, these ratios reached 63 per cent (firms) and 45 per cent (households) in 2000.[5]

---

[4] For general descriptions of the German financial system, see Krahnen and Schmidt (2002).

[5] See Supplement 1 to the *Monthly Report of the Deutsche Bundesbank*, table I.7.

Households raise funds solely in the form of loans, with bank loans making up nearly 94 per cent of total borrowing as at the end of 1998.[6] The share of bank loans in firms' total liabilities has decreased over time due to an ongoing securitisation process: from an average of 51 per cent in 1991 it fell to 37 per cent in 2000.[7] However, this development was caused almost solely by the very large firms: their ratio of bank loans to the balance sheet total decreased from 9 per cent in 1991 to 8 per cent in 1998, while it increased for small and medium-sized firms from 26 per cent to 29 per cent.[8] This indicates a growing importance of bank loans as a means of obtaining external finance for the large majority of small and medium-sized German firms, which are therefore of special interest in terms of the credit channel.[9]

The upper part of table 15.1 shows that credit cooperatives make up 70 per cent of all the German banks, whereas the savings banks make up about 18 per cent. All 'other banks' represent only around 12 per cent. This latter group is very heterogeneous and contains, for example, the four big banks, the thirteen head institutions of the savings banks' sector and the four head institutions of the cooperative sector,[10] foreign banks, private banks and banks with special functions. Despite the comparatively small number of institutions, this latter group accounts for almost three-quarters of all bank assets, while the many credit cooperatives together hold only 10 per cent. In terms of loans, the differences are not quite so striking, but still worth noting.

Table 15.1 also contains information on the size structure of the German banking system (the size groups are based on the distribution of total assets across all banks), 93 per cent of the credit cooperatives are small, while the majority of the savings banks are of medium size (74 per cent). The large banks consist only of 'other banks', i.e. this group contains neither savings banks nor credit cooperatives (but eleven of the thirteen head institutions of the savings banks' sector and two of the four head institutions of the cooperative sector). These thirty-two large banks alone comprise more than half of the total assets of all banks (55 per cent), the average bank size being about EUR 87.6 billion. However, the large banks' share of loans in total assets, at an average of 27 per cent, is far lower than that of the small and medium-sized banks. The lending business to domestic private non-banks seems to be of far greater importance

---

[6] See Deutsche Bundesbank (2000:34).

[7] See Deutsche Bundesbank (2000). For more information, see Worms (2003).

[8] See Deutsche Bundesbank (2001) and Friderichs, Paranque and Sauvé (1999).

[9] See Hackethal (2001), who also finds that in Germany the importance of banks as financiers of small and medium-sized enterprises (SMEs) increased during the 1990s.

[10] In October 2001 the number of cooperative central banks was reduced to two.

Table 15.1 *Structure of the German banking system, December 1998[a]*

	No. of banks	Sum of total assets (EUR billion)	Loans to domestic firms and individuals (EUR billion)	Loans to total assets (%)	Total assets per bank (mean) (EUR billion)
Total:	**3,228**	**5,138**	**1,886**	37	**1.6**
Of which:					
savings banks	594	910	510	56	1.5
credit coops	2,256	520	306	59	0.3
'other banks'[b]	378	3,708	1,070	29	9.8
Size groups:					
Small (bottom 75%)	**2,421**	**390**	**229**	59	**0.2**
Of which:					
savings banks	157	54	31	58	0.4
credit coops	2,087	303	185	61	0.2
'other banks'[b]	177	33	13	38	0.2
Medium-sized (75–99%)	**775**	**1,943**	**893**	46	**2.5**
Of which:					
savings banks	437	856	478	56	1.9
credit coops	169	217	122	56	1.3
'other banks'[b]	169	870	293	34	5.2
Large (top percentile) (only 'other banks')	**32**	**2,805**	**764**	27	**87.6**

[a] Based on the bank balance sheet statistics of the Deutsche Bundesbank. Some figures differ slightly from the data published in Supplement 1 to the *Bundesbank Monthly Report* (*Banking Statistics*) because a small number of banks were excluded in a data screening process. For more detailled information, see Worms (2001a).
[b] The head institutions of the savings banks' sector and the cooperative sector are assigned to the 'other banks'.

for the smaller banks, i.e. for credit cooperatives and for savings banks, than for the large banks.

There has been a strong consolidation process in Germany which – in terms of the number of banks – was concentrated primarily on the co-operative and the savings bank sector: The number of cooperative banks decreased from almost 2,800 at the end of 1993 to 1,800 at the end of 2000.[11] During the same period, the number of savings banks decreased from 717 to 575 institutions. This reduction in the overall number of banks was to a large extent due to mergers. But, despite this consolidation

[11] See Deutsche Bundesbank (2001:59) and Worms (2001b).

process, the degree of concentration on the German banking market must still be rated small by international standards.[12]

The savings bank sector and the cooperative sector consist of a few large head institutions, which are the *Landesbanken* in the case of the savings banks and the cooperative central banks in case of the cooperatives, and a large number of smaller affiliated institutions.[13] As for their interbank relationships, the cooperative banks and – to a lesser degree – the savings banks transact mainly with their head institutions:[14]

- On average, a savings bank holds almost two-thirds of its interbank *deposits vis-à-vis* the head institutions of its sector. In the case of the credit cooperatives, this share amounts to as much as 90 per cent (December 2000). Most of these interbank deposits held with the head institutions have a maturity of up to one year only: 58 per cent in the case of the savings banks and 67 per cent in the case of the credit cooperatives.
- 59 per cent of the interbank *loans* of the average savings bank, and 73 per cent of those of the average cooperative bank were granted by the head institutions of their respective system (December 2000). While savings banks and credit cooperatives therefore hold mainly short-term deposits with their head institutions, they obtain mainly long-term loans from these bodies. This illustrates that a strong maturity transformation takes place within these two networks.

As a mirror image of these strong intra-sectoral links, savings banks and credit cooperatives hold only a small share of their interbank assets *vis-à-vis* banks outside their own system. However, the links of the head institutions to banks outside their system are stronger. Both systems therefore incorporate a kind of 'internal interbank market', with the head institutions providing the external links of their respective network.

Therefore, while the German banking system is in fact characterised by a comparatively large share of small banks, it is far from clear whether this feature really leads to a strong credit channel. The fact that almost all the small and medium-sized banks belong to either the savings banks' or the cooperative banks' network – which are characterised by close interbank ties – could instead imply that the size of a single bank may not be important for its reaction to monetary policy. Hence, the role of interbank relationships will be explicitly taken into account in the subsequent econometric analysis.

---

[12] See European Central Bank (2000) and Hempell (2002).
[13] See Upper and Worms (2001a, tables 2a and 2b), and Ehrmann and Worms (2001).
[14] See Deutsche Bundesbank (2001).

3   The database

The monthly balance sheet data available for this analysis spans the period 1992–1998[15] and comprises all German banks (around 4,400). In order to match these with quarterly macro data and the quarterly borrowers statistics of the Deutsche Bundesbank, quarterly values were taken by using end-of-quarter values. In order to cope with the comparatively large number of mergers that took place during the observation period, the balance sheet positions of merging banks are aggregated backwards to the beginning of the sample period.[16] After taking end-of-quarter values and applying the merger and outlier procedure,[17] about 2,800 banks and 75,000 observations remain in the sample.

Preliminary estimations indicate the existence of bank-specific seasonal patterns. If not properly accounted for, these tend to worsen the quality of the estimation. Moreover, neglecting them creates differences in the loan movements across banks that may falsely be attributed to a differential reaction to monetary policy. Therefore, all bank-specific variables are seasonally adjusted bank-individually by applying a multiplicative method which is based on a moving average.[18]

4   Estimation specification

The test for a differential response of bank loans to monetary policy across banks of different size is essentially based on the approach described in Ehrmann *et al.* (chapter 14 in this volume). Despite the problems associated with using capitalisation and liquidity as discriminating variables for the identification of loan supply effects,[19] we nevertheless assume that these variables determine a bank's reaction to monetary policy. The test will be performed by applying dynamic panel-estimation techniques (GMM according to Arellano and Bond, 1991) to (1), which can be

---

[15] There was a change in data definitions created by the harmonisation procedure in the run-up to EMU. The data used in this study therefore ends in 1998 because the additionally available quarters from 1999 onwards would be too few to appropriately handle this statistical break.

[16] For a discussion of alternative methods for the treatment of mergers, see Worms (2001b).

[17] For a description of the outlier procedure, see Worms (2001a, 2001b).

[18] See Worms (2001b) for more details on the bank-individual seasonal adjustment.

[19] Both capitalisation and liquidity may be endogenous with respect to a bank's access to external finance. For instance, a high degree of capitalisation may not (only) indicate a bank's health, but (also) the riskiness of its loan portfolio (risk adjusted capital ratios are not available). Those banks that suffer most from informational imperfections may also hold large stocks of liquid assets. Moreover, more liquid banks may be those that are more risk averse and, therefore, have tighter lending standards.

derived from a simple model of a profit-maximising bank (see Ehrmann *et al.*, chapter 14 in this volume):

$$\Delta \log L_{it} = a_i + \sum_{j=1}^{l} b_j \cdot \Delta \log L_{it-j} + f \cdot x_{it-1}$$

$$+ \sum_{j=1}^{l} g_j \cdot (x_{it-1} \cdot \Delta r_{t-j}) + \sum_{j=1}^{l} \Phi_j \cdot \Delta \mathbf{X}_{it-j} + d_t + \varepsilon_{it}$$

$$(1)$$

L_{it} is the stock of loans to domestic private non-banks of bank i in quarter t (Δ indicates first differences), r_t is the short-term interest rate – which serves as the indicator of monetary policy – and ε_{it} is the error term. Equation (1) allows for a bank-specific constant a_i (which amounts to a bank-specific trend in $\log L_{it}$). Since the hypothesis test consists of looking for *differences* in the loan reaction of banks, we eliminate the overall effect of pure time variables by including a set of time dummies d_t. While this has the drawback that the (average) level effect of monetary policy is also captured by these dummies, i.e. that r_t cannot be included as such, it guarantees a perfect control for the time effect on the endogenous variable and thereby enhances the power of the hypothesis test.

A bank's loan reaction to monetary policy is assumed to depend linearly on a bank-characterising variable x_{it-1} (which could be size, liquidity or capitalisation). This is captured by the 'interaction terms' $(x_{it-1} \cdot \Delta r_{t-j}) \cdot x_{it-1}$ is also included in a non-interacted fashion in order to prevent possible direct effects of this variable on $\Delta \log L_{it}$ being captured by the coefficients of the interaction terms.

$\mathbf{X}_{it}$ is a matrix of bank-specific variables that serve to capture determinants of loan movements that are not caused by monetary policy-induced shifts in loan supply. It consists of (the logarithm of) a bank-individual income variable, and (the logarithm of) a bank-individual default-risk measure. The income of bank i's loan customers y_{it} – which serves as a bank-specific scaling factor for loan demand – is approximated by an average of sectoral real incomes (of nine production sectors and the private households), with a sector's real income being weighted by its share in bank i's loan portfolio. The bank's default risk is approximated by $risk_{it}$, which is constructed in the same way as a sectoral average of the number of insolvencies.[20] The long-run coefficient of y_{it} should be positive and that of $risk_{it}$ negative.

---

[20] Within the *balance sheet channel*, a monetary policy-induced interest rate increase may, in principle, reduce loan supply by (a) (endogenously) increasing the average probability of default, and (b) by lowering the amount paid to the bank in case of a (exogenous) default, where, typically, net worth serves as the indicator of this amount. Including $risk_{it}$ as an explanatory variable may capture a possible differential reaction of banks'

Liquidity liq_{it} is defined as the percentage share of liquid assets in total assets (35 per cent on average across all banks and periods), where liquid assets consist of cash and balances with the central bank (7 per cent on average across all banks and periods), short-term interbank deposits (32 per cent), debt securities (58 per cent) and shares (3 per cent). The capitalisation variable cap_{it} is constructed in the same way, using the bank's capital (as it appears on the balance sheet) instead of liquid assets. The size variable siz_{it} is the sum of total assets taken as a logarithm.[21]

5   Estimation results

In the following regressions, the three-month interest rate is used as the indicator of monetary policy. As the maximum lag length l of the variables entering the regression, four lags proved to be sufficient. Table 15.2a presents the results. To save space, only the long-run coefficients of the respective interaction terms, of the income and of the risk variable are reported.[22] The statistical tests indicate that an adequate set of instruments has been used in all cases.[23] Moreover, in no case do the long-run coefficients of the control variables show a significantly unexpected sign.

The long-run coefficient of the size interaction is negative and insignificant (reg. 1), indicating that a bank's reaction to monetary policy does not directly depend on its size – which contrasts with the results of the existing empirical literature on the US and on many other countries.[24]

In the case of liq (reg. 2), the long-run coefficient of the interaction term is significantly positive, indicating that the long-run effect of an increase in the interest rate on bank lending is the smaller, the more liquid a bank is: the decrease of the volume of loans in reaction to a 1-percentage point increase in the short-term interest rate r will on average be 0.035 percentage points smaller if, *ceteris paribus*, the liquidity ratio of a bank increases by 1 percentage point. According to reg. 3, a comparable result also holds in the case of capitalisation: the better capitalised a bank, the less its lending declines in response to a restrictive monetary policy measure.

loan supply to monetary policy caused by (a), which would otherwise be captured by the interaction term in (1). Therefore, the inclusion of $risk_{it}$ may lead to an under-estimation of possible loan-supply effects of monetary policy by the interaction term. However, the effect of monetary policy on $risk_{it}$ is probably only of minor relevance (compared to the influence of exogenous changes in default risk on loans).

[21] The x-variables are demeaned in order to make sure that the estimates of the coefficients of the interaction terms are not biased by the level effect of Δr on loan growth.

[22] For the short-run coefficients, see A. Worms (2001a).

[23] For a discussion of the choice of instrumental variables and the interpretation of the statistical tests, see Worms (2001b).

[24] See, for example, deBondt (1999a).

Table 15.2 *Loan equations: long-run coefficients,[a] Germany*

(a) Single-interaction regressions

Regression → Variable ↓ x →	1 siz	2 liq	3 cap	4 ibk	5 oli
$\Delta r \cdot x_{-1}$	−0.045	0.035**	0.136**	0.098**	−0.017**
	(0.025)	(0.006)	(0.041)	(0.012)	(0.006)
Δy	1.193**	0.756	0.960*	1.129*	1.249*
	(0.488)	(0.493)	(0.492)	(0.507)	(0.555)
$\Delta risk$	−0.691**	−0.733**	−0.566**	−0.912**	−0.822**
	(0.119)	(0.122)	(0.119)	(0.130)	(0.142)
AR1 (*p*-val, 1st step)	0.000**	0.000**	0.000**	0.000**	0.000**
AR2 (*p*-val, 1st step)	0.405	0.557	0.348	0.262	0.677
Sargan (*p*-val, 2nd step)	1.000	1.000	1.000	1.000	0.998
Lags of IVs	2−7	2−7	2−7	2−7	2−6
No. of observations	57,615	58,276	58,374	52,565	57,341
No. of banks	2,625	2,654	2,659	2,397	2,611

(b) Double-interaction regressions

Regression → Variable ↓ x →	6 siz	7 cap	8 liq	9 siz
$\Delta r \cdot x_{-1}$	0.101**	0.122**	0.009	0.114**
	(0.026)	(0.046)	(0.038)	(0.032)
$\Delta r \cdot ibk_{-1}$	0.099**	0.077**	0.181**	0.109**
	(0.009)	(0.011)	(0.006)	(0.012)
$\Delta r \cdot ibk_{-1} \cdot x_{-1}$	0.009	0.016	−0.003**	0.012
	(0.005)	(0.009)	(0.001)	(0.006)
Δy	0.996*	0.776	0.374	1.793*
	(0.422)	(0.711)	(0.629)	(0.833)
$\Delta risk$	−0.778**	−0.395**	−0.370*	−0.389*
	(0.103)	(0.160)	(0.159)	(0.172)
Δr				−1.550**
				(0.171)
Δy^{aggr}				0.118
				(0.110)
Δp^{aggr}				5.959**
				(0.657)
AR1 (*p*-val, 1st step)	0.000**	0.000**	0.000**	0.000**
AR2 (*p*-val, 1st step)	0.263	0.559	0.619	0.327
Sargan (*p*-val, 2nd step)	1.000	1.000	1.000	1.000
Lags of IVs	2−6	2−5	2−5	2−6
No. of observations	51,597	52,334	52,422	49,241
No. of banks	2,353	2,386	2,390	2,353

Notes: [a] Coefficients and standard errors of the bank individual income and risk variable multiplied by 100.
* Significant at the 5% level; ** significant at the 1% level (standard errors in parenthesis). Based on second estimation step.

The result that bank loan supply effects of monetary policy cannot be identified (solely) by bank size as the discriminating variable can be explained by the structure of the German banking system. As already discussed in part 2, the many small banks mainly belong to either the cooperative or the savings bank's network (see table 15.1). Ehrmann and Worms (2001) show that after a restrictive monetary policy shock, funds flow from the head institutions to the smaller banks of their respective systems. These flows are mainly reductions of short-term deposits held by the small banks with the head institutions. It seems that small banks do so in order to cushion the effect of a restrictive monetary policy on their loans.

In order to test this hypothesis, the liquidity variable is split into two parts: the share of short-term interbank deposits in total assets, *ibk*, and the share of the remaining other liquid assets in total assets, *oli*. The regressions are repeated with these variables as the bank characterising variables (reg. 4 and 5; the control variables show significantly the expected signs in both regressions). While the long-run coefficient of the interaction term is significantly positive in the case of *ibk*, it is significantly negative in the case of *oli*. Despite the fact that the latter result is difficult to explain at first glance – one would rather expect that a high share of securities, shares and cash in total assets tends to dampen and not to amplify a bank's loan reaction to a restrictive monetary policy[25] – it nevertheless strongly indicates that the significantly positive coefficient of the *liq*-interaction term in reg. 2 is mainly driven by *ibk*.

Therefore, a bank's share of short-term interbank deposits in total assets is crucial for its loan reaction to monetary policy – and not its size. Against the background of the credit channel theory – which assumes a stronger effect of monetary policy on the external finance premia of banks (and firms) with more pronounced informational problems – this result implies that short-term interbank deposits serve as a device to protect small banks from the risk that monetary policy-induced interest rate increases may increase their external finance premium by more than that of other banks.

Given the strong evidence in favour of short-term interbank deposits, the weak result for size leads to the question of whether there is a size effect if we control for the influence of *ibk*. In order to test for this,

---

[25] Splitting *oli* into its components and re-running the regressions reveals that the negative coefficient is driven by debt securities which make up more than 80 per cent of the assets contained in *oli*. One factor behind this could be that a significant part of these debt securities have already been pledged as collateral in repo operations with other banks and are therefore no longer available for a further procurement of funds. On this issue, see Upper and Worms (2001b).

the estimation equation is enhanced to include both interaction terms, size and short-term interbank deposits. Table 15.2b presents the results (reg. 6; the coefficients of the control variables are significant and show the expected signs). The coefficient of the *ibk*-interaction term is significantly positive as in reg. 4. Interestingly, the size-interaction term is now also significantly positive – which is consistent with the credit channel theory. However, given that such a significant coefficient does not show up in reg. 1, it can be concluded that the size effect is dominated by the influence exerted by *ibk*.[26]

Table 15.2b also contains the results of using *ibk* and *cap* simultaneously (reg. 7). Here again, the interaction term with short-term interbank deposits is positive, which adds to the impression that this influence is very strong. Additionally, the coefficient of the *cap*-interaction term is significantly positive (as in reg. 2): other things being equal, loans of well capitalised banks decline less strongly than loans of less capitalised banks if the interest rate is increased.[27]

Including *ibk* and *liq* simultaneously can be interpreted as a test for the dominance of one over the other: The 'weaker' of the two should drop out if it does not contain additional information. Table 15.2b shows that the coefficient of the *liq* interaction is indeed insignificant (reg. 8). This indicates that for the average bank *liq* does not contain relevant information that is not already contained in *ibk*. Only the double-interaction term with monetary policy is significantly negative. This indicates that the effect of short-term interbank deposits on a bank's reaction to monetary policy decreases with an increasing degree of liquidity, i.e. the more other liquid assets the bank has.

Besides these basic regressions, a number of robustness checks were carried out. The results can be summarised as follows:

• *Monetary policy indicator*

  If the residuals of the short-term interest rate equation of a VAR[28] are used as the monetary policy indicator, then the coefficient of the *ibk*-interaction term still significantly shows the expected positive

---

[26] The insignificance of the coefficient of the double interaction with Δr indicates that the strength of the effect of *ibk* on the reaction of a bank to monetary policy does not depend on its size and vice versa.

[27] The estimation of the 'triple-interaction' equation simultaneously containing the respective variables for size, short-term interbank deposits and capitalisation was not feasible, because no adequate set of instrumental variables could be found for applying the Arellano and Bond (1991) procedure.

[28] The VAR was estimated by F. Smets and R. Wouters, whom I would like to thank for supplying me with their data and results. See Smets and Wouters (1999) for more information.

sign. However, the coefficient of the size-interaction term becomes significantly negative, which is the opposite of what the credit channel theory would predict. Re-estimating double-interaction reg. 6 with the VAR shock confirms the dominance of short-term interbank deposits once again: the coefficient of the *ibk*-interaction term remains significantly positive. But there is no significant influence of size. Therefore, the significantly positive size effect found in reg. 6 is not robust against to change in the monetary policy indicator.

- *Treatment of mergers*
If mergers are ignored (instead of applying the backward aggregation procedure), then the estimations yield the same qualitative results with respect to the interaction terms in all cases. If we allow for the possibility that a merger creates a completely new bank, then again the qualitative results with respect to the interaction terms do not differ from those obtained in the single-interaction regressions (table 15.2a): only in the case of *cap* does the coefficient become insignificant. As regards the double-interaction regressions (table 15.2b), the significantly positive coefficient of the *ibk*-interaction remains, while a significant size effect cannot be found.

- *Large banks only*
In order to test whether the results hold if the least important banks in terms of the loan market share are excluded, the regressions are repeated with only those larger banks that together constitute 75 per cent of the loan market (about 90 per cent of all banks are excluded). The results for the interaction terms with *liq*, *cap* and *ibk* presented in table 15.2a hold qualitatively. Moreover, even the coefficients of those interaction terms that were either insignificant (*siz*) or had an implausible sign (*oli*) when using the whole sample, now show significantly the expected signs. This is especially interesting in the case of size: obviously, the insignificance of the size-interaction coefficient in reg. 1 (see table 15.2a) has been caused by the small banks that belong either to the savings banks' or the cooperative banks' network – indicating that they do not behave like the credit channel theory would predict.

- *Including time series*
In order to enhance the power of the hypothesis test, a complete set of time dummies is used in (1). This prevents the inclusion of variables that are varying only over time, and not over banks, like macroeconomic time series. However, in order to test the robustness of the results, reg. 6 is repeated with a set of time series (GDP growth, inflation and the monetary policy indicator) instead of time dummies. It turns out that all results concerning the interaction terms and the bank-individual

control variables are confirmed (see table 15.2b, reg. 9).[29] This similarity indicates that the chosen time series are able to adequately capture the time effect on loan growth.

Concerning the long-run coefficients of the time series, it turns out that a higher rate of inflation Δp^{aggr} tends to increase loan growth. Aggregate real GDP growth Δy^{aggr} has no significant effect, which can be explained by the fact that the bank-individual income variable has also been included. As should be expected, the long-run coefficient of the short-term interest rate r – which serves as the monetary policy indicator – is significantly negative: overall, the loan growth of the average bank declines in reaction to a monetary policy tightening.[30]

This estimation can be used to assess the overall response of the loan market to monetary policy by weighting the banks' individual reaction coefficients by their average loan market shares and aggregating them across all banks. It turns out that an increase in the short-term interest rate by 1 percentage point lowers overall loan growth by 0.94 percentage points in the long run.

6   Summary and conclusions

This chapter shows that the average bank's response to monetary policy in Germany depends mainly on its share of short-term interbank deposits in total assets: the higher this share, the less strongly does the average bank reduce its loans in reaction to an interest rate increase. This is compatible with the hypothesis that small banks – most of which are organised in either the cooperative or the savings banks' network – draw on their short-term interbank deposits to shield their loans to private non-banks from restrictive monetary policy measures.[31] This is consistent with the existence of long-term lending relationships between those banks and their loan customers ('house-bank relationships').

A significant dependence of a bank's reaction to monetary policy on its size can be found only if, at the same time, there is an appropriate control

---

[29] In order to capture at least some 'standard time effects', a linear trend and quarterly seasonal dummies are also included. For more information and the detailed regression results, see Worms (2001b).

[30] For a comparable result, see Ehrmann et al. (chapter 14 in this volume).

[31] Given that the Austrian and the German banking sector are very much alike (most of the Austrian banks belong to either the savings banks' or the credit cooperatives' sector), it is interesting to compare this result with the one obtained by Kaufmann (chapter 21 in this volume). Applying a time-varying estimation specification, she finds that during recessions the lending from banks with more liquid assets is significantly less affected by monetary policy than that of banks with less liquid assets. This points to the importance of banking networks and relationship lending also in the Austrian case.

for this strong influence exerted by short-term interbank deposits. But this results depends on the choice of the monetary policy indicator. While a significant size effect can be found if the three-month interest rate is chosen, this is not the case if the interest rate shocks from a VAR are used. Moreover, the result of a significant size effect is not robust against a change in the treatment of bank mergers. However, the dependence on short-term interbank deposits is robust to all these variations.

16 Is there a bank-lending channel of monetary policy in Spain?

I. Hernando and J. Martínez-Pagés

1 Introduction

This chapter explores the response of bank-loan supply to monetary policy changes in Spain. Results in Ehrmann *et al.* (chapter 14 in this volume) show that, after a tightening in monetary policy, those Spanish banks with less liquid assets, relative to total assets, reduce their loan growth by more than more liquid banks, whereas no difference is found in the response of big and small banks and well- and poorly capitalised banks. Under the usual assumption that more and less liquid banks face the same loan demand function, this differential response can be interpreted as a loan-supply movement, implying the existence of a bank-lending channel of monetary policy transmission in Spain.

However, in the case of Spain, because of the important differences in the composition of bank lending, the differential response across banks may be reflecting either a genuine difference in loan-supply behaviour or a difference induced by the diverse demand-side behaviour of the different types of loans. Moreover, since monetary policy affects both loan supply and loan demand, all tests based on monetary policy shocks are potentially subject to the criticism of not having controlled adequately for differences in loan demand. Fortunately, we have, in the Spanish case, a significant exogenous shock to bank deposits, arising from the tax-induced development of mutual funds during the 1990s, that permits us to carry out an experiment to check whether bank-loan supply is affected by changes in the availability of deposits.[1]

The authors wish to thank J. Ayuso, J. Galí, L. Gambacorta, F. Restoy, T. Sastre and J. Vallés for their useful comments and suggestions.

[1] This is a critical condition for the existence of a bank-lending channel. According to the theory behind this channel, a monetary policy tightening reduces the amount of deposits available to banks, and this reduces the supply of loans, the more so the more costly it is for the bank to compensate for this loss of deposits by raising other non-insured funds or drawing on its stock of liquid assets. See, for example, Kashyap and Stein (1995) or Stein (1998).

Therefore, in this chapter, we perform two additional tests for the existence of a bank-lending channel for the Spanish economy. First, we check whether the results in Ehrmann *et al.* change when looking at the behaviour of three different categories of bank loans: business loans, consumer loans and mortgage loans. Second, we check whether the tax-induced shift from deposits to mutual fund shares reduces the loan supply of (at least some) banks. As we have already said, the advantage of this 'mutual funds shock' is that, being a deposit-reducing shock, there is no reason to expect it to affect loan demand. Thus, any impact of the shock on loan growth can be safely interpreted as a supply effect.

The remainder of the chapter is organised as follows. Section 2 introduces the main developments and characteristics of the Spanish economy and banking system in the period under study (1991–8). Section 3 describes the database and the variables used. Section 4 then presents some results for the basic harmonised equations used in Ehrmann *et al.*, as a reference for the results of the additional tests presented in section 5. Section 6 draws some conclusions.

2   The Spanish banking system and its development during the 1990s

The Spanish financial system underwent a profound structural change after 1980.[2] It was deregulated and opened up to foreign competition. Securities markets developed considerably, but credit institutions still dominated the system, with two-thirds of the total assets of financial institutions and a dominant role as shareholders of companies in the growing businesses of investment and pension funds management and life insurance.

Among the Spanish institutions that are allowed to raise funds from the public in the form of deposits (deposit-money institutions), three different institutional groups can be distinguished: commercial banks, savings banks and cooperative banks. Commercial banks are public limited companies, more focused on corporate business. The traditional business of savings banks and cooperative banks has been, in contrast, that of collecting savings, mainly from households, and granting loans to households and small and medium-sized firms (SMFs); in the first case, particularly in the form of mortgage loans. Savings banks are private foundations controlled – to different degrees in each institution – by representatives of regional government, employees, depositors and founding institutions.

---

[2] See Banco de España (2000b) and Pérez, Maudos and Pastor (1999) for a detailed overview of recent developments in the Spanish banking system.

Although this means some degree of governmental control, there are no special government guarantees or – since 1989 – special regulations affecting these banks. As regards cooperative banks, these are owned by their members and subject to some limited restrictions on their operations. Generally, they are very small and, despite their number, account for less than 5 per cent of total assets. Savings banks, by contrast, had a 53 per cent share of the deposit market and 42 per cent of the loan market in 1998, around 10 percentage points above the levels of a decade earlier.

Competition between Spanish banks increased considerably during the 1990s, stimulated by the entry of foreign banks, the removal of the remaining restrictions on the geographical expansion of savings banks in 1989, technological advances and the process of integration of the Spanish economy in Europe. As a result of this, the average net interest margin (net interest income as a percentage of total assets) fell from around 4 per cent at the beginning of the 1990s to slightly above 2 per cent at the end. There was also a process of consolidation leading to a decline in the number of institutions operating in Spain, from 334 in 1988 to 281 in 2001, in spite of the entry of some foreign banks.

The 1990s, in Spain, was also a period of steadily declining inflation rates. Monetary policy was very tight at the beginning of the decade, but it was progressively relaxed.[3] This trend was broken only twice in the decade. The first time, in 1992, was associated with the crises in the European Monetary System (EMS) of that year. The second time, in the first half of 1995, was associated with some signs of inflationary pressure just as the new inflation-targeting monetary policy strategy of the Bank of Spain began to be applied. In both cases, monetary policy tightening was relatively limited and short-lived. Short-term interest rates went up by between 1.5 and 2 percentage points, and returned to their original level in less than eighteen months.

Loan growth was clearly pro-cyclical, with real growth of above 10 per cent in the expansionary phases at the beginning and end of the decade, and negative growth around the trough in 1993–4. However, different types of loan behaved differently. In particular, mortgage loans were less pro-cyclical. They never grew by less than 14 per cent (in nominal terms), averaging annual growth of 21.4 per cent over the whole period.

Bank deposits were also less pro-cyclical. Very important, in this respect, was the intense process of substitution of mutual fund shares for bank deposits in the portfolios of non-financial firms and households (see figure 16.1). This process was triggered by changes in the tax treatment

---

[3] From 1990 to 1998, the three-month interbank nominal interest rate fell by 11 percentage points (from 15 per cent to 4 per cent), and the inflation rate by 5 percentage points (from 7 per cent to 2 per cent).

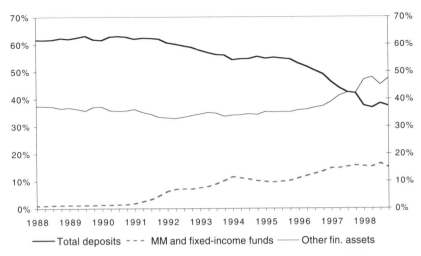

Figure 16.1 Spanish mutual funds and deposits, 1988–1998, percentage of total financial assets of non-financial firms and households

of capital gains on mutual fund shares, with tax rates being lowered twice during the decade; first in 1991 and then in 1996. During the sample period analysed in this chapter, growth in mutual funds is almost entirely explained by the growth of money market and fixed income mutual funds. Moreover, owing to the poor development of private debt markets in Spain, the funds channelled to these mutual funds were invested almost exclusively in public debt – either directly or through repos – and frequently the portfolio had a very short duration.

Consequently, these mutual funds were very liquid and safe and their after-tax return (taking into account management fees) was not significantly different from the return on bank time deposits. Therefore, most of the explanation for the surge in mutual funds during the decade should be attributed to the tax reforms of 1991 and 1996.

3   The data

The data used in this chapter is the same as that in Ehrmann *et al.* (chapter 14 in this volume), with some minor differences.[4] We analyse total loans to the domestic non-financial sector and, for those banks for which such a breakdown is available, we distinguish between loans to firms, consumer

---

[4] The differences are in the definition of liquidity and the treatment of mergers and outliers. See Hernando and Martínez-Pagés (2001) for more details.

Table 16.1 Descriptive statistics on the Spanish banking sector; 1991–1998[a]

	All	Type			Size		Liquidity		Capitalisation	
		Commer. banks	Savings banks	Cooper. banks	Small (<p75)	Large (>p90)	Low (<p30)	High (>p70)	Low (<p30)	High (>p70)
No. of institutions	216	61	57	98	171	23	119	107	106	95
No. of obs.	5,551	1,339	1,637	2,575	4,175	539	1,679	1,649	1,679	1,649
Average total assets (EUR million)	3,026	6,867	4,257	246	550	20,916	3,299	461	6,263	645
Market share (%) of										
Total assets	100.0	54.7	41.5	3.8	13.7	67.1	33.0	4.5	62.6	6.3
Loans	100.0	49.7	45.7	4.6	16.6	61.5	40.8	3.4	57.7	7.9
Deposits	100.0	41.7	52.4	5.9	18.6	59.6	39.2	4.4	58.0	7.4
Asset composition (% year-end total)										
Loans	50.6	56.9	54.2	45.0	49.2	50.7	62.9	36.1	53.0	44.9
Liquidity	32.0	25.1	21.9	42.0	35.2	24.5	15.8	50.9	25.9	41.3
Other assets	17.5	18.0	24.0	13.0	15.6	24.7	21.4	13.0	21.1	13.9

Liabilities composition (% year-end total)

Deposits	72.7	55.5	73.4	81.2	76.1	56.7	68.2	79.6	69.1	75.9
Sight deposits	*32.1*	*26.3*	*33.9*	*34.1*	*32.8*	*28.9*	*32.0*	*33.0*	*31.2*	*31.7*
Other deposits	*40.5*	*29.2*	*39.5*	*47.1*	*43.4*	*27.7*	*36.2*	*46.6*	*37.9*	*44.1*
Borrowing[b]	6.1	15.3	5.2	1.9	3.9	17.3	9.0	2.3	10.2	2.3
Capital and reserves	9.0	9.4	7.2	9.9	9.4	7.3	8.6	10.3	6.0	12.8
Other liabilities	12.2	19.7	14.2	6.9	10.6	18.7	14.3	7.8	14.7	9.0

Loan portfolio composition (% year-end total)

No. of obs.[c]	3,552	1,339	1,637	576	2,177	539	1,552	504	1,436	640
(% of the total)	*64.0*	*100.0*	*100.0*	*22.4*	*52.1*	*100.0*	*92.4*	*30.6*	*85.5*	*38.8*
Business loans	58.0	72.9	47.6	52.6	58.5	60.0	54.5	60.1	53.7	59.9
Mortgage loans	25.4	13.7	35.4	24.2	23.5	26.0	29.0	19.1	29.6	19.7
Consumer loans	7.8	5.6	8.9	9.6	8.0	7.2	8.2	8.4	8.2	8.2
Other loans to households	8.8	7.8	8.1	13.6	10.0	6.8	8.3	12.4	8.5	12.2

Notes: [a] The analysis is performed on the whole sample period, so that statistics are averages for the 1991–8 period. For this purpose, percentiles are calculated period by period, and each observation assigned to the corresponding group in each period. This means that one bank can appear in different groups at different times. Hence, the number of institutions per group do not necessarily sum up to the total.
[b] Interbank non-collateralised borrowed funds plus securities other than shares issued.
[c] This information is not available for all cooperative banks. Hence, we report the number of observations with data in each group and the percentage it represents of the total observations in the group.
Source: Banco de España.

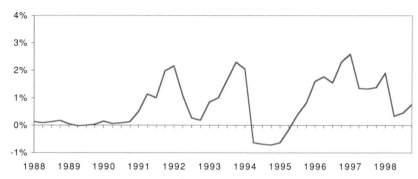

Figure 16.2 Spanish mutual funds shock, 1988–1998, change in the ratio of the net worth of money market and fixed income mutual funds to GDP

loans, mortgage loans and other loans. Our measure of monetary policy is the change in the three-month interbank nominal interest rate and, as in Ehrmann *et al.*, we consider three bank characteristics: size, liquidity and capitalisation.

To capture the impact of the shift from deposits to mutual fund shares, we use the change in the ratio of the net worth of money market and fixed income mutual funds to GDP (see figure 16.2).[5] In Hernando and Martínez-Pagés (2001) it is shown how this variable has a clear negative contemporaneous effect on deposit growth for all banks, although the impact is greater for large, less liquid banks.[6] Despite the somewhat different responses, mutual funds development creates a growing gap between loans and deposits for all banks (see table 7 in Hernando and Martínez-Pagés, 2001). As this process can be considered as an exogenous deposit-reducing shock without any impact on loan demand, we think this is a valid basis for a test of the assumptions underlying the bank-lending channel.

Table 16.1 shows the main descriptive statistics of the final sample used in this chapter. Small banks tend to have more liquid assets and capital, and to be more dependent on deposit financing. Thus, while only

[5] This is preferable to a dummy variable owing to the long duration of the process of substitution. To the extent that the timing of the shift towards mutual funds could have been affected by changes in interest rates, this would be controlled by the inclusion of the interest rate in the loan equation.

[6] Large banks are also less liquid on average. Hence, both results may stem from the same cause. These banks may have put more effort into promoting mutual funds because of the higher share of their groups in the market for mutual fund management and their lower share in the market for low-cost deposits. Also, small banks might have been less affected because of lower interest rate sensitivity on the part of their depositors. It is interesting to note that, if the latter were the case, the same would apply to a monetary policy shock.

4 per cent of bank liabilities for the group of smaller banks corresponds to borrowing (interbank borrowed funds plus securities other than shares issued), this figure is 17 per cent for banks in the upper 10 percentiles. This may indicate that smaller banks have difficulty resorting to uninsured sources of funds, owing to informational asymmetries, potentially leading to the existence of a bank-lending channel of monetary policy. On the other hand, the higher liquidity and capitalisation of smaller banks may be an endogenous response to such asymmetric information problems, thus reducing their impact on the monetary policy response of small banks. Cooperative banks are particularly well capitalised and liquid.

As regards the loan portfolio composition, mortgage loans and loans to households in general are much more important for savings banks and cooperative banks than for commercial banks (the latter channel, on average, 73 per cent of their lending to firms).

4   The response of total loans to monetary policy changes

In this section we report some results for the estimated response of bank loans in Spain to monetary policy changes, using the baseline regression equation presented in more detail in section 3 of Ehrmann *et al.* (chapter 14 in this volume) and our slightly different sample and variables.[7]

Results are presented in table 16.2. The residual-autocorrelation and Sargan tests are passed in all cases and the effects of the macroeconomic variables are robust across the different models. The long-run elasticity of credit to GDP is always significant and larger than one, the response of credit to prices always negative and significant[8] and the long-run monetary policy multiplier has the expected negative sign and is significantly different from zero for the average bank in the sample (according to each of the bank characteristics considered).

Following Kashyap and Stein (1995), if there is a bank-lending channel, we should expect small (illiquid and poorly capitalised) banks to reduce their lending by more after a monetary policy shock, i.e. a positive coefficient for the interaction of the monetary policy measure with each of the bank characteristics in the loan equation. In the cases of size and capitalisation, we do not find a significant differential effect of money

---

[7] As in Ehrmann *et al.*, we estimate the baseline equation in first seasonal differences using a GMM estimator based on orthogonality conditions that take into account the seasonal properties of the data. See Hernando and Martínez-Pagés (2001) for more details on the econometric approach and for additional exercises.

[8] This coefficient picks up both the positive effect of inflation on nominal loan growth and the potential negative effects of higher inflation via higher nominal interest rates. This second effect is important in our sample since inflation fell significantly during the 1990s (see section 2).

Table 16.2 *Baseline loan equations, Spain, dependent variable: first difference of total loans to non-financial private sector*[a]

GMM estimation. No. of obs.: 4,035. No. of banks: 216

Long-run coefficients	Bank charact.: SIZE		Bank charact.: LIQ		Bank charact.: CAP	
	Coeff.	Std error	Coeff.	Std error	Coeff.	Std error
Real GDP growth	1.710 ***	0.355	2.027 ***	0.377	1.870 ***	0.358
Inflation (CPI)	−0.989 ***	0.325	−1.691 ***	0.437	−0.790 **	0.377
Monetary policy (MP)	−1.566 ***	0.423	−2.579 ***	0.512	−1.547 ***	0.466
Bank char.*MP:	−0.132	0.109	3.403 *	1.997	−6.045	6.979
Residual autocorr. tests						
p-value, Sargan test:	0.741		0.811		0.796	
p-value, MA1, MA2:	0.833, 0.778		0.865, 0.988		0.716, 0.813	
p-value, MA4, MA8:	0.000, 0.819		0.000, 0.768		0.000, 0.679	

Notes: *, ** and *** denotes significance at the 10%, 5% and 1% level.
[a] The regressors are four lags of the endogenous variable, the bank characteristic at $t-1$, the contemporaneous value and four lags of the macroeconomic variables (GDP growth, inflation and quarterly change in the three-month interest rate as an indicator of monetary policy changes) and the interactions of the bank characteristic, at $t-1$, with the contemporaneous and lagged values of the three-month interest rate changes.

The model is estimated in first seasonal differences to eliminate bank-specific seasonal components. Therefore, we expect negative residual autocorrelation of order four, but not of other orders.

Instruments: macroeconomic variables, lags 5 to 8 of the endogenous variable and of the bank characteristic, and the interactions of the three-month interest rate with the bank characteristic at $t-5$.

shocks across banks. However, the loan response of banks with a lower share of liquid assets is found to be significantly stronger than that of more liquid banks. These results are consistent with those reported in Ehrmann *et al.* and somewhat conflicting with respect to the existence of a bank-lending channel in Spain.

5   Additional tests on the existence of the bank-lending channel

A possible objection to the results of the estimation of the baseline equation for total loans is that, because of the important differences across banks in the composition of bank lending – i.e. different types of banks concentrate on (specialise in) different categories of loans – we might be inadequately controlling for loan demand in the baseline model.[9] For instance, the stronger response of banks with less liquid assets might actually be reflecting differential loan-supply behaviour or might be explained by the fact that banks with less liquid assets have a higher share of mortgage loans (see table 16.1), the demand for which is more sensitive to monetary policy changes.

To address this objection, we focus on the analysis of three different categories of bank loans separately: business loans, consumer loans and mortgage loans.[10] The main drawback of this approach comes from the fact that the information on these loan categories is not available, on a quarterly basis, for all the banks. In particular, this is the case of most cooperative banks, for which the information requirements are less demanding. When we remove from the sample those banks for which the composition of lending is not available, the size of the sample is substantially reduced.[11]

The first row of panel A in table 16.3 reports the estimates of the long-run coefficients for the interaction terms, for total loans, using the reduced sample.[12] In spite of the significant reduction in the sample, the results do not substantially differ from those reported in table 16.2. The interaction with liquidity is again positive and significant and the interaction with capitalisation is now also significant but with the wrong sign.

The remaining rows in panel A of table 16.3 summarise the long-run differential impact on each type of bank loan of the monetary policy shock (proxied again by the first difference of the three-month money market rate).[13] For all types of loan, we never find any significant differential impact of the monetary policy shock. More precisely, in the case of the models including the interaction of monetary policy and liquidity, the

---

[9] The importance of differences in bank specialisation for the analysis of their behaviour is well documented in Saéz, Sánchez and Sastre (1994) and Sánchez and Sastre (1995). Manzano and Galmés (1996) show how this affects, in particular, the pricing policies of Spanish banks. See also Sastre (1998).

[10] These three categories account for over 90 per cent of total loans to the domestic non-financial private sector. Only other loans to households are excluded from this analysis.

[11] Whereas in the estimates with the complete sample (section 4) we make use of 4,035 observations corresponding to 216 banks, in the estimates with this reduced sample, only 2,100 observations corresponding to 116 banks are available. Nevertheless, it is noteworthy that, although in a smaller proportion, the reduced sample also contains observations corresponding to small banks, banks with a high level of liquid assets and highly capitalised banks, these being the standard attributes of the cooperative banks.

[12] To analyse the response of the different loan categories, we have slightly modified the baseline specification, the main reason being the difficulty in finding adequate demand-scale variables for the different loan categories. See notes to table 16.3.

[13] Although not reported to save space, the statistical properties of these estimates are satisfactory.

Table 16.3 *Additional tests on the bank-lending channel in Spain*

Panel A   Analysis of loan portfolio composition.[a] Long-run coefficients of the interaction of monetary policy with the bank characteristic by type of loan
GMM estimation. No. of obs.: 2,100. No. of banks: 116

| | Bank characteristic | | | | | |
| | SIZE | | LIQ | | CAP | |
Dependent variable	Coeff.	Std error	Coeff.	Std error	Coeff.	Std error
Total loans	0.009	0.156	4.629*	2.479	−9.000*	4.727
Loans to firms	−0.494	0.628	5.406	4.842	−11.380	9.650
Consumer loans	0.466	1.036	10.483	17.849	−19.131	30.413
Mortgage loans	−0.028	0.573	6.225	8.940	−24.014	19.449

Panel B   The impact of the mutual funds shock.[b] Dependent variable: first difference of total loans to non-financial private sector
GMM estimation. No. of obs.: 4,035. No. of banks: 216

| | Bank characteristic | | | | | |
| | SIZE | | LIQ | | CAP | |
Long-run coefficients	Coeff.	Std error	Coeff.	Std error	Coeff.	Std error
Mutual funds shock (MF)	−0.062	0.142	−0.222	0.149	−0.083	0.142
Bank char. *MF:	0.018	0.057	−1.155	0.960	−0.888	3.801

Notes: *, ** and *** denotes significance at the 10%, 5% and 1% level.
[a] The results reported in this panel are based on the sample of banks for which the composition of lending is available. The estimated model is also slightly different. First, the dependent variable is defined as the growth rate of loans of type k granted by bank i minus the growth rate of loans of type k granted by all banks. Second, a complete set of time dummies is added among the regressors, instead of the macroeconomic variables.
   Instruments: time dummies, lags 5 to 8 of the endogenous variable and of the bank characteristic and the interactions of the three-month interest rate change with the bank characteristic at $t-5$.
[b] Baseline model augmented with the mutual funds shock and with its interaction with the bank characteristics. Instruments: macroeconomic variables (including the mutual funds shock), lags 5 to 8 of the endogenous variable and of the bank characteristics, and the interactions of the monetary policy indicator and of the mutual funds shock with the bank characteristics at $t-5$.

interaction terms are always positive but never significant. This suggests that the differential response of total loans among more and less liquid banks, reported in section 4, reflects mostly a loan portfolio composition effect rather than a genuine difference in the loan-supply response.

However, this result is not immune from criticism. As mentioned before, all tests of the bank-lending channel based on the analysis of the cross-sectional differences in the response of loans to a monetary policy shock are potentially subject to the criticism of not having controlled adequately for differences in loan demand. Therefore, we perform an additional test, which is based on the response of bank loans to an exogenous shock to deposits arising from the tax-induced growth of mutual funds in the period under consideration (see section 2).

The importance of this 'mutual funds shock' in the sample period analysed in this chapter makes it very informative. Moreover, its main advantage is that, since it stems mainly from tax considerations, it can be considered as an exogenous negative shock to bank deposit demand, without any impact on loan demand while, under the assumptions of the bank-lending-channel theory, it should affect loan supply. Thus, any impact of the shock on loan growth can be safely interpreted as evidence in favour of the bank-lending channel.

To implement this testing strategy we estimate the loan equation considered in section 4 but enlarged by including the contemporaneous mutual funds shock defined in section 3 and the interactions of this shock with the bank characteristics (size, liquidity and capitalisation). Panel B of table 16.3 reports the results.[14] This table shows that the expansion of mutual funds has not led to a fall in bank lending growth in any case. The interaction terms are never significant.

Therefore, contrary to what the bank-lending theory assumes, it appears that even those banks which are more prone to suffer from an adverse shock to deposit demand (the small, less liquid and poorly capitalised ones) have been able to offset the fall in deposits in some way. Thus, there is no impact on banks' supply of loans. This is very surprising since, as mentioned before, the shock to deposits was quite big. A clue to the results is given in Hernando and Martínez-Pagés (2001), where it is shown how medium-sized and small banks were able to withstand the growing gap between loans and deposits by reducing their stock of liquid assets. Only large banks – and, to a lesser extent, some medium-sized banks – resorted significantly to securities issuance and interbank borrowing.

6   Conclusions

This chapter investigates the existence of a bank-lending channel in the Spanish economy using alternative methodological approaches to overcome the identification problem of disentangling loan-supply effects from loan-demand effects.

---

[14] The long-run coefficients for GDP growth, CPI inflation and the monetary policy shock, not reported to save space, are similar to those displayed in table 16.2. Again, the statistical properties of the estimates are satisfactory.

To this end, the finding, in Ehrmann *et al.* (chapter 14 in this volume), that less liquid banks in Spain display a stronger response to monetary policy than banks with a higher degree of liquidity is submitted to additional testing. We find that the previous result can be explained mostly by a loan portfolio composition effect rather than by a genuine difference in the loan-supply response.

Moreover, we perform an alternative test, based on the response to an exogenous deposit-reducing shock arising from the tax-induced development of mutual funds in the Spanish economy during this period. This shock has the advantage of better identifying loan-supply movements and of being of greater importance in our sample period. We find no evidence that the sizeable reduction in deposits due to the shifts towards mutual fund shares affected the ability of even the smaller, less liquid and less capitalised banks to satisfy loan demand.

Overall, our results are mostly against the existence of an operative bank-lending channel in the Spanish economy in the 1990s. However, we also find some evidence consistent with small banks being less able to resort to market financing than large banks. It has been the high levels of liquid assets of Spanish banks – and, particularly, of small banks – that has allowed them to offset even very significant shocks to their traditional sources of funds. Whether this characteristic of the Spanish banking system will persist in the future and, consequently, whether the results found in this chapter will still be valid is an open question.

17 Is there a bank-lending channel in France? Evidence from bank panel data

C. Loupias, F. Savignac and P. Sevestre

1 Introduction

The French monetary and financial markets were largely restructured in the 1980s, to allow in particular a better access of economic agents to market finance. However, bank-lending still remains a major source of finance for French firms and households. Then, a bank-lending channel is worth considering. Indeed, the population of Monetary and Financial Institutions (MFIs) is, in France as in many other countries, quite heterogeneous. Strong discrepancies can be observed across banks (e.g. in terms of legal structure, size and structure of their balance sheet) and information asymmetries between banks and their funds providers cannot be ruled out.

Unfortunately, previous work, based either on macro VAR models or on microeconometric estimates, is not very conclusive. In particular, Favero, Giavazzi and Flabbi (2001), in their comparative multinational study based on bank balance sheets from the BankScope database, do not find strong evidence of a bank lending channel in France. On the contrary, Martin and Rosenwald (1996) and Rosenwald (1998), using information about the rates at which banks issue CDs, find some differences across banks and thus cannot reject the existence of a lending channel. However, the latter find it to be of a rather small magnitude.

The present chapter fits, partly, in this literature. Its aim is to add a piece to the available evidence by looking at the way, depending on the

We wish to thank A. Duchateau and S. Matherat, for having allowed us the access to the individual bank data from the Commission Bancaire, as well as I. Odonnat (formerly head of the Service des Analyses et des Statistiques Monétaires) for his help in this respect. Thanks also to the Service des Synthèses Conjoncturelles for data from the Cost of Credit Survey and to L. Baudry and S. Tarrieu for their wonderful research assistance. This chapter also owes a lot to comments and suggestions made by S. Avouyi-Dovi, J. Dermine and A. Kashyap and to informal discussions with J. L. Cayssial, C. Cortet, M. Ehrmann, L. Gambacorta, B. Longet, J. Martínez-Pagés and A. Worms. We also thank P. Blanchard for the SAS-IML program used to estimate the model.

banks' characteristics, the outstanding amount of bank loans responds to policy shocks. Using a panel of more than 300 banks observed over the years 1993–2000, we estimate a dynamic reduced form model close to that proposed in Kashyap and Stein (1995, 2000). This model, fully described in another chapter of this book (see Ehrmann *et al.*, chapter 14 in this volume), allows asymmetries in loan supply across banks, depending on their size, liquidity and capitalisation. In addition to the results provided in Ehrmann *et al.*, we provide robustness checks related to different liquidity measures, as liquidity appears to be a key variable in our results.

The structure of the chapter is as follows: section 2 proposes a brief description of the French population of banks. Section 3 is devoted to the presentation of some data and econometric issues. In section 4, the existence of a bank lending channel is discussed. Section 5 draws some conclusions.

2   French banks: a brief presentation

At the end of 1998, there were 1,191 Credit Institutions (CIs) having an activity in France, among which 369 'commercial banks', 120 'mutual and cooperative banks' (which in fact belong to four large networks), thirty-one 'savings and provident institutions', twenty-two municipal credit banks and 649 financial companies (see Loupias, Savignac and Sevestre, 2001, for a description of those different groups of CIs).[1] This figure has to be compared with the 1,630 CIs that existed in March 1993. Indeed, stemming from the banking system law of 1984, the suppression of the state direct control over credit volumes (1985), the creation of a true capital market (including commercial paper) (1986), and the end of the currency exchange controls (1990), the rationalisation of the structure of the French banking industry and the more intense competition that followed have resulted in a steady decline in the number of credit institutions over the last decade (see Commission Bancaire, 2000). In particular, these reforms have improved the access of economic agents to capital markets and induced an increase in the availability of market finance which, in turn, has increased competition between banks. However, this better access to market finance has been essentially significant for large firms. The financing of small businesses and households still mainly rests on bank lending (e.g. see Kremp and Sevestre, 2000).

---

[1] The Caisse des Dépôts et Consignations is not included in this population.

'Commercial banks' clearly play a prominent role in the French banking system as their market share was, in 1998, around 50 per cent in terms of both bank lending and deposits.[2] The cooperative and savings banks come in second position. However, while those banks collect almost all the remainder of deposits (their market share is 42 per cent), their position is less strong on the loan market as they granted about 28 per cent of loans in 1998.[3]

Given the particular importance of size as an indicator for information asymmetries between banks and their funds providers, it is worth comparing the characteristics of small and large banks (see table 17.1).

It must be mentioned that, for the sake of comparability with other countries, institutions with deposits representing less than 10 per cent of their total assets have been discarded from our sample. Financial companies have thus been excluded from the sample as well as some other financial institutions which had almost no deposits despite their legal classification as banks (among which were numerous foreign banks' affiliates). Moreover, because of their particular nature, municipal credit banks have been also discarded and regional banks of three of the four mutual or cooperative bank networks have been replaced by their corresponding global entities. This has left us with 332 banks before the necessary trimming of the sample (see p. 301).

The share of credit in small banks' balance sheets (38 per cent) is higher than that for large banks (34 per cent). Small banks' balance sheets include a lot more liquidity (in the stricter sense, i.e. *Liquid1*) than the ones of large banks. The share of cash and interbank operations in total assets is indeed of 45 per cent (resp. 32 per cent) for small (resp. for large) banks while this share of securities is 13 per cent (resp. 31 per cent) for securities. Thus, small banks are more liquid than large banks. This could help small banks to shield their loan portfolio by making it easier for them to get funds by selling some of their liquid assets after a monetary policy tightening. On the liabilities side, small banks have slightly more deposits than large banks. The share of deposits in total assets is, respectively, 55 per cent for small banks against 49 per cent for large banks. The share of interbank liabilities in total assets equals 25 per cent for both small and large banks, but the share of security liabilities is only 4 per cent for small banks, against 20 per cent for large banks. These figures might indicate that small banks face stronger asymmetric information problems and have more difficulties for issuing bonds than large banks. Then, smaller

---

[2] Except where indicated, all subsequent figures in this section refer to the situation at the end of 1998.
[3] For a more detailed description of the population of French banks, see Loupias, Savignac and Sevestre (2001).

Table 17.1 *French banks' characteristics with respect to size, December 1998[a]*

Banks' characteristics	Absolute size[e]		Relative size[f]		
	Small	Large	Small	Large	Total
No. of banks	182	24	249	16	332
Mean assets (billion Euro)	0.313	66.741	0.770	92.326	6.398
Fraction of total assets	0.027	0.754	0.090	0.695	1
Mean deposits[b]	0.182	33.000	0.492	44.885	3.393
Fraction of total deposits	0.029	0.703	0.109	0.638	1
Mean loans	0.124	26.788	0.343	37.907	2.576
Fraction of total loans	0.026	0.752	0.100	0.709	1
Loans/total assets	0.379	0.335	0.411	0.358	0.403
Deposits/total assets	0.549	0.491	0.581	0.438	0.585
Capital and reserves/total assets	0.123	0.034	0.106	0.037	0.089
Liquid1[c]	0.455	0.317	0.416	0.294	0.401
Liquid2	0.523	0.491	0.481	0.454	0.481
Liquid3	0.236	0.095	0.216	0.034	0.203
Securities holding ratio[d]	0.132	0.311	0.140	0.304	0.163
Interbank liabilities ratio	0.246	0.246	0.226	0.281	0.227
Security liabilities ratio	0.040	0.196	0.046	0.206	0.062

Notes: [a] *Source:* Authors' calculations based on data from bank reports to the bank Supervisory Authority (Commission Bancaire).
[b] Deposits include certificates of deposits (CDs) and medium-term notes (MTNs).
[c] Liquid1 is the ratio of the sum of cash and interbank assets to total assets, Liquid2 is the ratio of the sum of cash, interbank assets and the so-called 'transaction' and 'short-term investment' securities to total assets. Those two categories are made up of securities that the bank does not consider as 'long-term investments' and can thus be considered to be a part of the banks' liquidity. Liquid3 is a measure aiming at taking account of the banks' net interbank position. It is defined as the ratio of the difference 'interbank assets – interbank liabilities' to the difference 'total assets – min(interbank assets, interbank liabilities)'.
[d] The securities holding and liabilities lines include other items 'divers'. Securities liabilities do not include CDs and MTNs. The last three ratios are relative to total assets.
[e] Absolute size: 'Small' banks have assets less than 1 billion, while 'large' banks have assets more than 10 billion.
[f] Relative size: A 'small' bank has the average size of the banks below the third quartile, while a 'large' bank has the average size of the banks above the 95th percentile.

banks would be more affected by a monetary policy tightening than large banks. However, if one looks at capitalisation, one may notice that small banks are a lot more capitalised than large banks. The capitalisation ratio is indeed 12.3 per cent for small banks while it is only 3.4 per cent for large banks. This might counterbalance the previous asymmetric information effect.

3   Data and econometric issues

3.1   Data issues

As stated above, we have had to discard some groups of CIs from our sample in order to ensure the comparability of our results with those for other countries. This has left us with a sample of 332 banks. However, as is often the case with individual data, this sample contained some outliers that could have led us to get unsound econometric estimates. Those outliers have been discarded from the sample in the following way. For quarterly growth rates of total assets, loans and deposits, all observations below the second and above the 98th percentiles have been treated as outliers. For the first difference in the capitalisation and liquidity ratios, the thresholds have been set to the first and 99th percentiles. In addition, a bank had to have at least six successive observations in levels, i.e. five in growth rates, in order to be kept in the sample. We have then been left with an unbalanced panel comprising 312 banks over the years 1993–2000 and 5,327 observations.

3.2   Econometric issues

We have estimated the same kind of model as Ehrmann *et al.* (chapter 14 in this volume), inspired by a generalisation of the textbook IS-LM model described in Bernanke and Blinder (1988), re-written in first differences:

$$
\Delta \log(L_{it}) = \sum_{j=1}^{4} b_j \Delta \log(L_{it-j}) + \sum_{j=0}^{4} c_j \Delta r_{t-j}
$$

$$
+ \sum_{j=0}^{4} d_j \Delta \log(GDP)_{t-j} + \sum_{j=0}^{4} e_j INFL_{t-j} + f x_{it-1}
$$

$$
+ \sum_{j=0}^{4} g_{1j} x_{it-1} \Delta r_{t-j} + \sum_{j=0}^{4} g_{2j} x_{it-1} \Delta \log(GDP)_{t-j}
$$

$$
+ \sum_{j=0}^{4} g_{3j} x_{it-1} INFL_{t-j} + \Delta \varepsilon_{it} \tag{1}
$$

where $i = 1, \ldots, N$ indexes banks and $t = 1, \ldots, T_i$ indexes time periods (quarters). L_{it} represents the loans of bank i in quarter t to the non-financial private sector. Δr_t represents the first difference of a nominal short-term interest rate, namely the three-month interbank interest rate. $\Delta \log(GDP)_t$ is the growth rate of real GDP,[4] and $INFL_t$ the inflation rate

[4] GDP evaluated at 1995 prices.

Table 17.2 Loan equations: long-run coefficients, France[a]

	Model 1 Liquid1		Model 2 Liquid1		Model 1 Liquid2		Model 1 Liquid3	
	Coeff. (1)	Std error (2)	Coeff. (3)	Std error (4)	Coeff. (5)	Std error (6)	Coeff. (7)	Std error (8)
Direct coefficients								
Sum of lags	0.289***	0.050	0301***	0.056	0.307***	0.053	0.381***	0.053
Monetary policy(MP)	−1.400***	0.403			−1.350***	0.432	−0.433	0.410
Real GDP	2.115***	0.318			2.392***	0.343	2.352***	0.338
Prices(CPI)	−2.615***	0.393			−2.716***	0.401	−2.492***	0.412
Interaction coefficients								
Monetary policy(MP) × size	−0.045	0.156	−0.093	0.163	−0.166	0.164	−0.257	0.174
Monetary policy(MP) × liquidity	5.762***	1.389	5.743***	1.539	2.810**	1.104	4.176***	0.856
Monetary policy(MP) × capitalisation	1.638	4.969	1.546	5.271	3.875	5.097	−10.840**	4.978
Long-run interaction coefficients[a]								
Monetary policy(MP) × size	−0.063	0.218	−0.132	0.233	−0.240	0.236	−0.416	0.287
Monetary policy(MP) × liquidity	8.106***	1.931	8.211***	2.102	4.055**	1.588	6.750***	1.482
Monetary policy(MP) × capitalisation	2.304	7.007	2.210	7.537	5.593	7.395	−17.530**	7.999
	Stat.	p-value	Stat.	p-value	Stat.	p-value	Stat.	p-value
m1	−3.588	0.000	−3.584	0.000	−3.260	0.001	−4.224	0.000
m2	−0.863	0.388	−1.058	0.290	−0.751	0.453	−0.717	0.474
Sargan test (2nd step)	122.669	0.231	105.892	0.376	126.309	0.168	137.486	0.051
No. of banks	312		312		312		313	
No. of obs.	5327		5327		5320		5279	

Notes: [a] Long-run interaction coefficients are computed as the interaction coefficients given above (themselves being the sum over lags of all the corresponding coefficients) over one minus the sum over lags of the endogenous variable.

computed as the growth rate of the consumer price index. x accounts for banks' characteristics that may affect directly or indirectly their loan supply through their reaction to monetary policy changes (as well as their reaction to GDP or price changes). We have decided to introduce three banks' characteristics together: size, liquidity and capitalisation. Indeed, these characteristics are not independent of each other. Then, including them separately in a model was likely to generate an omitted variable bias. Indeed, estimating models including only one characteristic at once led to unsatisfactory results (see chapter 14).

We first estimated the model including four lags of the three macroeconomic variables and their interactions with all bank characteristics. However, this led to unsatisfactory results. Indeed, we faced a strong multicollinearity problem, implying a lack of significance of almost all the estimated coefficients. We then decided to keep the interactions of monetary policy with size, liquidity and capitalisation but to discard all interactions with GDP growth and inflation, which were much less significant than the ones with the monetary policy indicator. The validity of this choice was confirmed by the fact that when the model included only one bank characteristic, we got insignificant coefficient estimates for the interactions with GDP and inflation, but significant ones for the monetary policy interactions.[5] In other words, it seems that one can accept the assumption that loan-demand elasticities with respect to GDP and inflation are homogeneous across banks. This set of estimates is referred to as model 1. In another set of regressions, time dummies were substituted for macroeconomic variables. This estimation, referred to as model 2, was aimed at checking for the proper isolation of asymmetries in banks' response to monetary policy changes. It is worth pointing out that, as regards the monetary policy interaction coefficients, the estimates obtained from model 1 (column (1) in table 17.2), are very similar to those obtained from model 2, including time dummies (column (2)). This reassures us that our interpretation of these interaction coefficients as indications of the existence of some heterogeneity in banks' lending behaviour is robust.

In order to account for the autoregressive nature of the model and for the possible endogeneity of banks' characteristics, the GMM estimator has been used with the following instruments: the second and third lags of the quarterly growth rate of loans, the second lag of the bank characteristics and the first difference of the three-month interbank interest rate. Moreover, to increase efficiency, this instrument set has been expanded

---

[5] The results associated with the estimation of a model with only one characteristic at a time are not reported here, but can be found in Ehrmann et al. (chapter 14 in this volume).

following Arellano and Bond's (1991) procedure, i.e. all instruments have been multiplied by time dummies. According to the Sargan test statistics we get, the instruments used are valid. Then, one cannot reject the assumption that the three month interbank interest rate is exogenous. Moreover, this statistic together with the p-values of the m1 (disturbance serial correlation of order 1) and m2 (disturbance serial correlation of order 2) statistics confirm our interpretation of the model as the first difference of a 'theoretical' specification in log levels. Indeed, the disturbances appear to be MA(1), and thus to be uncorrelated with bank-specific variables dated $t - 2$ or less and with lags 2 and 3 of the endogenous variable.

The results presented in table 17.2 are the GMM second-step estimates. However, first-step estimates with robust standard errors do not significantly differ from these. Moreover, robustness checks have been done as regards seasonality. Neither the inclusion of seasonal dummies nor the inclusion of the fourth lag of the growth rate of loans in the instrument set indicated any significant seasonality, besides that implicitly taken into account by the macro variables. Other robustness checks, specific to the particular treatment we applied to mutual and cooperative bank networks, did not indicate any quantitatively significant impact.[6]

4   Is there a bank-lending channel?

In our model, the existence of a bank-lending channel can be assessed through the sign and significance of the interaction coefficients measuring the differential impact of monetary policy on bank lending according to banks' size, liquidity, and/or capitalisation. If small/illiquid/under-capitalised banks faced stronger difficulties in finding external finance, after a monetary policy tightening, they would reduce their loans by more than large/liquid/highly capitalised ones. Given the negative impact of an interest rate increase on bank lending, this should translate into a positive and significant estimate of the interaction coefficients between monetary policy and banks' characteristics.

4.1   The impact of liquidity

Contrary to Favero, Giavazzi and Flabbi (2001), who carried out a multinational comparative study using BankScope data, we find some evidence

---

[6] For more details, see Loupias, Savignac and Sevestre (2001).

of a lending channel in France. Indeed, the existence of a lending channel can be assessed since our econometric results show that more liquid banks do not respond to a monetary policy tightening as strongly as less liquid banks. Indeed, they use their liquidity to compensate the effects of a monetary policy tightening: the interaction coefficient with liquidity is positive and highly significant. Banks appear to draw on their short-term interbank assets to dampen the consequences of an interest rate increase on their loan supply.

As liquidity appears to be important, robustness checks have been done by considering three alternative measures of the liquidity. *Liquid1* is a very simple measure of liquidity as it takes into account only cash and interbank assets on a gross basis. It is the one used in Ehrmann *et al.* (chapter 14 in this volume) and is our benchmark. The second measure of liquidity (*Liquid2*) is almost as simple but it includes, on top of cash and interbank assets, transaction securities and short-term investment securities. These securities are supposed to be easily marketable, and thus relatively liquid. The third measure of liquidity (*Liquid3*) aims at taking account of the banks' net interbank position. It is defined as the ratio of the difference 'interbank assets–interbank liabilities' to the difference 'total assets–min(interbank assets, interbank liabilities)'. The purpose of this measure is to get rid of the interbank activity of a bank in order to measure its 'truly disposable' liquidity. Indeed, one can imagine situations in which banks with a high level of interbank liquid assets cannot necessarily shield their loan portfolio from a monetary policy tightening by selling those assets. Banks with large commitments on the interbank market may have to use their interbank assets to fulfil their obligations. This phenomenon seems to be important for mutual and cooperative banks, owing to their particular management of liquidity (see Worms, chapter 15 in this volume, for a comparable observation for Germany).

Column (3) in table 17.2 presents a regression with the second measure of liquidity. The results are qualitatively not quite different from the ones with a more restricted definition of liquidity. Nevertheless, although still significantly positive, the magnitude of the monetary policy liquidity interaction coefficient appears to be about one half of that with the first definition of the liquidity ratio. This is an indication that the impact of a restrictive monetary policy on the banks' securities portfolio is less important than that on their interbank assets. This result is consistent with Baumel and Sevestre (2000) who found that, in order to finance more loans, banks use only marginally the possibility they have to sell the long-term securities they own. It is also in line with the results of Worms (chapter 15 in this volume) for German banks. The third definition of the liquidity ratio, aimed at taking account of the net liquidity position of banks, also leads to qualitatively similar results (column (4) in table 17.2). In other words, even taking account of their possibly particular management of liquidity, one cannot dismiss the conclusion that banks insulate their loan portfolio from a monetary policy tightening by first selling part of their most liquid assets portfolio.

4.2   The impact of size

Contrary to the results obtained by Kashyap and Stein (1995, 2000) for the USA, size does not appear to have any impact on the way banks respond to an increase in the monetary policy interest rate. This result is similar to the one obtained for several other European countries (see Ehrmann *et al.*, chapter 14 in this volume). One possible explanation rests in the fact that, as previously shown, small banks are significantly more liquid and capitalised than large ones.[7] This might counter-balance the effect of size, as far as size is taken as an indicator for information problems faced by banks when they look for external finance to compensate the decrease in deposits they may experience after a monetary policy tightening. A second explanation might come from the fact that small banks are often owned by larger ones. Thus, their size does not necessarily reflect their ability to raise funds nor their potential solvency problems. Another possible explanation comes from the identification problem we might have. Indeed, the interaction coefficients we get account for differences in the loan-supply behaviour of banks as long as one assumes that all banks face the same demand function as regards the interest rate elasticity. However, Baumel and Sevestre (2000) have shown that the elasticity of demand addressed to large banks is higher than that of the demand faced by small banks. Then, the interaction coefficient we get in our reduced form model results from the composition of two different effects of interest rate variations, which exhibit opposite magnitudes: for large banks (resp. small banks), the elasticity of supply may be low (resp. high) while that of demand is large (resp. small). This might explain why we get a non-significant impact of size on bank lending.

4.3   The impact of capitalisation

The third bank characteristic we have considered, namely capitalisation, does not seem to impact significantly on bank lending behaviour,

---

[7] Those differences exist in the USA, too. However, they are of a much smaller magnitude.

everything else being equal. This result cannot be explained by a lack of precision due to the correlations between size, liquidity and capitalisation. If this were the case, one would obtain significant coefficients when only one interaction is included in the model (see chapter 14). Again, most banks with a low capitalisation ratio are large banks, which may explain why this characteristic does not appear to impact on banks' loan supply. However, it might be the case that capitalisation matters for small banks only. In that case, one would expect to get a significant positive coefficient when introducing the double-interaction size-capitalisation in the model. This is not what we have found when we have estimated a model with a double-interaction size-capitalisation with monetary policy, as we got an insignificant coefficient for this double interaction. Finally, the absence of influence of the capitalisation ratio might also stem from the drawback of our accounting capitalisation measure. Indeed, this ratio is quite different from the one used in the prudential regulation.[8]

5   Conclusion

The aim of this chapter was to check for the possible existence of a bank-lending channel in France. For that purpose, we have estimated a dynamic reduced form model allowing for asymmetries in loan supply across banks, depending on their size, liquidity and capitalisation. We have used a panel of 312 French banks observed quarterly over the period 1993–2000.

We find some asymmetry between liquid and illiquid banks, the latter being more sensitive to a monetary policy tightening. This result is in accordance with that obtained for several other countries of the Euro area (see Ehrmann et al., chapter 14 in this volume). It constitutes an indication that, as far as they can, French banks sell part of their liquid assets in order to shield their loan portfolio from the effects of increases in the interest rate.

Contrary to what has been found for the USA (e.g. see Kashyap and Stein (1995, 2000) and Kishan and Opiela (2000)), we do not find the two other banks' characteristics we consider (size and capitalisation) to have any significant impact on bank lending.

Nevertheless, some more work needs to be done to get a better assessment of the influence of monetary policy decisions on bank lending. First, it would be probably more satisfactory to get an evaluation of the

---

[8] The so-called 'Basle capitalisation requirement' (see Ehrmann et al., Gambacorta, chapters 14 and 19 in this volume).

impact of those decisions on new loans granted by banks rather than on their outstanding amount. Indeed, banks cannot easily adjust their loan portfolio downwards, at least for long-term loans which represent a significant proportion of bank lending. Second, one should also have a look at the impact of monetary policy on the interest rate charged by banks to their customers.

18   Is there a bank-lending channel of monetary policy in Greece? Evidence from bank-level data

*S. N. Brissimis, N. C. Kamberoglou
and G. T. Simigiannis*

1   Introduction

This chapter examines the implications of differential bank characteristics for the loan supply behaviour of Greek banks, using monthly panel data that cover the second half of the 1990s, and assesses the importance of these cross-sectional differences for the operation of the bank-lending channel. Implicit in this approach, namely that the response of banks to changes in monetary policy could differ depending on their characteristics (such as size or liquidity), is the assumption that, when asymmetries are present, loan-supply shifts – a necessary condition for the operation of the lending channel – may be identified. The empirical results derived from bank-level data indicate that bank-specific characteristics were found to systematically shift the loan-supply function. This result is consistent with previous time-series evidence (Brissimis and Kastrissianakis, 1997) according to which the bank-lending channel operates in Greece although its importance diminished in the 1990s with the financial liberalisation.

The remainder of the chapter is divided as follows. Section 2 presents an overview of recent developments in the Greek banking system and its characteristics that may be pertinent to the operation of the lending channel. Section 3 uses two approaches for analysing the role of banks in monetary transmission. One employs a reduced form equation linking monetary policy and distributional variables to bank loans in the spirit of Kashyap and Stein's (1995) work. The other, which in general yields more satisfactory results, brings together some of the features of the Bernanke–Blinder (1988) model with a method for assessing the impact of differential balance sheet characteristics on banks' ability to supply loans and investigates directly the behaviour of bank-loan supply. This section also discusses data issues and presents estimation results by

We would like to thank Ignazio Angeloni, Claudio Borio, Anil Kashyap, Benoît Mojon and Andreas Worms for their useful comments and suggestions.

applying panel cointegration methods, which indicate the importance of the lending channel for the Greek economy and of bank-specific characteristics in accounting for a differentiated response of loans to monetary policy changes. Finally, section 4 summarises the main conclusions.

2   The structure of the Greek banking sector

Banks in Greece have historically played a dominant role in channelling financial savings from surplus to deficit economic units, whereas the relative importance of other financial institutions, such as mutual funds and insurance companies, in financial intermediation was until recently very limited, but is currently increasing. The special role of banks in financial intermediation was further enhanced by the following features of the financial system. First, banks were highly regulated, and detailed selective rules and restrictions governed the distribution of bank credit to economic sectors until the mid-1980s.[1] Moreover, until December 1990, commercial banks were required to invest 40 per cent of their drachma deposits in government securities, mainly three-month Treasury bills. This investment requirement was phased out at the margin by end-1993 and banks converted their accumulated Treasury bill holdings into negotiable medium-term government bonds. However, the relatively thin market for government securities did not allow banks to sell a large part of their portfolio of these securities without incurring substantial capital losses. Second, the scope for financing through the capital market was also very limited, as the stock exchange was not very developed until the beginning of the 1990s. Third, various restrictions had been imposed on external transactions and in particular on capital flows. Important developments in financial markets abroad, and the need to transpose the relevant EU Directives into domestic law and modernise the Greek financial system led to the gradual liberalisation of financial markets and external transactions, a process that was essentially complete by the mid-1990s. As a result, bank intermediation has relatively declined, whereas the stock market and mutual funds have displayed very rapid growth.

Banks have tried to counter these trends through financial innovations. Examples of this are the development of synthetic swaps[2] and the increase

---

[1] For a description of the regulated financial system and its subsequent deregulation, see Central Banking (1995–6) and Garganas and Tavlas (2001).

[2] Synthetic swaps were developed in the early 1990s mainly for tax avoidance reasons. A synthetic swap involved the transfer of an amount of funds to a term deposit account denominated in a foreign currency with a bank abroad and the simultaneous forward selling of the principal and the interest for drachmas. The difference between the spot and the forward exchange rates is treated as capital gains by tax authorities and is not taxed.

in banks' off-balance sheet items,[3] which mainly reflects the fast growth of financial derivatives. To a considerable extent, financial innovations were driven by tax avoidance motives, as well as by the desire of banks to circumvent reserve requirements, given the relatively high reserve requirement ratio (12 per cent, as against the 2 per cent currently applied by the Eurosytem) and the significantly low rates, compared with market rates, at which reserves were remunerated. The response of the Bank of Greece to these developments was to broaden the reserve base, by including all types of bank liabilities to residents and non-residents, arising from deposits or credits or, in general, associated with asset management agreements. This system of reserve requirements remained in place until June 2000, when it was harmonised with that of the Eurosystem, with transitory arrangements for the release of the accumulated reserves in excess of the new requirement. It should be also noted that a special regime applied to the bulk of deposits in foreign currencies, for which the reserve requirement ratio was effectively 100 per cent. Again, a gradual harmonisation brought the reserve requirement ratio for these deposits down to that applied by the Eurosystem.

The above discussion suggests that, prior to the harmonisation of the reserve requirement system, banks operating in Greece had only very limited possibilities to isolate their fund-raising activities from the effects of monetary policy shocks and thus to maintain their loan supply unchanged. The only possibility open to them was to resort to the stock market for raising share capital, but this procedure could not be used flexibly, given the institutional procedures that had to be followed for increasing share capital. On the other hand, the scope for substituting loans for securities appears to have been minimal until the mid-1990s, but it increased considerably after financial liberalisation was completed. Thus, the bank-lending channel is expected to have been especially potent in the period before the liberalisation of the banking system, but to have weakened thereafter.

Table 18.1 provides information on the structure of the Greek banking system according to various characteristics at the end of 1998. Commercial banks constitute the most important segment of the Greek banking sector, their share in total bank assets being 88.2 per cent, while the share of specialised credit institutions is a little above 10 per cent. Cooperative banks hold a very low percentage (0.3 per cent) of total bank assets, although their number has been increasing in recent years.

---

[3] Greek commercial banks' off-balance sheet items as a percentage of total assets: 1993: 53 per cent, 2000: 154 per cent.

Table 18.1 *Structure of the Greek banking sector, December 1998*

	All banks	Type			Size		Capitalisation		Liquidity	
		Commercial	Cooperative	Other	Small[a]	Large[a]	Low[b]	High[b]	Low[c]	High[c]
Size indicators										
No. of institutions	60	43	12	5	30	3	6	6	6	6
No. of bank branches	2757	2562	31	164	119	1249	52	18	22	144
No. of bank employees	57898	55112	244	2542	2423	25789	1729	508	1007	1580
Average total assets (million Euros)	2198	2704	29.4	3052	166.6	21321.3	916.5	315.3	654.5	1902.8
Median total assets (million Euros)	593.5	795	12	1852	593.5	10045.5	360.5	3.5	42	520
Market share (percentage of total assets)	100	88.2	0.3	11.6	3.8	48.5	4.2	1.4	3.0	8.6
Asset structure (percentage of year-end total assets)										
Cash	0.8	0.8	1.1	0.7	0.4	0.9	0.4	0.0	2.7	0.0
Loans to general government	2.6	2.2	0.3	6.0	0.7	3.7	0.2	26.4	8.4	0.6
Loans to non-MFI private sector	31.4	32.6	71.3	22.0	35.9	30.4	27.3	41.3	49.0	8.6
Loans to non-financial corporations	29.4	30.7	71.3	18.2	32.3	29.1	24.4	37.6	44.7	6.2
Loans to households	7.6	7.0	27.2	12.0	8.0	6.9	8.9	0.9	30.4	5.0
of which:										
House purchase	5.3	4.4	6.1	11.9	4.2	5.8	0.8	0.8	29.1	5.0
Securities	23.8	21.3	2.5	42.8	7.7	25.0	8.8	12.9	3.6	54.7
of which:										
Money market paper	0.0	0.0	0.0	0.0	0.0	0.0	0.0	0.0	0.0	0.0
Other securities issued by MFIs	0.2	0.3	0.0	0.0	0.0	0.4	0.0	0.0	0.0	0.0
Securities issued by general government	23.3	20.8	2.5	42.7	7.5	24.4	8.2	12.1	3.6	54.7
Securities issued by non-financial corporations	0.3	0.3	0.0	0.1	0.1	0.3	0.6	0.8	0.0	0.0

of which:									
Maturity of less than two years	3.1	3.3	0.0	1.1	1.1	4.1	1.5	0.3	1.5	1.0
Maturity of more than two years	20.7	18.0	2.5	41.7	6.5	20.9	7.3	12.6	2.1	53.7
Shares and other equity	3.3	3.1	1.0	4.9	0.4	3.3	0.2	9.0	9.2	1.2
Assets denominated in foreign currencies	26.8	29.7	0.1	5.6	45.6	22.6	59.5	32.0	14.5	9.1
Assets denominated in non-euro area currencies	18.2	20.2	0.0	2.8	28.5	12.8	56.3	19.3	9.9	7.7
Liabilities structure (percentage of year-end total assets)									
Overnight deposits	7.8	8.4	4.6	3.3	7.6	7.1	5.8	0.0	13.1	0.4
Time deposits										
Maturity of less than two years	62.4	63.3	59.2	55.7	38.5	70.5	55.4	0.6	19.7	73.2
Maturity of more than two years	1.0	0.3	1.2	6.5	1.8	0.2	0.1	0.0	25.3	0.0
Debt securities	0.4	0.4	0.0	0.0	0.1	0.8	0.0	0.2	0.0	0.0
of which:									
Money market paper	0.0	0.0	0.0	0.0	0.0	0.0	0.0	0.0	0.0	0.0
Other	0.4	0.4	0.0	0.0	0.1	0.8	0.0	0.2	0.0	0.0
Denominated in non-EMU currencies										
Liabilities denominated in foreign currencies	32.5	35.7	0.5	8.4	47.7	29.8	67.1	35.0	15.2	15.3
Liabilities denominated in non-euro area currencies	23.5	25.8	0.0	6.6	34.3	18.8	59.7	22.9	11.1	13.8
Capital and reserves	8.3	6.6	29.5	20.2	7.7	5.5	0.8	56.1	17.1	12.0

Notes: [a] Small (large) banks are defined as the bottom (top) 50th (5th) percentile of the distribution of total assets.
[b] Defined as the bottom/top 10th percentile of the capital–asset ratio.
[c] Defined as the bottom/top 10th percentile of the liquid asset ratio.

The degree of concentration of the Greek banking system is relatively high, given that the share of the three larger banks in total bank assets is almost 50 per cent, while that of the banks at the bottom 50 per cent of the distribution of their total assets is only 3.8 per cent. As shown in table 18.1, loans to the non-MFI private sector as a percentage of total assets is higher in the case of small banks. On the contrary, holdings of securities represent a smaller percentage of the total assets in smaller banks rather than in larger banks, indicating that the latter are relatively more liquid. Furthermore, the share of deposits in total liabilities is higher in the case of larger banks, but smaller banks are better capitalised.

As regards capitalisation, poorly capitalised banks rely on deposits more than well-capitalised banks. However, the ratio of loans to the non-MFI private sector to total assets of well-capitalised banks is higher, indicating that capital-adequacy considerations may have been more binding for poorly capitalised banks.

3   Theoretical framework and empirical evidence

The role of banks in the transmission process and the importance of differential bank characteristics as regards the response of bank loans to a monetary tightening is empirically investigated by using first the following specification based on Kashyap and Stein (1995) and derived by Ehrman *et al.* (chapter 14 in this volume) from a simple model of a profit-maximising bank:

$$\Delta L_{it} = \sum_j a_j \Delta L_{i,t-j} + \sum_j b_j \Delta r_{t-j} + \sum_j c_j Z_{i,t-1} \Delta r_{t-j}$$

$$+ d Z_{i,t-1} + \sum_j e_j \Delta W_{t-j} + v_i + \epsilon_{it} \tag{1}$$

where $L_{i,t}$ are real loans (in logs), r_t is a monetary policy interest rate, Z_{it} is a bank-specific characteristic, W_t is a vector of control variables, v_i represents individual bank effects, and ϵ_{it} is the error term. Subscripts i and t refer to specific banks and time periods, respectively. This specification is broadly similar to the baseline regression equation used in this volume.

Equation (1) is a typical reduced form equation which is compatible with the existence of a bank-lending channel and in which differential bank characteristics play an important role in shifting the banks' loan-supply function. The parameters of interest in this equation are the b_js and c_js, which are assumed to be the same across banks. A monetary tightening is expected to reduce lending, hence $\Sigma_j b_j$ should be negative. Large and liquid banks are expected to be able to better shield their loans from monetary shocks by using their buffer of liquid assets and/or by attracting funds from non-deposit sources (see, e.g., Favero, Giavazzi and Flabbi, 2001; Kashyap and Stein, 1995, 2000 and Kishan and Opiela, 2000). Thus, $\Sigma_j c_j$ is expected to be positive. Individual bank characteristics other than those represented by Z_i are captured by the fixed effect term v_i.

Panel data on balance sheet items for Greek banks have been used to estimate (1). The sample includes monthly observations covering the period January 1995 to December 1999 for twelve commercial banks representing all sizes. Although the sample contains only 20 per cent of all banks operating in Greece, at end-1999 the share of these banks in total assets, loans and deposits of the banking system was 57 per cent, 59 per cent and 68 per cent, respectively. Bank data had to be adjusted for two mergers that occurred in the later part of 1999. Merged banks were assumed to remain independent and the relevant data after the merger were allocated to each of the banks according to the pattern observed immediately prior to their merging.[4] All balance sheet variables were deflated by the consumer price index (CPI), seasonally adjusted and expressed in logs. The three-month money market rate (Athibor) is used as the monetary policy variable. As a control variable we used an index of real GDP constructed on the basis of annual national accounts data and available monthly indicators of economic activity for the main sectors of the economy.[5]

The effects of bank-specific characteristics are examined by using a balance sheet strength (liquidity) and a size variable. Liquidity is defined as the ratio of liquid assets $LQ_{i,t}$ (cash, deposits held with other banks and securities) to total assets $A_{i,t}$. Bank size is measured by total assets. The bank-characteristic variables are defined as deviations from the cross-sectional mean at each time period in the case of the size variable, so as to remove its trend, or the overall mean in the case of the bank strength variable, which does not have a trend:[6]

$$B_{i,t} = LQ_{i,t}/A_{i,t} - \sum_t \left[\left(\sum_i LQ_{i,t}/A_{i,t} \right) \Big/ N \right] \Big/ T \qquad (2)$$

$$S_{i,t} = \ln A_{i,t} - \left(\sum_i \ln A_{i,t} \right) \Big/ N \qquad (3)$$

---

[4] This treatment of mergers was adopted as a backward aggregation of merging banks would have resulted in a considerable loss of information, while the bias introduced by allocating data to the particular banks after their merger is small since, as mentioned above, the two mergers occurred only in the second half of the last year of the sample period.

[5] See Brissimis et al. (2001).   [6] See also section 3 of chapter 14 in this volume.

The system of equations (1) was estimated by using SUR weighted least squares (sometimes referred to as the Parks estimator) which is appropriate when residuals are both cross-section heteroscedastic and contemporaneously correlated.[7] Furthermore, in order to reduce possible multicollinearity problems, we discarded the inflation rate and the interaction terms with inflation which were much less significant. We ended up retaining three lags for the other variables. Also, we included the twelfth lag of the rate of growth of loans in order to capture any seasonality that had not been removed. Finally, a dummy variable was included to account for the impact of the turbulence in the foreign exchange market in November 1997 that followed the financial crisis in Russia.

The estimation results are shown in table 18.2. The direct impact of monetary policy on loans has the correct sign but is not significant in either equation. The effect of the interaction of the monetary policy variable with each bank characteristic also has the correct sign and is significant only in the case of the liquidity variable, indicating that more liquid banks can better shield their loan portfolio from monetary policy changes.

Empirical work based on (1) appears to have two limitations: first, it relies on a reduced form relating loans to a monetary policy variable, which does not permit the identification of the parameters of the structural model – the Bernanke–Blinder (1988) model – that are relevant to the existence of the lending channel. Moreover, measurement biases may be introduced from the use of explanatory variables, such as GDP, data on which have only a time dimension. Second, variables are expressed in first-difference form, not taking into account possible equilibrium relationships.

An alternative approach would consist in trying to estimate directly the banks' loan supply function. The identification of this function is critical to the empirical investigation of the bank-lending channel and panel data can be useful in uncovering certain aspects of bank behaviour which may be related to its existence.

Assuming that the loan market is competitive, we can specify the following equilibrium loan-supply function for the individual bank i:

$$L_{it} = \alpha + \beta(\rho_t - i_t) + \gamma D_{it} \quad \beta > 0, \quad \gamma > 0 \tag{4}$$

where L_{it} and D_{it} are real loans and deposits (in logs) of bank i in period t, and ρ_t and i_t are the lending rate and the bond rate in period t.

---

[7] This is the analogue to the Seemingly Unrelated Regression – GLS using an estimated cross-section residual covariance matrix.

Table 18.2 *Loan equations: baseline estimates, Greece*

Variable	(1) Bank characteristic: size			(1) Bank characteristic: balance sheet strength		
	Coefficient	t-statistic	Probability	Coefficient	t-statistic	Probability
ΔL_{t-1}	−0.134	−3.20	0.0014	−0.130	−3.14	0.0018
ΔL_{t-2}	−0.057	−1.38	0.1686	−0.047	−1.17	0.2426
ΔL_{t-3}	0.159	3.89	0.0001	0.176	4.38	0.0000
ΔL_{t-12}	−0.156	−4.26	0.0000	−0.148	−4.05	0.0001
$\Delta r_{t-1}+\Delta r_{t-2}+\Delta r_{t-3}$	−0.034	−0.65	0.5129	−0.064	−1.24	0.2134
S_{t-1}	−0.031	−0.44	0.6612			
B_{t-1}				−0.031	−0.63	0.5301
$\Delta \log Y_{t-1}+\Delta \log Y_{t-2}$ $+ \Delta \log Y_{t-3}$	0.000	0.38	0.7039	0.000	0.29	0.7735
$S_{t-1}{}^{*}\Delta r_{t-1}$	1.706	0.44	0.6614			
$S_{t-1}{}^{*}\Delta r_{t-2}$	−5.981	−1.40	0.1620			
$S_{t-1}{}^{*}\Delta r_{t-3}$	−2.409	−0.62	0.5386			
$B_{t-1}{}^{*}\Delta r_{t-1}$				23.546	0.81	0.4193
$B_{t-1}{}^{*}\Delta r_{t-2}$				42.320	1.30	0.1953
$B_{t-1}{}^{*}\Delta r_{t-3}$				97.221	3.37	0.0008
$S_{t-1}{}^{*}\Delta \log Y_{t-1}$	0.000	0.00	0.9967			
$S_{t-1}{}^{*}\Delta \log Y_{t-2}$	−0.092	−1.28	0.2009			
$S_{t-1}{}^{*}\Delta \log Y_{t-3}$	−0.031	−0.40	0.6901			
$B_{t-1}{}^{*}\Delta \log Y_{t-1}$				0.000	0.47	0.6393
$B_{t-1}{}^{*}\Delta \log Y_{t-2}$				−0.022	−0.43	0.6674
$B_{t-1}{}^{*}\Delta \log Y_{t-3}$				−0.078	−1.44	0.1496
Dummy for 11/97	0.004	0.84	0.4002	0.026	2.69	0.0073
Sample	Feb. 1996–Dec. 1999			Feb. 1996–Dec. 1999		
Total panel obs.	564			564		
Adjusted R^2	0.129			0.140		

Equation (4) is consistent with the aggregate loan-supply function in the Bernanke–Blinder (1988) model. In this specification, loans depend on the interest rate spread, assuming that there is rate of return homogeneity of degree zero which implies that, when all interest rates rise by the same amount, banks do not change the composition of their portfolios. Furthermore, the lending rate variable has only a time dimension, since in a competitive market the individual bank takes the price (interest rate) as given.[8] The sensitivity of loan supply to the interest

---

[8] This implies that for the estimation of the loan-supply function of the individual bank the simultaneity problem arising from the interaction of loan demand and loan supply and the identification problem do not exist. Of course, to the extent that the bank loan market is imperfectly competitive the results will suffer from unknown estimation biases. However, the perfect competition assumption is commonly made in most studies of the bank-lending channel.

rate spread (i.e. the parameter β) is one of the three parameters in the Bernanke–Blinder model which determine the lending channel's potency. When $\beta \to \infty$, loans and bonds are perfect substitutes for banks ($\rho = i$) and there is no bank-lending channel. Deposits are the scale variable in (4).

The effect of bank characteristics can be introduced *via* the coefficient on ($\rho_t - i_t$) or D_{it}. Assuming that bank characteristics affect loan supply by differentiating the loan response to changes in deposits, we can assume that:

$$\gamma_i = \gamma_0 + \gamma_1 Z_{it} \tag{5}$$

where Z_{it} is a bank-specific characteristic, for example its balance sheet strength. In terms of the Bernanke–Blinder model, this is translated into shifts of the loan-supply function and, consequently, of the CC curve according to cross-sectional differences.[9] Substituting (5) into (4) we obtain:

$$L_{it} = \alpha + \beta(\rho_t - i_t) + \gamma_0 D_{it} + \gamma_1 D_{it} Z_{it} \tag{6}$$

As in the previous model, distributional effects will be explored by using the same balance sheet and size variables. The effect of asset size on the sensitivity of loan supply to policy-induced shifts in deposits is expected to be negative ($\gamma_1 < 0$): larger banks may find it easier to raise non-deposit finance and thus partly offset the effects of contractionary policy on loans. This makes the shift parameter γ_i smaller, implying a weakened lending channel. Similarly, banks which hold higher ratios of liquid to total assets can better insulate their loan portfolio against monetary shocks. This means that the response of loans to monetary policy would be smaller for these banks and, as a result, the lending channel would be less important. As noted above, for a bank of a given size, the tightening of monetary policy would cause loans to decline less, the more liquid is the bank. To capture this effect, the interaction term $Z_{it} B_{it}$ will be introduced in (5) with an expected positive coefficient.

Equation (6) can be considered as a loan-supply function incorporating the effects of differential bank characteristics and will be the basis for the empirical analysis.[10] To deal with the issue of non-stationarity of the variables involved and the possible existence of a cointegrating

---

[9] Had we introduced the effect of differentiated bank characteristics through the coefficient on the interest rate spread, this would have affected both the slope and the position of the CC curve.

[10] A similar approach to ours is followed by Farinha and Robalo Marques (chapter 22 in this volume).

relationship between them we estimated a linear single-equation error correction model:[11]

$$\Delta L_{i,t} = \phi_{i,0} - \phi_1 ECT_{i,t-1} + \phi_3 \Delta L_{i,t-1} + \Gamma \Delta X_{i,t-1} + u_{i,t} \quad \phi_1 > 0 \quad (7)$$

where $\phi_{i,0}$ is a bank-specific constant capturing the effect of bank-specific variables not included in the cointegrating relationship, ECT is the residual of the cointegrating equation and X is the vector of the right-hand side variables in (6). In order to have a parsimonious representation of the error correction model, the lag length was restricted to one,[12] which was sufficient to ensure that residuals were not autocorrelated. We estimated the cointegrating relationship without bank-specific effects in the constant term and with homogeneity imposed across the slope coefficients. The cointegrating vector defines residuals that are stationary. To test for stationarity, the differenced residual is regressed on the lagged residual and bank dummies:

$$\Delta ECT_{i,t} = \delta ECT_{i,t-1} + \text{bank dummies} + u_{i,t} \quad \delta > 0 \quad (8)$$

The t-statistic on the δ-coefficient is then compared to the critical value given in table 5 of Levin and Lin (1992). If the t-statistic is significant, then the null hypothesis of non-stationarity and hence of no cointegration can be rejected.

The estimated cointegrating relationships with distributional effects are shown in table 18.3. As with the previous model, SUR weighted least squares were used in all estimations. The t-statistic for testing for cointegration is given at the bottom of this table. It indicates that the null hypothesis of no-cointegration can be rejected in all cases. As already mentioned, bank characteristics included in the regressions are the bank size (S_{it}) and the balance sheet strength (B_{it}). The interaction terms of these variables with deposits (D_{it}) give an indication of the importance of distributional effects in shifting the loan-supply function. Interaction terms always have the expected sign and in most of the cases are significant. Equation (1) in table 18.3 shows that large banks are able partly to insulate their loan portfolio from a monetary policy tightening. Similar results are found for the more liquid banks (table 18.3 (2)). Furthermore, the equations which use both the size and balance sheet strength variables

---

[11] Alternatively, the non-linear least squares (NLS) single-equation estimation method for the simple ECM specification, suggested by Phillips and Loretan (1991), could be used, which gives asymptotically efficient and median-unbiased estimates of long-run equilibrium relationships. For an application of this method, see Chinn (1997) and Chinn and Johnston (1997).

[12] With the exception of the dependent variable for which the lag length was three. Also the twelfth lag was added to capture any seasonality that had not been removed.

Table 18.3 *Loan equations: additional estimates, Greece*

Variable	(1)	(2)	(3)	(4)	(5)
Constant	0.124	0.804	0.201	0.891	0.281
	(0.47)	(6.63)	(0.77)	(7.23)	(1.08)
$\rho_t - i_t$	3.478	2.735	2.779	2.161	3.027
	(2.65)	(2.21)	(2.15)	(1.74)	(2.37)
D_{it}	0.880	0.807	0.876	0.801	0.865
	(34.35)	(108.21)	(34.95)	(104.90)	(34.49)
$S_{it}{}^*D_{it}$	−0.010		−0.010		−0.008
	(−3.42)		(−3.53)		(−2.67)
$B_{it}{}^*D_{it}$		−0.051		−0.038	−0.032
		(−6.37)		(−4.21)	(−3.51)
$S_{it}{}^*B_{it}{}^*D_{it}$			0.038	0.024	0.026
			(5.83)	(3.26)	(3.55)
Short-run dynamics with fixed effects					
$ECT_{i,t-1}$	−0.021	−0.018	−0.019	−0.020	−0.018
	(−2.75)	(−2.17)	(−2.56)	(−2.38)	(−2.23)
$\Delta L_{i,t-1}$	−0.120	−0.124	−0.124	−0.132	−0.132
	(−2.88)	(−2.96)	(−3.00)	(−3.17)	(−3.15)
$\Delta L_{i,t-2}$	−0.061	−0.057	−0.062	−0.054	−0.059
	(−1.47)	(−1.39)	(−1.52)	(−1.31)	(−1.43)
$\Delta L_{i,t-3}$	0.158	0.159	0.152	0.151	0.147
	(3.89)	(4.53)	(3.75)	(3.73)	(3.61)
$\Delta L_{i,t-12}$	−0.163	−0.164	−0.154	−0.151	−0.149
	(−4.51)	(−4.53)	(−4.24)	(−4.17)	(−4.11)
$\Delta(\rho_{t-1} - i_{t-1})$	0.038	0.030	0.088	0.064	0.077
	(0.25)	(0.20)	(0.58)	(0.42)	(0.50)
$\Delta D_{i,t-1}$	−0.020	−0.012	−0.019	−0.010	−0.019
	(−1.47)	(−0.89)	(−1.38)	(−0.79)	(−1.36)
$\Delta(S_{i,t-1}{}^*D_{i,t-1})$	0.003		0.003		0.003
	(1.81)		(2.29)		(2.23)
$\Delta(B_{i,t-1}{}^*D_{i,t-1})$		−0.001		−0.003	−0.003
		(−0.49)		(−1.66)	(−1.60)
$\Delta(S_{i,t-1}{}^*B_{i,t-1}{}^*D_{i,t-1})$			0.003	0.004	0.004
			(2.41)	(2.63)	(2.98)
Adjusted R^2	0.133	0.136	0.131	0.132	0.128
N	564	564	564	564	564
t-statistic for cointegration test	−7.07*	−6.87*	−7.11*	−6.76*	−7.03*

Notes: Numbers in parenthesis are *t*-statistics.
* Indicates rejection of hypothesis of no-cointegration at the 1% significance level.

confirm the hypothesis that the sensitivity of lending volume to monetary policy is greater for smaller banks with weaker balance sheets.

In all estimated equations, the coefficient of the spread variable is positive and significant (at the 5 per cent level[13]), providing evidence of imperfect substitutability between loans and securities in bank

[13] At the 10 per cent level in (4).

portfolios.[14] Thus, the panel data permit the identification of the loan-supply function, which is critical to the operation of the lending channel. Finally, the estimated coefficient of reversion (ϕ_1) is statistically significant and implies that the half-life of a deviation from equilibrium is about two years. This is a plausible result given that during the sample period about 40 per cent of total bank loans to the private sector were long term with an estimated average maturity of about eight years.

A second issue on which we focus is the possible bias owing to the endogeneity of the deposits variable. To correct for such bias, we used an instrumental variable estimator for deposits. The instruments used were lagged values of loans and deposits and the contemporaneous and lagged values of the interest rate spread and GDP. Correcting for endogeneity bias does not essentially alter the basic conclusions derived from the above estimation, although the importance of the bank-lending channel appears to have strengthened somewhat, as judged by the size of the estimated coefficient of the spread and the significance of shift factors represented by bank differential characteristics.[15]

4   Conclusions

The use of bank-level data has recently supplemented the empirical analysis of the role of bank lending in monetary transmission with aggregate data. Moving away from the aggregate data, a number of studies have addressed the issue that monetary policy actions may affect banks' loan-supply function, by testing the cross-sectional implications of the lending view.

In this chapter, two approaches have been taken. One employs a reduced form equation linking monetary policy and distributional variables, as well as their interaction, to bank loans in the spirit of Kashyap and Stein's (1995, 2000) work. This equation was estimated by using panel data for Greek banks covering the second half of the 1990s and two indicators of cross-sectional differences: a size indicator, differentiating large from small banks, and an indicator of the health of bank balance sheets. The results, while compatible with the existence of a bank-lending channel, were in general not satisfactory. In an alternative approach, it was argued that bank heterogeneity, though useful in interpreting loan supply shifts, is not the only element on which to base the analysis of the effectiveness of the lending channel. By bringing together some of

---

[14] This would imply the existence of a bank-lending channel, provided that there is also imperfect substitutability between loans and bonds on the part of borrowers.

[15] The relevant results are available on request.

the features of the Bernanke–Blinder model (1988) with a methodology for assessing the impact of differential balance sheet characteristics on banks' ability to supply loans, we investigated directly the behaviour of bank loan supply.

The empirical results of this second approach show that monetary policy clearly has a significant impact on the supply of bank loans and, through shifts in supply, on aggregate economic activity in Greece. Bank data helped us identify a loan-supply function, a task that presents well-known difficulties for researchers. The response of loan supply to the interest rate spread is one of the critical parameters in the Bernanke–Blinder model that relates to the degree of substitutability between loans and securities (for banks) and thus to the significance of the lending channel. In addition, bank-specific characteristics were found to systematically shift the loan supply function. The results showed that large banks can, to a certain extent, shield their loan portfolio from monetary policy changes. Similar results hold for the more liquid (healthy) banks.

19 The Italian banking system and monetary policy transmission: evidence from bank-level data

L. Gambacorta

1 Introduction

This chapter tests cross-sectional differences in the effectiveness of the bank-lending channel of monetary policy transmission in Italy from 1986 to 1998. Several studies (including Angeloni *et al.*, 1995; Bagliano and Favero, 1995; Buttiglione and Ferri, 1994; Chiades and Gambacorta, 2003; Fanelli and Paruolo, 1999) have shown that the bank-lending channel was at work in Italy.[1] However, the cross-sectional predictions of the lending channel have not been systematically explored.

Panel data are used to study the response of bank deposits and loans to monetary shocks, and tests are proposed to see if these responses depend on the size, the liquidity position, or the capitalisation of banks. Such tests have not previously been conducted using comprehensive data on Italian banks. The main difference with respect to Ehrmann *et al.* (chapter 14 in this volume) lies in the additional tests that are conducted regarding deposits and liquidity: according to the bank-lending channel hypothesis, deposits and liquid assets, together with bank loans, should also fall after a monetary restriction. These tests therefore allow us to identify a loan-supply shock correctly.

The remainder of the chapter is organised as follows. Section 2 analyses the institutional characteristics of the Italian economy in the 1980s and 1990s. After a brief description of the data in section 3, section 4 presents evidence on the response of lending to a monetary shock, while section 5 analyses the effects on deposits and liquidity. Section 6 summarises the main conclusions.

I wish to thank Gabe J. de Bondt, Claudio Borio, Alessio De Vincenzo, Dario Focarelli, Eugenio Gaiotti, Andrea Generale, Giorgio Gobbi, Simonetta Iannotti, Anyl Kashyap, Paolo Emilio Mistrulli, Benoît Mojon, Fabio Panetta and Alberto Franco Pozzolo for helpful discussions and comments. Roberto Felici provided excellent research assistance.
[1] Conflicting results are presented by Bagliano and Favero (1996), de Bondt (1999) and Favero *et al.* (2001).

2   The Italian banking sector

Before discussing the econometric analysis of banks' behaviour, we briefly analyse the important measures of liberalisation of the markets and deregulation of the intermediaries implemented since the 1980s (Ciocca, 2000).

At the beginning of the 1980s the Italian banking system was quite tightly regulated: (1) foreign exchange controls were in place; (2) the establishment of new banks and the opening of new bank branches were subject to authorization;[2] (3) competition was curbed by mandatory maturity specialisation, with special credit institutions operating at medium- and long-term and commercial banks at short-term maturities; (4) the quantity of bank lending was subject to a ceiling.

All these restrictions were gradually removed between the mid-1980s and the early 1990s (Angelini and Cetorelli, 2000; Cottarelli, Ferri and Generale 1995; Passacantando, 1996): (1) the lending ceiling was definitely removed in 1985; (2) foreign exchange controls were lifted between 1987 and 1990; (3) branching was liberalised in 1990; (4) the 1993 Banking Law allowed banks and special credit institutions to perform all banking activities.[3]

The deregulation has broadened the range of options available to banks in defining their corporate strategies. There is not a unique model that characterises Italian banks. While some have pursued their traditional lines of business, others have opted to organise in groups. Still others have attempted to become 'universal banks' (Ciocca, 2000).

The rationalisation of the structure of the Italian banking system, and the more intense competition that followed (Angelini and Cetorelli, 2000), has resulted in a steady decline in the number of credit institutions since the late 1990s. In the period 1998–2000 the number of banks in Italy declined from 921 to 841. Most of the decrease was accounted for by mutual banks (banche di credito cooperativo), which fell from 563 to 499 (at the end of 2000 their market share was around 5 per cent in terms of loans against 82 per cent for limited liability banks).

---

[2] Before 1987 the Bank of Italy authorised the opening of new branches on the basis of a four-year plan reflecting estimated local needs for banking services.

[3] The 1993 Banking Law completed the enactment of the institutional, operational and maturity despecialisation of the Italian banking system and ensured the consistency of supervisory controls and intermediaries' range of operations with the single market framework. The business restriction imposed by the 1936 Banking Law, which distinguished between banks that could raise short-term funds ('aziende di credito') and those that could not ('Istituti di credito speciale'), was eliminated. For more details see the *Annual Report of the Bank of Italy* for 1993. The potential impact of this regulation on the results of the study has been checked in section 4.

Mergers also played an important role in this transformation. Between 1996 and 2000, bank mergers accounted for nearly 40 per cent of the total value of merger activity in Italy, a value higher than that recorded in the euro area in the same period (22 per cent). At the end of 2000, the five biggest institutions accounted for 23 per cent of total assets, although the five largest banking groups accounted for 54 per cent of total assets, a figure comparable with those found in the other main euro area countries.[4]

Finally, as regards the internationalisation of the banking industry, at the end of 2000, fifty-eight foreign banks were operating in Italy, with ninety-nine branches. Italian subsidiaries of foreign groups numbered thirteen, ten of them belonging to EU groups. The presence of Italian banks abroad was extended, thanks notably to the acquisition of foreign banks. Twenty-six Italian banking groups operated abroad; seventy-three were foreign banking subsidiaries, while there were ninety-four foreign branches of Italian banks. Branches and subsidiaries located in non-EU countries numbered forty-four and forty-nine, respectively.

At the end of 2000, the ratio of total banks assets over GDP was around 150 per cent in Italy against 260 for the average of the euro area. In particular, there are four balance sheet components that are relatively under-developed for Italian banks compared to those of the other euro area countries: interbank activities, securities portfolio, foreign assets and loans to households (Gambacorta, Gobbi and Panetta, 2001).[5]

Other features of the Italian banking system are important to analyse the distributional effects of monetary policy on banks: market concentration, size structure, state influence, ownership structure, deposit insurance, bank failures, bank networks (see Ehrmann et al., chapter 14 in this volume, for a comparison among the main European countries). We will see that another important characteristic is relationship lending: there are close customer relationships between small firms and small banks in Italy (Angelini, Di Salvo and Ferri, 1998) that could attenuate the distributional effects due to banks' dimension traditionally detected by the literature for the USA.

---

[4] The number of banks listed on the stock exchange has doubled since 1990: on a consolidated basis, at the end of 2000, the forty banks whose shares were traded on the main market accounted for 80 per cent of the banking system's total assets.

[5] The difference in interbank accounts reflects the existence in Italy from the beginning of the 1990s of an efficient market for interbank deposits (Mercato Interbancario dei Depositi, MID) that reduces the number of bilateral accounts. The internalisation of the Italian banking system remains modest by comparison with the other main euro area countries also considering BIS data for secured and unsecured foreign loans by Italian banks. The difference regarding loans to households can be mainly ascribed to consumer credit. For more details see Gambacorta, Gobbi and Panetta (2001).

Table 19.1 *Description of the data set used for Italian lending regression*[a]

	Big	Small	Liquid	Low liquid	Well cap.	Poorly cap.	Total
No. of banks	29	440	59	57	59	57	587
Mean assets (billion Euro)	32.974	0.152	0.138	15.630	0.227	9.592	2.189
Fraction of total assets	0.744	0.052	0.006	0.693	0.010	0.425	–
Mean deposits (billion Euro)	11.225	0.077	0.076	5.320	0.106	3.405	0.795
Fraction of total deposits	0.698	0.073	0.010	0.650	0.013	0.416	–
Mean lending (billion Euro)	14.343	0.063	0.036	6.997	0.082	3.963	0.942
Fraction of total lending	0.752	0.050	0.004	0.721	0.009	0.408	–
Liquidity/total assets	0.239	0.418	0.563	0.227	0.466	0.339	0.392
Loans/total assets	0.418	0.392	0.279	0.478	0.331	0.424	0.400
Deposits/total assets	0.355	0.551	0.618	0.385	0.542	0.476	0.520
Deposits/loans	0.851	1.406	2.215	0.807	1.636	1.123	1.302
Capital and reserves/total assets	0.069	0.113	0.135	0.077	0.156	0.059	0.105
Short-term/total lending	0.593	0.487	0.434	0.617	0.486	0.569	0.519
Public securities/total securities	0.572	0.867	0.892	0.662	0.895	0.714	0.814
Bad debts/(loans and bad debts)	0.080	0.073	0.084	0.071	0.098	0.082	0.074
Bonds/(deposits and bonds)	0.257	0.206	0.123	0.276	0.184	0.228	0.213
No. of branches per province	15	5	3	12	4	9	7

Note: [a] Data refer to the end of December 1998. A 'small' bank has the average size of the banks below the third quartile, while a 'big' bank has the average size of the banks above the 95th percentile. A 'low-liquid' bank has the average liquidity ratio of the banks below the 10th percentile, a 'liquid' bank has the average liquidity ratio of the banks above the 90th percentile. A 'poorly capitalised' bank has the average capital ratio below the 10th percentile, a 'well-capitalised' bank has the average capitalisation of the banks above the 90th percentile. Since the characteristics of each bank could change through time, percentiles have been worked out on mean values.
Source: Bank of Italy supervisory returns.

3   The data

A partial description of the data set, the filtering process and some variable definitions are reported in the statistical appendix of Ehrmann *et al.* (chapter 14 in this volume). Several points are worth stressing regarding the variables used in this chapter. First, the series for deposits includes certificate of deposits (longer-term CDs were subject to the reserve requirement until May 1994). Second, the data are quarterly and are not seasonally adjusted (therefore three seasonal dummies and a constant are also included). The sample goes from the 1986:4 to 1998:4. This sample period covers mainly one monetary regime. Misspecification tests reveal the presence of a structural break around the middle of the 1980s, coinciding with the end of the lending ceiling and the emergence of the 'hard' EMS.[6] The sample ends with the start of stage 3 of EMU.

Third, the interest rate taken as monetary policy indicator is that on repurchase agreements between the Bank of Italy and credit institutions.[7] The sample eventually represents 92 per cent of total system assets.

Table 19.1 gives some basic information on what bank balance sheets look like after the trimming procedure implemented on the variables entering the loan regressions.[8] The first three parts of the table split the sample with respect to size, liquidity and capitalisation, while the last gives information on the whole data set. Several clear patterns emerge.

First, the table shows that small banks are more liquid and better capitalised. This result fits with the standard idea that smaller banks need buffer stocks of securities to compensate their limited ability to raise external finance on the capital market. This interpretation is confirmed on the liability side, where the percentage of deposits (overnight deposits, CDs and savings accounts) is greater among small banks, while their bonds issues are more limited than those of large banks. The high capitalisation of small banks is also due, at least in part, to the fact that credit

---

[6] To control for changes in supervisory regulations regarding the maturity range of assets and liabilities, special long-term credit sections of commercial banks have been considered part of the banks to which they belonged. To avoid breaks with foreign exchange control changes, only loans and deposits to residents have been taken into consideration. The liberalisation of branching in the early 1990s was *de facto* preceded by changes in supervisory actions, which, since the middle of the 1980s, were urged by competition motives (Ciocca, 2000).

[7] As pointed out by Buttiglione, Del Giovane and Gaiotti (1997), in the period under investigation the REPO rate mostly affected the short-term end of the yield curve and, as it influenced the cost of banks' refinancing, it represented the value to which market rates and bank rates eventually tended to converge.

[8] The characteristics of the data sets used for deposit and liquidity regressions are very similar and are not reported. For more details see the working-paper version of this study (Gambacorta, 2001b).

Table 19.2 Regression results: long-run coefficients, Italy

Dependent variable: quarterly growth rate of	(1) Lending		(2) Lending		(3) Short-term lending		(4) Deposits		(5) Liquidity	
	Coeff.	Std error	Coeff.	Std error	Coeff.	Std error	Coeff.	Std error	Coeff.	Std error
Monetary policy (MP)	−0.825***	0.127	−0.675***	0.113	−0.105	0.137	−0.839***	0.059	−0.329***	0.118
Real GDP growth	1.389***	0.213	1.084***	0.175	1.244***	0.284	−0.708***	0.110	−1.112***	0.300
Inflation (CPI)	−0.622	0.386	−0.264	0.310	−1.379***	0.504	4.260***	0.250	8.184***	0.928
Bank char.*MP										
Size	0.079	0.054	−0.046	0.073	0.082	0.062	0.272***	0.032	0.082**	0.040
Liquidity	2.278***	0.831	2.058***	0.574	3.192***	0.955	2.279***	0.474		
Capitalisation	3.616	3.099			3.052	3.260	−11.030***	1.589		
Double interaction			−1.238	0.845						
MP effect for:										
Large bank	−0.431*	0.258			0.303	0.292	0.472***	0.136	−0.314***	0.118
Small bank	−0.891***	0.147			−0.172	0.163	−1.060***	0.076	−0.345***	0.119
High-liquid	−0.414***	0.151			0.384	0.243	−0.426***	0.072		
Low-liquid	−1.285***	0.249			−0.615**	0.246	−1.300***	0.138		
Well-capitalised	−0.622***	0.223			0.056	0.222	−1.457***	0.113		
Poorly capitalised	−0.976***	0.017			−0.229	0.182	−0.375***	0.080		
Sargan test (2nd step; p-value)	0.000	0.077	0.000	0.062	0.000	0.078	0.000	0.080	0.000	0.203
MA(1), MA(2) (p-value)	0.000	0.128	0.000	0.156	0.000	0.726	0.000	0.324	0.000	0.579
No. of banks, no. of obs.	587	25,241	587	25,241	551	26,448	629	27,047	531	23,364

Note: The model is given by the following equation, which includes interaction terms that are the product of the monetary policy indicator and a bank-specific characteristic:

$$\Delta \ln x_{it} = \mu_i + \sum_{j=1}^{4} \alpha_j \Delta \ln x_{it-j} + \sum_{j=1}^{4} \beta_j \Delta MP_{t-j} + \sum_{j=1}^{4} \gamma_j Z_{it-1} \Delta MP_{t-j} + \lambda Z_{it-1} + \sum_{j=1}^{4} \varphi_j p_{t-j} + \sum_{j=1}^{4} \delta_j \Delta \ln y_{it-j} + \varepsilon_{it}$$

with $i = 1, \ldots, N$ and $t = 1, \ldots, T$ and where: $N =$ number of banks; $x_{it} =$ deposits, loans or liquidity of bank i in quarter t; $MP_t =$ monetary policy indicator; $y_{it} =$ real GDP; $p_{it} =$ inflation rate; $Z_{it} =$ bank-specific characteristic (size, liquidity, capitalisation). The model allows for fixed effects across banks, as indicated by the bank- specific intercept u_i. Four lags have been introduced in order to obtain white-noise residuals. The models have been estimated using the GMM estimator suggested by Arellano and Bond (1991) which ensures efficiency and consistency provided that the models are not subject to serial correlation of order two and that the instruments used are valid (which are tested for with the Sargan test). In the GMM estimation, instruments are the second and further lags of the growth rate of the dependent variable and of the bank-specific characteristics included in each Inflation, GDP growth rate and the monetary policy indicator are considered as exogenous variables.

cooperative banks, which dominate among small banks, are prevented from distributing net profits by banking legislation (art. 37 of the 1993 Banking Law).

Second, liquid banks are smaller and better capitalised than average. Their bond portfolio consists mainly of government paper. Banks with low holdings of liquid assets have fewer deposits and make more loans. They have also a higher percentage of short-term loans, which should increase the speed of the bank-lending channel transmission.

Third, the table shows that poorly capitalised banks make relatively more loans, particularly short-term loans, and hold fewer liquid assets. On the liability side, they raise less deposits and issue fewer bonds. They are larger than average.

4   The response of bank lending to a monetary shock

We first briefly review the estimates of our version of the baseline regression equation used in this volume: loan growth is regressed on changes of the interest rate controlled by the monetary authority, and on its interaction with the three bank characteristics (size, liquidity and capitalisation). The regression, which is presented in more detail in section 3 of Ehrmann *et al.* (chapter 14 in this volume), also includes inflation and GDP growth (see also the note to table 19.2). In section 5 the same type of regression is used to check the effects of a monetary tightening on deposits and liquidity. This will permit us to gain further insight on the bank-lending channel by reporting for the effects of changes in the interest rate on these other items of banks' balance sheet.

The main results regarding the impact of monetary policy on bank lending are given in table 19.2, which presents the long-run elasticities of the models.[9]

The results reported in column (1) of table 19.2 show that the long-run effect of monetary policy on lending has the expected negative sign and is significantly different from zero. A 1 per cent increase in the REPO rate leads to a loan reduction of around 0.8 per cent.[10]

---

[9] The complete set of coefficients of the models is available from the author upon request. Standard errors for the long-run effect have been approximated with the 'delta method' which expands a function of a random variable with a one-step Taylor expansion (Rao, 1973).

[10] The long-run elasticity of credit to GDP is always significant and larger than one. The sign of the response of lending to inflation is not significant at conventional levels. It is worth noting that this coefficient picks up both the positive effect of inflation on nominal loan growth and the potential negative effects due to higher interest rates. This second effect was important in the period under investigation since inflation (and interest rates) fell significantly during the 1980s and 1990s.

First, in contrast with the evidence for the USA (Kashyap and Stein, 1995), the interaction term between size and monetary policy is insignificant. The fact that lending volume of smaller banks is not more sensitive to monetary policy than that of larger banks may reflect features of the Italian banking system. As it is well documented in the literature, close customer relationships between small firms and small banks (Angelini, Di Salvo and Ferri, 1998) may increase the expected value to the bank of a continuation of the relationship and thus provide greater incentive to smooth the effect of a monetary squeeze on credit (Angeloni et al. 1995; Ferri and Pittaluga, 1996). Our results would then indirectly corroborate previous empirical evidence showing that the intensity of bank–firm relations does reduce the probability that a firm will be rationed (Conigliani, Ferri and Generale, 1997).[11]

Second, banks with a higher liquidity ratio are better able to buffer their lending activity from changes in monetary policy. The lending growth rate decreases by 0.4 per cent for more liquid banks and by 1.3 for less liquid banks.

Column (2) of table 19.2 reports the result of a regression that also includes a double-interaction between size and liquidity. Hence, it is possible to test whether the effect of liquidity is identical across banks regardless of size. As suggested by Kashyap and Stein (2000), we expect the double interaction to be negative because small banks have a higher degree of informational asymmetry. However, the double-interaction coefficient is not significant, which further confirms that, in the case of Italy, banks' size plays a limited role in shaping their response to interest rate shocks.

Bank capital interaction with monetary policy has the expected sign but is not significant at conventional values. This could be because the simple capital–asset ratio used here poorly approximates the relevant measure of capital constraint under the Basle standards.[12]

The distributional effects of size, liquidity and capitalisation have been also checked with respect to the maturity structure of banks' loan

[11] On the same lines, Angeloni et al. (1995) and Cottarelli, Ferri and Generale (1995) find that large banks tend to adjust lending rates more quickly than other banks. In their analysis, the dominant explanatory factor is the loan-concentration index at the local level, suggesting that cross-bank differences in price-setting can be related to the micro structure of the credit market.

[12] Gambacorta and Mistrulli (2003), define capitalisation as the amount of capital that banks hold in excess of the minimum required to meet prudential regulation standards, and perform a similar test over the period 1992–2001. They find that well-capitalised banks can better shield their lending from monetary policy shocks and that this appears to be due to their ability to raise non-deposit funding. In this respect, the banks' capitalisation effect is larger for non-cooperative banks which are more dependent on non-deposit forms of external funds.

portfolio. Column (3) of table 19.2 reports the result of a regression with the quarterly growth rate of short-term lending (less than eighteen months) as a dependent variable. The fact that the results are similar to those obtained for total loans is interesting in two respects. First, we can reject that small banks do not react differently from large banks to a monetary tightening because of the longer maturity of their loan portfolio (see table 19.1). Second, a much smaller proportion of short-term credit is backed by real guarantees than is the case for total loans. Hence, the effect of bank liquidity on loan supply and the lack of effect of bank size and bank capital are robust for two loan aggregates which also differ in terms of collateral (for more details see Gambacorta, 2001b).

To sum up, these results indicate that changes in monetary policy lead banks to modify their loan supply. The size of bank responses, however, is not related to the dimension of the bank or the level of a bank's capital. The strength of the lending response is instead related to a bank's holding of liquid assets.

5   The response of bank deposits and liquidity to a monetary shock

The second step of the analysis focuses on the response of deposits and liquidity to a monetary shock. According to the bank-lending channel hypothesis, deposits should fall after a monetary restriction and this is the trigger that spurs banks to cut back on their lending. Similarly, if banks' liabilities are shrinking in the wake of a monetary tightening, then we would expect to find some reductions in liquid asset holdings. Results reported in column (4) of table 19.2 show that the long-run effects of monetary policy on total deposits (which are subject to reserve requirements) are negative and significantly different from zero. These estimates roughly imply that a 1 per cent increase in the monetary policy indicator leads to a decline in deposits of around 0.8 per cent for the average bank in the long run.[13]

As shown in column (4) of table 19.2, the null hypothesis that monetary policy effects are equal for small and large banks and for well- and poorly

---

[13] The long-run coefficient on inflation is positive while that on the growth rate of real GDP is negative. The low pro-cyclicality of total deposits in the period under investigation is confirmed by the coefficient of simultaneous correlation between the two series (around −14 per cent). The correlation maintains the negative sign also with respect to lags of the growth rates of GDP (up to the fourth order). This pattern could have been caused by precautionary motives that increase the growth rate of deposits during periods of recession and decrease it during booms (when other forms of investment become more appealing). It is worth noting that the correlation between the level of deposits and real GDP is, as expected, positive (around 84 per cent).

capitalised banks can be rejected at the 95 per cent level of confidence. The effects of a monetary tightening on total deposits are greater for those banks that have less incentive to shield the effect of a monetary squeeze on this form of liability: small banks, characterised by deposits in excess of loans, and well-capitalised banks that have a higher capacity to raise other forms of external funds.

These results may actually reflect some specific institutional characteristics of the Italian financial system. Small Italian banks traditionally have a high capacity in local deposit markets, which reduces their need to raise other forms of external funds to counterbalance the effects of a monetary tightening.[14] As for capitalisation, well-capitalised banks are perceived by the market to be less risky and have less difficulty in issuing forms of non-reservable deposits. Therefore, for different reasons, these two kinds of banks do not have a great need to shield their deposits from the effect of a monetary tightening. In particular, the results on capitalisation indicate that agents do not withdraw their funds from low-capitalised banks after a monetary squeeze, meaning that they do not consider these deposits riskier than those at other banks. This has two main explanations. First, the impact of bank failures has been very small in Italy, especially with respect to deposits.[15] Second, the presence of deposit insurance insulates deposits of less-capitalised banks from the risk of default.[16] We also note that the interaction term between liquidity and monetary policy is positive: deposits of more liquid banks suffer less from a monetary tightening.

The last step of the analysis consists of measuring the effects of a monetary tightening on banks' liquidity. This check is important because a

[14] Apart from the reaction to monetary policy, the growth rate of deposits is higher for small banks. This can be checked through the scale variable in the equation, which is always highly significant. Other things equal, this coefficient captures the high capacity of small banks in local deposit markets.

[15] During our sample period, the share of deposits of failed banks to total deposits approached 1 per cent only twice, namely in 1987 and 1996 (Boccuzzi, 1998).

[16] Two explicit limited-coverage deposit insurance schemes (DISs) currently operate in Italy. Both are funded *ex post*; that is, member banks have a commitment to make available to the Funds the necessary resources should a bank default. All the banks operating in the country, with the exception of mutual banks, adhere to the main DIS, the 'Fondo Interbancario di Tutela dei Depositi' (FITD). Mutual banks ('Banche di Credito Cooperativo') adhere to a special Fund ('Fondo di Garanzia dei Depositanti del Credito Cooperativo') created for banks belonging to their category. The FITD, the main DIS, is a private consortium of banks created in 1987 on a voluntary basis. In 1996, as a consequence of the implementation of EU Directive 94/19 on deposit guarantee schemes, the Italian Banking Law regulating the DIS was amended, and FITD became a compulsory DIS. FITD performs its tasks under the supervision of and in cooperation with the banking supervision authority, Banca d'Italia. The level of protection granted to each depositor (slightly more than 103,000 Euros) is one of the highest in the European Union. FITD does not adopt any form of deposit coinsurance.

lending reduction following a monetary tightening does not reflect a simple reallocation of assets, with banks increasing their holdings of securities. If the bank-lending channel is at work, from an aggregate point of view, a contraction in deposits causes not only lending but also cash and securities holdings to decrease (Kashyap and Stein, 1995; Stein, 1998).

Column (5) of table 19.2 presents the results. The effects of the interest rate on liquidity parallel those for lending volume: a monetary restriction leads to a significant reduction in cash, securities and interbank accounts. The implication is twofold. First, liquidity is actually used by banks to shield their loan portfolio; second, we can reject that the lending reduction that follows a monetary tightening reflects a simple reallocation of assets towards holding more securities. Moreover, the drop in liquidity is greater for small banks which, as we have seen, have more incentive to shield their customer relationships.

The results of the additional equations on deposits and liquidity support the existence of a bank-lending channel in Italy. The effects of monetary policy on deposits differ among banks: after a tightening the decrease in deposits is more pronounced for small banks and well-capitalised banks. Hence a possible interpretation is that these two groups of banks are less likely to be constrained to downsize their supply of loans following a monetary squeeze.

6   Conclusions

This chapter investigates the existence of cross-sectional differences in the effectiveness of the bank-lending channel for monetary policy transmission in Italy from 1986 to 1998.

The main results are the following. At an aggregate level, after a monetary restriction deposits fall and banks reduce their lending. A simultaneous decrease in liquidity suggests that banks try to shield their loan portfolio by drawing down cash, securities and their net interbank position. All these effects are significant at conventional levels and are robust to changes in the empirical specification.[17]

---

[17] The working-paper version of the study (Gambacorta, 2001b) tests the robustness of these results in several ways: (1) considering as monetary policy indicator the interest rate residuals from a two–lag VAR estimated in Mojon and Peersman (2001); (2) introducing dummy variables to take account of the spikes in the change of the repo interest rate caused by the German re-unification and EMS crises; (3) introducing additional interaction terms combining the bank-specific characteristics with inflation and real output growth rates; (4) considering a model with a complete set of time dummies to test the possible presence of endogeneity between bank-specific characteristics and the cyclical indicators; (5) taking into account a geographical control dummy that takes the value of 1 if the main seat of the bank is in the North of Italy and 0 if elsewhere. In all cases the results of the study remained unchanged.

Comparing the effects of a monetary tightening on different kinds of banks, we find that the impact on deposits is greatest for the banks with less incentive to shield this form of liability: small banks, with a high ratio of deposits to lending and well-capitalised banks that have greater capacity to raise other forms of external funds.

Regarding lending bank size appears to be irrelevant, small banks are not more sensitive to monetary policy shocks than large banks. This finding can be explained by closer customer relationships, owing to which small banks, which tend to be more liquid, smooth the effect of a monetary tightening on their supply of credit. This result, which differs from the conclusions of studies for the USA (Gertler and Gilchrist, 1994; Kashyap and Stein, 1995; Kishan and Opiela, 2000), is consistent with previous works on Italian lending rates (Angeloni *et al.*, 1995 and Cottarelli, Ferri and Generale, 1995).

Banks' liquidity is the most critical factor determining whether a deposit contraction carries over to lending. Less-capitalised banks suffer more from a monetary tightening, but this result is not significant at conventional values because the measure of capitalisation used, the capital–asset ratio, is noisy.

20 The impact of monetary policy on bank lending in the Netherlands

L. de Haan

1   Introduction

For the Netherlands there is some evidence on the bank-lending channel from both VAR and panel data analysis. VAR analysis generally indicates that the lending channel is not very relevant in the Netherlands from a macroeconomic viewpoint. According to Garretsen and Swank (1998), van Ees, Garretsen and Sterken (1999) and Kakes (2000) the lending channel is partly offset because banks use their holdings of securities as a buffer to shield their loan portfolios from negative monetary shocks. However, the analysis by De Bondt (1999) does not confirm this buffer function. The evidence from the relatively scarce panel data analysis of the cross-sectional differences in bank-lending behaviour is somewhat mixed for the Netherlands. De Bondt (2000) finds some evidence for a lending channel in the Netherlands, while Schuller (1998) does not.

The present chapter contributes to the latter type of empirical evidence of the bank-lending channel for the Netherlands, using individual bank data. Following Ehrmann et al. (chapter 14 in this volume), the investigation concerns the response of bank lending to monetary shocks, together with the influence on this response of bank size, liquidity and capitalisation. The contributions of the present chapter are the following. First, consolidated data representing the Dutch banking population are used on a quarterly basis. Previous studies for the Netherlands have analysed BankScope data, which is biased towards large-sized banks, is available only at an annual frequency, and covers unconsolidated data.[1] Second, the present study extends the analysis to several segments of the bank credit market. Specifically, a distinction is made between loans with and without government guarantees and between lending to households and

I would like to thank Ignazio Angeloni, Gabe de Bondt, Michael Ehrmann, Jan Kakes, Anil Kashyap, Benoît Mojon, Marga Peeters, Elmer Sterken and Jukka Topi for their comments and suggestions.

[1] Schuller (1998) and De Bondt (2000) use data from BankScope. See Ehrmann et al. (chapter 14 in this volume) on the disadvantages of using BankScope for the present type of analysis.

firms. The relevance of the latter distinction is underpinned by a factor analysis of the sample.

The chapter is organised as follows. Section 2 describes the main macroeconomic developments in the Dutch bank credit market in the 1990s. Section 3 gives some facts about the banking structure in the Netherlands. Section 4 presents the empirical results, after which section 5 draws some conclusions.

2   The Dutch credit market in the 1990s

In the period between 1990 and 1997, the period under review in this chapter, the Dutch guilder was tied to the Deutsche Mark. During the 1970s and 1980s, the Netherlands had gradually moved from a combination of money supply- and exchange rate-targeting toward full reliance on the peg to the Mark as the benchmark for its monetary policy in the 1990s. The reason for the abandonment of money supply-targeting was the increased competition, innovation and integration of the financial markets.[2] In the 1990s active credit control policies were no longer undertaken, unlike in previous periods. The exchange rate target was maintained by using the interest rate as an instrument. The short-term interest rate was still relatively high during the years 1990–1 but came down considerably between 1992 and 1997. Inflation stabilised from the beginning of the 1990s at a level of around 2 per cent. Economic growth was 2.7 per cent on average between 1990 and 1997, including one period of economic slowdown in 1991–3 with an average growth rate of 1.7 per cent.

Developments in the Dutch credit market during the 1990s were remarkable in several respects. Figure 20.1 shows bank lending to the private sector over time, and a split between loans to non-financial firms and households, respectively. Households' bank borrowing consists mainly of mortgage loans. The 1990s witnessed an accelerating growth of mortgage lending to households, reaching 20 per cent in 1997. Subsequently, there was some slowdown in growth but nevertheless growth rates remained well above 10 per cent.

The rise in mortgage lending went hand in hand with a boom in Dutch house prices (DNB, 1999, 2000c). House prices more than doubled during the 1990s (figure 20.2), partly driven by a decrease in mortgage interest rates from around 9 per cent to 5 per cent. The demand push on the market for existing houses was reflected in a drop in the median selling period for houses on sale. However, the boom in the Dutch housing and

---

[2] See Wellink (1994) and Hilbers (1998).

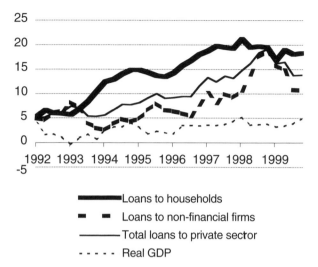

Figure 20.1 Bank lending to the private sector, 1992–1999 quarterly changes year-on-year

Figure 20.2 Dutch housing market, 1992–1999

mortgage markets has not only been caused by economic fundamentals such as income and interest rate developments. It has certainly also been triggered by the easing of banks' mortgage lending criteria, especially in the mid-1990s. The institutions also eased their mortgage acceptance criteria in the mid-1990s. This mainly entailed the inclusion of second and temporary incomes in determining borrowing capacity and raising the permissible mortgage debt service–income ratio as well as the ratio of loans granted to the collateral value of the mortgaged properties.

Bank lending to non-financial firms initially lagged behind that of mortgage lending, with growth rates of no more than a few percentage points above those of GDP. However, a clear acceleration took place in 1998, which could not be fully attributed to fundamental factors such as the low interest rate and the favourable economic developments. There are indications that the surge in lending to firms at the time was related to the financing of mergers, acquisitions and management buyouts (DNB, 2000b). Business investment growth, at a stable rate of 6–8 per cent after 1995, accounted less convincingly for the sudden rise in lending in 1998.

3   Structure of the Dutch banking sector

Among the 135 banks in the sample are 107 commercial banks (including four cooperative banks), seventeen savings banks, and eleven securities banks.[3] These three groups of banks aim at partly overlapping and partly different segments of the deposit and loan market. The commercial banks are really universal banks, involved in all market segments. Among those are the largest banks. One of the most striking characteristics of the Dutch banking sector is its high degree of concentration. The seven largest banks in the sample take account of no less than 79 per cent of total assets. They operate in both the wholesale and the retail market and have large amounts of households' deposits. Savings banks are typically smaller banks and are heavily involved in the retail market. They lend mainly to households (especially mortgage loans) and less to firms, compared to

---

[3] Data are taken from balance sheets of Dutch banks reporting to the DNB for the compilation of aggregate monetary statistics. The sample used in this study covers the period of 1990:Q4 until 1997:Q4, just before the European harmonisation of the monetary statistics and its consequential cut of the number of reporting banks to a mere twenty-five in the case of the Netherlands. The original, unbalanced panel data set contains 143 banks. When possible, mergers and acquisitions were corrected backwards by aggregation of the merging banks. If not, the time series were curtailed so that the remaining series referred to one and the same bank. In several cases, where there were multiple mergers in a row, banks had to be deleted from the sample completely. After this cleaning, the data set counted 135 banks.

commercial banks, and they lend often with government guarantees. In the Netherlands there is a system of government guarantees on mortgage loans for lower-income households, aimed to promote house ownership. Also government guarantees back bank loans to semi-state owned companies such as hospitals. Savings banks hold relatively large portfolios of government securities and fund their activities to a large extent with households' deposits, especially savings deposits. Securities banks, on the other hand, are more involved in the corporate market, especially in the pre-financing of the issuance and/or purchase of securities by firms. They hold their clients' securities as collateral.

Owing to the openness of the Dutch financial market, there are a lot of foreign banks in the sample: no less than sixty-two out of the total of 135. Foreign banks are relatively small, accounting for only 11 per cent of the Dutch market.[4] These banks are typically involved in wholesale banking. They do not lend to households and neither do they attract deposits from them. Among their depositors are many foreign firms.

As the majority (80 per cent) of the banks in the sample are universal banks, which are more or less involved in all segments of the market, a factor analysis can help to get a clearer picture of the market segmentation of the banking sector. Factor analysis aims at finding a 'common factor', x_k, which is an unobservable, hypothetical variable that contributes to the variance of several (at least two) observed variables, y_j. The equation of the common factor model (Mulaik, 1972) is:

$$y_{ij} = \sum_{k=1}^{q} x_{ik} b_{kj} + e_{ij} \tag{1}$$

where i denotes the observation. There are q common factors in this equation, which are conveniently assumed to be uncorrelated with each other. b_{kj} is the regression coefficient for predicting observed variable j using the kth common factor. e_{ij} are residuals and are defined to be uncorrelated both with each other and with the common factors. In matrix notation it reads:

$$Y = XB + E \tag{2}$$

B is the factor pattern, which lends itself to interpretation of the meanings of the common factors, as we shall see.

For the observed variables, Y, we take a set of potential proxy variables for banks' susceptibility to monetary policy shocks. First, the list of variables starts with the proxies already mentioned by Ehrmann *et al.*

---

[4] The balance sheet data of the foreign banks relate only to their activities in the Netherlands.

Table 20.1 *Factor pattern of the Dutch banks' panel* [a]

	Factor 1 Retail banking	Factor 2 Foreign banking	Factor 3 Wholesale banking
Size	−0.009	−0.027	0.004
Capital/assets	−0.027	−0.021	−0.006
Cash/assets	**0.291**	0.074	0.067
Interbank deposits/assets	−0.080	0.081	−0.023
Securities/assets	−0.006	−0.033	0.000
Loans to firms/assets	**−0.157**	−0.009	**0.992**
Loans to households/assets	**0.532**	0.015	0.128
Secured loans/assets	0.059	−0.017	0.015
Deposits of households/assets	**0.149**	−0.043	0.038
Deposits of firms/assets	0.110	**0.503**	0.004
Deposits of foreigners/assets	0.054	**0.435**	−0.006
Cumulative proportion of common variance	0.527	0.765	0.950

Note: [a] Number of banks (obs.) is ninty-nine (2,519).

(chapter 14 in this volume), i.e. bank size, capital ratio and liquidity ratio. However, liquid assets are split into their components: cash, securities and interbank deposits. Second, the set of variables is extended with other variables, especially representing the market segment orientation: loans to households, loans to non-financial firms, loans under government guarantee, deposits of households, deposits of non-financial firms and deposits of foreigners, all scaled by total assets. The goal of factor analysis is to cluster these variables into factors on the basis of their correlations. Consequently, three factors are retained in the analysis, together accounting for 95 per cent of the common variance in the data.

The resulting factor pattern is presented in table 20.1. Substantial factor loadings, conveniently set equal to or higher than 0.13, are printed in bold letters for easier interpretation. Loans to households show the highest positive loading on the first factor, while loans to firms have a negative loading. The large positive loading of cash holdings indicates that these types of banks carry a lot of cash for daily operations. Households' deposits also carry a significant loading in this factor. Since these characteristics point towards banks being heavily involved in the retail market, the first factor is labelled 'Retail banking'. Deposits of firms and foreigners dominate the second factor – i.e. the depositors are mostly foreign firms. Thus, the second factor is labelled 'Foreign banking'. The third factor is dominated by loans to firms and is labelled 'Wholesale banking'.

The conclusion from the factor analysis is that three types of banks can be distinguished: retail, foreign and wholesale banks. This distinction will be taken up when assessing monetary policy responses in different segments of the banking market.

4   Estimation results

This section presents the results of the estimation of loan equation (10) from Ehrmann *et al.* (chapter 14 in this volume) for our sample of Dutch banks.[5] We present the estimation results using the bank-characteristic variables size, liquidity and capitalisation, as defined in Ehrmann *et al.* to differentiate the lending behaviour between different types of banks. The model is then re-estimated with the three alternative bank-characteristic variables retail, foreign and wholesale banking derived from the factor analysis in section 3.

For further details on the empirical model and the estimation method (GMM) the reader is referred to Ehrmann *et al.* As for the estimation, our chosen set of instruments, apart from the usual lags of the model variables, contains lagged values of the seasonal differences of the logs of the house price, the average selling period for houses on sale, real consumption and real investment expenditure. This controls for the strong relationship between the house and credit market developments during the 1990s in the Netherlands (cf. section 2). The first difference of the short-term (three-month) interest rate is used as the monetary policy indicator.

4.1   The role of size, liquidity and capitalisation of banks

The top panel of table 20.2 gives the long-term coefficients of the equation for total loans to the private non-financial sector, which include 47 per cent of total assets of all banks in the sample. The coefficient of the monetary policy indicator is negative in all cases, though not significantly (at the 5 per cent level) in the equation with liquidity and capitalisation. The expected positive sign for the coefficients of the interaction terms is found to be significant for capitalisation only. Hence, there is no equation for total loans where both the coefficient of the monetary policy indicator and the coefficient of the interaction term are significant and have the signs that are to be expected from the lending-channel theory.

Further investigation reveals that in the case of the Netherlands it is important to make a distinction between bank loans with and without

---

[5] Before estimation, banks for which the available time series are shorter than twelve quarters are removed. After this selection step the sample includes ninety-nine banks.

Table 20.2 *Loan equations: long-run coefficients, bank loans to the private sector, with and without guarantee, the Netherlands*[a,b]

	Bank-characteristic variables					
	Size		Liquidity		Capitalisation	
Total loans (47% of total assets)						
Monetary policy (MP)	−4.849***		−1.798*		−0.969	
Real GDP	1.353		−2.027**		−2.569*	
Prices	3.724**		1.896		−2.220*	
Bank characteristic × MP	−0.462		5.645		94.71***	
Bank characteristic × GDP	3.922***		−35.39***		−171.87***	
Bank characteristic × Prices	−0.219		−28.74***		−58.86***	
Bank characteristic	−0.592***		2.653***		9.481***	
Sargan (*p*-value)	1.000		1.000		1.000	
MA1, MA2 (*p*-values)	0.001	0.869	0.000	0.949	0.001	0.857
No. of banks, observations	98	1,563	98	1,563	98	1,563
Loans with guarantee (10% of total assets)						
Monetary policy (MP)	20.15***		13.68		−0.449	
Real GDP	−23.25**		−33.58**		−21.39	
Prices	−8.637		−17.43		−19.81*	
Bank characteristic × MP	−13.42***		−102.75*		−162.06	
Bank characteristic × GDP	18.14***		53.76		−74.229	
Bank characteristic × Prices	−1.814		80.41**		3.110	
Bank characteristic	−0.884***		−3.215*		5.197	
Sargan (*p*-value)	1.000		1.000		1.000	
MA1, MA2 (*p*-values)	0.127	0.626	0.079	0.949	0.075	0.814
No. of banks, observations	54	725	54	725	54	725
Loans without guarantee (37% of total assets)						
Monetary policy (MP)	−10.91***		−7.395***		−2.411	
Real GDP	18.20***		13.91***		6.338***	
Prices	4.658*		1.044		4.700	
Bank characteristic × MP	1.852**		24.29***		202.67***	
Bank characteristic × GDP	−2.621*		−49.12***		−336.42***	
Bank characteristic × Prices	1.441		−72.29***		80.594**	
Bank characteristic	−0.410***		4.037***		8.942***	
Sargan (*p*-value)	1.000		1.000		1.000	
MA1, MA2 (*p*-values)	0.002	0.684	0.001	0.735	0.002	0.909
No. of banks, obs.	95	1,478	95	1,478	95	1,478

Notes: [a] The benchmark equation is equation (10) in Ehrmann *et al.* (chapter 14 in this volume).
[b] The numbers of banks in the respective samples differ as some banks do not have all types of loans on their balance sheets and consequently drop out of the sample.
*, **, and *** denote significance at the 10%, 5% and 1% level.

government guarantees, when investigating the lending channel of monetary policy. The second and third panels in table 20.2 present estimates for loans with and without government guarantees, or in other words secured and unsecured bank debt, respectively. Secured debt accounts for 10 per cent of total assets of the banks in the sample, unsecured debt 37 per cent. There are some striking outcomes:

- First, a significantly negative monetary policy effect on lending is totally absent in the case of secured lending, while it is present in all cases for unsecured lending except in the equation with capitalisation as the interaction variable. Hence, monetary policy tightening does not appear to have any negative effect on secured bank lending. A reason could be that loans with guarantees get special treatment by banks. In fact, they earn a special interest rate, which is generally lower than the market rate. This reflects the lower credit risk on secured debt for which the government stands surety.

- Second, the expected positive coefficient of the interaction term is found to be significant for unsecured loans in all cases while for secured lending the interaction term has the opposite sign and is moreover not always significant.

- Third, the coefficients of the control variables ('Real GDP' and 'Prices'), when they are significant, are of opposite signs for secured and unsecured debt. For unsecured debt the coefficients have the intuitively expected positive sign, while for secured debt the sign is negative although not always significantly so. Hence, secured lending moves counter to the macroeconomic cycle. The positive coefficients of real GDP are quite large for unsecured lending. This probably reflects the extraordinary high credit growth during the sample period, often exceeding the GDP growth rate, as mentioned in section 2.

All in all, these results show that in the case of the Netherlands it is highly important to look at unsecured bank credit, i.e. loans without any government guarantees, when investigating the lending channel of monetary policy. For unsecured debt the results are in accordance with expectations: there is a negative monetary policy effect on lending which is stronger for smaller, less-liquid and less-capitalised banks. This is in line with the lending-channel theory according to which such banks are less able to attract non-deposit funds or use their buffer of liquid assets to shield their loan portfolios from monetary policy tightening.[6] Therefore, in what follows the focus will remain on unsecured debt.

---

[6] The results show that small banks are more susceptible to monetary policy shocks than large banks. As several very large banks hold practically the whole market in the Netherlands, the macroeconomic impact of the lending channel may not be that great.

4.2   The influence of market orientation

The factor analysis results in section 3 showed that the banks in the sample could be split into three categories: retail banks, wholesale banks and foreign banks. This classification will be used to assess whether the market segments affect the lending responses to monetary shocks. The factors derived from the factor analysis lend themselves to be used as bank-characteristic variables, to interact with the monetary policy variable. The values of these factors measure the extent to which a particular bank can be characterised exclusively as a retail bank, a foreign bank or a wholesale bank.

It should be noted beforehand that the research question in this subsection is different. It is unlikely that the signs of the coefficients of the three factors (that are the new interaction variables in the equation) can be predicted *a priori* on the basis of the lending-channel theory. For example, that theory does not predict whether banks dealing with households cut down their loan supply differently after monetary tightening than banks dealing with firms. The research question posed here is just whether there is evidence that banks in different market segments respond differently to monetary policy. This is an interesting question because it gives insight into the distributional effects of monetary policy over the different groups of bank borrowers (households and firms).

Table 20.3 singles out the estimated long-run coefficients with respect to the monetary policy indicator.[7] The three columns represent the equations with the three factors from section 3 as the bank-characteristic variables, i.e. retail, foreign and wholesale banking. The table presents the long-term coefficients for total unsecured loans to the private sector, with splits into households and firms. The coefficients of the monetary policy indicator confirm that bank lending is affected negatively by monetary tightening. The values of the estimated coefficients for the interaction terms in the equation are not significant, however. Hence, these results seem not to be conclusive as to the question whether banks in different market segments respond differently to monetary policy. It is true that both the significance and magnitude of the negative monetary policy coefficient is consistently larger for lending to firms than it is for lending to households. However, this does not have to indicate that bank-dependent households are affected less by monetary tightness than bank-dependent firms. Instead these results could partly reflect the special circumstances

---

[7] The other coefficients can be found in De Haan (2001).

Table 20.3 *Loan equations: selected long-run coefficients with respect to the monetary policy indicator for unsecured Dutch loans to the private sector, households and firms*[a]

	Bank-characteristic variables					
	Retail banking		Foreign banking		Wholesale banking	
Private sector (37% of total assets)						
Monetary policy (MP)	−9.532***		−13.55***		−9.269***	
Bank characteristic × MP	−3.621		1.013		−0.049	
No. of banks, obs.	95	1,478	95	1,478	95	1,478
Of which:						
Households (14% of total assets)						
Monetary policy (MP)	−0.294		−6.132**		−5.215**	
Bank characteristic × MP	−3.671		3.099		−3.104	
No. of banks, obs.	62	962	62	962	62	962
Non-financial firms (23% of total assets)						
Monetary policy (MP)	−8.701***		−7.688***		−7.325***	
Bank characteristic × MP	−1.036		1.021		0.826	
No. of banks, obs.	95	1,468	95	1,468	95	1,468

Notes: [a] The numbers of banks in the respective samples differ as some banks do not have all types of loans on their balance sheets and consequently drop out of the sample.
*, **, and *** denote significance at the 10%, 5%, and 1% level.

in which the market for mortgage credit found itself during the 1990s (section 2).

5   Conclusion

This chapter contributes to the empirical evidence on the lending channel in the Netherlands, using individual bank data. The analysis focuses on the differential response of the loan supply to monetary policy changes across several bank categories. Two categorisation devices are used in this chapter: first, banks' financial strength (measured by size, liquidity and capitalisation) and, second, banks' market orientation (retail banking, wholesale banking and foreign banking).

The results for loan supply suggest that a lending channel is operative in the Netherlands. However, for the Netherlands it appears to be important to make a distinction between bank loans with and without government guarantees. Particularly, there is strong evidence that the lending channel is operative only for unsecured bank debt. The results show that monetary tightening does not have any negative effect on secured bank lending. A reason could be that loans with guarantees get special treatment by banks. For unsecured debt the results are in accordance with expectations: there is a negative monetary policy effect on lending which is stronger for smaller, less-liquid and less-capitalised banks. This is in line with the lending-channel theory according to which such banks are less able to attract non-deposit funds or use their buffer of liquid assets to shield their loan portfolios from monetary policy tightening.

A contribution of this chapter is that it explores the question whether the monetary policy impact on bank lending also depends on the market segment in which a bank is active.

21   The cross-sectional and the time dimension of the bank-lending channel: the Austrian case

S. Kaufmann

1   Introduction

In the same line of research as in other empirical work (see de Bondt, 1999, Kashyap and Stein, 1995 and the contributions in the present volume), the evidence for cross-sectional differences in Austrian banks' lending reaction is investigated here with individual bank balance sheet data. Additionally, I try to capture a potential asymmetric response of bank lending over time as recent models of credit cycles suggest it. Kiyotaki and Moore (1997a, 1997b), for example, develop a model of the credit market that amplifies initial liquidity shocks to the system and propagates them to the real economy. Moreover, during a recession, the probability of debt repayment default increases and the response of the economy is amplified.

So far, the bank-lending channel in Austria has not been thoroughly investigated. There is one other study (Frühwirth-Schnatter and Kaufmann, 2003), that uses a different approach but the same data set as in this chapter. Therein, similarly to the present study, the authors find only weak evidence for cross-sectional differences in bank-lending reaction and a significant time-varying effect of interest rate changes. Evidence on the balance sheet channel, which forms the other part of the credit channel, is rather strong, however. Wesche (2000) and in particular Valderrama (chapter 13 in this volume) find that balance sheet effects are amplified for financially constrained firms. Finally, asymmetric effects of monetary policy over time on GDP growth have been investigated at the aggregate level in Kaufmann (2002) using a Markov switching specification for the time-varying parameters (Hamilton, 1989, 1990). Here, I will use the same framework for parameters subject to unobservable regime

I thank Ernst Baltensperger, who commented on the paper at the conference on 'Monetary policy transmission in the euro area', and the editors of this volume and Michael Ehrmann, Helene Schuberth and Maria Valderrama who provided comments and suggestions that helped improve the paper a lot.

shifts. The latent state specification accounts for the usual uncertainty about the overall (relevant) state of the economy, whereas Markov switching captures the different persistence of each regime.

The panel of quarterly individual bank data used covers the period 1990:1 to 1998:2. As a measure for monetary policy, I use the first difference of the three-month Austrian interest rate. In view of the exchange rate regime that pegged the Austrian Schilling to the German Mark, the use of the domestic interest rate is justified given the high correlation with the German interest rate of over 0.9 for the levels and the first differences, too. The main results, summarised in the last section of the chapter, are interpretable in the light of the Austrian banking sector's specificities which are very similar to the German bank-based financial system (see Worms, chapter 15 in this volume).

Section 2 provides a brief look at the data characterising the structure of the Austrian banking sector. It also summarises the macroeconomic background of the analysis, and comments briefly on data cleaning. Section 3 reproduces some representative results of the comprehensive study (Kaufmann, 2001). Section 4 draws some conclusions.

2   The data

2.1   Structure of the banking sector

At the end of 2000, 934 banks were operating in Austria, of which 130 had been newly founded during the 1990s. To compile table 21.1, these 130 banks and five additional ones with recorded liquidity shares above 100 per cent are removed from the original data set, leaving us with 799 banks representing 82 per cent of the banking market in terms of total assets.[1]

Overall, three sectors dominate the market, and the relative importance of each has not changed much to date (OeNB, 2001b). The savings banks (*Sparkassen*) form the largest sector, accounting for roughly 31 per cent of lending to non-financial institutions. The *Sparkassen* are organised in a two-tier system, with the *Erste Bank* serving as the central institution. Most savings banks are owned either by a municipality or a foundation (*Privatstiftung*).[2] Publicly owned savings banks are, moreover, backed by

---

[1] In the subsequent analysis I work with a balanced sample. Owing to missing values at the beginning of the sample period, these 130 banks are removed from the sample. Data from 1996:1 are chosen to compile the table because it is the only quarter throughout the sample in which no merger occurred.

[2] The 1999 amendment to the Saving Bank Act allows holding companies of joint savings banks to convert into foundations, implying that no new municipal guarantees will be extended (the guarantee remains in place for old liabilities only) (see also IMF, 2000).

Table 21.1 *Structure of the Austrian banking sector, 1996, million Euro*

	No. of inst.	Assets (% of total)	Loans (% of total)
Joint stock and private banks	36	101,257 (31.3)	40,150 (26.1)
Sparkassen (savings banks)	68	97,625 (30.2)	47,487 (30.8)
Erste Bank (central inst.)	1	16,953 (5.2)	7,671 (5.0)
Raiffeisenkassen (agricult. credit coop.)	604	71,665 (22.1)	30,540 (19.8)
Raiffeisen Zentralbank (central inst.)	1	16,785 (5.2)	5,408 (3.5)
Raiffeisenlandesbanken (regional inst.)	8	20,537 (6.3)	6,330 (4.1)
Volksbanken (industrial credit coop.)	67	16,139 (5.0)	8,979 (5.8)
Oesterreichische Volksbanken AG	1	5,262 (1.6)	2,590 (1.7)
State mortgage banks and building societies	11	30,857 (9.5)	23,602 (15.3)
Other banks	13	6,253 (1.9)	3,310 (2.1)
Total	799	32,3797	15,4069

a public guarantee which is underpinned by a mutual assistance obliga-tion. Mainly joint stock banks and the Postal Savings Bank (*Postsparkasse*) form the commercial banks' sector, which follows with a market share of 26 per cent. The cooperatives' banking sector, with a 25.7 per cent market share, consists of two bank groups, agricultural and industrial credit co-operatives (*Raiffeisenkassen* and *Volksbanken*, respectively). Most of the very small banks, where depositors are the shareholders, are found in this last sector. The former group is characterised by a three-tier system with *Raiffeisen Zentralbank* and eight *Raiffeisenlandesbanken* as central and regional institutions, respectively. *Oesterreichische Volksbanken AG* is the central institution of the two-tier *Volksbanken* sector. A mutual assistance arrangement similar to that of the savings banks' sector links the *Raiffeisen* banks and the *Volksbanken*.

Typical business activities (as well as the business activities of the small savings banks) are restricted on a local area and focus on retail banking on a small to medium-sized scale. All inter-regional or large-scale financing lending or foreign exchange activities are channelled through the cen-tral or regional institutions. A feature that has developed also in Austria is that of the house bank, typical for the German bank-based financial system (see Worms, chapter 15 in this volume); in this system, firms or households rely on a single bank for most of their financial needs.

State mortgage banks mainly do business in mortgages and issue mortgage bonds (*Pfandbriefe*) guaranteed by the respective state (*Bundesland*), while building societies (*Bausparkassen*) are used to channel subsidised savings into mortgages. Together, both groups reach a market share of 15 per cent. Finally, other banks, with a market share of only 2 per cent, comprise special-purpose banks such as foreign banks, factoring companies or companies specialising in long-term or leasing financing.

Owing to the intensive merger activity during the 1990s,[3] the distinction between the sectors became blurred, in particular that between commercial and savings banks. The large-scale mergers reflected the ongoing privatisation process taking place throughout the 1990s. The first cross-sector merger took place in 1991, when the *Länderbank* merged with *Zentralsparkasse* after having encountered financial difficulties to form *Bank Austria*, a savings bank. *Bank Austria* thus became the largest bank in Austria ahead of the *Creditanstalt*. In 1997 the federal government sold its stake in the *Creditanstalt*, a commercial bank, to *Bank Austria*. At the same time, *Erste Bank* (formerly *Erste SparCasse*) was established, and became the second largest bank by fully integrating *GiroCredit*, the former central institution of the *Sparkassen* sector. Most of the 182 mergers (where 268 banks were taken over), however, involved small banks without influencing significantly the banking sector's business activities. In particular, 118 mergers took place in the *Raiffeisenkassen* sector, followed by thirty and eighteen mergers in the *Sparkassen* and the *Volksbanken* sector, respectively.

The characteristic of the Austrian banking sector, many small banks doing business locally, is reflected in the statistical properties of the pooled data set. The top five banks' market share is not higher than 50 per cent,[4] even the top twenty-one banks cover only around 70 per cent of the banking market, which is not much for a small EU country. A further typical feature of the data (found in most European countries) is the fact that smaller banks are more liquid than larger banks. The median liquidity share of the top twenty-one banks amounts to less than 8 per cent while the 50 per cent smallest banks have a median liquidity share of 22 per cent. Finally, the market distribution of the asset total is mirrored in the loans' market distribution, implying that the median loan share of

---

[3] Triggered to improve efficiency and diversify into new business segments (see Mooslechner, 1989, 1995; Waschiczek, 1999).

[4] OeNB (2001b). Further large-scale mergers at the end of the 1990s led to an increase in the top five banks' market share above 50 per cent, however (see OeNB, 2002).

big banks (56 per cent) is not very different from the one of small banks (51 per cent).

Given the typical features of Austrian banking, it is not easy to form expectations on the results to be obtained from the subsequent analysis. With the market mainly populated by small banks that do business primarily on a local scale, and given their ownership structure, Austrian banks tend to face smaller informational problems.[5] Moreover, the multitier system alleviates banks' exposure to liquidity constraints during periods of restrictive monetary policy.[6] What follows is that the size of a bank might not be decisive for its lending reaction to monetary policy moves. Moreover, the house bank system leads to close customer relationships permitting banks to insulate their customers from the full effects of tight monetary policy. Thus, monetary policy effects might be muted and as such not observable in the lending reaction of banks.

2.2   Macroeconomic background and aggregate loan behaviour

Figure 21.1 provides a snapshot of the macroeconomic environment in which aggregate lending behaviour was embedded during the observation period. It depicts yearly GDP and loans growth rates along with the Austrian three-month interest rate. The shaded area refers to the recession period that turned out to be quite mild in Austria. As no official business cycle dating is available for Austria, the turning points are identified here by visual inspection.

The main interest rate changes occurred during the first half of the 1990s, with interest rate rises mainly observable through mid-1992. Interest rates were then broadly declining throughout the observation period. The last rise of nearly 37 bps is registered for the last quarter of 1997, followed by a decrease of 18 bps in the next quarter, however. By the time monetary union was established, interest rate moves cease to be significant, with the decline being less than 10 bps in the last two quarters of 1998, respectively. At the aggregate level, the loans growth rate fell from 10 per cent at the beginning of the sample period to about 5 per cent in 1994, with a transitory growth acceleration in 1995–6 to above 7 per cent. The initial high of around 10 per cent growth is a

---

[5] On the borrowers' side as well as on the creditors' side. Throughout the 1990s, banks did not experience big swings in deposits. In particular, deposits' share in loans has been constantly quite high in the Austrian banking sector, ranging from around 125 per cent until 1995 and declining to 105 per cent at the end of 1998 (OeNB, 2001a).

[6] The possibility for small banks to refinance at the central institution is reflected in the fairly closed sub-systems of interbank liabilities of the three multi-tier bank sectors (Elsinger, Lehar and Summer, 2002).

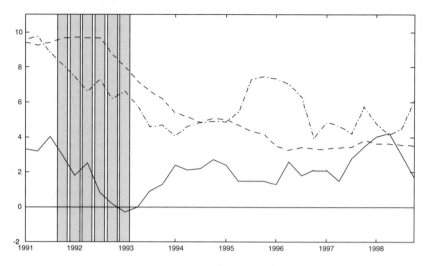

Figure 21.1 Austrian annual GDP growth rates (solid, computed by summing quarterly growth rates), annual loans growth rates (dash-dotted, fourth difference of the log levels) and interest rate level (dashed). The shaded area identifies the recession period at the beginning of the 1990s

reminiscence of the completed capital market liberalisation at the end of the 1980s which triggered a spurt in asset and real estate prices leading to a significant credit expansion (Braumann, 2002).

Over the whole observation period, the correlations between lagged interest rate changes and quarterly/yearly loans growth rates turn out to be insignificant/positive (see Kaufmann, 2001, table 3). However, the correlations turn negative when restricting the sample to the recovery period beginning in mid-1993. Indeed, in figure 21.1, total loans and the interest rate move in the same direction throughout 1993, while they move in opposite directions during 1995–6. This intuitively calls for time-varying effects of monetary policy.

2.3   Data-cleaning/data-compilation

The analysis is performed with a balanced sample of quarterly data running from 1990:1 through 1998:2. Outliers are identified in several steps (see Kaufmann, 2001, for details) and for computational reasons all banks involved in a merger or having some outliers in their series have to be removed from the sample. Additionally, I exclude banks specialised in leasing and foreign banks as their business does not depend primarily on domestic monetary policy. A total of 665 banks covering approximately 50 per cent of the Austrian banking sector's balance sheet total finally enter the analysis.

The variables are defined and transformed in the usual way (Ehrmann *et al.*, chapter 14 in this volume). However, the break in the series of the banks' liquidity share that is due to changing reporting definitions has to be accounted for by a dummy variable. Accordingly, *Liq95* denotes the liquidity share up to 1995, and *Liq96* the liquidity share from 1996 onwards. The investigation period begins in the 1990:2 and is restricted to end in the 1998:2 in order to include the second largest bank (*Creditanstalt AG*) in the sample. Its series display a break in 1998:3 because the bank was taken over at that time by *Bank Austria AG*. For comparison, the equation is estimated for total loans and loans to firms, as the latter are potentially the ones with a larger share granted without collateral.[7]

3   Results

3.1   Extending the bank-lending equation

To allow for changing effects of monetary policy over time, the basic reduced form lending equation ((10) in Ehrmann *et al.*, chapter 14 in this volume) is extended to allow for state-dependent parameters:

$$
\Delta\log(L_{it}) = a_0 + \sum_{j=1}^{3} a_j D_{jt} + \sum_{j=1}^{l} b_j \Delta\log(L_{i,t-j}) + \sum_{j=1}^{l} c_{j,S_t} \Delta r_{t-j}
$$
$$
+ d\,\Delta\log(GDP_t) + e\,(infl_t) + f_1 Liq95_{i,t-1}
$$
$$
+ f_2 Liq96_{i,t-1} + \sum_{j=1}^{l} g_{1j,S_t} Liq95_{i,t-1} \Delta r_{t-j}
$$
$$
+ \sum_{j=1}^{l} g_{2j,S_t} Liq96_{i,t-1} \Delta r_{t-j} + \varepsilon_{it} \tag{1}
$$

where ε_{it} is i.i.d. $N(0, \sigma^2)$, and quarterly dummy variables (D_{jt}) are included to account for seasonality. The equation is basically the same as in Ehrmann *et al.* as all variables except for the interest rate change and its interaction with the liquidity share are assumed to have a state-independent effect on lending. The coefficients on Δr_{t-j}, $Liq95_{i,t-1}\Delta r_{t-j}$

---

[7] Owing to the significant changes in the variables' reporting definitions at the end of 1995, a further breakdown of loans is not sensible because consistent more disaggregated time series cannot be constructed for the whole observation period.

and $Liq96_{i,t-1}\Delta r_{t-j}$, however, are time-varying according to the value that the state variable S_t takes on. If $S_t = k$, then $c_{j,S_t} = c_{j,k}$, $g_{1j,S_t} = g_{1j,k}$ and $g_{2,j,S_t} = g_{2j,k}$, $k = 1,2$, thus capturing changing effects of monetary policy over time.[8] S_t itself may be specified in different ways. As liquidity constraints may be more binding during periods of economic slowdown, we expect to observe a stronger reaction of bank lending to monetary policy during these times. Ad hoc, one might define S_t to equal 1 during the period of recovery and to equal 2 during the slowdown identified in figure 21.1 (p. 352) at the beginning of the sample period. However, it may well be that periods of binding liquidity constraints are leading (or lagging) the economic cycle, or that they may not even be related to the performance of the real economy at all. Therefore, the inference on S_t is part of the model estimation, i.e. it is assumed to be unobservable. Moreover, I assume it to follow a Markov process of order one with transition probabilities $\eta_{lk} = P(S_t = k \mid S_{t-1} = l)$, and $\sum_{k=1}^{2} \eta_{lk} = 1$, to account for the potential difference in persistence of the states.

The estimation of the model is cast into a Bayesian framework (see also Frühwirth-Schnatter and Kaufmann, 2002, 2003), which amounts to interpreting the path of S_t, $S^T = (S_1, \ldots, S_T)$, as an additional random variable and leads to the augmented parameter vector, $\psi = (\theta, S^T)$, where θ gathers all model parameters. An inference on the posterior distribution of ψ is obtained using Markov chain Monte Carlo simulation methods by iteratively simulating out of the conditional posterior distributions $S^T|\theta$ and $\theta|S^T$ (see Kaufmann, 2001, appendices A and B for the sampling scheme, the prior specification and the post-processing to identify state-specific parameters, respectively).

3.2   Results

Various specifications of (1) were investigated including alternatively interaction terms with size and liquidity and both simultaneously. In each specification, five lags of the endogenous variable proved enough to capture the dynamics in the panel. Alternatively, a linear and a Markov switching specification were estimated for each combination of interaction terms. In terms of marginal (or model) likelihood,[9] the specification

---

[8] The investigation revealed only two states present in the data. The extension to more than two states is straightforward, however.

[9] The marginal or 'model' likelihood represents the likelihood of the data (y) under a certain model M, $L(y/M)$, and as such is independent of specific parameter values. Model specification tests can then be made by means of the Bayes factor. In the present chapter, all marginal likelihoods were estimated using the optimal bridge sampler (Frühwirth-Schnatter, 1999, Meng and Wong, 1996).

including the interaction with liquidity proved to perform best. Moreover, the interaction with size remained insignificant irrespective of the state specification (justifying the hypothesis that size is not relevant to characterise cross-sectional asymmetry). Therefore, the results for total and corporate loans with the liquidity interaction are presented here (see Kaufmann, 2001 for detailed results and for the results on an ad hoc specification for S_t).

Table 21.2 reports mean estimates (with t-values) of the relevant parameters. In the linear specification, bank lending reacts positively to interest rate changes, and the evidence for cross-sectional asymmetry in banks' lending reaction is rather weak, the liquidity share being significant for lending to firms only from 1996 onwards. Nevertheless, the equation for total loans appears to be quite well specified as only 7 per cent of the banks have remaining autocorrelation at the 5 per cent significance level, and second-order residual autocorrelation does not seem to be a problem. For loans to firms, 8 per cent and 6 per cent of the banks have remaining first- and second-order autocorrelation, respectively. Several arguments might address the issue of the positively estimated coefficient on the interest rate, one being a bias introduced by time-varying effects of interest rate changes not accounted for in the linear specification.

Indeed, in the Markov switching specification, we can discriminate between two different states, where lending does not react significantly to interest rate changes in state 1 and (still) reacts positively when state 2 prevails. Cross-sectional asymmetry is not significant in state 1, while in state 2 there is a positive liquidity effect in both total lending and lending to firms. The estimation of a specification restricting the liquidity effect to be state-independent from 1996 onwards yielded nearly unchanged coefficients. Clearly, the marginal likelihood favours the switching specification, twice the difference between the log marginal likelihood of the linear and the latent specification being above 20 in each case.[10] To get an idea of what the estimated state variable tracks, the posterior probabilities of state 2 are depicted in figure 21.2. The state variable relates to the business cycle. State 2 identifies the turning point in 1991:3 and tracks the slowdown in the first half of 1992. For loans to firms, the sampler additionally identifies state 2 prevailing for another six months, in particular 1995:4 and 1996:1. A measure for the correlation of the state variable with the GDP growth rate indicates that the former leads the

---

[10] The difference between two marginal log likelihoods is equal to the log of the Bayes factor, twice the difference is interpretable on the same scale as the familiar likelihood ratio statistic.

Table 21.2 *Loan equations: total loans and loans to firms, Austria, Linear and Markov switching specification (with t-values)[c]*

state	Total loans			Loans to firms		
	Linear	Markov switching		Linear	Markov switching	
		1	2		1	2
Δr_{t-1}	0.50*	0.18	4.67*	0.54*	0.16	5.54*
	(5.43)	(1.73)	(7.66)	(3.25)	(1.04)	(10.73)
Δr_{t-2}				0.40*		
				(2.47)		
$Liq95_{i,t-1}\Delta r_{t-1}$	0.00	−0.02	0.21*	−0.02	−0.02	0.17*
	(0.20)	(−1.83)	(3.73)	(−1.07)	(−1.13)	(3.21)
$Liq95_{i,t-1}\Delta r_{t-2}$				0.04*		
				(1.97)		
$Liq96_{i,t-1}\Delta r_{t-1}$	−0.01	−0.01	0.01	−0.05	−0.03	0.41
	(−0.19)	(−0.22)	(0.01)	(−1.14)	(−0.68)	(1.76)
$Liq96_{i,t-1}\Delta r_{t-2}$				0.14*		
				(3.53)		
Log marginal likelihood	−48763.95	−48750.21		−53967.29	−53940.42	
η_{11}		0.95			0.87	
		(0.82 1.00)			(0.67 0.98)	
η_{22}		0.69			0.63	
		(0.31 0.95)			(0.32 0.90)	
AR(1) significance at 5% level[a]	0.07	0.07		0.08	0.07	
AR(2) significance at 5% level	0.04	0.04		0.06	0.05	
Maximum lead 'correlation' of state 2 with GDP growth[b]		3 leads/0.88			2 leads/0.85	

Notes: [a] The AR test is based on the *AC* index, $A = \sqrt{T}(\rho + [1/(T-1)])$, where ρ is the empirical autocorrelation coefficient of the transformed *P*-scores $v_t = \Phi^{-1}(u_t)$, where Φ is the standard normal distribution, and u_t is the one-step-ahead predictive distribution of the dependent variable in t (see e.g., Kaufmann, 2000).

[b] The maximum lead 'correlation', $H(-i)$, refers to the (maximum) frequency of correctly specified quarters for state 2 with respect to a reference series SR_t, $(SR_t = 0$ if $\Delta\log(GDP_t) \geq 0$ *and* $SR_t = 1$ if $\Delta\log(GDP_t) < 0$): $H(-i) = 1/T\sum_{t=1}^{T-i}|(S_t - 1) + SR_{t+i} - 1|$.

[c] The liquidity share is interacted with a dummy variable to account for the break in the level and the standard deviation due to changing reporting definitions. The *AR*(1) and *AR*(2) statistics denote the percentage of banks that have remaining autocorrelation in the residuals at the 5% significance level.

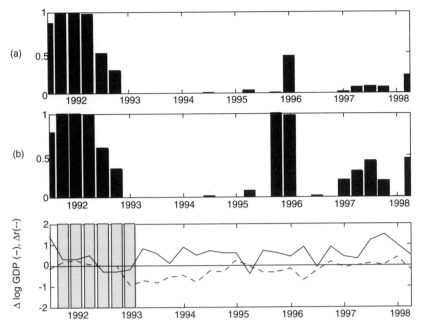

Figure 21.2 Austrian total loans (a) and loans to firms (b), 1992–1998: posterior probabilities of being in state 2, obtained by averaging over all simulated vectors S^T; bottom panel: GDP growth rate ($\Delta\log$ GDP) and lagged interest rate changes (Δ r_{t-1}); the shaded area refers to the economic slowdown of 1992–3

latter by three and two quarters in the case for total and corporate loans, respectively (see the bottom line of table 21.2).

4   Conclusions

The results obtained in the present investigation document a weak evidence for cross-sectional differences in banks' lending reaction after monetary policy changes which is driven by each bank's liquidity share rather than by its size. Moreover, the Markov switching specification adopted here reveals that the direct and the distributional effects of interest rate changes are asymmetric over time. In one state, lasting from the second half of 1992 (the last half-year of the mild slowdown) through the end of the sample period, monetary policy does not significantly affect banks' lending behaviour, for both total and corporate loans. In the other state during the first half of the economic slowdown lasting through mid-1992, interest rate changes and the liquidity effect are significantly positive, however.

These effects are interpretable if one takes into consideration the specificities of the Austrian banking sector which are much like the German banking system (see Worms, chapter 15 in this volume). Most banks are small and operate on a local level; therefore, they tend to be less exposed to informational asymmetry, on the borrowers' side as well as on the creditors' side. Furthermore, the multi-tier system in which they are embedded and which enables refinancing at the central institutions alleviates binding liquidity constraints. Owing to close business relationships, banks are willing to shield their customers from the effects of monetary policy. This explains the insignificant lending reaction in state 1. Finally, intertemporal smoothing of liquidity in a bank-based financial system (Allen and Gale, 2000) enables banks to assist customers especially during periods of tight liquidity or during periods of economic slack, which might explain the positive lending reaction in periods identified by state 2.

22　The bank-lending channel of monetary policy: identification and estimation using Portuguese micro bank data

L. Farinha and C. Robalo Marques

1　Introduction

This chapter investigates the existence of the bank-lending channel in the transmission of monetary policy using Portuguese micro bank data. In contrast to the conventional approach, which addresses the identification issue by resorting to reduced form equations for bank credit with variables in differences, we directly estimate loan-supply schedules with variables in levels, thereby exploiting recent results on cointegration for panel data.[1]

The main conclusion is that there is a banking lending channel in the transmission of monetary policy in the Portuguese economy and that the importance of this channel is larger for the less capitalised banks. Size and liquidity do not appear to be relevant bank characteristics in determining the importance of the lending channel.

The remainder of the chapter is organised as follows. Section 2 briefly characterises the main changes undergone by the Portuguese banking sector during the 1980s and 1990s. Section 3 describes the new approach aimed at identifying and estimating the importance of the bank-lending channel. Section 4 reports the empirical results for Portugal and section 5 summarises the main conclusions.

2　Monetary policy and banking sector developments in Portugal during the 1990s

Since the early 1980s the Portuguese financial system underwent a fundamental liberalisation process beginning with the opening up of the

This chapter represents the authors' personal opinions and does not necessarily reflect the views of the institution to which they are affiliated. We would like to thank the members of the Eurosystem's Monetary Transmission Network (MTN) and to the participants in the conference 'Monetary Policy Transmission in the Euro Area' for helpful discussions and feedback, and especially to Ignazio Angeloni, Anil Kashyap, Michael Ehrmann, Vitor Gaspar, Leo de Haan, Ferreira Machado, Maximiano Pinheiro and Nuno Ribeiro, for their comments and suggestions. All errors and shortcomings are our responsibility alone.
[1] For technical details on this chapter the interested reader is referred to Farinha and Marques (2001).

banking sector to private initiative in 1983.[2] In this period the first steps towards the elimination of the administrative controls on interest rates and credit growth were also taken. Moreover the explicit restrictions on the composition of banks' assets were removed and the legally imposed segmentation of banking activities was gradually eliminated, culminating in the establishment of universal banking in 1992.

Under a significantly more competitive environment the number of banks increased from fourteen in 1984 to twenty-seven 1989 and fifty-eight in 1997.[3] As in the other European countries, international competition stimulated several waves of takeovers, especially after 1994. However, the number of banks continued to increase, with entry largely dominated by foreign institutions.

Another important step in the liberalisation of the Portuguese banking system was the re-privatisation process that started in 1989, gradually transferring most of the banking business to private management. Since 1993, the main reforms have been directed at the harmonisation of procedures and regulations within the European Union, namely the capital adequacy rules.

On the monetary and exchange rate policy front, after having abandoned the crawling peg regime in October 1990, the escudo joined the European Exchange Rate Mechanism (ERM) in April 1992.[4] In December of the same year the remaining restrictions on international capital flows were removed.

The continuous decline of inflation since the early 1990s and the stability of the exchange rate after 1993 permitted the sustained reduction of interest rates. The process of nominal convergence increased the prospects of EMU participation, which in turn facilitated exchange rate stability and convergence. These developments were reflected in a substantial decrease in the exchange risk premium of the escudo after mid-1995.

The sustained and significant reduction of both short- and long-run nominal interest rates, perceived as being permanent, reduced the liquidity constraints of the economic agents thus contributing to the strong growth in overall credit demand observed in this period.

Figure 22.1 shows aggregate quarterly figures on the evolution of bank loans granted to the private non-financial sectors of the economy as well as

---

[2] The establishment of private investment companies, which were later transformed into investment banks, was authorised in 1979. For details on the institutional changes in the Portuguese banking sector during the 1980s and 1990s the reader is referred to Leite and Ribeiro (1997).

[3] Excluding the cooperative institutions, whose number is relatively large (160 in 1998), but account only for nearly 3 per cent of the credit institutions' total assets.

[4] For details on the Portuguese convergence process the reader is referred to Abreu (2001).

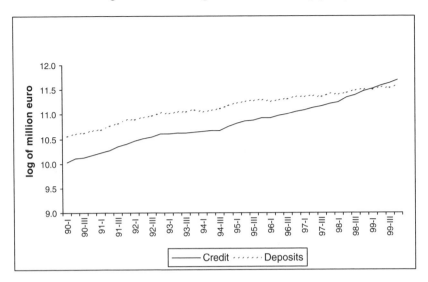

Figure 22.1 Portuguese credit and deposits, 1990–1999

the evolution of aggregate deposits held with the banks by the private non-financial sectors.[5] After the deceleration in the recession period between 1992 and 1994, in 1995–7 credit resumed the upward trend of the early 1990s (average annual growth rate in real terms of 14 per cent in this period compared to 16 per cent in 1991) and strongly accelerated in 1998 and 1999 (annual growth rate in real terms of 24 per cent). Until 1994 deposits behaved very much like credit, but from 1995/1996 onwards they clearly exhibited a much smaller growth rate (5.2 per cent in real terms during the period 1995–7 and 6 per cent in 1998–9).

These apparently diverging developments in credit and deposits were the consequence of the elimination of controls on the international capital flows, on the one hand, and a significant reduction of the exchange risk of the escudo on the other, that enhanced the integration between the Portuguese and the international money markets.

Figure 22.2 presents the evolution of the main non-deposits financing sources. It can be seen that the increase in the growth rate of loans coincided with a decrease of the government bonds in banks' portfolios

[5] The figures analysed in this section have been computed from non-consolidated data on the sample of eighteen bank conglomerates for which consistent series throughout the period 1990–8 may be obtained. In December 1998, the credit and deposits in these eighteen banks amounted to 96 per cent and 98 per cent of the total credit and total deposits, respectively. This is also the sample of banks used in the econometric estimations presented below.

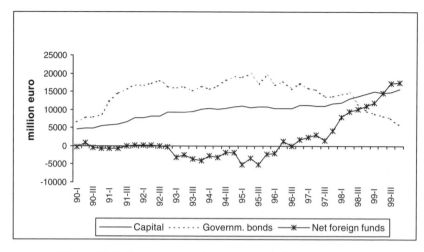

Figure 22.2 Portuguese main non-deposit financing sources, 1990–1999

and an increase in the (net) funds obtained in the international money markets. Banks partly substituted their investment in government securities by credit to private non-financial sectors. This whole process seems basically to have started in 1995 and accelerated in 1998. In fact, the weight of government securities in banks' balance sheets declined significantly from 19.5 per cent of total assets in 1992 to 5.7 per cent in 1998 (13.4 per cent in 1995).

3   Identifying the bank-lending channel: an alternative approach

At the empirical level, the bulk of the most relevant literature has tried to uncover the lending channel through the estimation of a reduced form equation for the bank credit market, with variables in differences (see, for instance, Ehrmann *et al.*, chapter 14 in this volume, Favero, Giavazzi and Flabbi, 1999 and Kashyap and Stein, 1995). The estimated equation is generally a dynamic version (in differences) of the static model:

$$\ln(C/P)_t = \theta_0 + \theta_1 \ln y_t + \theta_2 \ln y_t z_{it} + \theta_3 r_t + \theta_4 r_t z_{it} \\ + \theta_5 \pi_t + \theta_6 \pi_t z_{it} + \theta_7 z_{it} \tag{1}$$

where $(C/P)_t$ stands for bank loans (in real terms), y_t for a scale variable (usually GDP), π_t for the inflation rate, r_t for the monetary policy interest rate and z_{it} for a measure of a bank-specific characteristic (size, liquidity or capitalisation).

Under this approach, which we shall denote as the 'reduced form approach', the fact that the estimated θ_3 is (significantly) negative and θ_4 is (significantly) positive is taken as evidence of the existence of the bank-lending channel. The idea is that if the effect of monetary policy on bank lending is larger for the smaller, less-liquid or less-capitalised banks this can be due only to the existence of the bank-lending channel.

In order to motivate the alternative econometric approach we develop a simple IS-LM model for the money and credit markets, which draws heavily on Bernanke and Blinder (1988). The model, which in our view permits a better understanding of the identifying restrictions underlying the reduced form equation (1), is composed of four equations: money-demand (total deposits held with a typical bank), money-supply, loan-demand and loan-supply schedules. For space reasons we skip the details of the model and discuss only the loan-supply schedule, which reads as follows (below each coefficient is the corresponding expected sign according to economic theory):

$$\ln(C/P)^s_{it} = \alpha_{0i} + \alpha_1\ln(D/P)_{it} + \alpha_2\ln(D/P)_{it}Z_{it} + \alpha_3 l_t + \alpha_4 i_t + \alpha_5 \pi_t$$
$$(+)(-)(+)(-)(-)(2)$$

Equation (2) postulates that banks' loan-supply in real terms, (C/P), depends on the level of total deposits in real terms held by the private sector with the banks, (D/P), on the inflation rate, π_t, as a measure of uncertainty in the economy as well as on the loan, l_t, and bond, i_t, interest rates.[6] Assets held by banks in the form of bonds are seen as substitutes for loans, held mainly for liquidity reasons.

The null $\alpha_1 \neq 0$ in (2) captures the idea that banks cannot shield their loan portfolios from changes in monetary policy, i.e., from changes in deposits brought about by monetary policy and plays a central role in our analysis as it constitutes a key necessary condition for the existence of the lending channel. If banks were able to replace lost deposits with other sources of funds, such as certificates of deposits or new equity issues, or by selling securities, we would expect α_1 not to be significantly different from zero.

The term $\alpha_2 \ln(D/P)_{it}z_{it}$ intends to capture the idea that shifts in the supply curve brought about by monetary policy changes depend on some banks' specific characteristics (size, liquidity, capitalisation, etc.)

---

[6] As explained below this supply schedule may be justified in theoretical terms in the context of a profit-maximising bank, in which the amount of deposits is out of the control of the bank, being determined by central bank monetary policy.

measured by z_{it}. In principle we expect that $\alpha_2 < 0$ so that loan-supply shifts are larger for small, less-liquid or less-capitalised banks.

To see how the lending channel operates in the model, let us assume, for instance, that the central bank increases the discount rate. This will reduce the equilibrium quantity of money in the economy, i.e., deposits in our model, through the interaction between money supply and money demand. In turn, the drop in deposits held by the private sector with the banks shifts the loan-supply schedule inwards if $\alpha_1 > 0$ in (2). It is this additional transmission mechanism – the inward shift in supply of loans – which is known in the literature as the bank-lending channel.

Also important is the coefficient α_3 as it determines the slope of the supply curve. Of course for that inward shift to occur the supply curve cannot be horizontal. In other words we need the additional assumption that α_3 in (2) is finite. Thus to test the existence of the credit channel and evaluate its importance we need to estimate α_1 and α_3 in (2). The credit channel is the more important the larger α_1 (the larger the extent to which banks rely on deposit financing) and the smaller α_3.

Solving the model one obtains a reduced form equation for bank credit that looks very much like (1). From such an equation it is possible to discuss the restrictions on the coefficients of both money- and loan-demand and supply schedules, which are necessary in order to guarantee that proper conclusions on the existence of the lending channel can be drawn from a reduced form equation such as (1).[7]

In our opinion, some of these restrictions are very stringent. For this reason we will follow a different approach which consists of directly estimating the supply curve (2). This alternative approach has the advantage of allowing one to get direct point estimates of the relevant coefficients, which is not the case with the 'reduced form' approach.

We assume that deposits as well as the bond interest rate are exogenous at the bank level, so that we may stick to a 'structural model' consisting only of a loan-demand equation and a loan-supply equation. The assumption of deposits' exogeneity is probably the major limitation of our approach, but, in fact, this seems to be an issue also deserving further research at the theoretical level.

Of course, our model also raises an identification as well as an estimation issue. The identification of demand and supply schedules is discussed, for instance, in Intrilligator, Bodkin and Hsiao (1996) and in Zha (1997). The basic idea is that the supply curve is identified provided the loan demand curve includes at least one explanatory variable that does

---

[7] For a lengthy discussion of these 'identifying' restrictions see Farinha and Marques (2001).

not enter the supply equation. Under the assumption that deposits and the bond interest rate are exogenous at the bank level, we see that the supply curve (2) is identified provided we assume that the demand curve includes a scale variable (GDP, for instance) as an additional regressor (in turn, the demand curve would be identified because the supply curve includes $\ln(D/P)$ as an additional regressor).

Let us now address the estimation issue. So far in the literature the empirical models, using panel data, have been estimated with variables in first differences to circumvent the potential non-stationarity problem arising from the time-series dimension of the data. However it is well known that in most cases this approach does not solve the inconsistency problem, especially if the estimated model still includes specific effects and lagged endogenous variables.[8]

On the other hand, this approach neglects from the start the possibility of a levels' relation among the relevant variables. In other words this approach discards the possibility of a long-run effect of monetary policy on deposits and credit. This is at odds with the usual approach in the literature, which postulates a levels' relationships for the money and credit equations.

We estimate our model in levels using recently developed cointegration techniques for panel data. Some of these techniques allow obtaining (super) consistent estimators for the parameters of our supply equations even when some of the regressors are correlated with the residuals.[9] These, being static equations, should be seen as cointegrating relations, whose coefficients are the long-run effects.

Our estimated loan-supply functions are generalisations of (2) in that they include two additional regressors: bank capital and the cost of external financing alternative to deposits and capital, s_t. The basic equation reads as:

$$\ln(C/P)^s_{it} = \alpha_{0i} + \alpha_1 \ln(D/P)_{it} + \alpha_2 \ln(K/P)_{it} + \alpha_3 l_t + \alpha_4 i_t + \alpha_5 s_t + \alpha_6 \pi_t$$
$$\quad\quad (+) \quad\quad\quad (+) \quad\quad\quad (+) \quad (-) \quad (-) \quad (-)$$
$$(3)$$

We may justify this generalisation on econometric as well as on economic grounds. From an econometric point of view the introduction of capital in (3) aims at preventing deposits appearing as the single 'scale' variable,

---

[8] See Alvarez and Arellano (1998) for a survey on the asymptotic properties of various estimators, in dynamic panels, with stationary regressors.

[9] On this issue, see for instance, Binder, Hsiao and Pesaran (2000); Kao and Chiang (2000); Pedroni (1996); Pesaran and Shin (1995); Pesaran, Shin and Smith (1999); and Phillips and Moon (1999). Interesting surveys on the subject are Baltagi and Kao (2000); Banerjee (1999); and Phillips and Moon (2000).

which could bias the results towards favouring the conclusion of the existence of the credit channel. From an economic point of view we may justify (3) in the context of the model developed in Courakis (1988), in which banks maximise profits (by deciding on the amounts of assets and liabilities they control) conditional on the items they cannot control (capital and/or deposits, for instance). Under this framework our loan supply can be seen as resulting from a profit-maximising behaviour of a bank in which both deposits and capital are treated as exogenous. The bank is assumed to choose the volume of credit, securities and external finance, in order to maximise the expected profits for a given level of deposits and capital.

The possibility of other forms of external financing alternative to deposits and capital (money market funds, certificates of deposits, etc.) is taken into account by introducing into the credit equation an interest rate representing the cost of such funds s_t.[10]

4   Empirical evidence using Portuguese micro bank data

In the estimations we use balance sheet information on a sample of eighteen bank conglomerates for which consistent quarterly data throughout 1990:1–1998:4 are available.[11]

As expected, given the evolution of credit and deposits described in section 2, some preliminary tests showed that in the last years of the sample the relation between credit granted to private sector and deposits underwent a huge structural break. In order to minimise the corresponding damaging consequences for the estimated models we excluded the data for 1998 from the sample. So, we finally used eight years of quarterly data for eighteen bank conglomerates.

We estimated our equations by POLS (Pooled OLS), PCOLS (Panel corrected OLS), DPOLS (Dynamic panel OLS) and the PFMOLS (Panel fully modified OLS) estimators (see Kao and Chiang, 2000).[12] The results obtained by the first three estimators are basically similar. In such regressions most coefficients appear non-significantly different from zero or wrong signed. In contrast, the results supplied by the PFMOLS estimator are quite reasonable in terms of both sign and magnitude. The

---

[10] Actually the reported equations in section 4 only include two (and not three interest rates). Owing to strong colinearity we are not able to separately estimate the three coefficients. We dropped i_t from the equation, as in fact it turned out not to be significant in preliminary regressions.

[11] During the 1990s a process of takeovers took place. However many of the institutions involved did not effectively merge, but rather constituted bank conglomerates.

[12] We used the NPT 1.2 econometric package developed by Chiang and Kao (2001).

fact that we are using a small sample, the correlation in the residuals as well as the endogeneity of some of the regressors probably explains these differences. For this reason, below we present and comment only on the PFMOLS results[13].

The estimated equations are displayed in table 22.1. Below each co-efficient is the computed t-statistic, which is asymptotically normal distributed. For each equation several cointegration tests were computed. The null of a unit root in the residuals was always rejected, so that all the equations presented in table 22.1 are valid cointegrating relations.[14]

Column (1) displays the results of our basic specification (3). It can readily be seen that all the coefficients are statistically significant and exhibit the expected sign for a loan-supply function. Even though the estimated coefficients of l_t and s_t do not seem to be much different in absolute terms, the null hypothesis of their being equal in magnitude is statistically rejected. In fact the t-statistics for this restriction are always larger than two (see, bottom line of table 22.1).

Given that the coefficient of $\ln(D/P)$, α_1, is significantly positive and the coefficient of l_t, α_3, is finite we conclude that there is evidence of the existence of a bank-lending channel in the transmission of monetary policy in Portuguese bank data.

By comparing the results in columns (1) and (2) we also see that the conclusion on the existence of the credit channel does not depend on whether or not the estimated regression includes bank capital as an additional regressor.

The remaining regression results reported in table 22.1 interact the explanatory variables in our basic equation with three bank-specific characteristics, which are usually seen as potential important sources of bank heterogeneity: size, liquidity and capitalisation. These three variables are denoted by z_{it} in table 22.1. In the case of size and capitalisation the z_{it} variable is taken in the form of differences from each time period average, i.e.

$$z_{it} = x_{it} - \frac{1}{N} \sum_{i=1}^{N} x_{it} = x_{it} - \bar{x}_t \qquad (4)$$

---

[13] The use of the PFMOLS estimator was suggested by Phillips and Moon (1999) for the case of a homogeneous panel (the same coefficients for all the individuals) with endogenous regressors. We note that the PFMOLS estimator is superconsistent ($\sqrt{NT}$ consistent) and has a normal limit distribution, even when the regressors are correlated with the residuals.

[14] The panel cointegration tests computed by the NPT 1.2 package include the five panel cointegration tests developed in Kao (1999) and four panel cointegration tests developed in Pedroni (1997).

Table 22.1 Loan equation (3): PFMOLS estimates, Portugal

Regressors	Size				Liquidity		Capitalisation	
	(1)	(2)	(3)	(4)	(5)	(6)	(7)	(8)
$\ln(D/P)_{it}$	0.615	0.721	0.676	0.490	0.633	0.717	0.409	0.713
	(24.83)	(28.99)	(14.61)	(10.86)	(18.38)	(21.34)	(14.97)	(26.26)
$\ln(D/P)_{it} \cdot z_{it}$			0.156	0.049	−0.051	0.027	−3.947	−0.747
			(8.16)	(2.80)	(−0.75)	(0.54)	(−16.23)	(−6.97)
$\ln(K/P)_{it}$	0.156		−0.525		0.130		0.470	
	(3.00)		(−10.11)		(2.74)		(7.89)	
$\ln(K/P)_{it} \cdot z_{it}$			−0.101		0.022		6.462	
			(−3.03)		(0.13)		(12.14)	
l_t	19.318	16.734	17.953	22.262	14.787	12.839	22.187	16.617
	(15.00)	(12.96)	(16.14)	(18.91)	(12.10)	(10.34)	(18.01)	(12.40)
$l_t z_{it}$			0.523		101.926	111.513	24.639	
			(0.81)		(8.40)	(9.30)	(1.79)	
s_t	−15.905	−14.442	−11.767	−16.110	−11.835	−10.801	−17.096	−13.595
	(−11.85)	(−10.77)	(−10.22)	(−13.24)	(−9.55)	(−8.59)	(−13.63)	(−10.08)
$s_t z_{it}$			−1.410		−72.969	−79.466	13.953	
			(−2.26)		(−6.38)	(−7.10)	(1.04)	
π_t	−2.504	−1.114	−7.538	−6.476	−0.470	0.635	−5.114	−3.069
	(−2.24)	(−1.02)	(−7.66)	(−6.45)	(−0.45)	(0.61)	(−4.70)	(−2.76)
z_{it}			0.411	0.214	−8.213	−9.005	−6.589	−0.444
			(5.04)	(3.55)	(−13.27)	(−14.26)	(−5.15)	(−1.32)
Spread restriction	(4.30)	(2.98)	—	(8.79)	—	—	—	(3.81)

Notes: t-statistics in parenthesies.
$\ln(D/P)$ = natural log of total deposits deflated by the CPI.
$\ln(K/P)$ = natural log of total capital deflated by the CPI.
l_t = interest rate on long-term loans in decimals (five-year loans).
s_t = short-term interest rate on Portuguese money market in decimals.
π_t = inflation rate in decimals (fourth differences of log CPI).
z_{it} = measure of bank-specific characteristic (size, liquidity or capitalisation).

where x_{it} stands for the log of total assets, as a measure of size and for the capital ratio as a capitalisation indicator. By defining size and capitalisation in this way we ensure that the z_{it} variable captures pure differential effects. In case of liquidity the z_{it} variable is taken in the form of differences from a per-bank average, i.e.

$$z_{it} = x_{it} - \frac{1}{T}\sum_{t=1}^{T} x_{it} = x_{it} - \overline{x}_i \qquad (5)$$

where x_{it} stands for the liquidity ratio as a measure of bank liquidity.[15] This definition allows one to account for periods of general (positive or negative) excess liquidity for the banking sector as whole, which is likely to have been the case in the Portuguese banking system, during most of the sample.

Let us now take the model in column (3) of table 22.1. The fact that the coefficient on $\ln(D/P)_{it}z_{it}$ is positive means that the coefficient on deposits is lower for small banks, and so in the Portuguese case the supply of loans of small banks is less deposit-dependent than that of large banks. In other words, everything else equal, we would conclude that the credit channel is less important for small banks. However, we saw in section 3 that in order to evaluate the relative importance of the bank lending channel we need to look at the coefficient of deposits as well as at the coefficient of the loans interest rate. Thus, in terms of table 22.1, to evaluate the relative magnitude of the lending channel for two different banks one has to look both at the coefficient of $\ln(D/P)_{it}z_{it}$ and the coefficient of $l_t z_{it}$, as the effect of a decrease in the coefficient of deposits could be offset by an increase on the coefficient of the loans interest rate, and vice versa.

As it turns out that the coefficients on the interaction terms $l_t z_{it}$ and $s_t z_{it}$ are both not statistically different from zero we may definitely conclude that small Portuguese banks are less dependent on deposits than large banks or, in other words, the bank-lending channel appears to be less important for small banks.[16] We recognise that the lack of evidence of larger non-deposit external financing costs for smaller banks does not come as a large surprise in the Portuguese case. Portugal is a small country with a few banks in which even the smaller banks are large enough not to be discriminated in the access to markets for non-deposits' external funds.

[15] The rational for (5) is explained in Farinha and Marques (2001).
[16] We note that the coefficient of $\ln(K/P)$ in column (3) is wrong signed, but the above conclusion still holds for the model in column (4), which was estimated after dropping $\ln(K/P)_{it}$ and $\ln(K/P)_{it}z_{it}$ and after checking that the coefficients on $l_t z_{it}$ and $s_t z_{it}$ were still statistically not different from zero. However in column (4) the estimated coefficient of $\ln(D/P)_{it}zit$ is much smaller and the t-statistic is not very high in relative terms.

Columns (5) and (6) in table 22.1 display the models with liquidity as the bank-specific characteristic. The first important point to note is that the coefficient of $\ln(D/P)_{it}z_{it}$ and that of $\ln(K/P)_{it}z_{it}$ are not statistically different from zero. The fact that the coefficient of $\ln(D/P)_{it}z_{it}$ is zero means that in the Portuguese case the dependence of banks on deposits does not vary with the bank liquidity ratio.[17] On the other hand, it turns out that the coefficient of the loans interest rate is lower for illiquid banks[18] (as the coefficient of $l_t z_{it}$ is positive) and this means that the supply curve is flatter. This reduces the importance of the credit channel for the illiquid banks. This apparently counterintuitive result is not surprising because the Portuguese banks displayed a huge liquidity ratio at the beginning of the sample period owing to the existence of credit ceilings and compulsory minimum ratios of public debt. Moreover, there is some evidence suggesting that it might have been the case that the banking system as a whole operated under overall excess liquidity conditions during most of the sample period. So, it may well be the case that the coefficients of $l_t z_{it}$ and of $s_t z_{it}$ appear significantly different from zero because they are capturing the effects of a potential structural break occurring in the period, as we shall see below. All in all, a sensible conclusion, in this case, seems to be that liquidity in the Portuguese banks, during the 1990s did not play the role of a shield against monetary policy shocks.

Columns (7) and (8) in table 22.1 display the two models estimated with the capitalisation ratio as the interaction variable. In this case we have the coefficient of $\ln(D/P)_{it}z_{it}$ negative and the coefficients of $l_t z_{it}$ and $s_t z_{it}$ equal to zero, and thus we can definitely conclude that the lending channel appears to be more important for less-capitalised banks.

Of course, these conclusions are valid under the implicit assumption that the models estimated in table 22.1 are stable. But if we look again at figures 22.1 and 22.2 we immediately realise that during 1996 and 1997 the credit growth rate increased relative to the deposits growth rate, coinciding with the increase in the external non-deposits funds coming from abroad. This fact raises the question of whether the conclusions above still apply once we allow for the possibility of a structural break in the last two years of the sample.

To investigate this issue we 'interacted' the variables in our basic specification (3) with a dummy variable, which is zero for the first six years of

---

[17] We note that this conclusion depends on the fact that the liquidity variable is defined as in (5). If we rather define liquidity as in (4) the coefficient of $\ln(D/P)_{it}z_{it}$ appears significantly different from zero and negative. This result shows that the way the z_{it} is defined really matters for the empirical analysis.

[18] Note that an illiquid bank is one for which the current liquidity ratio is below the sample average liquidity ratio.

data (1990:1–1995:4) and equals one for the two last years of the sample (1996:1–1997:4).

The evidence strongly suggests the existence of a structural break occurring in the two last years of the sample, as the coefficients of the variables of the model interacted with the dummy variable are in general significantly different from zero. However the most important point is that all the relevant conclusions drawn above from table 22.1 remain valid. In particular, we still conclude that the dependence of banks on deposits does not vary with the bank liquidity ratio and that the lending channel is more important for the less-capitalised banks.[19]

5   Conclusions

This chapter investigates the existence of a bank-lending channel using quarterly data on the Portuguese banks for the period 1990–7.

In contrast to previous approaches which basically resort to (dynamic) reduced form equations for bank credit with variables in differences, this chapter proposes an alternative approach by estimating directly a loan supply schedule with variables in levels, thereby exploring recent cointegration results for non-stationary panel data.

We conclude for the existence of a bank-lending channel in Portuguese data and that the importance of this channel is larger for the less-capitalised banks. Size as well as liquidity do not appear to be relevant bank characteristics to determine the importance of the bank-lending channel.

[19] For a full discussion of the results see Farinha and Marques (2001).

23 Transmission of monetary policy shocks in Finland: evidence from bank-level data on loans

J. Topi and J. Vilmunen

1 Introduction

In this chapter we show evidence that bears on the existence of the credit channel of monetary policy in Finland.[1] We estimate reduced form dynamic equations for bank loans that were initially proposed by Kashyap and Stein (1995), using a panel of Finnish banks. A more detailed analysis of the issues can be found in Topi and Vilmunen (2001).

A number of studies have addressed the relationship between financial structure and economic performance in Finland (Brunila, 1994; Honkapohja and Koskela, 1999; Kajanoja, 1995; Kinnunen and Vihriälä 1999; Mörttinen 2000; Saarenheimo, 1995; Vihriälä, 1997; Vilmunen 2002). However, none of these focuses specifically on identifying the effects of monetary policy on bank-lending supply.[2] Our contribution is to test the existence of the bank-lending channel in Finland. More precisely, we estimate the response of individual bank loans to monetary policy shocks and we use the cross-sectional differences between banks to test whether this response depends significantly on the size, liquidity and capitalisation of banks.

The rest of the chapter is structured as follows. Section 2 gives a brief account of the economic development prior to the onset of the banking crisis in early 1990s and reviews the post-crisis – in-sample – evolution of the Finnish banking sector. It also presents the data and informs the reader about estimation method used in the empirical analysis. Section 3 presents the estimation results and section 4 draws some conclusions.

We would like to thank Luigi Guiso for helpful discussions and feedback. Also we are very grateful to Ignazio Angeloni, Anil Kashyap and Benoît Mojon for their comments and suggestions.
[1] For surveys, see, e.g., Cecchetti (2001) and Trautwein (2000).
[2] Vihriälä (1997) focuses on the behaviour of the Finnish savings banks during the credit cycle, while Mörttinen (2000), coming closest to our chapter, seeks evidence on the credit channel using a panel of large Finnish firms. Vilmunen (2002), using essentially the same data as Mörttinen (2000), explores the relationship between firms' investment behaviour and financial structure.

Tables summarising the data as well as the estimation results are relegated to an appendix.

2   Financial markets in Finland

Before going into the details of the econometric analysis of the behaviour of bank lending, we will briefly discuss some of the most important features of the financial markets in Finland, with a focus on the evolution of the markets over the sample period – i.e. the post-crisis period of the latter half of the 1990s. The characteristics of the financial system are important from the point of view of analysing the distributional effects on monetary policy in Finland.

Financial markets were poorly developed and tightly regulated untill about 1986–87.[3] At that time most of the controls on capital imports were lifted. Also, the cap on average lending rate was abolished (summer 1986). An interbank money market was created in early 1987 as the Bank of Finland started to use certificate of deposits (CDs) in its intervention operations in the interbank market. Thereafter, during the latter half of the 1980s, the evolution of the financial markets in Finland speeded up. Most notably, disintermediation at an increasing rate, greatly assisted by the buoyant real economy and rapid developments in the stock market contributed to the weakening of the role of banks in the financial markets, which, so far, had been so dominant. The role of the stock market, in particular, continued to increase throughout the 1990s, and by the end of the decade it was the most important source of finance for firms and companies.[4]

In 1991–2 the real economy plummeted, after being hit by a combination of adverse external shocks.[5] At the onset of the recession in late 1991 and collapse of the fixed exchange rate regime in late 1992, Finnish banks experienced growing liquidity and solvency problems.[6] A major commercial bank (Skopbank), which also functioned as a 'central bank' for some

---

[3] For a survey of the evolution of the financial markets in Finland, see Mörttinen and Virolainen (2002), and for an account of the evolution of the structure of credit and other financial institutions in Finland from 1996 to 2001, see Alhonsuo and Pesola (2002).

[4] Mörttinen and Virolainen (2002).

[5] On top of the cyclical downturn in 1990, there was a collapse in the trade with the former Soviet Union. The subsequent recession was very deep; in 1991–3 output (and private consumption) losses amounted to 13 per cent and unemployment quintupled from around 4 per cent in 1991 to 20 per cent in 1993. For an assessment of the crisis and economic policy see, e.g., Bordes, Currie and Söderström (1993)

[6] Banks saw debt service difficulties mounting, an ever-increasing share of their outstanding credits becoming non-performing as well as the number of bankruptcies multiplying. The number of bankruptcies doubled during the 1990–2 period are remained persistently high till 1995 (Kinnunen and Vihriälä, 1999).

of the savings banks, failed in the autumn of 1991 and was subsequently taken over by the Bank of Finland. The government started to intervene more heavily, initially in the form of establishing asset management companies to manage insolvent banks. Later it provided a guarantee that despite the crisis the banks could continue to honour their commitments. More specifically, a state guarantee on the contractual commitments of the Finnish deposit banks was introduced as a result of the parliamentary resolution in early 1993, which was rescinded only in December 1998.[7] In addition to the general guarantees the government also provided banks with capital support. The basic idea underlying these support measures was to prevent a generalised credit crunch emerging from the difficulties in the banking sector. In total the bank support commitments[8] amounted to about 16 per cent of GDP (FIM 80 billion or €16 billion).

The Finnish banking market is characterised by the existence of both a small number of dominant players and a large number of small (local) banks.[9] The post-crisis recovery of the Finnish economy has been associated with restructuring of the financial sector in general and the banking sector in particular. Currently the number of major players in the banking sector has gone down to three (Nordea, the OKO Bank Group with local cooperative banks and Sampo), with a combined market share of about 80 per cent.[10] Also as a result of the post-crisis restructuring, the Finnish banking sector is nowadays more international. For example, the biggest bank, Nordea, is owned by a holding company Nordea, which is registered in Sweden. On the other hand, the structure of the banking sector has in recent years also been characterised by the emergence of financial conglomeration.[11] Consequently, it is increasingly more difficult to draw the line between traditional deposit banking and other services provided by these new institutions.

The ratio of total bank assets to GDP was, in 2001, approximately 120 per cent, up from 100 per cent a year earlier, and in any case much lower than the euro area average of 260 per cent. One reason for such a low

---

[7] The Finnish deposit insurance scheme was revised at the start of 1998. Depositors' claims in the new scheme are protected by means of a new deposit guarantee fund. Instead of the previous full protection, there is now an upper limit – FIM 150 000 or €25 000 – on the guarantee per depositor per bank (see e.g. Valori and Vesala, 1998).

[8] Include capital injections to asset management companies.

[9] For more information on the size distribution of banks, see table 23A.2 in the appendix.

[10] The Herfindahl concentration index for the Finnish banking sector for the year 2000 is 0.208. It is interesting to note that Nordea's contribution to this index value is about 83.6 per cent (0.174 of 0.208). See chapter 14 for a comparison among some of the European countries.

[11] Or by the emergence of bank assurance, since the merger of the insurance company Sampo and Leonia bank was the impetus for the considerations concerning financial conglomeration (e.g. Alhonsuo and Pesola, 2002).

ratio seems to be that the rate of indebtedness of firms and households in Finland is, by international standards, low.[12]

3   The data

Our quarterly data on Finnish banks as well as on inflation, GDP growth and monetary policy indicator covers the period from the beginning of 1995 to the end of 2000. The maximum length of an individual time series is thus 24 whereas the cross-sections of the panel include around 340 banks. Hence, the full capacity of the panel exceeds 8,200, but since ours is an unbalanced panel, the effective number of observations is less. Information on nine banks altogether was removed from the panel.[13] More precisely, six of the nine banks that were removed visited the sample for only one year. No information was available on two banks and, finally, for one of the banks the panel contained information only from 1998:4. Furthermore, since some of the individual time series contain observations that were extreme, a rule for purging the data for these extreme values was adopted. Specifically, all cross-section observations of loan growth rates (log differences of bank loans) that were located in the lower or upper 1 per cent tail of the distribution were excluded in the estimations. All these measures and characteristics of the data amount to having, effectively, 5,500–5,600 observations in the estimations.

All of the individual cooperative banks belonging to the OKO Bank Group (roughly 240 banks) consequently entered our panel of banks as different, independent entities. These cooperative banks act as independent entities in the credit market, although they have been in closer cooperation since 1997 when a reorganisation of the group was carried out. At that time, some of the cooperative banks (about forty) rejected the proposed form of cooperation in the OKO Bank Group and established another group for cooperation.[14]

From 1995:1 to 1998:4 we use quarterly changes in the Bank of Finland tender rate as the monetary policy indicator, which is thereafter extended by quarterly changes in the ECB's main refinancing rate. Furthermore, the data are not seasonally adjusted, so three seasonal dummies and a constant are also included. Table 23.2 summarises the main features of our sample on Finnish banks. Clearly, the size distribution of banks,

---

[12] The debt:GDP ratio was around 45 per cent and 30 per cent for firms and households, respectively, in 2000 (Mörttinen and Virolainen, 2002). As such, 'loans to euro area residents' is the largest component in banks' balance sheets.

[13] The principal reasons for purging the panel this way were exit, too short time series and, simply, lack of information.

[14] Estimation results on data without the OKO Bank Group or on data with a consolidated OKO Bank Group are very similar to the ones reported in this chapter.

Table 23.1 Loan equations: long-run coefficients, Finland[a]

Dependent variable: quarterly growth rate of bank lending	Lending I (1)	Lending II: size (2)	Lending II: liquidity (3)	Lending II: capitalisation (4)
Sum of AR coefficients	0.1950**	0.0405	0.1635**	0.1495**
Sum of coeffs on:				
Monetary policy (MP)	−4.477***	−4.290***	−4.509***	−4.315***
Real GDP growth	0.7215**	0.6666**	0.7247**	0.6747**
GDP inflation	1.0056***	0.8759**	1.015**	0.9299**
Bank characteristics				
Size		−0.0584 ***		
Liquidity			0.0495***	
Capitalisation				0.2007**
Bank Char MP*				
Size		0.0895		
Liquidity			4.443*	
Capitalisation				10.14*
Policy dummy D98	0.0020 ***	0.0023***	0.0024***	0.0024***
Wald (joint) $\chi 2(25)$ (*p*-value)	1094 (*0.000*)***	1102 (*0.000*)***	1135 (*0.000*)***	1162 (*0.000*)***
Sargan $\chi 2(221)$ (*p*-value)	244.6 (*0.132*)	246.9 (*0.076*)*	243.9 (*0.139*)	246.6 (*0.114*)
AR(1) N(0,1) (*p*-value)	−10.93 (*0.000*)***	−10.71 (*0.000*)***	−10.85 (*0.000*)***	−10.86 (*0.000*)***
AR(2) N(0,1) (*p*-value)	−0.6394 (*0.523*)	−0.6761 (*0.499*)	−0.6953 (*0.487*)	−0.7109 (*0.477*)

[a] The estimated model is

$$\Delta \log L_{it} = a_{it} + \sum_{k=1}^{3} b_k \Delta \log L_{i(t-k)} + \sum_{k=1}^{4} c_k \Delta r_{t-k} + \gamma z x_{i(t+1)} + \sum_{k=1}^{4} g_{jk} [\Delta r_{t-k} - r_{i(t-1)}] + \sum_{k=1}^{4} g_{2k} \Delta \log(GDP_{t-k}) + \sum_{k=1}^{4} g_{3k} inf_{t-k} + D_t + \varepsilon_{it}$$

where L, r, GDP and $infl$ denote, respectively, the stock of bank loans, Bank of Finland tender rate (ECB's main refinancing rate), real GDP and inflation. Δ stands for quarterly difference, D signifies deterministic regressors, i.e. seasonal dummies as well as the policy dummy D98. x_i is the cross-sectionally demeaned bank-specific variable (size, liquidity and capitalisation). The model permits individual fixed effects, captured by the bank-specific intercept terms a_i. Column (1) 'Lending I' present the estimation results for the 'benchmark' model, i.e. that without the bank-specific variables ($\gamma_z = 0$ for all z). Columns (2)–(4) 'Lending II', introduce a bank characteristic into the benchmark model, starting from size (Column (2)), which is then replaced by liquidity (Column (3)), which, in turn, is finally replaced by capitalisation (Column (4)). The table gives us the sum of the coefficients of each explanatory variable together with the sum of the AR coefficients.

*, ** and *** significant at the 10%, 5% and 1% level.

as measured by total assets, is very skewed. Also, note that while the share of liquid assets in total assets displays a hump-shaped time profile during the sample period, the share of capital in total assets grew, at a rate of about 10 per cent per year.

4   The effects of monetary policy on bank lending

In this section we review the estimation results of our model, which is a version of the baseline regression model given in (10) in chapter 14 of this volume. Consequently, the growth rate of loans is regressed on an indicator of monetary policy on its interaction with bank size, liquidity and capitalisation. This regression also includes inflation and the growth rate of aggregate real GDP as control variables. More importantly, a step dummy enters our version of the baseline model to capture the effects of the government's support measures, discussed above, on the growth rate of bank lending.[15] Table 23.1 presents a summary of the estimation results. Only estimated long-run effects – sum of the various estimated coefficients – are reported in table 23.1.[16]

The second column of table 23.1 reports the parameter estimates of a model without the bank characteristics. This serves as a useful starting point for the subsequent analysis, where we present the results from estimating more complex models. The last three columns of table 23.1 present the estimation results of the model with bank characteristics.[17]

As for the specifications, the robust autocorrelation tests, AR(1) and AR(2) tests, respectively,[18] do not provide evidence to suggest that the assumption of serially uncorrelated errors in the equation for the growth rate of bank loans is inappropriate in the present context. The Sargan tests generally agree with this conclusion, given that the p-value for the observed test statistics is marginal in only one case.[19]

Most of the estimated coefficients appear reasonable, in terms of both size and sign. In particular, loan growth is not very persistent, implying that shocks to banks' loan growth die out rapidly. Furthermore, estimated (long-run) effects of monetary policy are of the expected negative sign

---

[15] Formally, the step dummy, D98, is defined as D98 = 1, for 1995.1 $\leq t \leq$ 1998.4, and D98 = 0, for t $\geq$ 1999.1.

[16] Here we present the two-step GMM estimates using the Arellano–Bond (1991) procedure in PcGive 10.0. See Topi and Vilmunen (2001) for the full set of estimation results.

[17] See the footnote to table 23.1 for further details. The estimated constant and centred seasonal dummies are not reported in table 23.1. The constant did not enter significantly, whereas some of seasonal dummies did.

[18] The famous m_1 and m_2 tests of Arellano and Bond (1991).

[19] I.e. $p = 0.076$ in the regression with bank size included.

Table 23.2 *Structure of the Finnish banking system, 1995–2000[a]*

	Descriptive statistics on the Finnish banking sector					
	1995	1996	1997	1998	1999	2000
Obs.	347	346	343	340	337	333
Loans						
Mean	143,153	139,656	142,384	160,149	173,236	195,983
Median	21,324	22,113	22,195	23,509	26,315	27,645
P25	11,994	12,257	12,683	13,080	14,788	15,937
P75	39,147	40,477	41,509	45,611	50,652	54,381
Max	23,550,647	22,313,706	22,195,902	24,949,840	26,228,131	28,755,218
Min	651	608	438	537	431	390
Std dev.	1,324,520	1,262,960	1,273,644	1,444,393	1,517,680	1,742,364
Deposits						
Mean	149,237	145,503	152,235	156,222	165,937	172,668
Median	27,789	27,568	28,738	29,896	31,240	33,361
P25	16,154	16,081	17,378	18,153	18,550	19,632
P75	49,639	50,805	53,357	56,791	59,711	61,494
Max	22,609,479	21,314,093	22,325,488	22,909,110	23,413,413	25,054,403
Min	1,603	1,436	1,933	1,803	1,689	0
Std dev.	1,297,410	1,227,823	1,288,682	1,323,902	1,369,998	1,442,910
Total assets						
Mean	289,571	285,769	306,031	307,705	338,240	380,274
Median	34,606	34,591	36,471	37,921	39,620	42,453
P25	20,869	21,624	22,327	22,524	23,694	25,236
P75	62,456	62,735	66,905	68,388	72,920	77,902
Max	45,715,954	44,571,638	49,195,440	50,582,984	52,471,370	61,141,488
Min	1,861	1,657	2,181	2,036	1,908	1,916
Std dev.	2,684,095	2,642,598	2,906,583	2,941,895	3,132,433	3,630,006
Liquid assets/total assets						
Mean	0.111	0.132	0.132	0.123	0.104	0.087
Median	0.096	0.118	0.125	0.111	0.090	0.068
P25	0.055	0.056	0.054	0.046	0.035	0.030
P75	0.158	0.190	0.186	0.180	0.152	0.125
Max	0.418	0.504	0.803	0.458	0.421	0.683
Min	0.004	0.003	0.000	0.005	0.000	0.000
Std dev.	0.077	0.094	0.095	0.089	0.080	0.076
Capital/total assets						
Mean	0.066	0.075	0.085	0.091	0.098	0.107
Median	0.062	0.072	0.081	0.087	0.094	0.103
P25	0.049	0.053	0.059	0.063	0.067	0.076
P75	0.080	0.095	0.110	0.114	0.120	0.127
Max	0.138	0.156	0.177	0.437	0.639	0.719
Min	0.026	0.029	0.003	0.021	0.028	0.030
Std dev.	0.021	0.027	0.032	0.038	0.048	0.055

Notes: [a] Observations: the number of banks with loans reported; End-of-year observations; Loans, deposits and total assets in thousand Euros.

as well as significantly different from zero. A 1-percentage point increase in the Bank of Finland tender rate reduces the growth rate of loans approximately by $5\frac{1}{2}$ percentage points.[20]

The dummy for the state guarantee of banks' (deposit and non-deposit) commitments, D98, enters very significantly. It also has the expected positive sign, implying that the policy measures taken to counteract the adverse effects of the crisis on banks' loan supply appear to have been successful. More specifically, these measures were effective in preventing, on their part, bank lending from falling further during the years immediately after the onset of the banking crisis in early 1990s.

The interaction between monetary policy and bank size does not enter the model significantly, as can be readily seen from column (2) of table 23.1 ('Size'). Here 'bank size' is defined in terms of a bank's assets. This is clearly in contrast to, for example, the results by Kashyap and Stein (1995) on the US data. Since the size variable has the well-favoured interpretation of being a proxy for the information frictions faced by different banks, our results suggest that heterogeneity in the implied information costs does not induce differences in banks' lending response to monetary policy shocks. Hence, small banks do not respond more strongly to changes in monetary policy. However, given that the coefficient is correctly signed, we can speculate that the information costs may not be irrelevant, but that our data is just too noisy for us to be able to pick significant differential effects.

The estimated (long-run) coefficients on the interaction of monetary policy shocks with liquidity and capitalisation in columns (3) and (4) ('Liquidity' and 'Capitalisation') are borderline significant. 'Liquidity' is here measured in terms the sum of cash, short-term interbank deposits and government bonds, while 'capitalisation' is defined in terms of each bank's equity–asset ratio. Anyway, the conclusion is that heterogeneity in terms of liquidity and capitalisation may thus not be irrelevant for policy transmission, but the signal of their potential importance in our sample is relatively weak.

Finally, as for the estimated *linear* effects of the bank-specific variables, they are also correctly signed. Liquidity and capitalisation both support stronger loan growth, whereas the bank size impinges negatively on banks'

---

[20] The implied long-run elasticity of loan growth w.r.t. GDP growth is below one across the specifications, while it exceeds one w.r.t. inflation. A unit long-run inflation elasticity would mean that our model reduces to a model for the growth rate of real credit, whereas a unit elasticity w.r.t. both GDP growth and inflation implies a model for the change in the (inverse of the) credit velocity L/PY. The specification tests, however, decisively rejected these restrictions on the model. The results are available from the authors upon request.

loan growth. Consequently, more-liquid and better-capitalised bank tend to grow faster than the less-liquid and poorly capitalised ones. Also, since bank size affects the growth rate of bank loans negatively, we can conclude that the market for bank loans in Finland does not have a tendency to get monopolised.

Across the board, changes in monetary policy have a relatively strong effect on banks' loan supply. However, the size of the response of banks to monetary policy shocks is not related to the size of banks and is only weakly related to the banks liquidity and rate of capitalisation.

5   Summary and discussion

This chapter investigates the existence of a bank-lending channel for monetary policy transmission in Finland using a panel of quarterly observations on loans of individual banks from 1995 to 2000. Our results indicate that after a contractionary monetary policy shock, bank lending falls. A reduction in liquidity as well as a lower rate of capitalisation similarly implies that the growth rate of bank loans tends to fall. These direct, linear effects of banks' liquidity and capitalisation on banks' loan growth are consistently positive and statistically significant. On the other hand, bank size is estimated to have a significantly negative effect on banks' loan growth, so that the loan stock of smaller banks is growing more rapidly than that of larger banks.

When it comes to comparing the effects of contractionary monetary policy shocks on different kinds of banks, we find statistically weak and marginal evidence in favour of heterogeneity in the banks' response to these shocks. There is a weaker effect of monetary policy shocks on more-liquid and better-capitalised banks, whereas no differential response can be identified among banks of different size. Consequently, since size is the proxy for informational frictions, we do not find evidence indicating that small banks, simply because they face higher informational costs, tend to respond more strongly to monetary tightening.

Finally, and importantly, we find evidence that the support measures introduced by the government in early 1993 to prevent a generalised credit crunch were effective. More precisely, the dummy for parliamentary guarantee on banks' deposit and non-deposit commitments, taking a value 1 while effective from early 1993 to late 1998 and 0 thereafter, enters the model significantly. These measures seem to have prevented, bank lending from falling further in the difficult years after the onset of the banking crisis in the early 1990s.

Part 4

Monetary policy in the euro area: summary
and discussion of the main findings

24 Monetary policy transmission in the euro area: where do we stand?

I. Angeloni, A. K Kashyap, B. Mojon and D. Terlizzese

1 Introduction

This chapter selectively brings together the main findings presented in the preceding ones to offer a characterisation of the monetary policy transmission in the euro area.

We organise our overview of the macro and micro evidence around one main question, namely, whether *monetary policy transmission in the euro area can broadly be described as taking place through the classical interest rate channel (IRC)*. By 'IRC' we mean the response of aggregate demand components, GDP and prices to the change in the policy controlled interest rate that would take place if there were no capital market imperfections.[1] Equivalently, the question we ask is whether accounting for such imperfections is necessary to understand the main features of monetary transmission in the euro area.

We focus on this specific 'null hypothesis' for several reasons. First, since the IRC is the conventional way in which monetary policy is presumed to operate in a large, fairly closed economy with a developed financial system, it is logical to ask whether it can explain the facts before looking at alternatives. Second, the commonly accepted – if not always fully accurate – picture of the euro area financial market is one in which banks play a prominent role. To check whether this prominence has implications for the transmission mechanism it is methodologically sound to start with a working assumption that denies any such implication. Third, much of the concern that has been voiced about the potentially asymmetric effects of the single monetary policy appears to be grounded in

Anil Kashyap thanks the ECB, the Houblon Norman Fund and the National Science Foundation (through a grant administered by the National Bureau of Economic Research) for financial support. We thank A. Dieppe, M. Ehrmann and L. Monteforte for helping us assemble some of the data and S. Sommaggio for editing the text.

[1] The IRC would be the only channel through which monetary policy would affect aggregate spending in a closed economy where: (1) the central bank was able to influence the term structure of market real interest rates; and (2) all agents were able to borrow and lend at those rates. In this world, there would be no balance sheet or lending channel.

observed asymmetries in the financial structure of firms or banks, as well as in their vulnerability to informational problems. These features would be clearly of little relevance if the IRC were to account for the bulk of the transmission mechanism. Finally, taking IRC dominance as the null hypothesis provides a disciplined way to look for alternative explanations. Highlighting the places where the interest rate effects do not appear to be the whole story helps identify where other channels (such as balance sheet, liquidity constraints, bank credit supply, and the like) may be important. This in turn can help guide the measurement and monitoring of the most relevant information for policymakers.

In reaching our assessment about the channels of transmission, we place relatively little weight on the exchange rate channel. One reason for doing so is that we expect domestic channels of monetary policy transmission to become more important for the euro area economy (which is relatively closed to international trade) than was previously true for the member countries. In addition, estimates of the exchange rate channel for the period prior to the euro should be more affected by the regime shift of EMU than estimates of domestic channels. Finally, the empirical evidence on the effects of monetary policy on exchange rates is very mixed: the response of exchange rates to monetary policy is notoriously hard to predict. For all these reasons, we will mainly focus on domestic channels in our analysis.

The chapter is organised into six further sections. In section 2 we briefly explain the logic underlying our analysis, focusing in particular on how we intend to bring the various pieces of empirical evidence to bear on the issue.

Section 3 summarises, as a background, the overall response to a monetary policy shift of both prices and quantities for the euro area as a whole. This section draws upon evidence from both Vector Autoregressive (VAR) models and structural euro area models and includes some comparisons between the euro area and the USA

The macro country-level evidence is sketched in section 4, including both results from VARs and from structural econometric models. We first present results concerning the potency of monetary policy across countries. We then check whether the interest-sensitive components of GDP – those components of aggregate demand that are traditionally taken to be most subject to intertemporal substitution effects (fixed investment and, in principle, durable consumption) – appear to be able to account for the bulk of the GDP response.

Section 5 introduces the microeconomic evidence on non-financial firms' behaviour. These data are used to determine whether a prominent role in the transmission of interest-sensitive components is also matched by a prominent role of the interest rate (or of the cost of capital) in driving the movements of those components.

Section 6 looks for evidence on banks' lending that would be consistent with non-interest channels of monetary transmission, to complement the assessment so far reached concerning the prominence of the IRC.

Section 7 contains our summary of the analysis. We first summarise our understanding of how policy effects appear to be transmitted in each euro area country, before reviewing the main findings for the overall euro area.

2   Combining disparate pieces of evidence

Ideally, one would like to test for the dominance of the IRC in a sharp statistical sense, using a single encompassing model with the appropriate data. Unfortunately, a spate of structural changes (most recently, the introduction of the euro) and well-known data limitations preclude this for the euro area. Hence we need to draw upon rather disparate pieces of evidence, trying to make them comparable in order to discover similarities and to corroborate findings, but eventually we will need to use our judgement in deciding what they tell us. Our 'testing strategy' thus yields a suggested interpretation of the empirical results; alternative interpretations may be possible, and we will flag them when appropriate.

The intuition for our approach is relatively simple. We will try to build up the case in favour of our 'null hypothesis' that the IRC is the dominant channel of monetary transmission by checking whether we find evidence of conditions that should be true, or at least probable, if our null were true; the more of these conditions we are able to verify, and the more robust is the evidence in their favour – being confirmed by different approaches and data sets – the more confident we will be about our 'null'.[2]

In particular, we will start checking whether interest-sensitive spending categories (which we will take to be represented by investment)[3] account for the bulk of the spending changes that occur after a shift in

---

[2] This corresponds to one of the main 'patterns of plausible inference' expounded by Polya (1954): 'if a certain circumstance is more credible with a certain conjecture than without it, the proof of that circumstance can only enhance the credibility of that conjecture.' This is essentially an application of Bayes' threorem.

[3] Theory suggests that interest rates should influence other spending categories besides investment, notably durable consumption and inventory investment. Unfortunately, the lack of homogeneous data for many euro area countries prevents a fully satisfactory statistical measurement of these categories. Durable consumption is measured separately only in Italy, France and Finland. Likewise, in all countries but France and the Netherlands inventory investment is computed as a residual in the national income and product accounts. Thus, there is little one can do to systematically study how interest rate changes influence these variables. See Angeloni *et al.* (2003) for details.

monetary policy. This is a natural question to ask when assessing the role of the IRC. Plainly, if the IRC is important we should see important movements of those components of the expenditure that are traditionally taken to be more interest-sensitive. However, it is also a question whose discriminatory power is rather weak. First, interest-sensitive spending might move responding to channels different from the IRC. Second, even non-interest-sensitive spending might move in reaction to changes of the interest-sensitive components. Finally, the dichotomy between interest-sensitive and non-interest-sensitive is not as sharp as the economy textbooks would suggest. For all these reasons we see the analysis of the composition of the output response to a monetary policy shift as a suggestive first step in analysing the role that is played by the IRC.

We will then move on to ask a few more specific questions, using micro data on firms and banks. The first of these tries to address one of the difficulties in interpreting the composition of the output response mentioned above. We will ask whether there is evidence that the spending shifts appear to be due *directly* to changes in interest rates, not just *indirectly* because other determinants of such spending categories are affected by policy. We will also ask, in connection with the possible role of financial factors, whether any sub-sets of firms where one might think liquidity problems should be more acute show stronger sensitivities of investment to liquidity. A further kind of question moves from the idea that if financial frictions are important it can be expected that banks play a role in amplifying and transmitting their effect throughout the economy. We will therefore also ask whether there is evidence of a strong role of bank loan-supply shifts in amplifying the effects of interest rates.

The evidence we compile – first, by asking whether the response of interest-sensitive components of spending account for the bulk of observed changes in aggregate demand; second, by checking whether such response can be explained, to a sufficiently large extent, by the direct effect of interest rate changes on investment; third, by checking for the presence of cash-flow or liquidity effects on investment and for independent evidence regarding banks' behaviour following changes in monetary policy – allows us to pass judgement about the nature of the transmission mechanism in the various countries and in the euro area as a whole.

3   Monetary transmission to the aggregate euro area

As a first step we present, in this section, some results concerning the aggregate effects of monetary policy on the euro area as a whole. These results provide useful background for the more disaggregated analyses to follow. All estimates are assembled from other chapters of this volume, which should be consulted for more detail.

3.1   Stylised facts on the euro area business cycle

Agresti and Mojon (chapter 1 in this volume) provide descriptive statistics that illustrate the main time-series properties of the euro area data, and also report comparative results for the USA.[4] All together these statistics constitute the first complete, albeit simple and preliminary, investigation of how the aggregate euro area cycle compares with the USA. This comparison is particularly relevant, for at least two reasons. First, the euro area economy shares certain broad structural features with the USA (particularly: size, degree of openness, composition of output by sector), which make the comparison natural from the viewpoint of the transmission mechanism. Second, the business cycle characteristics and the transmission of monetary policy in the USA are well documented. This makes the comparison with the euro area potentially interesting and fruitful.

Tables 1.3 and 1.4 (pp. 28 and 29) present a set of descriptive statistics for the (de-trended) euro area data along with similar statistics for the USA, which serve as a benchmark. The euro area data are available only from 1970 onwards, so for comparison purposes we show findings for both regions from this date through 2000 – when presenting further results we take advantage of earlier US data where available.

Three main features of these results stand out. First, the absolute level of the volatility of GDP in the euro area is lower than in the USA. Second, if measured relative to GDP, the volatility of the main domestic demand components appears to be broadly similar in the two economies; of relevance for our later findings is the fact that the relative volatilities of consumption and income are similar in both currency areas. This does not appear to be true for inflation (as measured by consumer price indices), whose volatility appears to be much lower in the euro area (both absolutely and relative to GDP). Third, the dynamic cross- and autocorrelations between the main macro variables display many striking similarities and some interesting differences across the two economies. The degree of persistence of the GDP and price series, as well as the lead–lag patterns of GDP components, interest rates and credit aggregates with respect to GDP are remarkably similar.

A few differences between the euro area and the USA are worth stressing. First, stock prices appear to be strongly positively correlated with

---

[4] Similar results for the UK are presented in chapter 6 of this volume.

future output in the USA, contrary to what is found for the euro area. This could result from the small size of the stock market in continental Europe over most of the sample period. Second, bank lending is also more strongly correlated with GDP in the USA than in Europe, which could be due to the prevalence of relationship lending in Europe. Third, the correlation between past GDP and current inflation tends to be lower in the euro area; this could reflect stronger rigidity in the wage–price formation process in the euro area. Finally, we also note some differences for which we don't necessarily have any, even tentative, interpretations. For example, the sign of the correlation between current inflation and future GDP growth quickly becomes negative in the USA, while it remains positive in the euro area; and M1 seems a better leading indicator of output in the euro area than in the USA.

3.2   VAR *estimates of the effects of monetary policy*

A set of basic VAR models for the euro area are estimated by Peersman and Smets (chapter 2 in this volume). In their models, an average short-term interest rate for the euro area is used as a proxy of the area-wide stance of monetary policy over the period. The main results can be seen in figure 2.1. There, the impulse responses from two different models of the euro area (one without and one with M3 as an endogenous variable) and one model for the USA (that uses an identification scheme quite similar to that of Christiano, Eichenbaum and Evans, 1999) are compared.

In both economies, the interest rate increase reduces output for a few quarters; the recovery starts within roughly one and a half years. Both in the USA and in the euro area, the price level gradually falls after a monetary tightening. The decline is not significant in either region for several quarters, but eventually the effect becomes strongly significant and permanent. The magnitudes of the responses are comparable if one corrects for the differences in the size of the initial interest rate shock. The similarity between the impulse responses in the euro area and the USA increases if one focuses on the euro area model with M3 rather than the one without it. The latter model may be more appropriate for the euro area over our sample period, in light of the prominence assigned to monetary aggregates by a number of central banks.

3.3   *Evidence from structural econometric models*

Alternative estimates of the impact of shocks to the short-term interest rate based on central banks structural econometric models are presented in table 24.1. The table compares the results for the euro area presented

Table 24.1 *Effects on the euro area and the USA of monetary policy shocks in structural models (deviation from baseline in%)*

| | USA | | | Euro area | | | | | |
| | FRB-US[a] | | | NCBs | | | AWM | | |
Models Horizon in years	1	2	3	1	2	3	1	2	3
Short-term rate	1.00	1.00	0.00	1.00	1.00	0.00	1.00	1.00	0.00
Long-term rate	0.16	0.06	0.00	0.16	0.06	0.00	0.16	0.06	0.00
Effective exchange rate	1.60	0.63	0.00	1.60	0.63	0.00	1.60	0.63	0.00
CPI	−0.07	−0.41	−1.01	−0.09	−0.21	−0.31	−0.15	−0.30	−0.38
GDP	−0.35	−1.28	−1.37	−0.22	−0.38	−0.31	−0.34	−0.71	−0.71
Consumption	−0.37	−1.35	−1.44	−0.12	−0.23	−0.19	−0.27	−0.58	−0.54
Contribution to GDP[b]	*0.70*	*0.70*	*0.69*	*0.33*	*0.36*	*0.37*	*0.48*	*0.49*	*0.46*
Investment	−0.31	−1.79	−3.16	−0.34	−1.04	−1.22	−0.81	−2.37	−2.96
Contribution to GDP	*0.13*	*0.21*	*0.35*	*0.31*	*0.55*	*0.79*	*0.48*	*0.67*	*0.83*

Notes: [a] FRB Federal Reserve Board.
[b] Contribution to GDP: see note to table 24.3 (p. 395).
Sources: Euro area, van Els *et al.* (2001); USA, private correspondance with Flint Brayton.

in van Els *et al.* (chapter 5 in this volume), which are based on simulations of the Area Wide Model (AWM) of Fagan, Henry and Mestre (2001) and of the national central banks' macroeconometric models (NCBs), with those for the USA, based on simulations of the Federal Reserve Board model.[5] Table 24.1 shows the percentage deviations from the baseline following an exogenous change in the short-term rate (by 100 basis points for eight quarters, returning to the baseline afterwards) and associated paths for the exchange rate and the long-term interest rate, consistent with arbitrage relationships (see section 3 of chapter 5 for a discussion).

The qualitative pattern of the response of output and prices already seen in the VAR response (see Peersman and Smets, chapter 2 in this volume) is broadly confirmed by the structural model simulations, despite the differences in the models, in the profiles of the shocks and in the methodological nature of the exercise. Specifically, in both economies one observes a relatively quick and strong output response whereas the price response is muted.[6]

[5] We are grateful to Flint Brayton at the Federal Reserve Board for providing us with these simulations.
[6] See also table 2 of Angeloni *et al.* (2003) and van Els *et al.* (2002) for comparisons of monetary policy shocks simulations with structural models and VARs.

Concerning the breakdown of the GDP response, we study the ratios between the derivatives with respect to the interest rate of investment and consumption, on the one hand, and GDP on the other. Equivalently, this statistic can be described as the total dollar (euro) change in investment (or consumption) following a shift in monetary policy relative to the total dollar (euro) change in GDP. We refer to this measure as the *contribution* of investment (or consumption) to the overall GDP change. The idea is that these contributions can more easily be compared across models and countries, thus sidestepping the problems of comparability among VARs and structural models. This is because, since we are comparing how much one variable moves relative to another following a policy shift, the nature of the shock moving both should be less relevant. The same intuition suggests that any differences in policy shocks across countries should also be less influential when comparing the respective contributions.

Moving to the results, we note that, in the FRB-US model, consumption is responsible for the bulk of the GDP adjustment following an interest rate shock, after both one and three years, whereas in the AWM and in the NCB models, the contributions of consumption and investment are initially balanced, and at three years the latter dominates. In other words, it seems that in the transmission of monetary policy a relatively greater role is played by consumption in the USA, and by investment in the euro area. This is consistent with the strength of wealth effects on consumer behaviour in the USA, as embodied in the FRB model[7] (see table 24.3 for the composition of the GDP response in VARs and Angeloni *et al.* (2003b) for a deeper analysis of these results, together with robustness checks).

3.4   The exchange rate channel

Before further describing the domestic channels of transmission, we briefly compare the effects of an exchange rate shock in the euro area and the USA. In chapter 5, the decomposition of the effects of monetary policy shocks showed that, up to one year, the exchange rate channel of monetary policy was the dominant mover of euro area GDP and prices. Table 24.2, which shows the percentage changes relative to the baseline following a permanent exogenous change in the nominal effective exchange rate (by 5 percent), puts this result in perspective by comparing it with what happens in the USA. This 'pure' exchange rate shock shows that, again most markedly in the short run, the euro area GDP and prices are more sensitive to changes in the exchange rate than their

---

[7] See, for example, Reifschneider, Tetlow and Williams (1999).

Table 24.2 *Effects of exchange rate-sustained shocks on the euro area and the USA (deviation from baseline in %)*

	5% NEER[a] appreciation					
Horizon in years	1			3		
	Euro area		USA	Euro area		USA
	NCBs	AWM	FRB-US[b]	NCBs	AWM	FRB-US
CPI	−0.12	−0.37	−0.07	−0.41	−1.08	−0.44
Real GDP	−0.23	−0.47	−0.05	−0.35	−1.24	−1.01
Private consumption	−0.01	−0.28	−0.04	−0.03	−1.02	−0.33
Gross fixed capital formation	−0.14	−0.49	−0.06	−0.46	−1.71	−1.40

Notes: [a] NEER stands the nominal effective exchange rate.
[b] FRB Federal Reserve Board.
Sources: NCBs: Authors' calculations based on the Eurosystem macroeconometric models simulations presented in van Els *et al.* (chapter 5 in this volume); AWM: ECB area-wide model calculations; FRB-US model calculations were kindly provided to us by Flint Brayton at the Federal Reserve Board.

US counterparts. While these responses to the exchange rate obviously need to be factored in the evaluation of the monetary policy stance, it is not obvious what is the appropriate way to do so nor that, in practice, the exchange rate channel is large in the transmission of monetary policy. The path of the exchange rate in the simulation designed in chapter 5 and table 24.2 is *assumed* to respect an uncovered interest rate parity (UIP) condition. However, as discussed in the introduction, the strong link between interest rates and exchange rates that are assumed in these models, and that are central to establishing the importance of the exchange rate channel in the transmission mechanism, cannot be taken for granted.

3.5   Overall summary of the euro aggregate evidence

We read the evidence in this section as suggesting three broad conclusions. First, consumption, investment and GDP in the euro area display broadly similar time-series characteristics over the business cycle as the corresponding series for the USA. The dynamic cross-correlation among key demand components is remarkably similar.

Second, VAR and structural model analyses for the euro area confirm plausible monetary policy effects on output and prices. In the VARs, an unexpected increase in the short-term interest rate temporarily reduces output, with the peak effects occurring after roughly one year. Prices respond more slowly, hardly moving during the first year and then falling gradually over the next few years. Again, these VAR properties are similar to those reported for the USA. The structural models of the USA and the euro area broadly confirm this picture.

Third, there are two interesting differences between the euro area and the USA. Changes in the exchange rates have, in the short run, larger effects on GDP and prices in the euro area. The composition of the GDP response to a monetary policy shock appears to be different between the two areas. In the USA, much of the output adjustment appears to be due to changes in consumption, whereas in the euro area investment changes are more important. We will see in section 4 that this finding is confirmed in a VAR-based analysis.

4   Macroeconomic evidence on monetary transmission in individual euro area countries

We move on, in this section, to explore the importance of the IRC using country-level data. The basic information we use on the responses of prices (as measured by the rate of CPI inflation), GDP and investment to a monetary policy changes is obtained with VAR models by Mojon and Peersman (chapter 3 in this volume) and with structural models by van Els *et al.* (chapter 5 in this volume).

We first briefly recall, in parallel with what we did in section 3, the pattern of GDP and price responses for the various countries. We must stress that, given the methodological differences between impulse responses from VARs and simulations from structural models, comparisons of the quantitative results across the techniques are not warranted. But qualitative comparisons are still valid and several results follow from a direct comparison of the findings in chapters 3 and 5. First, both econometric techniques suggest that a monetary tightening leads to a reduction in output and inflation in virtually all countries and in the euro area as a whole.[8] While this is not surprising, since this prediction was undoubtedly one of the things that the model builders considered in settling on their preferred specifications, it is nevertheless reassuring to observe that this presumption is confirmed by the data. A second observation, probably more informative, is that the peak response of inflation comes after the peak response in output for essentially all the estimates.

---

[8] These results are available in table 4 of Angeloni *et al.* (2003). The VAR results are also presented in figure 3.1 (for GDP and prices) and Figure 3.3 (for investment) (Mojon and Peersman, chapter 3 in this volume) while the structural model simulations are presented in figure 5.4 (van Els *et al.*, chapter 5 in this volume) for GDP and prices and van Els *et al.* (2001) for investment.

A third observation is that a close examination of the VARs reveals a few counter-intuitive results. The VAR point estimates for Austria, Greece, Ireland and the Netherlands imply that a monetary tightening is expected to raise either output or investment or both at some point in the first three years. However, once uncertainty is accounted for, these estimates are almost never significantly different from zero. We therefore put more weight on structural models for these countries in forming our judgements.

4.1   The contribution of interest-sensitive spending to monetary policy-induced GDP movements

Following the strategy briefly sketched in section 2, we now move to analyse the composition of the output response following a monetary shock, to check how much of that is attributable to interest-sensitive spending shifts. However, several practical problems arise in doing so.

One problem (alluded to earlier) is that we cannot measure all the components of spending that we expect to be interest-sensitive. At this point, all that we can consistently study is private consumption and total investment. This means that we cannot parse out the effects of changes in durable consumption expenditure from the rest of consumption. Similarly, the investment responses that we measure include the movements in government investment, but exclude shifts in inventories.

A second problem is what to do about exchange rate channel effects. As mentioned earlier, we expect this channel in the future to be less powerful than before the creation of the currency area. But we cannot deny the fact that this channel could have been important in some episodes of the 1980s and 1990s.

To address these issues we compute the investment contribution (IC) introduced in section 3.3 in two different ways, first comparing the investment response to the full response of GDP, and then comparing it to only the changes in final domestic demand (consumption plus investment).[9]

We also note that the magnitudes of the IC must be interpreted recognising that the investment response we record is a conservative estimate of the IRC effects (since durable consumption and inventory investment are omitted, and government investment is included). This is obviously more of problem for the comparisons where investment movements are

---

[9] In the case of VAR simulations, the contribution is based on the cumulated responses of GDP and investment because the interest rate shocks are temporary. In this way the interpretation is the same as given before: the total dollar (euro) change in investment (or consumption) following a shift in monetary policy relative to the total dollar (euro) change in GDP (or domestic demand).

compared to investment plus consumption, since the misattribution of the durables responses is magnified in this case.

We show results for the first three years after the shift because the bulk of the output adjustments had occurred in all the euro area countries by this time. The results are shown in table 24.3. Overall, there is a noticeable degree of correspondence between the estimates of the IC coming from the VARs (neglecting Greece, Ireland and Austria, which produce the previously mentioned counter-intuitive results) and those coming from structural models. Aside from France, in the other countries where meaningful comparisons can be made (Belgium, Germany, Finland, Italy and Spain) the VARs and structural models yield broadly similar conclusions. However, it should be noted that for a few cases, the two contribution measures are rather different. When looking at structural model, in Belgium and Germany IC is much larger when defined in terms of 'consumption plus investment', while the opposite is true in Portugal. When looking at VARs, in Italy and Spain the contributions are much larger when defined in terms of GDP.

Taking into account the measurement problems mentioned above, we view the estimated investment contributions as being relatively large in most cases. For instance, according to the national structural models, after twelve quarters, investment contributions are greater than 0.6 (relative to GDP) in nine of the twelve countries while five of the seven reliable VARs give the same reading. These same large responses are true for the weighted average response for the euro area, for the AWM and for the euro area VAR. Overall, the investment contributions in the euro area countries appear to be much larger than in the USA.

Turning to the specific countries, we judge aggregate demand shifts to be by and large dominated by investment in Austria, Finland, Ireland, Italy, Luxembourg, the Netherlands and Spain. Investment contributions are somewhat smaller in Germany and much smaller in Greece. Finally, the French, Belgian and Portuguese evidence is ambiguous. This assessment is reached by neglecting suspicious VAR results for Greece, Ireland, Austria and the Netherlands (see figure 3.1 and 3.3) and by checking whether the majority of the reliable measures of the IC are above 60 per cent. Indeed, in Ireland, Italy, Luxembourg and Spain, the contribution of investment often accounts for more than 100 per cent of the response of GDP. This is actually because net trade provides an offsetting contribution due to a sharp decline of imports.[10] For Germany,

---

[10] The strong reaction of net trade results in surprisingly large investment contributions not only for very small and open economies such as Luxembourg and Ireland, but also in the VAR simulation for Spain and Italy (in the latter case, the structural model simulation for year 3 after the shock also yields a very large IC).

Table 24.3 *Contribution[a] of investment to the aggregate demand response to policy shocks*

	Based on NCBs' structural models (van Els *et al.*, chapter 5 in this volume)					
	I/GDP			I/(C + I)		
Horizon in years	1	2	3	1	2	3
Belgium	0.45	0.57	0,31	1.19	1.23	2.03
Germany	0.14	0.18	0.25	0.50	0.63	1.35
Greece	0.20	0.47	0.65	0.21	0.39	0.50
Spain	2.22	1.17	0.96	0.92	0.80	0.72
France	0.13	0.21	0.27	0.17	0.24	0.32
Ireland	0.89	1.35	1.91	0.63	0.79	0.94
Italy	0.40	0.83	1.29	0.54	0.69	0.87
Luxembourg	0.13	1.20	1.58	0.20	0.61	0.63
Netherlands	0.41	0.70	0.88	0.68	0.78	0.71
Austria	0.87	0.90	0.66	0.78	0.60	0.42
Portugal	1.03	0.93	0.72	0.40	0.48	0.42
Finland	0.59	0.87	0.83	0.65	1.13	1.85
Euro area aggregate[c]	0.31	0.55	0.79	0.49	0.60	0.68
Euro area AWM	0.48	0.67	0.83	0.50	0.58	0.65
USA	0.13	0.21	0.35	0.16	0.23	0.33

	Based on VARs (Mojon and Peersman, chapter 3 in this volume)					
	I/GDP			I/(C + I)		
Horizon in years	1	2	3	1	2	3
Belgium	0.24	0.52	0.64	0.93	0.66	0.60
Germany	0.52	0.44	0.37	0.52	0.53	0.47
Greece	−0.18	−0.11	−0.12	−0.35	−0.24	−0.21
Spain	1.33	1.13	0.98	0.55	0.56	0.55
France	0.89	0.81	0.73	0.76	0.68	0.63
Ireland	−0.21	−0.32	−0.28	0.48	0.65	0.77
Italy	1.02	0.99	0.92	0.37	0.38	0.36
Luxembourg						
Netherlands	0.45	0.54	0.36	0.59	0.86	−0.49
Austria	0.15	−0.02	−0.01	0.95	−0.07	−0.01
Portugal						
Finland	0.50	0.65	0.77	0.60	0.58	0.58
Euro area aggregate	0.75	0.69	0.62	0.57	0.53	0.42
Euro area VAR	1.89	0.99	0.71	0.78	0.67	0.65
USA[b]	0.42	0.53	0.51	0.32	0.44	0.42

Note: [a] The contribution is computed on to the ratio of the relative deviations from baseline, cumulated up to quarter 4, 8 and 12 in the case of the VARs, of investment and of GDP (consumption plus investment, $C + I$) times the average share of investment relative to $GDP (C + I)$.
[b] Structural model simulations for the USA are shown in table 24.1. US VARs correspond to the Christiano, Eichenbaum and Evans (1999) baseline model augmented with consumption and investment (see Angeloni *et al.*, 2003, for a presentation).
[c] Euro area aggregate is the weighted average of country results, using PPP 1995 GDP weights.

model-based simulations show a discrepancy between the contribution of investment to GDP (which is small) and to domestic demand (which is large). VAR-based contributions are roughly consistent and point to a relatively small IC. For France, Belgium, and Portugal the available measures of the IC are evenly split, some suggesting a large value and some a small one. We do not see any clear basis for deciding which assessment is more reliable.

Putting all this together, the evidence seems supportive of a dominant role of the investment in the transmission of monetary policy in seven of the twelve euro area countries. The share of investment in the GDP response to monetary policy shocks is somewhat smaller in Germany, although in the structural model it still appears dominant when compared only to consumption. The situation in France, Belgium and Portugal is unclear. As mentioned in section 2, the key question becomes whether the strong observed investment responses are attributable to the interest rate channel or are reflecting transmission via balance sheet, bank-lending or other channels. We will address this question in section 5.

5   Firm-level estimates of the effect of interest rates on investment

The aim of this section is to link the movements in investment to changes in interest rates – the direct test of the critical link in the IRC. As explained in the introduction to the volume, there are a number of reasons for suspecting that this connection can be better estimated with firm-level data than with aggregate data. That said, there are still plenty of challenges to consistently estimating this effect; see the thorough discussion on this point in Chatelain *et al.* (chapter 7 in this volume).

These challenges notwithstanding, we do not have any *a priori* reasons to suspect that these potential biases differ much across countries. Yet, there are countries where liquidity and cash-flow effects appear to be very important and countries where they appear hardly to matter. It is these differences, rather than the exact size of any coefficient estimates, that drive our assessment. In section 6 we will attempt to cross-validate and to further qualify the conclusions that emerge from this analysis.

5.1   *Linking the policy rate to the determinants of investment*

In order to identify the full effects of monetary policy on investment, it is necessary to map the instrument controlled by the monetary authority into the determinants of investment. The investment equations that we rely upon, described in detail in Chatelain *et al.* (chapter 7 in this volume) are specified so that firms' investment rate is determined by current and lagged values of sales growth, the growth of the user cost of capital and the ratio of cash flow to capital. Our assessment thus depends on a set of estimates that relate the policy interest rate to sales, the user cost of capital and cash flow.

There are several ways to establish the linkages between the policy rate and these variables. While Chatelain *et al.* take an 'analytic' approach, Gaiotti and Generale (chapter 11 in this volume) use estimates from a structural econometric model for Italy. However, the analytic approach has some drawbacks (it neglects the intrinsic dynamics of the linkages as well as indirect effects), while the approach taken by Gaiotti and Generale was not easily replicable for all the countries.

We use aggregate data for Germany, France, Italy, and Spain to estimate these linkages. We computed the three determinants of investment in a similar way for each country, and then sought to correlate them with the relevant policy rate. We experimented with simple, single-equation estimates and with VAR estimates obtained appending those variables to the VARs described in section 4. Fortunately, the three main conclusions presented below are relatively robust to these different approaches (the results shown in table 24.4 use our single-equation estimates).

First, the user cost was most strongly affected by the policy rate in Spain, and its influence was fairly similar in the other three countries. Second, sales seemed to be well described as a near-random walk in each of the countries and there was a weak connection between the policy rate and sales. We view this conclusion as clearly unsatisfactory, most likely driven by the simultaneity between sales and interest rates, prominent in the aggregate data. However, while this might bias towards zero the measure of the overall interest rate elasticity of investment, it is unlikely to significantly affect our assessment of the relative role of cash flow, which is our main focus of interest. Finally, the policy rate was more strongly related to cash flow in Italy and to a lesser extent in France than in Spain or Germany. Changing the details of the regression specifications never changed the general properties of the linkages that we estimated.

For the other countries for which we have micro estimates of the investment equations (Belgium, Luxembourg, Austria and Finland), owing to data shortages we calibrated the coefficients of the linkage equations to be the average values estimated for the other four countries, but also cross-checked the results with other estimates of the linkages.

The elasticities of user cost, sales and cash flow to the policy interest rate at years 1, 2 and 3 (these are reported in table 6 of Angeloni *et al.*, 2003) are used to combine the elasticity of investment to the user cost, to sales and to cash flow, estimated on micro data, to get the overall elasticity of investment to the policy rate: we simulate the microeconomic

Table 24.4 *Elasticities of investment with respect to the policy rate in eight countries of the euro area[a]*

Horizon in years		1	2	3
Germany[b]	Full elasticity (1)	−0.13	−0.18	−0.16
	Elasticity suppressing cash flow (2)	−0.13	−0.17	−0.14
Spain[b]	Full elasticity (1)	−0.58	−0.45	−0.15
	Elasticity suppressing cash flow (2)	−0.57	−0.46	−0.17
Finland[c]	Full elasticity (1)	−0.01	−0.03	−0.09
	Elasticity suppressing cash flow (2)	−0.01	−0.03	−0.07
Luxembourg[c,d,e]	Full elasticity (1)	−0.57	−0.29	−0.10
	Elasticity suppressing cash flow (2)	−0.57	−0.17	0
France[b]	Full elasticity (1)	−0.03	−0.15	−0.22
	Elasticity suppressing cash flow (2)	0	−0.05	−0.06
Italy[b]	Full elasticity (1)	−0.30	−0.54	−0.43
	Elasticity suppressing cash flow (2)	−0.15	−0.21	−0.15
Belgium[c]	Full elasticity (1)	−0.02	−0.09	−0.15
	Elasticity suppressing cash flow (2)	−0.01	−0.04	−0.05
Austria[d]	Full elasticity (1)	−0.57	−0.46	−0.34
	Elasticity suppressing cash flow (2)	−0.25	−0.14	−0.04

Notes: [a] For each country, the entries are the elasticities of investment with respect to the short-term interest rate calculated by simulating the various investment equations and described in the text.
[b] The investment equations for Germany, France, Italy and Spain are taken from Chatelain *et al.* (chapter 7 in this volume), table 7.4.
[c] Equations similar to these were used for the other four countries, with the Belgium estimates taken from Butzen, Fuss and Vermeulen (2001, table 4, large manufacturing firms), the Austrian estimates taken from Valderrama (2001b, table 3, benchmark model), the Finnish estimates were kindly provided by Topi and Vilmunen, and the Luxembourg estimates taken from Lünnemann and Mathä (2001, table 4, within estimates). The baseline data for the calculation of the elasticities is constructed from micro summary statistics, mean values.
[d] Since the model includes the cash stock, rather than the cash flow, the relative link equation is not the average of those of the four largest countries, but is imposed to be what is mechanically implied by the duration of the stock of cash, which is assumed to be equal to four months (one-third of a year, implying a constant elasticity of −0.33).
[e] The estimates underlying our calculations are WITHIN (and not GMM as in all other cases).

regression equations together with the linkage equations, assuming that the economies start in a steady state (that is consistent with the sample properties of the micro data sets) and are hit by an increase in the policy interest rate. We then compute the implied elasticity of investment.

Our assessment turns on the importance of cash flow in the estimated investment elasticities. In particular, we compare the estimate of the overall elasticity when all the linkages between the policy rate and the determinants of investment are permitted and the estimate obtained when the cash-flow effects are suppressed. If the cash-flow effects are important in explaining the overall elasticity then we argue that the IRC does not provide a full explanation of the monetary transmission.

Importantly, for cash-flow effects to matter, two conditions must hold. First, the cash-flow coefficients in the investment equation must be substantial. Second, the link between the policy rate and cash flow must be significant. If either of these conditions fails then liquidity effects cannot play an important role in how monetary policy influences investment.

5.2   *Parsing the interest rate effects*

The elasticities of investment with respect to the policy rate (with and without cash-flow effects) are shown, for the seven countries where we have micro estimates, in table 24.4 (again, we refer to Angeloni *et al.*, 2003, for further details).

In Finland and Spain the pair of investment elasticities (overall and with cash-flow effects blocked out) are virtually identical. Also in Luxembourg, the role of the liquidity variable appears rather limited. This leads us to conclude that interest rate effects alone are responsible for the influence of the policy rate. Combined with our prior evidence, these countries appear to be cases where the IRC might be sufficient to explain monetary transmission.

Germany is a case, along with Greece, where the investment contributions to GDP responses were somewhat lower than for other countries. The data in table 24.4 show that in Germany the cash-flow effects on investment are minimal. Similar conclusions are reached by von Kalckreuth (chapter 9 in this volume). While he finds that firms with a low credit score (as assigned by the Bundesbank) have a relatively high investment sensitivity to cash flow, his calibrations suggest that these effects are not quantitatively large.

Overall, we conclude that for the purposes of modelling investment in Germany, the IRC is a satisfactory characterisation, but that some non-interest channels could be operative for other components of spending. We will look for confirmation of this conjecture in the banking data. In particular, we will see whether bank lending to households is more importantly affected by monetary policy than elsewhere.

In Belgium and France the aggregate evidence previously examined was ambiguous as to the role of investment. When looking at micro data, we see that in Belgium a sizeable part of the investment elasticity to the policy rate appears to operate through cash-flow effects. As the linkage equations were arbitrarily set equal to the average of the four main countries, we cross-checked this conclusion picking different sets of linkage coefficients. The result appears to be somewhat sensitive to the selection of the linkage equation, and in particular the role of cash flow appears substantially diminished assuming that the links are those estimated for Germany or Spain (the two countries where the interest rate elasticity of cash flow is estimated to be the smallest). While this casts some doubts about the role of financial factors in Belgium, Butzen, Fuss and Vermeulen (chapter 8 in this volume) find some evidence of a stronger effect of monetary policy on small firms, a finding usually interpreted as supportive of financial factors being at work in the transmission mechanism. Overall, we conclude that financial factors seem to matter for investment, and possibly for other components of GDP, given our agnostic conclusion about the aggregate role of investment in explaining aggregate demand movements.

As for France, table 24.4 shows that the cash-flow effects are large, accounting for roughly half of the total investment response. Indeed, Chatelain and Tiomo (chapter 10 in this volume) find that adding cash flow to their equation eliminates the statistical significance of the user cost for their full sample of firms. These cash-flow effects, however, are not uniformly strong across all firms, with equipment producers showing the highest sensitivity. Collectively these findings suggest that interest rate-induced changes in investment are unlikely to be the whole story in France. However, as in the case of Belgium, the prior ambiguity means that we cannot say whether any financial effects should be expected only for investment or for both investment and consumption.

Finally, Austria and Italy are cases where the aggregate evidence shows a predominant role of investment in the composition of the output response, but IRC dominance appears doubtful in light of the data in table 24.4. In both these countries the cash-flow effects appear to be relatively large, possibly more important than the interest rate effects. As with Belgium, the results for Austria were cross-checked using alternative choices for the linkage equations. The relative importance of the liquidity measure remains sizeable even when picking the links estimated for Italy or Spain (where the interest elasticity of user cost is highest). In addition, Valderrama (chapter 13 in this volume) finds for Austria stronger effects of monetary policy on small and young firms, and smaller effects for firms that have a tighter credit relationship with a bank ('*house bank*'). Both findings seem supportive of an important role of the credit channel in shaping the transmission of monetary policy. A similar supportive evidence for the role of financial factors is reported for Italy by Gaiotti and Generale (chapter 11 in this volume): they find that the effect of cash flow on investment is stronger for small firms and for firms with a larger share of intangible assets. Overall, we provisionally conclude that financial factors, by influencing investment, appear to play, both in Italy and in Austria, a noticeable role in monetary transmission, and we will look for more evidence supporting this conclusion in section 6.

6   The role of banks in the transmission of monetary policy

To complete our assessment, we now examine the evidence on banks. While we have identified in a number of countries a role for financial factors, this does not necessarily imply a role for banks. Balance sheet or broad credit channel effects could be quite important. These balance sheet effects could operate *in addition* to any effects attributable to banks, or even *in the absence* of effects generated by bank loan supply. The evidence that follows therefore can be viewed as a cross-check to see whether the provisional assignments made in section 5 should be refined to include a role for banks in the transmission mechanism.

In considering the refinement, we draw on three types of evidence. Whenever possible we rely on the findings of the country-specific, individual bank-level analyses, abridged versions of which appeared in the earlier chapters of this book. To summarise these findings succinctly, table 24.5 reports a verbal description of their results. In cases where the country-level data are missing or inconclusive we examine institutional features of the euro area national banking systems that might affect the strength of the bank-lending channel. In particular, as emphasised by Ehrmann *et al.* (chapter 14 in this volume), four aspects could matter for monetary transmission: the importance of state influences in determining credit flows, the prevalence of relationship lending, the size of deposit insurance guarantees and the extent of bank networks. We would expect that each of these features would reduce the sensitivity of bank lending to changes in monetary policy.

We begin by considering the countries for which the hypothesis of IRC dominance seemed to receive most support: Finland, Luxembourg and Spain. The two available country papers (Topi and Vilmunen, chapter 23 and Hernando and Martínez-Pagés, chapter 16 in this volume) do not find clear evidence of loan-supply effects on the monetary transmission. In the Spanish case this finding is reinforced by an interesting observation about the impact of the phenomenal growth of mutual funds in Spain. The deposit outflows that accompanied the growth were uneven across banks, but the lending changes that followed did not track the deposit shifts. This is unlikely to be due to any loan demand differences and is instead most naturally interpreted as showing that loan supply and deposits in Spain are not tightly linked. However, the structure of

Table 24.5 *Summary of country chapters testing for monetary policy induced loan supply shifts*

Country	Main conclusions regarding loan supply changes after a monetary policy shift
Austria	Loan-supply effects limited: lending responses appear to be asymmetric, during recessions loan supply does respond to monetary policy, but not during expansions
Belgium	n.a.
Finland	Loan-supply effects doubtful: size, liquidity nor capital level influence the amount of loan adjustment; the only caveat is that the sample is all post-banking crisis
France	Loan-supply effects present: banks with fewer liquid assets adjust loans more
Germany	Loan-supply effects present: banks with fewer liquid assets adjust loans more (interbank deposits are the key to the liquidity position)
Greece	Loan-supply effects present: smaller banks and banks with fewer liquid assets adjust loans more (small, illiquid banks adjust most)
Ireland	n.a.
Italy	Loan-supply effects present: banks with fewer liquid assets adjust loans more (also strong evidence of deposit shifts)
Luxembourg	n.a.
Netherlands	Loan-supply effects present: unsecured lending for small, illiquid, or poorly capitalised banks adjusts more; household lending is not affected
Portugal	Loan-supply effects present: less-capitalised banks adjust loans more (very small sample)
Spain	Loan-supply effects absent: no evidence of supply shifts, even following an institutional reform that squeezed deposits

Note: n.a. = Not available.

the Spanish banking system shows none of the institutional factors that might insulate lending decisions from monetary policy. In Finland, Topi and Vilmunen find that the main bank characteristics that might be expected to influence loan supply (size, capitalisation and liquidity) do not lead to any significant differences. A limited role of bank supply in the transmission appears broadly consistent with the presence, in Finland, of an important network for the many cooperative banks.

In Italy and Austria, the prior evidence identified financial factors as playing a role in explaining firms' responses to monetary policy. In Italy, the bank-level analysis presented in Gambacorta (chapter 19 in this volume) indicates that monetary policy does alter loan supply. Specifically, Gambacorta finds that the amount of liquidity on individual banks' balance sheets significantly influences the degree to which they change loans after a monetary shock: the lower the level of liquidity, the stronger the loan supply response. Overall, these findings are consistent with previous results and the VAR evidence we examined. Indeed, Gambacorta

(2001, table 2) reports that there is near-unanimity in the past literature that a broad credit channel exits.

The Austrian evidence is more ambiguous. Kaufmann (chapter 21 in this volume) finds cross-bank differences in lending responses only during recessions, when lending from banks with more liquid assets is significantly less affected than that from otherwise comparable banks. But the strength of this finding depends on how the recession periods are selected and also sometimes is accompanied by other anomalous findings (e.g. higher policy rates leading to higher lending). One possible explanation for the relatively weaker role of Austrian banks in the transmission process could be the importance of networks and relationship lending between firms and their banks.

Germany is the only country where our preliminary classification more clearly suggested that financial factors, if they were to matter, would operate through consumption, but not investment. Logically this would suggest investigating whether loan-supply effects (or other financial factors) are particularly important for households. We have no direct evidence on this question, but there are some suggestive pieces of information. The bank-level analysis of Worms (chapter 15 in this volume) shows significant loan-supply effects that are related to the liquidity position of the banks. A relevant aspect of chapter 15 is that it uses data on the customer mix of each bank to build a variable that reflects the average income of each bank's borrowers. As this income proxy should reliably control for loan demand, we expect lending changes genuinely to reflect supply shifts. At any rate, similar results are obtained when the standard controls for demand conditions employed by Ehrmann *et al.* (chapter 14 in this volume) are used. The general picture also seems to fit with certain structural features of Germany's banking system. On the one hand, the level of concentration is relatively low and banks are not particularly well capitalised. On the other hand, banks tend to belong to networks and the 'house bank' lending relations are often very strong. The latter feature could explain why corporate borrowers are insulated from credit restrictions, while households remain exposed.[11]

In our preliminary classification Belgium was the country where it was unclear as to how much weight to assign to investment movements in accounting for GDP movements, but it was clear that cash flow seemed important for observed investment responses. This suggests that liquidity effects would be expected to matter for business investment and possibly

---

[11] It is also worth stressing that the VAR simulations reported in the appendix of Mojon and Peersman (2001) show that household borrowing falls much more quickly after a monetary tightening than does business borrowing. Actually, business borrowing is estimated to rise in the first year.

household expenditure. As estimates based on bank-level data are not available, we are not able to draw any strong conclusions for Belgium.[12] It is worth stressing however that de Bondt (2000) suggests that bank loan supply may be affected by monetary policy.

Based on the macro and the micro evidence on firms in France, financial factors appear to play an important role in driving investment responses to monetary policy. The French evidence on micro bank data suggests that loan supply does shift when monetary policy changes. In particular, Loupias, Savignac and Sevestre (chapter 17 in this volume) show that less liquid French banks are more responsive to monetary policy. Previous studies using microeconomic data also find a role for banks – see Rosenwald (1998) and the literature review by Loupias, Savignac and Sevestre (2001). The evidence does not speak to the question of the relative importance of these effects for business as opposed to consumer lending (both of which might be expected to matter based on the evidence in sections 4 and 5).

Finally, we are left with the four countries (Ireland, Greece, the Netherlands and Portugal) where, absent firm-level evidence, our 'testing' of the IRC dominance hypothesis was only partially, if at all, implementable.

Among these, Greece stands out because the small share of GDP movements accounted for by investment already points to an important role for consumption adjustments in the transmission mechanism. This suggests looking for evidence of financial factors having a role for consumption (and only to a lesser extent for investment). Brissimis, Kamberoglou and Simigiannis (chapter 18 in this volume) find that both smaller banks and banks with lower levels of liquidity are more responsive to monetary policy. Smaller banks, with less liquid assets are estimated to be especially sensitive to policy changes. However, we do not have enough information to tell whether these loan-supply shifts are more relevant for households or businesses. Other evidence seems supportive of a non-negligible role of banks.[13]

In Portugal, the aggregate evidence was ambiguous about the role of investment. It appears that loan supply is affected by monetary policy

---

[12] The structural information is also ambiguous. On the one hand, the industry is concentrated (dominated by twelve banks) and the banks hold a relatively low percentage of assets in the form of loans. On the other hand, the lack of relationship lending, government guarantees, deposit insurance and bank networks means that there are few of the mechanisms that would cushion bank lending from monetary policy.

[13] For instance, the Greek banking system is characterised by banks holding relatively low levels of capital and liquid assets. Moreover neither networks nor relationship lending are believed to be significant. Finally, Brissimis and Kastrissianakis (1997) conclude that the bank-lending channel appears to exist in Greece, although it may have weakened in the 1990s.

changes. Farinha and Robalo Marques (chapter 22 in this volume) conclude that bank capital plays an important role in shaping banks' responses to monetary policy, with less-capitalised banks being more sensitive. This is consistent with the institutional characteristics of the banking
sector in Portugal, whereby networks are unimportant and relationship
lending is not typical, thus supporting the operation of a lending channel.

In the other two countries the aggregate evidence was broadly consistent with the hypothesis that investment is an important mover of aggregate demand in response to a monetary policy shift. In Ireland, we
lack a bank-level analysis and the indicators that are available provide
ambiguous readings so that we draw no firm conclusions.[14]

For the Netherlands, de Haan (chapter 20 in this volume) finds that
unsecured bank lending is responsive to monetary policy. These effects
are larger for small banks, banks with low liquidity and banks with low
capital – although the interactions between these characteristics do not
appear to be important. In contrast, secured lending seems to be unaffected by policy changes. Finally, household lending is little affected by
policy changes, and this reinforces the view that monetary policy operates primarily by affecting investment. This relatively clear-cut evidence,
however, contrasts with priors based on the fact that in the Dutch banking system liquidity, concentration and capital levels are relatively high
and relationship lending is prevalent.

7 Summary of the evidence for individual countries

Our survey of the country-by-country evidence leads to the two-way classification presented in table 24.6.

7.1 Austria

In Austria, interest-sensitive components of GDP seem to account for a
large part of the movements of GDP in the wake of a monetary shock.
But, firm panel results show that there is a non-negligible role for liquidity
variables in determining investment. Looking at the bank side, the results
from the panel estimates suggest that the lending channel of monetary
policy is not likely to be strong. This may be due to the strong bank networks and bank–firm relationships. Hence, any monetary policy effects

---

[14] Bank networks are prominent, with most banks belonging to one, and there is a lot of
relationship lending. But the largest banks control a relatively small share of the total
market, the share of loans in banks assets is very high and banks do not seem to carry
high levels of liquidity or capital.

Table 24.6 *Final assessment of monetary policy transmission in euro area countries*

Bank evidence	IRC dominance?				
	Data lacking to determine relevance of the IRC	Financial factors important for investment and potentially important for consumption	Some evidence against Financial factors potentially important for consumption only	Financial factors important for investment but not necessarily consumption	No evidence against No financial factors expected
Loan supply reacts	Netherlands, Portugal	Greece, France?	Germany	Italy, France?	Finland, Spain
Loan supply insensitive				Austria	
Loan-supply assessment not possible	Ireland	Belgium?		Belgium?	Luxembourg

Note: There is conflicting information about France and Belgium as to whether investment movements fully account for GDP responses to monetary policy. We express this ambiguity by showing two possible entries for each country.

beyond those going through the IRC should work largely through other channels (e.g. firm balance sheets).

7.2   Belgium

The evidence appears to point against IRC dominance in Belgium. The VAR and the structural models provide conflicting indications about the role of investment in accounting for aggregate demand movements (small for total demand, large for domestic final demand). The evidence on investment is that financial factors probably matter for investment. On the bank side, previous evidence concluded that the role of bank loan-supply shifts seem to play a role in the transmission of monetary policy in Belgium. We have no evidence that can be used to challenge that finding.

7.3   Finland

In Finland, the IRC seems to offer a satisfactory account of monetary transmission. The VAR and national econometric model suggest that this would be the case and we find the microeconomic evidence on investment to be consistent with this prediction as well. The prior banking evidence available on Finland was very limited. Our bank panel estimates (from the post-banking crisis period) signal that loan supply does not appear to be very responsive to monetary policy. In any case, considering that the IRC seems to be dominant, loan-supply behaviour of banks should not play an important role[15] in the overall mechanism.

7.4   France

As in Belgium, we had difficulty getting for France a consistent assessment of the role of interest-sensitive spending components. Traditionally, it has been difficult to identify cost-of-capital effects on investment in France. Our evidence confirms that, in keeping with the findings of previous studies, the cost of capital does not have a strong effect on investment, while financial factors – as captured by a cash-flow variable – appear important. On the bank side, the earlier literature placed France among the candidates for a strong bank-lending channel. The panel evidence on banks shows that the loan supply of the least liquid French banks is more sensitive to changes in the monetary policy stance.

---

[15] Our main caveat surrounding this conclusion is that much of the evidence comes in the post-banking crisis environment. Some prior studies had found that liquidity variables might matter for investment. We leave open the possibility that this may be the case again now that the adjustment to the crisis is over.

7.5   Germany

The German evidence is also complicated. On the one hand, investment spending plays a smaller than average role in accounting for GDP movements in the wake of a monetary policy shift. On the other hand, the IRC seems to be the dominant, indeed almost the only relevant channel in explaining monetary policy effects on investment. At the same time, as in France, the monetary shifts appear to have the strongest effects on the loan supply of the least-liquid banks. One possible reconciliation of the firm-level and bank-level evidence is that loan-supply effects influence consumption, but this cannot be independently checked using the evidence in this volume.

7.6   Greece

The large changes in the Greek economy since 1990 make it difficult for us to fit a stable VAR. But, based on the structural model of the Greek economy, it appears that consumption is an important component of the adjustment to a monetary shock. Earlier authors have pointed to Greece as a candidate for significant loan-supply effects, and the new econometric evidence we quote points in this direction.

7.7   Ireland

Ireland is the country where our evidence on monetary transmission is scarcest. The only available source comes from the structural model of the economy and it suggests that the IRC could be quite important. But we lack any findings about firms or banks that permit us to test this conjecture.

7.8   Italy

Interest-sensitive spending in Italy seems largely to account for output movements in the wake of a monetary policy shift. The investment response, however, shows clear signs of being affected by financial factors. This seems to reject the IRC dominance. Moreover, as in France and Germany, the effects of policy shifts on bank lending vary with the liquidity of the banks' assets. This picture is confirmed by a host of studies. Overall Italy is a country where the case for the presence of a lending channel seems strong.

7.9   Luxembourg

Our evidence for Luxembourg is somewhat incomplete. We do not have the data needed to fit a VAR, so relying solely on the structural econometric model we conclude that interest-sensitive spending movements dominate the monetary-induced changes in GDP. The firm-level evidence moreover suggests that investment does not appreciably depend on firms' liquidity holdings. The (limited) previously available evidence for Luxembourg suggests that bank loan supply is not likely to play a major role in monetary transmission. Our informal evidence supports this, though we lack any econometric evidence on bank behaviour in Luxembourg.

7.10   Netherlands

We also have incomplete information on the Netherlands. The macroeconometric-level evidence suggests that the investment plays an important role in accounting for output responses to monetary policy, but we lack the firm-level analysis to verify whether this corresponds to a dominant IRC. Past evidence is ambiguous as to whether investment responses can be fully explained by interest rate effects. There is clear evidence that bank loan supply changes following changes in monetary policy. The extension of household credit, however, does not appear affected. Thus, the outstanding question is whether the estimated change in unsecured business credit is relevant for Dutch corporate investment.

7.11   Portugal

As with Greece, Ireland and the Netherlands, the assessment of Portugal is impaired by lack of data. The structural changes in the economy limit our ability to estimate a VAR, while the evidence based on the econometric model was ambiguous about the role of investment. We lack the firm-level evidence needed to further sharpen this assessment. However, it appears that bank loan supply does change following a shift in monetary policy. As in the Netherlands, we cannot determine whether this is material for the transmission.

7.12   Spain

Spain is the case where the evidence most consistently points towards a pure IRC explanation for monetary transmission. Following a monetary policy shift, investment movements are substantial, yet they do not appear to be dependent on financial factors. Loan supply also appears to be disconnected from monetary policy; the evidence on how banks also shielded their lending after regulatory induced deposit outflows reinforces this presumption. This all fits together and suggests that financial factors do not play an important role in the Spanish monetary transmission.

8   Conclusions

Taken together, the findings from this project paint a rich, composite and, to some extent, surprising picture of the monetary transmission for the euro area as a whole. This picture can hopefully also serve as a point of departure when sufficient information to document, and measure, any changes in the transmission process resulting from the introduction of the single currency becomes available.

Starting with the unsurprising aspects, the VAR analysis suggests that an unexpected increase in the short-term interest rate temporarily reduces output, with the peak effects occurring after roughly one year. Prices respond more slowly, with inflation hardly moving during the first year and then falling gradually over the next few years. Structural econometric models, though not strictly comparable, provide a picture with similar qualitative features. Despite the somewhat artificial nature of the synthetic data for the area as a whole, these findings are theoretically sensible and broadly consistent with a large body of empirical literature analysing the other large currency area in the world, the USA. Moreover, the delayed response of prices relative to that of output suggests that studying the transmission of policy to spending and output is a logical step, even if the aim of monetary policy is defined primarily in terms of prices.

A further aspect of the assessment based on aggregate data at the area level is that both the VARs and the structural models highlight the importance of investment in driving output changes in the wake of a monetary policy tightening. This feature distinguishes the transmission mechanism in the euro area from that in the USA, where much of the output adjustment appears to be due to changes in consumption – a topic we explore further in Angeloni et al. (2003).

Moving to the main question posed in our introduction, our reading of the evidence is that the IRC, while not playing an exclusive role, is clearly a prominent channel of transmission in the euro area. For the area as a whole, investment accounts for the bulk of the GDP change after a monetary policy shift. In a group of countries, accounting for about 15 per cent of the euro area GDP, the IRC emerges as the nearly exclusive channel. In all other countries for which we have the evidence (covering, together with the first group, about 90 per cent of the euro area GDP) interest rate effects are always a sizeable, and sometimes the virtually unique, source of investment movements. It is interesting that there generally seems to be a significant effect of the user cost of capital on investment. These findings seem to contradict the oft-voiced presumption of an exclusive role of financial factors in the transmission of monetary policy in the euro area, based on the overarching role banks play as providers of finance.

This said, it is nonetheless clear that financial factors influence the transmission of monetary policy in several important ways. Significantly, the cases where the IRC dominance does not find much support do not point to a single, prevalent alternative. In most, but not all of these countries it looks as if the role of banks in supplying business credit to finance investment may be important. Thus, in terms of monitoring bank lending it is probably necessary to track both household and business lending. Moreover, there are also cases in which financial factors are important but banks are not likely to be an important ingredient in the picture.

Thirdly, the overall role of banks in the transmission mechanism is somewhat different, and perhaps smaller, than what might have been expected based on prior work. There are countries where bank lending appears irrelevant for transmission. In some, we suspect that government guarantees to support banks, the propensity of banks to operate in net-works and strong borrower–lender relationships may mitigate the strength of any loan-supply effects. Taken together this means that even though the banks dominate the supply of credit in all euro area countries, they do not appear to be uniformly important.

Lastly, in assessing the role that the banks do play in the transmission, the relevant characteristics that appear to affect the potency of the lend-ing channel are not always those that we (and probably others, too, based on our reading of the past literature) would have guessed at. Bank size and bank capital seems not to play much of a role in shaping loan-supply responses to monetary policy. We find the institutional reasons discussed by Ehrmann *et al.* (chapter 14 in this volume), and noted in section 6 of this chapter, to be a plausible explanation for this result. But this means that the vast heterogeneity in terms of size both across and within coun-tries is probably not very important. In contrast, bank liquidity positions seem to be important in virtually all the countries where loan-supply ef-fects appear to be present. But there are other potential supply effects that remain to be isolated.

All of our analysis has been based on the analysis of data from before the launch of the euro. Banks' balance sheets and pricing behaviour, cap-ital markets and the patterns of business financing have already changed substantially since 1998. One obvious caveat to our analysis is that we cannot say whether this has changed the operation of the monetary policy transmission channels, as a result, for example, of increased monetary and financial integration. Angeloni and Ehrmann (2003) explored these issues by looking at post-1999 data.

Whether or not our assessments are confirmed in future work, we hope they may provide some guidance about useful next steps in studying monetary transmission in the euro area. Among the many possibilities we see two as most urgent. First, it would be natural to ask why the composition of the output adjustment differs in the euro area and the USA. Angeloni *et al.* (2003) takes a step in this direction, trying to see whether the differences are more likely caused by differences in investment or consumption choices. Understanding why the transmission mechanism might differ between the world's two major currency areas strikes us as relevant for both academics and policymakers. Making progress on this issue will require an explicit investigation of consumption behaviour in the euro area. In pursuing this investigation, the possibility of again using micro and aggregate data is appealing.

A second critical issue is an explanation for the response of prices to monetary policy. As we have seen, aggregate data suggest that prices are slow to respond at the start, and then only gradually adjust over time. In light of the central importance of price stability in the ECB's mandate, determining the causes for this inertia and understanding whether it is likely to continue to hold is particularly important from a policy viewpoint.

25   Discussion of chapter 24

J. von Hagen, X. Freixas, B. Bernanke and V. Gaspar

Ben Friedman, chairman of the concluding session of the conference, opened the discussion by praising the Monetary Transmission Network (MTN) for its monumental achievement and the authors of the concluding chapter (chapter 24). He then invited the first three discussants to focus on one of the three different channels of monetary policy effectiveness that were discussed during the conference. Jürgen von Hagen was asked to focus on the classical interest rate channel, Javier Freixas on the bank-lending channel and Ben Bernanke on the broader balance sheet and credit channel. Finally, he invited Vítor Gaspar to give a more general evaluation of this summary of the MTN research.

Ben Friedman put forward two questions for the general discussion. First, one should get a sense of the relative contribution of the three channels of monetary policy to the overall effectiveness of monetary policy. Ideally we should get three figures that add up 100. Second, one should understand how the research of the MTN changes the priors of the researchers working on the transmission mechanism. To what extent should these priors be changed, and in what way should our earlier beliefs be adjusted because of the results of the MTN?

1   Jürgen von Hagen

The survey presented in chapter 24 skilfully and competently draws together the large amount of research into the transmission of monetary policy in the euro area undertaken by the Eurosystem in recent years and presented at the conference. The chapter presents evidence from euro area models, country models and country-specific microeconometric models, from VARs and from structural econometric models. The authors recognise that the comparability of these different approaches and techniques is not always straightforward. Nevertheless, they use them to look at the issue from different perspectives and to develop a coherent

413

and overarching interpretation of the transmission process in the euro area. This alone is a challenging exercise and the authors are to be complimented for their competent way of handling it.

The main purpose of the chapter is to identify the channels through which monetary policy affects output and price in the euro area. The authors cast their main research interest into the following question: can we reject the null hypothesis that the classical interest rate channel – IRC – dominates the transmission process in the euro area? They define the IRC as the response of aggregate demand components, GDP and prices, to changes in the interest rate controlled by the monetary authority that would take place, if there were no capital market imperfections. The authors propose to answer their main question by looking at three sub-questions:

- Question 1   Does the response of interest-sensitive spending account for the bulk of the response of GDP to monetary policy shocks?
- Question 2   Is the direct response of investment large enough to account for the response in interest-sensitive spending, or do we need financial market effects working through cash-flow constraints in addition to those working through sales and capital cost?
- Question 3   Does bank lending respond to changes in the controlled policy rate?

The research strategy then works as follows: if the answer to 1 is 'no', the IRC cannot dominate. If it is 'yes', we look at 2. If the answer to 2 is 'yes', we have identified a classical IRC as dominating. The process could stop here, but the authors review the evidence on 3 in these cases anyway. If the answer to 2 is 'no', the IRC does not dominate. The authors then look at 3 to see whether there is any evidence supporting the claim that financial market restrictions are important in the transmission of monetary policy.

I will concentrate on the following two questions:. First, is the evidence established in this chapter sufficient to declare the defendant, the IRC, not guilty of being the main transmitter of monetary policy impulses in the euro area? Second, is the evidence sufficient to establish that the defendant has important accomplices – i.e. that there are other channels at work as well?

Answering these questions raises problems of identification. Is the defendant properly identified? I have serious doubts. The authors define the IRC as a response to monetary policy shocks in the absence of capital market imperfections. There, it is key to carefully define what type of capital market imperfections the authors have in mind. For instance, the very existence of banks and central banks signals the presence of capital market imperfections, namely the well-known information asymmetries and principal–agent problems in credit relations, that we commonly refer to to explain the coexistence of banks and securitised credit. Thus, the reference point for identifying the IRC could become empirically undefined, since monetary systems with no capital market imperfections do not exist. Refining the definition to capital market imperfections apart from those that justify the existence of money obviously does not help, witness the large number of alternative approaches to modelling 'money'. It follows that the research programme although it produces a wealth of interesting evidence, may not be sufficiently precisely designed for answering the main question posed by the authors.

The logic of the answer they nevertheless offer us is essentially this: if the accumulated reaction of interest-sensitive spending to a policy shock, multiplied by the share of interest rate-sensitive spending in GDP, is equal to the accumulated response of GDP to the same shock, then the answer to 1 is 'yes'. But, if the accumulated response of GDP is larger, then the answer is 'no'. This poses two conceptual problems. First, assume that no individual spending component nor GDP as a whole responds to interest rate shocks. The logic of the authors then forces us to conclude that IRC is fully operative. This makes little sense. Second, and more importantly for the empirical results, assume that, following an interest rate shock, investment falls by 10 per cent, and let the share of investment in GDP be 20 per cent. Assume, further, that following the same interest rate shock, GDP falls by more than 2 per cent. The authors' logic then forces us to conclude that there are important non-IRC transmission channels at work. But this is a valid conclusion only if we are willing to assume that a monetary policy-induced drop in investment has no second-round effects on aggregate demand. Empirically, this seems almost certainly false in most European economies. But if multiplier effects exist, we can easily think of cases where GDP falls by more than 2 per cent in our experiment. Looking at the data reported in the chapter in this way, I see no good reason for the authors' conclusion that 1 must be answered negatively for Germany or even possibly for Belgium or France. At a minimum, one would want to see estimates of these multipliers, e.g. by looking at the response of output to GDP shocks. As it stands, the evidence is inconclusive for the question at hand.

The second identification problem is the monetary policy shock. The weaknesses of the Choleski-decompositions in this context are well known. It is surprising to see that within this huge research effort in the Eurosystem, no attempts seem to have been made to identify these shocks better.

The third identification problem relates to the notion of a dominant effect. The authors never tell us precisely what 'dominates' means. Looking at table 24.3, it seems that a ratio of the investment to GDP response around 50 per cent is not enough to conclude that the IRC 'dominates', since, if it did, the answer to 1 should be positive in the cases of Germany and Belgium.

In sum, the evidence presented for answering 1 is rather inconclusive. It may not convince us that the IRC alone explains everything, but it also does not allow us to conclude the opposite. This leaves us with the evidence regarding 2. Here the authors draw their main conclusions from table 24.4, which compares the reactions of investment to policy shocks with and without allowing for cash-flow effects. Again, the question of what they mean precisely by 'finding cash-flow effects important' is left open. But my main concern with their procedure is a different one. We typically think about cash-flow effects or capital market restrictions in general as amplifiers of the response of investment to policy shocks. This implies that, if the IRC is nil, capital market restrictions do not help explaining the observed reaction of investment to interest rate shocks either, since amplifying nil is still nothing. Thus, the results for France, Belgium and Finland, perhaps even for Germany, where the elasticities without cash-flow effects are very small, point to misspecifications of the econometric models more than to the importance of capital market restrictions. Italy and Austria are the two cases that convince me most in table 24.4.

Is there enough evidence to conclude that the defendant has important accomplices? As explained before, the evidence presented on 1 allows an affirmative answer only if we assume that multipliers are one. However, we don't know. For 2, the Austrian and Italian defendants may have accomplices. The German, Spanish and Luxembourg do not, the other cases are inconclusive.

What about the authors' question 3? Here again, the main difficulty relates to the underlying economic theory. The authors seem to argue that finding a negative reaction of bank lending to policy impulses means that capital market restrictions are important. Yet, conventional models of the banking firm predict that loan supply declines when the bank's cost of refinancing goes up. A further decline of lending may result from credit rationing and deteriorating collateral, but the evidence presented does not allow us to separate the normal from these additional, financial effects. Thus, apart from Italy and Austria, the case for important accomplices remains to be established.

To conclude, this chapter presents a wealth of interesting empirical results covering a broad range of different aspects of the transmission of monetary policy. These results should help the central banks predict how monetary policy actions will affect the economy. Yet, in view of the unresolved problems of identification, they are no basis to conclude that monetary policy transmission is shaped importantly by financial market effects beyond the IRC.

2   Xavier Freixas

First, I would like to emphasise that this is very interesting work, which really provides an overall picture of the monetary transmission mechanism in the euro area. The methodology has been selected in such a way that it is quite homogeneous. And this, indeed, is something that we miss and constitutes important added value for all of us. In particular, we – at least I – did not have a clear idea of what could be the countries where the monetary transmission mechanism could work mainly through the interest rate channel (IRC). It has been quite a surprise for me to learn that these countries were Spain, Finland and Luxembourg. This results should be taken with caution as it is a suggested interpretation that makes the authors of chapter 24 decide, depending on the distance between the VAR analysis and the structural modelling analysis, if the results are robust or not. Even so, it's a surprise when we think of Spain, where the banking sector is strong, to find that the interest rate channel is the main driving force for monetary policy. So, this answers Ben Friedman's question in terms of priors and posteriors. I personally would have bet on the Netherlands or on another Northern country. However, the results are there to prove that this is not so, or at least that things are somehow more complicated.

The idea of having a double test in cascade is a great contribution, even if the reader might be misled by some of the results. Indeed, in the first test, the fact that the contribution of investment to GDP response is larger than 100 per cent for some countries, is difficult to interpret. But this fact is due to a negative contribution of external trade to the response of GDP. So, in the end everything comes into place.

I would, however, like to mention that this exercise is all the more complex because during these three decades – the sample period spans mainly from 1971 to 2000 – all the countries in this sample have undergone incredible changes in their financial structure. So, what amazes me is that there are some positive consistent results and I find this spectacular when we think of Southern Europe. Spain under Franco in 1971 was quite different from Spain nowadays. Italy, Greece and Portugal were also countries where inflation and interest rate remained at 2 digits in the early 1990s. These countries now have sophisticated financial markets and are part of Euroland.

There is one small institutional aspect that should be mentioned in order to clarify the analysis. In some of these countries, such as France or Germany, variable interest rates are mainly unheard of. In other countries such as Spain it is the opposite: most loans in Spain are now granted on the basis of Euribor plus some spread. As a consequence, we have two kinds of countries. In the 'variable rate countries', we have an automatic immediate contractual effect of monetary policy, as it impacts the Euribor. In the 'fixed rate countries' this effect is non-existent. Hence, monetary policy will have different effects in countries where fixed rates are dominant from those where variable rates prevail.

I would like now to comment on the bank-lending channel and, first of all, to point out that, as we well know, not rejecting the interest rate channel hypothesis does not imply that the bank-lending channel has to be rejected. In fact, in Finland at least, one of the three countries – with Spain and Luxembourg – where the interest rate channel is not rejected, Topi and Vilmunen mention that there is weak evidence supporting the bank-lending channel. Hence, it makes sense that weak evidence supporting the bank-lending channel is consistent with a dominant interest rate channel. This result for Finland contrasts with others focused on the bank-lending channel. Loupias, Savignac and Sevestre on France (chapter 17), de Haan on the Netherlands (chapter 20), Worms on Germany (chapter 15), Farinha and Robalo Marques (chapter 22) on Portugal and Gambacorta on Italy (chapter 19) all underbook tests undertaken the results of which appear to support the existence of the bank-lending channel.

Let me now briefly discuss the difference I see between the bank-lending channel and the balance sheet channel. In order to do that, let me present a theoretical model. Consider a simple scheme in which we draw a horizontal line, to differentiate firms, for instance, with respect to their collateral, as in Holmstrom and Tirole (1997). If you prefer to have credit rating or the probability of success, as in Bolton and Freixas (2000), this could do as well, and if you think that riskiness is related to size, then we need sort of a partition of firms into small and large firms.

Good firms (e.g. which have more collateral, are safer or simply larger) will access the public debt market. This makes sense in Europe, where there are practically no junk bonds, and where firms have to be really large and safe in order to access the public debt market. How can we apprehend a monetary policy shock in this context, where we have a continuum of firms' instead of a unique representative firm? Suppose

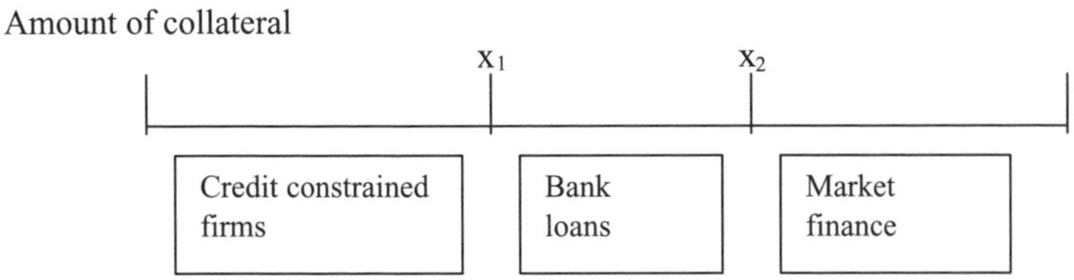

Amount of collateral

Figure 25.1 Collateral and financial constraint

there are two thresholds, x_1 and x_2. x_1 indicates the limit where a firm is out of the market and is denied credit and x_2 is the marginal firm that is just indifferent between obtaining a bank loan and issuing debt securities. It could be a firm which is simply the last one to have access to debt and which would, if anything, prefers public debt. Worsening of its conditions will lead this firm into the hands of bankers. And this implies paying a higher cost of borrowing, possibly because of the additional monitoring cost. A monetary contraction will always increase x_1 as the overall size of the market will be reduced. Small firms with weak collateral will be out of the market, supporting the available empirical evidence on the effect of monetary policy on heterogeneous firms. At the same time, since the market is to be reduced, corporate interest rates have to adjust and credit spreads have to adjust as well. This approach helps us to understand better the link between the two competing theories of the transmission mechanism: that is the bank-lending view and the balance sheet view (which relates to x_2) (figure 25.1).

Consider first the balance sheet view and assume an increase in interest rates. The effect will be a decrease in the value of firms' collateral. But a decrease in collateral implies a reduction in the market for corporate debt. So, the balance sheet view predicts the threshold x_2 will increase, with the corresponding decrease in debt issues and increase in bank loans. If instead the bank-lending channel operates, it is the bank supply that will be reduced and therefore the opposite effect will occur, and x_2 will decrease.

Consequently, the relevant test is not whether x_1 decreases, i.e. whether small firms are denied credit, since this is predicted by both theories. We all agree that a cash-flow effect on investment is consistent with the broad credit channel as well as with the bank-lending channel. It simply reflects the fact that when we have higher interest rates there are more firms that cannot access credit markets and therefore have to rely on their cash flows.

Turning to the interpretation of x_2, the key question is: what do firms do when they face a contractionary monetary shock? The paper that gives an answer is Kashyap, Stein and Wilcox (1993). This paper shows that when there is a monetary contraction, firms do change from bank loans into the commercial paper market. This means that x_2 is decreasing, i.e. that we are facing a downward shift in the supply of bank loans. Hence, while the empirical evidence presented in this conference brings support for the bank-lending view, it does not provide a quantification of the relative importance of the different channels to the transmission of monetary policy. Nevertheless, if we take into account Kashyap, Stein and Wilcox's (1993) contribution, it gives strong support to the lending view.

Now, why do we observe a bank-lending channel, as shown by the panel data analyses of banks' balance sheets? This is still a mystery to me. And I think it should be a mystery to you as well, for three reasons. First, inter-bank markets exist and work efficiently, allowing banks to exchange their liquidity. Second, because of the ability of a bank to restructure its liability and to react to deposits' shortage by raising all the types of debts. This criticism of the bank-lending channel is familiar, as it was originally formulated by Romer and Romer (1990). And the third reason is because the use of credit lines or loan commitment may be extended among firms, and therefore making them insensitive to these effects. Nonetheless, the empirical evidence confirms that the bank-lending channel seems to work. In addition, there is evidence regarding interbank market imperfection, since we know that large banks are less affected than small banks. But, why is it that the liquidity position of large banks is less important than the liquidity position of small banks? Well, I think we have to take a view on the interbank market. Large banks have a better access to interbank markets than small banks do. To sum up, we have a very strong support for the lending channel from the panel analysis of banks, confirming Kashyap, Stein and Wilcox's (1993) conclusions.

Yet, I'd like to point out a third effect. What is the effect of interest rates on the supply of bank loans? To start with, we should not discard the possibility that the existence of a strong banking sector should diminish the effect of monetary policy operations. The reason is simply that there is some room for retail bank rate stickiness. As shown in a paper by Berlin and Mester (2000), banks provide some kind of intertemporal insurance, isolating firms from interest rate or business cycle shocks. From that perspective, a strong banking sector should rather diminish the effect of monetary policy. So, taking these effects into account, how could monetary policy have so strong effects? This is a point originally noticed by Bernanke and Gertler (1995) and referred to as the *magnitude puzzle:* interest rate changes cannot lead to pronounced movements in output, while the cost of capital appears to be unchanged. The answer has to come from the lending view: if the lending view is correct, monetary policy could have important effects without moving open market interest rates by much. These effects cannot therefore be driven by the interest rate effects but by the bank's liquidity shortage, as the evidence on the data has shown.

To conclude I would like to add a final argument in favour of the lending channel. This is simply a result obtained by Mihov (2001). Mihov considers the cumulative deviation of output following a monetary policy shock and relates it to the ratio of bank loans to total liabilities. We observe that the larger the banking sector, the higher the overall effects of monetary policy. Hence, the bank-lending channel effect dominates the interest rate smoothing effect.

3   Ben Bernanke

To talk about the balance sheet channel, I thought it would be helpful if I put up a little model, which I use for teaching (originated in an article I coauthored with Mark Gertler and Simon Gilchrist, Bernanke, Gertler and Gilchrist, 1996). This is a simplified version of the Kiyotaki and Moore (1997) credit cycles model, and I think it will be useful for demonstrating what I think are the issues about the balance sheet channel.

When I tell the story in New Jersey, I talk about Joe the pretzel vendor, but here I'm going to talk about Hans the bratwurst vendor. Now the story of Hans is as follows: Hans owns a cart that he pushes through the streets of Frankfurt. The cart is his fixed capital, designated by K. There is a second-hand market for selling bratwurst carts, and today's price of a bratwurst cart is q per unit, and so the total value of Hans' cart is qK.

Every morning, Hans goes down to the butcher and buys some bratwurst in quantity X. X is his working capital, which he must buy fresh every day. Hans then takes the bratwurst and he goes out on the street and sells it to passing consumers. He earns a total revenue during the day of $a f(X)$. A higher stock of bratwurst is assumed to permit more sales – for example, a higher stock reduces the chance of selling out.

$f(X)$ is a constant returns production function which relates revenue to working capital (we assume the cart is necessary for any production to occur). Let 'a' be a productivity shock that depends (for example) on the weather or on whether there is a parade that day, or on whatever other considerations may affect the demand for bratwurst. Now, in case Hans needs to borrow in order to buy his bratwurst, he does have a loan market that he can go to, where he pays a gross interest rate R. The amount that he borrows is B. After selling his bratwurst Hans repays his debt, and the next day he goes through the whole process again.

What is Hans' economic problem? His budget constraint is:

$$X_1 = a_0 f(X_0) - R_0 B_0 + B_1$$

According to this budget constraint, the amount of bratwurst Hans can buy on day 1, X_1, equals total revenues from day zero, $a_0 f(X_0)$, less debt repayments plus new borrowing. Let's follow Kiyotaki and Moore and assume a capital market imperfection. Specifically, the borrower doesn't trust his ability to get payment out of Hans' proceeds, because Hans can easily slip his proceeds to his friend down the street. Instead, the lender insists on having collateral. And the collateral, of course, is Hans' cart, which can be sold and used to repay the loan. Assume we have a collateral-in-advance constraint, that is Hans' gross borrowings cannot exceed the value of his cart, or:

$$R_1 B_1 \leq q_1 K$$

What is the profit-maximising solution for Hans, who of course, being a bratwurst seller in Germany, is well acquainted with calculus? It turns out that there are two regimes – or even possibly three.

The first regime occurs when the collateral-in-advance constraint does not bind. In that case, for profit maximisation Hans will simply equate the marginal product of an extra link of bratwurst to the interest rate that he pays to purchase the bratwurst. That's simply the neo-classical first-order-condition for investment:

$$a_1 f'(X_1) = R_1$$

But what happens if, say, there have been several days of bad weather, for example, and Hans finds himself short of cash? In that case, let's assume that the collateral-in-advance-constraint binds. From that constraint we have the corner solution:

$$B_1 = \frac{q_1 K}{R_1}$$

Hans' purchases of bratwurst (and hence his economic activity) are determined by the borrowing constraint. Substituting the equation above into the budget constraint we find that Hans' working capital in period 1 is:

$$X_1 = a_0 f(X) - R_0 B_0 + \frac{q_1 K}{R_1}$$

This last equation is a useful one, because it summarises what I think of as the four basic ways in which the balance sheet channel of monetary policy can work. First of all is the cash flow effect. You can see there's a one to one relationship in a constrained environment between today's purchases of bratwurst X_1 and yesterday's cash flow $a_0 f(X_0)$, or what for empirical purposes might better be interpreted as the stock of liquidity. Monetary policy can affect cash flows, for example, by affecting the demand for bratwurst and thus the revenues that Hans can earn. Second is the debt overhang, $R_0 B_0$; the amount of debt that Hans has left over from yesterday affects the amount of net cash he has to buy bratwurst today. Large amounts of debt overhang will subtract from his available resources and will reduce his ability to invest in working capital today. In practice, monetary policy can affect the cost-of-carry of existing debt, with an impact on firm cash flows. Third is the asset or collateral effect, which is reflected by the value of the bratwurst cart, $q_1 K$. To the extent that monetary policy can affect asset prices, collateral and borrowing capacity will be affected. Finally, the fourth effect is the prospective interest rate effect, captured by R_1. A higher current interest rate reduces investment, not for the usual cost-of-capital reasons, but because high prospective interest payments increase the requisite amount of collateral.

Altogether, we see that there are in fact a number of ways in which monetary policy can affect balance sheets and hence economic activity. Yet another important lesson from this example is the possibility of non-linear relationships between balance sheet conditions and investment. In the first regime, with no binding constraint, the relationship between interest rates and investment is given by the neo-classical curvature of the production function. In the second, constrained regime, the production function is essentially irrelevant and investment is determined by the collateral-in-advance constraint. Additionally, one can imagine a third regime in which poor Hans is so credit constrained he can buy only a few links of sausage and it's not worth going out – in this range, Hans is out of business and investment is zero. In each of these three regimes, depending on the state of finance in this bratwurst economy, monetary policy will have different effects.

In the rest of my discussion, I want to talk about the chapter by Angeloni, Kashyap, Mojon and Terlizzese (chapter 24 in this volume). I'm taking the balance sheet point of view and I have some criticisms. But I do want to say that this is a very nice chapter, in the growing tradition of meta-analysis. The basic idea is to look critically at a large number of studies to try to distil overall conclusions. It's a very difficult thing to do, but I think it's potentially very informative. While the approach is promising, however, my bottom line is that unfortunately we still don't have enough hard information to make a clear call about the main channels of monetary transmission in the European economy. In particular, this chapter is set up to 'claim the residual' for the interest rate channel, or IRC. Since there is so much uncertainty in the estimates, the paper supports the IRC to a greater degree than I think is warranted.

Another concern is the extent to which the studies surveyed here provide independent information about policy channels. One difficulty with doing many studies in a similar framework, as has been the approach here, is that if there is a problem with one of them there is a problem with all of them. To varying degrees, I worry that all of the studies focusing on investment and on the cost of capital misidentify the cost of capital and neglect important channels of monetary policy. One important omission in virtually all the studies is collateral effects. Because of this omission, the tendency to find an effect of interest rates on investment, controlling for cash flow, is not necessarily conclusive. I would also add the small point that it's not quite right to specify these models as linear combinations of cash flow and interest rates. If the real world has two regimes, as in the bratwurst economy, then empirical work should try to estimate the probability the firm is in one regime or the other. As a given firm is never in both regimes at the same time, the linear specification misses something important.

Broadly, I would give two suggestions to the authors of this chapter. First, more attention should be paid to the role of collateral. A very simple thing that they could do would be to show and interpret some series of commercial real estate prices or other asset prices in the euro area. The other suggestion is to analyse the different components of investment, not just aggregate business fixed investment. US-based research suggests large differences in behaviour among investment components such as residential investment, structures, equipment and inventories, and also consumer durables for that matter. In fact, some of the key puzzles which the credit channel tries to explain have to do with the fact that housing has historically responded so strongly in the USA to monetary policy, while business structures respond barely at all. I understand that the data are a problem, but it would certainly be worthwhile to try to develop more evidence on this point, at least for the big countries.

Let me end with some free advice to the ECB. First of all, should we all be desperate because we don't know for sure what the monetary channel of transmission is in Europe? I would say 'no, not at all'. I very much enjoyed the chapter by Bean and his co-authors (chapter 6 in this volume) which showed some reasons for thinking about the relative influence of different channels. Nevertheless, it seems to me that, under normal conditions, knowing more or less the size of the policy effect, and the typical lags, is sufficient for making policy. For most purposes, it is sufficient just to keep a wary eye on financial conditions – the conditions of balance sheets and banks – to make sure that these are not such that the effects of policy will change discontinuously.

A second lesson for policymakers from this literature is to avoid deflation at all costs. Deflation kills financial systems and it kills economies. The relevance to the euro area is that inflation target ranges should have a clear minimum as well as a maximum. Remember Hans in his third state, when he can buy so few bratwurst that he stays home and watches the soccer matches on television instead. The only way that advanced economy can have a prolonged and extended depression such as Japan's is if the financial system is debilitated by deflation or other financial problems. My parting suggestion is to keep a close eye on the financial system, because its safety and soundness is very important to the health of the economy.

4   Vítor Gaspar

Before starting let me state that it is for me a true pleasure to participate in this conference and to discuss this chapter. The conference represents the summit of a huge effort carried out by research in the Eurosystem. Specifically, the work has been carried out within the Eurosystem's Monetary Transmission Network (MTN), with cooperation from the Monetary Policy Committee's Working Group on Econometric Modelling. Research in the Eurosystem is conducted in accordance with a fully decentralised model. This is in line with the autonomy of the institutions composing the System. Decentralisation, however, does not exclude concerted efforts when there is overlap of a clear common research interest with strong synergies associated with joint work.

Monetary Transmission was the topic of the first Eurosystem Research Network, for several reasons. First, there was a clear common interest of all participants in understanding monetary transmission, i.e. understanding the functioning of the euro area economy and, in particular, how monetary policy decisions affect economic outcomes. Second, given the indivisibility of monetary policy a clear euro area-wide focus was called for. Nonetheless that focus should be founded on deep knowledge of the institutional and structural characteristics of the national economies. Third, there were multiple data sets to be explored using a variety of approaches. Many of these were produced within the central banks themselves. After more than two years of work the MTN has to be considered a major success. It led to the first set of systematic evidence on the transmission mechanism in the euro area, drawing on both macro-level and micro-level data.

The findings permit a comparison between the characteristics of the transmission mechanism in the euro area and the USA. It also permits comparisons of impacts of monetary policy across different sectors of the economy and among member states. Evidence from micro-level data permits inferences about the importance of financial frictions and, in particular, the credit channel. Moreover the MTN made an impressive contribution to the visibility of research in the Eurosystem. One of the best examples is provided by this conference and its proceedings published by Cambridge University Press. Related papers will be forthcoming in journals such as the *Journal of the European Economic Association*, the *Journal of Money Credit, and Banking* and the *Oxford Review of Economic Policy*. As expected the work of the MTN has attracted the attention of policymakers and researchers alike.

Let me now come to my few remarks. The authors propose a testing strategy leading to a suggested interpretation. They try to answer to the question 'whether monetary policy transmission in the euro area can broadly be described as taking place through the classical interest rate channel (IRC)'. The authors recognise that a sharp rigorous statistical test is not possible. Instead they propose to exercise judgement to reach their suggested interpretation. The research strategy leads to a very interesting narrative that reads almost like a crime novel. The story starts with a crime: short-run monetary neutrality has been murdered. Anil Kashyap and Christopher Sims are prime suspects. The detectives will base their investigation assuming that Anil did it. The detectives think: if it was not Anil then it must have been Christopher; if Anil could not have done it alone then Christopher must have helped. Any such strategy is bound to lead to loose ends – even after a tremendous amount of detective work – and can, at best, deliver circumstantial evidence.

What are the most important difficulties facing the authors' research strategy? The authors themselves provide a list. No point in repeating those remarks here. However there are a few points that I believe are worth emphasising. First, the authors define IRC as 'the response of aggregate demand components, GDP and prices to the change in the policy controlled interest rate that would take place if there were no capital market imperfections'. The definition is vague. It does not permit identification of the IRC in a rigorous way. Here I very much agree with Jürgen von Hagen. 'No capital market imperfections' is a very loose concept. Some imperfection is, for instance, necessary to justify the existence of financial institutions. More generally it is reasonable to interpret perfect

capital markets as complete securities markets. The existence of complete
state-contingent securities contracts lead to resources allocations identical to those obtained under the Walrasian mechanism. Is the absence of
a precise notion of 'capital market imperfections' important? I think it
is, because it prevents a clear view of the alternative to the IRC. Coming
back to our crime story: the fact that Anil has an ironclad alibi is not sufficient to establish Chris' guilt. The fact that Anil could not have removed
the body alone is not sufficient to establish that Chris has helped. I believe that the authors had to rely on this kind of incomplete argument for
good reasons. Specifically the findings based on micro evidence – from
firms and banks – cannot easily translate into direct implications for the
aggregate behaviour of the economy. Circumstantial evidence is the best
that we can hope for.

My second observation is that the authors propose a sequential-testing
strategy. First, they ask if interest rate-sensitive components of spending
can account for the observed changes in output. Second, they ask whether
the changes in the interest rate-sensitive components can be explained by
the direct influence of interest rate changes. Third, in case they answer
'no' to at least one of the first two questions they look at evidence of
financial factors. Some remarks are, in order. (1) On the basis of euro
area-wide aggregate evidence one could feel comfortable with the aggregate characterisation of the transmission mechanism. Moreover there is
no robust evidence that the effects of monetary policy are asymmetric
across countries. After a (temporary) policy tightening there is a (temporary) contraction of output (with a lag) and a (permanent) reduction of
prices from baseline (after an even longer lag). (2) The approach followed
by the authors does not allow for the distinction between impact effects
and propagation mechanisms. This has the potential to create very serious identification problems in the presence of forward-looking optimising
economic agents. (3) There are potentially many effects which have not
been explicitly accounted for: (a) expectations; (b) intertemporal substitution in the labour supply; (c) intertemporal substitution in non-durable
consumption; (d) the role of housing (with potential impacts on households' wealth and collateral values), and more. (4) In order to obtain an
answer to their second question the authors need estimates of interest
rate elasticity of investment. However there is a problem. Caballero, in
his survey of aggregate investment (Caballero, 1999) shows that a downward bias in the estimated elasticity of investment to the cost of capital
should be expected. Accounting for this has the potential to make the
answer to the second question inconclusive.

To finish let me return to the spirit of the crime story and make a
confession. All my critical remarks were motivated by envy. I think that

the authors made the best possible case based on the available evidence. In my view, the case they make is a very persuasive one.

5   General discussion

The general discussion focused mainly on the link between the response of non-durable consumption and its relation with the importance of the IRC and on the potential importance of 'omitted channels'.

About the link between the response of non-durable consumption and the importance of the IRC, **Daniele Terlizzese** first reacted to the suggestion by Jürgen von Hagen that chapter 24 may over-reject the IRC by neglecting multiplier effects from investment and income to consumption. In his view, the important issue is to understand why such income effects on consumption would exist. In a world of perfect capital market, a temporary change in the real interest rate induced by monetary policy should not have a permanent effect on the stock of capital and hence on potential output and on lifetime resources. And with forward-looking consumers constrained only by their lifetime resources these multiplier effects, at least to a first approximation, should not exist. **Chris Sims** (Princeton University) and **Frank Smets** objected that multiplier effects on consumption could be due to real frictions or to nominal rigidities and not necessarily to financial rigidities. Chris Sims further explained why he thought that lack of large adjustment of non-interest rate-sensitive components of demand did not necessarily imply a weak interest rate channel. True, the fact that, in the USA, consumption is sensitive to the interest rates and that consumption adjustments correspond to a substantial fraction of the effects on GDP following monetary policy shocks, would be consistent with smaller degree of imperfection in US capital markets. US consumers, that have more access to asset markets, are more likely to be sensitive to changes in interest rates. However, either in Europe or in the USA, he would expect the main interest rate effects on consumption to work through the discount of future labour income. Country differences in the share of consumption in the response of GDP to monetary policy shocks may reflect different degree of price stickiness or other more general non-neutralities, and not necessarily differences in the strength of the bank-lending channels. Finally, Chris Sims stressed that distributional effects of a monetary contraction, for instance owing to a bank reselling the capital of bankrupt firms on a secondary market, should not have a significant impact on the aggregate. **Anil Kashyap** first recalled that assuming a low interest rate elasticity of non-durable consumption was backed by both theory and empirical studies. He then refuted Chris Sims' argument that the resale of capital from bankrupt firms on a secondary market should have no aggregate impact, precisely because these resale may happen in a state of the world where nobody would want to invest in such goods.

Several comments were made on the issue of 'omitted' channels. **Carlo Monticelli** (Deutsche Bank) regretted that the conference did not put more emphasis on the expectations and the real balances channels, as the latter would open the door for an explicit role of monetary aggregates, consistent with the ECB strategy. He asked whether the omission reflected the view that these channels were not relevant for the transmission of monetary policy in the euro area. **Ignazio Angeloni** said that money neutrality would hold both in an IRC-does-it-all type of world and in an IRC-plus-something-else type of world. The difference between the two worlds is that in the second, if we have financial factors operating, it's more likely that money, or credit aggregates, may have an active role in the transmission. So, it is the interpretation of the role of money which would be different according to whether we are in a pure IRC type of world, or whether we are in an IRC-plus-financial-factors type of world? **Daniele Terlizzese** answered to the point raised both by Vítor Gaspar and Jürgen von Hagen, that chapter 24 should have analysed the effect of monetary policy on housing and the associated wealth effects on consumption. He said that the evidence in the euro area, at least for some countries, is that these effects would be small. House price changes have substantial redistribution effects. Some of the consumers are feeling wealthier because the price of their house has gone up. However, the consumers that have to buy a house will feel poorer and increase their saving. And so, the overall effect usually tends to be relatively small.

Frank Smets then argued that the results of the chapter showing a relatively smaller share of investment in GDP adjustment in Germany were puzzling. There is no German institutional feature that could explain that households would be more liquidity constrained than firms or than households in other countries of the area. **Benoît Mojon** said that the results showing a relatively less important role of investment than in other countries, although consistent in the set of VAR models used in the MTN, might be questioned by future research. In all cases, the country classification proposed in chapter 24, would remain useful even if one or two countries were to be reallocated in the light of new research results.

Finally, **Reint Gropp** (ECB) regretted that chapter 24 seemed to imply that in cases where the interest rate channel was dominant, monetary policymakers should not be too concerned with financial frictions. While it is obvious that markets are not perfect, the research presented at the conference also indicated that somehow there are institutions or other factors that are able to offset these financial imperfections. For instance in

Germany, where, *ex ante*, everybody would have thought that the lending channel must be very important, there are active bank networks that protect small banks from adverse monetary policy and other shocks. This means that policymakers should be very much aware that reforms of financial markets, such as the current European Commission proposal to limit the publicly guarantees of some of the German banks, could have important implications for the transmission mechanism.

Appendix

26 The euro area economic and financial structure: an overview

A.-M. Agresti and J. Claessens

1 Introduction

Monetary policy transmission involves the adjustment of financial and real variables following a change in the policy-related short-term interest rate. Most the chapters in this volume analyse these adjustments, evaluating their relevance and measuring their economic importance. Economic and financial structures are potentially relevant factors in shaping monetary policy transmission. Accordingly, this chapter presents a set of stylised facts on the euro area. An extensive or complete account of the euro area's structural features is, however, beyond our scope here; we will concentrate only on the aspects that we believe are most important for the findings of this volume.[1]

The information is summarised in five tables, structured in a way that facilitates cross-country comparisons both within the euro area and, whenever available, with two other large world economies, Japan and the USA. Table 26.1 (p. 434) presents information on macroeconomic characteristics, the relative importance of markets and financial intermediaries. Table 26.2 (p. 438) reports indicators on the banking sectors and table 26.3 (p. 440) shows the balance sheet structures. Finally, the financial structure of the corporate and the household sector are depicted in tables 26.4 and 26.5 (pp. 444 and 447). All these aspects are relevant for the transmission mechanism and the tables give an overview of their relative importance in the euro area, for its member states and for the USA and Japan. The chapter is organised in four sections. Section 1 highlights the major macroeconomic and financial features. Section 2 describes in more detail the national banking sector. Section 3 discusses the financial accounts of the non-financial corporate sector, and section 4 concentrates on the household sector

We would like to thank Ignazio Angeloni, Jesper Berg, Stephano Borgioli, Peter Bull, Andrea Generale, Celestino Giron Pastor, Anil Kashyap and Benoît Mojon for comments on previous drafts of this chapter.

[1] More detailed information can be found in European Central Bank (2002), Erhman *et al.* (chapter 14 in this volume) and Chatelain *et al.* (chapter 7 in this volume).

Table 26.1 Overview of national accounts and financial structures in the euro area, the USA and Japan, 2001

	Euro area	Austria	Belgium	Finland	France	Germany	Greece	Ireland	Italy	Luxembourg	Netherlands	Portugal	Spain	USA	Japan
1 Population (millions of habitants)	306.4	8.1	10.3	5.2	60.9	82.3	10.9	3.8	57.9	0.4	16.0	10.0	40.3	284.8	127.3
2 Nominal per capita GDP (thousands of euros)	22.3	25.9	25.0	26.2	24.0	25.2	11.9	30.2	21.0	47.4	26.5	12.2	16.1	30.6	22.6
National accounts															
3 Nominal GDP (billion of euros)	6819.7	210.7	256.6	136.0	1463.7	2071.2	130.4	115.4	1216.7	21.2	424.8	122.7	650.2	9029.6	4602.6
GDP components (% of GDP)															
4 Private consumption	56.3	55.7	53.1	47.7	54.4	57.5	68.9	45.5	59.7	39.8	48.9	59.2	58.1	69.3	54.7
5 Investment	21.0	22.8	20.9	19.8	20.2	20.1	23.2	23.1	19.8	21.3	22.0	27.5	25.1	19.7	27.0
6 Exports	31.0	37.5	78.2	35.5	24.7	30.8	8.8	80.3	22.1	54.3	60.7	21.8	18.8	10.3	10.5
7 Imports	29.5	39.6	73.4	26.8	25.1	26.6	24.2	49.0	21.4	64.1	54.8	34.6	24.5	13.7	8.6
8 Exports extra euro area	15.4	16.9	27.7	23.7	12.6	17.5	6.0	49.2	12.1	12.1	21.7	7.2	7.7	–	–
9 Imports extra euro area	14.7	14.2	29.3	15.2	11.2	14.5	12.8	36.3	10.8	16.7	31.9	11.3	10.9	–	–
Sectoral decomposition of output (% of GDP)															
10 Agriculture and fishing	2.2	2.0	1.3	3.0	2.6	1.1	6.4	–	2.5	0.7	2.4	3.3	3.2	1.4	1.4
11 Manufacturing	19.8	23.1	21.0	26.7	18.8	22.5	11.8	–	17.3	13.5	17.3	17.7	17.9	21.9	30.8
12 Construction	5.1	7.0	4.6	5.1	4.3	4.4	6.6	–	4.6	6.3	5.4	6.9	8.3	–	–
13 Services	64.5	62.3	67.2	57.1	66.8	64.9	66.2	–	64.9	78.6	65.5	61.0	63.7	76.7	67.7
Capital markets (% of GDP)															
14 Stock-market capitalisation	71.7	13.4	72.6	157.3	90.6	58.1	71.9	73.3	48.7	125.9	131.2	42.4	80.9	137.1	60.1
Bonds issued by															
15 Government	53.4	50.4	95.4	38.6	46.7	38.6	–	–	89.9	–	42.3	42.1	46.7	45.3	10.4
16 Credit institutions	37.5	38.9	29.0	12.8	30.7	65.6	–	–	27.1	199.9	29.2	19.1	8.7	–	–
17 Non-financial enterprises	6.5	1.9	8.2	5.5	17.0	2.8	–	–	2.4	–	9.8	11.2	2.6	28.9	16.9

Money market paper
issued by

#																
18	Government	4.0	0.5	10.9	5.2	–	1.1	–	–	9.4	–	1.4	1.1	5.6	–	–
19	Credit institutions	3.5	0.7	2.5	9.9	10.3	1.5	–	–	0.0	57.6	2.8	0.1	1.8	–	–
20	Non-financial enterprises	1.4	0.0	1.8	2.6	3.8	1.0	–	–	0.0	–	0.0	6.0	0.7	–	–

Monetary and credit aggregates (% of GDP)

#																
21	M3	79.7	70.9	99.7	52.5	73.8	70.8	107.4	82.1	66.5	961.5	95.1	103.2	96.0	80.7	226.4
22	inc. Currency in circulation	3.5	3.9	2.8	1.9	2.0	3.3	5.5	3.2	4.7	2.0	2.0	3.5	6.6	5.8	13.3
23	inc. Overnight deposits	28.9	24.2	24.2	28.7	25.7	25.8	12.4	16.3	37.1	240.7	35.5	38.2	26.2	3.3	43.0
24	inc. Deposits with maturities up to 2 years (M2–M1)	36.1	42.1	68.1	16.8	25.5	37.0	69.4	62.4	15.4	465.3	54.6	60.8	43.0	42.4	78.1
25	inc. Marketable instruments (M3–M2)	11.2	0.7	4.7	5.1	20.6	4.8	20.1	0.2	9.2	253.5	2.9	0.8	20.2	25.5	94.3
26	Time deposits issued by MFIs with maturity over 2 years	18.8	24.1	9.3	1.6	19.1	38.0	2.6	8.7	0.5	25.5	14.8	2.9	7.7	–	–
27	Debt securities issued by MFI, maturities over 2 years	36.5	56.3	25.2	6.9	24.4	63.5	0.1	10.9	26.5	178.9	41.3	18.6	7.6	–	–
28	MFI loans to non-financial private sector	88.7	88.5	66.4	53.9	70.5	106.5	55.1	75.3	63.6	73.5	117.7	120.1	94.4	47.8	133.3
29	Loans to non-financial corporations	42.6	59.7	34.0	22.6	35.7	38.9	36.9	34.8	42.3	34.8	48.6	58.2	46.4	18.8	109.9
30	inc. < 1 year	14.9	19.0	14.1	3.8	9.1	11.3	24.5	13.5	22.0	15.6	14.9	29.8	14.7	–	–
31	Loans to households	45.6	27.9	31.8	30.7	34.2	66.9	18.2	39.5	20.7	38.0	69.1	61.4	47.5	–	–
32	House purchase	29.6	12.8	21.8	20.1	21.8	43.5	11.9	30.1	8.4	28.8	60.9	46.8	29.6	17.7	20.8
33	Consumer credit	7.3	12.2	3.3	4.7	8.0	10.7	6.0	9.4	2.0	3.1	3.2	6.6	7.5	8.1	2.6

Note: -: not available.

and its composition of wealth. Notes on the tables are contained in an appendix.

2   Major economic and financial features of the euro area

2.1   Output structure

Table 26.1 gathers summary statistics on population, the level and the composition of aggregate demand, the sectoral composition of output, the size of capital markets and the size of monetary and credit aggregates in the euro area and the member states, as well as in the euro area, the USA and Japan. Most figures relate to the year 2001.[2] Euro area countries diverge significantly in size but they are quite uniform in terms of *per capita* income. The four largest countries account for 79 per cent of its population and produce 79 per cent of the output in the euro area. *Per capita* GDP measured at PPP exchange rate in the euro area amounts to €22,300, lower than in the USA (€30,600) and close to Japan (€22,600).

The sectoral composition of GDP is quite similar for Germany, France and Italy. On the demand side, private consumption in these countries is between 54 and 60 per cent of GDP. These countries have investment shares close to 20 per cent of GDP. Export and import of goods in these countries are also roughly comparable. Exports (imports) of goods *vis-à-vis* outside the euro area range from 12 (11) per cent of GDP in Italy and France to 18 (15) per cent of GDP in Germany. The other euro area economies show higher contrasts in their GDP composition. For instance, in Greece private consumption is significantly larger than in the whole euro area, while in Finland and Ireland it is significantly lower. The euro area's private consumption represents a lower share of GDP than in the USA: 56 per cent against 69 per cent in the USA.[3] Finally, the euro area economy is somewhat more open to international trade than the USA and Japan.

The sectoral composition of output on the supply side is quite similar across the euro area member states. The services sector is by far the largest and accounts for 65 per cent of euro area GDP. Only Luxembourg, which holds the largest service sector owing to its high concentration of financial institutions, and Finland, whose manufacturing sector remains relatively large, differ markedly from the euro area average.

---

[2] Exceptions are flagged in the notes on the tables.
[3] One should note, however, that the share of consumption in GDP in the USA was exceptionally high in 2001. It was 62 per cent in 1999 and 64 per cent in 2000.

2.2   Financial structure

As is well known, the financial structure of the euro area is more bank-oriented and less financial market-oriented than that of the USA (see chapters 7 and 14 of this volume and European Central Bank, 2002). The dominant role of banks is still a salient feature of the euro area in spite of the ongoing structural changes towards more market-based finance and the resulting growing availability of alternative financial instruments for investors.

The third and fourth panel of table 26.1 illustrate the dominance of banks in the euro area by reporting statistics on the major outstanding financial instruments. The stock market capitalisation amounts in the euro area to 72 per cent of GDP. In comparison, stock market capitalisation represents 137 per cent of GDP in the USA and 60 per cent in Japan. Some inter-regional differences between the euro area countries exist; the stock market capitalisation ratio is especially high in Finland, Luxembourg and the Netherlands (in all cases much above 100 per cent of GDP), and is particularly low in Austria (13 per cent of GDP). Although the volume of private debt securities has increased over time, governments of the euro area still dominate among debt securities issuers. At the end of 2001 government bonds were equal to 53 per cent of GDP in the euro area. Higher than average figures are observed in Belgium and Italy. The outstanding value of corporate debt securities in the euro area remains lower than in the USA and Japan. France, Portugal, Belgium and the Netherlands have more developed markets for bonds issued by the corporate sector: 17, 11, 8 and 10 per cent of GDP, respectively. However, even in these countries, firms still depend much more on banks for their external financing than firms in the USA. In the euro area loans to non-financial corporations account for 43 per cent of GDP; in Austria and Portugal the ratio is more than 50 per cent, in Finland about 23 per cent. In the USA the ratio of loans to non-financial corporations to GDP accounts for 19 per cent, whereas in Japan the ratio is 110 per cent.

Credit institutions of the euro area collect funds both on financial markets and through traditional deposits, but the latter remain dominant. Bond and money market paper debt, 38 and 4 per cent of GDP, respectively, are way smaller than the aggregate of overnight and time deposits. In the euro area bond issues by credit institutions are higher in Germany, where the outstanding value is 66 per cent of GDP. On the other hand, money market paper issued by credit institutions is relatively high in Finland, where it represents 10 per cent of GDP.

Table 26.2 Structure of the banking sector in the euro area, the USA and Japan, 2001

	Euro area	Austria	Belgium	Finland	France	Germany	Greece	Ireland	Italy	Luxembourg	Netherlands	Portugal	Spain	US	Japan
Capacity indicators															
1 Total number of Credit institutions (CIs)	7230	836	112	366	1056	2529	61	88	849	195	561	212	365	11677	2630
2 Total number of Credit institutions (CIs) (per millions of inhabitants)	23.6	102.9	10.9	70.5	17.3	30.7	5.6	23.2	14.7	435.2	35.0	21.1	9.1	41	21
3 Total number of CIs branches (per millions of inhabitants)	559.1	561.5	599.9	229.4	427.7	655.0	272.3	–	505.2	–	326.0	704.6	969.2	272	327
4 Total number of CIs employees (per millions of inhabitants)	6614.3	9184.1	7401.6	4738.4	–	9302.9	5472.9	–	5935.9	53330.5	7936.0	5589.2	6079.8	6626	3629
Penetration of credit institutions from other EEA countries															
5 Number of subsidiaries of CIs (per millions of inhabitants)	1.0	2.0	1.9	0.0	1.7	0.3	0.2	7.1	–	198.6	0.9	0.9	1.1	–	–
6 Proportion of banks branches (% of total branches)	0.2	0.3	0.5	–	0.2	0.1	0.4	97.0	0.3	–	0.4	0.3	0.1	–	–
7 Share of total assets (% of total assets of all MFIs)	3.0	0.8	3.8	5.7	3.0	1.4	4.4	11.0	3.7	16.0	2.2	4.2	3.9	–	–
Penetration of credit institutions from nom EEA countries															
8 Number of subsidiaries of CIs (per millions of inhabitants)	0.43	0.86	0.68	0.00	0.38	0.39	0.18	3.42	–	78.12	1.06	0.30	0.30	–	–
9 Proportion of banks branches (% of total branches)	0.06	0.00	0.16	–	0.11	0.04	0.27	3.03	0.05	–	0.17	0.02	0.03	–	–
10 Share of total assets (% of total assets of all MFIs)	0.48	0.00	0.57	0.00	0.52	0.61	4.40	0.22	0.59	0.86	0.17	0.24	0.21	–	–

Concentration															
11 Herfindahl index	–	0.06	0.16	0.21	–	0.02	0.11	0.05	0.03	0.03	0.18	0.10	0.08	–	–
12 Market share of five largest banks (% of total)	–	44.88	78.27	80.00	47.05	20.16	66.00	42.50	29.00	28.19	82.49	59.57	53.20	–	–
13 *Total assets (% of GDP)*	267.1	272.1	303.0	122.6	276.7	304.3	155.4	460.8	154.4	3847.8	298.0	287.2	199.6	85.6	299.9
Bank profit and loss account structure															
14 Number of banks covered	6290	907	112	342	1067	2370	20	55	821	189	84	42	281	8130	124
Income statement (in % of total assets)															
15 Interest income	5.6	4.6	7.6	4.5	5.8	5.3	5.7	5.6	5.1	7.3	5.7	6.2	5.2	6.3	1.9
16 Interest expenses	4.3	3.4	6.6	2.9	5.1	4.0	3.2	4.1	2.6	6.7	4.2	4.4	2.8	2.9	0.5
17 Net interest income	1.4	1.2	1.0	1.6	0.7	1.3	2.6	1.4	2.5	0.6	1.4	1.8	2.3	3.3	1.4
18 Non-interest income	1.0	1.2	0.9	2.9	1.3	0.7	1.4	0.7	1.1	0.5	1.2	0.8	0.9	2.5	-0.5
19 Gross income	2.3	2.4	1.9	4.6	2.0	2.0	4.0	2.2	3.6	1.1	2.6	2.6	3.2	5.9	0.9
20 Operating expenses	1.5	1.6	1.2	1.7	1.3	1.4	2.3	1.2	2.0	0.5	1.8	1.5	1.8	3.5	0.9
21 inc. staff costs	0.6	0.8	0.6	0.7		0.7	1.4	0.4	1.1	0.3	1.0	0.7	1.1	1.5	0.4
22 Net income	0.9	0.8	0.7	2.8	0.8	0.6	1.7	1.0	1.6	0.6	0.8	1.1	1.4	2.4	-0.1
23 provisions (net)	0.3	0.2	0.1	0.1	0.2	0.4	0.3	0.1	0.6	0.1	0.2	0.4	0.6	0.7	0.6
24 inc. provisions on loans	0.2	0.4	0.1			0.4	0.3	0.1	0.4		0.2	0.3	0.3	0.7	0.6

Note:–not available.

Table 26.3 *Structure of the Monetary Financial Institutions (MFIs) in the euro area, the USA and Japan, 2001*

		Euro area	Austria	Belgium	Finland	France	Germany	Greece	Ireland	Italy	Luxembourg	Netherlands	Portugal	Spain	USA	Japan
Assets composition (% of year-end total assets)																
1	Loans to residents	61.1	65.0	43.5	58.1	56.9	65.8	50.6	39.9	66.5	46.8	65.8	60.2	67.8	61.8	44.5
2	MFIs	20.8	23.3	14.3	11.9	26.2	21.6	12.4	10.7	13.6	35.9	16.8	13.2	16.5	4.5	–
3	General government	4.5	5.0	3.1	1.6	3.0	7.9	1.9	2.5	3.1	0.7	2.6	1.0	2.6	–	–
4	Other residents	35.8	36.7	26.1	44.6	27.8	36.3	36.3	26.6	49.9	10.2	46.4	46.0	48.7	–	36.6
5	Non-financial corporations	15.9	21.9	11.2	18.4	12.9	12.8	23.8	7.6	27.4	0.9	16.3	20.3	23.3	–	–
6	inc. < 1 year	5.6	7.0	4.6	3.1	3.3	3.7	15.8	2.9	14.3	0.4	5.0	10.4	7.3	–	7.8
7	Households	17.1	10.2	10.5	25.1	12.4	22.0	11.7	8.6	13.4	1.0	23.2	21.4	23.8	–	–
8	inc. < 1 year	1.5	1.2	0.9	1.2	0.7	1.7	2.9	1.7	2.5	0.1	1.6	1.9	1.5	–	–
9	Securities issued by residents	18.6	15.3	27.7	12.8	19.7	19.7	26.9	16.3	16.5	19.2	11.4	10.9	17.6	23.0	19.2
10	Securities other than shares	13.3	10.0	24.7	7.3	11.6	14.6	21.4	13.9	11.7	17.0	8.1	5.9	13.0	–	–
11	MFIs	5.5	4.7	2.4	0.7	2.9	10.2	0.1	6.5	2.5	9.1	1.5	1.9	1.3	–	–
12	General government	5.9	3.5	20.1	5.3	5.3	3.4	20.4	4.7	8.2	5.3	5.8	1.9	9.1	12.9	13.9
13	Other residents	1.8	1.8	2.1	1.2	3.3	1.0	0.9	2.7	1.1	2.6	0.8	2.1	2.6	–	–
14	Money market paper	0.8	0.1	0.0	4.0	3.0	0.2	0.0	1.3	0.0	0.9	0.0	0.0	0.0	–	–
15	Shares/other equity issued by residents	4.4	5.2	3.0	1.6	5.1	4.9	5.5	1.1	4.8	1.3	3.3	4.9	4.6	–	0.3
16	inc. MFIs	1.4	1.8	1.5	0.4	2.1	0.9	1.3	0.2	2.6	0.8	0.9	0.8	1.0	–	–
17	inc. other residents	3.1	3.4	1.5	1.2	3.0	4.0	4.2	0.9	2.2	0.5	2.4	4.2	3.7	–	–
18	External assets	13.2	14.8	18.5	24.0	12.5	11.5	8.4	36.9	4.5	28.8	18.9	8.7	7.6	–	–
19	Fixed assets	0.9	0.9	0.5	1.4	0.8	0.6	1.6	0.4	2.6	0.4	0.5	1.0	1.6	–	–
20	Remaining assets	6.2	4.1	9.8	3.7	10.1	2.4	12.6	6.6	9.8	4.7	3.4	19.3	5.3	7.4	–

Liabilities composition (% of year-end total liabilities)

21	Deposits of residents	53.2	56.3	48.4	49.5	49.7	56.4	73.0	37.0	50.7	47.9	51.6	52.2	63.2	70.7	73.6
	Breakdown by holder															
22	MFIs	21.0	22.4	14.7	10.0	25.1	22.5	5.5	17.8	16.1	27.8	16.2	15.4	18.0	–	–
23	Central government	0.6	0.6	0.1	1.0	0.1	0.8	0.7	0.3	0.4	1.1	0.1	1.2	1.5	–	–
24	Other gen. gov./other residents	31.7	33.3	33.6	38.5	24.4	33.2	66.7	18.9	34.2	19.0	35.2	35.6	43.8	–	–
	Breakdown by instrument															
25	Overnight	10.3	8.9	7.9	23.4	7.5	8.5	7.8	3.5	23.9	6.2	11.9	13.3	12.3	10.6	–
26	Time deposits with maturities up to 2 years	13.1	15.5	22.5	13.7	9.2	12.1	44.5	13.4	5.8	12.1	18.3	21.2	21.6	–	–
27	Time deposits with maturities over 2 years	7.1	8.9	3.1	1.3	6.9	12.5	1.7	1.9	0.3	0.7	5.0	1.0	3.8	–	–
28	Repurchase agreements	1.2	0.1	0.1	0.0	0.8	0.1	12.9	0.1	4.1	0.0	0.0	0.1	6.1	–	–
29	Money market fund shares/units	2.4	–	0.2	1.8	6.3	0.5	0.0	2.5	1.4	6.8	–	0.0	3.3	–	–
30	Debt securities issued	14.7	21.2	10.0	7.2	9.3	22.5	0.1	3.9	17.8	5.7	15.1	6.6	5.0	–	6.2
31	inc.up to 2 years	1.1	0.5	1.7	1.5	0.4	1.6	0.1	1.5	0.6	1.0	1.3	0.2	1.2	–	–
32	inc. over 2 years	13.6	20.7	8.3	5.6	8.8	20.9	0.1	2.4	17.2	4.6	13.9	6.5	3.8	–	–
33	Money market paper	1.1	–	–	5.7	3.6	0.5	0.0	–	0.0	1.5	–	–	0.0	–	–
34	Capital and reserves	5.7	5.1	4.5	10.2	6.7	4.4	9.6	5.9	7.1	4.6	4.8	7.0	8.4	–	–
35	External liabilities	14.7	12.8	26.0	21.5	12.0	11.0	5.4	43.9	9.1	29.7	23.6	16.8	13.8	–	0.6
36	Remaining liabilities	8.1	4.6	10.9	4.2	12.5	4.8	11.9	6.8	13.9	3.9	4.8	17.4	6.2	6.1	0.5

Note:-: not available.

Turning to the maturity of the MFIs' liabilities,[4] we observe that time deposits and debt securities issued at maturity over two years are generally smaller than M3. This is the case for the euro area aggregate and for all member states except Austria and Germany. We also note that the Japanese monetary aggregates are dramatically larger than in their euro area and US counterparts.

In general, MFI loans to the non-financial private sector are far above the euro area average in the Netherlands (118 per cent of GDP), Portugal (120 per cent of GDP) and Germany (107 per cent of GDP). MFI loans to non-financial private sector are rather low in Finland, where they amount to about 54 per cent of GDP. We also note that, with the exception of for Greece, Italy and Portugal, over half of this funding is at maturity of more than one year.

Finally, households' borrowing is mainly related to house purchase. House purchase loans represent in the euro area 30 per cent of GDP while home mortgages in the USA account for 18 per cent. In the USA, consumer credit accounts for 8 per cent of GDP, not far from the euro area average (7 per cent).

3   National banking sectors in the euro area

This section describes some more details on the structure of the banking sector in the euro area. Tables 26.2 and 26.3 contain information on competition, openness and specialisation. All these factors may influence the response of banks to monetary policy. Further insight on the characteristics of the banking sectors in the euro area is available in section 2 of chapter 14 (p. 241).

While the banking sector in the euro area is, on the whole, comparatively fragmented, there are differences in concentration across the national banking sectors. The penetration of credit institutions both across euro area countries and from non-euro area countries remains limited.[5] Moreover, Austria, Germany, Luxembourg and the Netherlands are characterised by a number of institutions and number of bank employees far

---

[4] MFIs comprise resident credit institutions as defined in Community law (a credit institution is defined as 'an undertaking whose business is to receive deposits or other repayable funds from the public (including the proceeds arising from the sales of bank bonds to the public) and to grant credit for its own account') and of all other resident financial institutions whose business is to receive deposits and/or close substitutes for deposits from entities other than MFIs and, for their own account (at least in economic terms), to grant credits and/or to invest in securities (this group comprises mostly money market funds (MMFs)). Of course, monetary aggregates also include the Eurosystem monetary liabilities.

[5] More detailed data on cross-border banking are provided in Angeloni and Ehrmann (2003).

above the euro area average. In contrast, these countries are not necessarily the ones where the density of banks' branches is the highest, with the exception of Germany, or the lowest, for example, the Netherlands.

Bank profitability in the euro area is much smaller than in the USA. This is because both of low non-interest income and high interest expenses. The divergence of the Japanese banking system is also striking. Not only is interest income very low but the Japanese non-interest income is also negative owing to losses on market operations.

Inside the euro area, the profitability of most national banking is equally low, with the notable exception of Finland, while Greece, Italy and Spain in 2001 were somewhat more profitable than the euro area average.

Table 26.3 presents the structure of the MFIs' consolidated balance sheet excluding the Eurosystem. The structure of the MFIs' assets in the euro area is fairly similar to that observed in the USA. Loans account for about 60 per cent of the assets and securities for about 20 per cent. The euro area mainly differs from the USA and Japan with respect to the high level of interbank loans and securities. This difference may be due to large interbank loans across countries of the euro area.

Two-thirds of the loans granted to firms and households and about four-fifths of the debt securities held by euro area MFIs have a maturity higher than one year. Countries such as Greece, Italy, Portugal and Spain, which experienced higher and more volatile inflation and interest rates until the mid-to-late 1990s have significantly higher levels of short-term loans.

Turning to the MFIs' liabilities, deposits remain the main source of funding in the USA, Japan and the euro area. This feature is common to all member states. Moreover, the proportions of deposits of governments, deposits of other euro area residents, which include households and non-financial corporations, and deposits of MFIs, show a similar pattern in all euro area countries. We note however that the proportion of deposits in relation to total liabilities differs somewhat across the member states.

The second largest component of liabilities comprises securities other than shares (excluding money market paper), which accounts in the euro area for 15 per cent of the year-end total. Austria, Germany and Italy show a figure markedly above the euro area average. Bank-issued securities tend to be mostly long term; this contributes to close the maturity mismatch generated by the coexistence of long-term loans and short-term deposits.

4   The non-financial enterprise sector

Table 26.4 summarises the information on the non-financial enterprise sector. It focuses on differences on firm-size distribution, main

Table 26.4 Non-financial corporations: size, financial structure and access to capital markets in the euro area, the USA and Japan, 2001

	Euro area	Austria	Belgium	Finland	France	Germany	Greece	Ireland	Italy	Luxembourg	Netherlands	Portugal	Spain	USA	Japan
Size distribution of firms (% of total private sector employment)															
Firms with numbers of employees															
1 0 to 9	33	25	48	23	32	24	–	18	48	19	26	38	47	11	28
2 10 to 49 (99 US)	19	19	14	16	19	20	–	16	21	26	19	23	19	25	36
3 50 to 249 (EU), 299 (JP), 499 (US)	14	21	11	17	15	14	–	14	11	29	15	18	12	14	25
4 250 (EU), 300 (JP), 500 (US) and more	33	35	27	44	34	43	–	51	20	29	40	21	21	50	12
Financial accounts of non-financial corporations (% of GDP)															
5 **Assets**	147.5	50.9	232.5	164.6	218.1	104.4	–	–	114.3	–	150.7	134.2	182.4	105.5	136.8
6 Shares and other equity	76.7	23.8	145.3	67.4	125.4	52.9	–	–	69.6	–	36.6	36.5	81.8	–	21.1
7 other accounts receivable	29.6	3.5	8.5	25.7	38.6	16.6	–	–	25.4	–	29.6	47.3	72.4	–	–
8 Trade credits and advances	15.6	2.6	2.0	–	34.4	–	–	–	–	–	–	43.8	70.7	19.5	43.5
9 **Liabilities**	240.2	122.5	324.1	413.4	348.3	162.4	–	–	185.6	–	281.6	258.1	285.9	282.3	222.7
10 Securities other than shares	8.6	8.9	13.8	12.6	20.3	3.0	–	–	3.4	–	13.0	10.3	3.5	27.3	16.9
11 Short-term	2.3	0.0	7.4	1.4	6.7	0.9	–	–	0.2	–	0.0	4.6	0.6	1.9	–
12 Long-term	5.8	8.8	6.4	10.8	12.3	2.1	–	–	2.4	–	13.0	5.7	2.8	25.4	–
13 Loans	67.8	81.4	68.0	90.4	66.7	64.9	–	–	56.7	–	98.9	85.8	68.0	39.8	87.7
14 Short-term	24.3	21.5	23.3	28.8	20.2	21.0	–	–	32.8	–	36.9	32.6	18.1	–	–
15 Long-term	43.6	59.9	44.7	61.7	46.4	43.9	–	–	23.9	–	62.0	53.2	49.9	–	–
16 Shares and other equity	132.8	29.6	231.2	289.1	223.4	74.5	–	–	96.3	–	136.9	108.3	146.2	155.4	68.1
17 Other accounts payable	27.2	2.7	11.1	21.2	37.5	12.3	–	–	22.6	–	32.7	49.8	68.0	68.0	0.6
18 Trade credits and advances	14.7	1.7	–	–	34.5	–	–	–	–	–	–	36.0	63.7	15.3	38.0
Access to capital markets															
19 Number of firms issuing shares (per millions of inhabitants)[a]	16.0	13.9	13.0	29.9	13.0	11.9	28.7	22.7	5.1	573.6	13.0	9.9	36.8	25.6	16.8
20 Average cap. of firms issuing shares (millions of euros)[a]	998.9	250.5	1829.0	1380.0	1829.0	1252.0	266.7	972.0	2015.0	103.9	1829.0	525.7	355.3	3061.8	1275.5

Notes: -: not available.

[a] France, Belgium and Netherlands are grouped in a common Stock Exchange: Euronext.

financial balance sheet positions and access to capital markets. The financial account data for the euro area refer to the aggregation of the nine countries for which financial data are available.

As can be seen in table 26.4, employment in the euro area is concentrated in small firms. Even in Ireland, Finland, Germany and the Netherlands, where companies with a size exceeding 250 employees account for the largest share of employment, these proportions are smaller than the share of US employment in companies with more than 500 employees. Firms are of smaller size especially in Italy, Portugal, Spain, Belgium and Japan.

The financial assets of non-financial corporations amount in the euro area to 148 per cent of GDP. Financial investments in shares and other equities represent the bulk of the assets of euro area enterprises, accounting for 77 per cent of GDP; this reflects the more complex corporate ownership structure in the euro area (relative to, for example, Japan, where the corresponding figure is 21 per cent), characterised by the widespread presence of holding companies. Belgium and France surpass the euro area average by far, with proportions of 145 and 125 per cent of GDP, respectively. Total financial assets of non-financial corporations in the USA are 106 per cent of GDP. In comparison with the euro area aggregate, trade credit is relatively more important in Portugal (44 per cent of GDP) and especially Spain (71 per cent of GDP).

Table 26.4 also describes the financing of non-financial corporations by showing major liability categories and, where applicable, their maturity. In the euro area, financial liabilities were in 2001 equal to 240 per cent of GDP, which clearly shows how much the sector depends on the use of external finance. A higher level is observed in the USA, where it accounts for 282 per cent, whereas Japan has a level of 223 per cent.

Securities (other than shares) are still a minor component (though growing) in external financing and account for 9 per cent of GDP in the euro area. Debt securities are the highest in France, Belgium, Finland and the Netherlands and are relatively low in Italy, Germany and Spain. Loans, as noted, play an important role in the corporate sector finance. The amount outstanding in the euro area equals 68 per cent of GDP in 2001.[6] The ratios are higher in the Netherlands (99 per cent of GDP), Finland (90 per cent of GDP) and Portugal (86 per cent of GDP). In Italy, loans to the corporate sector account for only 57 per cent of GDP. The amount of loans in the USA is significantly lower (40 per cent of GDP). In Japan, by contrast, loans account for 88 per cent of GDP.

---

[6] About a third of these loans are granted by non-MFI financial institutions, government and non-residents.

In most of the euro area countries, long-term borrowing was in 2001 twice as important as short-term borrowing. To the extent that long-term loans are based on fixed interest rates, the impact of monetary policy on the liquidity situation of the corporate sector could be limited. Short-term borrowing by the corporate sector remains relatively high in the Netherlands, Finland and Portugal.

Shares and other equities constitute another substantial portion of euro area firms' financial liabilities. However, the proportion of shares and other equities that are quoted is much larger in the USA than in the euro area. And the very high level of shares and other equities observed in some countries such as Belgium and France reflects the somewhat artificial valuation of non-quoted shares on the basis of the stock market prices.[7]

The last panel of table 26.4 gives further information on the access of firms to capital markets. Such access reflects both the low average size of euro area corporations, and their lower propensity to access stock markets. In particular, the average market capitalisation of firms that are quoted is much smaller in the euro area relative to the USA. But the number of firms issuing shares (expressed in *per capita* terms in table 26.4) is much smaller.

5   The household sector

Table 26.5 indicates that the proportion of people between 40 and 59 years, who have the highest propensity to save, is quite homogeneous among euro area countries. Some divergence, however, occurs in the euro area countries when considering the proportion of people above 60 years. Ireland and the Netherlands show a lower proportion than the euro area average. Japan has a similar population pyramid. Proportions of people above 60 years are smaller in the USA than in the euro area.

Table 26.5 also provides summary data for the assets and liabilities set of households in relation to GDP. The data provide insights into cross-country differences in the composition of portfolio and wealth of households, which might affect the relative importance of the different channels of monetary policy transmission. The table also reports the asset composition of insurance companies and pension funds as a proxy of the households' indirect holdings of financial assets.

---

[7] In this respect, it is remarkable that the volume of shares issued by non-financial corporations are nearly three times as large as the stock market capitalisation (row 14 in table 26.1) in several euro area countries.

Table 26.5 *Households: demography, access to housing and financial accounts in the euro area, the USA and Japan, 2001*

	Euro area	Austria	Belgium	Finland	France	Germany	Greece	Ireland	Italy	Luxembourg	Netherlands	Portugal	Spain	US	Japan
Demographic determinants of savings (% of total population)															
1 Proportion of population aged 40–59 years	26.0	26.3	26.6	29.3	26.2	26.7	25.2	23.7	26.1	26.7	27.7	25.0	24.8	27.0	28.0
2 Proportion of population above 60 years	22.0	21.0	21.9	20.0	20.6	23.0	23.2	15.1	24.3	19.1	18.2	20.8	21.6	16.6	24.2
Access to housing															
3 Ownership of accommodation (% of households)	61.0	55.0	65.0	60.8	54.0	41.0	–	80.0	78.0	–	52.0	–	78.0	67.5	50.2
4 Total housing debt (% of GDP)	29.6	12.8	21.8	20.1	21.8	43.5	11.9	30.1	8.4	28.8	60.9	46.8	29.6	53.4	21.9
Financial accounts of households (% of GDP)															
5 **Assets**	201.7	133.4	286.7	154.6	213.9	177.1	–	–	212.6	–	279.1	198.8	180.5	321.4	207.5
6 Currency and deposits	61.5	73.7	77.8	34.1	58.4	60.9	–	–	58.3	–	57.4	89.8	68.7	47.9	154.1
7 Securities other than shares	19.3	9.9	61.5	2.4	4.6	18.4	–	–	47.6	–	6.4	8.5	2.8	23.5	16.8
8 Short-term	0.7	0.1	0.9	0.1	0.6	0.1	–	–	2.2	–	0.0	0.3	0.4	–	–
9 Long-term	18.7	9.8	60.6	2.4	3.9	18.3	–	–	45.4	–	6.4	8.2	2.4	–	–
10 Shares and other equity	67.2	20.7	107.8	95.3	88.8	44.1	–	–	75.5	–	54.5	64.4	78.6	137.9	20.5
11 Shares and other equity, excluding MFS	44.6	5.9	63.3	89.9	69.4	23.4	–	–	42.7	–	40.7	50.3	57.0	108.6	12.3
12 Mutual funds shares (MFS)	22.6	14.8	44.5	5.4	19.4	20.7	–	–	32.8	–	13.8	14.1	21.6	29.3	–
13 Insurance technical reserves (inc. pension funds)	50.1	28.9	40.3	20.2	55.0	51.3	–	–	30.0	–	154.0	32.8	24.7	99.5	81.6
14 **Liabilities**	56.8	40.5	45.2	33.8	46.8	73.3	–	–	30.8	–	96.5	77.9	60.9	79.8	75.9
15 Bank loans	51.6	40.4	38.5	32.3	37.7	72.9	–	–	23.0	–	96.5	61.7	49.9	76.2	65.8
16 Short-term	4.2	3.8	2.8	2.4	3.1	5.3	–	–	4.6	–	4.7	6.6	3.1	16.9	–
17 Long-term	47.3	36.6	35.8	29.9	34.6	67.6	–	–	18.4	–	91.8	55.1	46.8	–	–
18 **Assets of insurance corporations and pension funds**	56.6	30.1	38.6	29.1	69.0	61.1	–	–	23.7	–	167.2	33.2	29.8	81.9	88.5
19 Currency and deposits	7.4	1.3	1.0	0.7	1.1	19.3	–	–	1.0	–	4.9	3.5	4.1	0.6	3.4
20 Securities other than shares	18.1	8.9	18.5	12.5	33.6	4.4	–	–	13.9	–	56.8	16.7	14.0	32.9	41.6
21 Loans	4.8	4.3	2.3	1.4	3.3	6.0	–	–	0.1	–	27.8	0.0	1.0	–	18.5
22 Shares and other equity	23.1	13.8	16.1	13.1	29.3	25.1	–	–	8.6	–	72.1	8.6	8.5	36.3	10.9

Note: -: not available.

Euro area countries appear dissimilar in terms of house ownership. While in the euro area the rate of household ownership of accommodation is 61 per cent, Belgium, Italy, Ireland and Spain display higher proportions. Interestingly, in Belgium, Italy and Spain housing indebtedness is lower than average, which accounts for 30 per cent of GDP. The housing-related debt is, in contrast, above the euro area average in Germany, the Netherlands and Portugal. Ownership of accommodation in the USA is larger (68 per cent) than in the euro area and Japan (50 per cent). Moreover, housing-related debt in the USA (53 per cent of GDP) is far above the euro area and Japan (22 per cent of GDP).

Euro area countries also appear dissimilar in terms of total personal asset holdings. While in the euro area households' net financial assets equal 202 per cent of GDP, substantially higher figures are observed in France (214 per cent), in Belgium (287 per cent) and in the Netherlands (279 per cent). Lower values are observed in Austria, Finland, Portugal and Spain. On the other side, assets holdings of households, are larger in the USA than in the euro area as a whole.

Euro area household direct holdings of shares amount to 67 per cent of GDP.[8] In addition, claims on insurance corporations and pension funds amount to about 50 per cent of GDP. Currency and deposits represent the second biggest component in financial assets holdings. In Germany and Austria, currency and deposits holdings are even more important than holdings of shares and other equities. This is true also for Japan, where currency and deposit holdings reach 154 per cent of GDP.

Finally, long-term securities are also a significant part in the assets of the household sector in most euro area countries. Securities held by households in Italy and Belgium are larger than the euro area average, which reflects the high government debt in those countries.

The bulk of household indebtedness is issued as bank loans. Household sector holdings of debt claims are relatively high in Germany (73 per cent of GDP), the Netherlands (97 per cent) and Portugal (62 per cent). At the other end we find Finland and Italy. Another common feature in the euro area household indebtedness is the fact that a large part of the debt is at long-term maturity, including substantial amounts of long-term mortgages.

Altogether, the household sector in the euro area has a net position of interest-bearing assets of about 62 per cent of GDP, which compares to 48 per cent of GDP in the USA and 154 per cent in Japan.[9] This net

---

[8] Again including non-quoted shares.
[9] Defined as direct and indirect holdings of deposits and securities other than shares minus loans issued.

position is much higher for Italian and Belgian households while it is the lowest for the Finish, the Dutch and the Germans.

Notes on the tables

The euro area was composed of the following twelve EU Member States in 2001: Belgium, Greece, Germany, Spain, France, Ireland, Italy, Luxembourg, The Netherlands, Austria, Portugal and Finland. Data, where applicable, are in current prices. Owing to differences in the underlying definitions, data for the euro area, the USA and Japan are in many cases not fully comparable. All tables have been based on currently used statistical definitions and denominations. The notes below give details of the closest equivalent for the USA and Japan when the same denomination is not directly available.

Table 26.1 Overview of national accounts and financial structures in the euro area, the USA and Japan

Sources

Population: euro area: Eurostat (ESA95); USA: US Census Bureau (United States Department of Commerce); Japan: Statistics Bureau & Statistics Center (Ministry of Public Management, Home Affairs, Posts and Telecommunications). **National Accounts**: euro area: Eurostat (ESA95, TRADE); USA and Japan: IMF. **Sectoral composition**: OECD, OEO database. **Capital markets**: De Nederlandsche Bank, Euronext Brussels, World Federation of Exchanges (FIBV), European Central Bank, IMF, Board of Governors of the Federal Reserve System, Bank of Japan. **Monetary and credit aggregates**: European Central Bank, Board of Governors of the Federal Reserve System, Bank of Japan, BIS, Guide to Japan's Money Stock Statistics.

Rows

2	GDP is at market prices. Data for the USA and Japan converted into Euro at OECD purchasing power parities (PPPs) for 2001 (1 EUR = 1.1587 USD = 173.8123 JY). Ratio of nominal GDP to population.
3	GDP is at market prices. Data for the USA and Japan converted into Euro at market exchange rates (annual average 2001: 1 EUR = 0.8956 USD = 108.6824 JY).
4–33	Ratio to total GDP.
6–7	The figures are taken from the TRADE database and consider only exports and imports of goods.

8–9	Euro area: data are taken from ESA95.
10–13	Ratio of the sectoral output to total output. Sectoral classification: euro area: Statistical Classification of Economic Activities in the European Community, Revision 1 (NACE Rev.1). USA: North American Industry Classification System (NAICS); Japan: National Accounts. The figures for the euro area do not add up to 100 per cent of nominal GDP owing to the differences of the entries 'statistical discrepancy' and 'taxes less subsidies on products'. USA: figures for year 2000; Japan: figures for year 1999.
14	Data on market capitalisation exclude investment funds, rights, warrants, convertibles, foreign companies and include common and preferred shares, shares without voting rights. End-of-year data.
15	Euro area: euro-denominated securities. USA: sum of securities issued by state and local government and federal government. Japan: Securities other than shares issued by General Government. Ratio of amounts outstanding to nominal GDP. Amounts outstanding: end-of-year data.
16	Amounts outstanding: end-of-year data.
20	Japan: domestic non-financial sector.
21	Japan:, National concepts M3 + CDs.
22	USA and Japan: notes and coins.
23	USA: demand deposits. Japan: sight deposits.
24	USA: savings deposits, balances in small-denomination time deposits (amounts of less than \$100,000), and balances in retail money market mutual funds; Japan: sum of time deposits, fixed savings, instalment saving, non-resident Yen deposits, foreign currency deposits and CDs.
25	USA: large-denomination time deposits (in amounts of \$100,000 or more), balances in institutional money funds, RP liabilities (overnight and term) issued by all depository institutions, and Eurodollars (overnight and term) held by US residents at foreign branches of US banks world-wide and at all banking offices in the UK and Canada; Japan: Sum of Post Offices, other savings and deposits with financial institution and money trust.
26–27	Euro area: national aggregated balance sheet items of the euro area MFIs, excluding the Eurosystem.
28	USA: sum of total loans held on commercial banks' assets, other loans and mortgages held on savings institutions assets and home mortgages and consumer credit held on credit unions assets; Japan: depository corporations: sum of loans by private financial institutions and loans by public financial institutions.
29	USA: sum of loans n.e.c., other loans and advances and the 'non-home' mortgages (either multi-family, commercial or farm) issued by businesses and held by commercial banks, savings institutions or credit unions. Japan: depository corporations: loan to companies and government (the latter component is marginal).
32	USA: home mortgages held on the assets of commercial banks, savings institutions and credit unions; Japan: depository corporations: sum of housing loans by private and public financial institutions.
33	USA: consumer credit held on the assets of commercial banks, savings institutions and credit unions; Japan: depository corporations: consumer credit by private financial institutions.

Table 26.2 Structure of the banking sector in the euro area, the USA and Japan

Source

European Central Bank (ECB-Banking Structural Statistical Indicators), Eurostat (ESA95), OECD (Bank profitability), Banco do Portugal, Bank of Japan.

Rows

1–2	USA: year 1999; Japan: year 1999.
2–5	Ratio to millions of inhabitants.
3–4	USA: year 1999; Japan: year 1999, the figures have to be taken with caution since information was not available for the whole financial system.
6	Japan: the figure has to be taken with caution since information was not available for the whole financial system. Ratio to total branches.
7	Ratio to total assets.
8	Ratio to million inhabitants.
9	Japan: the figure has to be taken with caution since information was not available for the whole financial system. Ratio to total of branches.
10	Ratio to total assets.
13	Euro area: national aggregated Balance Sheet items of the euro area MFIs, excluding Eurosystem; USA; total assets held by commercial banks, savings institutions or credit unions; Japan: total assets of depository corporations. Ratio to nominal GDP.
14–24	OECD Bank profitability statistics. refer to commercial banks for Greece, Luxembourg, Portugal, the USA and Japan and to all banks for other countries. Euro area, ratios of the sum of the items of the twelve national banking systems denominated in euro divided by the sum of the total assets of national banking systems also denominated in euro.

Table 26.3 Structure of the Monetary Financial Institutions (MFIs) in the euro area, the USA and Japan

Sources

Euro area: European Central Bank (ECB, Monetary Financial Institutions); USA: Board and Governors of the Federal Reserve System (assets and liabilities of commercial banks in the USA); Japan: Bank of Japan (assets and liabilities of domestically licensed banks). All figures reported are percentages of total assets/liabilities. The nomenclature follows that of table 2.2 of the ECB Monthly Bulletin.

Rows

1	Euro area and member states: loans to euro area residents. USA: loans and leases in bank credit; Japan: depository corporations: sum of loans by private and public financial institutions.
2	USA: interbank loans.
5	Japan: depository corporations: sum of loans to companies and government by private financial institutions.
7	Japan: depository corporations: sum of housing loans and consumer credit.
9	Euro area and euro area countries: sum of rows 10, 14 and 15; USA: securities in bank credit; Japan: depository corporations: securities other than shares.
12	USA: Treasury and agency credits; Japan: depository corporations: sum of financing bills, central and local government securities and public corporations securities.
15	Japan: depository corporations: shares and other equities.
20	USA: other assets.
21	USA: total deposits; Japan: depository corporations: deposits.
25	USA: transaction deposits.
26	Sum of deposits agreed maturity up to two years and deposits redeemable at notice up to three months.
27	Sum of deposits with agreed maturity over two years and deposits redeemable at notice over three months.
30	Japan: depository corporations: securities other than shares.
35	Japan: depository corporations: other external claims and debts.
36	USA: other liabilities; Japan: depository corporations: others.

Table 26.4 Non-financial corporations: size, financial structure and access to capital markets in the euro area, the USA and Japan

Sources

Size distribution of firms: euro area: Eurostat (European survey on small and medium enterprises); USA: US Census Bureau (United States Department of Commerce); Japan: Statistics Bureau & Statistics Centre (Ministry of Public Management, Home Affairs, Posts and Telecommunications). **Financial accounts of non-financial corporations**: euro area: Eurostat (Monetary Union Financial Accounts; ESA95); USA: Board of Governors of the Federal Reserve System (Flow of Funds Matrix), OECD; Japan: Bank of Japan (Flow of Funds Accounts), OECD. **Access to capital markets**: World Federation of Exchanges (FIBV), Banco de España.

Rows

1–4	Euro area: figures for 1996; USA: 1999; Japan: 2001. Ratio of employment in firms with indicated number of employees to total employment in the private sector.
5–18	Ratio to nominal GDP. Euro area: figures correspond to EU9 as financial accounts for Greece, Ireland and Luxembourg are not available. Data for Portugal relate to the year 2000.
6	USA: the figure is negligible.
8	USA: trade receivable; Japan: trade credits and foreign trade credits.
9	USA: total financial liabilities of non-financial business, sum of rows 9, 12, 15 and 17. Japan: private non-financial corporations.
10	USA: sum of rows 11 and 12.
11	USA: open market paper.
12	USA: corporate and foreign bonds.
13	Euro area: loans taken from euro area MFIs and other financial corporations. USA: sum of bank loans, other loans and advances and mortgages. This sum is larger than the bank loans to firms show in table 26.1 because some of the loans initially granted by banks and that are still in the liabilities of the non-financial corporate sector have been securitised and hence are not any longer counted on banks' assets.
16	USA: sum of corporate equities and equity in non-corporate business.
18	USA: trade payables; Japan: trade credits and foreign trade credits.
19	The figure for France represents Euronext, the stock exchange that groups Euronext Paris, Euronext Amsterdam and Euronext Brussels. The ratio to the inhabitants considers the inhabitants of France, the Netherlands and Belgium. Ratio of firms issuing shares to millions of inhabitants. End-of-year data.
20	The figure for France represents Euronext, the stock exchange that groups Euronext Paris, Euronext Amsterdam and Euronext Brussels. Ratio of market capitalisation of firms issuing shares to number of firms issuing shares. End-of-year data.

Table 26.5 Households: demography, access to housing and financial accounts in the euro area, the USA and Japan

Sources

Euro area: Eurostat (New Cronos), Eurostat (Monetary Union Financial Accounts; ESA95), European Central Bank (Balance Sheet Items and Financial Accounts), Hypostat and Fannie Mae Foundation; USA: US Census Bureau (United States Department of Commerce) and Board of Governors of the Federal Reserve System (Flow of Funds Accounts); Japan: Statistics Bureau & Statistics Centre (Ministry of Public Management, Home Affairs, Posts and Telecommunications) and Bank of Japan.

Rows

1–2	Euro area: data for the euro area and Greece relate to the year 2000; USA: projections of the total resident population (1 July 2001); Japan: estimate of total population (October 2001). Ratio to total population.
3	Euro area: figure corresponds to EU15. Ratio to total households. Data relate to the year 2000.
4–22	Ratios to nominal GDP.
4	USA: home mortgages.
5–22	Euro area: figures correspond to EU9 as financial accounts for Greece, Ireland and Luxembourg are not available. Data for Portugal relate to the year 2000.
7	USA: sum of open market paper, US government securities, municipal securities, corporate and foreign bonds and mortgages; Japan: sum of central government securities and FILP bonds, local government securities, public corporations securities, bank debentures, industrial securities, securities investment trusts trust beneficiary rights and mortgage securities.
10	USA: corporate equities.
13	USA: sum of life insurance reserves, pension fund reserves, investment in bank personal trusts; Japan: sum of insurance reserves and pension reserves.
14	Euro area: loans taken from euro area MFIs and other financial corporations.
15	USA: credit instruments.
16	USA: Consumer credit.
18–22	USA: sum of assets of life insurance companies, other insurance companies and private pension funds; Japan: financial institutions: insurance and pension funds.
19	USA: Checkable deposits.
20	USA: Credit market instruments.
22	USA: Corporate equities and mutual funds shares.

References

Abel, A. B. and J. C. Eberly (1996), Optimal investment with costly reversibility, *Review of Economic Studies* 63, 581–93

Abreu, M. (2001), From EC accession to EMU participation: the Portuguese disinflation experience in the period 1984–1988, *Banco de Portugal Economic Bulletin*, December

Adams, F. G. and L. R. Klein (1991), Performance of quarterly econometric models of the United States: a new round of model comparisons, in L. R. Klein (ed.), *Comparative performance of US econometric models*, New York and Oxford: Oxford University Press, 18–68

Agresti, A. M. and B. Mojon (2001), Some stylised facts on the euro area business cycle, ECB Working Paper 95

Alhonsuo, S. and J. Pesola (2002), Credit and other financial institutions, ch. 3 in H. Koskenkylä (ed.), *Financial Markets in Finland*, forthcoming in Bank of Finland publication series A

Allen, F. and D. Gale (2000), *Comparing Financial Systems*, Cambridge, MA: MIT Press

Altissimo, F., A. Bassanetti, R. Cristodoro, M. Forni, M. Lippi, L. Reichlin and G. Veronese (2001), A real time coincident indicator of the euro area business cycle, presented at the Banca d'Italia/CEPR Conference – Monitoring the Euro Area Business Cycle, Rome, 7–8 September, mimeo

Altissimo, F., A. Locarno and S. Siviero (2001), Dealing with forward-looking expectations and policy rules in quantifying the channels of transmission of monetary policy, mimeo

Altissimo, F., D. J. Marchetti and G. P. Oneto (2000), The Italian business cycle: coincident and leading indicators and some stylized facts, Banca d'Italia, Temi di discussione 377

Altunbas, Y., O. Fazylow and P. Molyneux (2002), Evidence on the Bank lending channel in Europe, *Journal of Banking and Finance* 26(11), 2093–2110

Alvarez, J. and M. Arellano (1998), The time series and cross-section asymptotics of dynamic panel data estimators, mimeo

Andrews, D. (1999), Consistent moment selection procedures for generalised method of moments estimation, *Econometrica* 67(3), 543–64

Angelini, P. and N. Cetorelli (2000), Bank competition and regulatory reform: the case of the Italian banking industry, Banca d'Italia, Temi di discussione 380

Angelini, P., P. Di Salvo and G. Ferri (1998), Availability and cost of credit for small businesses: customer relationships and credit cooperatives, *Journal of Banking and Finance* 22(6–8), 925–54

Angeloni, I., L. Buttiglione, G. Ferri and E. Gaiotti (1995), The credit channel of monetary policy across heterogeneous banks: the case of Italy, Banca d'Italia, Temi di discussione 256

Angeloni, I. and L. Dedola (1999), From the ERM to the euro: new evidence on economic and policy convergence among EU countries, ECB Working Paper 4

Angeloni, I. and M. Ehrmann (2003), Monetary policy transmission in the euro area: early evidence, *Economic Policy* n. 37

Angeloni, I., A. Kashyap, B. Mojon and D. Terlizzese (2003), The output composition puzzle: a difference in the monetary transmission mechanism in the Euro area and US, ECB Working Paper 268, forthcoming: *Journal of Money, Credit and Banking*

Aoki, K., J. Proudman and G. Vlieghe (2001), Houses as collateral: has the link between house prices and consumption in the UK changed?, Federal Reserve Bank of New York, *Economic Policy Review*, 8(1), 163–77

Arellano, M. and S. R. Bond (1991), Some tests of specification for panel data: Monte Carlo evidence and an application to employment equations, *Review of Economic Studies* 58, 277–97

Artis, M., H. M. Krolzig and J. Toro (1999), The European business cycle, EUI Working Paper ECO 99/24

Artus, P., F. Legros and J.-P. Nicolaï (1989), Consommation et richesse perçue par les ménages, Document de travail 6, Service des Etudes Economiques et Financières, Caisse des Dépôts et Consignation

Ashcraft, A. B. (2001), New evidence on the lending channel. Federal Reserve Bank of New York Staff Reports 136

Assouline, M. et al. (1998), Structures et propriétés de cinq modèles macroéconomiques français, *Economie et Prévision* 134(3), 1–97

Auerbach, A. J. (1983), Taxation, corporate financial policy and the cost of capital, *Journal of Economic Literature* 21, 905–40

Bagliano, F. C. and C. A. Favero (1995), The credit channel of monetary transmission: the case of Italy, Università Cattolica del Sacro Cuore, Milan, mimeo

   (1996), Monetary policy, credit shocks and the channels of monetary transmission. The Italian experience: 1982–1994, Università Bocconi, Working Paper 103

Bagliano, F. C. and A. Sembenelli (2001), The cyclical behavior of inventories: European cross-country evidence from the early 1990s recession, mimeo

Baltagi, B. H. (1995), *Econometric Analysis of Panel Data*, Chichester: John Wiley

Baltagi, B. H. and C. Kao (2000), Nonstationarity panels, cointegration in panels and dynamic panels: a survey, mimeo

Banca d'Italia (1986), Modello trimestrale dell'economia italiana, Banca d'Italia, Temi di discussione 80

Banco de España (2000a), Results of non-financial corporations, Annual Report 1999, Central Balance Sheet Office, Banco de España

   (2000b), Spanish financial markets and intermediaries, *Economic Bulletin*, Banco de España, January

Banerjee, A. (1999), Panel data unit roots and cointegration: an overview, *Oxford Bulletin of Economics and Statistics, Special Issue*, 607–29

Bank for International Settlements (BIS) (1995), Financial structure and the monetary policy transmission mechanism, Basel: Bank for International Settlements

Banque centrale du Luxembourg (BCL) (2002a), *Rapport Annuel 2001*, Luxembourg: BCL

(2002b), A descriptive analysis of the Luxembourg financial structures: 1998–2001, Bulletin 2002, 3, Luxembourg: BCL

Barnett, S. A. and P. Sakellaris (1998), Nonlinear response of firm investment to Q: testing a model of convex and non-convex adjustment costs, *Journal of Monetary Economics* 42, 261–88

Barran, F., V. Coudert and B. Mojon (1997), The transmission of monetary policy in the European countries, in S. Collignon (ed.), *European Monetary Policy*, London and Washington: Pinter Press

Barran, F. and M. Peeters (1998), Internal finance and corporate investment, Belgian evidence with panel data, *Economic Modelling* 15, 67–89

Batini, N. and A. Haldane (1999), Forward looking rules for monetary policy, Bank of England, Working Paper 91

Batini, N. and E. Nelson (2000), Optimal horizons for inflation targeting, Bank of England, Working Paper 119

Baumel, L. and P. Sevestre (2000), La relation entre le taux des crédits et le coût des ressources bancaires. Modélisation et estimation sur données individuelles de banques, *Annales d'Economie et de Statistique* 59, 199–226

Baxter, M. (1995), International trade and business cycles, in G. M. Grossman and K. Rogoff (eds.), *Handbook of International Economics 3*, Amsterdam: Elsevier, 1801–64

Baxter, M. and R. G. King (1999), Measuring business cycles: approximate Band-pass filters for economic time series, *Review of Economics and Statistics* 81(4), 575–93

Bayoumi, T. and B. Eichengreen (1996), Operationalizing the theory of optimum currency areas, Centre for Economic Policy Research, Discussion Paper 1484

Bean, C. (1998), The new UK monetary arrangements: a view from the literature, *Economic Journal* 108, 1795–1809

Bean, C., J. Larsen and K. Nikolov (2002), Financial frictions and the monetary transmission mechanism: theory, evidence and policy implications, European Central Bank, Working Paper 113

Beaudu, A. and T. Heckel (2001), Le canal du crédit fonctionne-t-il en Europe? Une étude de l'hétérogénéité des comportements d'investissement à partir de données de bilan agrégées, *Economie et Prévision* 147, 117–41

Bentoglio, G., J. Fayolle and M. Lemoine (2001), Unité et pluralité du cycle européen, *Revue de L'OFCE* 78 9–73, July

Berlin, M. and L. Mester (2000), Deposits and relationship lending, *Review of Financial Studies* 12 (3)

Bernanke, B. (1986), Alternative explanation of the money–income correlation, in K. Brunner and A. Meltzer (eds.), *Real Business Cycles, Real Exchange*

Rates, and Actual Policies, Princeton Econometric Research Program Memorandum 321, 49–99

Bernanke, B. and A. Blinder (1988), Credit, money, and aggregate demand, *American Economic Review* 78, 435–9

(1992), The federal funds rate and the channels of monetary transmission, *American Economic Review*, 82, 901–21

Bernanke, B. S. and M. Gertler (1995), Inside the black box: the credit channel of monetary policy transmission, *Journal of Economic Perspectives* 9, 27–48

Bernanke, B., M. Gertler and S. Gilchrist (1996), The financial accelerator and the flight to quality, *Review of Economics and Statistics* 78(1), 1–15

(1999), The financial accelerator in a quantitative business cycle framework, in J. B. Taylor and M. Woodford (eds.), *Handbook of Macroeconomics*, 1C, Amsterdam: North-Holland 1341–96

Bernanke, B. and I. Mihov (1997), What does the Bundesbank target?, *European Economic Review* 41, 1025–54

Bester, H. (1985), Screening vs rationing in credit markets with imperfect information, *American Economic Review* 75 (4), 850–5

Beyer, A., J. Doornik and D. F. Hendry (2001), Constructing historical euro-zone data, *Economic Journal* 111, 308–27

Bianco, M. (1997), Vincoli finanziari e scelte reali delle imprese italiane: gli effetti di una relazione stabile con una banca, in I. Angeloni, V. Conti and F. Passacantando (eds.), *Le banche e il finanziamento delle imprese*, Bologna: Il Mulino

Binder, M., C. Hsiao and M. H. Pesaran (2000), Estimation and inference in short panel vector autoregressions with unit roots and cointegration, mimeo

Bischoff, C. (1969), Hypothesis testing and the demand for capital goods, *Review of Economics and Statistics* 51, 354–68

Blanchard, O. and D. Quah (1989), The dynamic effects of aggregate demand and supply disturbances, *American Economic Review* 79, 655–73

Boccuzzi, G. (1998), *La crisi dell'impresa bancaria. Profili economici e giuridici*, Milano: Giuffrè

Boivin, J. and M. Giannoni (2001), The monetary transmission mechanism: has it changed?, mimeo

Bolton, P. and X. Freixas (2000), Equity bonds and bank debt: capital structure and financial market equilibrium under asymmetric information, *Journal of Political Economy* 108, 324–51

Bond, S. and J. G. Cummins (2000), Noisy share prices and the Q model of investment, University of Oxford and Federal Reserve Board, mimeo

Bond, S., J. Elston, J. Mairesse and B. Mulkay (1997), A comparison of empirical investment equations using company panel data for France, Germany, Belgium and the UK, NBER Working Paper 5900

Bond, S. and C. Meghir (1994a), Dynamic investment models and the firm's financial policy, *Review of Economic Studies* 61, 197–222

(1994b), Financial constraints and company investment, *Fiscal Studies* 15(2), 1–18

Bonnet, X. and E. Dubois (1995), Peut-on comprendre la hausse imprévue du taux d'épargne des ménages depuis 1990?, *Economie et Prévision* 121(5), 39–58

Bordes, C., D. Currie and H.-T. Söderström (1993), Three assessments of Finland's economic crisis and economic policy, Suomen Pankki publication C:009

Borio, E. V. (1996), Credit characteristics and the monetary policy transmission mechanism in fourteen industrial countries: facts, conjectures and some econometric evidence, in K. Alders et al. (eds.), *Monetary Policy in a Converging Europe*, Boston: Kluwer Academic

Brainard, W. (1967), Uncertainty and the effectiveness of monetary policy, *American Economic Review, Papers and Proceedings* 57, 411–25

Braumann, B. (2002), Financial liberalization in Austria, Oesterreichische Nationalbank, mimeo

Brissimis, S. N. and E. C. Kastrissianakis (1997), Is there a credit channel in the Greek economy? (in Greek), *Bank of Greece Economic Bulletin* 10, 91–111

Brissimis, S. N. and N. S. Magginas (2002), Changes in financial structure and asset price substitutability: a test of the Bernanke–Blinder model, Bank of Greece, mimeo

Brissimis, S. N., N. S. Magginas, G. T. Simigiannis and G. S. Tavlas (2001), Issues in the transmission of monetary policy, in R. C. Bryant, N. C. Garganas and G. S. Tavlas (eds.), *Greece's Economic Performance and Prospects*, Athens: Bank of Greece and the Brookings Institution

Brunila, A. (1994), Investment and financing considerations: evidence from Finnish panel data, Suomen Pankki Dp 4/94

Buiter, W. and I. Jewitt (1981), Staggered wage setting with real wage relativities: variations on a theme of Taylor, *Manchester School of Economic and Social Studies* 49(3), 211–28

Buttiglione, L., P. Del Giovane and E. Gaiotti (1997), The role of different central bank rates in the transmission of monetary policy, Banca d'Italia, Temi di discussione 305

Buttiglione, L. and G. Ferri (1994), Monetary policy transmission via lending rates in Italy: any lessons from recent experience?, Banca d'Italia, Temi di discussione 224

Butzen, P., C. Fuss. and P. Vermeulen (2001), The interest rate and credit channel in Belgium: an investigation with micro-level firm data, ECB Working Paper 107

Caballero, R. (1999), Aggregate investment, in J. Taylor and M. Woodford (eds.), *Handbook of Macroeconomics*, Amsterdam: North-Holland

Campello, M. (2002), Internal capital markets in financial conglomerates: evidence from small bank responses to monetary policy, *Journal of Finance*, 576, 2773–2805

Carlstrom, C. T. and T. S. Fuerst (2000), Monetary shocks, agency costs and business cycles, Federal Reserve Bank of Cleveland, Working Paper 0011

Cecchetti, S. (1995), Distinguishing theories of the monetary transmission mechanism, in *Federal Reserve Bank of St. Louis Review*, May–June, 83–100

(1999), Legal structure, financial structure and the monetary policy transmission mechanism, *Federal Reserve Bank of New York Economic Policy Review*, July; NBER Working paper 7151

(2000), Legal structure, financial structure, and the monetary policy transmission mechanism, in *The Monetary Transmission Process: Recent Developments and Lessons for Europe*, Basingstoke: Palgrave for the Deutsche Bundesbank

(2001), Financial structure, macroeconomic stability and monetary policy, National Bureau of Economic Research Working Paper 8354

Cecchetti, S. and R. W. Rich (2001), Structural estimates of the US sacrifice ratio, *Journal of Business and Economic Statistics*, 19(4), 416–27

Central Banking (1995–6), *Financial Reform and the Banking System* 6(3), 66–71

Chatelain, J. B. (2001), Investment, the cost of capital and upward testing procedures for instrument selection on panel data, Banque de France, mimeo

(2002), Structural modelling of financial constraints on investment: where do we stand?, National Bank of Belgium Working Paper 28

Chatelain, J. B. and J. C. Teurlai (2000), Comparing several specifications of financial constraints and of adjustment costs in investment Euler Equation, Banque de France, mimeo, presented at the European Meeting of the Econometric Society

(2001), Investment and the cost of external finance: an empirical investigation according to the size of firms and their use of leasing, Banque de France, mimeo, presented at the Money, Macro and Finance Conference

Chatelain, J. B. and A. Tiomo (2001), Investment, the Cost of Capital and Monetary Policy in the Nineties in France: A Panel Data Investigation, ECB Working Paper, 106

Chenells, L. and R. Griffith (1997), Taxing profits in a changing world, London: Institute for Fiscal Studies

Chiades, P. and L. Gambacorta (2003), The Bernanke and Blinder Model in an open economy: The Italian case, *German Economic Review* 4

Chiang, M.-H. and C. Kao (2001), Nonstationary panel time series using NPT 1.2 – a user guide, Center for Policy Research, Syracuse University

Chinn, M. (1997), Sectoral productivity, government spending and real exchange rates: empirical evidence for OECD countries, NBER Working Paper 6017

Chinn, M. D and L. Johnston (1997), Real exchange rate levels, productivity and demand shocks: evidence from a panel of 14 countries, IMF Working Paper 66

Chirinko, R. S. (1993), Business fixed investment: a critical survey of modeling strategies, empirical results and policy implications, *Journal of Economic Literature* 31, 206–10

Chirinko, R. S., S. M. Fazzari and A. P. Meyer (1999), How responsive is business capital formation to its user cost? An exploration with micro data, *Journal of Public Economics* 74, 53–80

Christ, C. F. (1968), A simple macroeconomic model with a government budget restraint, *Journal of Political Economy* 76, 53–67

Christiano, L. J., M. Eichenbaum and C. L. Evans (1997), Sticky price and limited participation models of money: a comparison, *European Economic Review* 41, 1201–49

(1999), Monetary policy shocks: what have we learned and to what end?, in J. Taylor and M. Woodford (eds.), *Handbook of Macroeconomics*, Amsterdam: North-Holland

(2001), Nominal rigidities and the dynamic effects of a shock to monetary policy, National Bureau of Economic Research, Working Paper 8403

Church, K. B., J. E. Sault, S. Sgherri and K. F. Wallis (2000), Comparative properties of models of the UK economy, *National Institute Economic Review* 171, 106–22

Ciccarelli, M. and A. Rebucci (2002), The transmission mechanism of European monetary policy: is there heterogeneity? Is it changing over time?, IMF Working Paper 02154

Ciocca, P. (2000), *La nuova finanza in Italia. Una difficile metamorfosi (1980–2000)*, Turin: Bollati Boringhieri

Clarida, R., J. Galí and M. Gertler (1999), The science of monetary policy: a new Keynesian perspective, *Journal of Economic Literature* 37, 1661–1707

Clarida, R. and M. Gertler (1997), How the Bundesbank conducts monetary policy, in D. Romer and C. Romer (eds.), *Reducing Inflation: Motivation and Strategy*, Chicago: University of Chicago Press

Clements, B., Z. Kontolemis and J. Levy (2001), Monetary policy under EMU: differences in the transmission mechanism?, IMF Working Paper 01/102

Coen, R. (1969), Tax policy and investment behavior: Comment, *American Economic Review* 59, 370–9

Coenen, G. and J. Vega (2001), The demand for M3 in the euro area, ECB Working Paper 6, forthcoming in *Journal of Applied Econometrics*, 16(6), 727–48

Commission Bancaire (2000), *Annual Report 1999*, Secrétariat Général de la Commission Bancaire

Conigliani, C., G. Ferri and A. Generale (1997), The impact of bank–firm relations on the propagation of monetary policy squeezes: an empirical assessment for Italy, *BNL Quarterly Review* 202, 271–99

Cooley, T., V. Quadrini and R. Marimon (2001), Aggregate consequences of limited contract enforceability, Harvard University and Universitat Pompeu Fabra, mimeo

Cooper, N., R. Hillman and D. Lynch (2001), Interpreting movements in high-yield corporate bond spreads?, *Bank of England Quarterly Bulletin* 41(1), 110–20

Corvoisier, S. and R. Gropp (2001), Bank concentration and retail interest rates, ECB Working Paper 72

Cottarelli, C., G. Ferri and A. Generale (1995), Bank lending rates and financial structure in Italy: a case study, IMF Working Papers 38

Courakis, A. S. (1988), Modelling portfolio selection, *Economic Journal* 98, 619–42

Crépon, B. and C. Gianella (2001), Fiscalité et coût d'usage du capital: incidence sur l'investissement, l'activité et l'emploi, *Economie et Statistique* 341–342, 107–28

Crépon, B. and F. Rosenwald (2001), Des contraintes financières plus lourdes pour les petites entreprises, *Economie et Statistique* 341–342, 29–46

Cummins, G., K. Hassett and R. G. Hubbard (1994), A reconsideration of investment behavior using tax reforms on national experiments, *Brookings Papers on Economic Activity* 2, 1–59

(1996), Tax reforms and investment: a cross-country comparison, *Journal of Public Economics* 62, 237–73

Cummins, G., K. Hassett and S. D. Oliner (1999), Investment behavior, observable expectations, and internal funds, Board of Governors of the Federal Reserve System, Finance and Economics Discussion Paper 99/27

Cushman, D. O. and T. Zha (1997), Identifying monetary policy in a small open economy under flexible exchange rates, *Journal of Monetary Economics* 39, 433–48

De Bondt, G. J. (1999), Banks and monetary transmission in Europe: empirical evidence, *Banca Nazionale del Lavoro Quarterly Review* 52, 149–68

(2000), *Financial Structure and Monetary Transmission in Europe. A cross-country study*, Cheltenham and Northampton, MA: Edward Elgar

(2002), Euro area corporate debt securities market: first empirical evidence, ECB Working Paper 164

de Haan, L. (2001), The credit channel in the Netherlands: evidence from bank balance sheets, ECB Working Paper 98

De Mitri, S., D. J. Marchetti and A. Staderini (1998), Il costo d'uso del capitale nelle imprese italiane: un'analisi disaggregata, Banca d'Italia, mimeo

De Nederlandsche Bank DNB (1999), The Dutch housing and mortgage markets: a risk analysis, *Quarterly Bulletin* September, 23–33

(2000a), The importance of financial structure for monetary transmission in Europe, *Quarterly Bulletin*, March, 33–40

(2000b), The Nederlandsche Bank's analysis of bank lending, *Quarterly Bulletin* March, 64–71

(2000c), Survey among Dutch mortgage-holders on the use of mortgage credit, *Quarterly Bulletin*, June, 30–43

Dedola, L. and F. Lippi (2000), The monetary transmission mechanism: evidence from the industries of five OECD countries, Banca d'Italia, Temi di discussione 389

Degryse, H. and P. Van Cayseele (1998), Relationship lending within a bank-based system: evidence from European small business data, Discussion Paper Series 98.16, Center for Economic Studies

Delbreil, M., A. Esteban, H. Friderichs, B. Paranque, F. Partsch and F. Varetto (2000), Corporate finance in Europe from 1986 to 1996, Report of European Committee of Central Balance Sheet Offices, Own Funds Working Group, DG ECFIN

Dell'Ariccia, G. and R. Marquez (2001), Flight to quality or to captivity? Information and credit allocation, IMF Working Paper 20

Deloof, M. (1998), Internal capital markets, bank borrowing, and financing constraints. Evidence from Belgian firms, *Journal of Business Finance and Accounting* 25(7), 945–68

DeMeza, D. and D. Webb (1987), Too much investment: a problem of asymmetric information, *Quarterly Journal of Economics* 102(2), 281–92

Deutsche Bundesbank (1998), The methodological basis of the Deutsche Bundesbank's corporate balance sheet statistics, *Monthly Report* October, 49–64

Deutsche Bundesbank (1999), The Bundesbank's method of assessing the creditworthiness of business enterprises, *Monthly Report* January, 51–63

(2000a), The relationship between bank lending and the bond market in Germany, Monthly Report, January, 33–47

(2000b), Deposit protection and investor compensation in Germany, *Monthly Report* July, 29–45

(2001), Bank balance sheets, bank competition and monetary policy transmission, *Monthly Report* September, 51–70

(2002a), German enterprises' profitability and financing in 2000, *Monthly Report* April, 33–55

(2002b), Monetary policy and investment behaviour – an empirical investigation, *Monthly Report* July

Devereux, M. and F. Schiantarelli (1990), Investment, financial factors and cash flow from UK panel data, in G. Hubbard (ed.), *Information, Capital Markets and Investment*, Chicago: University of Chicago Press

Doms, M. and T. Dunne (1998), Capital adjustment patterns in manufacturing plants, *Review of Economic Dynamics* 1(2), 409–29

Dornbusch, R., C. A. Favero and F. Giavazzi, (1998), Immediate challenges for the ECB: issues in formulating a single monetary policy, *Economic Policy* 26, 15–64

Duhautois, R. (2001), Le ralentissement de l'investissement est plutôt le fait des petites entreprises tertiaires, *Economie et Statistiques* 341–342(1/2), 47–66

Edison, H. and T. Sloek (2001), Wealth effects and the new economy, International Monetary Fund, Working Paper WP/01/77

Ees, H. van, H. Garretsen and E. Sterken (1999), Some evidence on the relevance of bank behaviour for the lending channel in the Netherlands, *De Economist* 147, 19–37

Ehrmann, M. (2000a), Comparing monetary policy transmission across European countries, *Weltwirtschaftliches Archiv*, Band 136, 58–83

Ehrmann, M. (2000b), Firm size and monetary policy transmission: evidence from German business survey data, ECB Working Paper 21

Ehrmann, M., L. Gambacorta, J. Martínez-Pagés, P. Sevestre and A. Worms (2001), Financial systems and the role of banks in monetary policy transmission in the Euro area, ECB Working Paper 105

Ehrmann, M. and A. Worms (2001), Interbank lending and monetary policy transmission – evidence for Germany, ECB Working Paper 73

Eichenbaum, M. and C. Evans (1995), Some empirical evidence on the effects of shocks to monetary policy on exchange rates, *Quarterly Journal of Economics* November, 975–1009

Eisner, R. (1969), Tax policy and investment behavior: comment, *American Economic Review* 59, 379–88

(1970), Tax policy and investment behavior: further comment, *American Economic Review* 60, 746–52

Eisner, R. and M. Nadiri (1968), Investment behavior and the neo-classical theory, *Review of Economics and Statistics* 50, 369–82

(1970), Neoclassical theory of investment behavior: a comment, *Review of Economics and Statistics* 52, 216–22

Elliehausen, G. E. and J. D. Wolken (1993), The demand for trade credit: an investigation of motives for trade credit use by small businesses, *Federal Reserve Bulletin* October

Els, P. van, A. Locarno, J. Morgan and J. P. Villetelle (2001), Monetary policy transmission in the euro area: what do aggregate and national structural models tell us?, ECB Working Paper 94

Els, P. Van, A. Locarno, B. Mojon and B. Morgan (2002), New macroeconomic evidence on monetary policy transmission in the Euro area, European Central Bank, mimeo

Elsas, R. and J. P Krahnen (1998), Is relationship-lending special? Evidence from credit file data in Germany, *Journal of Banking and Finance* 22, 1283–1316

Elsinger, H., A. Lehar and M. Summer (2002), Risk assessment for banking systems, OeNB Working Paper 79

European Central Bank (ECB) (2000), Mergers and acquisitions involving the EU banking industry – facts and implications, *Monthly Report of the European Central Bank*, January, 33–47

(2001a), Characteristics of corporate finance in the euro area, *Monthly Bulletin* February

(2001b), Financing and financial investment in non-financial sector in the euro area, *Monthly Bulletin* May

(2002), *Report on Financial Structure* October

Evans, C. and D. Marshall (2002) Economic determinants of the nominal Treasury yield curve, Federal Reserve Bank of Chicago, mimeo

Fagan, G., J. Henry and R. Mestre (2001), An area-wide model (AWM) for the Euro area, ECB Working Paper 42

Fanelli, L. and P. Paruolo (1999), New evidence on the transmission mechanisms of monetary policy in Italy before Stage III of European Monetary Union, presented at the 9th Sadiba Conference Ricerche Quantitative per la Politica Economica, Perugia

Farinha, L. and C. R. Marques (2001), The bank lending channel of monetary policy: identification and estimation using Portuguese micro bank data, ECB Working Paper 102

Farinha, L. A. and J. A. C. Santos (2000), Switching from single to multiple bank lending relationships: determinants and implications, BIS Working Paper 83

Fase, M. and C. Winder (1993), The demand for money in the Netherlands and the other EC countries, *De Economist*, 141–4, 471–95

Favero, C. A., F. Giavazzi, L. Flabbi (2001), The transmission mechanism of monetary policy in Europe: evidence from banks' balance sheets, CEPR Discussion Paper 2303

Fazzari, S. M., G. R. Hubbard and B. C. Petersen (1988), Financing constraints and corporate investment, *Brookings Papers on Economic Activity* 1, 141–95

(2000), Investment-cash flow sensitivities are useful: a comment on Kaplan and Zingales, *Quarterly Journal of Economics* 115(2), 695–705

Fazzari, S. M. (1993), Investment and US fiscal policy in the 1990s, Public Policy Brief October

Federal Deposit Insurance Corporation (1998), Managing the crisis: the FDIC and RTC experience, 1980–1994, Washington, DC: FDIC

Ferri, G. and G. B. Pittaluga (1996), Il finanziamento delle imprese nelle fasi di restrizione monetaria. Il caso del credito cooperativo, *Cooperazione di Credito* 152–3, 473–506

Fisher, P. (1992), *Rational Expectations in Macroeconomic Models*, Boston: Kluwer Academic Press

Forni, M. and L. Reichlin (2001), Federal policies and local economies: Europe and the US, *European Economic Review*, 45(1), 109–34

Frankel, J. and A. Rose (2001), An estimate of the effect of currency union on trade and growth, NBER Working Paper 7857

Franzosi, A. M. (1999), Investment determinants: empirical evidence from a panel of Italian firms, IRS, *Contributi di ricerca* 44

Friderichs, H., and A. Sauvé (1999), The Annual Accounts Databases on Non-Financial Enterprises of the Banque de France and the Deutsche Bundesbank: methodological aspects and comparability, in A. Sauvé and M. Scheuer, (eds.), *Corporate Finance in Germany and France*, Deutsche Bundesbank and Banque de France, September, 33–62

Friderichs, H., B. Paranque and A. Sauvé (1999), Structures of corporate finance in Germany and France: a comparative analysis for West German and French incorporated enterprises with special reference to institutional factors, in A. Sauvé and M. Scheuer (eds.), *Corporate Finance in Germany and France*, Deutsche Bundesbank and Banque de France, September, 63–137

Frühwirth-Schnatter, S. (1999), Model likelihoods and Bayes factors for switching and mixture models, *Technical Report* 1999–71, revised version January 2001, Vienna University of Economics and Business Administration

Frühwirth-Schnatter, S. and S. Kaufmann (2002), Bayesian clustering of many short time series, Oesterreichische Nationalbank, mimeo

(2003), Investigating asymmetries in the bank lending channel. An analysis using Austrian banks' balance sheet data, Oesterreichische Nationalbank, mimeo

Fry, M., D. Julius, L. Mahadeva, S. Roger and G. Sterne (2000), in L. Mahadeva and G. Sterne (eds.), *Monetary Policy Frameworks in a Global Context*, Centre for Central Banking Studies, Bank of England

Fuhrer, J. and G. Moore (1995), Inflation persistence, *Quarterly Journal of Economics*, 110(1), 127–59

Gaiotti, E. (1999), The transmission of monetary policy shocks in Italy, 1967–1997, Banca d'Italia, Temi di discussione, 363

Gaiotti, E. and A. Generale (2001), Does monetary policy have asymmetric effects? A look at the investment decisions of Italian firms, ECB Working Paper 110

(2002), Does monetary policy have asymmetric effects? A look at the investment decisions of Italian firms, *Giornale degli Economisti e Annali di Economia* 61, 29–59

Galeotti, M., F. Schiantarelli and F. Jaramillo (1994), Investment decisions and the role of debt, liquid assests and cash flow: evidence from Italian Panel Data, *Applied Financial Economics* 4(2), 121–32

Galí, J. (1992), How well does the IS-LM model fit postwar US data?, *Quarterly Journal of Economics* May, 709–38

Galí, J., J. D. Lopez-Salido and J. Valles (2000), Technology shocks and monetary policy: assessing the Fed's performance, mimeo

Gambacorta, L. (2001a), Gli effetti di asimmetrie strutturali nella domanda aggregata per la politica monetaria delle BCE (The effects of structural asymmetries in aggregate demand on ECB monetary policy), *Economia Politica*, 18(2), 217–47

(2001b), Bank-specific characteristics and monetary policy transmission: the case of Italy, ECB Working Paper 103

(2003), Asymmetric bank lending channels and ECB monetary policy, *Economic Modelling* 20, 25–46

Gambacorta, L., G. Gobbi and F. Panetta (2001), Il sistema bancario italiano nell'area dell'euro, *Bancaria* 57(3), 21–32

Gambacorta, L. and P. E. Mistrulli (2003), Bank capital and lending behavior: empirical evidence for Italy. Banca d'Italia, Tenni di discussione, forthcoming

Garganas, N. and G. S. Tavlas (2001), Monetary regimes and inflation performance: the case of Greece, in R. C. Bruyant, N. C. Garganas and G. S. Tavlas (eds.), *Greece's Economic Performance and Prospects*, Athens: Bank of Greece and Brookings Institution, 43–96

Garretsen, H. and J. Swank (1998), The transmission of interest rate changes and the role of bank balance sheets: a VAR analysis for the Netherlands, *Journal of Macroeconomics*, 20(2), 325–39

Gérard, M. and F. Verschueren (2000), The neoclassical synthesis of investment behaviour and the co-integration challenge, an experimentation with Belgian industry data, *Cahiers Economiques de Bruxelles* 167, 299–344

Gerlach, S. and F. Smets (1995), The monetary transmission mechanism: evidence from the G7 countries, CEPR Discussion Paper 1219

Gertler, M. and R. G. Hubbard (1988), Financial factors in business fluctuations, Columbia First Boston Series in Money, Economics and Finance Working Paper FB-88-37, 71

Gertler, M. and S. Gilchrist (1994), Monetary policy, business cycles, and the behavior of small manufacturing firms, *Quarterly Journal of Economics* 109, 309–40

Giannetti, M. (2000), Do better institutions mitigate agency problems? Evidence from corporate finance choices, Banca d'Italia, Temi di discussione, 376

Giannoni, M. (2001), Robust optimal monetary policy in a forward-looking model with parameter and shock uncertainty, Federal Reserve Bank of New York, mimeo

Gilchrist, S. and C. P. Himmelberg (1995), Evidence on the role of cash flow for investment, *Journal of Monetary Economics* 36(3), 541–72

(1998), Investment: fundamentals and finance, *NBER Macroeconomics Annual*, 13; Cambridge and London: MIT Press (1999), 223–62

Gilchrist, S. and E. Zakrajsek (1995), The importance of credit for macro-economic activity: identification through heterogeneity, in J. Peek and E. Rosengreen, *Is Bank Lending Important for the Transmission of Monetary Policy?*, Conference Series 39, Boston: Federal Reserve Bank of Boston, 129–58

Glück, H. (1995), Transmission processes in the Austrian economy, in Bank for International Settlements (ed.), *Financial Structure and the Monetary Transmission Mechanism*, Basle: BIS, 278–87

Gnan, E. (1995), Austria's hard currency policy and European monetary integration, OeNB Working Paper 19

Gropp, R., J. Vesala and G. Vulpes (2001), Equity and bond market signals as leading indicators of bank fragility, ECB Working Paper 150

Guender, A. and Moersch, M. (1997), On the existence of a credit channel of monetary policy in Germany, *Kredit und Kapital* 30, 173–85

Gugler, K. (1997), Investment spending in Austria: asymmetric information versus managerial discretion, Department of Economics, University of Vienna

Guiso, L. (1997), High-tech firms and credit rationing, CEPR Discussion Paper 1696

Guiso L., A. Kashyap, F. Panetta and D. Terlizzese (2000), Will a common European monetary policy have asymmetric effects?, Banca d'Italia, Temi di discussione, 384; *Federal Reserve Bank of Chicago Economic Perspectives* 23(4), 56–75

(2002), How interest sensitive is investment? Very (when the data are well measured), Banca d'Italia, mimeo

Guiso, L. and G. Parigi (1999), Investment and demand uncertainty, *Quarterly Journal of Economics* 114, 185–227

Guiso, L., L. Pistaferri and F. Schivardi (2001), Insurance within the firm, CEPR Discussion Paper, 2793

Guiso, L., P. Sapienza and L. Zingales (2002), Does local financial development matter?, NBER Working Paper 8923

Hackethal, A. (2001), How unique are US banks? The role of banks in five major financial systems, *Jahrbücher für Nationalökonomie und Statisik* 221(5/6), 592–619

Hall, B., J. Mairesse and B. Mulkay (1999), Firm-level investment in France and the United States: an exploration of what we have learned in twenty years, *Annales d'Economie et de Statistique* 55–56, 27–67

(2001), Investissement des entreprises et contraintes financières en France et aux Etats-Unis, *Economie et Statistique* 341–342, 67–84

Hall, R. E. (1988), Intertemporal substitution in consumption, *Journal of Political Economy* 96, 339–57

Hall, R. E. and D. W. Jorgenson (1967), Tax policy and investment behavior, *American Economic Review* 57, 391–414

(1969), Tax policy and investment behavior: reply and further results, *American Economic Review* 59, 388–401

(1971), Application of the theory of optimum capital accumulation, in G. Fromm (ed.), *Tax Incentives and Capital Spending*, Washington, DC: Brookings Institution, 9–60

Hamilton, J. (1989), A new approach to the economic analysis of nonstationary time series and the business cycle, *Econometrica* 57, 357–84

(1990), Analysis of time series subject to changes in regime, *Journal of Econometrics* 45, 39–70

(1994), *Time Series Analysis*, Princeton: Princeton University Press

Hansen, L. (1982), Large sample properties of generalized method of moments estimators, *Econometrica* 50, 1029–54

Hansen, L. and T. Sargent (2001), Robust control and model uncertainty, *American Economic Review* 91(2), 60–6

Harhoff, D., and T. Körting (1998), Lending relationships in Germany – empirical evidence from survey data, *Journal of Banking and Finance* 22, 1317–53

Harhoff, D. and F. Ramb (2001), Investment and taxation in Germany: evidence from firm-level panel data, in Deutsche Bundesbank (ed.), *Investing Today for the World of Tomorrow*, Berlin, Heidelberg and New York: Springer Verlag

Hayashi, F. (1982), Tobin's marginal Q and average Q: a neoclassical interpretation, *Econometrica* 50, 213–24

(2000), The cost of capital, Q, and the theory of investment demand, in L. J. Lau (ed.), *Econometrics and the Cost of Capital: Essays in Honor of Dale W. Jorgenson*, Cambridge, MA: MIT Press, 55–83

Hempell, H. S. (2002), Testing for competition among German banks, Deutsche Bundesbank Discussion Paper 04/02, January

Herbet, J. B. (2001), Peut-on expliquer l'investissement à partir de ses déterminants traditionnels au cours de la décennie 90?, *Economie et Statistiques* 341–342, 85–106

Hernando, I. (2000), Identification of monetary policy in Spain, prepared for the MTN, mimeo

Hernando, I. and J. Martínez-Pagés (2001), Is there a bank lending channel of monetary policy in Spain, ECB Working Paper 99

Hilbers, P. (1998), Financial sector reform and monetary policy in the Netherlands, IMF Working Paper WP/98/19

Holmstrom, B. and J. Tirole (1997), Financial intermediation, loanable funds, and the real sector, *Quarterly Journal of Economics* 112(3), 663–91

Honkapohja, S. and E. Koskela (1999), The economic crisis of the 1990s in Finland, *Economic Policy*, 29, 400–36

Hsiao, C. (1986), *The Analysis of Panel Data*, Cambridge: Cambridge University Press

Hubbard, R. G. (1994), Is there a credit channel for monetary policy, NBER Working Paper 4977

(1998), Capital market imperfections and investment, *Journal of Economic Literature* 36, 193–225

Hülsewig, O., P. Winker and A. Worms (2001), Bank lending in the transmission of monetary policy: a VECM analysis for Germany, Working Paper 08/2001, School of Business Administration, International University in Germany, Bruchsal, December

International Monetary Fund (IMF) (1998), Austria, selected issues and statistical appendix, Staff Country Report 98/107, Washington, DC: IMF

(2000), Austria: selected issues and statistical appendix, Staff Country Report 00/107, Washington, DC: IMF

Intrilligator, M., R. Bodkin and C. Hsiao (1996), *Econometric Models, Techniques and Applications*, New York: Prentice-Hall International

Issing, O., V. Gapar, I. Angeloni and O. Tristani (2001), *Monetary Policy in the Euro Area*, Cambridge: Cambridge University Press

Jorgenson, D. (1963), Capital theory and investment behavior, *American Economic Review*, 43, 247–59

Kajanoja, L. (1995), Aggregate investment and corporate indebtedness: some empirical evidence from Finland, Bank of Finland Dp 10/95

Kakes, J. (2000), *Monetary Transmission in Europe: The Role of Financial Markets and Credit*, Cheltenham: Edward Elgar

Kakes, J. and J.-E. Sturm (2001), Monetary policy and bank lending – evidence from German banking groups, De Nederlandsche Bank, January, mimeo

Kalckreuth, U. von (2000), Exploring the role of uncertainty for corporate investment decisions in Germany, Deutsche Bundesbank, Economic Research Centre Discussion Paper 5/00, September

(2001), Monetary transmission in Germany: new perspectives on financial constraints and investment spending, Deutsche Bundesbank, Economic Research Centre, Discussion Paper 19–01

(2002), Der finanzielle Akzelerator in der monetären Transmission (The financial accelerator in monetary transmission), Wirtschaftsdienst 82, August, 555–60

Kao, C. (1999), Spurious regression and residual-based tests for cointegration in panel data, *Journal of Econometrics* 90, 1–44

Kao, C. and M.-H. Chiang (2000), On the estimation and inference of a cointegrated regression in panel data, mimeo

Kaplan, S. N. and L. Zingales (1997), Do investment–cash flow sensitivities provide useful measures of finance constraints?, *Quarterly Journal of Economics* 112, 169–215

(2000), Investment–cash flow sensitivities are not valid measures of financing constraints, *Quarterly Journal of Economics* 115, 707–12

Kashyap, A. K. and J. C. Stein (1995), The impact of monetary policy on bank balance sheets, *Carnegie–Rochester Conference Series on Public Policy* 42, 151–95

(1997), The role of banks in monetary policy: a survey with implications for the European Monetary Union, *Federal Reserve Bank of Chicago Economic Perspectives*, September–October 2–18

(2000), What do a million observations on banks say about the transmission of monetary policy?, *American Economic Review*, 90(3), 407–28

Kashyap, A. K., J. C. Stein and D. W. Wilcox (1993), Monetary policy and credit conditions: evidence from the composition of external finance, *American Economic Review* 83, 78–98

(1996), Monetary policy and credit conditions: evidence from the composition of external finance: a reply, *American Economic Review* 86, 310–14

Kaufmann, S. (2000), Measuring business cycles with a dynamic Markov switching factor model: an assessment using Bayesian simulation methods, *The Econometrics Journal* 3, 39–65

(2001), Asymmetries in bank lending behavior: Austria during the 1990s, ECB Working Paper 97

(2002), Is there an asymmetric effect of monetary policy over time? A Bayesian analysis using Austrian data, *Empirical Economics* 99, 277–98

Kieler, M. and T. Saarenheimo (1998), Differences in monetary policy transmission? A case not closed, Economic Papers, European Commission, Directorate-General for Economic and Financial Affairs, 132

Kim, S. and N. Roubini (1995), Liquidity and exchange rates: a structural VAR approach, mimeo

King, M. (1977), *Public Policy and the Corporation*, London: Chapman & Hall

King, M. and D. Fullerton (eds.) (1984), *The Taxation of Income from Capital. A Comparative Study of the United States, the United Kingdom, Sweden and West Germany*, Chicago and London: University of Chicago Press

King, S. (2000), A credit channel in Europe: evidence from banks' balance sheets, University of California, Davis, mimeo

Kinnunen, H. and V. Vihriälä (1999), Bank relationships and small-business closures during the Finnish recession of the 1990s, Bank of Finland DP 13/99

Kishan, R. and T. Opiela (2000), Bank size, bank capital and the bank lending channel, *Journal of Money, Credit, and Banking* 32(1), 121–41

Kiyotaki, N. and J. Moore (1997a), Credit cycles, *Journal of Political Economy* 105, 211–48

(1997b), Credit chains, London School of Economics, mimeo

Kocherlakota, N. (2000), Creating business cycles through credit constraints, *Federal Reserve Bank of Minneapolis Quarterly Review* 24(3), 2–10

Kohler, M., E. Britton and T. Yates (2000), Trade credit and the monetary transmission mechanism, Bank of England, Working Paper 115

Krahnen, J. P. and R. H. Schmidt (2003), *The German Financial System*, Oxford: Oxford University Press, forthcoming

Kremp, E. and P. Sevestre (2000), L'appartenance à un groupe facilite le financement des entreprises, *Economie et Statistique* 336, 79–92

Kremp, E. and E. Stöss (2000), Estimating the borrowing behaviour of French and German firms, mimeo

Küppers, M. (2001), Curtailing the black box: German banking groups in the transmission of monetary policy, *European Economic Review* 45, 1907–30

La Porta, R., F. Lopez-de-Silanes and A. Shleifer (2002), Government Ownership of Banks, *Journal of Finance* 57(1), 265–301

Labhard, V., O. Weeken and P. Westaway (2001), Characterising macroeconomic behaviour in the Euro area: are statisticians more influential then econometricians?, presented at the Banca d'Italia/CEPR Conference – Monitoring the Euro Area Business Cycle, Rome, 7–8 September, mimeo

Leeper, E., C. Sims and T. Zha (1998), What does monetary policy do?, *Brookings Papers on Economic Activity* 2, 1–78

Leite, A. N. and N. Ribeiro (1997), Portuguese banking and the euro, mimeo

Levin, A. and C. Lin (1992), Unit root tests in panel data: asymptotic and finite-sample properties, University of California, San Diego, Department of Economics, Discussion Paper 23

Loupias, C., F. Savignac and P. Sevestre (2001), Monetary policy and bank lending in France: are there asymmetries?, ECB Working Paper 101

Lucas, R. (1976), Econometric policy evaluation: a critique, *Carnegie–Rochester Conference Series on Public Policy*; *Journal of Monetary Economics* 1(2), 19–46

Lünnemann, P. and T. Mathä (2001), Monetary transmission: empirical evidence from Luxembourg firm-level data, ECB Working Paper 111

Manzano, M. and S. Galmés (1996), Credit institutions, price policies and type of customer: impact on the monetary transmission mechanism, Banco de España Working Paper 9605

Marchetti, D. and F. Nucci (2001), Price stickiness and contractionary technology shocks, Ente Einaudi, Temi di Ricerca 25

Marotta, G. (1997), Does trade credit redistribution thwart monetary policy? Evidence from Italy, *Applied Economics* 29, 1619–29

Martin, C. and F. Rosenwald (1996), Le marché des certificats de dépôt. Ecarts de taux à l'Emission; l'Influence de la relation émetteurs-souscripteurs initiaux. *Notes et études de recherche* 37, Banque de France

McAdam, P. and J. Morgan (2001), The monetary transmission mechanism at the euro-area level: issues and results using structural macroeconomic models, ECB Working Paper Series 93

McCallum, B. and E. Nelson (1999), Timeless perspective vs. discretionary monetary policy in forward-looking models, Carnegie Mellon University, mimeo

McConnell, M. M. and G. Perez-Quiros (2000), Output fluctuations in the United States: what has changed since the early 1980s?, *American Economic Review* 90(5), 1464–76

Meese, R. A. and K. Rogoff (1983), Empirical exchange rate models of the seventies: do they fit out of sample?, *Journal of International Economics* 14(1–2), 3–24

Meng, X.-L. and W. H. Wong (1996), Simulating ratios of normalising constants via a simple identity, *Statistica Sinica* 6, 831–60

Mihov, I. (2001), Monetary policy implementation and transmission in the European Monetary Union, *Economic Policy*, 33, 369–402

Mishkin, F. S. (1995), Symposium on the monetary transmission mechanism, *Journal of Economic Perspectives* 9(4), 3–10

Mitchell, P. R., J. E. Sault, P. N. Smith and K. F. Wallis (1998), Comparing global economic models, *Economic Modelling* 15, 1–48

Modigliani, F. and M. H. Miller (1958), The cost of capital, corporate finance and the theory of investment, *American Economic Review* 48, 261–97

Mojon, B. (1999), Monetary policy under a quasi-fixed exchange rate regime: the case of France between 1987 and 1996, *Banca Nationale del Lavoro Quarterly Review* December, 403–30

   (2000), Financial structure and the interest rate channel of ECB monetary policy, ECB Working Paper 40

Mojon, B. and G. Peersman (2001), A VAR description of the effects of monetary policy in countries of the Euro area, ECB Working Paper 92

Mojon, B., F. Smets and P. Vermeulen (2002), Investment and monetary policy in the Euro area, *Journal of Banking and Finance* 28, 2111–29

Monticelli, C. and O. Tristani (1999), What does the single monetary policy do? A SVAR benchmark for the European Central Bank, ECB Working Paper 2

Mooslechner, P. (1989), Österreichs Banken: Zu klein für Europa?, *WIFO-Monatsberichte* 62, 90–8

(1995), Die Ertragslage des Bankensystems in Österreich und Deutschland, Study by the Austrian Institute of Economic Research commissioned by Bank Austria AG

Mörttinen, L. (2000), Essays on loan pricing and the credit channel of monetary policy, Research Report 85:2000, Department of Economics, University of Helsinki

Mörttinen, L. and K. Virolainen (2002), Characteristics of the evolution of financial markets in Finland, in *Financial Markets in Finland 2002*, Bank of Finland Publication Series A, forthcoming

Mulaik, S. A. (1972), *The Foundations of Factor Analysis*, New York: McGraw-Hill

Nelson, E. and K. Nikolov (2002), Monetary policy and stagflation in the UK, Bank of England Working Paper 155

Nickell, S. (1981), Biases in dynamic models with fixed effects, *Econometrica* 54, 1417–25

Nicoletti Altimari, S., R. Rinaldi, S. Siviero and D. Terlizzese (1995), Monetary policy and the transmission channels in the Bank of Italy's quarterly econometric model, Bank for International Settlements, *Financial Structure and the Monetary Policy Transmission Mechanism*, Basle: BLS

NIESR (2001), NiGEM Model Manual, mimeo

Nilsen, J. (1999), Trade credit and the bank lending channel, Swiss National Bank, Study Center Gerzensee, Working Paper 4

Oesterreichische Nationalbank (OeNB) (2001a), Financial markets in Austria, *Financial Stability Report* 1, Oesterreichische Nationalbank

(2001b), Financial markets in Austria, *Financial Stability Report* 2, Oesterreichische Nationalbank

(2002), Financial intermediaries in Austria, *Financial Stability Report* 3, Oesterreichische Nationalbank

Oliner, S. D. and G. D. Rudebusch (1995), Is there a bank lending channel for monetary policy?, Federal Reserve Bank of San Francisco, *Economic Review* 2, 3–20

(1996), Is there a broad credit channel for monetary policy?, *Federal Reserve Bank of San Francisco-Economic Review*, 1, 3–13

Organisation for Economic Cooperation and Development (OECD) (1991), *Taxing Profits in a Global Economy, Domestic and International Issues*, Paris: OECD

Pagano, M., F. Panetta and L. Zingales (1998), Why do companies go public? An empirical analysis, *Journal of Finance* 53, 27–64

Parigi, G. and S. Siviero (2000), An investment function-based measure of capacity utilisation. Potential output and utilised capacity in the Bank of Italy's quarterly model, Banca d'Italia, Temi di discussione 367

Passacantando, F. (1996), Building an institutional framework for monetary stability, *BNL Quarterly Review* 49(196), 83–132

Pech, H., (1994), The interest rate policy transmission mechanism – the case of Austria, in Bank for International Settlements, *National Differences in Interest Rate Transmission*, Basle: BIS

Pedroni, P. (1996), Fully modified OLS for heterogeneous cointegrated panels and the case of purchasing power parity, Working Paper, Department of Economics, Indiana University

(1997), Panel cointegration: asymptotic and finite sample properties of pooled time series tests with an application to the PPP hypothesis, Working Paper, Department of Economics, Indiana University

Peek, J. and E. S. Rosengren (1995), Bank lending and the transmission of monetary policy; in J. Peek and E. S. Rosengren (eds.), *Is Bank Lending Important for the Transmission of Monetary Policy?*, Federal Reserve Bank of Boston Conference Series 39, 47–68

Peersman, G. (2001), The transmission of monetary policy in the euro area: implications for the European Central Bank, PhD dissertation, Ghent University

Peersman, G. and F. Smets (1999), The Taylor Rule: a useful monetary policy benchmark for the Euro Area?, *International Finance*, 2(1), 85–116

Pérez, F., J. Maudos and J. M. Pastor (1999), Sector bancario español (1985–1997): cambio estructural y competencia, Instituto Valenciano de Investigaciones Económicas, Valencia

Pesaran, M. H. and Y. Shin (1995), Estimating long-run relationships from dynamic heterogeneous panels, *Journal of Econometrics* 68, 79–113

Pesaran, M. H., Y. Shin and R. Smith (1999), Pooled mean group estimation of dynamic heterogeneous panels, *Journal of the American Statistical Association* 94(446), 621–34

Petersen, M. and R. Rajan (1994), The benefits of lending relationships: evidence from small business data, *Journal of Finance* 49, 3–37

Phillips, P. C. B. and M. Loretan (1991), Estimating long-run economic equilibria, *Review of Economic Studies* 58, 407–36

Phillips, P. and H. Moon (1999), Linear regression limit theory for nonstationary panel data, *Econometrica* 67(5), 1057–1111

(2000), Nonstationary panel data analysis: an overview of some recent developments, *Econometric Reviews* 19(3), 263–86

Polya, G. (1954), *Patterns of Plausible Inference*, Volume II of *Mathematics and Plausible Reasoning*, Princeton: Princeton University Press

Pozzolo, A. and F. Nucci (2001), Investment and the exchange rate: an analysis with firm-level data, *European Economic Review* 45(2), 259–83

Quehenberger, M. (1997), The influence of the Oesterreichische Nationalbank on the financing conditions of Austrian enterprises, *Focus on Austria*, 3, Vienna

Rajan, R. and L. Zingales (1998), Which capitalism? Lessons from the East Asian crisis, University of Chicago, mimeo

Ramaswamy, R. and T. Sloek (1997), The real effects of monetary policy in the European Union: what are the differences?, IMF Working Paper 160

Ramb, F. (2003), Steuersystem und Investitionstätigkeit, Eine panelökonometrische Untersuchung für Deutschland (Taxation and Investment. A Panel

Econometric Investigation for Germany), Baden-Baden: Nomos Verlag, forthcoming

Rao, C. (1973), *Linear Statistical Inference and its Applications*, New York: John Wiley

Reifschneides, D., D. R. Tetlow and J. Williams (1999), Aggregate disturbances, monetary policy, and the macroeconomy: the FRB/US Perspective, Federal Reserve Bulletin, 85(1), 1–19

Romer, C. and D. Romer (1990), New evidence on the monetary transmission mechanism, *Brookings Papers on Economic Activity* 1, 149–98

Rondi, L., A. Sembenelli and G. Zanetti (1994), Is excess sensitivity of investment to financial factors constant across firms? Evidence from panel data on Italian companies, *Journal of Empirical Finance* 1, 343–64

Rondi, L., B. Sack, F. Schiantarelli and A. Sembenelli (1998), Firms' financial and real responses to monetary tightening: evidence for large and small Italian companies, *Giornale degli Economisti e Annali di Economia* 57(1), 35–64

Rosenwald, F. (1998). Coût des crédits et montants des prêts, une interprétation en termes de canal large des crédit, *Revue économique* 49, 1103–1127

Rosolia, A. and R. Torrini (2001), The investment decisions of small and large Italian manufacturing firms, Banca d'Italia, mimeo

Rotemberg, J. (2002), Stochastic technical progress, nearly smooth trends and distinct business cycles, NBER Working Paper W8919

Rotemberg, J. and M. Woodford (1997), An optimisation-based econometric framework for the evaluation of monetary policy, *NBER Macroeconomics Annual*, 12, 297–346

(1998), Cout du crédit et montant des prêts: une interpretation en termes de canal large du credit, *Revue Economique* 49, 1003–27

Rothschild, M. and J. Stiglitz (1996), Equilibrium competitive insurance markets: an essay on the economics of imperfect information, *Quarterly Journal of Economics* 90(4), 630–49

Saarenheimo, T. (1995), Credit crunch caused investment slump? An empirical analysis using Finnish data, Bank of Finland DP 6/95

Sáez, F. J., J. M. Sánchez and T. Sastre (1994), The markets for banking operations in Spain: productive specialisation and competition, *Economic Bulletin*, Banco de España, July

Sala, L. (2000), Monetary transmission in the euro area: a common factor approach, ECARES, mimeo

(2001), Monetary transmission in the euro area: a factor model approach, ECARES, Université Libre de Bruxelles, mimeo

Sánchez, J. M. and T. Sastre (1995), ¿Es el tamaño un factor explicativo de las diferencias entre entidades bancarias?, Banco de España Working Paper 9512

Sargan, J. D. (1958), The estimation of economic relationships using instrumental variables, *Econometrica* 26, 393–415

Sastre, T. (1998), The role of the banking system in the monetary transmission mechanism, in J. L. Malo de Molina *et al.* (eds.) *Monetary Policy and Inflation in Spain*, London: Macmillan

Schiantarelli, F. (1995), Financial constraints and investment: a critical review of methodological issues and international evidence, in J. Peek and E. Rosengren (eds.), *Is Bank Lending Important for the Transmission of Monetary Policy?*, Federal Reserve Bank of Boston Conference Series 39

Schiantarelli, F. and A. Sembenelli (2000), Form of ownership and financial Constraints, *Empirica* 27(2), 175–92

Schuller, M. (1998), The impact of monetary policy on bank balance sheets in Germany and the Netherlands, mimeo

Sevestre, P. and A. Trognon (1985), A note on autoregressive error components models, *Journal of Econometrics* 28, 231–45

Sims, C. (1980), Macroeconomics and reality, *Econometrica* 48(1), 1–48

(1986), Are forecasting models usable for policy analysis?, *Federal Reserve Bank of Minneapolis Quarterly Review* 10

(1992), Interpreting the macro-economic time series facts: the effects of monetary policy, *European Economic Review* 36, 975–1011

Sims, C., J. Stock and M. Watson (1990), Inference in linear time series models with some unit roots, *Econometrica* 58(1), 113–44

Sims, C. and T. Zha (1998), Does monetary policy generate recessions?, Federal Reserve Bank of Atlanta, Working Paper 98–12

Sinn, H.-W. (1984), Systeme der Kapitaleinkommensbesteuerung: Ein allokationstheorethischer Vergleich (Systems of capital income taxation. A comparison with respect to allocation), in D. Bös, M. Rose and C. Seidl (eds.), *Beiträge zur neueren Steuertheorie. Referate des finanztheoretischen Seminars im Kloster Neustift bei Brixen 1983*, Berlin, Heidelberg, New York and Tokyo: Springer Verlag, 209–38

(1987), *Capital Income Taxation and Resource Allocation*, Amsterdam and Tokyo: North-Holland; New York: Elsevier; published in German as *Kapitaleinkommensbesteuerung*, Tübingen: Mohr, 1984

Smets, F. (1995), Central bank macroeconometric models and the monetary policy transmission mechanism, Bank for International Settlements (ed.), *Financial Structure and the Monetary Policy Transmission Mechanism*, Basel: BIS, CB 394, 225–66

(1997), Measuring monetary policy shocks in France, Germany and Italy: the role of the exchange rate, *Swiss Journal of Economics and Statistics* 133(3), 597–616

Smets, F. and R. Wouters (1999), The exchange rate and the monetary transmission mechanism in Germany, *De Economist* 147(4), 489–521

Spence, A. (1973), Job market signalling, *Quarterly Journal of Economics* 87(3), 355–74

Staderini, A. (2001), Tax reforms to influence corporate financial policy: the case of the Italian business tax reform of 1997–98, Banca d'Italia, Temi di discussione 423

Stein, J. (1998), An adverse-selection model of bank asset and liability management with implications for the transmission of monetary policy, *RAND Journal of Economics* 29(3), 466–86

Stiglitz, J. and A. Weiss (1981), Credit rationing in markets with imperfect information, *American Economic Review* 71, 393–410

476   References

Stock, J. and M. Watson (1999), Business cycle fluctuations in US macroeconomic time series, in J. Taylor and M. Woodford (eds.), *Handbook of Macroeconomics* I, Amsterdam: North-Holland

Stöss, E. (1996), Enterprises' financial structure and their response to monetary policy stimuli – an analysis based on the Deutsche Bundesbank's corporate balance sheet statistics, Deutsche Bundesbank Discussion Paper 9/96

(2001), Deutsche Bundesbank's corporate balance sheet statistics and areas of application, *Schmollers Jahrbuch (Journal of Applied Social Science Studies)* 121, 131–7

(1995), The monetary transmission mechanism: an empirical framework, *Journal of Economic Perspectives* 9, 11–26

Taylor, J. B. (1995), The monetary transmission mechanism: an empirical framework, *Journal of Economic Perspectives* 9, 11–26

Topi, J. and J. Vilmunen (2001), Transmission of monetary policy shocks in Finland: evidence from bank-level data on loans, ECB Working Paper 100/01

Trautwein, H.-M. (2000), The credit view, old and new, *Journal of Economic Surveys* 4(2), 155–89

Tsatsaronis, C. (1995), Is there a credit channel in the transmission of monetary policy? Evidence from four countries; Bank for International Settlements (ed.), *Financial Structure and the Monetary Policy Transmission Mechanism* Barel: BIS, CB 394, 154–87

Tychon, P. (1997), The structure of corporate finance in Belgium: an empirical investigation, IRES Discussion Paper 9719

US Census Bureau (2001), *Statistical Abstract of the United States: 2001*, Washington, DC

Upper, C. and A. Worms (2001a), Estimating bilateral exposures in the German interbank market: is there a danger of contagion?, in Bank for International Settlements (ed), *Marrying the Macro- and Microprudential Dimensions of Financial Stability*, Papers 1, Basel: BIS, 211–29

(2001b), Banken als Bindeglied zwischen Geld- und Kapitalmarkt in Deutschland, B. Schefold (ed.), *Exogenität und Endogenität – Die Geldmenge in der Geschichte des ökonomischen Denkens und in der modernen Politik*, Verlag Metropolis, 93–132

Valderrama, M. T. (2001a), Balance sheet and bank lending channels: some evidence from Austrian firms, *Focus on Austria*, 3–4

(2001b), Credit channel and investment behaviour in Austria: a microecomometric approach, ECB Working Paper 108

Valori, V.-P. and J. Vesala (1998), Reform of the Finnish deposit guarantee scheme, *Bank of Finland Quarterly Bulletin* 72(3), 11–13

Van den Heuvel, S. (2001), The bank capital channel of monetary policy, University of Pennsylvania, Wharton School, mimeo

Vermeulen, P. (1998), Detecting the influence of financing constraints on fixed investment, mimeo

(2000), Business fixed investment: evidence of a financial accelerator in Europe, ECB Working Paper 37

Vihriälä, V. (1997), Banks and the Finnish credit cycle 1986–1995, Bank of Finland Publication E:7

Vilmunen, J. (2002), Dynamics of investment behaviour in Finland: aggregate and firm level evidence, Bank of Finland Dp 22/02

Waschiczek, W. (1999), The Austrian banks at the beginning of monetary union, *Focus on Austria* 3, 79–108

Wellink, A. (1994), Experience gained with monetary instruments in the Netherlands, in *Monetary Policy Instruments, National Experiences and European Perspectives*, Bankhistorisches Archiv, Zeitschrift zur Bankengeschichte 27, 22–41

Wesche, K. (2000), Is there a credit channel in Austria? The impact of monetary policy on firms' investment decisions, Oesterreichische Nationalbank Working Paper 41

Woodford, M. (1999), Commentary: how should monetary policy be conducted in an era of price stability?, *New Challenges for Monetary Policy*, Federal Reserve Bank of Kansas City, 277–316

Worms, A. (1998), Bankkredite an Unternehmen und ihre Rolle in der geldpolitischen Transmission in Deutschland, Peter Lang-Verlag, Reihe Europäische Hochschulschriften, Reihe V: Volks- und Betriebswirtschaft 2244

(2001a), The reaction of bank lending to monetary policy measures in Germany, ECB Working Paper 96

(2001b), Monetary policy effects on bank loans in Germany: a panel-econometric analysis, Deutsche Bundesbank Discussion Paper 17/01

(2003), The financial system and monetary transmission in Germany, in J. P. Krahnen and R. H. Schmidt (eds.), *The German Financial System*, Oxford: Oxford University Press. forthcoming

Wynne, M. A. and J. Koo (2000), Business cycles under mnetary union: a comparison of the EU and USA, *Economica*, 67(267), 347–74

Zha, T. (1997), Identifying monetary policy: a primer, *Economic Review*, Federal Bank of Atlanta, second quarter

Figures

Tables

Subject index

1993 Banking Law, *see* Second Banking Directive
ADL, *see* Autoregressive Distributed Lag model
aggregates, euro area 18, 24–6
Amadeus model 187, 213, 214
Area Wide Model (European Central Bank) 18, 75, 76–7, 89–90, 389–90, 389–97
  exchange rate determination 77
  simulation experiments 80–7, 95–7
asset prices 50
autoregressive distributed lag model 44, 145–9

BACH European database 187
balance sheet channel 242, 276, 347, 418–19, 421
  see also broad credit channel
bank
  bankruptcies, Finland 373
  capitalization 268, 290, 291, 300, 306–7, 314, 327–9, 332, 334, 341, 367–9, 370, 379–80, 411
  failures 245–6, 332
  lending by sector 340, 344–5, 346, 348–9
  liquidity 260–2, 263, 264, 290, 292, 296, 298, 299–300, 304–6, 307, 309, 327–9, 330, 334, 341, 355, 367–9, 370, 379–80, 411
  monetary policy restriction, response to 8–9, 257, 263, 264, 277, 291, 298, 329–31
  size, relevance of 271, 277, 279–80, 281, 291, 296, 306, 307, 322, 327–30, 331, 334, 338, 350–1, 355, 367–9, 379–80, 411; BankScope definition 268
  see also banking systems
bank concentration 243–4

bank lending channel 110–11, 113–14, 248, 249, 255, 259, 284, 285, 290, 292–5, 401–5, 418, 419, 420, 421
  Austria 348–51, 401–5
  Finland 377–80, 401–5
  France 297, 304–8, 401–5
  Germany 275–82, 401–5
  Greece 316–22, 401–5
  Italy 329–34, 401–5
  Netherlands 341–6, 401–5
  Portugal 359, 362–6, 367, 366–71, 401–5
  Spain 291–6, 401–5
  see also loan supply
bank mergers
  Austria 350, 350, 352
  Germany 281, 273, 281, 283
  Greece 315
  Italy 324, 325
  Netherlands 338
  Spain 286
bank networks 237–40, 246–9
  Austria 349
  Finland 375
  Germany 274, 279, 282
  Italy 325
Banking sector, structure of 442–3
  see also banking systems
banking statistics
  BankScope database 254, 264
  Austria 349
  Finland 378
  France 244, 255, 300
  Germany 244, 255, 273
  Greece 312–13
  Italy 244, 255, 326
  Netherlands 340
  Spain 244, 255
banking systems
  Austria 223–4, 348–51
  bank dominance in Germany 174–5, 271–2

Author index